The Experience of America

Edited by

LOUIS D. RUBIN, Jr.

The University of North Carolina

and

R. H. W. DILLARD

Hollins College

THE MACMILLAN COMPANY

THE
EXPERIENCE
OF
AMERICA

A
BOOK
OF READINGS

COLLIER-MACMILLAN LIMITED, LONDON

Library of Congress catalog card number: 69-10457

THE MACMILLAN COMPANY
COLLIER-MACMILLAN CANADA, LTD., TORONTO, ONTARIO

Printed in the United States of America

Preface

This book of readings consists of one hundred selections which relate the experience of the American people from the earliest colonial settlements to the present day. The readings reflect the attitudes, ideas, and experiences of Americans as expressed in essays, excerpts from books, speeches, sermons, legislation, letters, newspapers, songs, testimonies, magazines, court decisions, diaries, journals, and the public and private writings of persons some of whom are well known and others who are all but forgotten. They do not add up to a complete and comprehensive coverage of American experiences—no single book could do that—but the editors hope they have managed to touch on the more important topics.

Although the editors are teachers of American literature, material strictly literary in nature is not included. Our idea was to compile material on American life in a single volume that could be used to complement the numerous anthologies of American literature. The very word "American," when placed in front of "literature," implies a relationship between literature and culture that includes the history, politics, philosophy, economics, and sociology of American life. American literature has been shaped by American experience (it has also helped shape that experience), and without seeking any literal, one-for-one correlation between events and works of art, one can profitably draw on the historical experience to help in understanding the literature. And the reverse is true as well.

We believe this book about America and Americans can be read with profit and enjoyment by anyone interested in American life. We hope our choice of selections encourages the reader to seek other material and thereby to use our book as a guide to the subject as well as an introduction.

We have purposely omitted some important material which is easily and generally accessible. Thus, we did not include passages from Emerson's *Nature,* the Federalist Papers, the Constitution of the United States, the Gettysburg Address, Woodrow Wilson's Fourteen Points, Turner's essay on the significance of the frontier, Henry George's *Progress and Poverty,* or Whitman's *Democratic Vistas.* Such works are indispensable to the student of American life but are readily available, while a good deal of the material we have included is not. On the other hand, we could not bring ourselves to omit the Declaration of Independence, the "House Divided" speech and Lincoln's Second Inaugural Address, de Tocqueville on the poetry of America, Paine's

Crisis, Mencken on Bryan and on the South, Faulkner's Nobel Prize speech, and Kennedy's Inaugural Address. So some of the "standard" pieces are here, others are not. Ideally, each person should compile his own selections; those in this book are ours.

We should like to express our gratitude to the staffs of the Fishburn Library of Hollins College and the Louis Round Wilson Library of the University of North Carolina, for their helpfulness in the preparation of this book, and to Mrs. Faye Ivanhoe for her efficient clerical assistance.

L. D. R.

R. H. W. D.

Contents

3

GOD AND MAN IN COLONIAL AMERICA 35

4

REBELS AND NATIONALISTS 58

8

SLAVERY AND SECESSION   *160*

9

THE GILDED AGE   *198*

10

POPULIST AND LABOR UNREST 230

11

OUR BROTHER IN BLACK 248

12

COMMERCE FOLLOWS THE FLAG 275

16

THE SHADOW OF TOTALITARIANISM

17

OLD PROBLEMS AND NEW

1

VIEWS OF THE
AMERICAN CHARACTER

What is America? What is an American? What should he be, and what should his country be? A new nation, founded on a new continent, heralding its independence with the statement that "all men are created equal," and creating a Constitution designed "to secure the blessings of liberty to ourselves and to our posterity"—here was something rare and new in human history, and filled with promise. But of what did such promise consist, and what ideals should Americans set for themselves and their country?

Americans have debated the question, have disagreed considerably over the nature of the good life; visitors from the Old World, having come to see for themselves, have had their own ideas about what was taking place. Hopes have usually been high; and sometimes when realization appeared especially far away, disappointment has been keen. Recurrently Americans have felt it necessary to redefine their country's nature and purpose in the light of new conditions. Each generation has had its ideals, its problems, its disappointments. To translate the aspirations of the founding fathers into reality, to equate ideals of freedom with the economic, social, and political conditions of an expanding, productive, infinitely complex nation, has been a continuing challenge, made more difficult by shrinking distances in a world beset with tremendous problems. To the solution of those problems the United States has been inextricably drawn. Where is America going? The question lives today, as throughout our history.

In the selections that follow, five observers discuss the American situation.

1

J. HECTOR ST. JOHN DE CRÈVECOEUR
Thus Europeans Become Americans

The Letters From An American Farmer *of Michel-Guillaume Jean de Crèvecoeur (1735–1813), a Frenchman who became a citizen of New York before the American Revolution, under the name of Hector St. John, pronounced in stirring fashion the dream of what the American freeman would be, once free of the burdens and restrictions of centuries of European caste and class. Crèvecoeur wrote from France, during the Revolution; his book was published in 1782.*

An European, when he first arrives, seems limited in his intentions, as well as in his views; but he very suddenly alters his scale; two hundred miles formerly appeared a very great distance, it is now but a trifle; he no sooner breathes our air than he forms schemes, and embarks in designs he never would have thought of in his own country. There the plenitude of society confines many useful ideas, and often extinguishes the most laudable schemes which here ripen into maturity. Thus Europeans become Americans.

But how is this accomplished in that crowd of low, indigent people, who flock here every year from all parts of Europe? I will tell you; they no sooner arrive than they immediately feel the good effects of that plenty of provisions we possess: they fare on our best food, and they are kindly entertained; their talents, character, and peculiar industry are immediately enquired into; they find countrymen everywhere disseminated, let them come from whatever part of Europe.

Let me select one as an epitome of the rest; he is hired, he goes to work, and works moderately; instead of being employed by a haughty person, he finds himself with his equal, placed at the substantial table of the farmer, or else at an inferior one as good; his wages are high, his bed is not like that bed of sorrow on which he used to lie: if he behaves with propriety, and is faithful, he is caressed, and becomes, as it were, a member of the family. He begins to feel the effects of a sort of resurrection; hitherto he had not lived, but simply vegetated; he now feels himself a man, because he is treated as such; the laws of his own country had overlooked him in his insignificancy; the laws of this cover him with their mantle. Judge what an alteration there must arise in the mind and thoughts of this man; he begins to forget his former servitude and dependence; his heart involuntarily swells and glows; this first swell inspires him with those new thoughts which constitute an

FROM *Letters From An American Farmer*, by J. Hector St. John de Crèvecoeur, A Farmer in Pennsylvania (Philadelphia: Carey, 1793), pp. 62–65.

American. What love can he entertain for a country where his existence was a burthen to him! if he is a generous good man, the love of this new adoptive parent, will sink deep into his heart. He looks around, and sees many a prosperous person, who but a few years before was as poor as himself. This encourages him much; he begins to form some little scheme, the first, alas, he ever formed in his life. If he is wise, he thus spends two or three years, in which time he acquires knowledge, the use of tools, the modes of working the lands, felling trees, etc. This prepares the foundation of a good name, the most useful acquisition he can make. He is encouraged; he has gained friends; he is advised and directed; he feels bold; he purchases some land; he gives all the money he has brought over, as well as what he has earned, and trusts to the God of harvests for the discharge of the rest. His good name procures him credit; he is now possessed of the deed, conveying to him and his posterity the fee simple, and absolute property of two hundred acres of land, situated on such a river. What an epocha in this man's life! He is become a freeholder, from perhaps a German boor—he is now an American, a Pennsylvanian. He is naturalized; his name is enrolled with those of the other citizens of the province. Instead of being a vagrant, he has a place of residence; he is called the inhabitant of such a county, or of such a district, and for the first time in his life counts for something; for hitherto he has been a cypher. I only repeat what I have heard many say, and no wonder their hearts should glow, and be agitated with a multitude of feelings, not easy to describe. From nothing to start into being; from a servant to the rank of a master; from being the slave of some despotic prince, to become a free man, invested with lands, to which every municipal blessing is annexed! What a change indeed! It is in consequence of that change, that he becomes an American.

This great metamorphosis has a double effect; it extinguishes all his European prejudices; he forgets that mechanism of subordination, that servility of disposition which poverty had taught him; and sometimes he is apt to forget too much, often passing from one extreme to the other. If he is a good man, he forms schemes of future prosperity; he proposes to educate his children better than he has been educated himself; he thinks of future modes of conduct, feels an ardour to labour he never felt before. Pride steps in and leads him to everything that the laws do not forbid: he respects them; with a heartfelt gratitude he looks toward that government from whose wisdom all his new felicity is derived, and under whose wings and protection he now lives. These reflections constitute him the good man and the good subject.

Ye poor Europeans, ye, who sweat, and work for the great—ye, who are obliged to give so many sheaves to the church, so many to your lords, so many to your government, and have hardly any left for yourselves—ye, who are held in less estimation than favourite hunters or useless lap-dogs—ye, who only breathe the air of nature, because it cannot be withheld from you; it is here that ye can conceive the possibility of those feelings I have been describing; it is here the laws of naturalization invite every one to partake of our great labours and felicity, to till unrented, untaxed lands!

Many, corrupted beyond the power of amendment, have brought with them all their vices, and disregarding the advantages held to them, have gone on in their former career of iniquity, until they have been overtaken and punished by our laws. It is not every emigrant who succeeds; no, it is only the sober, the honest, and industrious: happy those to whom this transition has served as a powerful spur to labour, to prosperity, and to the good establishment of children, born in the days of their poverty; and who had no other portion to expect but the rags of their parents, had it not been for their happy emigration. . . .

ALEXIS DE TOCQUEVILLE
The Hidden Nerve Which Gives Vigor to the Frame

As the American people "views its own march across these wilds—drying swamps, turning the course of rivers, peopling solitudes, and subduing nature," there is subject enough for American poets to celebrate. So deduced Alexis, Comte de Tocqueville in his classic analysis of the profits and losses of American democracy, published in 1835. De Tocqueville (1805–1859), who came to the United States from France to report on the prison system, produced the first important study of the nature of democracy as exemplified in American life. Not too many years later, the poet Walt Whitman would try, and with remarkable success, to make the very experience that de Tocqueville noted into the stuff of poetry.

Various different significations have been given to the word "poetry." It would weary my readers if I were to lead them into a discussion as to which of these definitions ought to be selected: I prefer telling them at once that which I have chosen. In my opinion, poetry is the search and the delineation of the ideal. The poet is he who, by suppressing a part of what exists, by adding some imaginary touches to the picture, and by combining certain real circumstances, but which do not in fact concurrently happen, completes and extends the work of nature. Thus the object of poetry is not to represent what is true, but to adorn it, and to present to the mind some loftier imagery. Verse, regarded as the ideal beauty of language, may be eminently poetical; but verse does not, of itself, constitute poetry.

FROM *Democracy in America,* by Alexis de Tocqueville. Translated by Henry Reeve (New York: P. F. Collier and Son, 1900), Vol. II, pp. 75–80.

I now proceed to inquire whether, amongst the actions, the sentiments, and the opinions of democratic nations, there are any which lead to a conception of ideal beauty, and which may for this reason be considered as natural sources of poetry. It must in the first place, be acknowledged that the taste for ideal beauty, and the pleasure derived from the expression of it, are never so intense or so diffused amongst a democratic as amongst an aristocratic people. In aristocratic nations it sometimes happens that the body goes on to act as it were spontaneously, whilst the higher faculties are bound and burdened by repose. Amongst these nations the people will very often display poetic tastes, and sometimes allow their fancy to range beyond and above what surrounds them. But in democracies the love of physical gratification, the notion of bettering one's condition, the excitement of competition, the charm of anticipated success, are so many spurs to urge men onwards in the active professions they have embraced, without allowing them to deviate for an instant from the track. The main stress of the faculties is to this point. The imagination is not extinct; but its chief function is to devise what may be useful, and to represent what is real.

The principle of equality not only diverts men from the description of ideal beauty—it also diminishes the number of objects to be described. Aristocracy, by maintaining society in a fixed position, is favorable to the solidity and duration of positive religions, as well as to the stability of political institutions. It not only keeps the human mind within a certain sphere of belief, but it predisposes the mind to adopt one faith rather than another. An aristocratic people will always be prone to place intermediate powers between God and man. In this respect it may be said that the aristocratic element is favorable to poetry. When the universe is peopled with supernatural creatures, not palpable to the senses but discovered by the mind, the imagination ranges freely, and poets, finding a thousand subjects to delineate, also find a countless audience to take an interest in their productions. In democratic ages it sometimes happens, on the contrary, that men are as much afloat in matters of belief as they are in their laws. Scepticism then draws the imagination of poets back to earth, and confines them to the real and visible world. Even when the principle of equality does not disturb religious belief, it tends to simplify it, and to divert attention from secondary agents, to fix it principally on the Supreme Power. Aristocracy naturally leads the human mind to the contemplation of the past, and fixes it there. Democracy, on the contrary, gives men a sort of instinctive distaste for what is ancient. In this respect aristocracy is far more favorable to poetry; for things commonly grow larger and more obscure as they are more remote; and for this twofold reason they are better suited to the delineation of the ideal.

After having deprived poetry of the past, the principle of equality robs it in part of the present. Amongst aristocratic nations there are a certain number of privileged personages, whose situation is, as it were, without and above the condition of man; to these, power, wealth, fame, wit, refinement, and distinction in all things appear peculiarly to belong. The crowd never sees them very closely, or does not watch them in minute details; and little is needed to make the description of such men poetical. On the other hand, amongst the same people, you will meet with classes so ignorant, low, and enslaved, that they are no less fit objects for poetry from the excess of their rudeness and wretchedness, than the former are from their greatness and refinement. Besides, as the different classes of which an aristocratic community is composed are widely separated, and imperfectly acquainted with each other, the imagination may always represent them with some addition to, or some subtraction from, what they really are. In democratic communities, where men are all insignificant and very much alike, each man instantly sees all his fellows when he surveys himself. The poets of democratic ages can never, therefore, take any man in particular as the subject of a piece; for an object of slender importance, which is distinctly seen on all sides, will never lend itself to an ideal conception. Thus the principle of equality, in proportion as it has established itself in the world, has dried up most of the old springs of poetry. Let us now attempt to show what new ones it may disclose.

When scepticism had depopulated heaven, and the progress of equality had reduced each individual to smaller and better known proportions, the poets, not yet aware of what they could substitute for the great themes which were departing together with the aristocracy, turned their eyes to inanimate nature. As they lost sight of gods and heroes, they set themselves to describe streams and mountains. Thence originated in the last century, that kind of poetry which has been called, by way of distinction, the descriptive. Some have thought that this sort of delineation, embellished with all the physical and inanimate objects which cover the earth, was the kind of poetry peculiar to democratic ages; but I believe this to be an error, and that it only belongs to a period of transition.

I am persuaded that in the end democracy diverts the imagination from all that is external to man, and fixes it on man alone. Democratic nations may amuse themselves for a while with considering the productions of nature; but they are only excited in reality by a survey of themselves. Here, and here alone, the true sources of poetry amongst such nations are to be found; and it may be believed that the poets who shall neglect to draw their inspirations hence, will lose all sway over the minds which they would enchant, and will be left in the end with none but unimpassioned spectators of their transports. I have shown how the ideas of progression and of the indefinite perfectibility of the human race belong to democratic ages. Democratic nations care but little for what has been, but they are haunted by visions of what will be; in this direction their unbounded imagination grows and dilates beyond all measure. Here then is the wildest range open to the genius of poets, which allows them to remove their performances to a sufficient distance from the eye. Democracy shuts the past against the poet, but opens the future before him. As all the citizens who compose a democratic community are nearly equal and alike, the poet cannot dwell upon any one of them; but the nation itself invites the exercise of his powers. The general similitude of individuals, which renders any one of them taken separately an improper subject of poetry, allows poets to include them all in the same imagery, and to take a general survey of the people itself. Democratic nations have a clearer perception than any others of their own aspect; and an aspect so imposing is admirably fitted to the delineation of the ideal.

I readily admit that the Americans have no poets; I cannot allow that they have no poetic ideas. In Europe people talk a great deal of the wilds of America, but the Americans themselves never think about them: they are insensible to the wonders of inanimate nature, and they may be said not to perceive the mighty forests which surround them till they fall beneath the hatchet. Their eyes are fixed upon another sight: the American people views its own march across these wilds—drying swamps, turning the course of rivers, peopling solitudes, and subduing nature. This magnificent image of themselves does not meet the gaze of the Americans at intervals only; it may be said to haunt every one of them in his least as well as in his most important actions, and to be always flitting before his mind. Nothing conceivable is so petty, so insipid, so crowded with paltry interests, in one word so anti-poetic, as the life of a man in the United States. But amongst the thoughts which it suggests there is always one which is full of poetry, and that is the hidden nerve which gives vigor to the frame.

In aristocratic ages each people, as well as each individual, is prone to stand separate and aloof from all others. In democratic ages, the extreme fluctuations of men and the impatience of their desires keep them perpetually on the move; so that the inhabitants of different countries intermingle, see, listen to, and borrow from each other's stores. It is not only then the members of the same community who grow more alike; communities are themselves assimilated to one another, and the whole assemblage presents to the eye of the spectator one vast democracy, each citizen of which is a people. This displays the aspect of mankind for the first time in the broadest light. All that belongs to the existence of the human race taken as a whole, to its vicissitudes and to its future, becomes an abundant mine of poetry. The poets who lived in aristocratic ages have been eminently successful in their delineations of certain incidents in the life of a people or a man; but none of them ever ventured to include within his performances the destinies of mankind—a task which poets writing in democratic ages may attempt. At that same time at which every man, raising his eyes above his country, begins at length to discern mankind at large, the Divinity is more and more manifest to the human mind in full and entire majesty. If in democratic ages faith in positive religions be often shaken, and the belief in intermediate agents, by whatever name they are called, be overcast; on the other hand men are disposed to conceive a far broader idea of Providence itself, and its interference in human affairs assumes a new and more imposing appearance to their eyes. Looking at the human race as one great whole, they easily conceive that its destinies are regulated by the same design; and in the actions of every individual they are led to acknowledge a trace of that universal and eternal plan on which God rules our race. This consideration may be taken as another prolific source of poetry which is opened in democratic ages. Democratic poets will always appear trivial and frigid if they seek to invest gods, demons, or angels, with corporeal forms, and if they attempt to draw them down from heaven to dispute the supremacy of earth. But if they strive to connect the great events they commemorate with the general providential designs which govern the universe, and, without showing the finger of the Supreme Governor, reveal the thoughts of the Supreme Mind, their works will be admired and understood, for the imagination of their contemporaries takes this direction of its own accord. . . .

WOODROW WILSON
A Vision Has Been Vouchsafed Us

In 1912 a Democrat, Woodrow Wilson (1856–1924), was elected President of the United States, and with his inauguration the reform spirit of twentieth-century America came of age. In his inaugural address Wilson outlined his views and ideals, declaring that "our duty is to cleanse, to reconsider, to restore, to correct the evil without impairing the good, to purify and humanize every process of our common life without weakening or sentimentalizing it." Born in Virginia, raised in South Carolina and Georgia, and elected to the presidency after a distinguished career as educator and political theorist at Princeton and governor of New Jersey, Wilson seemed to many to symbolize what was best in American political life as the nation prepared to enter what many were confident would be a period of unparalleled prosperity and accomplishment.

There has been a change of government. It began two years ago, when the House of Representatives became Democratic by a decisive majority. It has now been completed. The Senate about to assemble will also be Democratic. The offices of President and Vice-President have been put into the hands of Democrats. What does the change mean? That is the question that is uppermost in our minds to-day. That is the question I am going to try to answer, in order, if I may, to interpret the occasion.

It means much more than the mere success of a party. The success of a party means little except when the Nation is using that party for a large and definitive purpose. No one can mistake the purpose for which the Nation now seeks

FROM "First Inaugural Address," by Woodrow Wilson in *Inaugural Addresses of the Presidents of the United States from George Washington 1789 to Harry Truman 1949. Committee on House Administration,* 1952. H.R. 726, pp. 189–92.

to use the Democratic Party. It seeks to use it to interpret a change in its own plans and point of view. Some old things with which we had grown familiar, and which had begun to creep into the very habit of our thought and of our lives, have altered their aspect as we have latterly looked critically upon them, with fresh, awakened eyes; have dropped their disguises, and shown themselves alien and sinister. Some new things, as we look frankly upon them, willing to comprehend their real character, have come to assume the aspect of things long believed in and familiar, stuff of our own convictions. We have been refreshed by a new insight into our own life.

We see that in many things that life is very great. It is incomparably great in its material aspects, in its body of wealth, in the diversity and sweep of its energy, in the industries which have been conceived and built up by the genius of individual men and the limitless enterprise of groups of men. It is great, also, very great, in its moral force. Nowhere else in the world have noble men and women exhibited in more striking forms the beauty and the energy of sympathy and helpfulness and counsel in their efforts to rectify wrong, alleviate suffering, and set the weak in the way of strength and hope. We have built up, moreover, a great system of government, which has stood through a long age as in many respects a model for those who seek to set liberty upon foundations that will endure against fortuitous change, against storm and accident. Our life contains every great thing, and contains it in rich abundance.

But the evil has come with the good, and much fine gold has been corroded. With riches has come inexcusable waste. We have squandered a great part of what we might have used, and have not stopped to conserve the exceeding bounty of nature, without which our genius for enterprise would have been worthless and impotent, scorning to be careful, shamefully prodigal as well as admirably efficient. We have been proud of our industrial achievements, but we have not hitherto stopped thoughtfully enough to count the human cost, the cost of lives snuffed out, of energies overtaxed and broken, the fearful physical and spiritual cost to the men and women and children upon whom the dead weight and burden of it all has fallen pitilessly the years through. The groans and agony of it all had not yet reached our ears, the solemn, moving undertone of our life, coming up out of the mines and factories and out of every home where the struggle had its intimate and familiar seat. With the great Government went many deep secret things which we too long delayed to look into and scrutinize with candid, fearless eyes. The great Government we loved has too often been made use of for private and selfish purposes, and those who used it had forgotten the people.

At last a vision has been vouchsafed us of our life as a whole. We see the bad with the good, the debased and decadent with the sound and vital. With this vision we approach new affairs. Our duty is to cleanse, to reconsider, to restore, to correct the evil without impairing the good, to purify and humanize every process of our common life without weakening or sentimentalizing it. There has been something crude and heartless and unfeeling in our haste to succeed and be great. Our thought has been "Let every man look out for himself, let every generation look out for itself," while we reared giant machinery which made it impossible that any but those who stood at the levers of control should have a chance to look out for themselves. We had not forgotten our morals. We remembered well enough that we had set up a policy which was meant to serve the humblest as well as the most powerful, with an eye single to the standards of justice and fair play, and remembered it with pride. But we were very heedless and in a hurry to be great.

We have come now to the sober second thought. The scales of heedlessness have fallen from our eyes. We have made up our minds to square every process of our national life again with the standards we so proudly set up at the beginning and have always carried at our hearts. Our work is a work of restoration. . . .

The firm basis of government is justice, not pity. These are matters of justice. There can be no equality or opportunity, the first essential of justice in the body politic, if men and women and children be not shielded in their lives, their very vitality, from the consequences of great industrial and social processes which they can not alter, control, or singly cope with. Society must see to it that it does not itself crush or weaken or damage its own constituent parts. The first duty of law is to keep sound the society it serves. Sanitary laws, pure food laws, and laws determining conditions of labor which individuals are powerless to determine for themselves are intimate parts of the very business of justice and legal efficiency.

These are some of the things we ought to do, and not leave the others undone, the old-fashioned, never-to-be-neglected, fundamental safeguarding of property and of individual right. This is the high enterprise of the new day: To lift everything that concerns our life as a Nation to the light that shines from the hearthfire of every man's conscience and vision of the right. It is inconceivable that we should do this as partisans; it is inconceivable we should do it in ignorance of the facts as they are or in blind haste. We shall restore, not destroy. We shall deal with our economic system as it is and as it may be modified, not as it might be if we had a clean sheet of paper to write upon; and step by step we shall make it what it should be, in the spirit of those who question their own wisdom and seek counsel and knowledge, not shallow self-satisfaction or the excitement of excursions whither they can not tell. Justice, and only justice, shall always be our motto.

And yet it will be no cool process of mere science. The Nation has been deeply stirred, stirred by a solemn passion, stirred by the knowledge of wrong, of ideals lost, of government too often debauched and made an instrument of evil. The feelings with which we face this new age of right and opportunity sweep across our heartstrings like some air out of God's own presence, where justice and mercy are reconciled and the judge and the brother are one. We know our task to be no mere task of politics but a task which shall search us through and through, whether we be able to understand our time and the need of our people, whether we be indeed their spokesmen and interpreters, whether we have the pure heart to comprehend and the rectified will to choose our high course of action.

This is not a day of triumph; it is a day of dedication. Here muster, not the forces of party, but the forces of humanity. Men's hearts wait upon us; men's lives hang in the balance; men's hope call upon us to say what we will do. Who shall live up to the great trust? Who dares fail to try? I summon all honest men, all patriotic, all forward-looking men, to my side. God helping me, I will not fail them, if they will but counsel and sustain me!

H. L. MENCKEN
A Commonwealth of Third-Rate Men

The idealism of Woodrow Wilson's New Freedom seemed to become lost in the debacle of World War I, and the decade that followed was one in which, despite considerable material prosperity, the hopes that had characterized much American thought seemed very far from realization. Assailing his fellow countrymen for their complacency, their materialism, their mediocrity, H. L. Mencken (1880–1956) mounted a full-scale attack on the American scene shortly after World War I in his scathing essay, "On Being an American." Though Mencken excoriated the national mores with rage, perhaps that rage reflected an equally high standard of conduct which Mencken wanted Americans to meet. The disappointment and disillusionment that young American writers felt over the materialism of the post-World War I years is also profoundly reflected in the writings of such authors as F. Scott Fitzgerald, Ernest Hemingway, Sinclair Lewis, John Dos Passos, T. S. Eliot, and others.

All of which may be boiled down to this: that the United States is essentially a commonwealth of third-rate men—that distinction is easy here because the general level of culture, of information, of taste and judgment, of ordinary competence is so low. No sane man, employing an American plumber to repair a leaky drain, would expect him to do it at the first trial, and in precisely the same way no sane man, observing an American Secretary of State in negotiation with Englishmen and Japs, would expect him to come off better than second best. Third-rate men, of course, exist in all countries, but it is only here that they are in full control of the state, and with it of all the national stand-

FROM "On Being an American," in *Prejudices: Third Series* by H. L. Mencken, pp. 22–25. Copyright 1922 by Alfred A. Knopf, Inc., and renewed 1950 by H. L. Mencken. Reprinted by permission of the publisher.

ards. The land was peopled, not by the hardy adventurers of legend, but simply by incompetents who could not get on at home, and the lavishness of nature that they found here, the vast ease with which they could get livings, confirmed and augmented their native incompetence. No American colonist, even in the worst days of the Indian wars, ever had to face such hardships as ground down the peasants of Central Europe during the Hundred Years War, nor even such hardships as oppressed the English lower classes during the century before the Reform Bill of 1832. In most of the colonies, indeed, he seldom saw any Indians at all: the one thing that made life difficult for him was his congenital dunderheadedness. The winning of the West, so rhetorically celebrated in American romance, cost the lives of fewer men than the single battle of Tannenberg, and the victory was much easier and surer. The immigrants who have come in since those early days have been, if anything, of even lower grade than their forerunners. The old notion that the United States is peopled by the offspring of brave, idealistic and liberty loving minorities, who revolted against injustice, bigotry and medievalism at home—this notion is fast succumbing to the alarmed study that has been given of late to the immigration of recent years. The truth is that the majority of non-Anglo-Saxon immigrants since the Revolution, like the majority of Anglo-Saxon immigrants before the Revolution, have been, not the superior men of their native lands, but the botched and unfit: Irishmen starving to death in Ireland, Germans unable to weather the *Sturm und Drang* of the post-Napoleonic reorganization, Italians weed-grown on exhausted soil, Scandinavians run to all bone and no brain, Jews too incompetent to swindle even the barbarous peasants of Russia, Poland and Roumania. Here and there among the immigrants, of course, there may be a bravo, or even a superman—*e.g.,* the ancestors of Volstead, Ponzi, Jack Dempsey, Schwab, Daugherty, Debs, Pershing—but the average newcomer is, and always has been simply a poor fish.

Nor is there much soundness in the common assumption, so beloved of professional idealists and wind-machines, that the people of America constitute "the youngest of the great peoples." The phrase turns up endlessly; the average newspaper editorial writer would be hamstrung if the Postoffice suddenly interdicted it, as it interdicted "the right to rebel" during the war. What gives it a certain specious plausibility is the fact that the American Republic, compared to a few other existing governments, is relatively young. But the American Republic is not necessarily identical with the American people; they might overturn it to-morrow and set up a monarchy, and still remain the same people. The truth is that, as a distinct nation, they go back fully three hundred years, and that even their government is older than that of most other nations, *e.g.,* France, Italy, Germany, Russia. Moreover, it is absurd to say that there is anything properly describable as youthfulness in the American outlook. It is not that of young men, but that of old men. All the characteristics of senescence are in it: a great distrust of ideas, an habitual timorousness, a harsh fidelity to a few fixed beliefs, a touch of mysticism. The average American is a prude and a Methodist under his skin, and the fact is never more evident than when he is trying to disprove it. His vices are not those of a healthy boy, but those of an ancient paralytic escaped from the *Greisenheim*. If you would penetrate to the causes thereof, simply go down to Ellis Island and look at the next shipload of immigrants. You will not find the spring of youth in their step; you will find the shuffling of exhausted men. From such exhausted men the American stock has sprung. It was easier for them to survive here than it was where they came from, but that ease, though it made them feel stronger, did not actually strengthen them. It left them what they were when they came: weary peasants, eager only for the comfortable security of a pig in a sty. Out of that eagerness has issued many of the noblest manifestations of American *Kultur:* the national hatred of war, the pervasive suspicion of the aims and intents of all other nations, the short way with heretics and disturbers of the peace, the unshakable belief in devils, the implacable hostility to every novel idea and point of view.

JOHN F. KENNEDY
Ask What You Can Do for Your Country

In 1961, having in his still young lifetime lived through an economic boom, a depression, two world wars, and a period of Cold War in which the United States reluctantly but firmly took over the leadership of the free world, John Fitzgerald Kennedy (1917–1963) took the oath of office as thirty-fifth President of the United States. He then delivered an address which for many Americans was a restatement of their country's dedication to the principles upon which the United States of America was founded. Reviewing the complex problems of national and international existence that faced the United States in the second half of the twentieth century, he declared that "the energy, the faith, the devotion which we bring to this endeavor will light our country and all who serve it—and the glow from that fire can truly light the world."

. . . we observe today not a victory of party, but a celebration of freedom—symbolizing an end, as well as a beginning—signifying renewal, as well as change. For I have sworn before you and Almighty God the same solemn oath our forebears prescribed nearly a century and three-quarters ago.

The world is very different now. For man holds in his mortal hands the power to abolish all forms of human poverty and all forms of human life. And yet the same revolutionary beliefs for which our forebears fought are still at

FROM "Inaugural Address," by John F. Kennedy in *Inaugural Addresses of the Presidents of the United States from George Washington 1789 to John F. Kennedy 1961.* House Document No. 218 (Washington, D.C.: U.S. Govt. P. O., 1961), pp. 267–70.

issue around the globe—the belief that the rights of man come not from the generosity of the state but from the hand of God.

We dare not forget today that we are the heirs of that first revolution. Let the word go forth from this time and place, to friend and foe alike, that the torch has been passed to a new generation of Americans—born in this century, tempered by war, disciplined by a hard and bitter peace, proud of our ancient heritage—and unwilling to witness or permit the slow undoing of those human rights to which this nation has always been committed, and to which we are committed today at home and around the world.

Let every nation know, whether it wishes us well or ill, that we shall pay any price, bear any burden, meet any hardship, support any friend, oppose any foe, in order to assure the survival and the success of liberty.

This much we pledge—and more.

To those old allies whose cultural and spiritual origins we share, we pledge the loyalty of faithful friends. United, there is little we cannot do in a host of cooperative ventures. Divided, there is little we can do—for we dare not meet a powerful challenge at odds and split asunder.

To those new states whom we welcome to the ranks of the free, we pledge our words that one form of colonial control shall not have passed away merely to be replaced by a far more iron tyranny. We shall not always expect to find them supporting our view. But we shall always hope to find them strongly supporting their own freedom—and to remember that, in the past, those who foolishly sought power by riding the back of the tiger ended up inside.

To those peoples in the huts and villages across the globe struggling to break the bonds of mass misery, we pledge our best efforts to help them help themselves, for whatever period is required—not because the Communists may be doing it, not because we seek their votes, but because it is right. If a free society cannot help the many who are poor, it cannot save the few who are rich.

To our sister republics south of our border, we offer a special pledge—to convert our good words into good deeds, in a new alliance for progress, to assist free men and free governments in casting off the chains of poverty. But this peaceful revolution of hope cannot become the prey of hostile powers. Let all our neighbors know that we shall join with them to oppose aggression or subversion anywhere in the Americas. And let every other power know that this hemisphere intends to remain the master of its own house.

To that world assembly of sovereign states, the United Nations, our last best hope in an age where the instruments of war have far outpaced the instruments of peace, we renew our pledge of support—to prevent it from becoming merely a forum for invective—to strengthen its shield of the new and the weak —and to enlarge the area in which its writ may run.

Finally, to those nations who would make themselves our adversary, we offer not a pledge but a request: that both sides begin anew the quest for peace, before the dark powers of destruction unleashed by science engulf all humanity in planned or accidental self-destruction.

We dare not tempt them with weakness. For only when our arms are sufficient beyond doubt can we be certain beyond doubt that they will never be employed.

But neither can two great and powerful groups of nations take comfort from our present course—both sides overburdened by the cost of modern weapons, both rightly alarmed by the steady spread of the deadly atom, yet both racing to alter that uncertain balance of terror that stays the hand of mankind's final war.

So let us begin anew—remembering on both sides that civility is not a sign of weakness, and sincerity is always subject to proof. *Let us never negotiate out of fear. But let us never fear to negotiate.*

Let both sides explore what problems unite us instead of laboring those problems which divide us.

Let both sides, for the first time, formulate serious and precise proposals for the inspection and control of arms—and bring the absolute power to destroy other nations under the absolute control of all nations.

Let both sides seek to invoke the wonders of science instead of its terrors. Together let us explore the stars, conquer the deserts, eradicate disease, tap the ocean depths, and encourage the arts and commerce.

Let both sides unite to heed in all corners of the earth the command of Isaiah—to "undo the heavy burdens and to let the oppressed go free."

And if a beach-head of cooperation may push back the jungle of suspicion, let both sides join in creating a new endeavor, not a new balance of power, but a new world of law, where the strong are just and the weak secure and the peace preserved.

All this will not be finished in the first 100 days. Nor will it be finished in the first 1,000 days, nor in the life of this administration, nor even perhaps in our lifetime on this planet. But let us begin.

In your hands, my fellow citizens, more than in mine, will rest the final success or failure of our course. Since this country was founded, each generation of Americans has been summoned to give testimony to its national loyalty. The graves of young Americans who answered the call to service are found around the globe.

Now the trumpet summons us again—not as a call to bear arms, though arms we need; not as a call to battle, though embattled we are; but a call to bear the burden of a long twilight struggle, year in, and year out, "rejoicing in hope, patient in tribulation"—a struggle against the common enemies of man: tyranny, poverty, disease, and war itself.

Can we forge against these enemies a grand and global alliance, North and South, East and West, that can assure a more fruitful life for all mankind? Will you join in that historic effort?

In the long history of the world, only a few generations have been granted the role of defending freedom in its hour of maximum danger. I do not shrink from this responsibility—I welcome it. I do not believe that any of us would exchange places with any other people or any other generation. The energy, the faith, the devotion which we bring to this endeavor will light our country and all who serve it—and the glow from that fire can truly light the world.

And so, my fellow Americans, ask not what your country can do for you: Ask what you can do for your country.

My fellow citizens of the world: Ask not what America will do for you, but what together we can do for the freedom of man.

Finally, whether you are citizens of America or citizens of the world, ask of us the same high standards of strength and sacrifice which we ask of you. With a good conscience our only sure reward, with history the final judge of our deeds, let us go forth to lead the land we love, asking His blessing and His help, but knowing that here on earth God's work must truly be our own.

2

COLONIAL EXPERIENCE

The colonial experience, whether in Virginia, Massachusetts or elsewhere, marked Englishmen and others. They became, at some point in their endeavors, not Europeans but Americans. Where, why, and how did it happen? No one can say exactly. Certainly the Englishmen who went ashore at Jamestown to establish the first permanent English colony in the New World did not intend to become anything other than loyal English subjects in a new land, and not for many years did they think of themselves as anything other than that. Yet long before the time of William Byrd of Westover, the change had taken place.

In Massachusetts, settled by Dissenters from the Established Church, there were religious differences that set the colony apart from the royal government. Yet in South Carolina, where no such differences existed, the process that made Americans out of Europeans was just as inevitable.

The selections that follow do not concern themselves with the process of separation. All were written by Englishmen who considered themselves Englishmen, and record the conditions under which colonial life began. They show both the economic and social problems involved in creating communities amid new and unprecedented surroundings. In them we can observe the confrontation of the European settler with the geographical and social realities of life on the new continent which would become his home and, ultimately, his country.

17

CAPTAIN JOHN SMITH
Each Houre Expecting the Fury of the Salvages

Poorly supplied, ill-suited either by training or inclination for the rigors of life in the New World, the first Englishmen to set up a permanent colony in America went ashore at Jamestown in 1607. Their sufferings were intense, and would have been even worse but for the determination and good sense of Captain John Smith, as related in this account, probably written by Thomas Studley and Anas Todkill, of what happened during the first season in the new continent.

Being thus left to our fortunes, it fortuned that, within tenne daies, scarse ten amongst vs could either goe, or well stand, such extreame weaknes and sicknes oppressed vs. And thereat none need mervaile, if they consider the cause and reason, which was this:

Whilest the ships staied, our allowance was somewhat bettered by a daily proportion of bisket which the sailers would pilfer to sell, give, or exchange with us, for mony, saxefras, furres, or love. But when they departed, there remained neither taverne, beere-house, nor place of rel[e]ife but the common kettell. Had we beene as free from all sinnes as gluttony and drunkenes, we might have bin canonized for Saints. But our President would never have bin admitted, for ingrossing to his privat [i.e., his own use]. Otemeale, sacke, oile, aquavitæ, beefe, e[g]gs, or what not, but the kettel; that indeede he allowed equally to be distributed: and that was halfe a pinte of wheat, and as much barly, boyled with water, for a man a day; and this having fryed some 26. weekes in the ships hold, contained as many wormes as graines, so that we might truely call it rather so much bran than corne. Our drinke was water, our lodgings, castles in the air [i.e., in the trees].

With this lodging and diet, our extreame toile in bearing and planting pallisadoes, so strained and bruised vs, and our continuall labour in the extremity of the heate had so weakened us, as were cause sufficient to have made vs as miserable in our native country, or any other place in the world.

From May to September, those that escaped lived upon Sturgion and sea-Crabs.

50. in this time we buried.

The rest seeing the Presidents projects to escape these miseries in our Pinnas by flight (who all this time, had neither felt want nor sicknes) [this] so

FROM "The Proceedings of the English Colony in Virginia," in *Capt. John Smith . . . Works, 1608–1631*, edited by Edward Arber, Birmingham, England, 1884, pp. 94–99.

moved our dead spirits, as we deposed him; [10 Sept. 1607] and established *Ratcliffe* in his place: *Gosnoll* being dead, [22 Aug. 1607] [and] *Kendall* deposed [? Sept. 1607] *Smith* newly recovered; *Martin* and *Rat[c]liffe* was, by his care, preserved and relieved.

But now was all our provision spent, the Sturgeon gone, all helps abandoned, each houre expecting the fury of the Salvages; when God, the patron of all good indeavours, in that desperate extreamity, so changed the harts of the Salvages, that they brought such plenty of their fruits and provision, as no man wanted.

And now where some affirmed it was ill done of the Councel to send forth men so badly provided, this incontradictable reason will shew them plainely they are too ill advised to nourish such il conceipts. First, the fault of our going was our owne. What could bee thought fitting or necessary wee had: but what wee should finde, what we should want, where we shoulde bee, we were all ignorant [of]. And supposing to make our passage in two monthes, with victuall to live, and the advantage of the spring to worke: we weare at sea 5. monthes, where we both spent our victuall and lost the opportunity of the time and season to plant.

Such actions have ever since the worlds beginning beene subject to such accidents, and every thing of worth is found full of difficulties: but nothing [is] so difficult as to establish a common wealth so farre remote from men and meanes; and where mens mindes are so untoward as neither do well themselves, nor suffer others. But to proceed.

The new President, and *Martin,* being little beloved, of weake judgement in dangers and lesse industry in peace, committed the managing of all things abroad [i.e., out of doors] to captaine *Smith:* who, by his owne example, good words, and faire promises, set some to mow, others to binde thatch; some to build houses, others to thatch them; himselfe alwaies bearing the greatest taske for his own share: so that, in short time, he provided most of them lodgings, neglecting any for himselfe.

This done, seeing the Salvages superfluity beginne to decrease, [he] (with some of his workemen) shipped himselfe in the shallop, to search the country for trade. The want of the language, knowledge to mannage his boat without sailers, the want of a sufficient power [forces] (knowing the multitude of the Salvages), [of] apparell for his men, and [of] other necessaries, [these] were infinite impediments, yet no discouragement.

Being but 6 or 7 in company, he went down the river to *Kecoughtan;* where at first they scorned him, as a starved man: yet he so dealt with them, that the next day they loaded his boat with corne. And in his returne, he discovered and kindly traded with the *Weraskoyks.*

In the meane time, those at the fort so glutted the Salvages with their commodities, as they became not regarded.

Smith perceiving (notwithstanding their late miserie) not any regarded but from hand to mouth, the company being well recovered, caused the Pinas to bee provided with things fitting to get provision for the yeare following. But in the interim, he made 3. or 4. journies, and discovered the people of *Chickahamine.* Yet what he carefully provided, the rest carelessly spent.

Wingfield and *Kendall* living in disgrace, (seeing al things at randome in the absence of *Smith,* the companies dislike of their Presidents weaknes, and their small love to *Martins* never-mending sicknes) strengthened themselves with the sailers and other confederates, to regaine their former credit and authority, or at least such meanes abord the Pinas (being fitted to saile as *Smith* had appointed for trade), to alter her course, and to go for England.

Smith unexpectedly returning, had the plot discovered to him. Much trouble he had to prevent it, till with store of fauken [Falcon balls] and musket shot, he forced them [i.e., by threats] [to] stay or sinke in the river. Which action cost the life of captaine *Kendall* [who was shot after trial . . .].

These brawles are so disgustfull, as some will say they were better forgotten: yet all men of good judgement will conclude, it were better their basenes should be manifest to the world, then the busines beare the scorne and shame of their excused disorders.

The President and captaine Archer not long after intended also to have abandoned the country; which project also was curbed and suppressed by *Smith.*

The Spanyard never more greedily desired gold then he victuall; which he found so plentiful in the river of *Chickahamine,* where hundreds of Salvages, in divers places, stood with baskets expecting his coming.

And now the winter approaching, the rivers became so covered with swans, geese, duckes, and cranes, that we daily feasted with good bread, Virginia pease, pumpions, and putchamins; fish, fowle, and diverse sorts of wild beasts as fat as we could eat them: so that none of our Tuftaffaty humorists desired to goe for England.

But our comædies never endured long without a Tragedie. Some idle exceptions being muttered against Captaine *Smith,* for not discovering the head of Chickahamine river; and taxed by the Councell, to bee too slow in so worthie an attempt: the next voyage, hee proceeded so farre that with much labour, by cutting of trees in sunder, he made his passage.

But when his Barge could passe no farther, he left her in a broad bay, out of danger of shot; commanding none should goe ashore till his returne. [He] himselfe, with 2 English and two Salvages, went up higher in a Canowe.

But hee was not long absent, but his men went ashore; whose want of government gave both occasion and opportunity to the Salvages, to surprise one *George Casson;* and much failed not to have cut of[f] the boat and all the rest.

Smith little dreaming of that accident, being got to the marshes at the rivers head, 20 myles in the desert, had his 2 men slaine (as is supposed) sleeping by the Canowe, whilst himselfe by fowling sought them victuall. Who finding he was beset with 200 Salvages, 2 of them hee slew, stil defending himselfe with the aid of a Salvage his guid[e], whome hee bounde to his arme and used as his buckler: till at last slipping into a bogmire, they tooke him prisoner.

When this newes came to the fort, much was their sorrow for his losse, fewe expecting what ensued.

A month those Barbarians kept him prisoner. Many strange triumphes and conjurations they made of him: yet hee so demeaned himselfe amongst them, as he not only diverted them from surprising the Fort; but procure his owne liberty, and got himselfe and his company such estimation amongst them, that those Salvages admired [wondered at] him as a demi-God. So returning safe to the Fort [on 8 Jan. 1608], [he] once more staied the Pinnas her flight for England; which, til his returne, could not set saile, so extreame was the weather, and so great the frost.

His relation of the plentie he had seene, especially at *Werowocomoco,* where inhabited *Powhatan* (that till that time was unknowne) [i.e., personally], so revived againe their dead spirits as all mens feare was abandoned.

Powhatan having sent with this Captaine, divers of his men loaded with provision; he had conditioned, and so appointed his trustie messengers to bring but 2 or 3 of our great ordenances: but the messengers being satisfied with the sight of one of them discharged, ran away amazed with feare, till meanes was used with guifts to assure them [of] our loves.

Thus you may see what difficulties stil crossed any good indeavour, and the good successe of the businesse; and being thus oft brought to the very period of destruction, yet you see by what strange meanes God hath still delivered it.

As for the insufficiencie of them admitted in commission, that errour could not be prevented by their electors; there being no other choice, and all were strangers each to others education, quallities, or disposition.

And if any deeme it a shame to our nation, to have any mention made of these enormities, let them peruse the histories of the Spanish discoveries and plantations: where they may see how many mutinies, discords, and dissentions have accompanied them and crossed their attempts; which being knowne to be particular mens offences, doth take away the generall scorne and contempt, [that] mallice and ignorance might else produce to the scandall and reproach of those whose actions and valiant resolution deserve a worthie respect.

Now whether it had beene better for Captaine *Smith* to have concluded with any of their severall projects to have abandoned the Countrie with some 10 or 12 of them [that] we cal the better sort; to have left Maister *Hunt* our preacher, Maister *Anthony Gosnoll* (a most honest worthy and industrious gentleman) with some 30 or 40 others, his countrie men, to the furie of the Salvages, famin, and all manner of mischiefes and inconveniences; or starved himselfe with them for company, for want of lodging; or but adventuring abroad to make them provision: or by his opposition, to preserve the action, and save all their lives; I leave to the censure of others to consider.

WILLIAM BRADFORD
In These Hard & Dificulte Beginings

Because their enterprise was undertaken in quest of religious liberty as well as economic opportunity, the landing of the Pilgrims at Plymouth Rock in 1620 and their subsequent survival amid the rigors of a New England winter has remained the classic American story of settlement in the New World, even though further South there was already a thriving English colony by then, with a legislature of its own. Here the story of the signing of the Mayflower Compact, the ordeal of illness, unfriendly Indians, and wintry weather, and the subsequent relief in the company's fortunes which came with the advent of an English-speaking Indian, Squanto, are related by William Bradford (1590-1657), who came to America on the Mayflower, *was elected governor of Plymouth Colony the next year, and served in that office for most of the remaining years of his life.*

The remainder of An°: 1620

I shall a litle returne backe and begine with a combination made by them before they came ashore, being ye first foundation of their govermente in this place; occasioned partly by ye discontented & mutinous speeches that some of the strangers amongst them had let fall from them in ye ship—That when they came a shore they would use their owne libertie; for none had power to comand them, the patente they had being for Virginia, and not for New-england, which belonged to an other Goverment, with which ye Virginia Company had nothing to doe. And partly that shuch an acte by them done (this their condition considered) might be as firme as any patent, and in some respects more sure.

The forme was as followeth.

In ye name of God, Amen. We whose names are under-writen, the loyall subjects of our dread soveraigne Lord, King James, by ye grace of God, of Great Britaine, Franc, & Ireland king, defender of ye faith, etc., haveing undertaken, for ye glorie of God, and advancemente of ye Christian faith, & honour of our king & countrie, a voyage to plant ye first colonie in ye Northerne parts of Virginia, doe by these presents solemnly & mutualy in ye presence of God, and one of another, covenant & combine our selves together into a civill body politick, for our better ordering & preservation & furtherance of ye ends aforesaid; and by vertue hearof to

FROM *Bradford's History "Of Plimoth Plantation," from the Original Manuscript.* Printed under the Direction of the Secretary of the Commonwealth, by Order of the General Court (Boston: Wright and Potter, 1898), pp. 109–16, 120–22.

enacte, constitute, and frame such just & equall lawes, ordinances, acts, constitutions, & offices, from time to time, as shall be thought most meete & convenient for ye generall good of ye Colonie, unto which we promise all due submission and obedience. In witnes whereof we have hereunder subscribed our names at Cap-Codd ye 11. of November, in ye year of ye raigne of our soveraigne lord, King James, of England, France, and Ireland ye eighteenth, & of Scotland ye fiftie fourth. An°: Dom. 1620.

After this they chose, or rather confirmed, Mr. John Carver (a man godly & well approved amongst them) their Governour for that year. And after they had provided a place for their goods, or comone store, (which were long in unlading for want of boats, foulnes of winter weather, and sicknes of diverce,) and begune some small cottages for their habitation, as time would admitte, they mette and consulted of lawes & orders, both for their civill & military Govermente, as ye necessitie of their condition did require, still adding therunto as urgent occasion in severall times, & as cases did require.

In these hard & difficulte beginings they found some discontents & murmurings arise amongst some, & mutinous speeches & carriags in other; but they were soone quelled & overcome by ye wisdome, patience, & just and equall carrage of things by ye Gov.r and better part, wch clave faithfully togeather in ye maine. But that which was most sadd & lamentable was, that in 2. or 3. moneths time halfe of their company dyed, espetialy in Jan: & February, being ye depth of winter, and wanting houses & other comforts; being infected with ye scurvie & other diseases, which this long vioage and their inacomodate condition had brought upon them; so as ther dyed some times 2. or 3. of a day, in ye foresaid time; that of 100. and odd persons, scarce 50. remained. And of these in ye time of most distres, ther was but 6. or 7. sound persons, who, to ther great comendations be it spoken, spared no pains, night or day, but with abundance of toyle and hazard of their owne health, fetched them woode, made them fires, drest them meat, made their beads, washed their lothsome cloaths, cloathed & uncloathed them; in a word, did all ye homly & necessarie offices for them wch dainty & quesie stomacks cannot endure to hear named; and all this willingly & cherfully, without any grudging in ye least, shewing herein their true love unto their freinds & bretheren. A rare example & worthy to be remembered. Tow of these 7. were Mr. William Brewster, ther reverend Elder, & Myles Standish, ther Captein & military comander, unto whom my selfe, & many others, were much beholden in our low & sicke condition. And yet the Lord so upheld these persons, as in this generall calamity they were not at all infected either with sicknes, or lamnes. And what I have said of these, I may say of many others who dyed in this generall vissitation, & others yet living, that whilst they had health, yea, or any strength continuing, they were not wanting to any that had need of them. And I doute not but their recompence is with ye Lord.

But I may not hear pass by an other remarkable passage not to be forgotten. As this calamitie fell among ye passengers that were to be left here to plant, and were hasted a shore and made to drinke water, that ye sea-men might have ye more bear, and one in his sicknes desiring but a small cann of beere, it was answered, that if he were their owne father he should have none; the disease begane to fall amongst them also, so as allmost halfe of their company dyed before they went away, and many of their officers and lustyest men, as ye boatson, gunner, 3. quarter-maisters, the cooke, & others. At wch ye m^{r} was something strucken and sent to ye sick a shore and tould ye Govr he should send for beer for them that had need of it, though he drunke water homward bound. But now amongst his company ther was farr another kind of carriage in this miserie then amongst ye passengers; for they that before had been boone companions in drinking and joyllity in ye time of their health and wellfare, begane now to deserte one another in this calamitie, saing they would not hasard ther lives for them, they should be infected by coming to help them in their cabins, and so, after they came to dye by it, would doe litle or nothing for them, but if they dyed let them dye. But shuch of ye passengers as were yet abord shewed them what mercy they could, wch made some of their harts relente, as ye boatson (& some others), who was a prowd yonge man, and would often curse and scofe at ye passengers; but when he grew weak, they had compassion on him and helped him; then he confessed he did not deserve it at their hands, he had abused them in word & deed. O! saith he, you, I now see, shew your love like Christians indeed one to another, but we let one another lye & dye like doggs. Another lay cursing his wife, saing if it had not ben for her he had never come this unlucky viage, and anone cursing his felows, saing he had done this & that, for some of them, he had spente so much, & so much, amongst them, and they were now weary of him, and did not help him, having need. Another gave his companion all he had, if he died, to help him in his weaknes; he went and got a litle spise & made him a mess of meat once or twise, and because he dyed not so soone as he expected, he went amongst his fellows, & swore ye rogue would cousen him, he would see him choaked before he made him any more meate; and yet ye pore fellow dyed before morning.

All this while ye Indians came skulking about them, and would sometimes show them selves aloofe of, but when any aproached near them, they would rune away. And once they stoale away their tools wher they had been at worke, & were gone to diner. But about ye 16. *of March,* a certaine Indian came bouldly amongst them, and spoke to them in broken English, which they could well understand, but marvelled at it. At length they understood by discourse with him, that he was not of these parts, but belonged to ye eastrene parts, wher some English-ships came to fhish, with whom he was aquainted, & could name sundrie of them by their names, amongst whom he had gott his language. He became profitable to them in aquainting them with many things concerning ye state of ye cuntry in ye east-parts wher he lived, which was afterwards profitable unto them; as also of ye people hear, of their names, number, & strength; of their situation & distance from this place, and who was cheefe amongst them. His name was *Samaset;* he tould them also of another Indian whos name was *Squanto,* a native of this place, who had been in England & could speake better English then him selfe. Being, after some time of entertainmente & gifts, dismist, a while after he came againe, & 5. more with him, & they brought againe all ye tooles that were stolen away before, and made way for ye coming of their great Sachem, called Massasoyt; who, about 4. *or* 5. *days after,* came with the cheefe of his freinds & other attendance, with the aforesaid *Squanto.* With whom, after frendly entertainment, & some gifts given him, they made a peace with him (which hath now continued this 24. years) in these terms.

1. That neither he nor any of his, should injurie or doe hurte to any of their peopl.

2. That if any of his did any hurte to any of theirs, he should send ye offender, that they might punish him.

3. That if any thing were taken away from any of theirs, he should cause it to be restored; and they should doe ye like to his.

4. If any did unjustly warr against him, they would aide him; if any did warr against them, he should aide them.

5. He should send to his neighbours confederats, to certifie them of this, that they might not wrong them, but might be likewise comprised in ye conditions of peace.

6. That when ther men came to them, they should leave their bows & arrows behind them.

After these things he returned to his place caled *Sowams,* some 40. mile from this place, but *Squanto* continued with them, and was their interpreter, and was a spetiall instrument sent of God for their good beyond their expectation. He directed them how to set their corne, wher to take fish, and to procure other comodities, and was also their pilott to bring them to unknowne places for their profitt, and never left them till he dyed. He was a *native of this place,* & scarce any left alive besids him selfe. He was caried away with diverce others by one Hunt, a m^r of a ship, who thought to sell them for slaves in Spaine; but he got away for England, and was entertained by a marchante in London, & imployed to New-foundland & other parts, & lastly brought hither into these parts by one Mr. *Dermer,* a gentle-man imployed by Sr. Ferdinando Gorges & others, for discovery, & other designes in these parts. Of whom I shall say some thing, because it is mentioned in a booke set forth An°: 1622. by ye Presidente & Counsell for New-England, that he made ye peace betweene ye salvages of these parts & ye English; of which this plantation, as it is intimated, had ye benefite. But what a peace it was, may apeare by what befell him & his men. . . .

Anno. 1621

They now begane to dispatch ye ship away which brought them over, which lay tille aboute this time, or ye begining of Aprill. The reason on their parts why she stayed so long, was ye necessitie and danger that lay upon them, for it was well towards ye ende of Desember before she could land any thing hear, or they able to receive any thing ashore. Afterwards, ye 14. of Jan: the house which they had made for a generall randevoze by casulty fell afire, and some were faine to retire abord for shilter. Then the sicknes begane to fall sore amongst them, and ye weather so bad as they could not make much sooner any dispatch. Againe, the Govr & cheefe of them, seeing so many dye, and fall downe sick dayly, thought it no wisdom to send away the ship, their condition considered, and ye danger they stood in from ye Indians, till they could procure some shelter; and therfore thought it better to draw some more charge upon them selves & freinds, then hazard all. The m^r and sea-men like-wise, though before they hasted ye passengers a shore to be goone, now many of their men being dead, & of ye ablest of them, (as is before noted,) and of ye rest many lay sick & weake, ye m^r durst not put to sea, till he saw his men begine to recover, and ye hart of winter over.

Afterwards they (as many as were able) began to plant ther corne, in which servise Squanto stood them in great stead, showing them both ye maner how to set it, and after how to dress & tend it. Also he tould them excepte they gott fish & set with it (in these old grounds) it would come to nothing, and he showed them y^t in ye midle of Aprill they should have store enough come up ye brooke, by which they begane to build, and taught them how to take it, and wher to get other provissions necessary for them; all which they found true by triall & experience. Some English seed they sew, as wheat & pease, but it came not to good, eather by ye badnes of ye seed, or latenes of ye season, or both, or some other defecte.

In this month of *Aprill* whilst they were bussie about their seed, their Govr (M^r. John Carver) came out of ye feild very sick, it being a hott day; he complained greatly of his head, and lay downe, and within a few howers his sences failed, so as he never spake more till he dyed, which was within a few days after. Whoss death was much lamented, and caused great heavines amongst them, as ther was cause. He was buried in ye best maner they could, with some vollies of shott by all that bore armes; and his wife, being a weak woman, dyed within 5. or 6. weeks after him.

Shortly after William Bradford was chosen Gove^r in his stead, and being not yet recoverd of his ilnes, in which he had been near ye point of death, Isaak Allerton was chosen to be an Asistante unto him, who, by renewed election every year, continued sundry years togeather, which I hear note once for all.

JOHN COTTON
It Is Necessary Therefore, That All Power That Is on Earth Be Limited

For all that the Massachusetts Bay Colony was a theocracy, and intolerant of free speech or freedom of worship in any modern sense of the words, there was implicit in seventeenth-century New England Puritanism certain concepts of individual liberty and sovereignty that, when the issues that produced the American Revolution caused such concepts to be translated into political terms, helped to produce the Boston Tea Party and Bunker Hill. In this excerpt from "Limitation of Government," a sermon by John Cotton (1584–1652), leader of the Boston church, one catches a hint of sentiments which a century later John Adams himself might have expressed in opposition to King George III and his ministers—a development which, it should be added at once, would doubtless have horrified John Cotton if he could have foreseen the political and social implications. For it was John Cotton whose autocratic views on liberty of worship inspired Roger Williams' The Bloudy Tenent of Persecution. *Two centuries later, a descendant of these Puritans, Nathaniel Hawthorne, would conduct a searching fictional investigation into the moral and social premises of the theocratic society of his ancestors, and throughout the nineteenth and twentieth centuries the continuing impact of puritanism upon the American mind and heart would reflect itself in the work of numerous writers.*

This may serve to teach us the danger of allowing to any mortall man an inordinate measure of power to speak great things, to allow to any man uncontrollableness of speech, you see the desperate danger of it: Let all the world learn to give mortall men no greater power then they are content they shall use, for use it they will: and unlesse they be better taught of God, they will use it ever and anon, it may be make it the passage of their proceeding to speake what they will: And they that have liberty to speak great things, you will finde it to be true, they will speak great blasphemies. No man would think what desperate deceit and wickednesse there is in the hearts of men: And that was the reason why the Beast did speak such great things, hee might speak, and no body might controll him: What, saith the Lord in *Jer.* 3. 5. *Thou hast spoken and done evill things as thou couldst.* If a Church or head of a Church could have done worse, he would have done it: This is one of the straines of nature, it affects boundlesse liberty, and to runne to the utmost extent: What ever power he hath received, he hath a corrupt nature that will

FROM "Limitations of Government," by John Cotton, in *The Puritans*, ed. Perry Miller and Thomas H. Johnson (New York: American Book, 1938), pp. 212–14.

improve it in one thing or other; if he have liberty, he will think why may he not use it. Set up the Pope as Lord Paramount over Kings and Princes, and they shall know that he hath power over them, he will take liberty to depose one, and set up another. Give him power to make Laws, and he will approve, and disprove as he list; what he approves is Canonicall, what hee disproves is rejected: Give him that power, and he will so order it at length, he will make such a State of Religion, that he that so lives and dyes shall never be saved, and all this springs from the vast power that is given to him, and from the deep depravation of nature. Hee will open his mouth, *His tongue is his owne, who is Lord over him,* Psal. 12. 3, 4. It is therefore most wholsome for Magistrates and Officers in Church and Common-wealth, never to affect more liberty and authority then will do them good, and the People good; for what ever transcendant power is given, will certainly over-run those that give it, and those that receive it: There is a straine in a mans heart that will sometime or other runne out to excesse, unlesse the Lord restraine it, but it is not good to venture it: It is necessary therefore, that all power that is on earth be limited, Church-power or other: If there be power given to speak great things, then look for great blasphemies, look for a licentious abuse of it. It is counted a matter of danger to the State to limit Prerogatives; but it is a further danger, not to have them limited: They will be like a Tempest, if they be not limited: A Prince himselfe cannot tell where hee will confine himselfe, nor can the people tell: But if he have liberty to speak great things, then he will make and unmake, say and unsay, and undertake such things as are neither for his owne honour, nor for the safety of the State. It is therefore fit for every man to be studious of the bounds which the Lord hath set: and for the People, in whom fundamentally all power lyes, to give as much power as God in his word gives to men: And it is meet that Magistrates in the Commonwealth, and so Officers in Churches should desire to know the utmost bounds of their own power, and it is safe for both: All intrenchment upon the bounds which God hath not given, they are not enlargements, but burdens and snares; They will certainly lead the spirit of a man out of his way sooner or later. It is wholsome and safe to be dealt withall as God deales with the vast Sea; *Hitherto shalt thou come, but there shalt thou stay thy proud waves:* and therefore if they be but banks of simple sand, they will be good enough to check the vast roaring Sea. And so for Imperiall Monarchies, it is safe to know how far their power extends; and then if it be but banks of sand, which is most slippery, it will serve, as well as any brazen wall. If you pinch the Sea of its liberty, though it be walls of stone or brasse, it will beate them downe: So it is with Magistrates, stint them where God hath not stinted them, and if they were walls of brasse, they would beate them downe, and it is meet they should: but give them the liberty God allows, and if it be but a wall of sand it will keep them: As this liquid Ayre in which we breath, God hath set it for the waters of the Clouds to the Earth; It is a Firmament, it is the Clouds, yet it stands firme enough, because it keeps the Climate where they are, it shall stand like walls of brasse:

So let there be due bounds set, and I may apply it to Families; it is good for
the Wife to acknowledg all power and authority to the Husband, and for the
Husband to acknowledg honour to the Wife, but still give them that which
God hath given them, and no more nor lesse: Give them the full latitude that
God hath given, else you will finde you dig pits, and lay snares, and cumber
their spirits, if you give them lesse: there is never peace where full liberty is
not given, nor never stable peace where more then full liberty is granted: Let
them be duely observed, and give men no more liberty then God doth, nor
women, for they will abuse it: The Devill will draw them, and Gods providence leade them thereunto, therefore give them no more then God gives. And
so for children; and servants, or any others you are to deale with, give them
the liberty and authority you would have them use, and beyond that stretch
not the tether, it will not tend to their good nor yours: And also from hence
gather, and goe home with this meditation; That certainly here is this dis-
temper in our natures, that we cannot tell how to use liberty, but wee shall
very readily corrupt our selves: Oh the bottomlesse depth of sandy earth! of a
corrupt spirit, that breaks over all bounds, and loves inordinate vastnesse; that
is it we ought to be carefull of.

ROBERT HORNE (?)
Worshipping God After Their Own Way

*Unlike Puritan New England, the Southern colonies founded by Englishmen
in the New World were in no sense theocratic; though there was an Established Church, religious freedom was generally practiced and even, in the List
of Privileges for the Carolina Colony, made into a cornerstone of government.
Several years after this "Brief Description of the Province of Carolina" was
written, the Lords Proprietors of the Carolina Colony issued (1669) a Fundamental Constitution, written by John Locke for his patron Sir Anthony Ashley
Cooper, in which religious freedom was guaranteed.*

The chief of the Privileges are as follows

First, There is full and free Liberty of Conscience granted to all, so that
no man is to be molested or called in question for matters of Religious Concern; but every one to be obedient to the Civil Government, worshipping God
after their own way.

Secondly, There is freedom from Custom, for all Wine, Silk, Raisins, Cur-

---

FROM "A Brief Description of the Province of Carolina," by Robert Horne (?), 1666; in *Historical
Collections of South Carolina,* comp. by B. R. Carroll (New York: Harper and Bros.), 1836,
Vol. II, pp. 15–18.

rance, Oyl, Olives, and Almonds, that shall be raised in the Province for 7. years, after 4 Ton of any of those commodities shall be imported in one Bottom.

Thirdly, Every Free-man and Free-woman that transport themselves and Servants by the 25 of March next, being 1667. shall have for Himself, Wife, Children, and Men-servants, for each 100 Acres of Land for him and his Heirs for ever, and for every Woman-servant and Slave 50 Acres, paying at most ½d. per acre, *per annum,* in lieu of all demands, to the Lords Proprietors: Provided always, That every Man be armed with a good Musquet full bore, 10l. Powder, and 20l. of Bullet, and six Months Provision for all, to serve them whilst they raise Provision in that Countrey.

Fourthly, Every Man-Servant at the expiration of their time, is to have of the Country a 100 Acres of Land to him and his heirs for ever, paying only ½d. per Acre, *per annum,* and the Women 50. Acres of Land on the same conditions; their Masters also are to allow them two Suits of Apparrel and Tools such as he is best able to work with, according to the Custom of the Countrey.

Fifthly, They are to have a Governour and Council appointed from among themselves, to see the Laws of the Assembly put in due execution; but the Governour is to rule but 3 years, and then learn to obey; also he hath no power to lay any Tax, or make or abrogate any Law, without the Consent of the Colony in their Assembly.

Sixthly, They are to choose annually from among themselves, a certain Number of Men, according to their divisions, which constitute the General Assembly with the Governour and his Council, and have the sole power of Making Laws, and Laying Taxes for the common good when need shall require.

These are the chief and Fundamental privileges, but the Right Honourable Lords Proprietors have promised (and it is their Interest so to do) to be ready to grant what other Privileges may be found advantageous for the good, of the Colony.

Is there therefore any younger Brother who is born of Gentile blood, and whose Spirit is elevated above the common sort, and yet the hard usage of our Country hath not allowed suitable fortune; he will not surely be afraid to leave his Native Soil to advance his Fortunes equal to his Blood and Spirit, and so he will avoid those unlawful ways too many of our young Gentlemen take to maintain themselves according to their high education, having but small Estates; here, with a few Servants and a small Stock a great Estate may be raised, although his Birth have not entituled him to any of the Land of his Ancestors, yet his Industry may supply him so, as to make him the head of as famous a family.

Such as are here tormented with much care how to get worth to gain a Livelyhood, or that with their labour can hardly get a comfortable subsistance, shall do well to go to this place, where any man what-ever, that is but willing to take moderate pains, may be assured of a most comfortable subsistance, and be in a way to raise his fortunes far beyond what he could ever hope for in England. Let no man be troubled at the thoughts of being a Servant for 4 or 5 year, for I can assure you, that many men give mony with their children to serve 7 years, to take more pains and fare nothing so well as the Servants in this Plantation will do. Then it is to be considered, that so soon as he is out of his time, he hath Land, and Tools, and Clothes given him; and is in a way of advancement. Therefore all Artificers, as Carpenters, Wheelrights, Joyners, Coopers, Bricklayers, Smiths, or diligent Husbandmen and Labourers, that are willing to advance their fortunes, and live in a most pleasant healthful and fruitful Country, where Artificers are of high esteem, and used with all Civility and Courtesie imaginable, may take notice, that

There is an opportunity offers now by the Virginia Fleet, from whence Cape Feare is but 3 or 4 days sail, and then a small Stock carried to Virginia will purchase provisions at a far easier rate than to carry them from hence; also the freight of the said Provisions will be saved, and be more fresh, and there wanteth not conveyance from Virginia thither.

If any Maid or single Woman have a desire to go over, they will think themselves in the Golden Age, when Men paid a Dowry for their Wives; for if they be but Civil, and under 50 years of Age, some honest Man or other, will purchase them for their Wives.

Those that desire further advice, or Servants that would be entertained, let them repair to Mr. Matthew Wilkinson, Ironmonger, at the Sign of the Three Feathers, in Bishopsgate-Street, where they may be informed when the Ships will be ready, and what they must carry with them.

COLONEL WILLIAM BYRD
A People That Are Contented with Nature as They Find Her

In the new world the colonists found a previous inhabitant: the Red Man, and for the next several centuries the confrontation continued. Here Colonel William Byrd of Virginia (1674–1744), on an expedition into western North Carolina, interviews an Indian about his religious beliefs. Byrd, a planter, belle-lettrist, scientist, member of the Royal Society, had a library of more than 4,000 volumes in his estate at Westover on the James River. Commissioned to survey the boundary between Virginia and North Carolina, Byrd found much to amuse and much to astound him in the customs and habits of the whites and

FROM *The Writings of 'Colonel William Byrd of Westover in Virginia Esq'.*, ed. J. S. Bassett (New York: Doubleday, Page and Co.), 1901. pp. 139–43.

the Indians along the border. He recorded his views in a narrative, History of the Dividing Line, *which was found among his manuscripts and first published in 1841. The wilderness experience of Byrd and other Americans, and their confrontation with the Red Man, was to be profoundly reflected in American literature in the nineteenth and twentieth centuries, in the work of such writers as James Fenimore Cooper, William Gilmore Simms, William Faulkner, and Robert Penn Warren.*

1728, Oct. 13. This being Sunday, we rested for our Fatigue, and had leisure to reflect on the signal Mercies of Providence.

The great Plenty of Meat wherewith Bearskin furnisht us in these lonely Woods made us once more Shorten the men's allowance of Bread, from 5 to 4 Pounds of bisket a week. This was the more necessary, because we knew not yet how long our Business might require us to be out.

In the Afternoon our Hunters went forth, and return'd triumphantly with three brace of wild Turkeys. They told us they cou'd see the Mountains distinctly from every Eminence, tho' the Atmosphere was so thick with Smoak that they appear'd at a greater Distance than they really were.

In the Evening we examin'd our Friend Bearskin, concerning the Religion of his Country, and he explain'd it to us, without any of that Reserve to which his Nation is Subject.

He told us he believ'd there was one Supreme God, who had Several Subaltern Deities under Him. And that this Master-God made the World a long time ago. That he told the Sun, the Moon, and Stars, their Business in the Beginning, which they, with good looking after, have faithfully perform'd ever Since.

That the same Power that made all things at first has taken care to keep them in the same Method and Motion ever since.

He believ'd God had form'd many Worlds before he form'd this, but that those Worlds either grew old and ruinous, or were destroyed for the Dishonesty of the Inhabitants.

That God is very just and very good—ever well pleas'd with those men who possess those God-like Qualities. That he takes good People into his safe Protection, makes them very rich, fills their Bellies plentifully, preserves them from sickness, and from being surpriz'd or Overcome by their Enemies.

But all such as tell Lies, and Cheat those they have Dealings with, he never fails to punish with Sickness, Poverty and Hunger, and, after all that, Suffers them to be knockt on the Head and scalpt by those that fight against them.

He believ'd that after Death both good and bad People are conducted by a strong Guard into a great Road, in which departed Souls travel together for some time, till at a certain Distance this Road forks into two Paths, the one extremely Levil, and the other Stony and Mountainous.

Here the good are parted from the Bad by a flash of Lightening, the first being hurry'd away to the Right, the other to the Left. The Right hand Road leads to a charming warm Country, where the Spring is everlasting, and every Month is May; and as the year is always in its Youth, so are the People, and particularly the Women are bright as Stars, and never Scold.

That in this happy Climate there are Deer, Turkeys, Elks, and Buffaloes innumerable, perpetually fat and gentle, while the Trees are loaded with delicious Fruit quite throughout the four Seasons.

That the Soil brings forth Corn Spontaneously, without the Curse of Labour, and so very wholesome, that None who have the happiness to eat of it are ever Sick, grow old, or dy.

Near the Entrance into this Blessed Land Sits a Venerable Old Man on a Mat richly woven, who examins Strictly all that are brought before Him, and if they have behav'd well, the Guards are order'd to open the Crystal Gate, and let them enter into the Land of Delights.

The left Hand Path is very rugged and uneaven, leading to a dark and barren Country, where it is always Winter. The Ground is the whole year round cover'd with Snow, and nothing is to be seen upon the Trees but Icicles.

All the People are hungry, yet have not a Morsel of any thing to eat, except a bitter kind of Potato, that gives them the Dry-Gripes, and fills their whole Body with loathsome Ulcers, that Stink, and are insupportably painfull.

Here all the Women are old and ugly, having Claws like a Panther, with which they fly upon the Men that Slight their Passion. For it seems these haggard old Furies are intolerably fond, and expect a vast deal of Cherishing. They talk much and exceedingly Shrill, giving exquisite Pain to the Drum of the Ear, which in that Place of the Torment is so tender, that every Sharp Note wounds it to the Quick.

At the End of this Path sits a dreadful old Woman on a monstrous Toad-Stool, whose head is cover'd with Rattle-Snakes instead of Tresses, with glaring white Eyes, that strike a Terror unspeakable into all that behold her.

This Hag pronounces Sentence of Woe upon all the miserable Wretches that hold up their hands at her Tribunal. After this they are deliver'd over to huge Turkey-Buzzards, like harpys, that fly away with them to the Place above mentioned.

Here, after they have been tormented a certain Number of years, according to their several Degrees of Guilt, they are again driven back into this World, to try if they will mend their Manners, and merit a place the next time in the Regions of Bliss.

This was the Substance of Bearskin's Religion, and was as much to the purpose as cou'd be expected from a meer State of Nature, without one Glimpse of Revelation or Philosophy.

It contain'd, however, the three Great Articles of Natural Religion: The

Belief of a God; The Moral Distinction betwixt Good and Evil; and the Expectation of Rewards and Punishments in Another World.

Indeed, the Indian Notion of a Future Happiness is a little Gross and Sensual, like Mahomet's Paradise. But how can it be otherwise, in a People that are contented with Nature as they find Her, and have no other Lights but what they receive from purblind Tradition? . . .

3

GOD AND MAN
IN
COLONIAL AMERICA

The seventeenth century was a religious century, and not one of the new settlements along the Atlantic coast, no matter how materialistic its principal concerns, was founded without the church playing an important role in its civic life. The avowed intention of the founders of New England was to establish a theocracy, a community of the faithful who would proceed to create God's city upon a hill. But as settlements expanded, farmers pushed their way westward into the back-country, seaboard towns built up a thriving commerce, and material prosperity became the abundant reward of the labors of the Elect. Things of this world grew increasingly important, and community life became more and more secular in its principal manifestations. Meanwhile the intellectual and religious ideas of the Old World in the eighteenth century made their way across the ocean, and the rationalistic deism of a Newtonian universe soon clashed sharply with the Calvinistic doctrine of the innate depravity of man upon which the Massachusetts Bay Colony had been established.

Dissent had risen early within the Puritan Commonwealth itself; nearby Rhode Island was settled by men who refused to bow to the theocratic leadership of Boston. Later as Boston itself grew increasingly more prosperous and its religion became more formalized, the Congregational Church tended to become Unitarian in its theology. Thus the religious revivalism of eighteenth-century England among the working classes

35

posed new trouble when it reached New England, as it soon did. In western Massachusetts Jonathan Edwards exhorted his parishioners to return to the old Calvinist enthusiasm, and the evangelicism of the Awakening was much disliked and distrusted in respectable Boston.

The Great Awakening, as it was termed, spread throughout the colonies, especially in the back-country and the laboring districts of the seaport cities. There was consequent resentment of the Established Anglican Church, and of the taxes levied for its support. There was also much activity among Quakers, especially in Pennsylvania. Meanwhile the intellectual elite of the colonies was turning increasingly toward the rationalistic tenets of eighteenth-century deism.

The selections that follow illustrate some of the varieties of religious experience and expression in the years before the American Revolution.

JOHN WINTHROP
He Saw They Must Be Sent Away

When Anne Hutchinson, a gentlewoman of kindliness and forceful character, emigrated to Boston with her husband in 1634, she soon began asserting controversial doctrines, claiming that the Christian who was justified by faith and whose sins were redeemed by Christ need not give his allegiance to the State— not even the Puritan State modeled along Old Testament lines. Her views struck at the heart of the Puritan theocracy, and despite the support of powerful friends, she was tried for her beliefs and banished from the colony. Governor John Winthrop of Massachusetts (1588-1649), who took the lead in the trial and banishment, records the events in his Journal *for the years 1637-1638. No doubt Nathaniel Hawthorne was mindful of such problems when he created his great protagonist Hester Prynne in* The Scarlet Letter.

There was great hope that the late general assembly would have had some good effect in pacifying the troubles and dissensions about matters of religion; but it fell out otherwise. For though Mr. Wheelwright and those of his party had been clearly confuted and confounded in the assembly, yet they persisted in their opinions, and were as busy in nourishing contents (the principal of them) as before. Whereupon the general court, being assembled in the 2 of the 9th month, and finding, upon consultation, that two so opposite parties

FROM John Winthrop, *The History of New England from 1630 to 1649,* ed. James Savage (Boston: Little, Brown and Co., 1853), pp. 291–92, 294–95, 299, 300–01, 306–07, 309–11.

could not contain in the same body, without apparent hazard of ruin to the whole, agreed to send away some of the principal; . . .

Then the court sent for Mr. Wheelwright, and, he persisting to justify his sermon, and his whole practice and opinions, and refusing to leave either the place or his public exercisings, he was disfranchised and banished. Upon which he appealed to the king, but neither called witnesses, nor desired any act to be made of it. The court told him, that an appeal did not lie; for by the king's grant we had power to hear and determine without any reservation, etc. So he relinquished his appeal, and the court gave him leave to go to his house, upon his promise, that, if he were not gone out of our jurisdiction within fourteen days, he would render himself to one of the magistrates.

The court also sent for Mrs. Hutchinson, and charged her with divers matters, as her keeping two public lectures every week in her house, whereto sixty or eighty persons did usually resort, and for reproaching most of the ministers (viz., all except Mr. Cotton) for not preaching a covenant of free grace, and that they had not the seal of the spirit, nor were able ministers of the New Testament; which were clearly proved against her, though she sought to shift it off. And, after many speeches to and fro, at last she was so full as she could not contain, but vented her revelations; amongst which this was one, that she had it revealed to her, that she should come into New England, and should here be persecuted, and that God would ruin us and our posterity, and the whole state, for the same. So the court proceeded and banished her; but, because it was winter, they committed her to a private house, where she was well provided, and her own friends and the elders permitted to go to her, but none else. . . .

After this, many of the church of Boston, being highly offended with the governor for this proceeding, were earnest with the elders to have him called to account for it; but they were not forward in it, and himself, understanding their intent, thought fit to prevent such a public disorder, and so took occasion to speak to the congregation to this effect:—

. . . He did nothing in the cases of the brethren, but by the advice and direction of our teacher and other of the elders. For in the oath, which was administered to him and the rest, etc., there was inserted, by his advice, this clause,—In all causes wherein you are to give your vote, etc., you are to give your vote as in your judgment and conscience you shall see to be most for the public good, etc.; and so for his part he was persuaded, that it would be most for the glory of God, and the public good, to pass sentence as they did.

He would give them one reason, which was a ground for his judgment, and that was, for that he saw, that those brethren, etc., were so divided from the rest of the country in their judgment and practice, as it could not stand with the public peace, that they should continue amongst us. So, by the example of Lot in Abraham's family, and after Hagar and Ishmael, he saw they must be sent away. . . .

While Mrs. Hutchinson continued at Roxbury, divers of the elders and others resorted to her, and finding her to persist in maintaining those gross errors beforementioned, and many others, to the number of thirty or thereabout, some of them wrote to the church at Boston, offering to make proof of the same before the church, etc., 15; whereupon she was called, (the magistrates being desired to give her license to come), and the lecture was appointed to begin at ten. . . . When she appeared, the errors were read to her. . . . These were also clearly confuted, but yet she held her own; so as the church (all but two of her sons) agreed she should be admonished, and because her sons would not agree to it, they were admonished also.

Mr. Cotton pronounced the sentence of admonition with great solemnity, and with much zeal and detestation of her errors and pride of spirit. The assembly continued till eight at night, and all did acknowledge the special presence of God's spirit therein; and she was appointed to appear again the next lecture day. . . .

Mrs. Hutchinson appeared again; (she had been licensed by the court, in regard she had given hope of her repentance, to be at Mr. Cotton's house, that both he and Mr. Davenport might have the more opportunity to deal with her;) and the articles being again read to her, and her answer required, she delivered it in writing, wherein she made a retractation of near all, but with such explanations and circumstances as gave no satisfaction to the church; so as she was required to speak further to them. Then she declared, that it was just with God to leave her to herself, as he had done, for her slighting his ordinances, both magistracy and ministry; and confessed that what she had spoken against the magistrates at the court (by way of revelation) was rash and ungrounded; and desired the church to pray for her. This gave the church good hope of her repentance; but when she was examined about some particulars, as that she had denied inherent righteousness, etc., she affirmed that it was never her judgment; and though it was proved by many testimonies, that she had been of that judgment, and so had persisted, and maintained it by argument against divers, yet she impudently persisted in her affirmation, to the astonishment of all the assembly. So that, after much time and many arguments had been spent to bring her to see her sin, but all in vain, the church, with one consent, cast her out. Some moved to have her admonished once more; but, it being for manifest evil in matter of conversation, it was agreed otherwise; and for that reason also the sentence was denounced by the pastor, matter of manners belonging properly to his place.

After she was excommunicated, her spirits, which seemed before to be somewhat dejected, revived again, and she gloried in her sufferings, saying, that it was the greatest happiness, next to Christ, that ever befel her. Indeed, it was a happy day to the churches of Christ here, and to many poor souls, who had been seduced by her, who, by what they heard and saw that day, were (through the grace of God) brought off quite from her errors, and settled again in the truth. . . .

JONATHAN EDWARDS
Thy Wickedness Seems Good to Thee

Jonathan Edwards (1703–58) is best known as the New World's first great revivalist preacher. Sermons such as "Sinners in the Hands of an Angry God" and "The Future Punishment of the Wicked," part of which is reproduced below, sent fear of eternal punishment into the hearts of eighteenth-century New Englanders, for whom the ease and comfort of the secular commonwealth had long since come to replace the rigors of theocratic Calvinism. Edwards' preachings in the Great Awakening so stirred up his congregation that when a reaction against his emotionalism set in, he was deposed from his church and sent to a frontier post to work among the Indians. Late in his life he was called to be president of the college that is now Princeton University, but he died shortly afterward.

To modern readers what is most striking about Edwards is the way in which he infused the growing rationalism and scientific empiricism of the eighteenth century with the throbbing, vital emotional fervor of the imma- nence of the divine presence. Edwards' adaptation of Lockean sensationalism made little impact on the thinking of eighteenth-century Boston, which grew more rationalistic and Unitarian as the century progressed. But New England Transcendentalists of the nineteenth century could recognize in Edwards the same vibrant idealism that made Emerson and Thoreau find spirit in matter and soul in the rocks and trees of nature, for all that Edwards' own orthodox Calvinism had kept much pantheistic thinking rigorously in check.

Readers familiar with Robert Lowell's poem "Mr. Edwards and the Spider" will no doubt recognize numerous phrases used by Lowell in the excerpt from the sermon that follows. The evangelical fervor of an Edwards would likewise be profoundly reflected in the work of such twentieth-century authors as Flannery O'Connor.

. . . This subject may be applied in a use of awakening to impenitent sinners. What hath been said under this doctrine is for thee, O impenitent sinner, O poor wretch, who art in the same miserable state in which thou camest into the world, excepting that thou art loaded with vastly greater guilt by thine actual sins. These dreadful things which thou hast heard are for thee, who art yet unconverted, and still remainest an alien and stranger, without Christ and

FROM "The Future Punishment of the Wicked Unavoidable and Intolerable," Sermon X in *The Works of President Edwards in Eight Volumes* (London: James Black and Sons, 1817), Vol. VII, pp. 460–65.

without God in the world. They are for thee, who to this day remainest an enemy to God, and a child of the devil, even in this remarkable season, when others both here and elsewhere, far and near, are flocking to Christ; for thee who hearest the noise, the fame of these things, but knowest nothing of the power of godliness in thine own heart.

Whoever thou art, whether young or old, little or great, if thou art in a Christless, unconverted state, this is the wrath, this is the death to which thou art condemned. This is the wrath that abideth on thee; this is the hell over which thou hangest, and into which thou art ready to drop every day and every night.

If thou shalt remain blind, and hard, and dead in sin a little longer, this destruction will come upon thee: God hath spoken, and he will do it. It is vain for thee to flatter thyself with hopes that thou shalt avoid it, or to say in thine heart, perhaps it will not be; perhaps it will not be just so; perhaps things have been represented worse than they are. If thou wilt not be convinced by the word preached to thee by men in the name of God, God himself will undertake to convince thee. Ezek. xiv. 4, 7, 8.

Doth it seem to thee not real that thou shalt suffer such a dreadful destruction, because it seems to thee that thou dost not deserve it? And because thou dost not see any thing so horrid in thyself, as to answer such a dreadful punishment?—Why is it that thy wickedness doth not seem bad enough to deserve this punishment? The reason is, that thou lovest thy wickedness; thy wickedness seems good to thee; it appears lovely to thee; thou dost not see any hatefulness in it as to answer such misery.

But know, thou stupid, blind, hardened wretch, that God doth not see, as thou seest with thy polluted eyes: thy sins in his sight are infinitely abdominable.—Thou knowest that thou hast a thousand and a thousand times made light of the majesty of God. And why should not that majesty, which thou hast thus despised, be manifested in the greatness of thy punishment? Thou hast often heard what a great and dreadful God Jehovah is; but thou hast made so light of it, that thou hast not been afraid of him, thou hast not been afraid to sin against him, nor to go on day after day, by thy sins, to provoke him to wrath, nor to cast his commands under foot, and trample on them. Now why may not God, in the greatness of thy destruction, justly vindicate and manifest the greatness of that majesty, which thou hast despised?

Thou hast despised the mighty power of God; thou hast not been afraid of it. Now why is it not fit that God should show the greatness of his power in thy ruin. What king is there who will not show his authority in the punishment of those subjects that despise it! and who will not vindicate his royal majesty in executing vengeance on those that rise in rebellion? And art thou such a fool as to think that the great King of heaven and earth, before whom all other kings are so many grasshoppers, will not vindicate his kingly majesty on such contemptuous rebels as thou art? Thou art very much mistaken if thou thinkest so. If thou be regardless of God's Majesty, be it known to thee, God is not regardless of his own majesty; he taketh care of the honor of it, and he will vindicate it.

Think it not strange that God should deal so severely with thee, or that the wrath which thou shalt suffer should be so great. For as great as it is, it is no greater than that love of God which thou hast despised. The love of God, and his grace, condescension, and pity to sinners in sending his Son into the world to die for them, is every whit as great and wonderful as this inexpressible wrath. This mercy hath been held forth to thee, and described in its wonderful greatness hundreds of times, and as often hath it been offered to thee; but thou wouldst not accept Christ; thou wouldst not have this great love of God; thou despisedst God's dying love; thou trampledst the benefits of it under foot. Now why shouldst thou not have wrath as great as that love and mercy which thou despisest and rejectest? Doth it seem incredible to thee, that God should so harden his heart against a poor sinner, as so to destroy him, and to bear him down with infinite power and merciless wrath? And is this a greater thing than it is for thee to harden thy heart, as thou hast done, against infinite mercy, and against the dying love of God?

Doth it seem to thee incredible, that God should be so utterly regardless of the sinner's welfare, as so to sink him into an infinite abyss of misery? Is this shocking to thee? And is it not at all shocking to thee, that thou shouldst be so utterly regardless as thou hast been of the honour and glory of the infinite God?

It arises from thy foolish stupidity and senselessness, and is because thou hast a heart of stone, that thou art so senseless of thine own wickedness as to think thou hast not deserved such a punishment, and that it is to thee incredible that it will be inflicted upon thee. But if, when all is said and done, thou be not convinced, wait but a little while, and thou wilt be convinced: God will undertake to do the work which ministers cannot do. Though judgment against thine evil works be not yet executed, and God now let thee alone: yet he will soon come upon thee with his great power, and then thou shalt know what God is, and what thou art.

Flatter not thyself, that if these things shall prove true, and the worst shall come, thou wilt set thyself to bear it as well as thou canst. What will it signify to set thyself to bear, and to collect thy strength to support thyself, when thou shalt fall into the hands of that omnipotent King, Jehovah? He that made thee can make his sword approach unto thee. His sword is not the sword of man, nor is his wrath the wrath of man. If it were, possibly stoutness might be maintained under it. But it is the fierceness of the wrath of the great God, who is able to baffle and dissipate all thy strength in a moment. He can fill thy poor soul with an ocean of wrath, a deluge of fire and brimstone; or he can make it ten thousand times fuller of torment than ever an oven was full of fire; and at the same time, can fill it with despair of ever seeing any end to its torment, or any rest from its misery: and then where will be thy strength; what will become of thy courage then? what will signify thine attempts to bear?

What art thou in the hands of the great God, who made heaven and earth by speaking a word? What art thou, when dealt with by that strength, which manages all this vast universe, holds the globe of the earth, directs all the motions of the heavenly bodies from age to age, and, when the fixed time shall come, will shake all to pieces? There are other wicked beings a thousand times stronger than thou: there are the great leviathans, strong and proud spirits of gigantic stoutness and hardiness. But how little are they in the hands of the great God! they are less than weak infants; they are nothing, and less than nothing in the hands of an angry God, as will appear at the day of judgment. Their hearts will be broken; they will sink; they will have no strength nor courage left; they will be as weak as water; their souls will sink down into an infinite gloom, an abyss of death and despair. Then what will become of thee, a poor worm, when thou shalt fall into the hands of that God, when he shall come to show his wrath, and make his power known on thee?

If the strength of all the wicked men on earth, and of all the devils in hell, were united in one, and thou wert possessed of it all; and if the courage, greatness, and stoutness of all their hearts were united in thy single heart, thou wouldst be nothing in the hands of Jehovah. If it were all collected, and thou shouldst set thyself to bear as well as thou couldst, all would sink under his great wrath in an instant, and would be utterly abolished: thine hands would drop down at once and thine heart would melt as wax. The great mountains, the firm rocks, cannot stand before the power of God. He can tear the earth in pieces in a moment; yea, he can shatter the whole universe, and dash it to pieces at one blow. How then will thine hands be strong, or thine heart endure?

Thou canst not stand before a lion of the forest; an angry wild beast, if stirred up, will easily tear such a one as thou art in pieces. Yea not only so, but thou art crushed before the moth. A very little thing, a little worm or spider, or some such insect, is able to kill thee. What then canst thou do in the hands of God? It is vain to set the briers and thorns in battle array against glowing flames; the points of thorns, though sharp, do nothing to withstand the fire.

Some of you have seen buildings on fire; imagine therefore with yourselves, what a poor hand you would make at fighting with the flames, if you were in the midst of so great and fierce a fire. You have often seen a spider, or some other noisome insect, when thrown into the midst of a fierce fire, and have observed how immediately it yields to the force of the flames. There is no long struggle, no fighting against the fire, no strength exerted to oppose the heat, or to fly from it; but it immediately stretches forth itself and yields; and the fire takes possession of it, and at once it becomes full of fire, [and is burned into a bright coal]. Here is a little image of what you will be in hell, except you repent and fly to Christ. To encourage yourselves, that you will set yourselves to bear hell-torments as well as you can, is just as if a worm, that is about to be thrown into a glowing furnace, should swell and fortify itself, and prepare itself to fight the flames.

What can you do with lightnings? What doth it signify to fight with them? What an absurd figure would a poor weak man make, who in a thunder storm should expect a flash of lightning on his head or his breast, and should go forth sword in hand to oppose it; when a stream of brimstone would, in an instant, drink up all his spirits and his life, and melt his sword!

Consider these things, all you enemies of God, and rejecters of Christ, whether you be old men or women, Christless heads of families, or young people and wicked children. Be assured, that if you do not hearken and repent, God intends to show his wrath, and make his power known upon you. He intends to magnify himself exceedingly in sinking you down in hell. He intends to show his great majesty at the day of judgment, before a vast assembly, in your misery; before a greater assembly many thousandfold than ever yet appeared on earth; before a vast assembly of saints, and a vast assembly of wicked men, a vast assembly of holy angels, and before all the crew of devils. God will before all these get himself honor in your destruction; you shall be tormented in the presence of them all. Then all will see that God is a great God indeed; then all will see how dreadful a thing it is to sin against such a God, and to reject such a Saviour, such love and grace, as you have rejected and despised. All will be filled with awe at the great sight, and all the saints and angels will look upon you, and adore that majesty, and that mighty power, and that holiness and justice of God, which shall appear in your ineffable destruction and misery.

It is probable that here are some who hear me, are at this very moment unawakened, and are in a great degree careless about their souls. I fear there are some among us who are most fearfully hardened: their hearts are harder than the very rocks. It is easier to make impressions upon an adamant than upon their hearts. I suppose some of you have heard all that I have said with ease and quietness: it appears to you as great big sounding words, but doth not reach your hearts. You have heard such things many times: you [are old soldiers, and] have been too much used to the roaring of heaven's cannon, to be frightened at it. It will therefore probably be in vain for me to say anything further to you; I will only put you in mind that ere long God will deal with you. I cannot deal with you, you despise what I say; I have no power to make you sensible of your danger and misery, and of the dreadfulness of the wrath of God. The attempts of men in this way have often proved vain.

However, God hath undertaken to deal with such men as you are. It is his manner commonly first to let men try their utmost strength: particularly to let ministers try, that thus he may show ministers their own weakness and impotency; and when they have done what they can, and all fails, then God takes the matter into his own hands. So it seems by your obstinacy, as if God intended to undertake to deal with you. He will undertake to subdue you; he will see if he cannot cure you of your senselessness and regardlessness of his threatenings. And you will be convinced; you will be subdued effectually: your strength will be utterly broken, your courage and hope will sink. God will surely break those who will not bow.

Having girded himself with his power and wrath, he hath heretofore undertaken to deal with many hard, stubborn, senseless, obstinate hearts; and he never failed, he always did his work thoroughly.

It will not be long before you will be wonderfully changed. You who now hear of hell and the wrath of the great God, and sit here in these seats so easy and quiet, and go away so careless; by and by will shake, and tremble, and cry out, and shriek, and gnash your teeth, and will be thoroughly convinced of the vast weight and importance of these great things, which you now despise.

CHARLES CHAUNCY
We Were Made for Business

Jonathan Edwards' great antagonist in his dispute over the direction of eighteenth-century Calvinism in Massachusetts was the Rev. Charles Chauncy (1705–1787), pastor of the First Church of Boston and leader of the conservative theologians who opposed the emotionalism of the revival movement. Chauncy's sermon "Enthusiasm Described and Caution'd Against" (1742) expressed his entire distrust of the fervor and recklessness of the Great Awakening. In his later years Chauncy was one of the foremost advocates of American separation from Great Britain.

The sermon "The Idle-Poor Secluded from the Bread of Charity by the Christian Law" (1752) was preached before a society formed to promote industry in Massachusetts by establishing a linen manufacture. Much of it sounds peculiarly modern, in its inveighing against welfare schemes. Its conservative tenor, its implied belief in the importance of the material goods of this world are at a far remove from Edwards' intense spirituality; what Chauncy had to say was doubtless comforting to the respectable Boston society whose spokesman he was. In the nineteenth century young New England theologians and poets would protest strongly against the spirit of Boston Unitarianism as exemplified by Chauncy.

Some perhaps may think, that it ought to be interpreted universally, as extending to all, the Rich, as well as the Poor; insomuch that they ought neither of them to eat, if they will not work. But such an Interpretation does not fall in with the Design of the Apostle in this Place. For he is here speaking, not of those who are able, without Labour, to maintain themselves; but of poor

FROM "The Idle-Poor Secluded from the Bread of Charity by the Christian Law," by Charles Chauncy (Boston: Thomas Fleet, 1752). Reprinted in *Early American Sermons, 1729–1794*. California State Library, Sutro Branch, San Francisco, Occasional Papers Reprint Series No. 2 (1939), pp. 25–26, 28–32.

People, who, if they won't work, must have their Expectations of Relief from the Charities of others.

Not but that it is a shameful Thing for any to eat the Bread of Idleness. If Persons possess ever so great an Abundance, this gives them no Licence to be lazy. They may indeed reasonably exempt themselves from the lower and more servile Parts of Business: But still they ought not to be idle. Indulged habitual Idleness is a Reproach to any Man, whether he be high or low, rich or poor. We were made for Business. Both our Souls and Bodies are so constituted, as that Exercise is a great and necessary Means to keep them in an healthful and vigorous State; and without it we shall soon contract a strange Hebetude of Mind, as well as Inability of Body to all the Functions of Life. If the great and rich would but thoroughly realize this, it might happily tend to lessen their love of Ease, and put them upon Activity and Diligence in the Employment of their Time and Powers to some or other of the valuable Purposes of Life.

But the Rich, as I said, are not the Persons the Apostle has here to do with, but the Poor; whose Circumstances in the World are such as that, if they won't work, they have nothing to depend on but the Charities of their Friends and Neighbours. And it is with respect to this kind of Persons, in special, that the Apostle has commanded, if any will not work, neither should he eat. . . .

The positive Will of God has appointed Labour the Means in order to a Livelihood in the World. To this Purpose are those Words of the Almighty, which, tho' originally directed to Adam, are yet obligatory upon all his Posterity, Gen. 3. 19. In the Sweat of thy Face thou shalt eat Bread, till thou return to the Ground. As this Appointment of Heaven was published after the Fall of Man, and as a Punishment for Sin, it should seem as tho' humane Labour had but an ignoble Original. And so it had, if considered as to Kind and Degree: But as to the Thing itself, it was as truly the Requirement of God from Man in his innocent, as in his lapsed State. Even Adam in Paradise was not wholly provided with every Thing by the sole Bounty of Nature, but that it was necessary he should be employed in Labour. We therefore read, not only that he had Work to do in his innocent State, but what it was, namely, to dress and keep the Garden of Eden, Gen. 2. 15. If therefore Sin had not entered into the World, Men would not have lived without Labour; tho' it would have been of a nobler Kind, and in a less Degree. In these respects, Sin has made a difference. We must now sweat and toil. Nature calls for this Sort of Labour, and will not furnish us, upon any lower Terms, with such of her good Things as we stand in need of: And it is the express Will of God, that, in this Way, we should earn our Bread. Laborious Diligence is the Means by which he has ordained we should supply ourselves with Food, and other Necessaries of Life.

If any therefore indulge to Idleness, who have Ability for Labour, they virtually set aside the Method God has been pleased to direct to, and enjoin, in order to their being supported in Life. And is it reasonable they should be maintained in any other? Is it fit, if Men won't work, when they can, that a different Way, from what the Wisdom of God has instituted, should be taken for their Supply with Bread? And yet, by supporting the needy in Idleness, we constructively oppose the Appointment of God, and substitute a Method for their Maintenance of our own devising. And is this reasonable? Can it be justified? Ought Persons to be maintained in plain Contempt of the Constitution of God?

I am sensible, it has sometimes been pleaded, that, however it might be in former Days, the Cares of Religion now, in a great Measure, supersede the Affairs of the World; insomuch that if Men neglect their temporal Business, provided they do it that they may have Time to attend on the Spiritual Concerns of their Souls and another World, they ought to be considered and helped; and that it is a Christian Duty to support such pious Persons upon the Bread of Charity.

A specious Pretence this for Idleness, in contempt of the Government of God; but a very poor one; as being founded on intirely wrong Notions of the Christian Religion, which requires its Professors, not only to mind the Things of another World, but the Affairs of this also. And it is particularly observable, Christianity is so far from allowing Men to be slothful in the Business of their proper Callings, that it has reinforced the Law of Labour given to Adam, and in him to all Mankind, by adopting it into its Scheme of Morals. Says Paul, the Apostle of Jesus Christ, addressing himself to the Thessalonians, and in them to all Christians, We command and exhort, by our Lord Jesus Christ, that with Quietness they work, and eat their own Bread; as we read in the 12th v. of my Context. Very observable is the Manner, in which these Words are delivered, We command and exhort, by our Lord Jesus Christ. He does not satisfy himself with exhorting only; but he commands. And he does it by our Lord Jesus Christ, i.e. by his Authority, as commissioned, and empowered by him. So that whosoever, in this Article, despiseth, despiseth not Man, but God; for here the Contempt does finally terminate, as our Saviour himself has taught us, in Luke 10. 16. He that despiseth you, despiseth me; and he that despiseth me, despiseth him that sent me.

Industrious Labour is therefore the Law of Christianity. Instead of altering this Method appointed by God, from the Beginning, for the Support of Life, the Gospel has confirmed it. So that Idleness is a Reflection upon the governing Wisdom and Authority of God under the Christian, as well as former Dispensations. And to support Man in Sloth, tho' they should disguise their Guilt under the Cover of the most pious Pretences, is a virtual setting up our own Wisdom in opposition to the Wisdom of God, and subverting the Method he has established, both in the nature of Things, and by positive Revelation, for the supply of Mankind with the Necessaries and Conveniences of Life.

The Command, in my Text, is founded on the publick Good. For there cannot be a flourishing People, without Labour. It is by Improvement in Arts and Trade, that they must grow in Wealth, and Power, and become possessed of the various Emoluments tending to the Benefit and Pleasure of Life; and these Arts take their Rise from, and are carried on by, the Industry of particular Persons. And this is so evident, that while some Nations have increased in Riches, and Grandeur, and Power, by being industrious, tho' great Obstacles, and discouraging Difficulties have stood in the Way; others, thro' Sloth and Indolence, have been kept low, and sunk in Oblivion, tho' under great natural Advantages to have got into flourishing Circumstances: Or, it may be, they have become a Prey to other more active and enterprising Nations, who knew how to make a better Use of their Advantages. And the Truth is, the natural Advantages a People are favoured with, whether for Husbandry, Navigation, Fishery, Manufacturers, or any other Source of Wealth, will be, in a great Measure, lost, and, as it were, thrown away upon them, without Labour and Industry, in making a wise and good Use of them.

The Athenians were so sensible of this, that Idleness, in that State, subjected the guilty Person, whoever he was, to a Prosecution at Law, as an Injury to the Common-Wealth: And they made Inquiry of each Man and Woman, quà Arte se Alerent? By what Trade they supported themselves? And so long ago as the Days of Pharoah, it was taken for granted that a Man could not be without some Occupation, or other. Hence that Question of his to Joseph's Brethren, upon their coming into Egypt, Gen. 47. 3. What is your Occupation?

The Law, in my Text, is therefore connected with the publick Good; as it tends to encourage Industry, by restraining us from Distributions to the lazy and slothful. And it is indeed a great Hurt to a Community, when private Persons dispense their Charities to such, among the poor, as keep themselves so by an Indulgence to Idleness, while yet they are able to work. For the Public loses the whole Benefit of the Labour of those, who are thus supported in Idleness; and not only so, but is liable to suffer all the Inconveniences which are to be looked for, in Consequence of their indulging to Sloth and doing nothing.

And it is observable, the Apostle had it particularly in his View to guard against these public Inconveniences, when he gave the Command in my Text. Hence he adds, in the Words that immediately follow, giving the Reason, at least one Reason, of the Command, For we have heard, that there are some among you which walk disorderly, working not at all; but are Busy-bodies.

You observe, these Persons who did not work, and were the Occasion of the Command in the Text, were disorderly. And this, in a Sense, is always the Case. Whenever Persons are idle, they are disorderly: For an idle Life is, in the whole of it, a Disorder. It subverts the Order God has establish'd for the Support of Mankind, and would introduce another Method of Livelihood than that, infinite Wisdom has contrived and appointed.

Nor is this the only Sense in which idle Persons are disorderly. They are too often Tempters to others to neglect their Business. Having none of their own, and being inclined to none, they endeavour to find, or, if they can't do that, to make Persons as idle as themselves, to the great Detriment of the Public, and, many Times, the intire Ruin of their Companions in Sloth. And who are so much noted for the moral Disorders of Lying and Stealing, as those who have settled into an Habit of Laziness? Their Laziness reduces them to Straits and Difficulties; and these, as the readiest and easiest Way to supply their Wants, put them upon deceiving the kind and charitable by artfully invented Falsehoods, or else upon secretly robbing them of their Money, or their Goods. And who more given to Tipling than the Persons who have accustomed themselves to Idleness? The Drones in a Place are commonly the People who doze away their Time and Senses over their Cups. There are indeed no Disorders, but the idle are liable to them; and their Danger lies in their Idleness. Were they diligently employed in Business of one Kind or another, their Thoughts and Time would be properly taken up; but having settled into a Temper inclining them to sit idle and do nothing, they lie open to every Temptation, and are in danger of being betrayed into moral Disorders of every Kind.

And these idle Persons were not only disorderly, but Busy-bodies. We hear there are some who work not at all, but are Busy-bodies. This may seem an Inconsistency; but it is most commonly the Truth of the Case. None more ready to busy themselves in other Men's Matters, than those who neglect all Business of their own. Not minding their own Affairs, they have Leisure, and generally Inclination, to intrude into other Men's. Hence that Character of some, in the Apostolic Times, They learn to be idle; wandring about from House to House; and not only idle, but Tatlers also, and Busy-bodies, speaking Things which they ought not. I Tim. 5. 13. And none indeed are, usually, more free with their Tongues than idle Persons; none wander more about from House to House; none are more ready to meddle in Things which don't belong to them; acting in the Sphere of others, tho' they won't in their own. And I need not say that this intermeddling in other Men's Concerns, greatly tends to public Hurt; —for it kindles Contention, creates Feuds and Animosities; and is indeed a main Source of that Variance and Strife, which disturb the Peace of Society.

And is it any Wonder, when Idleness is connected with such Damage to the Public, which might be as much benefitted by Industry, that we should be restrained from supporting those who won't work, thro' Slothfulness of Disposition? It is certainly a most reasonable Restraint: And the Command that lays it, is so far from being hard and unjust, that it kindly and equitably consults the public Good. And it is an Honour to the Christian Religion, that it can boast, of this, and a great many other Commands, which, the more critically they are examined, the more wise and equitable they appear to be. . . .

JOHN WOOLMAN
I Believe Liberty Is Their Right

At a time when Negro slavery was largely taken for granted in the North as well as in the South, some of the strongest condemnation of the institution came from members of the Society of Friends. Quakers such as John Woodman (1720–1772) spoke out against the keeping of humans in bondage. Here Woolman describes a trip into the Southern colonies, and his discourses with slaveholding Quakers and others. In the century that followed, the moral and human problem of slavery was to occupy the attention of America's most important writers. In 1967 the year's outstanding novel, William Styron's The Confessions of Nat Turner, *would concern itself with the experience of Negro slavery.*

Feeling the exercise in relation to a visit to the Southern Provinces to increase upon me, I acquainted our Monthly Meeting therewith, and obtained their certificate. Expecting to go alone, one of my brothers who lived in Philadelphia, having some business in North Carolina, proposed going with me part of the way; but as he had a view of some outward affairs, to accept of him as a companion was some difficulty with me, whereupon I had conversation with him at sundry times. At length feeling easy in my mind, I had conversation with several elderly Friends of Philadelphia on the subject, and he obtaining a certificate suitable to the occasion, we set off in the Fifth Month, 1757. Coming to Nottingham week-day meeting, we lodged at John Churchman's, where·I met with our friend, Benjamin Buffington, from New England, who was returning from a visit to the Southern Provinces. Thence we crossed the river Susquehanna, and lodged at William Cox's in Maryland.

Soon after I entered this province a deep and painful exercise came upon me, which I often had some feeling of since my mind was drawn toward these parts, and with which I had acquainted my brother before we agreed to join as companions. As the people in this and the Southern Provinces live much on the labour of slaves, many of whom are used hardly, my concern was that I might attend with singleness of heart to the voice of the true Shepherd, and be so supported as to remain unmoved at the faces of men. . . .

The prospect of so weighty a work, and of being so distinguished from many whom I esteemed before myself, brought me very low, and such were the conflicts of my soul that I had a near sympathy with the Prophet, in the time of his weakness, when he said: "If thou deal thus with me, kill me, I pray

FROM *The Journal of John Woolman,* ed. J. G. Whittier (Glasgow: Robert Smead, 1883), pp. 99–106, 108–10.

thee, if I have found favour in thy sight." (Num. xi. 15.) But I soon saw that this proceeded from the want of a full resignation to the Divine will. Many were the afflictions which attended me, and in great abasement, with many tears, my cries were to the Almighty for his gracious and fatherly assistance, and after a time of deep trial I was favored to understand the state mentioned by the Psalmist more clearly than ever I had done before; to wit: "My soul is even as a weaned child." (Psalm cxxxi. 2.) Being thus helped to sink down into resignation, I felt a deliverance from that tempest in which I had been sorely exercised, and in calmness of mind went forward, trusting that the Lord Jesus Christ, as I faithfully attended to him, would be a counsellor to me in all difficulties, and that by His strength I should be enabled even to leave money with the members of society where I had entertainment, when I found that omitting it would obstruct that work to which I believed He had called me. As I copy this after my return, I may here add, that oftentimes I did so under a sense of duty. The way in which I did it was thus: when I expected soon to leave a Friend's house where I had entertainment, if I believed that I should not keep clear from the gain of oppression without leaving money, I spoke to one of the heads of the family privately, and desired them to accept of those pieces of silver, and give them to such of their negroes as they believed would make the best use of them; and at other times I gave them to the negroes myself, as the way looked clearest to me. Before I came out, I had provided a large number of small pieces for this purpose and thus offering them to some who appeared to be wealthy people was a trial both to me and them. But the fear of the Lord so covered me at times that my way was made easier than I expected; and few, if any, manifested any resentment at the offer, and most of them, after some conversation, accepted of them.

Ninth of Fifth Month.—A Friend at whose house we breakfasted setting us a little on our way, I had conversation with him, in the fear of the Lord, concerning his slaves, in which my heart was tender; I used much plainness of speech with him, and he appeared to take it kindly. We pursued our journey without appointing meetings, being pressed in my mind to be at the Yearly Meeting in Virginia. In my travelling on the road, I often felt a cry rise from the centre of my mind, thus: "O Lord, I am a stranger on the earth, hide not thy face from me." On the 11th, we crossed the rivers Patowmack and Rapahannock, and lodged at Port Royal. On the way we had the company of a colonel of the militia, who appeared to be a thoughtful man. I took occasion to remark on the difference in general betwixt a people used to labor moderately for their living, training up their children in frugality and business, and those who live on the labor of slaves; the former, in my view, being the most happy life. He concurred in the remark, and mentioned the trouble arising from the untoward, slothful disposition of the negroes, adding that one of our laborers would do as much in a day as two of their slaves. I replied, that free men, whose minds were properly on their business, found a satisfaction in improving, cultivating, and providing for their families; but negroes, laboring to support others who claim them as their propery, and expecting nothing but slavery during life, had not the like inducement to be industrious.

After some further conversation I said, that men having power too often misapplied it; that though we made slaves of the negroes, and the Turks made slaves of the Christians, I believed that liberty was the natural right of all men equally. This he did not deny, but said the lives of the negroes were so wretched in their own country that many of them lived better here than there. I replied, "There is great odds in regard to us on what principle we act;" and so the conversation on that subject ended. I may here add that another person, some time afterwards, mentioned the wretchedness of the negroes, occasioned by their intestine wars, as an argument in favor of our fetching them away for slaves. To which I replied, if compassion for the Africans, on account of their domestic troubles, was the real motive of our purchasing them, that spirit of tenderness being attended to, would incite us to use them kindly, that, as strangers brought out of affliction, their lives might be happy among us. And as they are human creatures, whose souls are as precious as ours, and who may receive the same help and comfort from the Holy Scriptures as we do, we could not omit suitable endeavours to instruct them therein; but that while we manifest by our conduct that our views in purchasing them are to advance ourselves, and while our buying captives taken in war animates those parties to push on the war, and increase desolation amongst them, to say they live unhappily in Africa is far from being an argument in our favour. . . .

Having travelled through Maryland, we came amongst Friends at Cedar Creek in Virginia, on the 12th; and the next day rode, in company with several of them, a day's journey to Camp Creek. As I was riding along in the morning, my mind was deeply affected in a sense I had of the need of Divine aid to support me in the various difficulties which attended me, and in uncommon distress of mind I cried in secret to the Most High, "O Lord be merciful, I beseech thee, to thy poor afflicted creature!" After some time, I felt inward relief, and, soon after, a Friend in company began to talk in support of the slave-trade, and said the negroes were understood to be the offspring of Cain, their blackness being the mark which God set upon him after he murdered Abel, his brother; that it was the design of Providence they should be slaves, as a condition proper to the race of so wicked a man as Cain was. Then another spake in support of what had been said. To all which I replied in substance as follows: that Noah and his family were all who survived the flood, according to Scripture; and as Noah was of Seth's race, the family of Cain was wholly destroyed. One of them said that after the flood Ham went to the land of Nod and took a wife; that Nod was a land far distant, inhabited by Cain's race, and that the flood did not reach it; and as Ham was sentenced to be a servant of servants to his brethren, these two families, being thus joined, were undoubtedly fit only for slaves. I replied, the flood was a judgment upon the world for their abominations, and it was granted that Cain's stock was the most wicked, and therefore unreasonable to suppose that they were spared.

As to Ham's going to the land of Nod for a wife, no time being fixed, Nod might be inhabited by some of Noah's family before Ham married a second time; moreover the text saith "That all flesh died that moved upon the earth." (Gen. vii. 21.) I further reminded them how the prophets repeatedly declare "that the son shall not suffer for the iniquity of the father, but every one be answerable for his own sins." I was troubled to perceive the darkness of their imaginations, and in some pressure of spirit said, "The love of ease and gain are the motives in general of keeping slaves, and men are wont to take hold of weak arguments to support a cause which is unreasonable. I have no interest on either side, save only the interest which I desire to have in the truth. I believe liberty is their right, and as I see they are not only deprived of it, but treated in other respects with inhumanity in many places, I believe He who is a refuge for the oppressed will, in His own time, plead their cause, and happy will it be for such as walk in uprightness before him." And thus our conversation ended. . . . .

The prospect of a way being open to the same degeneracy, in some parts of this newly settled land of America, in respect to our conduct towards the negroes, hath deeply bowed my mind in this journey, and though briefly to relate how these people are treated is no agreeable work, yet, after often reading over the notes I made as I travelled, I find my mind engaged to preserve them. Many of the white people in those provinces take little or no care of negro marriages; and when negroes marry after their own way, some make so little account of those marriages that with views of outward interest they often part men from their wives by selling them far asunder, which is common when estates are sold by executors at vendue. Many whose labor is heavy being followed at their business in the field by a man with a whip, hired for that purpose, have in common little else allowed but one peck of Indian corn and some salt, for one week, with a few potatoes; the potatoes they commonly raise by their labour on the first day of the week. The correction ensuing on their disobedience to overseers, or slothfulness in business, is often very severe, and sometimes desperate.

Men and women have many times scarcely clothes sufficient to hide their nakedness, and boys and girls ten and twelve years old are often quite naked amongst their master's children. Some of our Society, and some of the society called Newlights use some endeavours to instruct those they have in reading; but in common this is not only neglected, but disapproved. These are the people by whose labour the other inhabitants are in a great measure supported, and many of them in the luxuries of life. These are the people who have made no agreement to serve us, and who have not forfeited their liberty that we know of. These are the souls for whom Christ died, and for our conduct towards them we must answer before Him who is no respecter of persons. They who know the only true God, and Jesus Christ whom He hath sent, and are thus acquainted with the merciful, benevolent, gospel spirit, will therein perceive that the indignation of God is kindled against oppression and cruelty, and in beholding the great distress of so numerous a people will find cause for mourning.

ETHAN ALLEN
Reason Therefore Must Be the Standard

Because eighteenth-century rationalism and Deism presupposed an orderly, regulated universe, it is often thought that those who professed the new rationalism proposed a cold, passionless scientism in place of the fervor of revealed religious faith. Such a view overlooks the passion and excitement with which champions of Reason and Enlightenment set forth the claims of rationality and reason as the guide to human happiness and social good, as is evident in the concluding chapter of Reason the Only Oracle of Man *(1784) by Ethan Allen (1738–1789). Allen is best known to students of American history as leader of the Green Mountain Boys, who, with Benedict Arnold and a force of Connecticut soldiers captured Fort Ticonderoga in 1775. On that occasion Allen reportedly called for the surrender of the British garrison "in the name of the Great Jehovah and the Continental Congress."*

Of the Importance of the Exercise of Reason and Practice of Morality, in order to the Happiness of Mankind. The period of life is very uncertain, and at the longest is but short: a few years bring us from infancy to manhood, a few more to a dissolution; pain, sickness and death are the necessary consequences of animal life. Through life we struggle with physical evils, which eventually are certain to destroy our earthly composition; and well would it be for us did evils end here; but alas! moral evil has been more or less predominant in our agency, and though natural evil is unavoidable, yet moral evil may be prevented or remedied by the exercise of virtue. Morality is therefore of more importance to us than any or all other attainments; as it is a habit of mind, which, from a retrospective consciousness of our agency in this life, we should carry with us into our succeeding state of existence, as an acquired appendage of our rational nature, and as the necessary means of our mental happiness. Virtue and vice are the only things in this world, which, with our souls, are capable of surviving death; the former is the rational and only procuring cause of all intellectual happiness, and the latter of conscious guilt and misery; and therefore, our indispensible duty and ultimate interest is, to love, cultivate and improve the one, as the means of our greatest good, and to hate and abstain from the other, as productive of our greatest evil. And in order thereto, we

FROM *Reason the Only Oracle of Man, or A Compendious System of Natural Religion,* by Ethan Allen (Bennington, Vt.: Haswell and Russell, 1784), pp. 472–77.

should so far divest ourselves of the incumbrances of this world, (which are too apt to engross our attention) as to enquire a consistent system of the knowledge of religious duty, and make it our constant endeavour in life to act conformably to it. The knowledge of the being, perfections, creation and providence of GOD, and of the immortality of our souls, is the foundation of religion; which has been particularly illustrated in the four first chapters of this discourse. And as the Pagan, Jewish, Christian and Mahometan countries of the world have been overwhelmed with a multiplicity of revelations diverse from each other, and which, by their respective promulgators, are said to have been immediately inspired into their souls, by the spirit of God, or immediately communicated to them by the intervening agency of angels (as in the instance of the invisible Gabriel to Mahomet) and as those revelations have been received and credited, by far the greater part of the inhabitants of the several countries of the world (on whom they have been obtruded) as supernaturally revealed by God or Angels, and which, in doctrine and discipline, are in most respects repugnant to each other, it fully evinces their imposture, and authorizes us, without a lengthy course of arguing, to determine with certainty, that not more than one if any one of them, had their original from God; as they clash with each other; which is ground of high probability against the authenticity of each of them.

A revelation, that may be supposed to be really of the institution of God, must also be supposed to be perfectly consistent or uniform, and to be able to stand the test of truth; therefore such pretended revelations, as are tendered to us as the contrivance of heaven, which do not bear that test, we may be morally certain, was either originally a deception, or has since, by adulteration become spurious. Furthermore, should we admit, that among the numerous revelations on which the respective priests have given the stamp of divinity, some one of them was in reality of divine authority, yet we could no otherwise, as rational beings, distinguish it from others, but by reason.

Reason therefore must be the standard, by which we determine the respective claims of revelation; for otherwise we may as well subscribe to the divinity of the one as of the other, or to the whole of them, or to none at all. So likewise on this thesis, if reason rejects the whole of those revelations, we ought to return to the religion of nature and reason.

Undoubtedly it is our duty, and for our best good, that we occupy and improve the faculties, with which our Creator has endowed us, but so far as prejudice, or prepossession of opinion prevails over our minds, in the same proportion, reason is excluded from our theory or practice. Therefore if we acquire useful knowledge, we must first divest ourselves of those impediments; and sincerely endeavour to search out the truth; and draw our conclusions from reason and just argument, which will never conform to our inclination, interest or fancy; but we must conform to that if we would judge rightly. As certain as we determine contrary to reason, we make a wrong conclusion; therefore, our wisdom is, to conform to the nature and reason of things, as well in religious matters, as in other sciences. Preposterously absurd would it be, to negative the exercise of reason in religious concerns, and yet, be actuated by it in all other and less occurrences of life. All our knowledge of things is derived from God, in and by the order of nature, out of which we cannot perceive, reflect or understand any thing whatsoever; our external senses are natural and so are our souls; by the instrumentality of the former we perceive the objects of sense, and with the latter we reflect on them. And those objects are also natural; so that ourselves, and all things about us, and our knowledge collected therefrom, is natural, and not supernatural; as argued in the 6th chapter.

We may and often do, connect or arrange our ideas together, in a wrong or improper manner, for the want of skill or judgment, or through mistake or the want of application, or through the influence of prejudice; but in all such cases, the error does not originate from the ideas themselves, but from the composer; for a system, or an arrangement of ideas justly composed; always contain the truth; but an unjust composition never fails to contain error and falshood. Therefore an unjust connection of ideas is not derived from nature, but from the imperfect composition of man. Misconnection of ideas is the same as misjudging, and has no positive existence, being merely a creature of the imagination; but nature and truth are real and uniform; and the rational mind by reasoning, discerns the uniformity, and is thereby enabled to make a just composition of ideas, which will stand the test of truth. But the fantastical illuminations of the credulous and superstitious part of mankind, proceed from weakness, and as far as they take place in the world, subvert the religion of REASON and TRUTH.

THOMAS JEFFERSON
Truth Is Great and Will Prevail

Thomas Jefferson (1743–1826) was chosen governor of Virginia in 1779, and shortly thereafter wrote a bill for establishing religious freedom in that state. Jefferson, like other great figures of the Enlightenment, favored the strict separation of church and state. So, for entirely different reasons, did Baptists and others; they resented being taxed to pay for the Established Anglican Church. Thus as soon as the outbreak of the Revolution severed the royal control, public sentiment at once moved toward freedom of religion. The bill which follows, which was voted into law in 1786, guaranteed all Virginians the right "to profess, and by argument to maintain, their opinions in matters

FROM "Act Establishing Religious Liberty," in *Notes on the State of Virginia*, by Thomas Jefferson (Philadelphia: Richard and Hall, 1788), pp. 242–44.

of religion. . . ." Jefferson's ardent humanitarianism and optimistic view of human progress would be the subject of a searching examination of the great Virginian's beliefs in a long poem by Robert Penn Warren, entitled Brother to Dragons.

N° III

An ACT *for establishing* RELIGIOUS FREEDOM, *passed in the Assembly of Virginia in the beginning of the year* 1786.

Well aware that Almighty God hath created the mind free; that all attempts to influence it by temporal punishments or burthens, or by civil incapacitations, tend only to beget habits of hypocrisy and meanness, and are a departure from the plan of the Holy Author of our religion, who, being Lord both of body and mind, yet chose not to propagate it by coercions on either, as was in his Almighty power to do; that the impious presumption of legislators and rulers, civil as well as ecclesiastical, who, being themselves but fallible and uninspired men have assumed dominion over the faith of others, setting up their own opinions and modes of thinking as the only true and infallible, and as such endeavouring to impose them on others, hath established and maintained false religions over the greatest part of the world, and through all time; that to compel a man to furnish contributions of money for the propagation of opinions which he disbelieves, is sinful and tyrannical; that even the forcing him to support this or that teacher of his own religious persuasion, is depriving him of the comfortable liberty of giving his contributions to the particular pastor whose morals he would make his pattern, and whose powers he feels most persuasive to righteousness, and is withdrawing from the ministry those temporal rewards, which, proceeding from an approbation of their personal conduct, are an additional incitement to earnest and unremitting labours for the instruction of mankind; that our civil rights have no dependance on our religious opinions, more than on our opinions in physics or geometry; that therefore the proscribing any citizen as unworthy the public confidence by laying upon him an incapacity of being called to offices of trust and emolument, unless he profess or renounce this or that religious opinion, is depriving him injuriously of those privileges and advantages to which in common with his fellow citizens he has a natural right; that it tends also to corrupt the principles of that very religion it is meant to encourage, by bribing, with a monopoly of worldly honours and emoluments, those who will externally profess and conform to it; that though indeed these are criminal who do not withstand such temptation, yet neither are those innocent who lay the bait in their way; that to suffer the civil magistrate to intrude his powers into the field of opinion and to restrain the profession or propagation of principles, on supposition of their ill tendency, is a dangerous fallacy, which at once destroys all religious liberty, because he being of course judge of that tendency, will make his opinions the rule of judgment, and approve or condemn the sentiments of others only as they shall square with or differ from his own; that it is time enough for the rightful purposes of civil government for its officers to interfere when principles break out into overt acts against peace and good order; and finally, that truth is great and will prevail if left to herself, that she is the proper and sufficient antagonist to error, and has nothing to fear from the conflict, unless by human interposition disarmed of her natural weapons, free argument and debate, errors ceasing to be dangerous when it is permitted freely to contradict them.

Be it therefore enacted by the General Assembly, That no man shall be compelled to frequent or support any religious worship, place or ministry whatsoever, nor shall be enforced, restrained, molested, or burthened in his body or goods, nor shall otherwise suffer on account of his religious opinions or belief; but that all men shall be free to profess, and by argument to maintain, their opinions in matters of religion and that the same shall be in no wise diminish, enlarge, or affect their civil capacities.

And though we well know that this Assembly, elected by the people for the ordinary purposes of legislation only, have no power to restrain the acts of succeeding Assemblies, constituted with power equal to our own, and that therefore to declare this act irrevocable, would be of no effect in law, yet we are free to declare, and do declare, that the rights hereby asserted are of the natural rights of mankind, and that if any act shall be hereafter passed to repeal the present, or to narrow its operation, such act will be an infringement of natural right.

4

REBELS AND NATIONALISTS

By 1763, at the conclusion of the Seven Years' War, known on the American continent as the French and Indian War, England was supreme in North America. France ceded all claim to Acadia, Cape Breton, Canada, and the islands of the St. Lawrence, retaining only fishing rights on Newfoundland's banks and the city of New Orleans at the mouth of the Mississippi River. The American colonies, however, freed of the necessity for help from the mother country against the French, and impressed by the performance of their own militia against the French during the recent conflict, became increasingly resentful of British hegemony, and when Britain sought revenue to help defray the expenses of the late war and of maintaining an army in America, there was widespread resistance. Import duties, higher taxes, and the enforced quartering of British troops in American cities and towns resulted in a growing wave of protest against royal authority. After the port of Boston was closed in retaliation for the Boston Tea Party, in which Americans dressed as Indians destroyed tea imported by the East India Company, the colonies held a Continental Congress in Philadelphia to plan united resistance. Fighting broke out near Boston in 1775, and rebellion spread from New England to South Carolina and Georgia. In 1776 a Declaration of Independence was adopted, and after seven more years of increasingly ineffective attempts at coercion, England signed a treaty of peace with the United States of America. Following some years of weak government under the Articles of Confederation, a Constitution of the United States was ratified in 1789 and George Washington elected first president of the new nation.

Throughout these years patriotism and national feeling ran high, and

Americans looked to the future of their republic with high hopes. All anticipated a national culture separate and distinct from English and European origins. The War of 1812–14 emphasized the independence of the new country from English influence, and the ensuing years saw the new nation rapidly expanding its borders to the west, with the seaboard cities prospering and population increasing rapidly.

The selections that follow demonstrate the growth of sentiment for national independence in America, and the surge of nationalism that came with the Revolution.

GEORGE WASHINGTON
The Dastardly Behaviour of Those They Call Regular's

When in 1775 an army of 2,200 British and colonial troops under the command of Major General Edward Braddock moved against the French outpost of Fort Duquesne in western Pennsylvania, a Virginia militia officer, George Washington (1732–1799), went along with the Virginia troops as Braddock's aide-de-camp. Ambushed near the Monongahela River by French and Indian troops, Braddock's army was routed and the General himself mortally wounded. Washington led the remnants of the army back eastward. Subsequently he wrote the three letters which follow, describing the disgraceful conduct of the vaunted English regulars during the battle. His faith in the power of British military might was considerably weakened; in later years he would not forget what he learned that day along the Monongahela. And in the century ahead, an American novelist, James Fenimore Cooper, would write at great length about the performance of Britons and colonials in the wilderness against the Indians.

To ROBERT DINWIDDIE

Fort Cumberland, July 18, 1755.

Honbl. Sir: As I am favour'd with an oppertunity, I shou'd think myself excusable was I to omit giv'g you some acct. of our late Engagem't with the French on the Monongahela the 9th. Inst.

We continued our March from Fort Cumberland to Frazier's (which is within 7 Miles of Duquisne) with't meet'g with any extraordinary event, hav'g only a stragler or two picked up by the French Indians. When we came to this place, we were attack'd (very unexpectedly I must own) by abt. 300

FROM *The Writings of George Washington from the Original Manuscript Sources, 1745–1799,* ed. J. C. Fitzpatrick (Washington, D.C., U.S. Govt. P. O., 1931), Vol. I: 1745–1756, pp. 148–53.

French and Ind'ns; Our numbers consisted of abt. 1300 well arm'd Men, chiefly Regular's, who were immediately struck with such a deadly Panick, that nothing but confusion and disobedience of order's prevail'd amongst them: The Officer's in gen'l behav'd with incomparable bravery, for which they greatly suffer'd, there being near 60 kill'd and wound'd. A large proportion, out of the number we had! The Virginian Companies behav'd like Men and died like Soldiers; for I believe out of the 3 Companys that were there that day, scarce 30 were left alive: Captn. Peyrouny and all his Officer's, down to a Corporal, were kill'd; Captn. Polson shar'd almost as hard a Fate, for only one of his Escap'd: In short the dastardly behaviour of the English Soldier's expos'd all those who were inclin'd to do their duty to almost certain Death; and at length, in despight of every effort to the contrary, broke and run as Sheep before the Hounds, leav'g the Artillery, Ammunition, Provisions, and, every individual thing we had with us a prey to the Enemy; and when we endeavour'd to rally them in hopes of regaining our invaluable loss, it was with as much success as if we had attempted to have stop'd the wild Bears of the Mountains. The Genl. was wounded behind in the shoulder, and into the Breast, of w'ch he died three days after; his two Aids de Camp were both wounded, but are in a fair way of Recovery; Colo. Burton and Sir Jno. St. Clair are also wounded, and I hope will get over it; Sir Peter Halket, with many other brave Officers were kill'd in the Field. I luckily escap'd with't a wound tho' I had four Bullets through my Coat and two Horses shot under me. It is suppose that we left 300 or more dead in the Field; about that number we brought of wounded; and it is imagin'd (I believe with great justice too) that two thirds of both [?]* received their shott from our own cowardly English Soldier's who gather'd themselves into a body contrary to orders 10 or 12 deep, wou'd then level, Fire and shoot down the Men before them.

I tremble at the consequences that this defeat may have upon our back settlers, who I suppose will all leave their habitations unless there are proper measures taken for their security.

Colo. Dunbar, who commands at present, intends so soon as his Men are recruited at this place, to continue his March to Phila. into Winter Quarters: so that there will be no Men left here unless it is the poor remains of the Virginia Troops, who survive and will be too small to guard our Frontiers. As Captn. Orme is writg. to your honour I doubt not but he will give you a circumstantial acct. of all things, which will make it needless for me to add more than that I am, etc.

To MRS. MARY WASHINGTON

[Fort Cumberland, July 18, 1755.]

Honour'd Mad'm: As I doubt not but you have heard of our defeat, and perhaps have it represented in a worse light (if possible) than it deserves; I

---

* Two words obliterated.

have taken this earliest oppertunity to give you some acct. of the Engagement, as it happen'd within 7 miles of the French Fort, on Wednesday the 9th. Inst.

We March'd on to that place with't any considerable loss, having only now and then a stragler pick'd up by the French Scoutg. Ind'nd. When we came there, we were attack'd by a Body of French and Indns. whose number, (I am certain) did not exceed 300 Men; our's consisted of abt. 1,300 well arm'd Troops; chiefly of the English Soldiers, who were struck with such a panick, that they behav'd with more cowardice than it is possible to conceive; The Officers behav'd Gallantly in order to encourage their Men, for which they suffer'd greatly; there being near 60 kill'd and wounded; a large proportion out of the number we had! The Virginia Troops shew'd a good deal of Bravery, and were near all kill'd; for I believe out of 3 Companys that were there, there is scarce 30 Men left alive; Capt. Peyrouny and all his Officer's down to a Corporal was kill'd; Capt. Polson shar'd near as hard a Fate; for only one of his was left: In short the dastardly behaviour of those they call regular's expos'd all others that were inclin'd to do their duty to almost certain death; and at last, in dispight of all the efforts of the Officer's to the Contrary, they broke and run as Sheep pursued by dogs; and it was impossible to rally them.

The Genl. was wounded; of w'ch he died 3 Days after; Sir Peter Halket was kill'd in the Field where died many other brave Officer's; I luckily escap'd with't a wound, tho' I had four Bullets through my Coat, and two Horses shot under me; Captns. Orme and Morris two of the Genls. Aids de Camp, were wounded early in the Engagem't. which render'd the duty hard upon me, as I was the only person then left to distribute the Genl's. Orders which I was scarcely able to do, as I was not half recover'd from a violent illness, that confin'd me to my Bed, and a Waggon, for above 10 Days; I am still in a weak and Feeble cond'n; which induces me to halt here, 2 or 3 Days in hopes of recov'g. a little Strength, to enable me to proceed homewards; from whence, I fear I shall not be able to stir till towards Sept., so that I shall not have the pleasure of seeing you till then, unless it be in Fairfax; please to give my love to Mr. Lewis and my Sister, and Compts. to Mr. Jackson and all other Fds. that enquire after me. I am, Hon'd Madam Yr. most dutiful Son.

P.S. You may acqt. Priscilla Mullican that her Son Charles is very well, hav'g only rec'd a slight w'd in his Foot, w'ch will be cur'd with't detrimt. to him, in a very small time.

We had abt. 300 Men kill'd and as many, and more, wounded.

To JOHN AUGUSTINE WASHINGTON

Fort Cumberland, July 18, 1755.

Dear Jack: As I have heard since my arriv'l at this place, a circumstantial acct. of my death and dying speech, I take this early oppertunity of contradicting both, and of assuring you that I now exist and appear in the land of the living by the miraculous care of Providence, that protected me beyond all human expectation; I had 4 Bullets through my Coat, and two Horses shot under me, and yet escaped unhurt.

We have been most scandalously beaten by a trifling body of men; but fatigue and want of time prevents me from giving any of the details till I have the happiness of seeing you at home; which I now most ardently wish for, since we are drove in thus far. A Weak and Feeble state of Health, obliges me to halt here for 2 or 3 days, to recover a little strength, that I may thereby be enabled to proceed homewards with more ease; You may expect to see me there on Saturday or Sunday Se'night, which is as soon as I can well be down as I shall take my Bullskin Plantation's in my way. Pray give my Compl'ts to all my F'ds. I am Dr. Jack, y'r most Affect. Broth'r.

BENJAMIN FRANKLIN
O! This Will Work Admirably!

Born, like Jonathan Edwards, in Massachusetts just after the turn of the eighteenth century, Benjamin Franklin (1706–1790) was distinguished for his urbanity, scientific curiosity and inventiveness, and political wisdom. Franklin spent most of his life in Philadelphia, though he was resident in England for long periods as agent for the colonies and then in France as ambassador during the Revolution. At first an advocate of reconciliation between the Mother Country and the colonies, Franklin's zeal for liberty grew as the gap between England and her colonies widened during the 1760's and 1770's. It was in 1773 that he composed his satirical essay, "Rules By Which a Great Empire May Be Reduced to a Small One," in which he set forth the colonies' case against the Crown in tellingly oblique fashion.

Rules for reducing a Great Empire to a small one, presented to a late Minister, when he entered upon his Administration.[1]

An ancient sage valued himself upon this, that though he could not fiddle, he knew how to make a great city of a little one. The science, that I, a modern simpleton, am about to communicate, is the very reverse.

FROM "Rules By Which a Great Empire May Be Reduced to a Small One," in *Memoirs of Benjamin Franklin* (Philadelphia: McCarty and Davis, 1834), Vol. I, pp. 227–30.

---

[1] These rules first appeared in a London newspaper, about the beginning of the year 1774, and have several times since been introduced ,into the public prints.—The minister alluded to was the earl of Hillsborough. "The causes and motions of seditions (says lord Bacon) are, innovation in religion, taxes, alteration of laws and customs, breaking of privileges, general oppression, advancement of unworthy persons, strangers, dearths, disbanded soldiers, factions grown desperate, and whatsoever in offending people joineth and knitteth them in a common cause."

I address myself to all ministers, who have the management of extensive dominions, which, from their very greatness, are become troublesome to govern—because the multiplicity of their affairs leaves no time for fiddling.

I. In the first place, gentlemen, you are to consider, that a great empire, like a great cake, is most easily diminished at the edges. Turn your attention therefore first to your *remotest* provinces; that, as you get rid of them, the next may follow in order.

II. That the possibility of this separation may always exist, take special care the provinces are *never incorporated with the mother-country;* that they do not enjoy the same common rights, the same privileges in commerce, and that they are governed by severer laws, all of your enacting, without allowing them any share in the choice of the legislators. By carefully making and preserving such distinctions, you will (to keep to my simile of the cake) act like a wise gingerbread-baker; who, to facilitate a division, cuts his dough half through in those places, where, when baked, he would have it broken to pieces.

III. Those remote provinces have perhaps been acquired, purchased, or conquered, at the sole expense of the settlers or their ancestors, without the aid of the mother-country. If this should happen to increase her strength, by their growing numbers, ready to join in her wars; her commerce, by their growing demand for her manufactures; or her naval power, by greater employment for her ships and seamen, they may probably suppose some merit in this, and that it entitles them to some favour: you are therefore to *forget it all, or resent it,* as if they had done you injury. If they happen to be zealous whigs, friends of liberty, nurtured in revolution principles; remember all that to their prejudice, and contrive to punish it; for such principles, after a revolution is thoroughly established, are of no more use; they are even odious and abominable.

IV. However peaceably your colonies have submitted to your government, shown their affection to your interests, and patiently borne their grievances, you are to suppose them *always inclined to revolt,* and treat them accordingly. Quarter troops among them, who, by their insolence may provoke the rising of mobs, and by their bullets and bayonets suppress them. By this means, like the husband who uses his wife ill from suspicion, you may in time convert your suspicions into realities.

V. Remote provinces must have governors and judges, to represent the royal person, and execute every where the delegated parts of his office and authority. You, ministers, know, that much of the strength of government depends on the opinion of the people, and much of that opinion on the *choice of rulers* placed immediately over them. If you send them wise and good men for governors, who study the interest of the colonists, and advance their prosperity, they will think their king wise and good, and that he wishes the welfare of his subjects. If you send them learned and upright men for judges, they will think him a lover of justice. This may attach your provinces more to his government. You are therefore to be careful who you recommend for those offices.—If you can find prodigals, who have ruined their fortunes, broken gamesters, or stock-jobbers, these may do well as governors, for they will probably be rapacious, and provoke the people by their extortions. Wrangling proctors and petty-fogging lawyers too are not amiss, for they will be for ever disputing and quarrelling with their little parliaments. If withal they should be ignorant, wrong-headed and insolent, so much the better. Attorneys clerks and Newgate solicitors will do for chief justices, especially if they hold their places during your pleasure:—and all will contribute to impress those ideas of your government, that are proper for a people you would wish to renounce it.

VI. To confirm these impressions, and strike them deeper, whenever the injured come to the capital with complaints of mal-administration, oppression, or injustice, *punish such suitors* with long delay, enormous expense, and a final judgment in favour of the oppressor. This will have an admirable effect every way. The trouble of future complaints will be prevented, and governors and judges will be encouraged to farther acts of oppression and injustice, and thence the people may become more disaffected, and at length desperate.

VII. When such governors have crammed their coffers, and made themselves so odious to the people, that they can no longer remain among them with safety to their persons, *recal and reward* them with pensions. You may make them baronets too, if that respectable order should not think fit to resent it. All will contribute to encourage new governors in the same practice, and make the supreme government detestable.

VIII. If, when you are engaged in war, your colonies should vie in liberal aids of men and money against the common enemy, upon your simple requisition, and give far beyond their abilities,—reflect, that a penny, taken from them by your power, is more honourable to you, than a pound presented by their benevolence; *despise therefore, their voluntary grants,* and resolve to harrass them with *novel taxes.*—They will probably complain to your parliament, that they are taxed by a body in which they have no representative, and that this is contrary to common right. They will petition for redress. Let the parliament flout their claims, reject their petitions, refuse even to suffer the reading of them, and treat the petitioners with the utmost contempt. Nothing can have a better effect in producing the alienation proposed; for though many can forgive injuries, none ever forgave contempt.

IX. In laying these taxes, *never regard the heavy burdens* those remote people already undergo, in defending their own frontiers, supporting their own provincial government, making new roads, building bridges, churches, and other public edifices, which in old countries have been done to your hands, by your ancestors, but which occasion constant calls and demands on the purses of a new people.—Forget the restraint you lay on their trade for your own benefit, and the advantage a monopoly of this trade gives your exacting merchants. Think nothing of the wealth those merchants and your manufacturers acquire by the colony commerce, their increased ability thereby to pay taxes at home, their accumulating, in the price of their commodities, most of those taxes, and so levying them from their consuming customers: all this, and the employment and support of thousands of your poor by the colonists, you are entirely to forget. But remember to make your arbitrary tax more grievous to your provinces, by public declarations, importing, that your power of taxing them has *no limits,* so that when you take from them without their consent a shilling in the pound, you have a clear right to the other nineteen. This will probably weaken every idea of security in their property, and convince them, that under such a government they have nothing they can call their own; which can scarce fail of producing the happiest consequences!

X. Possibly indeed some of them might still comfort themselves, and say, "though we have no property, we have yet something left that is valuable, we have constitutional *liberty, both of person and of conscience.* This king, these lords, and these commons, who it seems are too remote from us to know us and feel for us, cannot take from us our *habeas corpus* right, or our right of trial by a jury of our neighbours: they cannot deprive us of the exercise of our religion, alter our ecclesiastical constitution, and compel us to be papists, if they please, nor Mahometans." To annihilate this comfort, begin by laws to perplex their commerce with infinite regulations, impossible to be remembered and observed: ordain seizures of their property for every failure, take away the trial of such property by jury, and give it to arbitrary judges of your own appointing, and of the lowest characters in the country, whose salaries and emoluments are to arise out of the duties or condemnations, and whose appointments are during pleasure. Then let there be a formal declaration of both houses, that opposition to your edicts is treason, and that persons suspected of treason in the provinces may, according to some obsolete law, be seized and sent to the metropolis of the empire for trial; and pass an act, that those there charged with certain other offences shall be sent away in chains from their friends and country, to be tried in the same manner for felony. Then erect a new court of inquisition among them, accompanied by an armed force, with instructions to transport all such suspected persons, to be ruined by the expense, if they bring over evidences to prove their innocence, or be found guilty and hanged, if they cannot afford it. And lest the people should think you cannot possibly go any farther, pass another solemn declaratory act, "that kings, lords, and commons had, have, and of right ought to have, full power and authority to make statutes of sufficient force and validity to bind the unrepresented provinces *in all cases whatsoever."* This will include spiritual with temporal, and taken together must operate wonderfully to your purpose, by convincing them, that they are at present under a power, something like that spoken of in the scriptures, which can not only kill their bodies, but damn their souls to all eternity, by compelling them, if it pleases, to worship the devil.

XI. To make your taxes more odious, and more likely to procure resistance, send from the capital a *board of officers* to superintend the collection, *com-*

posed of the most indiscreet, ill-bred, and insolent you can find. Let these have large salaries out of the extorted revenue, and live in open grating luxury upon the sweat and blood of the industrious, whom they are to worry continually with groundless and expensive prosecutions, before the above-mentioned arbitrary revenue-judges; all at the cost of the party prosecuted, though acquitted, because the king is to pay no costs. Let these men, by your order, be exempted from all the common taxes and burdens of the province, though they and their property are protected by its laws. If any revenue officers are suspected of the least tenderness for the people, discard them. If others are justly complained of, protect and reward them. If any of the under officers behave so as to provoke the people to drub them, promote those to better offices: this will encourage others to procure for themselves such profitable drubbings, by multiplying and enlarging such provocations, and all will work towards the end you aim at.

XII. Another way to make your tax odious is, to *misapply the produce of it.* If it was originally appropriated for the defence of the provinces, and the better support of government, and the administration of justice, where it may be necessary, then apply none of it to that defence, but bestow it, where it is not necessary, in augmenting salaries or pensions to every governor, who has distinguished himself by his enmity to the people, and by calumniating them to their sovereign. This will make them pay it more unwillingly, and be more apt to quarrel with those that collect it, and those that imposed it, who will quarrel again with them, and all shall contribute to your own purpose, of making them weary of your government.

XIII. If the people of any province have been accustomed to *support their own governors and judges to satisfaction,* you are to apprehend, that such governors and judges may be thereby influenced to treat the people kindly, and to do them justice. This is another reason for applying part of that revenue in larger salaries to such governors and judges, given, as their commissions are, during *your* pleasure only, forbidding them to take any salaries from their provinces; that thus the people may no longer hope any kindness from their governors, or (in crown cases) any justice from their judges. And as the money, thus misapplied in one province, is extorted from all, probably all will resent the misapplication.

XIV. If the parliaments of your provinces should dare to claim rights, or complain of your administration, order them to be harrassed with *repeated dissolutions.* If the same men are continually returned by new elections, adjourn their meetings to some country village, where they cannot be accommodated, and there keep them during pleasure; for this, you know, is your prerogative, and an excellent one it is, as you may manage it, to promote discontents among the people, diminish their respect, and increase their disaffection.

XV. Convert the brave honest officers of your *navy* into pimping tide-waiters and colony officers of the *customs.* Let those, who in time of war fought gallantly in defence of the commerce of their countrymen, in peace be taught to prey upon it. Let them learn to be corrupted by great and real smugglers;

but (to show their diligence) scour with armed boats every bay, harbour, river, creek, cove, or nook, throughout the coast of your colonies; stop and detain every coaster, every wood-boat, every fisherman, tumble their cargoes and even their ballast inside out, and upside down; and if a pennyworth of pins is found un-entered, let the whole be seized and confiscated. Thus shall the trade of your colonists suffer more from their friends in time of peace, than it did from their enemies in war. Then let these boats' crews land upon every farm in their way, rob their orchards, steal their pigs and poultry, and insult the inhabitants. If the injured and exasperated farmers, unable to procure other justice, should attack the aggressors, drub them, and burn their boats, you are to call this *high treason and rebellion,* order fleets and armies into their country, and threaten to carry all the offenders three thousand miles to be hanged, drawn, and quartered.—O! this will work admirably!

XVI. If you are told of *discontents* in your colonies, never believe that they are general, or that you have given occasion for them; therefore do not think of applying any remedy, or of changing any offensive measure. Redress no grievance, lest they should be encouraged to demand the redress of some other grievance. Grant no request, that this is just and reasonable, lest they should make another, that is unreasonable. Take all your informations of the state of the colonies from your governors and officers in enmity with them. Encourage and reward these leasing-makers, secrete their lying accusations, lest they should be confuted, but act upon them as the clearest evidence; and believe nothing you hear from the friends of the people. Suppose all *their* complaints to be invented and promoted by a few factious demagogues, whom if you could catch and hang, all would be quiet. Catch and hang a few of them accordingly, and the blood of the martyrs shall work miracles in favour of your purpose.[2]

XVII. If you see *rival nations* rejoicing at the prospect of your disunion with your provinces, and endeavouring to promote it, if they translate, publish and applaud all the complaints of your discontented colonies, at the same time privately stimulating you to severer measures, let not that alarm or offend you. Why should it? since you all mean the same thing?

XVIII. If any colony should *at their own charge erect a fortress,* to secure their *port* against the fleets of a foreign enemy, get your governor to betray that fortress into your hands. Never think of paying what it cost the country, for that would look, at least, like some regard for justice; but turn it into a citadel, to awe the inhabitants and curb their commerce. If they should have lodged in such fortress the very arms they bought and used to aid you in your conquests,

---

[2] An American writer affirmed, "That there has not been a single instance in which *they* have complained, without being rebuked, or in which they have been complained *against,* without being punished."—A fundamental mistake in the minister occasioned this. Every individual in New England (the peccant country) was held a coward or a knave, and the disorders, which spread abroad there, were treated as the result of the *too great lenity* of Britain! By the aid of this short and benevolent rule, judgment was ever wisely pre-determined, to the shutting out redress on the one hand, and enforcing every rigour of punishment on the other.

seize them all; it will provoke like ingratitude added to robbery. One admirable effect of these operations will be, to discourage every other colony from erecting such defences, and so their and your enemies may more easily invade them, to the great disgrace of your government, and of course the furtherance of your project.

XIX. Send armies into their country, under pretence of protecting the inhabitants; but, instead of garrisoning the forts on their frontiers with those troops, to prevent incursions, demolish those forts, and order the troops into the heart of the country, that the savages may be encouraged to attack the frontiers,[3] and that the troops may be protected by the inhabitants: this will seem to proceed from your *ill-will or your ignorance,* and contribute farther to produce and strengthen an opinion among them that you are no longer fit to govern them.[4]

XX. Lastly, invest the *general of your army in the provinces* with great and unconstitutional powers, and free him from the controul of even your own civil governors. Let him have troops enow under his command, with all the fortresses in his possession, and who knows but (like some provincial generals in the Roman empire, and encouraged by the universal discontent you have produced) he may take it into his head to set up for himself? If he should, and you have carefully practised these few excellent rules of mine, take my word for it, all the provinces will immediately join him—and you will that day (if you have not done it sooner) get rid of the trouble of governing them, and all the plagues attending their commerce and connexion from thenceforth and for ever.

[3] In April, 1778, the assembled chiefs of the western nations told one of our Indian agents, "that they remembered their father, the king of Great Britain's message delivered to them last fall, of demolishing Fort Pittsburg and removing the soldiers with their sharp-edged weapons out of the country:—this gave them great pleasure, as it was a strong proof of his paternal kindness towards them." (See Considerations on the Agreement with Mr. T. Walpole for Lands upon the Ohio, p. 9.) This is general history: the persons concerned are dead, and the application of facts would be personally invidious.

[4] As some readers may be inclined to divide their belief between the wisdom of the British ministry and the candour and veracity of Dr. Franklin, it may be observed that two contrary objections might be made to the truth of this representation. The first is, that the conduct of Great Britain is made *too* absurd for possibility, and the second, that it is not made absurd *enough* for fact. If we consider that this piece does not include the measures subsequent to 1773, the latter difficulty is easily set aside. The former can only be solved by the many instances in history, where the infatuation of individuals has brought the heaviest calamities upon nations.

PATRICK HENRY
The War Is Inevitable—and Let It Come!

Before most of his fellow colonists, Patrick Henry (1736–1799) realized that war between England and America was inevitable. His famous "Give Me Liberty or Give Me Death" oration was spoken before the Virginia House of Burgesses after his resolutions for arming the Virginia militia were opposed by conservatives. Henry's famous speech was not written down; it was reconstructed from the memories of some who heard it by William Wirt in his Life of Patrick Henry *(1817), but apparently there was general agreement on the phraseology of most of what Henry said on the historic occasion.*

Mr. President: It is natural for man to indulge in the illusions of hope. We are apt to shut our eyes against a painful truth, and listen to the song of that siren till she transforms us into beasts. Is this the part of wise men, engaged in a great and arduous struggle for liberty? Are we disposed to be of the number of those who, having eyes, see not, and having ears, hear not, the things which so nearly concern their temporal salvation? For my part, whatever anguish of spirit it may cost, I am willing to know the whole truth; to know the worst, and to provide for it.

I have but one lamp by which my feet are guided, and that is the lamp of experience. I know of no way of judging of the future but by the past. And, judging by the past, I wish to know what there has been in the conduct of the British ministry for the last ten years to justify those hopes with which the gentlemen have been pleased to solace themselves and the House? Is it that insidious smile with which our petition has been lately received? Trust it not, sir; it will prove a snare to your feet. Suffer not yourselves to be betrayed with a kiss. Ask yourselves how this gracious reception of our petition comports with those warlike preparations which cover our waters and darken our land. Are fleets and armies necessary to a work of love and reconciliation? Have we shown ourselves so unwilling to be reconciled that force must be called in to win back our love? Let us not deceive ourselves, sir. These are the implements of war and subjugation, the last arguments to which kings resort.

I ask the gentlemen, sir, what means this martial array, if its purpose be not to force us to submission? Can the gentlemen assign any other possible motive for it? Has Great Britain any enemy in this quarter of the world, to call for all this accumulation of navies and armies? No, sir, she has none. They are meant for us; they can be meant for no other. They are sent over to bind and

FROM *Sketches of the Life and Character of Patrick Henry,* by William Wirt (Philadelphia: Thomas, Cowperthwait and Co., 1838), pp. 138–42.

rivet upon us those chains which the British ministry has been so long forging. And what have we to oppose to them? Shall we try argument? Sir, we have been trying that for the last ten years. Have we anything new to offer upon the subject? Nothing. We have held the subject up in every light of which it is capable; but it has been all in vain.

Shall we resort to entreaty and humble supplication? What terms shall we find which have not been already exhausted? Let us not, I beseech you, sir, deceive ourselves longer. Sir, we have done everything that could be done, to avert the storm which is now coming on. We have petitioned, we have remonstrated, we have supplicated; we have prostrated ourselves before the throne, and have implored its interposition to arrest the tyrannical hands of the ministry and Parliament. Our petitions have been slighted; our remonstrances have produced additional violence and insult; our supplications have been disregarded; and we have been spurned, with contempt, from the foot of the throne. In vain, after these things, may we indulge the fond hope of peace and reconciliation. There is no longer any room for hope.

If we wish to be free; if we mean to preserve inviolate those inestimable privileges for which we have been so long contending; if we mean not basely to abandon the noble struggle in which we have been so long engaged, and which we have pledged ourselves never to abandon until the glorious object of our contest shall be obtained—we must fight! I repeat it, sir, we must fight! An appeal to arms, and to the God of hosts, is all that is left us.

They tell us, sir, that we are weak—unable to cope with so formidable an adversary. But when shall we be stronger? Will it be the next week or the next year? Will it be when we are totally disarmed, and when a British guard shall be stationed in every house? Shall we gather strength by irresolution and inaction? Shall we acquire the means of effectual resistance by lying supinely on our backs, and hugging the delusive phantom of hope, until our enemies shall have bound us hand and foot? Sir, we are not weak, if we make a proper use of those means which the God of nature hath placed in our power. Three millions of people, armed in the holy cause of Liberty, and in such a country as that which we possess, are invincible by any force which our enemy can send against us.

Besides, sir, we shall not fight our battles alone. There is a just God, who presides over the destinies of nations, and who will raise up friends to fight our battles for us. The battle, sir, is not to the strong alone; it is to the vigilant, the active, the brave. Besides, sir, we have no election. If we were base enough to desire it, it is now too late to retire from the contest. There is no retreat but in submission and slavery! Our chains are forged. Their clanking may be heard on the plains of Boston! The war is inevitable—and let it come! I repeat it, sir, let it come!

It is vain, sir, to extenuate the matter. The gentlemen may cry, Peace, peace! but there is no peace. The war has actually begun! The next gale that sweeps from the north will bring to our ears the clash of resounding arms!

Our brethren are already in the field! Why stand we here idle? What is it that the gentlemen wish? What would they have? Is life so dear or peace so sweet as to be purchased at the price of chains and slavery? Forbid it, Almighty God. I know not what course others may take, but as for me, give me liberty or give me death!

THOMAS JEFFERSON
Our Lives, Our Fortunes, and Our Sacred Honor

Thomas Jefferson was almost wholly responsible for the writing of America's first great political testament, the Declaration of Independence. He composed it in two days (July 2–3, 1776) and the day afterward, with few emendations, it was approved by the Continental Congress. The Declaration was publicly proclaimed in Philadelphia on July 8, and the next day read before General George Washington and his troops in New York City. Most of the "signers" actually affixed their signatures to the document almost a month after its adoption, on August 2, 1776.

When, in the Course of human events, it becomes necessary for one people to dissolve the political bands which have connected them with another, and to assume, among the Powers of the earth, the separate and equal station to which the Laws of Nature and of Nature's God entitle them, a decent respect to the opinions of mankind requires that they should declare the causes which impel them to the separation.

We hold these truths to be self-evident: that all men are created equal; that they are endowed by their Creator with certain unalienable Rights; that among these are Life, Liberty, and the pursuit of Happiness. That, to secure these Rights, Governments are instituted among Men, deriving their just powers from the consent of the governed; that, whenever any Form of Government becomes destructive of these ends, it is the Right of the People to alter or to abolish it, and to institute new Government, laying its foundation on such Principles, and organizing its Powers in such form, as to them shall seem most likely to affect their Safety and Happiness. Prudence, indeed, will dictate that Governments long established should not be changed for light and transient causes; and accordingly, all experience has shewn that mankind are more disposed to suffer, while evils are sufferable, than to right themselves by abolish-

FROM "A Declaration by the Representatives of the United States of America, in General Congress Assembled," *The Writings of Thomas Jefferson*, ed. A. E. Bergh (Washington, D.C.: Thomas Jefferson Memorial Association, 1905), Vol. I, pp. 28–38.

ing the forms to which they are accustomed. But, when a long train of abuses and usurpations, pursuing invariably the same Object, evinces a design to reduce them under absolute Despotism, it is their right, it is their duty, to throw off such Government, and to provide new Guards for their future security. Such has been the patient sufferance of these Colonies, and such is now the necessity which constrains them to alter their former Systems of Government. The history of the present King of Great Britain is a history of repeated injuries and usurpations, all having in direct object the establishment of an absolute Tyranny over these States. To prove this, let Facts be submitted to a candid world:

He has refused his Assent to Laws the most wholesome and necessary for the public good.

He has forbidden his Governors to pass Laws of immediate and pressing importance, unless suspended in their operation till his Assent should be obtained; and, when so suspended, he has utterly neglected to attend to them.

He has refused to pass other Laws for the accommodation of large districts of people, unless those people would relinquish the right of Representation in the Legislature; a right inestimable to them, and formidable to tyrants only.

He has called together legislative bodies at places unusual, uncomfortable, and distant from the depository of their Public Records, for the sole purpose of fatiguing them into compliance with his measures.

He has dissolved Representative Houses repeatedly for opposing, with manly firmness, his invasions on the rights of the people.

He has refused for a long time after such dissolutions to cause others to be elected; whereby the Legislative Powers, incapable of Annihilation, have returned to the People at large for their exercise; the State remaining, in the meantime, exposed to all the dangers of invasion from without, and convulsions within.

He has endeavored to prevent the Population of these States; for that purpose obstructing the Laws for Naturalization of Foreigners; refusing to pass others to encourage their migrations hither, and raising the conditions of new Appropriations of Lands.

He has obstructed the Administration of Justice by refusing his Assent to Laws for establishing Judiciary Powers.

He has made Judges dependent on his Will alone for the tenure of their offices, and the amount and Payment of their salaries.

He has erected a multitude of New Offices, and sent hither swarms of Officers to harrass our People and eat out their substance.

He has kept among us, in times of Peace, Standing Armies, without the Consent of our legislatures.

He has affected to render the Military independent of and superior to, the Civil Power.

He has combined with others, to subject us to a jurisdiction foreign to our constitution, and unacknowledged by our laws; giving his Assent to their Acts of pretended Legislation:

For quartering large bodies of armed troops among us;

For protecting them, by a mock Trial, from Punishment for any Murders which they should commit on the Inhabitants of these States;

For cutting off our Trade with all parts of the world;

For imposing Taxes on us without our Consent;

For depriving us, in many cases, of the benefits of Trial by Jury;

For transporting us beyond Seas to be tried for pretended offences;

For abolishing the free System of English Laws in a neighboring Province, establishing therein an Arbitrary government, and enlarging its Boundaries, so as to render it at once an example and fit instrument for introducing the same absolute rule into these Colonies;

For taking away our Charters, abolishing our most valuable Laws, and altering, fundamentally, the Forms of our Governments;

For suspending our own Legislatures, and declaring themselves invested with Power to legislate for us in all cases whatsoever.

He has abdicated Government here by declaring us out of his Protection, and waging War against us.

He has plundered our seas, ravaged our Coasts, burnt our towns, and destroyed the Lives of our People.

He is, at this time, transporting large Armies of foreign Mercenaries to complete the works of death, desolation, and tyranny, already begun with circumstances of Cruelty and Perfidy scarcely paralleled in the most barbarous ages, and totally unworthy the Head of a civilized nation.

He has constrained our fellow Citizens, taken Captive on the High Seas, to bear Arms against their Country, to become the executioners of their friends and Brethren, or to fall themselves by their Hands.

He has excited domestic insurrections amongst us, and has endeavored to bring on the inhabitants of our frontiers the merciless Indian Savages, whose known rule of warfare is an undistinguished destruction of all ages, sexes, and conditions.

In every stage of these Oppressions, We have Petitioned for Redress, in the most humble terms; Our repeated Petitions have been answered only by repeated injury. A Prince, whose character is thus marked by every act which may define a Tyrant, is unfit to be the ruler of a free People.

Nor have We been wanting in attentions to our British brethren. We have warned them, from time to time, of attempts by their Legislature to extend an unwarrantable jurisdiction over us. We have reminded them of the circumstances of our emigration and settlement here. We have appealed to their native justice and magnanimity, and we have conjured them, by the ties of our common kindred, to disavow these usurpations, which would inevitably interrupt our connections and correspondence, They, too, have been deaf to the voice of justice and of consanguinity. We must, therefore, acquiesce in the necessity which denounces our Separation, and hold them, as we hold the rest of mankind—Enemies in War—in Peace, Friends.

We, Therefore, the Representatives of the United States of America, in General Congress Assembled, appealing to the Supreme Judge of the world for the rectitude of our intentions, Do, in the Name and by the Authority of the good People of these Colonies, solemnly Publish and Declare, That these United Colonies are, and of Right ought to be, Free and Independent States; that they are Absolved from all Allegiance to the British Crown, and that all political connexion between them and the State of Great Britain is, and ought to be, totally dissolved; and that, as Free and Independent States, they have full Power to levy War, conclude Peace, contract Alliances, establish Commerce, and to do all other Acts and Things which Independent States may of right do. And, for the support of this Declaration, with a firm reliance on the Protection of Divine Providence, we mutually pledge to each other our Lives, our Fortunes, and our Sacred Honor.

THOMAS PAINE
Tyranny, Like Hell, Is Not Easily Conquered

"The American Crisis: I" was written by Thomas Paine (1737–1809) while with Washington's army in its retreat across New Jersey in 1776. It is credited not only with helping to inspire the army to win the Battle of Trenton a few days after it was written, but also with infusing new determination and resolve into the American cause throughout the embattled thirteen colonies. Though not a rich man, Paine refused all royalties for his series of Crisis pamphlets, giving the copyright to the United States.

These are the times that try men's souls. The summer soldier and the sunshine patriot will, in this crisis, shrink from the service of his country; but he that stands it *now,* deserves the love and thanks of man and woman. Tyranny, like hell, is not easily conquered; yet we have this consolation with us, that the harder the conflict, the more glorious the triumph. What we obtain too cheap, we esteem too lightly: 'tis dearness only that gives every thing its value. Heaven knows how to put a proper price upon its goods; and it would be strange indeed if so celestial an article as FREEDOM should not be highly rated. Britain, with an army to enforce her tyranny, has declared that she has a right (*not only* to tax) but *"to BIND us in ALL CASES*

FROM "The American Crisis: I," *The Political Writings of Thomas Paine* (New York: Solomon King, 1830), Vol. I, pp. 75–76, 78–82.

WHATSOEVER," and if being *bound in that manner* is not slavery, then is there not such a thing as slavery upon earth. Even the expression is impious, for so unlimited a power can belong only to God.

Whether the independence of the continent was declared too soon, or delayed too long, I will not now enter into as an argument; my own simple opinion is, that had it been eight months earlier, it would have been much better. We did not make a proper use of last winter, neither could we, while we were in a dependent state. However, the fault, if it were one, was all our own; we have none to blame but ourselves. But no great deal is lost yet; all that Howe has been doing for this month past, is rather a ravage than a conquest, which the spirit of the Jerseys a year ago would have quickly repulsed, and which time and a little resolution will soon recover.

I have as little superstition in me as any man living, but my secret opinion has ever been, and still is, that God Almighty will not give up a people to military destruction, or leave them unsupportedly to perish, who have so earnestly and so repeatedly sought to avoid the calamities of war, by every decent method which wisdom could invent.

Neither have I so much of the infidel in me, as to suppose that He has relinquished the government of the world, and given us up to the care of devils; and as I do not, I cannot see on what grounds the King of Britain can look up to heaven for help against us: a common murderer, a highwayman, or a housebreaker, has as good a pretence as he.

'Tis surprising to see how rapidly a panic will sometimes run through a country. All nations and ages have been subject to them: Britain has trembled like an ague at the report of a French fleet of flat bottomed boats, and in the fourteenth century the whole English army, after ravaging the kingdom of France, was driven back like men petrified with fear; and this brave exploit was performed by a few broken forces collected and headed by a woman, Joan of Arc. Would that heaven might inspire some Jersey maid to spirit up her countrymen, and save her fair fellow sufferers from ravage and ravishment! Yet panics, in some cases, have their uses; they produce as much good as hurt. Their duration is always short; the mind soon grows through them, and acquires a firmer habit than before. But their peculiar advantage is, that they are the touchstones of sincerity and hypocrisy, and bring things and men to light, which might otherwise have lain forever undiscovered. In fact, they have the same effect on secret traitors, which an imaginary apparition would have upon a private murderer. They sift out the hidden thoughts of man, and hold them up in public to the world. Many a disguised tory has lately shown his head, that shall penitentially solemnize with curses the day on which Howe arrived upon the Delaware. . . .

I shall not now attempt to give all the particulars of our retreat to the Delaware; suffice it for the present to say, that both officers and men, though greatly harassed and fatigued, frequently without rest, covering, or provision, the inevitable consequences of a long retreat, bore it with a manly and martial spirit. All their wishes centered in one, which was, that the country would turn out and help them to drive the enemy back. Voltaire has remarked that King William never appeared to full advantage but in difficulties and in action; the same remark may be made on General Washington, for the character fits him. There is a natural firmness in some minds which cannot be unlocked by trifles, but which, when unlocked, discovers a cabinet of fortitude; and I reckon it among those kind of public blessings, which we do not immediately see, that God has blessed him with uninterrupted health, and given him a mind that can even flourish upon care.

I shall conclude this paper with some miscellaneous remarks on the state of our affairs; and shall begin with asking the following questions: Why is it that the enemy have left the New England provinces, and made these middle ones the seat of war? The answer is easy: New England is not infested with tories, and we are. I have been tender in raising the cry against these men, and used numberless arguments to show them their danger, but it will not do to sacrifice a world either to their folly or their baseness. The period is now arrived, in which either they or we must change our sentiments, or one or both must fall. And what is a tory? Good God! what is he? I should not be afraid to go with a hundred whigs against a thousand tories, were they to attempt to get into arms. Every tory is a coward; for servile, slavish, self-interested fear is the foundation of toryism; and a man under such influence, though he may be cruel, never can be brave.

But, before the line of irrecoverable separation be drawn between us, let us reason the matter together: your conduct is an invitation to the enemy, yet not one in a thousand of you has heart enough to join him. Howe is as much deceived by you as the American cause is injured by you. He expects you will all take up arms and flock to his standard, with muskets on your shoulders. Your opinions are of no use to him, unless you support him personally, for 'tis soldiers, and not tories, that he wants.

I once felt all that kind of anger, which a man ought to feel, against the mean principles that are held by the tories: a noted one, who kept a tavern at Amboy, was standing at his door, with as pretty a child in his hand, about eight or nine years old, as I ever saw, and after speaking his mind as freely as he thought was prudent, finished with this unfatherly expression, *"Well! give me peace in my day."* Not a man lives on the continent but fully believes that a separation must some time or other finally take place, and a generous parent should have said, *"If there must be trouble, let it be in my day, that my child may have peace,"* and this single reflection, well applied, is sufficient to awaken every man to duty. Not a place upon earth might be so happy as America. Her situation is remote from all the wrangling world, and she has nothing to do but to trade with them. A man can distinguish in himself between temper and principle, and I am as confident, as I am that God governs the world, that America will never be happy till she gets clear of foreign dominion. Wars, without ceasing, will break out till that period arrives, and the continent must in the end be conqueror; for though the flame of liberty may sometimes cease to shine, the coal can never expire.

America did not, nor does not want force; but she wanted a proper application of that force. Wisdom is not the purchase of a day, and it is no wonder that we should err at the first setting off. From an excess of tenderness, we were willing to raise an army, and trusted our cause to the temporary defense of a well-meaning militia. A summer's experience has now taught us better; yet with those troops, while they were collected, we were able to set bounds to the progress of the enemy, and, thank God! they are again assembling. I always considered militia as the best troops in the world for a sudden exertion, but they will not do for a long campaign. Howe, it is probable, will make an attempt on this city; should he fail on this side of the Delaware, he is ruined: if he succeeds, our cause is not ruined. He stakes all on his side against a part on ours; admitting he succeeds, the consequence will be, that armies from both ends of the continent will march to assist their suffering friends in the middle states; for he cannot go everywhere; it is impossible. I consider Howe as the greatest enemy the tories have; he is bringing a war into their country, which, had it not been for him and partly for themselves, they had been clear of. Should he now be expelled, I wish with all the devotion of a Christian, that the names of whig and tory may never more be mentioned; but should the tories give him encouragement to come, or assistance if he come, I as sincerely wish that our next year's arms may expel them from the continent, and the congress appropriate their possessions to the relief of those who have suffered in well-doing. A single successful battle next year will settle the whole. America could carry on a two years' war by the confiscation of the property of disaffected persons, and be made happy by their expulsion. Say not that this is revenge, call it rather the soft resentment of a suffering people, who, having no object in view but the *good* of *all,* have staked their *own all* upon a seemingly doubtful event. Yet it is folly to argue against determined hardness; eloquence may strike the ear, and the language of sorrow draw forth the tear of compassion, but nothing can reach the heart that is steeled with prejudice.

Quitting this class of men, I turn with the warm ardor of a friend to those who have nobly stood and are yet determined to stand the matter out: I call not upon a few but upon all: not on *this* state or *that* state, but on *every* state; up and help us; lay your shoulders to the wheel; better have too much force than too little, when so great an object is at stake. Let it be told to the future world, that in the depth of winter, when nothing but hope and virtue could survive, that the city and the country, alarmed at one common danger, came forth to meet and to repulse it. Say not that thousands are gone, turn out your tens of thousands; throw not the burden of the day upon Providence, but *"show your faith by your works,"* that God may bless you. It matters not where you live, or what rank of life you hold, the evil or the blessing will reach you all. The far and the near, the home counties and the back, the rich and the poor, will suffer or rejoice alike. The heart that feels not now, is dead:

the blood of his children will curse his cowardice, who shrinks back at a time when a little might have saved the whole, and made *them* happy. I love the man that can smile in trouble, that can gather strength from distress, and grow brave by reflection. 'Tis the business of little minds to shrink, but he whose heart is firm, and whose conscience approves his conduct, will pursue his principles unto death. My own line of reasoning is to myself as straight and clear as a ray of light. Not all the treasures of the world, so far as I believe, could have induced me to support an offensive war, for I think it murder; but if a thief breaks into my house, burns and destroys my property, and kills or threatens to kill me, or those that are in it, and to *"bind me in all cases whatsoever"* to his absolute will, am I to suffer it? What signifies it to me, whether he who does it is a king or a common man; my countryman or not my countryman: whether it be done by an individual villain, or an army of them? If we reason to the root of things we shall find no difference; neither can any just cause be assigned why we should punish in the one case and pardon in the other. Let them call me rebel, and welcome, I feel no concern from it; but I should suffer the misery of devils, were I to make a whore of my soul by swearing allegiance to one whose character is that of a sottish, stupid, stubborn, worthless, brutish man. I conceive likewise a horrid idea in receiving mercy from a being, who at the last day shall be shrieking to the rocks and mountains to cover him, and fleeing with terror from the orphan, the widow, and the slain of America.

There are cases which cannot be overdone by language, and this is one. There are persons too who see not the full extent of the evil which threatens them, they solace themselves with hopes that the enemy, if he succeed, will be merciful. It is the madness of folly, to expect mercy from those who have refused to do justice; and even mercy, where conquest is the object, is only a trick of war; the cunning of the fox is as murderous as the violence of the wolf; and we ought to guard equally against both. Howe's first object is partly by threats and partly by promises, to terrify or seduce the people to deliver up their arms and receive mercy. The ministry recommended the same plan to Gage, and this is what the tories call making their peace, *"a peace which passeth all understanding"* indeed! A peace which would be the immediate forerunner of a worse ruin than any we have yet thought of. Ye men of Pennsylvania, do reason upon these things! Were the back counties to give up their arms, they would fall an easy prey to the Indians, who are all armed: this perhaps is what some tories would not be sorry for. Were the home counties to deliver up their arms, they would be exposed to the resentment of the back counties, who would then have it in their power to chastise their defection at pleasure. And were any one state to give up its arms, *that* state must be garrisoned by all Howe's army of Britons and Hessians to preserve it from the anger of the rest. Mutual fear is the principal link in the chain of mutual love, and wo be to that state that breaks the compact. Howe is mercifully inviting you to barbarous destruction, and men must be either rogues or fools that will not see it. I dwell not upon the powers of imagination; I bring reason to your ears; and in language as plain as A, B, C, hold up truth to your eyes.

I thank God that I fear not. I see no real cause for fear. I know our situation well, and can see the way out of it. While our army was collected, Howe dared not risk a battle, and it is no credit to him that he decamped from the White Plains, and waited a mean opportunity to ravage the defenseless Jerseys; but it is great credit to us, that, with a handful of men, we sustained an orderly retreat for near an hundred miles, brought off our ammunition, all our field pieces, the greatest part of our stores, and had four rivers to pass. None can say that our retreat was precipitate, for we were near three weeks in performing it, that the country might have time to come in. Twice we marched back to meet the enemy, and remained out till dark. The sign of fear was not seen in our camp, and had not some of the cowardly and disaffected inhabitants spread false alarms through the country, the Jerseys had never been ravaged. Once more we are again collected and collecting, our new army at both ends of the continent is recruiting fast, and we shall be able to open the next campaign with sixty thousand men, well armed and clothed. This is our situation, and who will may know it. By perseverance and fortitude we have the prospect of a glorious issue; by cowardice and submission, the sad choice of a variety of evils—a ravaged country—a depopulated city—habitations without safety, and slavery without hope—our homes turned into barracks and bawdy-houses for Hessians, and a future race to provide for, whose fathers we shall doubt of. Look on this picture and weep over it! and if there yet remains one thoughtless wretch who believes it not, let him suffer it unlamented.
December 23, 1776

NOAH WEBSTER
A Hundred Millions of Men, All Speaking the Same Language

A new nation requires a language of its own. Though Americans spoke English, such would not long be the case; just as English itself was continually evolving, so Americans would develop from it a language of their own, fit for a nation of free men. So contended Noah Webster (1758-1843), author, lawyer, Revolutionary soldier, and lexicographer, in the introduction to his Dissertations Upon The English Language *(1789). Webster is best known for his*

FROM *Dissertations Upon the English Language,* by Noah Webster (Boston: I. Thomas Co., 1789), pp. 18–30.

American Dictionary of the English Language (*1828*), *and few are the American dictionaries that do not bear his name in their title today.*

The English tongue, tho later in its progress towards perfection, has attained to a considerable degree of purity, strength and elegance, and been employed, by an active and scientific nation, to record almost all the events and discoveries of ancient and modern times.

This language is the inheritance which the Americans have received from their British parents. To cultivate and adorn it, is a task reserved for men who shall understand the connection between language and logic, and form an adequate idea of the influence which a uniformity of speech may have on national attachments.

It will be readily admitted that the pleasures of reading and conversing, the advantage of accuracy and business, the necessity of clearness and precision in communicating ideas, require us to be able to speak and write our own tongue with ease and correctness. But there are more important reasons, why the language of this country should be reduced to such fixed principles, as may give its pronunciation and construction all the certainty and uniformity which any living tongue is capable of receiving.

The United States were settled by emigrants from different parts of Europe. But their descendants mostly speak the same tongue; and the intercourse among the learned of the different States, which the revolution has begun, and an American Court will perpetuate must gradually destroy the differences of dialect which our ancestors brought from their native countries. This approximation of dialects will be certain; but without the operation of other causes than an intercourse at Court, it will be slow and partial. The body of the people, governed by habit, will still retain their respective peculiarities of speaking; and for want of schools and proper books, fall into many inaccuracies, which, incorporating with the language of the state where they live, may imperceptibly corrupt the national language. Nothing but the establishment of schools and some uniformity in the use of books, can annihilate differences in speaking and preserve the purity of the American tongue. A sameness of pronunciation is of considerable consequence in a political view; for provincial accents are disagreeable to strangers and sometimes have an unhappy effect upon the social affections. All men have local attachments, which lead them to believe their own practice to be the least exceptionable. Pride and prejudice incline men to treat the practice of their neighbors with some degree of contempt. Thus small differences in pronunciation at first excite ridicule—a habit of laughing at the singularities of strangers is followed by disrespect—and without respect friendship is a name, and social intercourse a mere ceremony.

These remarks hold equally true, with respect to individuals, to small societies and to large communities. Small causes, such as a nick-name, or a vulgar tone in speaking, have actually created a dissocial spirit between the inhabitants of the different states, which is often discoverable in private business and public deliberations. Our political harmony is therefore concerned in a uniformity of language.

As an independent nation, our honor requires us to have a system of our own, in language as well as government. Great Britain, whose children we are, and whose language we speak, should no longer be *our* standard; for the taste of her writers is already corrupted, and her language on the decline. But if it were not so, she is at too great a distance to be our model, and to instruct us in the principles of our own tongue.

It must be considered further, that the English is the common root or stock from which our national language will be derived. All others will gradually waste away—and within a century and a half, North America will be peopled with a hundred millions of men, *all speaking the same language.* Place this idea in comparison with the present and possible future bounds of the language in Europe—consider the Eastern Continent as inhabited by nations, whose knowledge and intercourse are embarrassed by differences of language; then anticipate the period when the people of one quarter of the world, will be able to associate and converse together like children of the same family.[1] Compare this prospect, which is not visionary, with the state of the English language in Europe, almost confined to an Island and to a few millions of people; then let reason and reputation decide, how far America should be dependent on a transatlantic nation, for her standard and improvements in language.

Let me add, that whatever predilection the Americans may have for their native European tongues, and particularly the British descendants for the English, yet several circumstances render a future separation of the American tongue from the English, necessary and unavoidable. The vicinity of the European nations, with the uninterrupted communication in peace, and the changes of dominion in war, are gradually assimilating their respective languages. The English with others is suffering continual alterations. America, placed at a distance from those nations, will feel, in a much less degree, the influence of the assimilating causes; at the same time, numerous local causes, such as a new country new associations of people, new combinations of ideas in arts and science, and some intercourse with tribes wholly unknown in Europe, will introduce new words into the American tongue. These causes will produce, in a course of time, a language in North America, as different from the future language of England, as the modern Dutch, Danish and Swedish are from the German, or from one another: Like remote branches of a tree springing from the same stock; or rays of light, shot from the same center, and diverging from each other, in proportion to their distance from the point of separation.

Whether the inhabitants of America can be brought to a perfect uniformity in the pronunciation of words, it is not easy to predict; but it is certain that no

---

[1] Even supposing that a number of republics, kingdoms or empires, should within a century arise and divide this vast territory; still the subjects of all will speak the same language, and the consequence of this uniformity will be an intimacy of social intercourse hitherto unknown, and a boundless diffusion of knowledge.

attempt of the kind has been made, and an experiment, begun and pursued on the right principles, is the only way to decide the question. Schools in Great Britain have gone far towards demolishing local dialects—commerce has also had its influence—and in America these causes, operating more generally, must have a proportional effect.

In many parts of America, people at present attempt to copy the English phrases and pronunciation—an attempt that is favored by their habits, their prepossessions and the intercourse between the two countries. This attempt has, within the period of a few years, produced a multitude of changes in these particulars, especially among the leading classes of people. These changes make a difference between the language of the higher and common ranks; and indeed between the *same* ranks in *different* states; as the rage for copying the English, does not prevail equally in every part of North America.

But besides the reasons already assigned to prove this imitation absurd, there is a difficulty attending it, which will defeat the end proposed by its advocates; which is, that the English themselves have no standard of pronunciation, nor can they ever have one on the plan they propose. The Authors, who have attempted to give us a standard, make the practice of the court and stage in London the sole criterion of propriety in speaking. An attempt to establish a standard on this foundation is both *unjust* and *idle*. It is unjust, because it is abridging the nation of its rights: The *general practice* of a nation is the rule of propriety, and this practice should at least be consulted in so important a matter, as that of making laws for speaking. While all men are upon a footing and no singularities are accounted vulgar or ridiculous, every man enjoys perfect liberty. But when a particular set of men, in exalted stations, undertake to say, "we are the standards of propriety and elegance, and if all men do not conform to our practice, they shall be accounted vulgar and ignorant," they take a very great liberty with the rules of the language and the rights of civility.

But an attempt to fix a standard on the practice of any particular class of people is highly absurd: As a friend of mine once observed, it is like fixing a light house on a floating island. It is an attempt to *fix* that which is in itself *variable;* at least it must be variable so long as it is supposed that a local practice has no standard but a *local practice;* that is, no standard but *itself*. While this doctrine is believed, it will be impossible for a nation to follow as fast as the standard changes—for if the gentlemen at court constitute a standard, they are above it themselves, and their practice must shift with their passions and their whims.

But this is not all. If the practice of a few men in the capital is to be the standard, a knowledge of this must be communicated to the whole nation. Who shall do this? An able compiler perhaps attempts to give this practice in a dictionary; but it is probable that the pronunciation, even at court, or on the stage, is not uniform. The compiler therefore must follow his particular friends and patrons; in which case he is sure to be opposed and the authority of his standard called in question; or he must give two pronunciations as the standard, which leaves the student in the same uncertainty as it found him. Both these events have actually taken place in England, with respect to the most approved standards; and of course no one is universally followed.

Besides, if language must vary, like fashions, at the caprice of a court, we must have our standard dictionaries republished, with the fashionable pronunciation, at least once in five years; otherwise a gentleman in the country will become intolerably vulgar, by not being in a situation to adopt the fashion of the day. The *new* editions of them will supersede the *old,* and we shall have our pronunciation to re-learn, with the polite alterations, which are generally corruptions.

Such are the consequences of attempting to make a *local* practice the *standard* of language in a *nation.* The attempt must keep the language in perpetual fluctuation, and the learner in uncertainty.

If a standard therefore cannot be fixed on local and variable custom, on what shall it be fixed? If the most eminent speakers are not to direct our practice, where shall we look for a guide? The answer is extremely easy; the *rules of the language itself,* and the *general practice of the nation,* constitute propriety in speaking. If we examine the structure of any language, we shall find a certain principle of analogy running through the whole. We shall find in English that similar combinations of letters have usually the same pronunciation; and that words, having the same terminating syllable, generally have the accent at the same distance from that termination. These principles of analogy were not the result of design—they must have been the effect of accident, or that tendency which all men feel towards uniformity.[2] But the principles, when established, are productive of great convenience, and become an authority superior to the arbitrary decisions of any man or class of men. There is one exception only to this remark: When a deviation from analogy has become the universal practice of a nation, it then takes place of all rules and becomes the standard of propriety.

The two points therefore, which I conceive to be the basis of a standard in speaking, are these; *universal undisputed practice,* and the *principle of analogy.* *Universal practice* is generally, perhaps always, a rule of propriety; and in disputed points, where people differ in opinion and practice, *analogy* should always decide the controversy.

These are authorities to which all men will submit—they are superior to the opinions and caprices of the great, and to the negligence and ignorance of the

---

[2] This disposition is taken notice of by Dr. Blair, Lect. 8. Where he observes, "that tho the formation of abstract or general conceptions is supposed to be a difficult operation of the mind, yet such conceptions must have entered into the first formation of languages"—"this invention of abstract terms requires no great exertion of metaphysical capacity"—"Men are *naturally* inclined to call all those objects which resemble each other by one common name—We may daily observe this practiced by children, in their first attempts towards acquiring language."

I cannot, with this great critic, call the process by which *similar* objects acquire the *same* name, an act of *abstraction,* or the name an *abstract term.* Logical distinctions may lead us astray. There is in the mind an *instinctive disposition,* or *principle of association,* which will account for all common names and the analogies in language.

multitude. The authority of individuals is always liable to be called in question —but the unanimous consent of a nation, and a fixed principle interwoven with the very construction of a language, coeval and coextensive with it, are like the common laws of a land, or the immutable rules of morality, the propriety of which every man, however refractory, is forced to acknowledge, and to which most men will readily submit. Fashion is usually the child of caprice and the being of a day; principles of propriety are founded in the very nature of things, and remain unmoved and unchanged, amidst all the fluctuations of human affairs and the revolutions of time.

It must be confessed that languages are changing, from age to age, in proportion to improvements in science. Words, as Horace observes, are like leaves of trees; the old ones are dropping off and new ones growing. These changes are the necessary consequence of changes in customs, the introduction of new arts, and new ideas in the sciences. Still the body of a language and its general rules remain for ages the same, and the new words usually conform to these rules; otherwise they stand as exceptions, which are not to overthrow the principle of analogy already established. . . .

GEORGE WASHINGTON
The Baneful Effects of the Spirit of Party

Having served for the better part of two terms as first President of his country, George Washington now prepared to step down and to gain the retirement from public affairs he had so long desired. He prepared a Farewell Address to the American people, in which he set forth his views on present and future. After discussing its contents with Alexander Hamilton, to whom he had submitted a draft, he handed it to David Claypoole for publication in the American Daily Advertiser *of September 9, 1796. Washington stressed the need for unity, called for the perpetuation of the Union, warned against the divisive effect of the spirit of party, and counselled neutrality in regard to European affairs, with no permanent alliances with other nations. Then he prepared to retire to his estate at Mount Vernon, to live out the three remaining years of his life as a private citizen.*

United States, September 19, 1796.

Friends, and Fellow-Citizens: The period for a new election of a Citizen, to Administer the Executive government of the United States, being not far

FROM "Farewell Address," *The Writings of George Washington From the Original Manuscript Sources, 1745–1799,* ed. J. C. Fitzpatrick (Washington, D.C.: U.S. Govt. P. O., 1940), Vol. XXXV: March 30, 1796–July 31, 1797, pp. 214–15, 218–24, 226–27, 229–38.

distant, and the time actually arrived, when your thoughts must be employed in designating the person, who is to be cloathed with that important trust, it appears to me proper, especially as it may conduce to a more distinct expression of the public voice, that I should now apprise you of the resolution I have formed, to decline being considered among the number of those, out of whom a choice is to be made.

I beg you, at the same time, to do me the justice to be assured, that this resolution has not been taken, without a strict regard to all the considerations appertaining to the relation, which binds a dutiful citizen to his country, and that, in with drawing the tender of service which silence in my situation might imply, I am influenced by no diminution of zeal for your future interest, no deficiency of grateful respect for your past kindness; but am supported by a full conviction that the step is compatible with both. . . .

Interwoven as is the love of liberty with every ligament of your hearts, no recommendation of mine is necessary to fortify or confirm the attachment.

The Unity of Government which constitutes you one people is also now dear to you. It is justly so; for it is a main Pillar in the Edifice of your real independence, the support of your tranquility at home; your peace abroad; of your safety; of your prosperity; of that very Liberty which you so highly prize. But as it is easy to foresee, that from different causes and from different quarters, much pains will be taken, many artifices employed, to weaken in your minds the conviction of this truth; as this is the point in your political fortress against which the batteries of internal and external enemies will be most constantly and actively (though often covertly and insidiously) directed, it is of infinite moment, that you should properly estimate the immense value of your national Union to your collective and individual happiness; that you should cherish a cordial, habitual and immoveable attachment to it; accustoming yourselves to think and speak of it as of the Palladium of your political safety and prosperity; watching for its preservation with jealous anxiety; discountenancing whatever may suggest even a suspicion that it can in any event be abandoned, and indignantly frowning upon the first dawning of every attempt to alienate any portion of our Country from the rest, or to enfeeble the sacred ties which now link together the various parts. . . .

The *North*, in an unrestrained intercourse with the *South*, protected by the equal Laws of a common government, finds in the productions of the latter, great additional resources of Maritime and commercial enterprise and precious materials of manufacturing industry. The *South* in the same Intercourse, benefitting by the Agency of the *North*, sees its agriculture grow and its commerce expand. Turning partly into its own channels the seamen of the *North*, it finds its particular navigation envigorated; and while it contributes, in different ways, to nourish and increase the general mass of the National navigation, it looks forward to the protection of a Maritime strength, to which itself is unequally adapted. The *East*, in a like intercourse with the West, already finds, and in the progressive improvement of interior communications, by land

and water, will more and more find a valuable vent for the commodities which it brings from abroad, or manufactures at home. The *West* derives from the *East* supplies requisite to its growth and comfort, and what is perhaps of still greater consequence, it must of necessity owe the *secure* enjoyment of indispensable *outlets* for its own productions to the weight, influence, and the future Maritime strength of the Atlantic side of the Union, directed by an indissoluble community of Interest as *one Nation.* Any other tenure by which the *West* can hold this essential advantage, whether derived from its own seperate strength, or from an apostate and unnatural connection with any foreign Power, must be intrinsically precarious.

While then every part of our country thus feels an immediate and particular Interest in Union, all the parts combined cannot fail to find in the united mass of means and efforts greater strength, greater resource, proportionably greater security from external danger, a less frequent interruption of their Peace by foreign Nations; and, what is of inestimable value! they must derive from Union an exemption from those broils and Wars between themselves, which so frequently afflict neighbouring countries, not tied together by the same government; which their own rivalships alone would be sufficient to produce, but which opposite foreign alliances, attachments and intriegues would stimulate and imbitter. Hence likewise they will avoid the necessity of those overgrown Military establishments, which under any form of Government are inauspicious to liberty, and which are to be regarded as particularly hostile to Republican Liberty: In this sense it is, that your Union ought to be considered as a main prop of your liberty, and that the love of the one ought to endear to you the preservation of the other. . . .

In contemplating the causes wch. may disturb our Union, it occurs as matter of serious concern, that any ground should have been furnished for characterizing parties by *Geographical* discriminations: *Northern* and *Southern; Atlantic* and *Western;* whence designing men may endeavour to excite a belief that there is a real difference of local interests and views. One of the expedients of Party to acquire influence, within particular districts, is to misrepresent the opinions and aims of other Districts. You cannot shield yourselves too much against the jealousies and heart burnings which spring from these misrepresentations. They tend to render Alien to each other those who ought to be bound together by fraternal affection. . . .

To the efficacy and permanency of Your Union, a Government for the whole is indispensable. No Alliances however strict between the parts can be an adequate substitute. They must inevitably experience the infractions and interruptions which all Alliances in all times have experienced. Sensible of this momentous truth, you have improved upon your first essay, by the adoption of a Constitution of Government, better calculated than your former for an intimate Union, and for the efficacious management of your common concerns. This government, the offspring of our own choice uninfluenced and unawed, adopted upon full investigation and mature deliberation, completely free in its principles, in the distribution of its powers, uniting security with energy, and containing within itself a provision for its own amendment, has a just claim to your confidence and your support. Respect for its authority, compliance with its Laws, acquiescence in its measures, are duties enjoined by the fundamental maxims of true Liberty. The basis of our political systems is the right of the people to make and to alter their Constitutions of Government. But the Constitution which at any time exists, 'till changed by an explicit and authentic act of the whole People, is sacredly obligatory upon all. The very idea of the power and the right of the People to establish Government presupposes the duty of every Individual to obey the established Government. . . .

I have already intimated to you the danger of Parties in the State, with particular reference to the founding of them on Geographical discriminations. Let me now take a more comprehensive view, and warn you in the most solemn manner against the baneful effects of the Spirit of Party, generally.

This spirit, unfortunately, is inseperable from our nature, having its root in the strongest passions of the human Mind. It exists under different shapes in all Governments, more or less stifled, controuled, or repressed; but, in those of the popular form it is seen in its greatest rankness and is truly their worst enemy.

The alternate domination of one faction over another, sharpened by the spirit of revenge natural to party dissention, which in different ages and countries has perpetrated the most horrid enormities, is itself a frightful despotism. But this leads at length to a more formal and permanent despotism. The disorders and miseries, which result, gradually incline the minds of men to seek security and repose in the absolute power of an Individual: and sooner or later the chief of some prevailing faction more able or more fortunate than his competitors, turns this disposition to the purposes of his own elevation, on the ruins of Public Liberty.

Without looking forward to an extremity of this kind (which nevertheless ought not to be entirely out of sight) the common and continual mischiefs of the spirit of Party are sufficient to make it the interest and the duty of a wise People to discourage and restrain it. . . .

'Tis substantially true, that virtue or morality is a necessary spring of popular government. The rule indeed extends with more or less force to every species of free Government. Who that is a sincere friend to it, can look with indifference upon attempts to shake the foundation of the fabric.

Promote then as an object of primary importance, Institutions for the general diffusion of knowledge. In proportion as the structure of a government gives force to public opinion, it is essential that public opinion should be enlightened.

As a very important source of strength and security, cherish public credit. One method of preserving it is to use it as sparingly as possible: avoiding occasions of expence by cultivating peace, but remembering also that timely disbursements to prepare for danger frequently prevent much greater disbursements to repel it; avoiding likewise the accumulation of debt, not only by shunning occasions of expence, but by vigorous exertions in time of Peace to discharge the Debts which unavoidable wars may have occasioned, not ungenerously throwing upon posterity the burthen which we ourselves ought to bear. The execution of these maxims belongs to your Representatives, but it is necessary that public opinion should cooperate. To facilitate to them the performance of their duty, it is essential that you should practically bear in mind, that towards the payment of debts there must be Revenue; that to have Revenue there must be taxes; that no taxes can be devised which are not more or less inconvenient and unpleasant; that the intrinsic embarrassment inseperable from the selection of the proper objects (which is always a choice of difficulties) ought to be a decisive motive for a candid constructon of the Conduct of the Government in making it, and for a spirit of acquiescence in the measures for obtaining Revenue which the public exigencies may at any time dictate.

Observe good faith and justice towds. all Nations. Cultivate peace and harmony with all. Religion and morality enjoin this conduct; and can it be that good policy does not equally enjoin it? It will be worthy of a free, enlightened, and, at no distant period, a great Nation, to give to mankind the magnanimous and too novel example of a People always guided by an exalted justice and benevolence. Who can doubt that in the course of time and things the fruits of such a plan would richly repay any temporary advantages wch. might be lost by a steady adherence to it? Can it be, that Providence has not connected the permanent felicity of a Nation with its virtue? The experiment, at least, is recommended by every sentiment which ennobles human Nature. Alas! is it rendered impossible by its vices?

In the execution of such a plan nothing is more essential than that permanent, inveterate antipathies against particular Nations and passionate attachments for others should be excluded; and that in place of them just and amicable feelings towards all should be cultivated. The Nation, which indulges towards another an habitual hatred, or an habitual fondness, is in some degree a slave. It is a slave to its animosity or to its affection, either of which is sufficient to lead it astray from its duty and its interest. Antipathy in one Nation against another, disposes each more readily to offer insult and injury, to lay hold of slight causes of umbrage, and to be haughty and intractable, when accidental or trifling occasions of dispute occur. Hence frequent collisions, obstinate envenomed and bloody contests. The Nation, prompted by illwill and resentment sometimes impels to War the Government, contrary to the best calculations of policy. The Government sometimes participates in the national propensity, and adopts through passion what reason would reject; at other times, it makes the animosity of the Nation subservient to projects of hostility instigated by pride, ambition, and other sinister and pernicious motives. The peace often, sometimes perhaps the Liberty, of Nations has been the victim. . . .

Against the insidious wiles of foreign influence, (I conjure you to believe me fellow citizens) the jealousy of a free people ought to be *constantly* awake; since history and experience prove that foreign influence is one of the most baneful foes of Republican Government. But that jealousy to be useful must be impartial; else it becomes the instrument of the very influence to be avoided, instead of a defence against it. Excessive partiality for one foreign nation and excessive dislike of another, cause those whom they actuate to see danger only on one side, and serve to veil and even second the arts of influence on the other. Real Patriots, who may resist the intriegues of the favourite, are liable to become suspected and odious; while its tools and dupes usurp the applause and confidence of the people, to surrender their interests.

The Great rule of conduct for us, in regard to foreign Nations is in extending our commercial relations to have with them as little *political* connection as possible. So far as we have already formed engagements let them be fulfilled, with perfect good faith. Here let us stop.

Europe has a set of primary interests, which to us have none, or a very remote relation. Hence she must be engaged in frequent controversies, the causes of which are essentially foreign to our concerns. Hence therefore it must be unwise in us to implicate ourselves, by artificial ties, in the ordinary vicissitudes of her politics, or the ordinary combinations and collisions of her friendships or enmities:

Our detached and distant situation invites and enables us to pursue a different course. If we remain one People, under an efficient government, the period is not far off, when we may defy material injury from external annoyance; when we may take such an attitude as will cause the neutrality we may at any time resolve upon to be scrupulously respected; when belligerent nations, under the impossibility of making acquisitions upon us, will not lightly hazard the giving us provocation; when we may choose peace or war, as our interest guided by our justice shall Counsel.

Why forego the advantages of so peculiar a situation? Why quit our own to stand upon foreign ground? Why, by interweaving our destiny with that of any part of Europe, entangle our peace and prosperity in the toils of European Ambition, Rivalship, Interest, Humour or Caprice?

'Tis our true policy to steer clear of permanent Alliances, with any portion of the foreign world. So far, I mean, as we are now at liberty to do it, for let me not be understood as capable of patronising infidelity to existing engagements (I hold the maxim no less applicable to public than to private affairs, that honesty is always the best policy). I repeat it therefore, let those engagements be observed in their genuine sense. But in my opinion, it is unnecessary and would be unwise to extend them.

Taking care always to keep ourselves, by suitable establishments, on a respectably defensive posture, we may safely trust to temporary alliances for extraordinary emergencies.

Harmony, liberal intercourse with all Nations, are recommended by policy, humanity and interest. But even our Commercial policy should hold an equal and impartial hand: neither seeking nor granting exclusive favours or preferences; consulting the natural course of things; diffusing and deversifying by gentle means the streams of Commerce, but forcing nothing; establishing with Powers so disposed; in order to give to trade a stable course, to define the rights of our Merchants, and to enable the Government to support them; conventional rules of intercourse, the best that present circumstances and mutual opinion will permit, but temporary, and liable to be from time to time abandoned or varied, as experience and circumstances shall dictate; constantly keeping in view, that 'tis folly in one Nation to look for disinterested favors from another; that it must pay with a portion of its Independence for whatever it may accept under that character; that by such acceptance, it may place itself in the condition of having given equivalents for nominal favours and yet of being reproached with ingratitude for not giving more. There can be no greater error than to expect, or calculate upon real favours from Nation to Nation. 'Tis an illusion which experience must cure, which a just pride ought to discard.

In offering to you, my Countrymen these counsels of an old and affectionate friend, I dare not hope they will make the strong and lasting impression, I could wish; that they will controul the usual current of the passions, or prevent our Nation from running the course which has hitherto marked the Destiny of Nations: But if I may even flatter myself, that they may be productive of some partial benefit, some occasional good; that they may now and then recur to moderate the fury of party spirit, to warn against the mischiefs of foreign Intriegue, to guard against the Impostures of pretended patriotism; this hope will be a full recompence for the solicitude for your welfare, by which they have been dictated. . . .

Though in reviewing the incidents of my Administration, I am unconscious of intentional error, I am nevertheless too sensible of my defects not to think it probable that I may have committed many errors. Whatever they may be I fervently beseech the Almighty to avert or mitigate the evils to which they may tend. I shall also carry with me the hope that my Country will never cease to view them with indulgence; and that after forty five years of my life dedicated to its Service, with an upright zeal, the faults of incompetent abilities will be consigned to oblivion, as myself must soon be to the Mansions of rest.

Relying on its kindness in this as in other things, and actuated by that fervent love towards it, which is so natural to a Man, who views in it the native soil of himself and his progenitors for several Generations; I anticipate with pleasing expectation that retreat, in which I promise myself to realize, without alloy, the sweet enjoyment of partaking, in the midst of my fellow Citizens, the benign influence of good Laws under a free Government, the ever favourite object of my heart, and the happy reward, as I trust, of our mutual cares, labours and dangers.

JAMES MADISON
To Interpose for Arresting the Progress of the Evil

*When in 1798 the Federalist-controlled Congress passed a series of Alien and
Sedition Acts designed to combat pro-French activities of the Jeffersonian Republicans, the arrest of editors, writers, and speakers charged with attacking
the government was authorized. Numerous Jeffersonian leaders and supporters
were arrested and convicted. The Republicans vigorously attacked the new
laws as despotic and unconstitutional, and in 1798 the state legislatures of
Kentucky and Virginia passed resolutions against them. The Kentucky resolutions were drafted by Jefferson and those of Virginia by James Madison
(1751–1836). Madison's resolutions, the text of which follows, declared that
when the national government exercises powers not specifically granted to it
in the Constitution, the states "have the right and are in duty bound to interpose for arresting the progress of the evil." When the Jeffersonians came into
power in 1801, they repealed the acts. Later Madison's strict constructionist
view of the Constitution was used by South Carolina as a justification for
nullification in 1832, whereupon Madison declared emphatically that the Virginia and Kentucky Resolutions had countenanced no such doctrine.*

IN THE HOUSE OF DELEGATES
Friday, December 21, 1798

Resolved, That the general assembly of Virginia doth unequivocally express
a firm resolution to maintain and defend the constitution of the United States,
and the constitution of this state, against every aggression either foreign or
domestic and that they will support the government of the United States in all
measures warranted by the former. . . .

The general assembly most solemnly declares a warm attachment to the
union of the states, to maintain which it pledges all its powers; and that, for
this end, it is their duty to watch over and oppose every infraction of those
principles which constitute the only basis of that union, because a faithful
observance of them can alone secure its existence and the public happiness. . . .

That this assembly doth explicitly and peremptorily declare, that it views
the powers of the federal government, as resulting from the compact, to which
the states are parties, as limited by the plain sense and intention of the instrument constituting that compact; as no farther valid than they are authorized

FROM "Resolutions of 1798," in *Resolutions of Virginia and Kentucky Penned by Madison and
Jefferson* (Richmond, Va.: Robert I. Smith, 1835), pp. 25–26, 30, 34, 58, 60–61.

by the grants enumerated in that compact; and that, in case of a deliberate, palpable, and dangerous exercise of other powers, not granted by the said compact, the states, who are parties thereto, have the right, and are in duty bound, to interpose for arresting the progress of the evil, and for maintaining within their respective limits, the authorities, rights, and liberties appertaining to them. . . .

That the general assembly doth also express its deep regret, that a spirit has in sundry instances, been manifested by the federal government, to enlarge its powers by forced constructions of the constitutional charter which defines them; and that indications have appeared of a design to expound certain general phrases, (which, having been copied from the very limited grant of powers in the former articles of confederation, were the less liable to be misconstrued) so as to destroy the meaning and effect of the particular enumeration which necessarily explains, and limits the general phrases; and so as to consolidate the states, by degrees, into one sovereignty, the obvious tendency and inevitable result of which would be, to transform the present republican system of the United States, into an absolute, or, at best, a mixed monarchy.

That the general assembly doth particularly protest against the palpable and alarming infractions of the constitution, in the two late cases of the "alien and sedition acts," passed at the last session of congress; the first of which exercises a power no where delegated to the federal government; and which, by uniting legislative and judicial powers to those of executive, subverts the general principles of a free government, as well as the particular organization and positive provisions of the federal constitution; and the other of which acts exercises, in like manner, a power not delegated by the constitution; but, on the contrary, expressly and positively forbidden by one of the amendments thereto: a power, which, more than any other, ought to produce universal alarm; because it is levelled against that right of freely examining public characters and measures, and of free communication among the people thereon, which has ever been justly deemed the only effectual guardian of every other right. . . .

That this state having by its convention, which ratified the federal constitution, expressly declared, that, among other essential rights, "the liberty of conscience and of the press cannot be cancelled, abridged, restrained or modified by any authority of the United States," and from its extreme anxiety to guard these rights from every possible attack of sophistry and ambition, having, with other states, recommended an amendment for that purpose, which amendment was, in due time, annexed to the constitution, it would mark a reproachful inconsistency, and criminal degeneracy, if an indifference were now shown, to the most palpable violation of one of the rights thus declared and secured, and to the establishment of a precedent, which may be fatal to the other. . . .

That the good people of this commonwealth, having ever felt and continuing to feel the most sincere affection for their brethren of the other states; the truest anxiety for establishing and perpetuating the union of all; and the most scrupulous fidelity to that constitution, which is the pledge of mutual friendship, and the instrument of mutual happiness; the general assembly doth solemnly appeal to the like dispositions of the other states, in confidence that they will concur with this commonwealth in declaring, as it does hereby declare, that the acts aforesaid are unconstitutional; and, that the necessary and proper measures will be taken by each, for co-operating with this state, in maintaining unimpaired, the authorities, rights, and liberties reserved to the states respectively, or to the people.

That the governor be desired to transmit a copy of the foregoing resolutions to the executive authority of each of the other states, with a request that the same may be communicated to the legislature thereof; and that a copy be furnished to each of the senators and representatives, representing this state in the congress of the United States. . . .

THOMAS JEFFERSON / JOHN ADAMS
We Ought Not to Die Before We Have Explained Ourselves to Each Other

In the years after 1808, when Thomas Jefferson left Washington and public life for a long retirement at his beloved Monticello, the once-strong friendship between Jefferson and John Adams (1735–1826), broken by political differences for many years, was renewed. The second and third Presidents of the United States engaged in a lengthy correspondence for the remaining years of their lives, ending only when both men died on July 4, 1826, exactly fifty years after enactment of the Declaration of Independence which Jefferson had written and both had signed. The Adams-Jefferson correspondence constitutes one·of the American nation's most precious spiritual heritages. In the two letters reprinted here (Jefferson to Adams, October 28, 1813; Adams to Jefferson, November 15, 1813), the two ex-Presidents speculate on aristocracy and democracy. The exchange between them, with its implied disagreement about the nature of man and society, was one that would be argued out by many an American writer in years to come.

Jefferson to Adams

Monticello, October 28, 1813

Dear Sir,

According to the reservation between us, of taking up one of the subjects of our correspondence at a time, I turn to your letters of August the 16th and September the 2nd.

FROM Jefferson to Adams, October 28, 1813, from *Memoir, Correspondence, and Miscellanies, from the Papers of Thomas Jefferson,* ed. Thomas Jefferson Randolph (Boston: Gray and Bowen, 1830), Vol. IV, pp. 226–31. Adams to Jefferson, November 15, 1813, from *The Works of Thomas Jefferson,* ed. H. A. Washington (New York: Townsend MacConn, 1884), Vol. VI, pp. 254–60.

The passage you quote from Theognis, I think has an ethical rather than a political object. The whole piece is a moral *exhortation,* παραίνεσις and this passage particularly seems to be a reproof to man, who, while with his domestic animals he is curious to improve the race, by employing always the finest male, pays no attention to the improvement of his own race, but intermarries with the vicious, the ugly, or the old, for considerations of wealth or ambition. It is in conformity with the principle adopted afterwards by the Pythagoreans, and expressed by Ocellus in another form; Περὶ δὲ τῆς ἐξ ἀλλήλων ἀνθρώπων γενέσεως &c. . . . . οὐχ ἡδονῆς ἕνεχα ἡ μίξις· which, as literally as intelligibility will admit, may be thus translated; 'Concerning the interprocreation of men, how, and of whom it shall be, in a perfect manner, and according to the laws of modesty and sanctity, conjointly, this is what I think right. First, to lay it down that we do not commix for the sake of pleasure, but of the procreation of children. For the powers, the organs, and desires for coition have not been given by God to man for the sake of pleasure, but for the procreation of the race. For as it were incongruous for a mortal born to partake of divine life, the immortality of the race being taken away, God fulfilled the purpose by making the generations uninterrupted and continuous. This, therefore, we are especially to lay down as a principle, that coition is not for the sake of pleasure.' But nature, not trusting to this moral and abstract motive, seems to have provided more securely for the perpetuation of the species, by making it the effect of the *œstrum* implanted in the constitution of both sexes. And not only has the commerce of love been indulged on this unhallowed impulse, but made subservient also to wealth and ambition by marriages, without regard to the beauty, the healthiness, the understanding, or virtue of the subject from which we are to breed. The selecting the best male for a Haram of well chosen females, also, which Theognis seems to recommend from the example of our sheep and asses, would doubtless improve the human, as it does the brute animal, and produce a race of veritable ἄριστοι [aristocrats]. For experience proves that the moral and physical qualities of man, whether good or evil, are transmissible in a certain degree from father to son. But I suspect that the equal rights of men will rise up against this privileged Solomon and his Haram, and oblige us to continue acquiescence under the 'Αμαύρωσις γένεος ἀστῶν [race's degeneration] which Theognis complains of, and to content ourselves with the accidental *aristoi* produced by the fortuitous concourse of breeders. For I agree with you, that there is a natural aristocracy among men. The grounds of this are virtue and talents. Formerly, bodily powers gave place among the *aristoi*. But since the invention of gunpowder has armed the weak as well as the strong with missile death, bodily strength, like beauty, good humor, politeness, and other accomplishments, has become but an auxiliary ground of distinction. There is also an artificial aristocracy, founded on wealth and birth, without either virtue or talents; for with these it would belong to the first class. The natural aristocracy I consider as the most precious gift of nature, for the instruction, the trusts, and government of society. And, indeed, it would have been inconsistent in creation to have formed man for the social state, and not to have provided virtue and wisdom enough to manage the concerns of the society. May we not even say, that that form of government is the best, which provides the most effectually for a pure selection of these natural *aristoi* into the offices of government? The artificial aristocracy is a mischievous ingredient in government, and provision should be made to prevent its ascendancy. On the question, what is the best provision, you and I differ; but we differ as rational friends, using the free exercise of our own reason, and mutually indulging its errors. You think it best to put the *pseudo-aristoi* into a separate chamber of legislation, where they may be hindered from doing mischief by their co-ordinate branches, and where, also, they may be a protection to wealth against the Agrarian and plundering enterprises of the majority of the people. I think that to give them power in order to prevent them from doing mischief, is arming them for it, and increasing instead of remedying the evil. For if the co-ordinate branches can arrest their action, so may they that of the co-ordinates. Mischief may be done negatively as well as positively. Of this, a cabal in the Senate of the United States has furnished many proofs. Nor do I believe them necessary to protect the wealthy; because enough of these will find their way into every branch of the legislation, to protect themselves. From fifteen to twenty legislatures of our own, in action for thirty years past, have proved that no fears of an equalization of property are to be apprehended from them. I think the best remedy is exactly that provided by all our constitutions, to leave to the citizens the free election and separation of the *aristoi* from the *pseudo-aristoi,* of the wheat from the chaff. In general, they will elect the really good and wise. In some instances, wealth may corrupt, and birth blind them; but not in sufficient degree to endanger the society.

It is probable that our difference of opinion may, in some measure, be produced by a difference of character in those among whom we live. From what I have seen of Massachusetts and Connecticut myself, and still more from what I have heard, and the character given of the former by yourself, who know them so much better, there seems to be in those two States a traditionary reverence for certain families, which has rendered the offices of government nearly hereditary in those families. I presume that from an early period of your history, members of these families happening to possess virtue and talents, have honestly exercised them for the good of the people, and by their services have endeared their names to them. In coupling Connecticut with you, I mean it politically only, not morally. For having made the Bible the common law of their land, they seem to have modeled their morality on the story of Jacob and Laban. But although this hereditary succession to office with you may, in some degree, be founded in real family merit, yet in a much higher degree, it has proceeded from your strict alliance of Church and State. These families are canonized in the eyes of the people on the common principle, 'You tickle me, and I will tickle you.' In Virginia, we have nothing of this. Our clergy, before the revolution, having been secured against rivalship by fixed salaries, did not give themselves the trouble of acquiring influence over the people. Of wealth, there were great accumulations in particular families, handed down from generation to generation, under the English law of entails. But the only object of ambition for the wealthy was a seat in the King's Council. All their court then was paid to the crown and its creatures; and they Phillipized in all collisions between the King and the people. Hence they were unpopular; and that unpopularity continues attached to their names. A Randolph, a Carter, or a Burwell must have great personal superiority over a common competitor, to be elected by the people, even at this day. At the first session of our legislature after the Declaration of Independence, we passed a law abolishing entails. And this was followed by one abolishing the privilege of primogeniture, and dividing the lands of intestates equally among all their children, or other representatives. These laws, drawn by myself, laid the axe to the root of pseudo-aristocracy. And had another which I prepared been adopted by the legislature, our work would have been complete. It was a bill for the more general diffusion of learning. This proposed to divide every county into wards of five or six miles square, like your townships; to establish in each ward a free school for reading, writing, and common arithmetic; to provide for the annual selection of the best subjects from these schools, who might receive, at the public expense, a higher degree of education at a district school; and from these district schools to select a certain number of the most promising subjects, to be completed at an University, where all the useful sciences should be taught. Worth and genius would thus have been sought out from every condition of life, and completely prepared by education for defeating the competition of wealth and birth for public trusts. My proposition had, for a further object, to impart to these wards those portions of self-government for which they are best qualified, by confiding to them the care of their poor, their roads, police, elections; the nomination of jurors, administration of justice in small cases, elementary exercises of militia; in short, to have made them little republics, with a warden at the head of each, for all those concerns which, being under their eye, they would better manage than the larger republics of the county or State. A general call of ward-meetings by their wardens on the same day through the State, would at any time produce the genuine sense of the people on any required point, and would enable the State to act in mass, as your people have so often done, and with so much effect, by their town-meetings. The law for religious freedom, which made a part of this system, having put down the aristocracy of the clergy, and restored to the citizen the freedom of the mind, and those of entails and descents nurturing an equality of condition among them, this on education would have raised the mass of the people to the high ground of moral respectability necessary to their own safety, and to orderly government; and would have completed the great object of qualifying them to select the veritable *aristoi,* for the trusts of government, to the exclusion of the pseudalists: and the same Theognis, who has furnished the epigraphs of your two letters, assures us that Οὐδεμίανπω, Κύρν, ἀγαθοί πόλιν ὤλεσαν ἄνδρες [good men have never brought harm to a city]. Although this law has not yet been acted on but in a small and inefficient degree, it is still considered as before the legislature, with other bills of the revised code, not yet taken up, and I have great hope that some patriotic spirit will, at a favorable moment, call it up, and make it the key-stone of the arch of our government.

With respect to aristocracy, we should further consider that before the establishment of the American States, nothing was known to history but the man of the old world, crowded within limits either small or overcharged, and steeped in the vices which that situation generates. A government adapted to such men would be one thing; but a very different one, that for the man of these States. Here every one may have land to labor for himself, if he chooses; or, preferring the exercise of any other industry, may exact for it such compensation as not only to afford a comfortable subsistence, but wherewith to provide for a cessation from labor in old age. Every one, by his property or by his satisfactory situation, is interested in the support of law and order. And such men may safely and advantageously reserve to themselves a wholesome control over their public affairs, and a degree of freedom, which, in the hands of the *canaille* of the cities of Europe, would be instantly perverted to the demolition and destruction of every thing public and private. The history of the last twenty-five years of France, and of the last forty years in America, nay, of its last two hundred years, proves the truth of both parts of this observation.

But even in Europe a change has sensibly taken place in the mind of man. Science had liberated the ideas of those who read and reflect, and the American example had kindled feelings of right in the people. An insurrection has consequently begun, of science, talents, and courage, against rank and birth, which have fallen into contempt. It has failed in its first effort, because the mobs of the cities, the instrument used for its accomplishment, debased by ignorance, poverty, and vice, could not be restrained to rational action. But the world will recover from the panic of this first catastrophe. Science is progressive, and talents and enterprise on the alert. Resort may be had to the people of the country, a more governable power from their principles and subordination; and rank and birth and tinsel-aristocracy will finally shrink into insignificance, even there. This, however, we have no right to meddle with. It suffices for us, if the moral and physical condition of our own citizens qualifies them to select the able and good for the direction of their government, with a recurrence of elections at such short periods as will enable them to displace an unfaithful servant, before the mischief he meditates may be irremediable.

I have thus stated my opinion on a point on which we differ, not with a view to controversy, for we are both too old to change opinions which are the result of a long life of inquiry and reflection; but on the suggestion of a former letter of yours, that we ought not to die before we have explained ourselves to each other. We acted in perfect harmony, through a long and perilous contest for our liberty and independence. A constitution has been acquired, which, though neither of us thinks perfect, yet both consider as competent to render our fellow-citizens the happiest and the securest on whom the sun has ever shone. If we do not think exactly alike as to its imperfections, it matters little to our country, which, after devoting to it long lives of disinterested labor we have delivered over to our successors in life, who will be able to take care of it and of themselves.

Of the pamphlet on aristocracy which has been sent to you, or who may be its author, I have heard nothing but through your letter. If the person you suspect, it may be known from the quaint, mystical, and hyperbolical ideas, involved in affected, newfangled, and pedantic terms, which stamp his writings. Whatever it be, I hope your quiet is not to be affected at this day by the rudeness or intemperance of scribblers; but that you may continue in tranquility to live and to rejoice in the prosperity of our country, until it shall be your own wish to take your seat among the *aristoi* who have gone before you.

Ever and affectionately yours.

Adams to Jefferson

Quincy, November 15, 1813
Dear Sir,

I cannot appease my melancholy commiseration for our armies in this furious snow storm, in any way so well as by studying your letter of Oct. 28.

We are now explicitly agreed upon one important point, viz., that there is a natural aristocracy among men, the grounds of which are virtue and talents. You very justly indulge a little merriment upon this solemn subject of aristocracy. I often laugh at it too, for there is nothing in this laughable world more ridiculous than the management of it by all the nations of the earth; but while we smile, mankind have reason to say to us, as the frogs said to the boys, what is sport to you, are wounds and death to us. When I consider the weakness, the folly, the pride, the vanity, the selfishness, the artifice, the low craft and mean cunning, the want of principle, the avarice, the unbounded ambition, the unfeeling cruelty of a majority of those (in all nations) who are allowed an aristocratical influence, and, on the other hand, the stupidity with which the more numerous multitude not only become their dupes, but even love to be taken in by their tricks, I feel a stronger disposition to weep at their destiny, than to laugh at their folly. But though we have agreed in one point, in words, it is not yet certain that we are perfectly agreed in sense. Fashion has introduced an indeterminate use of the word talents. Education, wealth, strength, beauty, stature, birth, marriage, graceful attitudes and motions, gait, air, complexion, physiognomy, are talents, as well as genius, science, and learning. Any one of these talents that in fact commands or influences two votes in society, gives to the man who possesses it the character of an aristocrat, in my sense of the word. Pick up the first hundred men you meet, and make a republic. Every man will have an equal vote; but when deliberations and discussions are opened, it will be found that twenty-five, by their talents, virtues being equal, will be able to carry fifty votes. Every one of these twenty-five is an aristocrat in my sense of the word; whether he obtains his one vote in addition to his own, by his birth, fortune, figure, eloquence, science, learning, craft, cunning, or even his character for good fellowship, and a *bon vivant*.

What gave Sir William Wallace his amazing aristocratical superiority? His strength. What gave Mrs. Clark her aristocratical influence—to create generals, admirals, and bishops? Her beauty. What gave Pompadour and Du Barry the power of making cardinals and popes? And I have lived for years in the hotel de Valentinois, with Franklin, who had as many virtues as any of them. In the investigation of the meaning of the word "talents," I could write 630 pages as pertinent as John Taylor's, of Hazlewood; but I will select a single example; for female aristocrats are nearly as formidable as males. A daughter of a green grocer walks the streets in London daily, with a basket of cabbage sprouts, dandelions, and spinage, on her head. She is observed by the painters to have a beautiful face, an elegant figure, a graceful step, and a *debonair*. They hire her to sit. She complies, and is painted by forty artists in a circle around her. The scientific Dr. William Hamilton outbids the painters, sends her to school for a genteel education, and marries her. This lady not only causes the triumphs of the Nile, Copenhagen, and Trafalgar, but separates Naples from France, and finally banishes the king and queen from Sicily. Such is the aristocracy of the natural talent of beauty. Millions of examples might be quoted from history, sacred and profane, from Eve, Hannah, Deborah, Susanna, Abigail, Judith, Ruth, down to Helen, Mrs. de Mainbenor, and Mrs. Fitzherbert. For mercy's sake do not compel me to look to our chaste States and territories to find women, one of whom to let go would in the words of Holopherne's guards, deceive the whole earth.

The proverbs of Theognis, like those of Solomon, are observations on human nature, ordinary life, and civil society, with moral reflections on the facts. I quoted him as a witness of the fact, that there was as much difference in the races of men as in the breeds of sheep, and as a sharp reprover and censurer of the sordid, mercenary practice of disgracing birth by preferring gold to it. Surely no authority can be more expressly in point to prove the existence of inequalities, not of rights, but of moral, intellectual, and physical inequalities in families, descents and generations. If a descent from pious, virtuous, wealthy, literary, or scientific ancestors, is a letter of recommendation, or introduction in a man's favor, and enables him to influence only one vote in addition to his own, he is an aristocrat; for a democrat can have but one vote. Aaron Burr has 100,000 votes from the single circumstance of his descent from President Burr and President Edwards.

Your commentary on the proverbs of Theognis, reminded me of two solemn characters; the one resembling John Bunyan, the other Scarron. The one John Torrey, the other Ben Franklin. Torrey, a poet, an enthusiast, a superstitious bigot, once very gravely asked my brother, whether it would not be better for mankind if children were always begotten by religious motives only? Would not religion in this sad case have as little efficacy in encouraging procreation, as it has now in discouraging it? I should apprehend a decrease of population, even in our country where it increases so rapidly.

In 1775, Franklin made a morning visit at Mrs. Yard's, to Sam Adams and John. He was unusually loquacious. "Man, a rational creature!" said Franklin. "Come, let us suppose a rational man. Strip him of all his appetites, especially his hunger and thirst. He is in his chamber, engaged in making experiments, or in pursuing some problem. He is highly entertained. At this moment a servant knocks. 'Sir, dinner is on the table.' 'Dinner! pox! pough! but what have you for dinner?' 'Ham and chickens.' 'Ham, and must I break the chain of my thoughts to go down and gnaw a morsel of damned hog's arse? Put aside your ham; I will dine to-morrow.'" Take away appetite, and the present generation would not live a month, and no future generation would ever exist; and thus the exalted dignity of human nature would be annihilated and lost, and in my opinion the whole loss would be of no more importance than putting out a candle, quenching a torch, or crushing a fire-fly, *if in this world we only have hope.* Your distinction between natural and artificial aristocracy, does not appear to me founded. Birth and wealth are conferred upon some men as imperiously by nature as genius, strength, or beauty. The heir to honors, and riches, and power, has often no more merit in procuring these advantages, than he has in obtaining a handsome face, or an elegant figure. When aristocracies are established by human laws, and honor, wealth, and power are made hereditary by municipal laws and political institutions, then I acknowledge artificial aristocracy to commence; but this never commences till corruption in elections become dominant and uncontrollable. But this artificial aristocracy can never last. The everlasting envies, jealousies, rivalries, and quarrels among them; their cruel rapacity upon the poor ignorant people, their followers, compel them to set up Cæsar, a demagogue, to be a monarch, a master; *pour mettre chacun à sa place* [to put each in his proper place]. Here you have the origin of all artificial aristocracy, which is the origin of all monarchies. And both artificial aristocracy and monarchy, and civil, military, political, and hierarchical despotism, have all grown out of the natural aristocracy of virtues and talents. We, to be sure, are far remote from this. Many hundred years must roll away before we shall be corrupted. Our pure, virtuous, public-spirited, federative republic will last forever, govern the globe, and introduce the perfection of man; his perfectibility being already proved by Price, Priestley, Condorcet, Rousseau, Diderot, and Godwin. Mischief has been done by the Senate of the United States. I have known and felt more of this mischief, than Washington, Jefferson, and Madison, all together. But this has been all caused by the constitutional power of the Senate, in executive business, which ought to be immediately, totally, and essentially abolished. Your distinction between the Aριστοι [aristocracy] and ψσεμδσ αριστγοι [pseudo-aristocracy], will not help the matter. I would trust one as well as the other with unlimited power. The law wisely refuses an oath as a witness in his own case, to the saint as well as the sinner. No romance would be more amusing than the history of your Virginian and our New England aristocratical families. Yet even in Rhode Island there has been no clergy, no church, and I had almost said no State, and some people say no religion. There has been a constant respect for certain old families. Fifty-seven or fifty-eight years ago, in company with Colonel, Counsellor, Judge, John Chandler, whom I have quoted before, a newspaper was brought in. The old sage asked me to look for the news from Rhode Island, and see how the elections had gone there. I read the list of Wanbous, Watrous, Greens, Whipples, Malboues, &c. "I expected as much," said the aged gentleman, "for I have always been of opinion that in the most popular governments, the elections will generally go in favor of the most ancient families." To this day, when any of these tribes—and we may add Ellerys, Channings, Champlins, &c.,—are pleased to fall in with the popular current, they are sure to carry all before them.

You suppose a difference of opinion between you and me on the subject of aristocracy. I can find none. I dislike and detest hereditary honors, offices, emoluments, established by law. So do you. I am for excluding legal, hereditary distinctions from the United States as long as possible. So are you. I only say that mankind have not yet discovered any remedy against irresistible corruption in elections to offices of great power and profit, but making them hereditary.

But will you say our elections are pure? Be it so, upon the whole; but do you recollect in history a more corrupt election than that of Aaron Burr to be President, or that of De Witt Clinton last year? By corruption here, I mean a sacrifice of every national interest and honor to private and party objects. I see the same spirit in Virginia that you and I see in Rhode Island and the rest of New England. In New York it is a struggle of family feuds—a feudal aristocracy. Pennsylvania is a contest between German, Irish and old England families. When Germans and Irish unite they give 30,000 majorities. There is virtually a white rose and a red rose, a Cæsar and a Pompey, in every State in this Union, and contests and dissensions will be as lasting. The rivalry of Bourbons and Noaillises produced the French revolution, and a similar competition for consideration and influence exists and prevails in every village in the world. Where will terminate the *rabies agri* [rage for land]? The continent will be scattered over with manors much larger than Livingston's, Van Renselaers's, or Philips's; even our Deacon Strong will have a principality among you Southern folk. What inequality of talents will be produced by these land jobbers. Where tends the mania of banks? At my table in Philadelphia, I once proposed to you to unite in endeavors to obtain an amendment of the constitution prohibiting to the separate States the power of creating banks; but giving Congress authority to establish one bank with a branch in each State, the whole limited to ten millions of dollars. Whether this project was wise or unwise, I know not, for I had deliberated little on it then, and have never thought it worth thinking of since. But you spurned the proposition from you with disdain. This system of banks, begotten, brooded and hatched by Duer, Robert and Gouverneur Morris, Hamilton and Washington, I have always considered as a system of national injustice. A sacrifice of public and private interest to a few aristocratical friends and favorites. My scheme could have had no such effect. Verres plundered temples, and robbed a few rich men, but he never made such ravages among private property in general, nor swindled so much out of the pockets of the poor, and middle class of people, as these banks have done. No people but this would have borne the imposition so long. The people of Ireland would not bear Wood's half-pence. What inequalities of talent have been introduced into this country by these aristocratical banks? Our Winthrops, Winslows, Bradfords, Saltonstalls, Quinceys, Chandlers, Leonards, Hutchinsons, Olivers, Sewalls, &c., are precisely in the situation of your Randolphs, Carters, and Burwells, and Harrisons. Some of them unpopular for the part they took in the late revolution, but all respected for their names and connections; and whenever they fell in with the popular sentiments are preferred *ceteris paribus* [all other things being equal], to all others. When I was young the *summum bonum* in Massachusetts was to be worth £10,000 sterling, ride in a chariot, be Colonel of a regiment of militia, and hold a seat in his Majesty's council. No man's imagination aspired to anything higher beneath the skies. But these plumbs, chariots, colonelships, and counsellorships, are recorded and will never be forgotten. No great accumulations of land were made by our early settlers. Mr. Baudoin, a French refugee, made the first great purchases, and your General Dearborne, born under a fortunate star, is now enjoying a large portion of the aristocratical sweets of them. As I have no amanuenses but females, and there is so much about generation in this letter that I dare not ask any of them to copy it, and I cannot copy it myself, I must beg of you to return it to me. Your old friend.

5

FRONTIERS

ON

LAND AND SEA

American life from the beginning
was one of frontiers, and the experience of the new American nation in
the nineteenth century was no different. The explorers and soldiers and
settlers pressed westward, while the eastern merchants began to send
their ships around the world. This continual presence of frontiers mark-
edly influenced American ideas and literature; activity, experience and
exploration, inward and outward, became hallmarks of distinctively
American thought. As reality and as metaphor, the frontier was always
present: Thoreau felt free only when walking westward, the forests
around Hawthorne's Salem were the haunt of the Black Man—the scene
of fear as well as freedom, Melville's Ahab sailed around the world after
Moby Dick and his fate, Poe's Pym sailed into the polar wastes, and
Cooper's heroes faced the perils and tasted the free joys of both forest
and sea. In Whitman's "Passage to India," the American spirit is urged
around the world and out into the universe to press on to the frontiers
of being itself. And where literature in America always sought metaphysical frontiers, the real frontiers were just as trying and exciting and
elusive. Frontier became too quickly familiar ground, and the clash of
cultures always ended in the loss of one as well as the enrichment, mate-
rially and spiritually, of the other.

The selections that follow are four accounts of different kinds of experiences of the frontiers, which give much of the flavor of an America
in a constant state of expansion in every way.

J. G. HECKEWELDER
I Know the *Long Knives;* They Are Not To Be Trusted

John Gottlieb Heckewelder (1743–1823) became a Moravian missionary to the Indians of Ohio and developed a strong interest in Indian life. In 1819 he pub-lished his History, Manners, and Customs of the Indian Nations, Who Once Inhabited Pennsylvania and the Neighboring States, *which was widely read throughout the country—and especially by James Fenimore Cooper, who drew heavily on Heckewelder in writing his* Leatherstocking Tales. *Here Hecke-welder describes the Indians' grievances against the white man.*

Long and dismal are the complaints which the Indians make of European ingratitude and injustice. They love to repeat them, and always do it with the eloquence of nature, aided by an energetic and comprehensive language, which our polished idioms cannot imitate. Often I have listened to these descriptions of their hard sufferings, until I felt ashamed of being a *white man.*

They are, in general, very minute in these recitals, and proceed with a great degree of order and regularity. They begin with the Virginians, whom they call the *long knives,* and who were the first European settlers in this part of the American continent. "It was we," say the Lenape, Mohicans, and their kindred tribes, "who so kindly received them on their first arrival into our country. We took them by the hand, and bid them welcome to sit down by our side, and live with us as brothers, but how did they requite our kindness? They at first asked only for a little land on which to raise bread for themselves and their families, and pasture for their cattle, which we freely gave them. They soon wanted more, which we also gave them. They saw the game in the woods, which the Great Spirit had given us for our subsistence, and they wanted that too. They penetrated into the woods, in quest of game; they dis-covered spots of land which pleased them; that land they also wanted, and because we were both loth to part with it, as we saw they had already more than they had need of, they took it from us by force and drove us to a great distance from our ancient homes."

"By and by the *Dutchemaan* arrived at *Manahachtánienk* . . . The great man wanted only a little, little land, on which to raise greens for his soup, just as much as a bullock's hide would cover. Here we first might have ob-served their deceitful spirit. The bullock's hide was cut up into little strips,

FROM "Indian Relations of the Conduct of the Europeans Towards Them," *History, Manners and Customs of the Indian Nations,* by J. G. Heckewelder (Philadelphia: Historical Society of Pennsylvania, 1881), pp. 76–81.

and did not cover, indeed, but encircled a very large piece of land, which we foolishly granted to them. They were to raise *greens* on it, instead of which they planted *great guns;* afterwards they built strong houses, made themselves masters of the Island, then went up the river to our enemies, the Mengwe, made a league with them, persuaded us by their wicked arts to lay down our arms, and at last drove us entirely out of the country. . . .

"When the *Yengeese* arrived at *Machtitschwanne,* they looked about everywhere for good spots of land, and they found one, they immediately and without ceremony possessed themselves of it; we were astonished, but still we let them go on, not thinking it worth while to contend for a little land. But when at last they came to our favourite spots, those which lay most convenient to our fisheries, then bloody wars ensued: we would have been contented that the white people and we should have lived quietly beside each other; but these white men encroached so fast upon us, that we saw at once we should lose all, if we did not resist them. The wars that we carried on against each other, were long and cruel. We were enraged when we saw the white people put our friends and relatives, whom they had taken prisoners, on board of their ships, and carry them off to sea, whether to drown or sell them as slaves, in the country from which they came, we knew not, but certain it is that none of them have ever returned or even been heard of. At last they got possession of the whole of the country which the Great Spirit had given us. One of our tribes was forced to wander far beyond Quebec; others dispersed in small bodies, and sought places of refuge where they could; some came to Pennsylvania; others went far to the westward and mingled with other tribes.

"To many of those, Pennsylvania was a last, delightful asylum. But here, again, the Europeans disturbed them, and forced them to emigrate, although they had been most kindly and hospitably received. On which ever side of the *Lenapewihittuck* the white people landed, they were welcomed as brothers by our ancestors, who gave them lands to live on, and even hunted for them, and furnished them with meat out of the woods. Such was our conduct to the white men who inhabited this country, until our elder brother, the great and good Miquon, came and brought us words of peace and good will. We believed his words, and his memory is still held in veneration among us. But it was not long before our joy was turned into sorrow: our brother Miquon died, and those of his good counsellors who were of his mind, and knew what had passed between him and our ancestors, were no longer listened to; the strangers who had taken their places, no longer spoke to us of sitting down by the side of each other as brothers of one family, they forgot that friendship which their great man had established with us, and was to last to the end of time; they now only strove to get all our land from us by fraud or by force, and when we attempted to remind them of what our good brother had said, they became angry, and sent word to our enemies the Mengwe, to meet them at a great council which they were to hold with us at *Læhauwake,* where they should take us by the hair of our heads and shake us well. The Mengwe came;

the council was held, and in the presence of the white men, who did not contradict them, they told us that we were women, and that they had made us such; that we had no right to any land, because it was all theirs; that we must be gone; and that as a great favour they permitted us to go and settle further into the country, at the place which they themselves pointed out at Wyoming."

Thus these good Indians, with a kind of melancholy pleasure, recite the long history of their sufferings. After having gone through these painful details, they seldom fail to indulge in bitter, but too just reflections, upon the men of Europe. "We and our kindred tribes," say they, "lived in peace and harmony with each other, before the white people came into this country; our council house extended far to the north and far to the south. In the middle of it we would meet from all parts to smoke the pipe of peace together. When the white men arrived in the south, we received them as friends; we did the same when they arrived in the east. It was we, it was our forefathers, who made them welcome, and let them sit down by our side. The land they settled on was ours. We knew not but the Great Spirit had sent them to us for some good purpose, and therefore we thought they must be a good people. We were mistaken; for no sooner had they obtained a footing on our lands, than they began to pull our council house down, first at one end and then at the other, and at last meeting each other at the centre, where the council fire was yet burning bright, they put it out, and extinguished it with our own blood! with the blood of those who with us had received them! who had welcomed them in our land! Their blood ran in streams into our fire, and extinguished it so entirely, that not one spark was left us whereby to kindle a new fire; we were compelled to withdraw ourselves beyond the great swamp, and to fly to our good uncle the *Delamattenos,* who kindly gave us a tract of land to live on. How long we shall be permitted to remain in this asylum, the Great Spirit only knows. The whites will not rest contented until they shall have destroyed the last of us, and made us disappear entirely from the face of the earth."

I have given here only a brief specimen of the charges which they exhibit against the white people. There are men among them, who have by heart the whole history of what took place between the whites and the Indians, since the former first came into their country; and relate the whole with ease and with an eloquence not to be imitated. On the tablets of their memories they preserve this record for posterity. I, at one time, in April 1787, was astonished when I heard one of their orators, a great chief of the Delaware nation, go over this ground, recapitulating the most extraordinary events which had before happened, and concluding in these words: "I admit there are good white men, but they bear no proportion to the bad; the bad must be the strongest, for they rule. They do what they please. They enslave those who are not of their colour, although created by the same Great Spirit who created us. They would make slaves of us if they could, but as they cannot do it, they kill us! There is no faith to be placed in their words. They are not like the

Indians, who are only enemies, while at war, and are friends in peace. They will say to an Indian, 'my friend! my brother!' They will take him by the hand, and at the same moment destroy him. And so you (addressing himself to the Christian Indians) will also be treated by them before long. Remember! that this day I have warned you to beware of such friends as these. I know the *long knives;* they are not to be trusted."

Eleven months after this speech was delivered by this prophetic chief, ninety six of the same Christian Indians, about sixty of them women and children, were murdered at the place where these very words had been spoken, by the same men he had alluded to, and in the same manner that he had described. . . .

RICHARD HENRY DANA, JR.
Enough to Make One Heartsick

American ships sailed the seven seas, and the American flag soon made its way to ports all over the world. New England led the way, but New York soon eclipsed Boston as the new nation's leading port of commerce. From New Bedford and Nantucket, whaling craft went forth to hunt down the sperm whale in the Atlantic and Pacific. Tall clipper ships set records for swift passage between China and Australia and New York and Boston. By the time of the Civil War the U.S. merchant marine totaled some five million tons. Conditions aboard many of the ships were appalling, however, for the crew, and seamen received very little justice indeed when they attempted to protest the cruelties of merchant captains. In 1834 young Richard Henry Dana, Jr. (1815–1882), son of a noted poet and journalist, interrupted his Harvard education to sail to California as a common seaman. The cruelties and mistreatment he saw, including the flogging of two seamen, made him vow to work to improve the treatment of seamen. In 1839 he published an article on cruelty to seamen, and in 1840 came Two Years Before the Mast, *his enthralling account of his years at sea, which was widely popular and helped to bring about needed reform legislation. In the concluding chapter, part of which is reproduced below, Dana discussed relationships on board ship. Though Dana specifically did not urge the abolition of flogging, the eventual outlawing of this form of punishment on board American ships was due in large part to the impact of his book. Among the many young Americans who read and admired Dana's book was one who would soon write some sea stories of his own—Herman Melville.*

FROM *Two Years Before the Mast, A Personal Narrative of Life at Sea,* by Richard Henry Dana, Jr. (New York: Harper and Bros., 1840), pp. 460–71, 476–77.

The romantic interest which many take in the sea, and in those who live upon it, may be of use in exciting their attention to this subject, though I cannot feel sure that all who have followed me in my narrative must be convinced that the sailor has no romance in his every-day life to sustain him, but that it is very much the same plain, matter-of-fact drudgery and hardship, which would be experienced on shore. If I have not produced this conviction, I have failed in persuading others of what my own experience has most fully impressed upon myself.

There is a witchery in the sea, its songs and stories, and in the mere sight of a ship, and the sailor's dress, especially to a young mind, which has done more to man navies, and fill merchantmen, than all the press-gangs of Europe. I have known a young man with such a passion for the sea, that the very creaking of a block stirred up his imagination so that he could hardly keep his feet on dry ground; and many are the boys, in every seaport, who are drawn away, as by an almost irresistible attraction, from their work and schools, and hang about the decks and yards of vessels, with a fondness which, it is plain, will have its way. No sooner, however, has the young sailor begun his new life in earnest, than all this fine drapery falls off, and he learns that it is but work and hardship, after all. This is the true light in which a sailor's life is to be viewed; and if in our books, and anniversary speeches, we would leave out much that is said about "blue water," "blue jackets," "open hearts," "seeing God's hand on the deep," and so forth, and take this up like any other practical subject, I am quite sure we should do full as much for those we wish to benefit. The question is, what can be done for sailors, as they are,—men to be fed, and clothed, and lodged, for whom laws must be made and executed, and who are to be instructed in useful knowledge, and, above all, to be brought under religious influence and restraint? It is upon these topics that I wish to make a few observations.

In the first place, I have no fancies about equality on board ship. It is a thing out of the question, and certainly, in the present state of mankind, not to be desired. I never knew a sailor who found fault with the orders and ranks of the service; and if I expected to pass the rest of my life before the mast, I would not wish to have the power of the captain diminished an iota. It is absolutely necessary that there should be one head and one voice, to control everything, and be responsible for everything. There are emergencies which require the instant exercise of extreme power. These emergencies do not allow of consultation; and they who would be the captain's constituted advisers might be the very men over whom he would be called upon to exert his authority. It has been found necessary to vest in every government, even the most democratic, some extraordinary, and, at first sight, alarming powers; trusting in public opinion, and subsequent accountability, to modify the exercise of them. These are provided to meet exigencies, which all hope may never occur, but which yet by possibility may occur, and if they should, and there were no power to meet them instantly, there would be an end put to the government at once. So it is with the authority of the shipmaster. It will not answer to say that he shall never do this and that thing, because it does not seem always necessary and advisable that it should be done. He has great cares and responsibilities; is answerable for everything; and is subject to emergencies which perhaps no other man exercising authority among civilized people is subject to. Let him, then, have powers commensurate with his utmost possible need; only let him be held strictly responsible for the exercise of them. Any other course would be injustice, as well as bad policy.

In the treatment of those under his authority, the captain is amenable to the common law, like any other person. He is liable at common law for murder, assault and battery, and other offences; and in addition to this, there is a special statute of the United States which makes a captain or other officer liable to imprisonment for a term not exceeding five years, and to a fine not exceeding a thousand dollars, for inflicting any cruel punishment upon, withholding food from, or in any other way maltreating a seaman. This is the state of the law on the subject; while the relation in which the parties stand, and the peculiar necessities, excuses, and provocations arising from that relation, are merely circumstances to be considered in each case. As to the restraints upon the master's exercise of power, the laws themselves seem, on the whole, to be sufficient. I do not see that we are in need, at present, of more legislation on the subject. The difficulty lies rather in the administration of the laws; and this is certainly a matter that deserves great consideration, and one of no little embarrassment.

In the first place, the courts have said that public policy requires the power of the master and officers should be sustained. Many lives and a great amount of property are constantly in their hands, for which they are strictly responsible. To preserve these, and to deal justly by the captain, and not lay upon him a really fearful responsibility, and then tie up his hands, it is essential that discipline should be supported. In the second place, there is always great allowance to be made for false swearing and exaggeration by seamen, and for combinations among them against their officers; and it is to be remembered that the latter have often no one to testify on their side. These are weighty and true statements, and should not be lost sight of by the friends of seamen. On the other hand, sailors make many complaints, some of which are well founded.

On the subject of testimony, seamen labor under a difficulty fully as great as that of the captain. It is a well-known fact, that they are usually much better treated when there are passengers on board. The presence of passengers is a restraint upon the captain, not only from his regard to their feelings and to the estimation in which they may hold him, but because he knows they will be influential witnesses against him if he is brought to trial. Though officers may sometimes be inclined to show themselves off before passengers, by freaks of office and authority, yet cruelty they would hardly dare to be guilty of. It is on long and distant voyages, where there is no restraint upon the captain, and none but the crew to testify against him, that sailors need most the protection of the law. On such voyages as these, there are many cases of outrageous cruelty on record, enough to make one heartsick, and almost disgusted with the sight of man; and many, many more, which have never come to light, and never will be known, until the sea shall give up its dead. Many of these have led to mutiny and piracy,—stripe for stripe, and blood for blood. If on voyages of this description the testimony of seamen is not to be received in favor of one another, or too great a deduction is made on account of their being seamen, their case is without remedy; and the captain, knowing this, will be strengthened in that disposition to tyrannize which the possession of absolute power, without the restraints of friends and public opinion, is too apt to engender.

It is to be considered, also, that the sailor comes into court under very different circumstances from the master. He is thrown among landlords, and sharks of all descriptions; is often led to drink freely; and comes upon the stand unaided, and under a certain cloud of suspicion as to his character and veracity, The captain, on the other hand, is backed by the owners and insurers, and has an air of greater respectability; though, after all, he may have but a little better education than the sailor, and sometimes, (especially among those engaged in certain voyages that I could mention) a very hackneyed conscience.

These are the considerations most commonly brought up on the subject of seamen's evidence; and I think it cannot but be obvious to every one that here, positive legislation would be of no manner of use. There can be no rule of law regulating the weight to be given to seamen's evidence. It must rest in the mind of the judge and jury; and no enactment or positive rule of court could vary the result a hair, in any one case. The effect of a sailor's testimony in deciding a case must depend altogether upon the reputation of the class to which he belongs, and upon the impression he himself produces in court by his deportment, and by those infallible marks of character which always tell upon a jury. In fine, after all the well-meant and specious projects that have been brought forward, we seem driven back to the belief, that the best means of securing a fair administration of the laws made for the protection of seamen, and certainly the only means which can create any important change for the better, is the gradual one of raising the intellectual and religious character of the sailor, so that as an individual, and as one of a class, he may, in the first instance, command the respect of his officers, and if any difficulty should happen, may upon the stand carry that weight which an intelligent and respectable man of the lower class almost always does with a jury. I know there are many men who, when a few cases of great hardship occur, and it is evident that there is an evil somewhere, think that some arrangement must be made, some law passed, or some society got up, to set all right at once. On this subject there can be no call for any such movement; on the contrary, I fully believe that any public and strong action would do harm, and that we must be satisfied to labor in the less easy and less exciting task of gradual improvement, and abide the issue of things working slowly together for good. Equally injudicious would be any interference with the economy of the ship. The lodging, food, hours of sleep, etc., are all matters which, though capable of many changes for the better, must yet be left to regulate themselves. And I am confident that there will be, and that there is now a gradual improvement in all such particulars. The forecastles of most of our ships are small, black, and wet holes, which few landsmen would believe held a crew of ten or twelve men on a voyage of months or years; and often, indeed in most cases, the provisions are not good enough to make a meal anything more than a necessary part of a day's duty;* and on the score of sleep, I fully believe that the lives of merchant seamen are shortened by the want of it. I do not refer to those occasions when it is necessarily broken in upon; but, for months, during fine weather, in many merchantmen, all hands are kept throughout the day, and, then, there are eight hours on deck for one watch each night. Thus it is usually the case that at the end of a voyage, where there has been the finest weather, and no disaster, the crew have a wearied and worn-out appearance. They never sleep longer than four hours at a time, and are seldom called without being really in need of more rest. There is no one thing that a sailor thinks more of as a luxury of life on shore, than a whole night's sleep. Still, all these things must be left to be gradually modified by circumstances. Whenever hard cases occur, they should be made known, and masters and owners should be held answerable, and will, no doubt, in time, be influenced in their arrangements and discipline by the increased consideration in which sailors are held by the public. It is perfectly proper that the men should live in a different part of the vessel from the officers; and if the forecastle is made large and comfortable, there is no reason why the crew should not live there as well as in any other part. In fact, sailors prefer the forecastle. It is their accustomed place, and in it they are out of the sight and hearing of their officers.

As to their food and sleep, there are laws, with heavy penalties, requiring a certain amount of stores to be on board, and safely stowed; and, for depriv-

---

* I am not sure that I have stated, in the course of my narrative, the manner in which sailors eat, on board ship. There are neither tables, knives, forks, nor plates, in a forecastle; but the kid (a wooden tub, with iron hoops) is placed on the floor, and the crew sit around it, and each man cuts for himself with the common jack-knife or sheath-knife, that he carries about him. They drink their tea out of tin pots, holding little less than a quart each.

These particulars are not looked upon as hardships, and, indeed, may be considered matters of choice. Sailors, in our merchantmen, furnish their own eating utensils, as they do many of the instruments which they use in the ship's work, such as knives, palms and needles, marine-spikes, rubbers, etc. And considering their mode of life in other respects, the little time they would have for laying and clearing away a table with its apparatus, and the room it would take up in a forecastle, as well as the simple character of their meals, consisting generally of only one piece of meat,—it is certainly a convenient method, and, as the kid and pans are usually kept perfectly clean, a neat and simple one. I had supposed these things to be generally known, until I heard, a few months ago, a lawyer of repute, who has had a good deal to do with marine cases, ask a sailor upon the stand whether the crew had "got up from table" when a certain thing happened.

ing the crew unnecessarily of food or sleep, the captain is liable at common law, as well as under the statute before referred to. Farther than this, it would not be safe to go. The captain must be the judge when it is necessary to keep his crew from their sleep; and sometimes a retrenching, not of the necessaries, but of some of the little niceties of their meals, as, for instance, *duff* on Sunday, may be a mode of punishment, though I think generally an injudicious one.

I could not do justice to this subject without noticing one part of the discipline of a ship, which has been very much discussed of late, and has brought out strong expressions of indignation from many,—I mean the infliction of corporal punishment. Those who have followed me in my narrative will remember that I was witness to an act of great cruelty inflicted upon my own shipmates; and indeed I can sincerely say that the simple mention of the word flogging, brings up in me feelings which I can hardly control. Yet, when the proposition is made to abolish it entirely and at once; to prohibit the captain from ever, under any circumstances, inflicting corporal punishment; I am obliged to pause, and, I must say, to doubt exceedingly the expediency of making any positive enactment which shall have that effect. If the design of those who are writing on this subject is merely to draw public attention to it, and to discourage the practice of flogging, and bring it into disrepute, it is well; and, indeed, whatever may be the end they have in view, the mere agitation of the question will have that effect, and, so far, must do good. Yet I should not wish to take the command of a ship to-morrow, running my chance of a crew, as most masters must, and know, and have my crew know, that I could not, under any circumstances, inflict even moderate chastisement. I should trust that I might never have to resort to it; and, indeed, I scarcely know what risk I would not run, and to what inconvenience I would not subject myself, rather than do so. Yet not to have the power of holding it up *in terrorem,* and indeed of protecting myself, and all under my charge, by it, if some extreme case should arise, would be a situation I should not wish to be placed in myself, or to take the responsibility of placing another in.

Indeed, the difficulties into which masters and officers are liable to be thrown, are not sufficiently considered by many whose sympathies are easily excited by stories, frequent enough, and true enough, of outrageous abuse of this power. It is to be remembered that more than three fourths of the seamen in our merchant vessels are foreigners. They are from all parts of the world. A great many from the north of Europe, beside Frenchmen, Spaniards, Portuguese, Italians, men from all parts of the Mediterranean, together with Lascars, Negroes, and, perhaps worst of all, the off-casts of British men-of-war, and men from our own country who have gone to sea because they could not be permitted to live on land.

As things now are, many masters are obliged to sail without knowing anything of their crews, until they get out at sea. There may be pirates or mutineers among them; and one bad man will often infect all the rest; and it is almost certain that some of them will be ignorant foreigners, hardly understanding a word of our language, accustomed all their lives to no influence but force, and perhaps nearly as familiar with the use of the knife as with that of the marline-spike. No prudent master, however peaceably inclined, would go to sea without his pistols and handcuffs. Even with such a crew as I have supposed, kindness and moderation would be the best policy, and the duty of every conscientious man; and the administering of corporal punishment might be dangerous, and of doubtful use. But the question is not, what a captain ought generally to do, but whether it shall be put out of the power of every captain, under any circumstances, to make use of, even moderate, chastisement. As the law now stands, a parent may correct moderately his child, and the master his apprentice; and the case of the shipmaster has been placed upon the same principle. The statutes, and the common law as expounded in the decisions of courts, and in the books of commentators, are express and unanimous to this point, that the captain may inflict moderate corporal chastisement, for a reasonable cause. If the punishment is excessive, or the cause not sufficient to justify it, he is answerable; and the jury are to determine, by their verdict in each case, whether, under all the circumstances, the punishment was moderate, and for a justifiable cause.

This seems to me to be as good a position as the whole subject can be left in. I mean to say, that no positive enactment, going beyond this, is needed, or would be a benefit either to masters or men, in the present state of things. This again would seem to be a case which should be left to the gradual working of its own cure. As seamen improve, punishment will become less necessary; and as the character of officers is raised, they will be less ready to inflict it; and, still more, the infliction of it upon intelligent and respectable men, will be an enormity which will not be tolerated by public opinion, and by juries, who are the pulse of the body politic. No one can have a greater abhorrence of the infliction of such punishment than I have, and a stronger conviction that severity is bad policy wtih a crew; yet I would ask every reasonable man whether he had not better trust to the practice becoming unnecessary and disreputable; to the measure of moderate chastisement and a justifiable cause being better understood, and thus, the act becoming dangerous, and in course of time to be regarded as an unheard-of barbarity—than to take the responsibility of prohibiting it, at once, in all cases, and in what ever degree, by positive enactment?

There is, however, one point connected with the administration of justice to seamen, to which I wish seriously to call the attention of those interested in their behalf, and, if possible, also of some of those concerned in that administration. This is, the practice which prevails of making strong appeals to the jury in mitigation of damages or to the judge, after a verdict has been rendered against a captain or officer, for a lenient sentence, on the grounds of their previous good character, and of their being poor, and having friends and families depending upon them for support. These appeals have been allowed a weight which is almost incredible and which, I think, works a greater hardship upon seamen than any one other thing in the laws, or the execution of them. . . .

There are many particulars connected with the manning of vessels, the provisions given to crews, and the treatment of them while at sea, upon which there might be a good deal said; but as I have, for the most part, remarked upon them as they came up in the course of my narrative, I will offer nothing further now, except on the single point of shipping men. This, it is well known, is usually left entirely to shipping-masters, and is a cause of a great deal of difficulty, which might be remedied by the captain, or owner, if he has any knowledge of seamen, attending to it personally. One of the members of the firm to which our ship belonged, Mr. S——, had been himself a master of a vessel, and generally selected the crew from a number sent down to him from the shipping-office. In this way he almost always had healthy, serviceable, and respectable men; for any one who has seen much of sailors can tell pretty well at first sight, by a man's dress, countenance, and deportment, what he would be on board ship. This same gentleman was also in the habit of seeing the crew together, and speaking to them previously to their sailing. On the day before our ship sailed, while the crew were getting their chests and clothes on board, he went down into the forecastle and spoke to them about the voyage, the clothing they would need, the provision he had made for them, and saw that they had a lamp and a few other conveniences. If owners or masters would more generally take the same pains, they would often save their crews a good deal of inconvenience, beside creating a sense of satisfaction and gratitude, which makes a voyage begin under good auspices, and goes far toward keeping up a better state of feeling throughout its continuance. . . .

DAVY CROCKETT
I Knowed They Had a Bear

The adventures of Davy Crockett (1786–1836) in the wilderness of the new nation have long fascinated Americans of all ages. Col. Crockett, who entered politics and went to Congress as "the coonskin Congressman," was first a Jacksonian and then, when he changed sides in 1829, a hero of the Whig faction, which used him and his largely ghostwritten autobiography as a device to combat Jackson's popularity with the masses of Americans. Here Davy Crockett gives an account of his prowess at bear hunting, his favorite form of recreation. The "tall tale" of the frontier, of which Crockett's narrative is an example, was a popular form of American humor in the nineteenth century, and in the work

FROM *The Life of David Crockett: An Autobiography* (New York: Grossett and Dunlap, 1902), pp. 137–42.

*of Samuel L. Clemens it would attain genuine literary stature. William
Faulkner's "The Bear" is squarely within this tradition.*

When I got home, one of my neighbors was out of meat, and wanted me to
go back, and let him go with me, to take another hunt. I couldn't refuse; but
I told him I was afraid the bear had taken to house by that time, for after they
get very fat in the fall and early part of the winter, they go into their holes, in
large hollow trees, or into hollow logs, or their cane-houses, or the harricanes;
and lie there till spring, like frozen snakes. And one thing about this will seem
mighty strange to many people. From about the first of January to about the
last of April, these varmints lie in their holes altogether. In all that time they
have no food to eat; and yet when they come out, they are not an ounce lighter
than when they went to house. I don't know the cause of this, and still I know
it is a fact; and I leave it for others who have more learning than myself to
account for it. They have not a particle of food with them, but they just lie and
suck the bottom of their paw all the time. I have killed many of them in their
trees, which enables me to speak positively on this subject. However, my neighbor, whose name was McDaniel, and my little son and me, went on down to
the lake to my second camp, where I had killed my seventeen bears the week
before, and I turned out to hunting. But we hunted hard all day without getting a single start. We had carried but little provision with us, and the next
morning was entirely out of meat. I sent my son about three miles off, to the
house of an old friend, to get some. The old gentleman was much pleased to
hear I was hunting in those parts, for the year before the bears had killed a
great many of his hogs. He was that day killing his bacon hogs, and so he gave
my son some meat, and sent word to me that I must come in to his house that
evening, that he would have plenty of feed for my dogs, and some accommodations for ourselves; but before my son got back, we had gone out hunting, and
in a large cane-brake my dogs found a big bear in a canehouse, which he had
fixed for his winter-quarters, as they sometimes do.

When my lead dog found him, and raised the yell, all the rest broke to him,
but none of them entered his house until we got up. I encouraged my dogs,
and they knowed me so well, that I could have made them seize the old serpent himself, with all his horns and heads, and cloven foot and ugliness into
the bargain, if he would only have come to light, so that they could have seen
him. They bulged in, and in an instant the bear followed them out, and I told
my friend to shoot him, as he was mighty wrathy to kill a bear. He did so, and
killed him prime. We carried him to our camp, by which time my son had
returned; and after we got our dinners we packed up, and cut for the house of
my old friend, whose name was Davidson.

We got there, and staid with him that night; and the next morning, having
salted up our meat, we left it with him, and started to take a hunt between the
Obion lake and the Red foot lake; as there had been a dreadful harricane,
which passed between them, and I was sure there must be a heap of bears in

the fallen timber. We had gone about five miles without seeing any sign at all; but at length we got on some high cany ridges, and, as we rode along, I saw a hole in a large black oak, and on examining more closely, I discovered that a bear had clomb the tree. I could see his tracks going up, but none coming down, and so I was sure he was in there. A person who is acquainted with bear-hunting, can tell easy enough when the varmint is in the hollow; for as they go up they don't slip a bit, but as they come down they make long scratches with their nails.

My friend was a little ahead of me, but I called him back, and told him there was a bear in that tree, and I must have him out. So we lit from our horses, and I found a small tree which I thought I could fall so as to lodge against my bear tree, and we fell to work chopping it with our tomahawks. I intended, when we lodged the tree against the other, to let my little son go up, and look into the hole, for he could climb like a squirrel. We had chopp'd on a little time and stopp'd to rest, when I heard my dogs barking mighty severe at some distance from us, and I told my friend I knowed they had a bear; for it is the nature of a dog, when he finds you are hunting bears, to hunt for nothing else; he becomes fond of the meat and considers other game as "not worth a notice," as old Johnson said of the devil.

We concluded to leave our tree a bit, and went to my dogs, and when we got there, sure enough they had an eternal great big fat bear up a tree, just ready for shooting. My friend again petitioned me for liberty to shoot this one also. I had a little rather not, as the bear was so big, but I couldn't refuse; and so he blazed away, and down came the old fellow like some great log had fell. I now missed one of my dogs, the same that I before spoke of as having treed the bear by himself sometime before, when I had started the three in the cane-brake. I told my friend that my missing dog had a bear somewhere, just as sure as fate; so I left them to butcher the one we had just killed, and I went up on a piece of high ground to listen for my dog. I heard him barking with all his might some distance off, and I pushed ahead for him. My other dogs hearing him, broke to him, and when I got there, sure enough again he had another bear ready treed; if he hadn't I wish I may be shot. I fired on him, and brought him down; and then went back, and help'd finish butchering the one at which I had left my friend. We then packed both to our tree where we had left my boy. By this time, the little fellow had cut the tree down that we intended to lodge, but it fell the wrong way; he had then feather'd in on the big tree, to cut that, and had found that it was nothing but a shell on the outside, and all dotted in the middle, as too many of our big men are in these days, having only an outside appearance. My friend and my son cut away on it, and I went off about a hundred yards with my dogs to keep them from running under the tree when it should fall. On looking back at the hole, I saw the bear's head out of it, looking down at them as they were cutting. I hollered to them to look up, and they did so; and McDaniel catched up his gun, but by this time the bear was out, and coming down the tree. He fired at it, and as soon as it touched the ground the dogs were all round it, and they had a roll-and-tumble fight to the foot of the hill, where they stopp'd him. I ran up, and putting my gun against the bear, fired and killed him. We had now three, and so we made our scaffold and salted them up.

CAPTAIN RANDOLPH B. MARCY
What Will Then Become of the Prairie Indian?

Much of the exploration of the West was first undertaken by expeditions sent out by the United States Army. In 1852 Captain Randolph B. Marcy (1812–1887) of the Fifth U.S. Infantry led a party on an expedition up the Red River of Louisiana and Texas. His report, published two years later, not only contained a graceful narrative of the trip and observations on the terrain and the Indians encountered, but extensive mineralogical, botanical, topographical, and geological data that was soon put to considerable commercial use. Accompanying Captain Marcy on his expedition was Brevet Captain George B. McClellan, who later became his son-in-law. During the Civil War, when McClellan was commander-in-chief of the Union forces in the East, Marcy served as his chief of staff. Marcy's book Thirty Years of Army Life on the Border *(1866) was widely read. Here, in an excerpt from the report of his Red River expedition of 1852, he describes the Comanche Indians he encountered and comments on the slaughter of bison then taking place by white hunters and its probable effect on the red man. The importance and the vitality of the image of the West, with its implications for all of American society, has been brilliantly analyzed in Henry Nash Smith's* Virgin Land.

The Comanche men are about the medium stature, with bright, copper-colored complexions and intelligent countenances, in many instances with aquiline noses, thin lips, black eyes and hair, but with little beard. They never cut the hair, but wear it of very great length, and ornament it upon state occasions with silver and beads. Their dress consists of leggins and moccasins, with a cloth wrapped around the loins. The body is generally naked above the middle, except when covered with the buffalo-robe, which is a constant appendage to their wardrobe. The women are short, with crooked legs, and are obliged to crop their hair close to their heads. They wear, in addition to the leggins and

FROM *Exploration of the Red River of Louisiana, in the Year 1852,* by Capt. Randolph B. Marcy. U.S. House of Rep., 33rd Cong., 1st Session, Executive Documents (Washington, D.C.: A. O. P. Nicholson, 1854), pp. 98–100, 102–108.

moccasins, a skirt of dressed deer-skin. They also tattoo their faces and breasts, and are far from being as good looking as the men.

Notwithstanding that these people are hospitable and kind to strangers, and apparently amiable in their dispositions, yet, when a warrior conceives himself injured, his thirst for revenge knows no satiety. Grave and dignified in his deportment, and priding himself upon his coolness of temper and the control of his passions, yet, when once provoked, he, like the majority of his race, is implacable and unrelenting; an affront is laid up and cherished in his breast, and nothing can efface it from his mind until ample reparation has been made. He has no idea of forgiveness; the insult must be atoned for by blood. With many tribes, quarrels can often be settled by presents to the injured party; but with the Comanches, their law of equity is of such a character that no reconciliation can take place until the reproach is wiped out with the blood of their enemy. They make no use of money except for ornaments. Like other tribes, they are fond of decking themselves with paint, beads, and feathers; and the young warrior often spends more time at his toilet than the most conceited coxcomb that can be found in civilized life. Bright red and blue are their favorite colors; and vermilion is an important article in the stock of goods of one of their traders. This they always carry about their persons; and whenever they expect to meet strangers, they always (provided they have time) make their toilet with care and paint their faces. Some few of their chiefs who have visited their Great Father at Washington, have returned strongly impressed with the numerical power and prosperity of the whites; but the great majority of them being entirely ignorant of everything that relates to us, and the most of them having never even seen a white man, believe the Comanches to be the most powerful nation in existence; and the relation of facts which conflict with this notion, by their own people, to the masses of the tribes at their prairie firesides, only subjects the narrator to ridicule, and he is set down as one whose brain has been turned by the necromancy of the pale-faces, and is thenceforth regarded as wholly unworthy of confidence.

Having upon one occasion a Delaware and a Comanche with me in the capacity of guides, I was much diverted with a conversation which passed between them in my presence, and which was interpreted to me by the Delaware. It appeared that the latter had stated to the other the fact of the sphericity of the earth's surface. This idea being altogether new and incomprehensible to the Comanche, was received with much incredulity, and, after gazing a moment intently at the Delaware to ascertain if he was sincere, he asked if that person took him for a child, or if he looked like an idiot. The Delaware said no; but that the white people, who knew all about these things, had ascertained such to be the fact; and added, that the world was not only round, but that it revolved in its orbit around the sun. The Comanche very indignantly replied, that any man of sense could, by looking off upon the prairie, see at a glance that the earth was perfectly level; and, moreover that his grandfather had been west to the end of it, where the sun disappeared behind a vertical wall. The

Delaware continued, in his simple but impressive manner, to describe to the Comanche the steam-engine, with other objects of interest he had seen among the whites, all of which the Comanche regarded as the product of a fertile imagination, expressly designed to deceive him; and the only reply that he deigned to make was an occasional exclamation in his own language, the interpretation of which the Delaware pronounced to be, "Hush, you fool!" I then endeavored to explain to the Delaware the operation of the magnetic telegraph, and, in illustration of its practical utility, stated to him that a message could be sent a distance of one thousand miles, and an answer returned, in the short space of ten minutes' time. He seemed much interested in this, and listened attentively to my remarks, but made no comments until I requested him to explain it to the Comanche, when he said, "I don't think I tell him that, Captain; for the truth is, I don't believe it myself." ...

The diet of these people is very simple; from infancy to old age their only food, with the exception of a few wild plants which they find on the prairies, is fresh meat, of which, in times of plenty, they consume enormous quantities. In common with many other tribes, they can, when necessity demands it, abstain from eating for several days without inconvenience, and they are enabled to make up at one meal the deficiency. All of them are extravagantly fond of tobacco, which they use for smoking, mixed with the dried leaves of the sumach, inhaling the smoke into their lungs and giving it out through their nostrils. Their language is verbal and pantomimic. The former consists of a very limited number of words—some of which are common to all the prairie tribes. The latter, which is exceedingly graceful and expressive, is the court language of the plains, and is used and understood with great facility and accuracy by all the tribes from the Gila to the Columbia; the motions and signs to express ideas being common to all. In contemplating the character of the prairie Indian, and the striking similarity between him and the Arab and Tartar, we are not less astonished at the absolute dissimilarity between these and the aboriginal inhabitants of the Eastern States. The latter, from the time of the discovery of the country, lived in permanent villages, where they cultivated fields of corn, and possessed strong attachment for their ancestral abodes and sepulchres: they did not use horses, but always made their hunting and war expeditions on foot, and sought the cover of trees on going into battle; while the former have no permanent abiding-places, never cultivate the soil, are always mounted, and never fight a battle except in the open prairie, where they charge boldly up to an enemy, discharge their arrows with great rapidity, and are away before their panic-stricken antagonist can prepare to resist or retaliate. In their treatment of prisoners of war there was also a very marked difference. The eastern tribes, although they put their prisoners to tortures of the most appalling character, seldom, if ever, violate the chastity of the females; while, on the contrary, the prairie Indians do not put their prisoners to death by prolonged tortures, but invariably compel the females to submit to their lewd embraces. There is at this time a white woman among the Middle

Comanches, by the name of Parker, who, with her brother, was captured while they were young children, from their father's house in the western part of Texas. This woman has adopted all the habits and peculiarities of the Comanches; has an Indian husband and children, and cannot be persuaded to leave them. The brother of the woman, who had been ransomed by a trader and brought home to his relatives, was sent back by his mother for the purpose of endeavoring to prevail upon his sister to leave the Indians and return to her family; but he stated to me that on his arrival she refused to listen to the proposition, saying that her husband, childen, and all she held most dear, were with the Indians, and there she should remain. As the prairie Indians depend almost entirely on the buffalo for a subsistence and for clothing, it becomes a question of much interest, what will be the fate of these people when these animals shall have become extinct? Formerly, buffaloes were found in countless herds over almost the entire northern continent of America, from the 28th to the 50th degree of north latitude, and from the shores of Lake Champlain to the Rocky mountains. As it is important to collect and preserve all facts connected with the history of this interesting and useful animal before the species becomes extinct, I trust I shall be pardoned for introducing a few quotations from authors, touching their early history, which to me appear highly interesting. In a work published at Amsterdam in 1637, called "New English Canaan," by Thomas Morton, one of the first settlers of New England, he says: "The Indians have also made description of great *heards* of well-growne beasts that live about the parts of this lake (Erocoise,) now Lake Champlain, such as the Christian world (until this discovery) hath not *bin* made acquainted with. These beasts are of the bigness of a *cowe*, their flesh being very good *foode*, their hides good leather; their fleeces very useful, being a kind of *woole*, as fine almost as the *woole* of the beaver; and the *salvages* do make garments thereof. It is *tenne yeares* since first the relation of these things came to the *eares* of the English."

It is stated by another author, (Purchas,) that as early as in 1613 the adventurers in Virginia discovered a "slow *kinde of cattell* as *bigge* as kine which were good *meate*."

The limit of the buffalo range on the north has been given differently by different writers. In a work published in London in 1589, by Hukluyt, it is stated, that in the island of New Foundland were found *"mightie beastes,* like to camels in greatness, and their *feete* were cloven." He then says: "I did see them *farre* off, not able to *discerne* them perfectly, but their steps showed that their *feete* were cloven, and *bigger* than the *feete* of camels. I suppose them to be a kind of *buffes,* which I read to *bee* in the *countreys* adjacent, and very many in the *firme* land."

It is supposed by some that these animals may have been the muskox. They were found by Captain Franklin as high as 60° north latitude. Although it is doubtful whether the buffalo ever ranged beyond the Rocky mountains, yet they have been found as far west as the western slope. They formerly ranged free and uninterrupted over the boundless plains of the West, only guided in their course by that faithful instinct which invariably led them to the freshest and sweetest pastures. Their only enemy then was the Indian, who supplied himself with food and clothing from the immense herds around his door; but would have looked upon it as sacrilege to destroy more than barely sufficient to supply the wants of his family. Thus this monarch of the plains was allowed free range from one end of the continent to the other. But this happy state of things was not destined to continue; an enemy appeared, who made great havoc among them, and in a short time caused a very sensible diminution in their numbers, and much contracted the limits of their wanderings. This enemy was the white man, who, in his steady march, causes the original proprietor of the soil to recede before him, and to diminish in numbers almost as rapidly as the buffalo. Thousands of these animals were annually slaughtered for their skins, and often for their tongues alone; animals whose flesh is sufficient to afford sustenance to a large number of men are sacrificed to furnish a "bon bouche" for the rich epicure. This wholesale slaughter on the part of the white man, with the number consumed by the Indians, who are constantly on their trail, migrating with them as regularly as the season comes round, with the ravenous wolves that are always at hand to destroy one of them if wounded, gives the poor beast but little rest or prospect of permanent existence. It is only eight years since the western borders of Texas abounded with buffaloes; but now they seldom go south of Red river, and their range upon east and west has also very much contracted within the same time; so that they are at present confined to a narrow belt of country between the outer settlements and the base of the Rocky mountains. With this rapid diminution in their numbers, they must in the course of a very few years become exterminated. What will then become of the prairie Indian, who, as I have already remarked, relies for subsistence, shelter, and clothing, on the flesh and hide of this animal? He must either perish with them, increase his marauding depredations on the Mexicans, or learn to cultivate the soil. As the first law of our nature is self preservation, it is not probable that he will sit down and quietly submit to starvation; he must, therefore, resort to one of the latter alternatives. But as he has no knowledge of agriculture, considers it the business of a slave, and very much beneath the dignity of a warrior, it appears reasonable to suppose that he will turn his attention to the Mexicans, over whom he has held the mastery for many years. Heretofore he has plundered these people to supply himself with animals for his own use and for traffic.

A number of Delawares, Shawnees, and Kickapoos, from Missouri and the borders of Arkansas, have for several years past been engaged in a traffic with the prairie Indians, which has had a tendency to defeat the efforts of the military authorities in checking their depredations upon the citizens of the northern provinces of Mexico. These traders, after procuring from the whites an outfit of such articles as are suited to the wants of the prairie Indians, visit all the different bands, and prosecute a very lucrative business. The goods they carry out consist of a few articles of small value, such as tobacco, paint, knives, calico, wampum, beads, &c., &c., which are of the utmost importance to the Indians, and which, if necessary, they will make great sacrifices to procure; but as they have no commodity for exchange that the traders desire except horses and mules, they must necessarily give these for the goods, and large numbers are annually disposed of in this manner. As I have before mentioned, nearly all these animals are pilfered from the Mexicans; and as the number they traffic away must be replaced by new levies upon their victims, of course all that the traders obtain causes a corresponding increase in the amount of depredations. Should the government of the United States feel disposed to make the prairie Indians annual donations of the same description of articles that the traders now supply them with, (which I am most happy to learn is now contemplated,) upon the express condition that they would continue only so long as they adhered strictly to all the requirements of the agents, it would in a measure obviate the necessity of their making long expeditions into Mexico, and would most undoubtedly have the effect of depreciating the value of the merchandise to such a degree that the traders would no longer find the traffic profitable. The Indians of the plains are accustomed, in their diplomatic intercourse with each other, to exchange presents, and they have no idea of friendship unaccompanied by a substantial token in this form: moreover, they measure the strength of the attachment of their friends by the magnitude of the presents they receive; and I am firmly convinced that a small amount of money annually expended in this way, with a proper and judicious distribution of the presents, would have a very salutary influence in checking the depredations upon the Mexicans. In a talk which I held with a chief of one of the bands of prairie Indians, I stated to him that the President of the United States was their friend, and wished to live in peace with them. He replied that he was much astonished to hear this; for, judging from the few trifling presents I had made his people, he was of opinion that the "Big Captain" held them in but little estimation. Trained up, as the prairie Indians have been from infancy, to regard the occupation of a warrior as the most honorable of all others, and having no permanent abiding-places or local attachments, they can without inconvenience move all their families and worldly effects from one extremity of the buffalo range to the other. With their numerous and hardy horses they travel with great rapidity; and possessing as intimate a knowledge as they do of the localities, it would give them a great advantage over any body of troops who should pursue them into the country. War would not, therefore, be as great a calamity to them as to other tribes who have permanent habitations. Some have supposed that a large body of these Indians could not obtain a sufficient amount of subsistence to enable them to remain together for any great length of time; but their numerous horses and mules, which they often make use of for food when game is scarce, would supply them with subsistence for a long time. It will be necessary to devise some measures to do away with the inveterate prejudices which the Comanches entertain against the habits and customs of the whites, before they will be induced to remain in any fixed abodes or cultivate the soil.

In common with most other Indians, they are very superstitious: they believe in dreams, the wearing of amulets, medicine-bags, &c., and the dedication of offerings to secure the favor of invisible agents; as also in the efficacy of music and dancing for the cure of diseases. They submit with the most imperturbable stoicism and apathy to misfortunes of the most serious character, and, in the presence of strangers, manifest no surprise or curiosity at the exhibition of novelties; yet this apparent indifference is assumed, and they are in reality very inquisitive people. In every village may be seen small structures, consisting of a framework of slight poles, bent into a semi-spherical form, and covered with buffalo-hides. These are called *medicine-lodges,* and are used as vaporbaths. The patient is seated within the lodge, beside several heated stones, upon which water is thrown, producing a dense hot vapor, which brings on a profuse perspiration, while, at the same time, the shamans, or medicine-men, who profess to have the power of communicating with the unseen world, and of propitiating the malevolence of evil spirits, are performing various incantations, accompanied by music, on the outside. Such means are resorted to for healing all diseases; and I am also informed that their young men are obliged to undergo a regular course of steam-bathing before they are considered worthy of assuming the responsible duties of warriors. The knowledge they possess of their early history is very vague and limited, and does not extend further back than a few generations. They say that their forefathers lived precisely as they do, and followed the buffalo: that they came from a country towards the setting sun, where they expect to return after death. They acknowledge the existence and power of a great supernatural agent, who directs and controls all things; but this power they conceive to be vested in the sun, which they worship and appeal to on all occasions of moment. They also anticipate a future state of existence similar to the present, and invariably bury with the warrior his hunting and war equipments. Thus far no efforts have ever been made to improve the moral or physical condition of these people; no missionaries have, to my knowledge, ever visited them, and they have no more idea of Christianity than they have of the religion of Mahomet. We find dwelling almost at our doors as barbarous and heathenish a race as exists on the face of the earth; and while our benevolent and philanthropic citizens are making such efforts to ameliorate the condition of savages in other countries, should we not do something for the benefit of these wild men on the prairies? Those dingy noblemen of nature, the original proprietors of all that vast domain included between the shores of the Atlantic and Pacific, have been despoiled, supplanted, and robbed of their just and legitimate heritage, by the avaricious and rapid encroachments of the *white man.* Numerous and powerful nations have already become exterminated by unjustifiable wars that he has waged with them, and by the effects of the vices he has introduced and inculcated; and of those that remain, but few can be found who are not contaminated by the pernicious influences of unprincipled and designing adventurers. It is not at this late day in our power to atone for all the injustice inflicted upon the *red men;* but it seems to me that a wise policy would dictate almost the only recompense it is now in our power to make—that of introducing among them the light of Christianity and the blessings of civilization, with their attendant benefits of agriculture and the arts.

6

LIBERTY AND UNION

By the beginning of the 1820's, sharp strains began to appear in the facade of the American Union. The Missouri Compromise of 1820 had found the states divided for the first time along lines of North and South, and thereafter the slavery issue was an increasingly important factor in American politics. Thomas Jefferson likened it to "a fire bell in the night . . . the knell of the Union." Westward the nation expanded its borders, with canals and then railroads linking the country beyond the mountains and the Mississippi to the seaboard. The advent of Andrew Jackson to the presidency in 1829 represented the triumph of the political alliance of the West and the South, together with the laboring classes of the Eastern cities. For three decades this combination dominated American politics, until the urgency of the slavery question in the 1850's split the Democratic Party in two. The years between Jackson's election and the Civil War were the years of Manifest Destiny, in which the republic's dominion was extended to the Pacific Ocean. Throughout the period, however, the slavery issue, even when least agitated, caused general unease. Though the Nullification crisis was ostensibly over the protective tariff, behind it lay the question of slavery. Much of the opposition to the Mexican War of 1846–47 came from the fear that its result would be to create new slave states for the Union.

The selections that follow consist of four political expressions of the issues that dominated the period.

DANIEL WEBSTER
One and Inseparable!

One of the splendid moments of nineteenth-century American political oratory came in the Senate of the United States on January 26, 1830, when Daniel Webster of Massachusetts (1782–1852) rose to defend the concept of an indissoluble Union of the states during his debate over the tariff with Senator Robert Y. Hayne of South Carolina. In a famous peroration, given below, Webster called for "Liberty and Union, now and forever, one and inseparable." Webster was to incur the wrath of Northern antislavery men two decades later for a speech of conciliation in which he defended the Compromise of 1850. His high-flown rhetoric, however, was for decades the admiration of his countrymen. It contrasts sharply with the simple, poetic sincerity of Abraham Lincoln, and today it is Lincoln's style which seems most effective. An interesting fictional depiction of Webster appears in Stephen Vincent Benet's story "The Devil and Daniel Webster."

Mr. President,

I have thus stated the reasons of my dissent to the doctrines which have been advanced and maintained. I am conscious, sir, of having detained you and the Senate much too long. I was drawn into the debate with no previous deliberation, such as is suited to the discussion of so grave and important a subject. But it is a subject of which my heart is full, and I have not been willing to suppress the utterance of its spontaneous sentiments. I cannot, even now, persuade myself to relinquish it without expressing once more my deep conviction that, since it respects nothing less than the Union of the States, it is of most vital and essential importance to the public happiness. I profess, Sir, in my career hitherto, to have kept steadily in view the prosperity and honor of the whole country, and the preservation of our federal Union. It is to that Union we owe our safety at home, and our consideration and dignity abroad. It is to that Union that we are chiefly indebted for whatever makes us most proud of our country. That Union we reached only by the discipline of our virtues in the severe school of adversity. It had its origin in the necessities of disordered finance, prostrate commerce, and ruined credit. Under its benign influences, these great interests immediately awoke, as from the dead, and sprang forth with newness of life. Every year of its duration has teemed with fresh proofs of its utility and its blessings, and although our territory has stretched out wider and wider, and our population spread farther and farther, they have

FROM "Second Speech on Foot's Resolution," *Writings and Speeches of Daniel Webster* (Boston: Little, Brown and Co., 1903), Vol. VI, pp. 616–18.

not outrun its protection or its benefits. It has been to us all a copious fountain of national, social, and personal happiness.

I have not allowed myself, Sir, to look beyond the Union, to see what might lie hidden in the dark recess behind. I have not coolly weighed the chances of preserving liberty when the bonds that unite us together shall be broken asunder. I have not accustomed myself to hang over the precipice of disunion, to see whether, with my short sight, I can fathom the depth of the abyss below; nor could I regard him as a safe counsellor in the affairs of this government, whose thoughts should be mainly bent on considering, not how the Union may be best preserved, but how tolerable might be the condition of the people when it shall be broken up and destroyed. While the Union lasts, we have high, exciting, gratifying prospects spread out before us, for us and our children. Beyond that I seek not to penetrate the veil. God grant that in my day, at least, that curtain may not rise. God grant that on my vision never may be opened what lies behind. When my eyes shall be turned to behold for the last time the sun in heaven, may I not see him shining on the broken and dishonored fragments of a once glorious Union; on states dissevered, discordant, belligerent; on a land rent with civil feuds, or drenched, it may be, in fraternal blood! Let their last feeble and lingering glance rather behold the gorgeous ensign of the republic, now known and honored throughout the earth, still full high advanced, its arms and trophies in their original lustre, not a stripe erased or polluted, nor a single star obscured, bearing for its motto no such miserable interrogatory as, "What is all this worth?" nor those other words of delusion and folly, "Liberty first and Union afterwards"; but everywhere, spread all over in characters of living light, blazing on all its ample folds, as they float over the sea and over the land, and in every wind under the whole heavens, that other sentiment, dear to every true American heart—Liberty *and* Union, now and for ever, one and inseparable!

UNITED STATES' TELEGRAPH
Our Union—It Must Be Preserved!

On April 13, 1830, at the height of the Nullification controversy, the Democratic Party held a Jefferson's Birthday Dinner at Brown's Indian Queen Hotel in Washington. All the prominent Democrats of the day were there, and a series of formal toasts was printed and distributed in advance. Precisely what happened at and before the dinner is disputed, but apparently the leading proponents of Nullification, led by the then Vice-President, John C. Calhoun of South Carolina, sought to shape the occasion into a celebration of states rights'

FROM "Jefferson's Birth Day," *United States' Telegraph*, April 17, 1830.

*philosophy, with President Andrew Jackson (1767–1845), whose stand on Nul-
lification was not yet known, being forced to take part. But when the formal
toasts were completed, and it was Jackson's turn to respond, he stood up,
looked the Nullification leader squarely in the eye, and declared:* "Our Union
—it must be preserved!" *Though Calhoun rejoined with a toast to the effect of
"our Union: next to our liberties, the most dear. May we always remember
that it can only be preserved by distributing equally the benefits and burdens
of the Union," Jackson had made his point quite emphatically. Later he was
asked to insert the word "Federal" in the printed version of his toast, and he
agreed; apparently he had intended the word to be there anyway. There was,
however, no question now of where Andrew Jackson stood on the question of
a state's being able to revoke any law of the nation it wanted. The* United
States' Telegraph *for July 17, a pro-Calhoun newspaper, carried the following
account of the many toasts offered during the evening, with Jackson's role
confined to two lines of type.*

*It was Jackson whom Herman Melville chose for his great apotheosis of
democracy in the famous invocation to the muses in the twenty-sixth chapter
of* Moby-Dick.

We are enabled, to-day, to lay before our readers an account of the Celebration
of the 13th inst. The venerable patriot, the Hon. John Roane, of Virginia, offi-
ciated as President of the Day, assisted by the Hon. Geo. M. Bibb, of Ky.,
Hon. Levi Woodbury, of New Hampshire, Hon. Felix Grundy, of Tennessee,
Hon. C. C. Cambreleng, of New York, Hon. Wm. F. Gordon, of Va., and the
Hon. Mr. Overton, of Louisiana, as Vice Presidents. The toasts and speeches
are worthy of the distinguished individuals who were present, and of the
occasion which they are designed to commemorate.

1. Thomas Jefferson: We celebrate the anniversary of his birth, not in the
spirit of personal idolatry, but from regard and reverence for his political
principles.

2. The Declaration of Independence: An enduring moment of that devotion to liberty, and abhorrence of tyranny, which stamp the character, and
mark the whole course of the life of its author.

3. "Thomas Jefferson: Author of the Declaration of American Independence; of the Statute of Virginia, establishing religious freedom, and Father of
the University of Virginia." (Memorandum of Mr. Jefferson, found in a
drawer containing his will.)

4. The Kentucky resolutions of '98: drawn by the same hand which drew
the Declaration of Independence; a practical illustration of Jeffersonian republican principles, and a correct definition of the relative powers of the State
and Federal Governments. . . .

By Mr. Bibb. The Federal Constitution: The charter of limits between
State and federal powers. Let us remember that the best constitutions will

degenerate into tyranny if there be not a power to watch, support, and defend them against usurpation.

5. The Virginia resolutions, and Madison's report of the year '98—Text books in the Jeffersonian school: when they cease to be read and admired, the days of Liberty will be numbered. . . .

6. Louisiana: The memory of him who *acquired* it, first honored, by an anniversary commemoration under the Presidency of him who *defended* it. . . .

(Mr. B. then gave the following toast, which was drunk with great applause:)

The Birth Day of Thomas Jefferson: May its anniversary celebration *extend* through all time, and *spread* through all the borders of the Republic.

7. "Peace, commerce, and honest friendship, with all nations; entangling alliances with none." (Jefferson's Inaugural Address.)

8. "The support of the State Governments in all their rights, as the most competent administrations for our domestic concerns." (The Same.)

9. "The preservation of the General Government in its whole constitutional vigor, as the sheet anchor of our peace at home and safety abroad." (The Same.)

10. "A jealous care of the right of election by the people; a mild and safe corrective of those abuses which are lopped by the sword of revolution in countries where peaceable remedies are unprovided." (Same.)

11. "Economy in the public expense, that labor may be lightly burdened." (Same.)

12. "A wise and frugal Government, which shall restrain men from injuring one another, shall leave them otherwise free to regulate their own pursuits of industry and improvement, and shall not take from the mouth of labor the bread it had earned: *this* is the sum of good government." (Same.)

13. Republicans of the Jeffersonian faith, wherever found—in the North, South, East, or West—all brethren of the same principle; unity of action in the great cause of good government their paramount obligation of duty and interest. . . .

14. The surviving associates and coadjutors of Jefferson in the civil revolution and political reformation of 1800.

15. The basis of the Union; equality of rights and duties—of benefits and of burdens.

16. The bane of the Union: oppression of minorities; unequal taxation; unequal distribution of public benefits.

Mr. Hubbard, of New Hampshire, then offered the following sentiment:

South Carolina: Her munificent liberality to the family of Jefferson—the most *feeling* evidence of her devotion to his principles.

After the applause which followed the annunciation of the foregoing toast had ceased,

Mr. Hayne, of South Carolina, rose and said: . . . The State of Georgia. By the firmness and energy of her *Troups,* she has achieved one great victory for *State rights;* the wisdom and eloquence of her sons, will secure her another proud triumph in the councils of the nation. . . .

17. Liberty of the Tongue, liberty of the Press, liberty of the Conscience, liberty of the hand—the last not least.

18. Virginia, the mother of the Gracchi; may her sons, not less patriotic than the Roman brothers, be more successful in resisting the encroachments of power.

19. Freedom of Industry: As sacred as the freedom of speech, or of the press—no wise government will restrain it.

20. The States: Their harmony and overruling consideration in the minds of all patriotic statesmen.

21. The States: Jefferson gave up the embargo, in 1808, to restore their harmony; can nothing be given up by the professors of his principles, for the same object in 1830?

22. The memory of Washington: The Father of his Country, and first in her affections—not less the friend of free Government, because the abusers of his name would have made him an enemy.

23. Taxes: As many as are necessary, and no more; as long as necessary; and no longer.

24. The Daughter and Descendants of Thomas Jefferson: Their happiness and prosperity is dear to the American people.

Volunteers

By the President of the United States. Our *Federal* Union: *It must be preserved.*

By the Vice President of the United States. The Union: Next to our liberty, the most dear; may we all remember that it can only be preserved by respecting the rights of the States and distributing equally the benefit and burden of the Union.

By Mr. Van Buren, Secretary of State. Mutual forbearance and reciprocal concession: Through their agency the Union was established. The patriotic spirit from which they emanated will forever sustain it.

· · ·

By Mr. Speaker Stevenson. The reserved Rights of the People! ! Let the character of their defence be—an *animated moderation* that *seeks only* its own, and will never *be satisfied with less!*

By Mr. Roane, President of the Day. The President of the United States. · · ·

By Mr. Grundy, third Vice President. The Republican party throughout the Nation: May they be as harmonious in action as they are united in principle.

. . .

Mr. William F. Gordon, the Fifth Vice President, being called on for a sentiment, said that the distinguished individual whose memory and public virtue we have met to commemorate, had directed that a plain granite tomb stone should be the only erection over his grave. He therefore gave—The granite tomb of Jefferson, a shrine to which the votaries of freedom will turn for ever.

By the fifth Vice President, Mr. Overton, Thomas Jefferson and the Declaration of Independence: The fame of the one is co-eval with the principles of the other.

By Mr. Haynes, Chairman of the Committee of Arrangements. The *Union* of the States, and the *Sovereignty* of the States.

By Mr. Desha, of Tennessee. Frequent recurrence to fundamental principles: an essential to the preservation of liberty.

By Mr. Monell, of New York. Democracy: Without regard to the place of its nativity or nourishment—alike the same—her motto, *Principles and Men*.

By Mr. Alexander, of Virginia. "The mind that founded, and the mind that reformed our system," and the man who follows them for his guide.

. . .

Mr. White, of Tennessee, who was prevented from attending by indisposition, sent the following toast, which was given:

"The Constitution of the United States: Intended for the benefit of all, may the Government under it never be so administered as to sacrifice the rights of any."

By Gen. Donelson, of Tennessee. The true American system: Hard fighting in war—low taxes in peace.

By Mr. Yancey, of Kentucky. Brethren of the North, South, East, and West: Let us unite as a band of brothers, in maintaining, and transmitting to our latest posterity, the equal rights of man, pure and uncontaminated, as inculcated by the illustrious Jefferson.

By Mr. Troup, of Georgia. The Government of the United States, with more limited powers than the Republic of San Marino, it rules an Empire more extended than the Roman, with the absoluteness of Tiberius, with less wisdom than Augustus, and less justice than Trajan or the Antonines.

By Gen. Mason. The patriot sage, who traced the foundation of our liberties, and labored during half a century in perfecting the superstructure—Peace to his manes!

Gen. Van Ness, after some other remarks, observed, that he had heard a great deal in the course of the evening about the rights and prosperity of the

States, but nothing about the *Territories.* He hoped the latter were not to be overlooked or neglected: and begged leave to offer as a toast.

The Territories of the United States: Whilst they are dutiful and obedient children, their parents will be kind and affectionate: and when they shall arrive at the age and maturity of manhood, the rights and advantages belonging to that condition will not be withheld from them.

By Mr. McDuffie. The memory of Patrick Henry: The first American statesman who had the soul to feel, and the courage to declare, in the face of an armed tyranny, that there is no treason in resisting oppression.

By Mr. Wm. S. Archer. The Union: The bond of reconcilement of Sectional Interests, not the instrument of exaction.

. . .

By Mr. Boulden, of Virginia. Our Federal Union must be preserved, *by doing equal justice to all its parts.*

. . .

By M. Davenport, of Virginia. Thomas Jefferson: His true disciples are those who act upon his precepts—faith without works, is dead.

. . .

By Mr. Carson, of North Carolina. The reserved sovereignty of the people. The fundamental principle of democracy, the ultimate tribunal, in the last resort, to decide all political contests.

. . .

By Dr. Robert Mayo. General Andrew Jackson, the President of the People: May he respond to the second call to finish the good work.

Mr. Benton presented, through the President of the day, the following toast from Mr. Nuckolls, of South Carolina, prevented by indisposition from attending:

The Union of the States and the liberties of the people: The *one* never to be dissevered until the *other* shall be endangered by the concentration here of a "government without limitation of powers."

By Mr. D. H. Lewis, of Alabama. The resurrection of the Constitution: The people will roll away the stone from the door of the sepulchre.

By Col. Rector, of Arkansas. General Andrew Jackson: The gentleman and the soldier, and the bravest of the brave.

By Henry G. Lamar, Pensions: "A system which has sent European laborers supperless to bed."—Jefferson's Notes on Virginia.

. . .

By Mr. Polk, of Tennessee. Public opinion: May it always perform one of its appropriate offices, by teaching the public functionaries of the States and of the Federal Government, that neither shall assume the exercise of powers entrusted by the Constitution to the other.

. . .

Mr. McKinley being called on, gave the following toast:

The Constitution of the United States: The compact of sovereign and independent States, instituted for national purposes only; limited and specific in its power; but supreme within the *prescribed sphere* of its action. The powers not delegated belonging to the States *exclusively*. Let not the unhallowed hand of avarice, or ambition, attempt to obliterate the line separating these powers.

By Mr. S. C. Potter, of Philadelphia. South Carolina: Her star is in the ascendant—may it reach the zenith and illumine the Union.

. . .

By Mr. N. P. Trist. State Rights: The *several* rights of the States INDEPENDENT—the *joint* rights of the States UNITED. Inviolability of the former, the duty of *all* to *each*—inviolability of the latter, the duty of *each* to *all*. Both equally *State* Rights—both essential to the preservation of "the primitive and precious model of what is to change the condition of man over the globe."

By Col. G. W. Tucker, of New Jersey. This day and assemblage verifies the truth of the saying of the author of the Declaration of Independence: "We are all Republicans, all Federalists."

. . .

By Mr. White, of New York. The Press: A vigilant Sentinel on the bulwarks of Liberty. The public will its guide—the public good its end. . . .

Governor Pope . . . May the sacred principles of human liberty embodied in the Declaration of Independence, be ever green in the memory and hearts of men, and spread throughout the earth.

. . .

Mr. Kane. 13th of April: Through all time a *national* jubilee. The feeling of this meeting the surest guarantee that it will never be polluted by an effort to divide the Jeffersonian party, nor to sanctify a spirit of disunion.

. . .

By H. L. White. The Constitution of the United States: Intended for the benefit of all, may it never be so construed as to sacrifice the rights of any.

By J. Orde Creighton. The distinguished Commander in Chief, who, on the 8th of January, 1814, possessed both the moral and physical courage to do his duty.

By A. L. Maginis, of Missouri: John Randolph, of Roanoke, a liberal son of Virginia, the champion of State Rights, the ascendant star of the Convention, the first proclaimer of the coincidence, that the Book of Kings follows next to the Book of Judges.

By H. Craig of New York. The Protecting Policy: While its evident tendency is to encourage industry, and lessen the price of its products, there can be no cause of complaint.

By S. P. Pettit. Mr. Jefferson's "Favorite Western Country": May she not disappoint his highest hopes or expectations—May his principles be her principles as long as time shall last or liberty be worth preserving.

By F. R. Conway, of Missouri. The people of the Untied States: May they manifest a determination to make this the greatest and most powerful nation in the world, by ever continuing to cherish that love of Liberty, which will give permanence to her Republican principles and the Union.

JOHN L. O'SULLIVAN
The Still Accumulating Momentum of Our Progress

Manifest Destiny—an American nation fated to stretch from ocean to ocean— was heady doctrine in the 1840's. Political orators proclaimed the might of the great democracy. It was the Democrats who most vociferously called for the annexation, if need be the conquest, of all the territory lying west of the Mississippi, and the Whigs, especially the New England conservatives who feared the extension of slave states into the Southwest, who were least enthusiastic about it. Here a Democratic editor, John Louis O'Sullivan (1813– 1895), editor of the United States Magazine and Democratic Review, *sets forth the claims of the United States to Texas and points west. O'Sullivan, who was the first person to use the expression "manifest destiny" in print, later helped to sponsor a filibustering expedition to Cuba. Another Democratic editor of the period, Walt Whitman, echoed such sentiments as O'Sullivan's in his prose and, far more convincingly, in* Leaves of Grass.

It is time now for opposition to the annexation of Texas to cease, all further agitation of the waters of bitterness and strife, at least in connection with this question—even though it may perhaps be required of us as a necessary condition of the freedom of our institutions that we must live on forever in a state of unpausing struggle and excitement upon some subject of party division or

FROM "Annexation," by John L. O'Sullivan in *United States Magazine and Democratic Review,* Vol. XVII (July, 1845), pp. 6–8, 12–14.

other. But, in regard to Texas, enough has now been given to party. It is time for the common duty of patriotism to the country to succeed—or, if this claim will not be recognized, it is at least time for common sense to acquiesce with decent grace in the inevitable and the irrevocable.

Texas is now ours. Already, before these words are written, her convention has undoubtedly ratified the acceptance, by her congress, of our proffered invitation into the Union and made the requisite changes in her already republican form of constitution to adapt it to its future federal relations. Her star and her stripe may already be said to have taken their place in the glorious blazon of our common nationality; and the sweep of our eagle's wing already includes within its circuit the wide extent of her fair and fertile land. She is no longer to us a mere geographical space—a certain combination of coast, plain, mountain, valley, forest, and stream. She is no longer to us a mere country on the map. She comes within the dear and sacred designation of our country; no longer a *"pays,"* she is a part of *"la patrie";* and that which is at once a sentiment and a virtue, patriotism, already begins to thrill for her too within the national heart. It is time then that all should cease to treat her as alien and even adverse—cease to denounce and vilify all and everything connected with her accession—cease to thwart and oppose the remaining steps for its consummation; or, where such efforts are felt to be unavailing, at least to embitter the hour of reception by all the most ungracious frowns of aversion and words of unwelcome. There has been enough of all this. It has had its fitting day during the period when, in common with every other possible question of practical policy that can arise, it unfortunately became one of the leading topics of party division, of presidential electioneering. But that period has passed, and with it let its prejudices and its passions, its discords and its denunciations, pass away too. The next session of Congress will see the representatives of the new young state in their places in both our halls of national legislation, side by side with those of the old thirteen. Let their reception into "the family" be frank, kindly, and cheerful, as befits such an occasion, as comports not less with our own self-respect than patriotic duty toward them. Ill betide those foul birds that delight to 'file their own nest, and disgust the ear with perpetual discord of ill-omened croak.

Why, were other reasoning wanting, in favor of now elevating this question of the reception of Texas into the Union, out of the lower region of our past party dissensions, up to its proper level of a high and broad nationality, it surely is to be found, found abundantly, in the manner in which other nations have undertaken to intrude themselves into it, between us and the proper parties to the case, in a spirit of hostile interference against us, for the avowed object of thwarting our policy and hampering our power, limiting our greatness and checking the fulfilment of our manifest destiny to overspread the continent allotted by Providence for the free development of our yearly multiplying millions. This we have seen done by England, our old rival and enemy; and by France, strangely coupled with her against us, under the influence of the Anglicism strongly tinging the policy of her present prime minister, Guizot. The zealous activity with which this effort to defeat us was pushed by the representatives of those governments, together with the character of intrigue accompanying it, fully constituted that case of foreign interference which Mr. Clay himself declared should and would unite us all in maintaining the common cause of our country against the foreigner and the foe. We are only astonished that this effect has not been more fully and strongly produced and that the burst of indignation against this unauthorized, insolent, and hostile interference against us has not been more general even among the party before opposed to annexation and has not rallied the national spirit and national pride unanimously upon that policy. We are very sure that if Mr. Clay himself were now to add another letter to his former Texas correspondence, he would express this sentiment and carry out the idea already strongly stated in one of them in a manner which would tax all the powers of blushing belonging to some of his party adherents. . . .

California will, probably, next fall away from the loose adhesion which, in such a country as Mexico, holds a remote province in a slight equivocal kind of dependence on the metropolis. Imbecile and distracted, Mexico never can exert any real governmental authority over such a country. The impotence of the one and the distance of the other must make the relation one of virtual independence; unless, by stunting the province of all natural growth, and forbidding that immigration which can alone develop its capabilities and fulfil the purposes of its creation, tyranny may retain a military dominion which is no government in the legitimate sense of the term. In the case of California this is now impossible. The Anglo-Saxon foot is already on its borders. Already the advance guard of the irresistible army of Anglo-Saxon emigration has begun to pour down upon it, armed with the plow and the rifle, and marking its trail with schools and colleges, courts and representative halls, mills and meeting-houses. A population will soon be in actual occupation of California, over which it will be idle for Mexico to dream of dominion. They will necessarily become independent. All this without agency of our government, without responsibility of our people—in the natural flow of events, the spontaneous working of principles, and the adaptation of the tendencies and wants of the human race to the elemental circumstances in the midst of which they find themselves placed. And they will have a right to independence—to self-government—to the possession of the homes conquered from the wilderness by their own labors and dangers, sufferings and sacrifices—a better and a truer right than the artificial title of sovereignty in Mexico a thousand miles distant, inheriting from Spain a title good only against those who have none better. Their right to independence will be the natural right of self-government belonging to any community strong enough to maintain it—distinct in position, origin, and character, and free from any mutual obligations of membership of a common political body, binding it to others by the duty of loyalty and compact of public faith. This will be their title to independence; and by this title, there can be no doubt that the population now fast streaming down upon California will both assert and maintain that independence. Whether they will then attach themselves to our Union or not is not to be predicted with any certainty. Unless the projected railroad across the continent to the Pacific be carried into effect, perhaps they may not; though, even in that case, the day is not distant when the empires of the Atlantic and Pacific would again flow together into one, as soon as their inland borders should approach each other. But that great work, colossal as appears the plan on its first suggestion, cannot remain long upbuilt. Its necessity for this very purpose of binding and holding together in its iron clasp our fast settling Pacific region with that of the Mississippi Valley—the natural facility of the route—the ease with which any amount of labor for the construction can be drawn in from the overcrowded populations of Europe, to be paid in the lands made valuable by the progress of the work itself—and its immense utility to the commerce of the world with the whole eastern coast of Asia, alone almost sufficient for the support of such a road—these considerations give assurance that the day cannot be distant which shall witness the conveyance of the representatives from Oregon and California to Washington within less time than a few years ago was devoted to a similar journey by those from Ohio; while the magnetic telegraph will enable the editors of the *San Francisco Union,* the *Astoria Evening Post,* or the *Nootka Morning News* to set up in type the first half of the President's Inaugural before the echoes of the latter half shall have died away beneath the lofty porch of the Capitol as spoken from his lips.

Away, then, with all idle French talk of *balances of power* on the American continent. There is no growth in Spanish America! Whatever progress of population there may be in the British Canadas, is only for their own early severance of their present colonial relation to the little island three thousand miles across the Atlantic; soon to be followed by annexation and destined to swell the still accumulating momentum of our progress. And whosoever may hold the balance, though they should cast into the opposite scale all the bayonets and cannon, not only of France and England, but of Europe entire, how would it kick the beam against the simple solid weight of the two hundred and fifty, or three hundred millions—and American millions—destined to gather beneath the flutter of the Stripes and Stars, in the fast-hastening year of the Lord 1945!

THOMAS HART BENTON
Into New Regions and Far Distant Climes

When the old Jacksonian Democrat Thomas Hart Benton (1782–1858) got up in the Senate and spoke on the subject of Texan independence and American relations with Mexico, the banner of Manifest Destiny waved in the breeze thus engendered. In his speech, part of which is reprinted below, Benton was careful not to counsel war against Mexico, which he did not favor, but he was sure that the revolt of Texas against Mexican domination was a noble deed, and that no sordid thought of the expansion of slavery and of future slave states should be allowed to sully the glory of the Texas story. It was a saga of Anglo-Saxons versus lesser breeds: "Just in its origin, valiant and humane in its conduct, sacred in its object, the Texan revolt has illustrated the Anglo-Saxon character, and given it new titles to the respect and admiration of the world." In Chapter 22 of The Adventures of Tom Sawyer *Samuel L. Clemens, who grew up in the Missouri that Benton represented in Congress, makes an amusing allusion to the Senator.*

Just in its origin, valiant and humane in its conduct, sacred in its object, the Texan revolt has illustrated the Anglo-Saxon character, and given it new titles to the respect and admiration of the world.

It shows that liberty, justice, valor—moral, physical, and intellectual power —discriminate that race wherever it goes. Let our America rejoice, let Old England rejoice, that the Brassos and Colorado, new and strange names— streams far beyond the western bank of the Father of Floods—have felt the impress, and witnessed the exploits of a people sprung from their loins, and carrying their language, laws, and customs, their *magna charta* and its glorious privileges, into new regions and far distant climes. Of the individuals who have purchased lasting renown in this young war, it would be impossible, in this place to speak in detail, and invidious to discriminate; but there is one among them whose position forms an exception, and whose early association with myself justifies and claims the tribute of a particular notice. I speak of him whose romantic victory has given to the Jacinto that immortality in grave and serious history which the diskos of Apollo had given to it in the fabulous pages of the heathen mythology. General Houston was born in the State of Virginia, county of Rockbridge: he was appointed an ensign in the army of the United States, during the late war with Great Britain, and served in the Creek campaign under the banners of Jackson. I was the lieutenant colonel of the regiment to which he belonged, and the first field officer to whom he re-

FROM *Thirty Years' View*, by Thomas Hart Benton (New York: D. Appleton and Co., 1854), pp. 675–76.

ported. I then marked in him the same soldierly and gentlemanly qualities which have since distinguished his eventful career; frank, generous, brave; ready to do, or to suffer, whatever the obligations of civil or military duty imposed; and always prompt to answer the call of honor, patriotism, and friendship. Sincerely do I rejoice in his victory. It is a victory without alloy, and without parallel, except at New Orleans. It is a victory which the civilization of the age, and the honor of the human race, required him to gain: for the nineteenth century is not the age in which a repetition of the Goliad matins could be endured. Nobly has he answered the requisition; fresh and luxuriant are the laurels which adorn his brow.

It is not within the scope of my present purpose, to speak of military events, and to celebrate the exploits of that vanguard of the Anglo-Saxons who are now on the confines of the ancient empire of Montezuma; but that combat of the San Jacinto! it must for ever remain in the catalogue of military miracles. Seven hundred and fifty citizens, miscellaneously armed with rifles, muskets, belt pistols, and knives, under a leader who had never seen service, except as a subaltern, march to attack near double their numbers—march in open day across a clear prairie, to attack upwards of twelve hundred veterans, the elite of an invading army of seven thousand, posted in a wood, their flanks secured, front intrenched; and commanded by a general trained in civil wars, victorious in numberless battles; and chief of an empire of which no man becomes chief except as conqueror. In twenty minutes, the position is forced. The combat becomes a carnage. The flowery prairie is stained with blood; the hyacinth is no longer blue, but scarlet. Six hundred Mexicans are dead; six hundred more are prisoners, half wounded; the President General himself is a prisoner; the camp and baggage all taken; and the loss of the victors, six killed and twenty wounded. Such are the results, and which no European can believe, but those who saw Jackson at New Orleans. Houston is the pupil of Jackson; and he is the first self-made general, since the time of Mark Antony, and the King Antigonus, who has taken the general of the army and the head of the government captive in battle. Different from Antony, he has spared the life of his captive, though forfeited by every law, human and divine.

I voted, in 1821, to acknowledge the absolute independence of Mexico; I vote now to recognize the contingent and expected independence of Texas. In both cases, the vote is given upon the same principle—upon the principle of disjunction where conjunction is impossible or disastrous. The Union of Mexico and Spain had become impossible; that of Mexico and Texas is no longer desirable or possible. A more fatal present could not be made than that of the future incorporation of the Texas of La Salle with the ancient empire of Montezuma. They could not live together, and extermination is not the genius of the age; and, besides, is more easily talked of than done. Bloodshed only could be the fruit of their conjunction; and every drop of that blood would be the dragon's teeth sown upon the earth. No wise Mexican should wish to have this Trojan horse shut up within their walls.

7

AMERICAN IDEALISM

Friedrich Nietzsche, in his *Twilight of the Idols,* spoke of Ralph Waldo Emerson as "One who instinctively nourishes himself only on ambrosia, leaving behind what is indigestible in things. . . . He simply does not know how old he is already and how young he is still going to be." He could well have been speaking of all the New England Transcendentalists of whom Emerson was the most brilliant and richly productive, for they developed, in reaction to what they felt was a sterile Christian Unitarianism, a philosophical and artistic movement which emphasized spiritual vitality, action, experience, and self-reliance. They opposed (in Emerson's terms) intuitive Reason to empirical Understanding, "man thinking" to systematic analysis and explanation, and sought God and a unity of spirit within the self rather than through revelation from without or logical examination of apparent reality. As such, they are the fountainhead of the mainstream of independent American philosophical thought which flows on through C. S. Peirce's early pragmatism, William James's radical empiricism, and John Dewey's instrumentalism to Santayana and Whitehead. Their impact on literature from Emerson, Thoreau, Whitman, Hawthorne, and Melville to Robinson, Frost, Stevens, and Henry Miller was as powerful an impetus as Poe's aestheticism or the realistic honesty of the western frontier.

American idealistic thought grew, as Floyd Stovall has said in his *American Idealism,* from such diverse sources as "the mysticism and moral power inherent in Puritanism, the rational liberalism and faith in human nature that developed in the thought of the eighteenth century, and the expansive spirit of the frontier, which gives to the whole its peculiarly American character." Stimulated by English and German romantic thought, the Transcendentalists established their own new and vital belief in spirit, in individual value and endeavor, in the mentally and physically active life, in the rich meaning of every living moment, which has remained essential to the American character ever since.

The following selections from Transcendentalist writings give some indication of their genuine radicalism, of their excesses, and of the real and lasting intellectual excitement which was stirring in America in the first half of the nineteenth century.

RALPH WALDO EMERSON
Let It Be One Cheerful Rational Voice

The excitement of Transcendentalism had so gripped its adherents in Boston by the late 1830's that it seemed essential that those who held with the new doctrines have a journal in which to promulgate their views. Thus Theodore Parker, Bronson Alcott, Orestes Brownson, Margaret Fuller, James Freeman Clarke, George Ripley, and Ralph Waldo Emerson came together and agreed upon the founding of a magazine, to be called The Dial, *with Margaret Fuller (1810–1850) as editor and Ripley in charge of finances. Miss Fuller prepared an editorial manifesto, which Emerson rewrote.* The Dial *would chronicle "the progress of a revolution," for like everything noble, it was "directed on life," and would seek to "give expression to that spirit which lifts men to a higher platform, restores to them the religious sentiment, brings them worthy aims and pure pleasures, purges the inward eye, makes life less desultory, and through raising men to the level of nature, takes away its melancholy from the landscape, and reconciles the practical with the speculative powers." Like all good "little" literary magazines,* The Dial *was short-lived; it survived only until 1844. But it was the first to publish Henry David Thoreau and other notable New England writers.*

We invite the attention of our countrymen to a new design. Probably not quite unexpected or unannounced will our Journal appear, though small pains have been taken to secure its welcome. Those, who have immediately acted in editing the present Number, cannot accuse themselves of any unbecoming forwardness in their undertaking, but rather of a backwardness, when they remember how often in many private circles the work was projected, how eagerly desired, and only postponed because no individual volunteered to combine and concentrate the freewill offerings of many coöperators. With some reluctance the present conductors of this work have yielded themselves to the wishes of their friends,

FROM "The Editors to the Reader," by Ralph Waldo Emerson, *The Dial*, Vol. I (July, 1840), pp. 1–4.

finding something sacred and not to be withstood in the importunity which urged the production of a Journal in a new spirit.

As they have not proposed themselves to the work, neither can they lay any the least claim to an option or determination of the spirit in which it is conceived, or to what is peculiar in the design. In that respect, they have obeyed, though with great joy, the strong current of thought and feeling, which, for a few years past, has led many sincere persons in New England to make new demands on literature, and to reprobate that rigor of our conventions of religion and education which is turning us to stone, which renounces hope, which looks only backward, which asks only such a future as the past, which suspects improvement, and holds nothing so much in horror as new views and the dreams of youth.

With these terrors the conductors of the present Journal have nothing to do,—not even so much as a word of reproach to waste. They know that there is a portion of the youth and of the adult population of this country, who have not shared them; who have in secret or in public paid their vows to truth and freedom; who love reality too well to care for names, and who live by a Faith too earnest and profound to suffer them to doubt the eternity of its object, or to shake themselves free from its authority. Under the fictions and customs which occupied others, these have explored the Necessary, the Plain, the True, the Human,—and so gained a vantage ground, which commands the history of the past and the present.

No one can converse much with different classes of society in New England, without remarking the progress of a revolution. Those who share in it have no external organization, no badge, no creed, no name. They do not vote, or print, or even meet together. They do not know each other's faces or names. They are united only in a common love of truth and love of its work. They are of all conditions and constitutions. Of these acolytes, if some are happily born and well bred, many are no doubt ill dressed, ill placed, ill made—with as many scars of hereditary vice as other men. Without pomp, without trumpet, in lonely and obscure places, in solitude, in servitude, in compunctions and privations, trudging beside the team in the dusty road, or drudging a hireling in other men's cornfields, schoolmasters, who teach a few children rudiments for a pittance, ministers of small parishes of the obscurer sects, lone women in dependent condition, matrons and young maidens, rich and poor, beautiful and hard-favored, without concert or proclamation of any kind, they have silently given in their several adherence to a new hope, and in all companies do signify a greater trust in the nature and resources of man, than the laws or the popular opinions will well allow.

This spirit of the time is felt by every individual with some difference,—to each one casting its light upon the objects nearest to his temper and habits of thought;—to one, coming in the shape of special reforms in the state; to another, in modifications of the various callings of men, and the customs of business; to a third, opening a new scope for literature and art; to a fourth, in philosophical insight; to a fifth, in the vast solitudes of prayer. It is in every form a protest against usage, and a search for principles. In all its movements, it is peaceable, and in the very lowest marked with a triumphant success. Of course, it rouses the opposition of which it judges and condemns, but it is too confident in its tone to comprehend an objection, and so builds no outworks for possible defence against contingent enemies. It has the step of Fate, and goes on existing like an oak or a river, because it must.

In literature, this influence appears not yet in new books so much as in the higher tone of criticism. The antidote to all narrowness is the comparison of the record with nature, which at once shames the record and stimulates to new attempts. Whilst we look at this, we wonder how any book has been thought worthy to be preserved. There is somewhat in all life untranslatable into language. He who keeps his eye on that will write better than others, and think less of his writing, and of all writing. Every thought has a certain imprisoning as well as uplifting quality, and, in proportion to its energy on the will, refuses to become an object of intellectual contemplation. Thus what is great usually slips through our fingers, and it seems wonderful how a life-like word ever comes to be written. If our Journal share the impulses of the time, it cannot now prescribe its own course. It cannot foretell in orderly propositions what it shall attempt. All criticism should be poetic; unpredictable; superseding, as every new thought does, all foregone thoughts, and making a new light on the whole world. Its brow is not wrinkled with circumspection, but serene, cheerful, adoring. It has all things to say, and no less than all the world for its final audience.

Our plan embraces much more than criticism; were it not so, our criticism would be naught. Everything noble is directed on life, and this is. We do not wish to say pretty or curious things, or to reiterate a few propositions in varied forms, but, if we can, to give expression to that spirit which lifts men to a higher platform, restores to them the religious sentiment, brings them worthy aims and pure pleasures, purges the inward eye, makes life less desultory, and, though raising men to the level of nature, takes away its melancholy from the landscape, and reconciles the practical with the speculative powers.

But perhaps we are telling our little story too gravely. There are always great arguments at hand for a true action, even for the writing of a few pages. There is nothing but seems near it and prompts it,—the sphere in the ecliptic, the sap in the apple tree,—every fact, every apparance seem to persuade to it.

Our means correspond with the ends we have indicated. As we wish not to multiply books, but to report life, our resources are therefore not so much the pens of practised writers, as the discourse of the living, and the portfolios which friendship has opened to us. From the beautiful recesses of private thought; from the experience and hope of spirits which are withdrawing from all old forms, and seeking in all that is new somewhat to meet their inappeasable longings; from the secret confession of genius afraid to trust itself to aught but sympathy; from the conversations of fervid and mystical pietists; from tear-stained diaries of sorrow and passion; from the manuscripts of young poets; and from the records of youthful taste commenting on old works of art; we hope to draw thoughts and feelings, which being alive can impart life.

And so with diligent hands and good intent we set down our Dial on the earth. We wish it may resemble that instrument in its celebrated happiness, that of measuring no hours but those of sunshine. Let it be one cheerful rational voice amidst the din of mourners and polemics. Or to abide by our chosen image, let it be such a Dial, not as the dead face of a clock, hardly even such as the Gnomon in a garden, but rather such a Dial as is the Garden itself, in whose leaves and flowers and fruits the suddenly awakened sleeper is instantly apprised not what part of dead time, but what state of life and growth is now arrived and arriving.

AMOS BRONSON ALCOTT
All Things Are Instinct with Spirit

Amos Bronson Alcott (1799–1888) contributed to the first issue of The Dial *a group of "Orphic Sayings" which make up in mystical fervor what they lack in coherence and rationality. Alcott was the High Priest of Transcendentalism; improvident, impractical, he was filled with the poetic vision of the glories of the transcendent world-soul, and loved to talk about it. In Perry Miller's words, "Of course, poor Alcott simply could not write. But that never worried him. He kept an immense Journal, and lived as an equal with such cosmic minds as Goethe, Coleridge, Plato and Plotinus, trusting that somehow food and clothing would be supplied to him, as proved to be the case." Not until Alcott's daughter, Louisa May (1832–1888) began writing such highly popular novels as* Little Women *and* Little Men, *however, was the Sage of Concord able to count on being amply supplied with "the fulness of plenty."*

I

Thou art, my heart, a soul-flower, facing ever and following the motions of thy sun, opening thyself to her vivifying ray, and pleading thy affinity with the celestial orbs. Thou dost

the livelong day
Dial on time thine own eternity.

FROM "Orphic Sayings," by Amos Bronson Alcott, *The Dial,* Vol. I (July, 1840), pp. 85–98.

II. Enthusiasm

Believe, youth, that your heart is an oracle; trust her instinctive auguries, obey her divine leadings; nor listen too fondly to the uncertain echoes of your head. The heart is the prophet of your soul, and ever fulfills her prophecies; reason is her historian; but for the prophecy the history would not be. Great is the heart: cherish her; she is big with the future, she forebodes renovations. Let the flame of enthusiasm fire always your bosom. Enthusiasm is the glory and hope of the world. It is the life of sanctity and genius; it has wrought all miracles since the beginning of time.

III. Hope

Hope deifies man; it is the apotheosis of the soul; the prophecy and fulfilment of her destinies. The nobler her aspirations, the sublimer her conceptions of the Godhead. As the man, so his God: God is his idea of excellence; the complement of his own being.

IV. Immortality

The grander my conception of being, the nobler my future. There can be no sublimity of life without faith in the soul's eternity. Let me live superior to sense and custom, vigilant always, and I shall experience my divinity; my hope will be infinite, nor shall the universe contain, or content me. But if I creep daily from the haunts of an ignoble past, like a beast from his burrow, neither earth nor sky, man nor God, shall appear desirable or glorious; my life shall be loathsome to me, my future reflect my fears. He alone, who lives nobly, oversees his own being, believes all things, and partakes of the eternity of God.

VI. Sensualism

He who marvels at nothing, who feels nothing to be mysterious, but must needs bare all things to sense, lacks both wisdom and piety. Miracle is the mantle in which these venerable natures wrap themselves, and he, who seeks curiously to rend this asunder, profanes their sacred countenance to enter by stealth into the Divine presence. Sanctity, like God, is ever mysterious, and all devout souls reverence her. A wonderless age is godless: an age of reverence, an age of piety and wisdom.

VII. Spiritualism

Pity is not scientific; yet embosoms the facts that reason develops in scientific order to the understanding. Religion, being a sentiment, is science yet in synthetic relations; truth yet undetached from love; thought not yet severed from action. For every fact that eludes the analysis of reason, conscience affirms its root in the supernatural. Every synthetic fact is supernatural and miraculous. Analysis by detecting its law resolves it into science, and renders it a fact of the understanding. Divinely seen, natural facts are symbols of spiritual laws. Miracles are of the heart; not of the head: indigenous to the soul; not freaks of nature, not growths of history. God, man, nature, are miracles.

VIII. Mysticism

Because the soul is herself mysterious, the saint is a mystic to the worldling. He lives to the soul; he partakes of her properties, he dwells in her atmosphere of light and hope. But the worldling, living to sense, is identified with the flesh; he dwells amidst the dust and vapors of his own lusts, which dim his vision, and obscures the heavens wherein the saint beholds the face of God.

X. Apotheosis

Every soul feels at times her own possibility of becoming a God; she cannot rest in the human, she aspires after the Godlike. This instinctive tendency is an authentic augury of its own fulfilment. Men shall become Gods. Every act of admiration, prayer, praise, worship, desire, hope, implies and predicts the future apotheosis of the soul.

XI. Discontent

All life is eternal; there is none other; and all unrest is but the struggle of the soul to reassure herself of her inborn immortality; to recover her lost intuition of the same, by reason of her descent amidts the lusts and worship of the idols of flesh and sense. Her discomfort reveals her lapse from innocence; her loss of the divine presence and favor. Fidelity alone shall instaurate the Godhead in her bosom.

XIV. Instinct and Reason

Innocent, the soul is quick with instincts of unerring aim; then she knows by intuition what lapsed reason defines by laborious inference; her appetites and affections are direct and trustworthy. Reason is the left hand of instinct; it is tardy, awkward, but the right is ready and dextrous. By reasoning the soul strives to recover her lost intuitions; groping amidst the obscure darkness of sense, by means of the fingers of logic, for treasures present alway and available to the eye of conscience. Sinners must needs reason; saints behold.

XV. Identity and Diversity

It is the perpetual effort of conscience to divorce the soul from the dominion of sense; to nullify the dualities of the apparent, and restore the intuition of the real. The soul makes a double statement of all the facts; to conscience and sense; reason mediates between the two. Yet though double to sense, she remains single and one in herself; one in conscience, many in understanding; one in life, diverse in function and number. Sense, in its infirmity, breaks this unity to apprehend in part what it cannot grasp at once. Understanding notes diversity; conscience alone divines unity, and integrates all experience in identity of spirit. Number is predictable of body alone; not of spirit.

XVI. Conscience

Ever present, potent, vigilant, in the breast of man, there is that which never became a party in his guilt, never consented to a wrong deed, nor performed one, but holds itself above all sin, impeccable, immaculate, immutable, the deity of the heart, the conscience of the soul, the oracle and interpreter, the judge and executor of the divine law.

XVII. Theocracy

In the theocracy of the soul majorities do not rule. God and the saints; against them the rabble of sinners, with clamorous voices and uplifted hand, striving to silence the oracle of the private heart. Beelzebub marshals majorities. Prophets and reformers are always special enemies of his and his minions. Multitudes ever lie. Every age is a Judas, and betrays its Messiahs into the hands of the multitude. The voice of the private, not popular heart, is alone authentic.

XVIII. Speech

There is a magic in free speaking, especially on sacred themes, most potent and resistless. It is refreshing, amidst the inane common-places bandied in pulpits and parlors, to hear a hopeful word from an earnest, upright soul. Men rally around it as to the lattice in summer heats, to inhale the breeze that flows cool and refreshing from the mountains, and invigorates their languid frames. Once heard, they feel a buoyant sense of health and hopefulness, and wonder that they should have lain sick, supine so long, when a word has power to raise them from their couch, and restore them to soundness. And once spoken, it shall never be forgotten; it charms, exalts; it visits them in dreams, and haunts them during all their wakeful hours. Great, indeed, is the delight of speech;

sweet the sound of one's bosom thought, as it returns laden with the fragrance of a brother's approval.

XIX. Thought and Action

Great thoughts exalt and deify the thinker; still more ennobling is the effect of great deeds on the actor. The dilation and joy of the soul at these visitations of God is like that of the invalid, again inhaling the mountain breeze after long confinement in chambers: she feels herself a noble bird, whose eyrie is in the empyrean that she is made to bathe her bosom and plume herself in the ether of thought; to soar and sing amidst the seraphim, beholding the faces of Apollo and Jove.

XX. Action

Action translates death into life; fable into verity; speculation into experience; freeing man from the sorceries of tradition and the torpor of habit. The eternal Scripture is thus expurgated of the falsehoods interpolated into it by the supineness of the ages. Action mediates between conscience and sense; it is the gospel of the understanding.

XXI. Originality

Most men are on the ebb; but now and then a man comes riding down sublimely in high hope from God on the flood tide of the soul, as she sets into the coasts of time, submerging old landmarks, and laying waste the labors of centuries. A new man wears channels broad and deep into the banks of the ages; he washes away ancient boundaries, and sets afloat institutions, creeds, usages, which clog the ever flowing Present, stranding them on the shores of the Past. Such deluge is the harbinger of a new world, a renovated age. Hope builds an ark; the dove broods over the assuaged waters; the bow of promise gilds the east; the world is again repeopled and replanted. Yet the sons of genius alone venture into the ark: while most pass the rather down the sluggish stream of usage into the turbid pool of oblivion. Thitherward the retreating tide rolls, and wafted by the gales of inglorious ease, or urged by the winds of passion, they glide down the Lethean waters, and are not. Only the noble and heroic outlive in time their exit from it.

XXIV. Bread

The hunger of an age is like a presentiment and pledge of its own supply. Instinct is not only prophetic but provident. When there is a general craving for bread, that shall assuredly be satisfied; bread is even then growing in the fields. Now, men are lean and famishing; but, behold, the divine Husbandman has driven his share through the age, and sown us bread that we may not perish; yea, the reapers even are going forth, a blithe and hopeful company, while yet the fields weep with the dews of the morning, and the harvests wave in yellow ripeness. Soon shall a table be spread, and the age rejoice in the fulness of plenty.

XXV. Prophet

The prophet, by disciplines of meditation and valor, faithful to the spirit of the heart, his eye purified of the notes of tradition, his life of the vestiges of usage, ascends to the heights of immediate intuition: he rends the veil of sense; he bridges the distance between faith and sight, and beholds spiritual verities without scripture or mediator. In the presence of God, he communes with him face to face.

XXVII. Balances

I am not partial to your man who always holds his balance in hand, and must weigh forthwith whatsoever of physical or metaphysical haberdashery chances to be laid on his counter. I have observed that he thinks more of the accuracy and polish of his scales, than of the quality of the wares in which he deals. He never questions his own levity. But yet these balance-men are useful: it is convenient to have standards of market values. These are the public's approved sealers of weights and measures, who determine the worth of popular wares by their favorite weights, lucre and usage. It is well for the ages, that Genius rectifies both scales and men by a truer standard, quite wide of marts or markets.

XXVIII. Prudence

Prudence is the footprint of Wisdom.

XXIX. Revelation

The standing problem of Genius is to divine the essential verity intimated in the life and literature of the Past, divesting it of historical interpolations; separating the foreign from the indigenous, and translating the letter of the universal scripture into the spirit of contemporaneous life and letters.

XXX. Criticism

To just criticism unity of mind is essential. The critic must not esteem difference as real as sameness, and as permanent in the facts of nature. This tendency is fatal to all sound and final thinking: it never penetrates to the roots of things. All creative minds have been inspired and guided by the law of unity: their problem is ever to pierce the coarse and superficial rind of diversity, and discover the unity in whose core is the heart and seed of all things.

XXXI. Calculus

We need, what Genius is unconsciously seeking, and, by some daring generalization of the universe, shall assuredly discover, a spiritual calculus, a novum organon, whereby nature shall be divined in the soul, the soul in God, matter in spirit, polarity resolved into unity; and that power which pulsates in all life, animates and builds all organizations, shall manifest itself as one universal deific energy, present alike at the outskirts and centre of the universe, whose centre and circumference are one; omniscient, omnipotent, self-subsisting, uncontained, yet containing all things in the unbroken synthesis of its being.

XXXIII. Each and All

Life eludes all scientific analysis. Each organ and function is modified in substance and varied in effect, by the subtile energy which pulsates throughout the whole economy of things, spiritual and corporeal. The each is instinct with the all; the all unfolds and reappears in each. Spirit is all in all. God, man, nature, are a divine synthesis, whose parts it is impiety to sunder. Genius must preside devoutly over all investigations, or analysis, with her murderous knife, will seek impiously to probe the vitals of being.

XXXIV. God

God organizes never his attributes fully in single structures. He is instant, but never extant wholly, in his works. Nature does not contain, but is contained in him; she is the memoir of his life; man is a nobler scripture, yet fails to outwrite the godhead. The universe does not reveal, eternities do not publish the mysteries of his being. He subjects his noblest works to minute and constant revision; his idea ever transcends its form; he moulds anew his own idols; both nature and man are ever making, never made.

XXXV. Nature

Nature seems remote and detached, because the soul surveys her by means of the extremest senses, imposing on herself the notion of difference and remoteness through their predominance, and thereby losing that of her own oneness with it. Yet nature is not separate from me; she is mine alike with my body; and in moments of true life, I feel my identity with her; I breathe, pulsate, feel, think, will, through her members, and know of no duality of being. It is in such moods of soul that prophetic visions are beheld, and evangeles published for the joy and hope of mankind.

XXXVI. Flux

Solidity is an illusion of the senses. To faith, nothing is solid: the nature of the soul renders such fact impossible. Modern chemistry demonstrates that nine tenths of the human body are fluid, and substances of inferior order in lesser proportion. Matter is ever pervaded and agitated by the omnipresent soul. All things are instinct with spirit.

XXXVII. Sepulture and Resurrection

That which is visible is dead: the apparent is the corpse of the real; and undergoes successive sepultures and resurrections. The soul dies out of organs; the tombs cannot confine her; she eludes the grasp of decay; she builds and unseals the sepulchres. Her bodies are fleeting, historical. Whatsoever she sees when awake is death; when asleep dream.

XXXVIII. Time

Organizations are mortal; the seal of death is fixed on them at birth. The young Future is nurtured by the Past, yet aspires to a nobler life, and revises, in his maturity, the traditions and usages of his day, to be supplanted by the sons and daughters whom he begets and ennobles. Time, like fabled Saturn, now generates, and, ere even their sutures be closed, devours his own offspring. Only the children of the soul are immortal; the births of time are premature and perishable.

XXXIX. Embryon

Man is a rudiment and embryon of God: eternity shall develop in him the divine image.

XLIII. Genesis

The popular genesis is historical. It is written to sense not to the soul. Two principles, diverse and alien, interchange the Godhead and sway the world by turns. God is dual. Spirit is derivative. Identity halts in diversity. Unity is actual merely. The poles of things are not integrated: creation globed and orbed. Yet in the true genesis, nature is globed in the material, souls orbed in the spiritual firmament. Love globes, wisdom orbs, all things. As magnet the steel, so spirit attracts matter, which trembles to traverse the poles of diversity, and rest in the bosom of unity. All genesis is of love. Wisdom is her form: beauty her costume.

XLIV. Gravitation

Love and gravity are a twofold action of one life, whose conservative instincts in man and nature preserve inviolate the harmony of the immutable and eternal law of spirit. Man and nature alike tend toward the Godhead. All seeming divergence is overruled by this omnipotent force, whose retributions restore universal order.

XLV. Love

Love designs, thought sketches, action sculptures the works of spirit. Love is divine, conceiving, creating, completing, all things. Love is the Genius of Spirit.

XLVI. Life

Life, in its initial state, is synthetic; then feeling, thought, action are one and indivisible: love is its manifestation. Childhood and woman are samples and instances. But thought disintegrates and breaks this unity of soul: action alone restores it. Action is composition; thought decomposition. Deeds executed in love are graceful, harmonious, entire; enacted from thought merely, they are awkward, dissonant, incomplete: a manufacture, not creations, not works of genius.

XLVII. Actual and Ideal

The actual and ideal are twins of one mother, Reality, who failing to incarnate her conceptions in time, meanwhile contents herself with admiring in each the complement of the other, herself integrant of both. Always are the divine Gemini intertwined; Pan and Psyche, man and woman, the soul and nature.

XLVIII. Beauty

All departures from perfect beauty are degradations of the divine image. God is the one type, which the soul strives to incarnate in all organizations. Varieties are historical: the one form embosoms all forms; all having a common likeness at the base of difference. Human heads are images, more or less perfect, of the soul's or God's head. But the divine features do not fix in flesh; in the coarse and brittle clay. Beauty is fluent; art of highest order represents her always in flux, giving fluency and motion to bodies solid and immovable to sense. The line of beauty symbolizes motion.

L. Prometheus

Know, O man, that your soul is the Prometheus, who, receiving the divine fires, builds up this majestic statue of clay, and moulds it in the deific image, the pride of gods, the model and analogon of all forms. He chiselled that god-like brow, arched those mystic temples from whose fanes she herself looks forth, formed that miraculous globe above, and planted that sylvan grove below; graved those massive blades yoked in armed powers; carved that heaven-containing bosom, wreathed those puissant thighs, and hewed those stable columns, diffusing over all the grandeur, the grace of his own divine lineaments, and delighting in this cunning work of his hand. Mar not its beauty, spoil not its symmetry, by the deforming lines of lust and sin: dethroning the divinity incarnated therein, and transforming yourself into the satyr and the beast.

ELIZABETH PALMER PEABODY
The Lowing of Cattle Is the Natural Bass to the Melody of Human Voices

The "Brook Farm Institute of Agriculture and Education," which was Transcendentalism's experiment in the practical application of its principles of life and society, was set up on a 200-acre farm in West Roxbury, Mass., in 1841. In 1842 Elizabeth Palmer Peabody (1804–1894) wrote for The Dial *this explanation of its existence and its principles. Emerson would have nothing to do with going to Brook Farm, but young Nathaniel Hawthorne, himself no Transcendentalist, was among its colonists—not the less for his interest in Miss Peabody's younger sister Sophia. The Farm foundered because the leading Transcendentalists proved to be less able farmers than conversationalists. After several years the Brook Farmers who remained became converted to the socialist doctrine of Fourierism, and the experiment entered a new phase, that of the Brook Farm Phalanx, which terminated when the uninsured "Central Phalanstery" burned down. Hawthorne describes life at Brook Farm in* The Blithedale Romance.

. . . A few individuals, who, unknown to each other, under different disciplines of life, reacting from different social evils, but aiming at the same object,—of being wholly true to their natures as men and women; have been made acquainted with one another, and have determined to become the Faculty of the Embryo University.

FROM "Plan of the West Roxbury Community," by Elizabeth Palmer Peabody, *The Dial*, Vol. II (January, 1842), pp. 361–65, 367, 372.

In order to live a religious and moral life worthy the name, they feel it is necessary to come out in some degree from the world, and to form themselves into a community of property, so far as to exclude competition and the ordinary rules of trade;—while they reserve sufficient private property, or the means of obtaining it, for all purposes of independence, and isolation at will. They have bought a farm, in order to make agriculture the basis of their life, it being the most direct and simple in relation to nature.

A true life, although it aims beyond the highest star, is redolent of the healthy earth. The perfume of clover lingers about it. The lowing of cattle is the natural bass to the melody of human voices.

On the other hand, what absurdity can be imagined greater than the institution of cities? They originated not in love, but in war. It was war that drove men together in multitudes, and compelled them to stand so close, and build walls around them. This crowded condition produces wants of an unnatural character, which resulted in occupations that regenerated the evil, by creating artificial wants. Even when that thought of grief,

> I know, where'er I go
> That there hath passed away a glory from the Earth, . . .

came to our first parents, as they saw the angel, with the flaming sword of self-consciousness, standing between them and the recovery of spontaneous Life and Joy, we cannot believe they could have anticipated a time would come, when the sensuous apprehension of Creation—the great symbol of God— would be taken away from their unfortunate children,—crowded together in such a manner as to shut out the free breath and the Universal Dome of Heaven, some opening their eyes in the dark cellars of the narrow, crowded streets of walled cities. How could they have believed in such a conspiracy against the soul, as to deprive it of the sun and sky, and glorious apparelled Earth! The growth of cities, which were the embryo of nations hostile to each other, is a subject worthy of the thoughts and pen of the philosophic historian. Perhaps nothing would stimulate courage to seek, and hope to attain social good, so much as a profound history of the origin, in the mixed nature of man, and the exasperation by society, of the various organized Evils under which humanity groans. . . .

The plan of the Community, as an Economy, is in brief this; for all who have property to take stock, and receive a fixed interest thereon; then to keep house or board in commons, as they shall severally desire, at the cost of provisions purchased at wholesale, or raised on the farm; and for all to labor in community, and be paid at a certain rate an hour, choosing their own number of hours, and their own kind of work. With the results of this labor, and their interest, they are to pay their board, and also purchase whatever else they require at cost, at the warehouses of the Community, which are to be filled by the Community as such. To perfect this economy, in the course of time they must have all trades, and all modes of business carried on among themselves, from the lowest mechanical trade, which contributes to the health and comfort of life, to the finest art which adorns it with food or drapery for the mind.

All labor, whether bodily or intellectual, is to be paid at the same rate of wages; on the principle, that as the labor becomes merely bodily, it is a greater sacrifice to the individual laborer, to give his time to it; because time is desirable for the cultivation of the intellect, in exact proportion to ignorance. Besides, intellectual labor involves in itself higher pleasures, and is more its own reward, than bodily labor.

Another reason for setting the same pecuniary value on every kind of labor is to give outward expression to the great truth that all labor is sacred, when done for a common interest. Saints and philosophers already know this but the childish world does not; and very decided measures must be taken to equalize labors in the eyes of the young of the community, who are not beyond the moral influences of the world without them. . . .

Besides, after becoming members of this community, none will be engaged merely in bodily labor. The hours of labor for the Association will be limited by a general law, and can be curtailed at the will of the individual still more; and means will be given to all for intellectual improvement and for social intercourse, calculated to refine and expand. The hours redeemed from labor by community, will not be reapplied to the acquisition of wealth, but to the production of intellectual goods. This community aims to be rich, not in the metallic representative of wealth, but in the wealth itself, which money should represent, namely, LEISURE TO LIVE IN ALL THE FACULTIES OF THE SOUL. As a community, it will traffic with the world at large, in the products of Agricultural labor; and it will sell education to as many young persons as can be domesticated in the families, and enter into the common life with their own children. In the end, it hopes to be enabled to provide—not only all the necessaries, but all the elegances desirable for bodily and for spiritual health; books, apparatus, collections for science, works of art, means of beautiful amusement. These things are to be common to all; and thus that object, which alone gilds and refines the passion for individual accumulation, will no longer exist for desire, and whenever the Sordid passion appears, it will be seen in naked selfishness. In its ultimate success, the community will realize all the ends which selfishness seeks, but involved in spiritual blessings, which only greatness of soul can aspire after.

And the requisitions on the individuals, it is believed, will make this the order forever. The spiritual good will always be the condition of the temporal. Every one must labor for the community in a reasonable degree, or not taste its benefits. The principles of the organization, therefore, and not its probable results in future time, will determine its members. These principles are coöperation in social matters, instead of competition or balance of interests; and individual self-unfolding, in the faith that the whole soul of humanity is in each man and woman. The former is the application of the love of man; the latter of the love of God, to life. Whoever is satisfied with society, as it is; whose sense of justice is not wounded by its common action, institutions, spirit of commerce, has no business with this community; neither has any one who is willing to have other men (needing more time for intellectual cultivation than himself) give their best hours and strength to bodily labor, to secure himself immunity therefrom. And whoever does not measure what society owes to its members of cherishing and instruction, by the needs of the individuals that compose it, has no lot in this new society. Whoever is willing to receive from his fellow men that, for which he gives no equivalent, will stay away from its precincts forever.

But whoever shall surrender himself to its principles, shall find that its yoke is easy and its burden light. Everything can be said of it, in a degree, which Christ said of his kingdom, and therefore it is believed that in some measure it does embody his Idea. For its Gate of entrance is straight and narrow. It is literally a pearl *hidden in a field.* Those only who are willing to lose their life for its sake shall find it. Its voice is that which sent the young man sorrowing away. "Go sell all thy goods and give to the poor, and then come and follow me." "Seek first the kingdom of Heaven, and its righteousness, and all other things shall be added to you."

This principle, with regard to labor, lies at the root of moral and religious life; for it is not more true that "money is the root of all evil," than that *labor is the germ of all good* . . .

There are some persons who have entered the community without money. It is believed that these will be able to support themselves and dependents, by less work, more completely, and with more ease than elsewhere; while their labor will be of advantage to the community. It is in no sense an eleemosynary establishment but it is hoped that in the end it will be able to receive all who have the spiritual qualifications.

It seems impossible that the little organization can be looked on with any unkindness by the world without it. Those, who have not the faith that the principles of Christ's kingdom are applicable to real life in the world, will smile at it, as a visionary attempt. But even they must acknowledge it can do no harm, in any event. If it realizes the hopes of its founders, it will immediately become a manifest blessing. Its moral *aura* must be salutary. As long as it lasts, it will be an example of the beauty of brotherly love. If it succeeds in uniting successful labor with improvement in mind and manners, it will teach a noble lesson to the agricultural population, and do something to check that rush from the country to the city, which is now stimulated by ambition, and by something better, even a desire for learning. Many a young man leaves the farmer's life, because only by so doing can he have intellectual companionship and opportunity; and yet, did he but know it, professional life is ordinarily more unfavorable to the perfection of the mind, than the farmer's life; if the latter is lived with wisdom and moderation, and the labor mingled as it might be with study. This community will be a school for young agriculturalists, who may learn within its precincts, not only the skilful practice, but the scientific reasons of their work, and be enabled afterwards to improve their art continuously. It will also prove the best of normal schools, and as such, may claim the interest of those, who mourn over the inefficiency of our common school system, with its present ill-instructed teachers . . .

There may be some persons, at a distance, who will ask, to what degree has this community gone into operation? We cannot answer this with precision, for we do not write as organs of this association, and have reason to feel, that if we applied to them for information, they would refuse it, out of their dislike to appear in public. We desire this to be distinctly understood. But we can see, and think we have a right to say, that it has purchased the Farm, which some of its members cultivated for a year with success, by way of trying their love and skill for agricultural labor;—that in the only house they are as yet rich enough to own, is collected a large family, including several boarding scholars, and that all work and study together. They seem to be glad to know of all, who desire to join them in the spirit, that at any moment, when they are able to enlarge their habitations, they may call together those that belong to them.

HENRY DAVID THOREAU
They Never *Were* Read, They Never *Were* Heard

Along with Emerson's, the writings of Henry David Thoreau (1817–1862) have best survived their century, and of all the representatives of pre-Civil War American idealism, it is Thoreau who perhaps most often speaks to modern audiences. Best known for Walden *and his essay "On the Duty of Civil Disobedience," Thoreau left several other works which contain chapters and passages of compelling relevance today. Of all the leading Transcendentalists, Thoreau was doubtlessly the most self-sufficient, and lived the solitary independence he advocated in his writings. In the passage which follows, from* A Week on the Concord and Merrimack Rivers, *Thoreau is typically iconoclastic in his attitude toward revealed Christianity, and in his recognition of the revolutionary implications of much that was painlessly institutionalized in Sunday church services. Reading this passage, one can understand why even the Liberal Unitarians of Boston were shocked by some of the manifestations of Transcendentalist thought.*

FROM *A Week on the Concord and Merrimack Rivers,* by Henry David Thoreau (Boston and New York: Houghton Mifflin Co., 1893), pp. 87–92.

Most people with whom I talk, men and women even of some originality and genius, have their scheme of the universe all cut and dried,—very *dry*, I assure you, to hear, dry enough to burn, dry-rotted and powder-post, methinks,—which they set up between you and them in the shortest intercourse; an ancient and tottering frame with all its boards blown off. They do not walk without their bed. Some to me seemingly very unimportant and unsubstantial things and relations, are for them everlastingly settled,—as Father, Son, and Holy Ghost, and the like. These are like the everlasting hills to them. But in all my wanderings, I never came across the least vestige of authority for these things. They have not left so distinct a trace as the delicate flower of a remote geological period on the coal in my grate. The wisest man preaches no doctrines; he has no scheme; he sees no rafter, not even a cobweb, against the heavens. It is clear sky. If I ever see more clearly at one time than at another, the medium through which I see is clearer. To see from earth to heaven, and see there standing, still a fixture, that old Jewish scheme! What right have you to hold up this obstacle to my understanding you, to your understanding me! You did not invent it; it was imposed on you. Examine your authority. Even Christ, we fear, had his scheme, his conformity to tradition, which slightly vitiates his teaching. He had not swallowed all formulas. He preached some mere doctrines. As for me, Abraham, Isaac, and Jacob are now only the subtilest imaginable essences which would not stain the morning sky. Your scheme must be the framework of the universe; all other schemes will soon be ruins. The perfect God in his revelations of himself has never got to the length of one such proposition as you, his prophets, state. Have you learned the alphabet of heaven, and can count three? Do you know the number of God's family? Can you put mysteries into words? Do you presume to fable of the ineffable? Pray, what geographer are you, that speak of heaven's topography? Whose friend are you that speak of God's personality? Do you, Miles Howard, think that he has made you his confidant? Tell me of the height of the mountains of the moon, or of the diameter of space, and I may believe you, but of the secret history of the Almighty, and I shall pronounce thee mad. Yet we have a sort of family history of our God,—so have the Tahitians of theirs,—and some old poet's grand imagination is imposed on us as adamantine everlasting truth, and God's own word! . . .

The New Testament is an invaluable book, though I confess to having been slightly prejudiced against it in my very early days by the church and the Sabbath school, so that it seemed, before I read it, to be the yellowest book in the catalogue. Yet I early escaped from their meshes. It was hard to get the commentaries out of one's head, and taste its true flavor. I think that Pilgrim's Progress is the best sermon which has been preached from this text; almost all other sermons that I have heard or heard of, have been but poor imitations of this. It would be a poor story to be prejudiced against the Life of Christ, because the book has been edited by Christians. In fact, I love this book rarely, though it is a sort of castle in the air to me, which I am permitted to dream.

Having come to it so recently and freshly, it has the greater charm, so that I cannot find any to talk with about it. I never read a novel, they have so little real life and thought in them. The reading which I love best is the scriptures of the several nations, though it happens that I am better acquainted with those of the Hindoos, the Chinese, and the Persians, than of the Hebrews, which I have come to last. Give me one of these Bibles, and you have silenced me for a while. When I recover the use of my tongue, I am wont to worry my neighbors with the new sentences, but commonly they cannot see that there is any wit in them. Such has been my experience with the New Testament. I have not yet got to the crucifixion, I have read it over so many times. I should love dearly to read it aloud to my friends, some of whom are seriously inclined; it is so good, and I am sure that they have never heard it, it fits their case exactly, and we should enjoy it so much together,—but I instinctively despair of getting their ears. They soon show, by signs not to be mistaken, that it is inexpressibly wearisome to them. I do not mean to imply that I am any better than my neighbors; for, alas! I know that I am only as good, though I love better books than they.

It is remarkable, that notwithstanding the universal favor with which the New Testament is outwardly received, and even the bigotry with which it is defended, there is no hospitality shown to, there is no appreciation of, the order of truth with which it deals. I know of no book that has so few readers. There is none so truly strange, and heretical, and unpopular. To Christians, no less than Greeks and Jews, it is foolishness and a stumbling block. There are, indeed, severe things in it which no man should read aloud more than once. "Seek first the kingdom of heaven." "Lay not up for yourselves treasures on earth." "If thou wilt be perfect, go and sell that thou hast, and give to the poor, and thou shalt have treasure in heaven." "For what is a man profited, if he shall gain the whole world, and lose his own soul? or what shall a man give in exchange for his soul?" Think of this, Yankees! "Verily I say unto you, if ye have faith as a grain of mustard seed, ye shall say unto this mountain, Remove hence to yonder place; and it shall remove; and nothing shall be impossible unto you." Think of repeating these things to a New England audience! thirdly, fourthly, fifteenthly, till there are three barrels of sermons! Who, without cant, can read them aloud? Who, without cant, can hear them, and not go out of the meeting-house? They never *were* read, they never *were* heard. Let but one of these sentences be rightly read from any pulpit in the land, and there would not be left one stone of that meeting-house upon another.

8

SLAVERY AND SECESSION

The slavery issue, a factor in the debates over the Constitution in 1789, brought into the open in the Missouri Controversy of 1819–1820, very much present though seldom alluded to during the Nullification crisis of 1832, became more and more unavoidable as the first half of the nineteenth century drew to a close. In Boston William Lloyd Garrison began publishing *The Liberator* in 1831; its first issue contained a manifesto to the effect that its editor would not rest until slavery was outlawed. The same year the bloody insurrection led by Nat Turner in tidewater Virginia brought a new urgency to the slavery question. Many factors, of course, contributed to the coming of the Civil War. The approximate political balance between North and South that had existed in the early years of the Republic was destroyed as immigrants flooded into the Northeast and settlers from the Northeast moved out into the territories of the Midwest, which soon became free states, until by the 1840's and 1850's the slaveholding South was very much a minority region. Railroads linked the Midwest to the industrial Northeast; the Mississippi River traffic that had drawn that region into economic relationship with the South became less important economically. Northeastern manufacturing interests pressed for a protective tariff to aid American industry; the agricultural South bitterly opposed such a move, desiring to sell its staple crops in the European market and to purchase European goods on an unrestricted basis. When in 1860 the Democratic Party split into Northern and Southern wings and a Republican President was elected, the lower South seceded from the Union, and was soon joined by the border states. A bloody Civil War resulted; ultimately the South was defeated at a cost of some 600,000 American soldiers killed in battle; and the slaves were freed.

Whether or not slavery actually caused the war, it was the principal

issue of public contention. Against the onslaught of Abolitionist sentiment the South attempted to create an ideological defense in which the
institution of slavery was justified. Each successive political crisis—the
Mexican War, the Wilmot Proviso, the Kansas-Nebraska Bill, the Dred
Scott Decision—inflamed passions higher.

The literature of the coming of Civil War is voluminous. The selections that follow attempt to show a few of the points at issue.

WILLIAM LLOYD GARRISON
I Will Be Heard

*William Lloyd Garrison (1805–1879), after an imprisonment for libel in Balti-
more in 1830, returned home to Massachusetts and on January 1, 1831, published the first issue of* The Liberator. *For the next thirty-four years he filled its
columns with the demand for immediate and complete emancipation of the
slaves. The United States Constitution, since it recognized slavery, was in his
words "a covenant with Death and an agreement with Hell." Though at first
his influence was slight and the circulation of his newspaper small, his impact
grew, until by the 1850's he was a figure of great political importance. The
selection which follows is his statement "To The Public" in the first issue of*
The Liberator.

In the month of August, I issued proposals for publishing "The Liberator"
in Washington City; but the enterprise, though hailed in different sections of
the country, was palsied by public indifference. Since that time, the removal of
the *Genius of Universal Emancipation* to the Seat of Government has rendered
less imperious the establishment of a similar periodical in that quarter.

During my recent tour for the purpose of exciting the minds of the people
by a series of discourses on the subject of slavery, every place that I visited gave
fresh evidence of the fact, that a greater revolution in public sentiment was to
be effected in the free States—*and particularly in New England*—than at the
South. I found contempt more bitter, opposition more active, detraction more
relentless, prejudice more stubborn, and apathy more frozen, than among slave-
owners themselves. Of course, there were individual exceptions to the contrary.
This state of things afflicted, but did not dishearten me. I determined, at every
hazard, to lift up the standard of emancipation in the eyes of the nation, *within
sight of Bunker Hill and in the birthplace of liberty.* That standard is now un-

FROM "To The Public," *The Liberator*, January 1, 1840, quoted in *William Lloyd Garrison, 1805–
1879, The Story of His Life Told By His Children* (New York: The Century Co., 1885), Vol. I:
1805–1835, pp. 294–96.

furled; and long may it float, unhurt by the spoliations of time or the missiles of a desperate foe—yea, till every chain be broken, and every bondman set free! Let Southern oppressors tremble—let their secret abettors tremble—let their Northern apologists tremble—let all the enemies of the persecuted blacks tremble.

I deem the publication of my original Prospectus unnecessary, as it has obtained a wide circulation. The principles therein inculcated will be steadily pursued in this paper, excepting that I shall not array myself as the political partisan of any man. In defending the great cause of human rights, I wish to derive the assistance of all religions and of all parties.

Assenting to the "self-evident truth" maintained in the American Declaration of Independence, "that all men are created equal, and endowed by their Creator with certain inalienable rights—among which are life, liberty and the pursuit of happiness," I shall strenuously contend for the immediate enfranchisement of our slave population. In Park-Street Church, on the Fourth of July, 1829, in an address on slavery, I unreflectingly assented to the popular but pernicious doctrine of *gradual* abolition. I seize this opportunity to make a full and unequivocal recantation, and thus publicly to ask pardon of my God, of my country, and of my brethren the poor slaves, for having uttered a sentiment so full of timidity, injustice, and absurdity. A similar recantation, from my pen, was published in the *Genius of Universal Emancipation* at Baltimore, in September, 1829. My conscience is now satisfied.

I am aware that many object to the severity of my language; but is there not cause for severity? I *will be* as harsh as truth, and as uncompromising as justice. On this subject, I do not wish to think, or speak, or write, with moderation. No! no! Tell a man whose house is on fire to give a moderate alarm; tell him to moderately rescue his wife from the hands of the ravisher; tell the mother to gradually extricate her babe from the fire into which it has fallen;—but urge me not to use moderation in a cause like the present. I am in earnest —I will not equivocate—I will not excuse—I will not retreat a single inch—AND I WILL BE HEARD. The apathy of the people is enough to make every statue leap from its pedestal, and to hasten the resurrection of the dead.

It is pretended, that I am retarding the cause of emancipation by the coarseness of my invective and the precipitancy of my measures. *The charge is not true.* On this question my influence,—humble as it is,—is felt at this moment to a considerable extent, and shall be felt in coming years—not perniciously, but beneficially—not as a curse, but as a blessing; and posterity will bear testimony that I was right. I desire to thank God, that he enables me to disregard "the fear of man which bringeth a snare," and to speak his truth in its simplicity and power. And here I close with this fresh dedication:

> Oppression! I have seen thee, face to face,
> And met thy cruel eye and cloudy brow;
> But thy soul-withering glance I fear not now—

For dread to prouder feelings doth give place
Of deep abhorrence! Scorning the disgrace
Of slavish knees that at thy footstool bow,
I also kneel—but with far other vow
Do hail thee and thy herd of hirelings base:—
I swear, while life-blood warms my throbbing veins,
Still to oppose and thwart, with heart and hand,
Thy brutalising sway—till Afric's chains
Are burst, and Freedom rules the rescued land,—
Trampling Oppression and his iron rod:
Such is the vow I take—SO HELP ME GOD!

NAT TURNER
The Impression That I Was Ordained
for Some Great Purpose

*In August, 1831, the county of Southampton in southern tidewater Virginia was
the scene of the only successful slave rebellion in American history. A Negro
preacher, Nat Turner, led a band of seventy-five Negroes in a three-day march
of slaughter, during which some fifty-five white men, women, and children
were murdered. Finally the whites rallied to capture and kill the insurrectionists, Nat Turner went into hiding, and white mobs roamed about the area and
killed almost two hundred Negroes in retaliation. When Turner finally surrendered, he was tried, convicted, and hanged. While awaiting trial and death
in his cell, he dictated a lengthy confession to a white lawyer, Thomas R.
Gray, who published it in 1831 as "The Confessions of Nat Turner."*

*The insurrection played a large part in the decision of the Virginia legis-
lature early the next year not to abolish slavery in the state. It also resulted in
the enactment of new and harsher slave laws throughout the Southern states.*

*In 1967 the Virginia novelist William Styron used Nat Turner's confession
as the basis for a novel,* The Confessions of Nat Turner.

The material that follows is excerpted from the original Confessions.

Sir: You have asked me to give a history of the motives which induced
me to undertake the late insurrection, as you call it. To do so I must go back
to the days of my infancy, and even before I was born.

I was 31 years of age the 2d of October last, and born the property of
Benj. Turner of this county. In my childhood, a circumstance occurred which

FROM "The Confessions of Nat Turner, the Leader of the Late Insurrection in Southampton,
Virginia, as fully and voluntarily made to Thomas R. Gray . . ." (Baltimore, 1831), pp. 7–12,
15–18.

made an indelible impression on my mind and laid the groundwork of that enthusiasm which has terminated so fatally to many, both white and black, and for which I am about to atone at the gallows. It is here necessary to relate this circumstance—trifling as it may seem, it was the commencement of that belief which has grown with time, and even now, sir, in this dungeon, helpless and forsaken as I am, I cannot divest myself of.

Being at play with other children when 3 or 4 years old, I was telling them something which, my mother overhearing, said it happened before I was born. I stuck to my story, however, and related some things which went, in her opinion, to confirm it. Others called on were greatly astonished, knowing that these things had happened and caused them to say in my hearing that I surely would be a prophet, as the Lord had shown me things that had happened before my birth. And my father and mother strengthened me in this, my first impression, saying in my presence I was intended for some great purpose, which they had always thought from certain marks on my head and breast.

My grandmother, who was very religious, and to whom I was much attached; my master, who belonged to the church, and other religious persons who visited the house, and whom I often saw at prayers, noticing the singularity of my manners, I suppose, and my uncommon intelligence for a child, remarked I had too much sense to be raised, and if I was, I would never be of any service to anyone as a slave. To a mind like mine, restless, inquisitive and observant, there was nothing that I saw or heard of to which my attention was not directed.

The manner in which I learned to read and write not only had great influence on my own mind (as I acquired it with the most perfect ease, so much so that I have no recollection whatever of learning the alphabet), but to the astonishment of the family, one day when a book was shown to me to keep me from crying, I began spelling the names of the different objects.

When I got large enough to go to work, while employed I was reflecting on many things that would present themselves to my imagination, and whenever an opportunity occurred of looking at a book, when the school children were getting their lessons, I would find many things that the fertility of my own imagination had depicted to me before. All my time not devoted to my master's service was spent either in prayer or in making experiments in casting different things in molds made of earth; in attempting to make paper, gunpowder and many other experiments that although I could not perfect, yet convinced me of its practicability if I had the means.

I was not addicted to stealing in my youth, nor have ever been, yet such was the confidence of the Negroes in the neighborhood even in this early period of my life in my superior judgment that they would often carry me with them when they were going on any roguery, to plan for them. Growing up among them, with this confidence in my superior judgment, and when this, in their opinions, was perfected by Divine inspiration, from the circumstances already alluded to in my infancy, and which belief was ever afterward zealously inculcated by the austerity of my life and manners, which became the subject of remark by white and black, having soon discovered to be great, I must appear so, and therefore studiously avoided mixing in society and wrapped myself in mystery, devoting my time to fasting and prayer.

By this time having arrived to man's estate and hearing the Scriptures commented on at meetings, I was struck with that particular passage which says: "Seek ye the Kingdom of Heaven and all things shall be added unto you." I reflected much on this passage and prayed daily for light on this subject. As I was praying one day at my plough, the Spirit spoke to me, saying: "Seek ye the Kingdom of Heaven and all things shall be added unto you."

And I was greatly astonished, and for two years prayed continually whenever my duty would permit; and then again I had the same revelation, which fully confirmed me in the impression that I was ordained for some great purpose in the hands of the Almighty.

Several years rolled round in which many events occurred to strengthen me in this, my belief. At this time I reverted in my mind to the remarks made of me in my childhood and the things that had been shown me, and as it had been said of me in my childhood by those by whom I had been taught to pray, both white and black, and in whom I had the greatest confidence, that I had too much sense to be raised and if I was, I would never be of any use as a slave.

Now, finding that I had arrived to man's estate and was a slave, and these revelations being known to me, I began to direct my attention to this great object, to fulfill the purpose for which by this time I felt assured I was intended. Knowing the influence I had obtained over the minds of my fellow servants (not by the means of conjuring and such like tricks, for to them I always spoke of such things with contempt) but by the communion of the Spirit, whose revelation I often communicated to them, and they believed and said my wisdom came from God, I now began to prepare them for my purpose by telling them something was about to happen that would terminate in fulfilling the great promise that had been made to me.

About this time I was placed under an overseer from whom I ran away and after remaining in the woods 30 days, I returned, to the astonishment of the Negroes on the plantation, who thought I had made my escape to some other part of the country as my father had done before. But the reason of my return was that the Spirit appeared to me and said I had my wishes directed to the things of this world and not to the Kingdom of Heaven, and that I should return to the service of my earthly master—"For he who knoweth his Master's will, and doeth it not, shall be beaten with many stripes, and thus have I chastened you."

And the Negroes found fault and murmured against me, saying if they had my sense they would not serve any master in the world. And about this time I had a vision, and I saw white spirits and black spirits engaged in battle, and the sun was darkened—the thunder rolled in the heavens and blood flowed in streams—and I heard a voice saying, "Such is your luck, such you are called to see, and let it come rough or smooth, you must surely bear it."

I now withdrew myself as much as my situation would permit from the intercourse of my fellow servants for the avowed purpose of serving the Spirit more fully; and it appeared to me and reminded me of the things it had already shown me, and that it would then reveal to me the knowledge of the elements, the revolution of the planets, the operation of tides and changes of the seasons. After this revelation in the year 1825, and the knowledge of the elements being made known to me, I sought more than ever to obtain true holiness before the great day of judgment should appear; and then I began to receive the true knowledge of the faith.

And from the first steps of righteousness until the last was I made perfect; and the Holy Ghost was with me and said, "Behold me as I stand in the Heavens"; and I looked and saw the forms of men in different attitudes, and there were lights in the sky to which the children of darkness gave other names than what they really were, for they were the lights of the Saviour's hands stretched forth from east to west, even as they were extended on the cross of Calvary for the redemption of sinners.

And I wondered greatly at these miracles, and prayed to be informed of a certainty of the meaning thereof, and shortly afterward, while laboring in the field, I discovered drops of blood on the corn, as though it was dew from heaven, and I communicated it to many, both white and black, in the neighborhood; and then I found on the leaves in the woods hieroglyphic characters and numbers, with the forms of men in different attitudes, portrayed in the blood, and representing the figures I had seen before in the heavens.

And now the Holy Ghost had revealed itself to me, for as the blood of Christ had been shed on this earth, and had ascended to Heaven for the salvation of sinners, and was now returning to earth again in the form of dew; and as the leaves on the trees bore the impression of figures I had seen in the heavens, it was plain to me that the Saviour was about to lay down the yoke he had borne for the sins of men and the great day of judgment was at hand.

About this time I told these things to a white man (Etheldred T. Brantley), on whom it had a wonderful effect, and he ceased from his wickedness and was attacked immediately with a cutaneous eruption, and blood oozed from the pores of his skin, and after praying and fasting nine days, he was healed; and the Spirit appeared to me again and said, "As the Saviour had been baptized, so should we be also"; and when the white people would not let us be baptized by the church, we went down into the water together, in the sight of many who reviled us, and were baptized by the Spirit.

After this I rejoiced greatly and gave thanks to God. And on the 12th of May, 1828, I heard a loud noise in the heavens and the Spirit instantly appeared to me and said the Serpent was loosened, and Christ had laid down the yoke he had borne for the sins of men, and that I should take it on and fight against the Serpent, for the time was fast approaching when the first should be last and the last should be first.

QUESTION: Do you not find yourself mistaken now?

ANSWER: Was not Christ crucified?

And by signs in the heavens that it would make known to me when I should commence the great work, and until the first sign appeared I should conceal it from the knowledge of men; and on the appearance of the sign (the eclipse of the sun last February) I should arise and prepare myself and slay my enemies with their own weapons.

And immediately on the sign appearing in the heavens, the seal was removed from my lips and I communicated the great work laid out for me to do to four in whom I had the greatest confidence (Henry, Hark, Nelson and Sam). It was intended by us to have begun the work of death on the 4th of July last.

Many were the plans formed and rejected by us, and it affected my mind to such a degree that I felt sick, and the time passed without our coming to any determination how to commence. Still forming new schemes and rejecting them when the sign appeared again, which determined me not to wait longer.

Since the commencement of 1830, I had been living with Mr. Joseph Travis, who was to me a kind master and placed the greatest confidence in me; in fact, I had no cause to complain of his treatment of me. On Saturday evening, the 20th of August, it was agreed between Henry, Hark and myself to prepare a dinner the next day for the men we expected, and then to concert a plan, as we had not yet determined on any. Hark, on the following morning, brought a pig, and Henry, brandy, and being joined by Sam, Nelson, Will and Jack, they prepared in the woods a dinner, where, about 3 o'clock I joined them.

QUESTION: Why were you so backward in joining them?

ANSWER: The same reason that had caused me not to mix with them for years before.

I saluted them on coming up, and asked Will how came he there. He answered, his life was worth no more than others, and his liberty as dear to him. I asked him if he thought to obtain it. He said he would, or lose his life. This was enough to put him in full confidence. Jack, I knew, was only a tool in the hands of Hark.

It was quickly agreed we should commence at home (Mr. J. Travis') on that night, and until we had armed and equipped ourselves and gathered sufficient force, neither age nor sex was to be spared (which was invariably adhered to). We remained at the feast until about two hours in the night, when we went to the house and found Austin; they all went to the cider press and drank except myself. . . .

[*There follows a detailed account of the insurrectionists as they proceeded from farmhouse to farmhouse, killing all the whites they found.*]

On reaching Mr. James W. Parker's gate, immediately on the road leading to Jerusalem, and about three miles distant, it was proposed to me to call there, but I objected, as I knew he was gone to Jerusalem and my object was to reach there as soon as possible; but some of the men having relations at Mr. Parker's, it was agreed that they might call and get his people. I remained at the gate on the road with seven or eight; the others going across the field to the house, about half a mile off.

After waiting some time for them, I became impatient, started to the house for them and on our return we were met by a party of white men, who had pursued our blood-stained track and who had fired on those at the gate and dispersed them, which I knew nothing of, not having been at that time re-joined by any of them. Immediately on discovering the whites, I ordered my men to halt and form, as they appeared to be alarmed.

The white men, 18 in number, approached us within about 100 yards, when one of them fired (this was against the positive orders of Capt. Alexander P. Peete, who commanded, and who had directed the men to reserve their fire until within 30 paces) and discovered about half of them retreating. I then ordered my men to fire and rush on them. The few remaining stood their ground until we approached within 50 yards, when they fired and retreated.

We pursued and overtook some of them, who we thought we left dead (they were not killed). After pursuing them about 200 yards, and rising a little hill, I discovered they were met by another party and had halted, and were reloading their guns, thinking that those who retreated first, and the party who fired on us at 50 or 60 yards distant, had all only fallen back to meet others with ammunition.

As I saw them reloading their guns and more coming up than I saw at first, and several of my bravest men being wounded, the others became panic-struck and squandered over the field; the white men pursued and fired on us several times. Hark had his horse shot under him and I caught another for him as it was running by me; five or six of my men were wounded, but none left on the field.

Finding myself defeated here, I instantly determined to go through a private way and cross the Nottoway River at the Cypress Bridge, three miles below Jerusalem, and attack that place in the rear, as I expected they would look for me on the other road, and I had a great desire to get there to procure arms and ammunition. After going a short distance in this private way, ac-companied by about 20 men, I overtook two or three who told me the others were dispersed in every direction.

After trying in vain to collect a sufficient force to proceed to Jerusalem, I determined to return, as I was sure they would make back to their old neigh-borhood, where they would rejoin me, make new recruits and come down again. On my way back I called at Mrs. Thomas', Mrs. Spencer's and several other places; the white families having fled, we found no more victims to gratify our thirst for blood. We stopped at Maj. Ridley's quarters for the night and being joined by four of his men, with the recruits made since my defeat, we mustered now about 40 strong.

After placing out sentinels, I laid down to sleep, but was quickly roused by a great racket. Starting up, I found some mounted and others in great confusion. One of the sentinels having given the alarm that we were about to be attacked, I ordered some to ride round and reconnoiter, and on their return, the others being more alarmed, not knowing who they were, fled in different ways, so that I was reduced to about 20 again. With this I determined to attempt to recruit and proceed to rally in the neighborhood I had left.

Dr. Blunt's was the nearest house, which we reached just before day. On riding up the yard, Hark fired a gun. We expected Dr. Blunt and his family were at Maj. Riley's, as I knew there was a company of men there, the gun was fired to ascertain if any of the family were at home. We were immediately fired upon, and retreated, leaving several of my men. I do not know what became of them, as I never saw them afterward.

Pursuing our course back, and coming in sight of Capt. Harris', where we had been the day before, we discovered a party of white men at the house, on which all deserted me but two (Jacob and Nat). We concealed ourselves in the woods until near night, when I sent them in search of Henry, Sam, Nelson and Hark and directed them to rally all they could at the place we had had our dinner the Sunday before, where they would find me, and I accordingly returned there as soon as it was dark and remained until Wednesday evening, when discovering white men riding around the place as though they were looking for someone, and none of my men joining me, I concluded Jacob and Nat had been taken and compelled to betray me.

On this, I gave up all hope for the present, and on Thursday night, after having supplied myself with provisions from Mr. Travis', I scratched a hole under a pile of fence rails in a field, where I concealed myself for six weeks, never leaving my hiding place but for a few minutes in the dead of night to get water, which was very near.

Thinking by this time I could venture out, I began to go about in the night and eavesdrop the houses in the neighborhood; pursuing this course for about a fortnight and gathering little or no intelligence, afraid of speaking to any human being, and returning every morning to my cave before the dawn of day, I know not how long I might have led this life if accident had not betrayed me.

A dog in the neighborhood passing by my hiding place one night while I was out, was attracted by some meat I had in my cave and crawled in and stole it, and was coming out just as I returned. A few nights after, two Negroes having started to go hunting with the same dog and passing that way, the dog came again to the place, and having just gone out to walk about, discovered me and barked, on which, thinking myself discovered, I spoke to them to beg concealment. On making myself known, they fled from me.

Knowing then they would betray me, I immediately left my hiding place and was pursued almost incessantly until I was taken a fortnight afterward by Mr. Benjamin Phipps in a little hole I had dug out with my sword, for the purpose of concealment, under the top of a fallen tree. On Mr. Phipps' discovering the place of my concealment, he cocked his gun and aimed at me. I requested him not to shoot, and I would give up, upon which he demanded my sword. I delivered it to him and he brought me to prison.

During the time I was pursued, I had many hairbreadth escapes which your time will not permit me to relate. I am here loaded with chains and willing to suffer the fate that awaits me.

GEORGE FITZHUGH
You Treat Your Horses and Hounds Better

In response to Abolitionist attacks, there were Southern defenses of slavery aplenty. Negro slavery, contended the Virginia writer George Fitzhugh (1806–1881), was but one form, and a more humane one at that, of human slavery. The wage slavery of the industrial Northeast, he argued, was less humane by far, since it realized the profits deriving from human chattels without accepting the responsibility for feeding, clothing, and housing the laborers who made wealth possible. Fitzhugh entitled his polemic Cannibals All!, *asserting that both the industrial capitalist and the planter alike existed through the ownership of the labors of less affluent human beings. Though motivated by very different reasons, denunciations of capitalistic wage-slavery would become frequent in the literature of the latter decades of the nineteenth century and in the century to follow.*

Probably, you are a lawyer, or a merchant, or a doctor, who has made by your business fifty thousand dollars, and retired to live on your capital. But, mark! not to spend your capital. That would be vulgar, disreputable, criminal. That would be, to live by your own labor; for your capital is your amassed labor. That would be, to do as common working men do; for they take the pittance which their employers leave them, to live on. They live by labor; for they exchange the results of their own labor for the products of other people's labor. It is, no doubt, an honest, vulgar way of living, but not at all a respectable way. The respectable way of living is, to make other people work for you, and to pay them nothing for so doing—and to have no concern about them after their work is done. Hence, white slave-holding is much more respectable than negro slavery—for the master works nearly as hard for the negro, as he for the

FROM *Cannibals All! Or, Slaves Without Masters*, by George Fitzhugh (Richmond: A. Morris, 1857), pp. 28–32.

master. But you, my virtuous, respectable reader, exact three thousand dollars per annum from white labor, (for your income is the product of white labor,) and make not one cent of return in any form. You retain your capital, and never labor, and yet live in luxury on the labor of others. Capital commands labor, as the master does the slave. Neither pays for labor; but the master permits the slave to retain a larger allowance from the proceeds of his own labor, and hence "free labor is cheaper than slave labor." You, with the command over labor which your capital gives you, are a slave owner—a master, without the obligations of a master. They who work for you, who create your income, are slaves, without the rights of slaves. Slaves without a master! Whilst you were engaged in amassing your capital, in seeking to become independent, you were in the White Slave Trade. To become independent, is to be able to make other people support you, without being obliged to labor for *them*. Now, what man in society is not seeking to attain this situation? He who attains it, is a slave owner, in the worst sense. He who is in pursuit of it, is engaged in the slave trade. You, reader, belong to the one or other class. The men without property, in free society, are theoretically in a worse condition than slaves. Practically, their condition corresponds with this theory, as history and statistics every where demonstrate. The capitalists, in free society, live in ten times the luxury and show that Southern masters do, because the slaves to capital work harder and cost less, than negro slaves.

The negro slaves of the South are the happiest, and, in some sense, the freest people in the world. The children and the aged and infirm work not at all, and yet have all the comforts and necessaries of life provided for them. They enjoy liberty, because they are oppressed neither by care nor labor. The women do little hard work, and are protected from the despotism of their husbands by their masters. The negro men and stout boys work, on the average, in good weather, not more than nine hours a day. The balance of their time is spent in perfect abandon. Besides, they have their Sabbaths and holidays. White men, with so much of license and liberty, would die of ennui; but negroes luxuriate in corporeal and mental repose. With their faces upturned to the sun, they can sleep at any hour; and quiet sleep is the greatest of human enjoyments. "Blessed be the man who invented sleep." 'Tis happiness in itself— and results from contentment with the present, and confident assurance of the future. We do not know whether free laborers ever sleep. They are fools to do so; for, whilst they sleep, the wily and watchful capitalist is devising means to ensnare and exploitate them. The free laborer must work or starve. He is more of a slave than the negro, because he works longer and harder for less allowance than the slave, and has no holiday, because the cares of life with him begin when its labors end. He has no liberty, and not a single right. We know, 'tis often said, air and water, are common property, which all have equal right to participate and enjoy; but this is utterly false. The appropriation of the lands carries with it the appropriation of all on or above the lands, *usque ad cœlum, aut ad inferos* [even to heaven or to hell]. A man cannot breathe the air, without a place to breathe it from, and all places are appro-priated. All water is private property "to the middle of the stream," except the ocean, and that is not fit to drink.

Free laborers have not a thousandth part of the rights and liberties of negro slaves. Indeed, they have not a single right nor a single liberty, unless it be the right or liberty to die. But the reader may think that he and other capi-talists and employers are freer than negro slaves. Your capital would soon vanish, if you dared indulge in the liberty and abandon of negroes. You hold your wealth and position by the tenure of constant watchfulness, care, and circumspection. You never labor; but you are never free.

Where a few own the soil, they have unlimited power over the balance of society, until domestic slavery comes in, to compel them to permit this balance of society to draw a sufficient and comfortable living from *terra mater*. Free society, asserts the right of a few to the earth—slavery, maintains that it belongs, in different degrees, to all.

But, reader, well may you follow the slave trade. It is the only trade worth following, and slaves the only property worth owning. All other is worthless, a mere *caput mortuum* [worthless residue], except in so far as it vests the owner with the power to command the labors of others—to enslave them. Give you a palace, ten thousand acres of land, sumptuous clothes, equipage, and every other luxury; and with your artificial wants, you are poorer than Robinson Crusoe, or the lowest working man, if you have no slaves to capital, or domestic slaves. Your capital will not bring you an income of a cent, nor supply one of your wants, without labor. Labor is indispensable to give value to property, and if you owned every thing else, and did not own labor, you would be poor. But fifty thousand dollars means, and is, fifty thousand dol-lars worth of slaves. You can command, without touching on that capital, three thousand dollars' worth of labor per annum. You could do no more were you to buy slaves with it, and then you would be cumbered with the cares of governing and providing for them. You are a slaveholder now, to the amount of fifty thousand dollars, with all the advantages, and none of the cares and responsibilities of a master.

"Property in man" is what all are struggling to obtain. Why should they not be obliged to take care of man, their property, as they do of their horses and their hounds, their cattle and their sheep. Now, under the delusive name of liberty, you work him "from morn to dewy eve"—from infancy to old age—then turn him out to starve. You treat your horses and hounds better. Capital is a cruel master. The free slave trade, the commonest, yet the cruellest of trades.

HARRIET BEECHER STOWE
The Frightful Reality of Scenes Daily and Hourly Acting on Our Shores

When Harriet Beecher Stowe (1811–1896) visited the White House during the Civil War, President Lincoln half-humorously referred to her as the lady who "made this great civil War." Such was the popularity of Uncle Tom's Cabin (1852), with its unforgettable picture of an old Negro slave being cruelly flogged. The novel has been translated into languages all over the world; it helped to bring about the liberation of the serfs of Russia. As literature Uncle Tom's Cabin cannot be said to enjoy any very high repute; yet the modern reader who encounters it will find scenes of surprising realism and vigor, mixed in with much sentimentality and an overriding didacticism. Today the name of Mrs. Stowe's protagonist has become an epithet in the civil rights struggle, used to describe Negroes who fail to be sufficiently vigorous in their insistence on equality before the law. In her afterword to the novel, Mrs. Stowe asks a question that is even today of much consequence: "Is man ever a creature to be trusted with wholly irresponsible power?"

The author hopes she has done justice to that nobility, generosity, and humanity, which in many cases characterize individuals at the South. Such instances save us from utter despair of our kind. But, she asks any person who knows the world, are such characters *common, anywhere?*

For many years of her life, the author avoided all reading upon or allusion to the subject of slavery, considering it as too painful to be inquired into, and one which advancing light and civilization would certainly live down. But, since the legislative act of 1850, when she heard, with perfect surprise and consternation, Christian and humane people actually recommending the remanding escaped fugitives into slavery, as a duty binding on good citizens,—when she heard, on all hands, from kind, compassionate and estimable people, in the free states of the North, deliberations and discussions as to what Christian duty could be on this head,—she could only think, These men and Christians cannot know what slavery is; if they did, such a question could never be open for discussion. And from this arose a desire to exhibit it in a *living dramatic reality.* She has endeavored to show it fairly, in its best and its worst phases. In its *best* aspect, she has, perhaps, been successful; but, oh!

FROM *Uncle Tom's Cabin; or, Life Among the Lowly,* by Harriet Beecher Stowe (Boston: Houghton Mifflin, 1886), pp. 493–97, 499–500.

who shall say what yet remains untold in that valley and shadow of death, that lies the other side?

To you, generous, noble-minded men and women, of the South,—you, whose virtue, and magnanimity and purity of character, are the greater for the severer trial it has encountered,—to you is her appeal. Have you not, in your own secret souls, in your own private conversings, felt that there are woes and evils, in this accursed system, far beyond what are here shadowed, or can be shadowed? Can it be otherwise? Is *man* ever a creature to be trusted with wholly irresponsible power? And does not the slave system, by denying the slave all legal right of testimony, make every individual owner an irresponsible despot? Can anybody fail to make the inference what the practical result will be? If there is, as we admit, a public sentiment among you, men of honor, justice and humanity, is there not also another kind of public sentiment among the ruffian, the brutal and debased? And cannot the ruffian, the brutal, the debased, by slave law, own just as many slaves as the best and purest? Are the honorable, the just, the high-minded and compassionate, the majority anywhere in this world?

The slave-trade is now, by American law, considered as piracy. But a slave-trade, as systematic as ever was carried on on the coast of Africa, is an inevitable attendant and result of American slavery. And its heart-break and its horrors, *can* they be told?

The writer has given only a faint shadow, a dim picture, of the anguish and despair that are, at this very moment, riving thousands of hearts, shattering thousands of families, and driving a helpless and sensitive race to frenzy and despair. There are those living who know the mothers whom this accursed traffic has driven to the murder of their children; and themselves seeking in death a shelter from woes more dreaded than death. Nothing of tragedy can be written, can be spoken, can be conceived, that equals the frightful reality of scenes daily and hourly acting on our shores, beneath the shadow of American law, and the shadow of the cross of Christ.

And now, men and women of America, is this a thing to be trifled with, apologized for, and passed over in silence? Farmers of Massachusetts, of New Hampshire, of Vermont, of Connecticut, who read this book by the blaze of your winter-evening fire,—strong-hearted, generous sailors and ship-owners of Maine,—is this a thing for you to countenance and encourage? Brave and generous men of New York, farmers of rich and joyous Ohio, and ye of the wide prairie states,—answer, is this a thing for you to protect and countenance? And you, mothers of America,—you who have learned, by the cradles of your own children, to love and feel for all mankind,—by the sacred love you bear your child; by your joy in his beautiful, spotless infancy; by the motherly pity and tenderness with which you guide his growing years; by the anxieties of his education; by the prayers you breathe for his soul's eternal good;—I beseech you, pity the mother who has all your affections, and not one legal right to protect, guide, or educate the child of her bosom! By the sick hour of your child; by those dying eyes, which you can never forget; by those last cries, that wrung your heart when you could neither help nor save; by the desolation of that empty cradle, that silent nursery,—I beseech you, pity those mothers that are constantly made childless by the American slave-trade! And say, mothers of America, is this a thing to be defended, sympathized with, passed over in silence?

Do you say that the people of the free states have nothing to do with it, and can do nothing? Would to God this were true! But it is not true. The people of the free states have defended, encouraged, and participated; and are more guilty for it, before God, than the South, in that they have *not* the apology of education or custom.

If the mothers of the free states had all felt as they should, in times past, the sons of the free states would not have been the holders, and, proverbially, the hardest masters of slaves; the sons of the free states would not have connived at the extension of slavery, in our national body; the sons of the free states would not, as they do, trade the souls and bodies of men as an equivalent to money, in their mercantile dealings. There are multitudes of slaves temporarily owned, and sold again, by merchants in northern cities; and shall the whole guilt or obloquy of slavery fall only on the South?

Northern men, northern mothers, northern Christians, have something more to do than denounce their brethren at the South; they have to look to the evil among themselves.

But, what can any individual do? Of that, every individual can judge. There is one thing that every individual can do,—they can see to it that *they feel right*. An atmosphere of sympathetic influence encircles every human being; and the man or woman who *feels* strongly, healthily and justly, on the great interests of humanity, is a constant benefactor to the human race. See, then, to your sympathies in this matter! Are they in harmony with the sympathies of Christ? or are they swayed and perverted by the sophistries of worldly policy?

Christian men and women of the North! still further,—you have another power; you can *pray!* Do you believe in prayer? or has it become an indistinct apostolic tradition? You pray for the heathen abroad; pray also for the heathen at home. And pray for those distressed Christians whose whole chance of religious improvement is an accident of trade and sale; from whom any adherence to the morals of Christianity is, in many cases, an impossibility, unless they have given them, from above, the courage and grace of martyrdom.

But, still more. On the shores of our free states are emerging the poor, shattered, broken remnants of families,—men and women, escaped, by miraculous providences from the surges of slavery,—feeble in knowledge, and, in many cases, infirm in moral constitution, from a system which confounds and confuses every principle of Christianity and morality. They come to seek a refuge among you; they come to seek education, knowledge, Christianity.

What do you owe to these poor unfortunates, O Christians? Does not every American Christian owe to the African race some effort at reparation for the wrongs that the American nation has brought upon them? Shall the doors of churches and school-houses be shut upon them? Shall states arise and shake them out? Shall the church of Christ hear in silence the taunt that is thrown at them, and shrink away from the helpless hand that they stretch out; and, by her silence, encourage the cruelty that would chase them from our borders? If it must be so, it will be a mournful spectacle. If it must be so, the country will have reason to tremble, when it remembers that the fate of nations is in the hands of One who is very pitiful, and of tender compassion.

Do you say, "We don't want them here; let them go to Africa"?

That the providence of God has provided a refuge in Africa, is, indeed, a great and noticeable fact; but that is no reason why the church of Christ should throw off that responsibility to this outcast race which her profession demands of her.

To fill up Liberia with an ignorant, inexperienced, half-barbarized race, just escaped from the chains of slavery, would be only to prolong, for ages, the period of struggle and conflict which attends the inception of new enterprises. Let the church of the north receive these poor sufferers in the spirit of Christ; receive them to the educating advantages of Christian republican society and schools, until they have attained to somewhat of a moral and intellectual maturity, and then assist them in their passage to those shores, where they may put in practice the lessons they have learned in America.

There is a body of men at the north, comparatively small, who have been doing this; and, as the result, this country has already seen examples of men, formerly slaves, who have rapidly acquired property, reputation, and education. Talent has been developed, which, considering the circumstances, is certainly remarkable; and, for moral traits of honesty, kindness, tenderness of feeling,—for heroic efforts and self-denials, endured for the ransom of brethren and friends yet in slavery,—they have been remarkable to a degree that, considering the influence under which they were born, is surprising.

The writer has lived, for many years, on the frontier-line of slave states, and has had great opportunities of observation among those who formerly were slaves. They have been in her family as servants; and, in default of any other school to receive them, she has, in many cases, had them instructed in a family school, with her own children. She has also the testimony of missionaries, among the fugitives in Canada, in coincidence with her own experience; and her deductions, with regard to the capabilities of the race, are encouraging in the highest degree. . . .

This is an age of the world when nations are trembling and convulsed. A mighty influence is abroad, surging and heaving the world, as with an earthquake. And is America safe? Every nation that carries in its bosom great and unredressed injustice has in it the elements of this last convulsion.

For what is this mighty influence thus rousing in all nations and languages those groanings that cannot be uttered, for man's freedom and equality?

O Church of Christ, read the signs of the times! Is not this power the spirit of HIM whose kingdom is yet to come, and whose will to be done on earth as it is in heaven?

But who may abide the day of his appearing? "for that day shall burn as an oven: and he shall appear as a swift witness against those that oppress the hireling in his wages, the widow and the fatherless, and that *turn aside the stranger in his right:* and he shall break in pieces the oppressor."

Are not these dread words for a nation bearing in her bosom so mighty an injustice? Christians! every time that you pray that the kingdom of Christ may come, can you forget that prophecy associates, in dread fellowship, the *day of vengeance* with the year of his redeemed?

A day of grace is yet held out to us. Both North and South have been guilty before God; and the *Christian church* has a heavy account to answer. Not by combining together, to protect injustice and cruelty, and making a common capital of sin, is this Union to be saved,—but by repentance, justice and mercy; for, not surer is the eternal law by which the millstone sinks in the ocean, than that stronger law, by which injustice and cruelty shall bring on nations the wrath of Almighty God!

DRED SCOTT v. *SANDFORD*
The Constitution Recognizes the Right of Property of the Master in a Slave

The most famous case ever to come before the United States Supreme Court was probably Dred Scott v. Sandford, 19 Howard, 393 *(1857). Scott, a Negro slave who lived in Missouri, a slave state, sued for his freedom on the grounds that he had been taken by his master to free territory for most of the period 1834–1838. When the case came to the Court, the question at issue was made into one of whether or not a slave, taken to live in a state with laws prohibiting slavery, became a freeman—that is, a citizen—or whether the right of owner-ship, under the Fifth Amendment prohibiting deprivation of property without due process of law, took precedence over state laws prohibiting slavery. In an historic decision, with two Justices dissenting, the Court held that the right of ownership was superior to state statutes. In effect this meant that the Missouri Compromise, which for more than thirty-five years had defined the limits of territorial expansion for slave states, was unconstitutional, since that arrange-ment had specified that slaves could not be owned in western territories north of a certain line. Chief Justice Roger B. Taney (1777–1864) delivered the deci-*

FROM *Dred Scott* v. *Sandford*, 19 Howard, 393 (1857).

sion which was held to speak for the majority of the Court. The storm of protest that followed the ruling included cries of "conspiracy," and the decision undoubtedly weakened the Supreme Court's prestige in the North and helped further to aggravate sectional tensions.

Before we speak of the pleas in bar, it will be proper to dispose of the questions which have arisen on the plea in abatement.

That plea denies the right of the plaintiff to sue in a court of the United States, for the reasons therein stated.

If the question raised by it is legally before us, and the court should be of opinion that the facts stated in it disqualify the plaintiff from becoming a citizen, in the sense in which that word is used in the Constitution of the United States, then the judgment of the Circuit Court is erroneous, and must be reversed. . . .

The question to be decided is, whether the facts stated in the plea are sufficient to show that the plaintiff is not entitled to sue as a citizen in a court of the United States.

This is certainly a very serious question, and one that now for the first time has been brought for decision before this court. But it is brought here by those who have a right to bring it, and it is our duty to meet it and decide it.

The question is simply this: Can a negro, whose ancestors were imported into this country, and sold as slaves, become a member of the political community formed and brought into existence by the Constitution of the United States, and as such become entitled to all the rights, and privileges, and immunities, guarantied by that instrument to the citizen? One of which rights is the privilege of suing in a court of the United States in the cases specified in the Constitution.

It will be observed, that the plea applies to that class of persons only whose ancestors were negroes of the African race, and imported into this country, and sold and held as slaves. The only matter in issue before the court, therefore, is, whether the descendants of such slaves, when they shall be emancipated, or who are born of parents who had become free before their birth, are citizens of a State, in the sense in which the word citizen is used in the Constitution of the United States. And this being the only matter in dispute on the pleadings, the court must be understood as speaking in this opinion of that class only, that is of persons who are the descendants of Africans who were imported into this country and sold as slaves. . . .

The words "people of the United States" and "citizens" are synonymous terms, and mean the same thing. They both describe the political body who, according to our republican institutions, form the sovereignty, and who hold the power and conduct the government through their representatives. They are what we familiarly call the "sovereign people," and every citizen is one of this people, and a constituent member of this sovereignty. The question before us is, whether the class of persons described in the plea in abatement compose a portion of this people, and are constituent members of this sovereignty? We think they are not, and that they are not included, and were not intended to be included, under the word "citizens" in the Constitution, and can, therefore, claim none of the rights and privileges which that instrument provides for and secures to citizens of the United States. On the contrary, they were at that time considered as a subordinate and inferior class of beings, who had been subjugated by the dominant race, and whether emancipated or not, yet remained subject to their authority, and had no rights or privileges but such as those who held the power and the government might choose to grant them. . . .

It is very clear . . . that no State can, by any Act or law on its own, passed since the adoption of the Constitution, introduce a new member into the political community created by the Constitution of the United States. It cannot make him a member of this community by making him a member of its own. And for the same reason it cannot introduce any person, or description of persons, who were not intended to be embraced in this new political family, which the Constitution brought into existence, but were intended to be excluded from it.

The question then arises, whether the provisions of the Constitution, in relation to the personal rights and privileges to which the citizen of a State should be entitled, embraced the negro African race, at that time in this country, or who might afterwards be imported, who had then or should afterwards be made free in any State; and to put it in the power of a single State to make him a citizen of the United States, and endue him with the full rights of citizenship in every other State without their consent. Does the Constitution of the United States act upon him whenever he shall be made free under the laws of a State, and raised there to the rank of a citizen, and immediately clothe him with all the privileges of a citizen in every other State, and in its own courts?

The court think the affirmative of these propositions cannot be maintained. And if it cannot, the plaintiff in error could not be a citizen of the State of Missouri, within the meaning of the Constitution of the United States, and, consequently, was not entitled to sue in its courts.

It is true, every person, and every class and description of persons, who were at the time of the adoption of the Constitution recognized as citizens in the several States, became also citizens of this new political body; but none other; it was formed by them, and for them and their posterity, but for no one else. And the personal rights and privileges guarantied to citizens of this new sovereignty were intended to embrace those only who were then members of the several state communities, or who should afterwards, by birthright or otherwise, become members, according to the provisions of the Constitution and the principles on which it was founded. . . .

In the opinion of the court, the legislation and histories of the times, and the language used in the Declaration of Independence, show, that neither the class of persons who had been imported as slaves, nor their descendants, whether they had become free or not, were then acknowledged as a part of the people, nor intended to be included in the general words used in that memorable instrument.

It is difficult at this day to realize the state of public opinion in relation to that unfortunate race, which prevailed in the civilized and enlightened portions of the world at the time of the Declaration of Independence, and when the Constitution of the United States was framed and adopted. . . .

They had for more than a century before been regarded as beings of an inferior order; and altogether unfit to associate with the white race, either in social or political relations; and so far inferior that they had no rights which the white man was bound to respect; and that the negro might justly and lawfully be reduced to slavery for his benefit. . . . This opinion was at that time fixed and universal in the civilized portion of the white race. It was regarded as an axiom in morals as well as in politics, which no one thought of disputing, or supposed to be open to dispute; and men in every grade and position in society daily and habitually acted upon it in their private pursuits, as well as in matters of public concern, without doubting for a moment the correctness of this opinion. . . .

The legislation of the different Colonies furnishes positive and undisputable proof of this fact. . . .

The language of the Declaration of Independence is equally conclusive. . . .

This state of public opinion had undergone no change when the Constitution was adopted, as is equally evident from its provisions and language. . . .

But there are two clauses in the Constitution which point directly and specifically to the negro race as a separate class of persons, and show clearly that they were not regarded as a portion of the people or citizens of the Government then formed.

One of these clauses reserves to each of the thirteen States the right to import slaves until the year 1808, if he thinks it proper. And the importation which it thus sanctions was unquestionably of persons of the race of which we are speaking, as the traffic in slaves in the United States had always been confined to them. And by the other provision the States pledge themselves to each other to maintain the right of property of the master, by delivering up to him any slave who may have escaped from his service, and be found within their respective territories. . . . And these two provisions show, conclusively, that neither the description of persons therein referred to, nor their descendants, were embraced in any of the other provisions of the Constitution; for certainly these two clauses were not intended to confer on them or their posterity the blessings of liberty, or any of the personal rights so carefully provided for the citizen. . . .

Indeed, when we look to the condition of this race in the several States at the time, it is impossible to believe that these rights and privileges were intended to be extended to them. . . .

But it is said that a person may be a citizen, and entitled to that character, although he does not possess all the rights which may belong to other citizens;

as, for example, the right to vote, or to hold particular offices; and that yet, when he goes into another State, he is entitled to be recognized there as a citizen, although the State may measure his rights by the rights which it allows to persons of a like character or class, resident in the State, and refuse to him the full rights of citizenship.

This argument overlooks the language of the provision in the Constitution of which we are speaking.

Undoubtedly, a person may be a citizen, that is, a member of the community who form the sovereignty, although he exercises no share of the political power, and is incapacitated from holding particular offices. . . .

So, too, a person may be entitled to vote by the law of the State, who is not a citizen even of the State itself. And in some of the States of the Union foreigners not naturalized are allowed to vote. And the State may give the right to free negroes and mulattoes, but that does not make them citizens of the State, and still less of the United States. And the provision in the Constitution giving privileges and immunities in other States, does not apply to them.

Neither does it apply to a person who, being the citizen of a State, migrates to another State. For then he becomes subject to the laws of the State in which he lives, and he is no longer a citizen of the State from which he removed. And the State in which he resides may then, unquestionably, determine his *status* or condition, and place him among the class of persons who are not recognized as citizens, but belong to an inferior and subject race; and may deny him privileges and immunities enjoyed by its citizens.

. . . But if he ranks as a citizen of the State to which he belongs, within the meaning of the Constitution of the United States, then, whenever he goes into another State, the Constitution clothes him, as to the rights of person, with all the privileges and immunities which belong to citizens of the State. And if persons of the African race are citizens of a state, and of the United States, they would be entitled to all of these privileges and immunities in every State, and the State could not restrict them; for they would hold these privileges and immunities, under the paramout authority of the Federal Government, and its courts would be bound to maintain and enforce them, the Constitution and laws of the State to the contrary notwithstanding. . . .

And upon a full and careful consideration of the subject, the court is of opinion that, upon the facts stated in the plea in abatement, Dred Scott was not a citizen of Missouri within the meaning of the Constitution of the United States, and not entitled as such to sue in its courts; and consequently, that the Circuit Court had no jurisdiction of the case, and that the judgment on the plea in abatement is erroneous. . . .

We proceed, therefore, to inquire whether the facts relied on by the plaintiff entitled him to his freedom. . . .

In considering this part of the controversy, two questions arise: 1st. Was he, together with his family, free in Missouri by reason of the stay in the territory of the United States hereinbefore mentioned? And 2d, If they were not, is

Scott himself free by reason of his removal to Rock Island, in the State of Illinois, as stated in the above admissions?

We proceed to examine the first question.

The Act of Congress, upon which the plaintiff relies, declares that slavery and involuntary servitude, except as a punishment for crime, shall be forever prohibited in all that part of the territory ceded by France, under the name of Louisiana, which lies north of thirty-six degrees, thirty minutes north latitude, and not included within the limits of Missouri. And the difficulty which meets us at the threshold of this part of the inquiry is, whether Congress was authorized to pass this law under any of the powers granted to it by the Constitution; for if the authority is not given by that instrument, it is the duty of this court to declare it void and inoperative, and incapable of conferring freedom upon any one who is held as a slave under the laws of any one of the States.

The counsel for the plaintiff has laid much stress upon that article in the Constitution which confers on Congress the power "to dispose of and make all needful rules and regulations respecting the territory or other property belonging to the United States;" but, in the judgment of the court, that provision has no bearing on the present controversy, and the power there given, whatever it may be, is confined, and was intended to be confined, to the territory which at that time belonged to, or was claimed by, the United States, and was within their boundaries as settled by the treaty with Great Britain, and can have no influence upon a territory afterwards acquired from a foreign Government. It was a special provision for a known and particular territory, and to meet a present emergency, and nothing more. . . .

If this clause is construed to extend to territory acquired by the present Government from a foreign nation, outside of the limits of any charter from the British Government to a colony, it would be difficult to say, why it was deemed necessary to give the Government the power to sell any vacant lands belonging to the sovereignty which might be found within it; and if this was necessary, why the grant of this power should precede the power to legislate over it and establish a Government there; and still more difficult to say, why it was deemed necessary so specially and particularly to grant the power to make needful rules and regulations in relation to any personal or movable property it might acquire there. For the words, *other property* necessarily, by every known rule of interpretation, must mean property of a different description from territory or land. And the difficulty would perhaps be insurmountable in endeavoring to account for the last member of the sentence, which provides that "nothing in this Constitution, shall be so construed as to prejudice any claims of the United States or any particular State," or to say how any particular State could have claims in or to a territory ceded by a foreign Government, or to account for associating this provision with the preceding provisions of the clause, with which it would appear to have no connection. . . .

But the power of Congress over the person or property of a citizen can never be a mere discretionary power under our Constitution and form of Government. The powers of the Government and the rights and privileges of the citizen are regulated and plainly defined by the Constitution itself. And when the Territory becomes a part of the United States, the Federal Government enters into possession in the character impressed upon it by those who created it. It enters upon it with its powers over the citizen strictly defined, and limited by the Constitution, from which it derives its own existence, and by virtue of which alone it continues to exist and act as a Government and sovereignty. It has no power of any kind beyond it; and it cannot, when it enters a Territory of the United States, put off its character, and assume discretionary or despotic powers which the Constitution has denied to it. It cannot create for itself a new character separated from the citizens of the United States, and the duties it owes them under the provisions of the Constitution. The Territory being a part of the United States, the Government and the citizen both enter it under the authority of the Constitution, with their respective rights defined and marked out; and the Federal Government can exercise no power over his person or property, beyond what that instrument confers, nor lawfully deny any right which it has reserved. . . .

The rights of private property have been guarded with equal care. Thus the rights of property are united with the rights of person, and placed on the same ground by the fifth amendment to the Constitution. . . . An Act of Congress which deprives a person of the United States of his liberty or property merely because he came himself or brought his property into a particular Territory of the United States, and who had committed no offense against the laws, could hardly be dignified with the name of due process of law. . . .

And this prohibition is not confined to the States, but the words are general, and extend to the whole territory over which the Constitution gives it power to legislate, including those portions of it remaining under territorial government, as well as that covered by States. It is a total absence of power everywhere within the dominion of the United States, and places the citizens of a territory, so far as these rights are concerned, on the same footing with citizens of the States, and guards them as firmly and plainly against any inroads which the general government might attempt, under the plea of implied or incidental powers. And if Congress itself cannot do this—if it is beyond the powers conferred on the Federal Government—it will be admitted, we presume, that it could not authorize a territorial government to exercise them. It could confer no power on any local government, established by its authority, to violate the provisions of the Constitution.

It seems, however, to be supposed, that there is a difference between property in a slave and other property, and that different rules may be applied to it in expounding the Constitution of the United States. And the laws and usages of nations, and the writings of eminent jurists upon the relation of master and slave and their mutual rights and duties, and the powers which governments may exercise over it, have been dwelt upon in the argument.

But . . . if the Constitution recognizes the right of property of the master in a slave, and makes no distinction between that description of property and other property owned by a citizen, no tribunal, acting under the authority of the United States, whether it be legislative, executive, or judicial, has a right to draw such a distinction, or deny to it the benefit of the provisions and guarantees which have been provided for the protection of private property against the encroachments of the Government.

Now . . . the right of property in a slave is distinctly and expressly affirmed in the Constitution. The right to traffic in it, like an ordinary article of merchandise and property, was guaranteed to the citizens of the United States, in every State that might desire it, for twenty years. And the Government in express terms is pledged to protect it in all future time, if the slave escapes from his owner. . . . And no word can be found in the Constitution which gives Congress a greater power over slave property, or which entitles property of that kind to less protection than property of any other description. The only power conferred is the power coupled with the duty of guarding and protecting the owner in his rights.

Upon these considerations, it is the opinion of the court that the Act of Congress which prohibited a citizen from holding and owning property of this kind in the territory of the United States north of the line therein mentioned, is not warranted by the Constitution, and is therefore void; and that neither Dred Scott himself, nor any of his family, were made free by being carried into this territory; even if they had been carried there by the owner, with the intention of becoming a permanent resident. . . .

ABRAHAM LINCOLN
Sooner or Later the Victory Is Sure to Come

Abraham Lincoln's "House Divided" Speech, delivered at Springfield, Illinois, on June 17, 1858, when he had been nominated by the Republican Party to oppose Stephen A. Douglas for the United States Senate, catapulted him into national prominence. In it Lincoln (1807–1865) made famous the idea that the Union, like a divided household, could not stay divided, and that it would be made up of states either all free or all slave. Lincoln also charged, without specifically saying so, that the delay of the Dred Scot decision until after the presidential election of 1856 had been the result of a "conspiracy" between outgoing President Pierce, incoming President Buchanan, Chief Justice Taney and Senator Douglas. Lincoln lost the election for the Senate against Douglas, but he so dramatized the slavery issue and his position that he became a prime candidate for the Republican nomination for President in 1860.

FROM "A House Divided," *Political Debates between Abraham Lincoln and Stephen A. Douglas* (Cleveland, Ohio: The Burrows Brothers Co., 1894, pp. 7–12).

Mr. President and Gentlemen of the Convention: If we could first know where we are, and whither we are tending, we could better judge what to do, and how to do it. We are now far into the fifth year since a policy was initiated with the avowed object and confident promise of putting an end to slavery agitation. Under the operation of that policy, that agitation has not only not ceased, but has constantly augmented. In my opinion, it will not cease until a crisis shall have been reached and passed. "A house divided against itself cannot stand." I believe this government cannot endure permanently half slave and half free. I do not expect the Union to be dissolved; I do not expect the house to fall; but I do expect it will cease to be divided. It will become all one thing, or all the other. Either the opponents of slavery will arrest the further spread of it, and place it where the public mind shall rest in the belief that it is in the course of ultimate extinction, or its advocates will push it forward till it shall become alike lawful in all the States, old as well as new, North as well as South.

Have we no tendency to the latter condition?

Let any one who doubts, carefully contemplate that now almost complete legal combination—piece of machinery, so to speak—compounded of the Nebraska doctrine and the Dred Scot decision. Let him consider, not only what work the machinery is adapted to do, and how well adapted, but also let him study the history of its construction, and trace, if he can, or rather fail, if he can, to trace the evidences of design, and concert of action, among its chief architects, from the beginning.

The new year of 1854 found slavery excluded from more than half the States by State Constitutions, and from most of the National territory by Congressional prohibition. Four days later, commenced the struggle which ended in repealing that Congressional prohibition. This opened all the National territory to slavery, and was the first point gained.

But, so far, Congress only had acted; and an indorsement by the people, real or apparent, was indispensable to save the point already gained, and give chance for more.

This necessity had not been overlooked, but had been provided for, as well as might be, in the notable argument of "squatter sovereignty," otherwise called "sacred right of self-government," which latter phrase, though expressive of the only rightful basis of any government, was so perverted in this attempted use of it as to amount to just this: That if any *one* man choose to enslave *another*, no *third* man shall be allowed to object. That argument was incorporated into the Nebraska bill itself, in the language which follows: "It being the true intent and meaning of this Act not to legislate slavery into any Territory or State, nor to exclude it therefrom, but to leave the people thereof perfectly free to form and regulate their domestic institutions in their own way, subject only to the Constitution of the United States." Then opened the roar of loose declamation in favor of "squatter sovereignty," and "sacred right of self-government." "But," said opposition members, "let us amend the bill so as to expressly declare that the people of the Territory may exclude slavery." "Not we," said the friends of the measure; and down they voted the amendment.

While the Nebraska bill was passing through Congress, a *law case,* involving the question of a negro's freedom, by reason of his owner having voluntarily taken him first into a free State, and then into a Territory covered by the Congressional prohibition, and held him as a slave for a long time in each, was passing through the United States Circuit Court for the District of Missouri; and both Nebraska Bill and lawsuit were brought to a decision in the same month of May, 1854. The negro's name was "Dred Scott," which name now designates the decision finally made in the case. Before the then next Presidential election, the law case came to, and was argued in, the Supreme Court of the United States; but the decision of it was deferred until after the election. Still, before the election, Senator Trumbull, on the floor of the Senate, requested the leading advocate of the Nebraska Bill to state *his opinion* whether the people of a Territory can constitutionally exclude slavery from their limits; and the latter answers: "That is a question for the Supreme Court."

The election came. Mr. Buchanan was elected, and the indorsement, such as it was, secured. That was the second point gained. The indorsement, however, fell short of a clear popular majority by nearly four hundred thousand votes, and so, perhaps, was not overwhelmingly reliable and satisfactory. The outgoing President, in his last annual message, as impressively as possible echoed back upon the people the weight and authority of the indorsement. The Supreme Court met again, did not announce their decision, but ordered a re-argument. The Presidential inauguration came, and still no decision of the court; but the incoming President, in his inaugural address, fervently exhorted the people to abide by the forthcoming decision, whatever it might be. Then, in a few days, came the decision.

The reputed author of the Nebraska bill finds an early occasion to make a speech at this capital indorsing the Dred Scott decision, and vehemently denouncing all opposition to it. The new President, too, seizes the early occasion of the Silliman letter to indorse and strongly construe that decision, and to express his astonishment that any different view had ever been entertained!

At length a squabble springs up between the President and the author of the Nebraska Bill, on the mere question of *fact,* whether the Lecompton Constitution was or was not in any just sense made by the people of Kansas; and in that quarrel the latter declares that all he wants is a fair vote for the people, and that he cares not whether slavery be voted *down* or voted *up*. I do not understand his declaration, that he cares not whether slavery be voted down or voted up, to be intended by him other than as an apt definition of the policy he would impress upon the public mind,—the principle for which he declares he has suffered so much, and is ready to suffer to the end. And well may he cling to that principle! If he has any parental feeling, well may he cling to it. That principle is the only shred left of his original Nebraska doctrine. Under the Dred Scott decision "squatter sovereignty" squatted out of existence, tumbled down like temporary scaffolding; like the mould at the foundry, served through one blast, and fell back into loose sand; helped to carry an election, and then was kicked to the winds. His late joint struggle with the Republicans, against the Lecompton Constitution, involves nothing of the original Nebraska doctrine. That struggle was made on a point—the right of a people to make their own constitution—upon which he and the Republicans have never differed.

The several points of the Dred Scott decision, in connection with Senator Douglas's "care not" policy, constitute the piece of machinery, in its present state of advancement. This was the third point gained. The working points of that machinery are:—

Firstly, That no negro slave, imported as such from Africa, and no descendant of such slave, can ever be a citizen of any State, in the sense of that term as used in the Constitution of the United States. This point is made in order to deprive the negro, in every possible event, of the benefit of that provision of the United States Constitution which declares that "The citizens of each State shall be entitled to all privileges and immunities of citizens in the several States."

Secondly, That, "subject to the Constitution of the United States," neither Congress nor a Territorial Legislature can exclude slavery from any United States Territory. This point is made in order that individual men may fill up the Territories with slaves, without danger of losing them as property, and thus to enhance the chances of permanency to the institution through all the future.

Thirdly, That whether the holding a negro in actual slavery in a free State, makes him free, as against the holder, the United States courts will not decide, but will leave to be decided by the courts of any slave State the negro may be forced into by the master. This point is made, not to be pressed immediately; but, if acquiesced in for awhile, and apparently indorsed by the people at an election, then to sustain the logical conclusion that what Dred Scott's master might lawfully do with Dred Scott, in the free State of Illinois, every other master may lawfully do with any other one, or one thousand slaves, in Illinois, or in any other free State.

Auxiliary to all this, and working hand in hand with it, the Nebraska doctrine, or what is left of it, is to educate and mould public opinion, at least Northern public opinion, not to care whether slavery is voted down or voted up. This shows exactly where we now are; and partially, also, whither we are tending.

It will throw additional light on the latter, to go back and run the mind over the string of historical facts already stated. Several things will now appear less dark and mysterious than they did when they were transpiring. The people were to be left "perfectly free," "subject only to the Constitution."

What the Constitution had to do with it, outsiders could not then see. Plainly enough now, it was an exactly fitted niche, for the Dred Scot decision to afterward come in, and declare the perfect freedom of the people to be just no freedom at all. Why was the amendment, expressly declaring the right of the people, voted down? Plainly enough now,—the adoption of it would have spoiled the niche for the Dred Scott decision. Why was the court decision held up? Why even a Senator's individual opinion withheld, till after the Presidential election? Plainly enough now, the speaking out then would have damaged the perfectly free argument upon which the election was to be carried. Why the outgoing President's felicitation on the indorsement? Why the delay of a re-argument? Why the incoming President's advance exhortation in favor of the decision? These things look like the cautious patting and petting of a spirited horse preparatory to mounting him, when it is dreaded that he may give the rider a fall. And why the hasty after-indorsement of the decision by the President and others?

We cannot absolutely know that all these exact adaptations are the result of preconcert. But when we see a lot of framed timbers, different portions of which we know have been gotten out at different times and places and by different workmen,—Stephen, Franklin, Roger, and James, for instance,—and when we see these timbers joined together, and see they exactly make the frame of a house or a mill, all the tenons and mortises exactly fitting, and all the lengths and proportions of the different pieces exactly adapted to their respective places, and not a piece too many or too few,—not omitting even scaffolding,—or, if a single piece be lacking, we see the place in the frame exactly fitted and prepared yet to bring such piece in,—in such a case, we find it impossible not to believe that Stephen and Franklin and Roger and James all understood one another from the beginning, and all worked upon a common plan or draft drawn up before the first blow was struck.

It should not be overlooked that by the Nebraska bill the people of a *State* as well as Territory were to be left "perfectly free," "subject only to the Constitution." Why mention a State? They were legislating for Territories, and not for or about States. Certainly the people of a State are and ought to be subject to the Constitution of the United States; but why is mention of this lugged into this merely Territorial law? Why are the people of a Territory and the people of a State therein lumped together, and their relation to the Constitution therein treated as being precisely the same? While the opinion of the court, by Chief Justice Taney, in the Dred Scott case, and the separate opinions of all the concurring Judges, expressly declare that the Constitution of the United States neither permits Congress nor a Territorial Legislature to exclude slavery from any United States Territory, they all omit to declare whether or not the same Constitution permits a State, or the people of a State, to exclude it. *Possibly*, this is a mere omission; but who can be quite sure, if McLean or Curtis had sought to get into the opinion a declaration of unlimited power in the people of a State to exclude slavery from their limits, just as

Chase and Mace sought to get such declaration, in behalf of the people of a Territory, into the Nebraska bill,—I ask, who can be quite sure that it would not have been voted down in the one case as it had been in the other? The nearest approach to the point of declaring the power of a State over slavery, is made by Judge Nelson. He approaches it more than once, using the precise idea, and almost the language, too, of the Nebraska Act. On one occasion, his exact language is, "Except in cases where the power is restrained by the Constitution of the United States, the law of the State is supreme over the subject of slavery within its jurisdiction." In what cases the power of the States is so restrained by the United States Constitution, is left an open question, precisely as the same question, as to the restraint on the power of the Territories, was left open in the Nebraska Act. Put this and that together, and we have another nice little niche, which we may, ere long, see filled with another Supreme Court decision, declaring that the Constitution of the United States does not permit a *State* to exclude slavery from its limits. And this may especially be expected if the doctrine of "care not whether slavery be voted down or voted up" shall gain upon the public mind sufficiently to give promise that such a decision can be maintained when made.

Such a decision is all that slavery now lacks of being alike lawful in all the States. Welcome or unwelcome, such decision is probably coming, and will soon be upon us, unless the power of the present political dynasty shall be met and overthrown. We shall lie down pleasantly dreaming that the people of Missouri are on the verge of making their State free, and we shall awake to the reality instead that the Supreme Court has made Illinois a slave State. To meet and overthrow the power of that dynasty is the work now before all those who would prevent that consummation. That is what we have to do. How can we best do it?

There are those who denounce us openly to their own friends, and yet whisper us softly that Senator Douglas is the aptest instrument there is with which to effect that object. They wish us to *infer* all, from the fact that he now has a little quarrel with the present head of the dynasty, and that he has regularly voted with us on a single point, upon which he and we have never differed. They remind us that he is a great man, and that the largest of us are very small ones. Let this be granted. But "a living dog is better than a dead lion." Judge Douglas, if not a dead lion, for this work is at least a caged and toothless one. How can he oppose the advances of slavery? He don't care anything about it. His avowed mission is impressing the "public heart" to *care nothing about it.* A leading Douglas Democratic newspaper thinks Douglas's superior talent will be needed to resist the revival of the African slave trade. Does Douglas believe an effort to revive that trade is approaching? He has not said so. Does he really think so? But if it is, how can he resist it? For years he has labored to prove it a sacred right of white men to take negro slaves into the new Territories. Can he possibly show that it is less a sacred right to buy them where they can be bought cheapest? And unquestionably they can be bought cheaper in Africa than in Virginia. He has done all in his power to reduce the whole question of slavery to one of a mere right of property; and, as such, how can he oppose the foreign slave trade,—how can he refuse that trade in that "property" shall be "perfectly free,"—unless he does it as a protection to the home production? And as the home producers will probably not ask the protection, he will be wholly without a ground of opposition.

Senator Douglas holds, we know, that a man may rightfully be wiser to-day than he was yesterday; that he may rightfully change when he finds himself wrong. But can we, for that reason, run ahead, and infer that he will make any particular change, of which he himself has given no intimation? Can we safely base our action upon any such vague inference? Now, as ever, I wish not to misrepresent Judge Douglas's position, question his motives, or do aught that can be personally offensive to him. Whenever, if ever, he and we can come together on principle so that our cause may have assistance from his great ability, I hope to have interposed no adventitious obstacles. But clearly he is not now with us; he does not pretend to be,—he does not promise ever to be.

Our cause, then, must be intrusted to, and conducted by, its own un-doubted friends,—those whose hands are free, whose hearts are in the work, who *do care* for the result. Two years ago the Republicans of the nation mustered over thirteen hundred thousand strong. We did this under the single impulse of resistance to a common danger, with every external circumstance against us. Of strange, discordant, and even hostile elements we gathered from the four winds, and formed and fought the battle through, under the constant hot fire of a disciplined, proud, and pampered enemy. Did we brave all then to falter now,—now, when that same enemy is wavering, dissevered, and belligerent? The result is not doubtful. We shall not fail; if we stand firm, we *shall not fail*. Wise counsels may accelerate, or mistakes delay it, but, sooner or later, the victory is sure to come.

JEFFERSON DAVIS
A People United in Heart

When the Southern states seceded from the Union to form their own Confederacy, they chose a distinguished Mississippian, Jefferson Davis (1808–1889), to be their President. Davis, U.S. Senator from Mississippi from 1847 to 1851 and again from 1857 to 1861, had been Secretary of War in the cabinet of President Franklin Pierce, and throughout most of the slavery and secession

FROM "Inaugural Address," by Jefferson Davis, in *The Memorial Volume of Jefferson Davis* by J. William Jones (Richmond, Va., 1890), pp. 302–06.

controversy he had been a moderate. Bidding farewell to the Senate in a moving speech (January 21, 1861), he proceeded homeward, to be called to the highest office of the new Confederacy. He took the oath of office at the provisional capital in Montgomery, Alabama, on February 18, and delivered there the inaugural address reproduced below, in which he called for peace between the Confederacy and the Union, but expressed the South's determination to resist to the last if its territories were invaded. Shortly thereafter Davis moved to Richmond when the capital was placed in that city, and for the next four years directed the South's resistance. Upon the collapse of the Confederacy, he was imprisoned for two years before being released.

Gentlemen of the Congress of the Confederate States of America, Friends and Fellow-Citizens: Called to the difficult and responsible station of Chief Executive of the Provisional Government which you have instituted, I approach the discharge of the duties assigned to me with an humble distrust of my abilities, but with a sustaining confidence in the wisdom of those who are to guide and aid me in the administration of public affairs, and an abiding faith in the virtue and patriotism of the people.

Looking forward to the speedy establishment of a permanent government to take the place of this, and which, by its greater moral and physical power, will be better able to combat with the many difficulties which arise from the conflicting interests of separate nations, I enter upon the duties of the office, for which I have been chosen, with the hope that the beginning of our career, as a Confederacy, may not be obstructed by hostile opposition to our enjoyment of the separate existence and independence which we have asserted, and, with the blessing of Providence, intend to maintain. Our present condition, achieved in a manner unprecedented in this history of nations, illustrates the American idea that governments rest upon the consent of the governed, and that it is the right of the people to alter or abolish governments whenever they become destructive of the ends for which they were established.

The declared purpose of the compact of union from which we have withdrawn, was "to establish justice, insure domestic tranquillity, provide for the common defense, promote the general welfare, and secure the blessings of liberty to ourselves and posterity"; and when in the judgment of the sovereign States now composing this Confederacy, it had been perverted from the purposes for which it was ordained, and had ceased to answer the ends for which it was established, a peaceful appeal to the ballot-box declared that so far as they were concerned, the government created by that compact should cease to exist. In this they merely asserted a right which the Declaration of Independence of 1776 had defined to be inalienable. Of the time and occasion for its exercise, they as sovereigns, were the final judges, each for itself. The impartial and enlightened verdict of mankind will vindicate the rectitude of our conduct, and He, who knows the hearts of men, will judge of the sincerity with which we labored to preserve the government of our fathers in its spirit. The right solemnly proclaimed at the birth of the States and which has been affirmed and re-affirmed in the bills of rights of States subsequently admitted into the Union of 1789, undeniably recognizes in the people the power to resume the authority delegated for the purposes of government. Thus the sovereign States, here represented, proceeded to form this Confederacy, and it is by abuse of language that their act has been denominated a revolution. They formed a new alliance, but within each State its government has remained, and the rights of person and property have not been disturbed. The agent, through whom they communicated with foreign nations, is changed; but this does not necessarily interrupt their international relations.

Sustained by the consciousness that the transition from the former Union to the present Confederacy has not proceeded from a disregard on our part of just obligations, or any failure to perform any constitutional duty; moved by no interest or passion to invade the rights of others; anxious to cultivate peace and commerce with all nations, if we may not hope to avoid war, we may at least expect that posterity will acquit us of having needlessly engaged in it. Doubly justified by the absence of wrong on our part, and by wanton aggression on the part of others, there can be no cause to doubt that the courage and patriotism of the people of the Confederate States will be found equal to any measure of defence which honor and security may require.

An agricultural people, whose chief interest is the export of a commodity required in every manufacturing country, our true policy is peace and the freest trade which our necessities will permit. It is alike our interest, and that of all those to whom we would sell and from whom we would buy, that there should be the fewest practicable restrictions upon the interchange of commodities. There can be but little rivalry between ours and any manufacturing or navigating community, such as the northeastern States of the American Union. It must follow, therefore, that a mutual interest would invite good and kind offices. If, however, passion or the lust of dominion should cloud the judgment or inflame the ambition of those States, we must prepare to meet the emergency, and to maintain, by the final arbitrament of the sword, the position which we have assumed among the nations of the earth. We have entered upon the career of independence, and it must be inflexibly pursued. Through many years of controversy with our late associates, the Northern States, we have vainly endeavored to secure tranquillity, and to obtain respect for the rights to which we were entitled. As a necessity, not a choice, we have resorted to the remedy of separation; and henceforth our energies must be directed to the conduct of our own affairs and the perpetuity of the Confederacy which we have formed. If a just perception of mutual interest shall permit us peaceably to pursue our separate political career, my most earnest desire will have been fulfilled; but if this be denied us, and the integrity of our territory and jurisdiction be assailed, it will but remain for us, with firm resolve, to appeal to arms and invoke the blessings of Providence on a just cause.

As consequence of our new condition, and with a view to meet anticipated wants, it will be necessary to provide for the speedy and efficient organization of branches of the Executive Department, having special charge of foreign intercourse, finance, military affairs, and the postal service.

For purposes of defence, the Confederate States may, under ordinary circumstances, rely mainly upon the militia; but it is deemed advisable, in the present condition of affairs, that there should be a well-instructed and disciplined army, more numerous than would usually be required on a peace establishment. I also suggest that, for the protection of our harbors and commerce on the high seas, a navy adapted to those objects will be required. These necessities have doubtless engaged the attention of Congress.

With a Constitution differing only from that of our fathers in so far as it is explanatory of their well-known intent, freed from the sectional conflicts which have interfered with the pursuit of the general welfare, it is not unreasonable to expect that States from which we have parted, may seek to unite their fortunes with ours under the government which we have instituted. For this your constitution makes adequate provision; but beyond this, if I mistake not, the judgment and will of the people, a reunion with the States from which we have separated is neither practicable nor desirable. To increase the power, develop the resources, and promote the happiness of the Confederacy, it is requisite that there should be so much of homogeneity that the welfare of every portion shall be the aim of the whole. Where this does not exist, antagonisms are engendered which must and should result in separation.

Actuated solely by the desire to preserve our own rights and promote our own welfare, the separation of the Confederate States has been marked by no aggression upon others, and followed by no domestic convulsion. Our industrial pursuits have received no check; the cultivation of our fields has progressed as heretofore; and even should we be involved in war, there would be no considerable diminution in the production of the staples which have constituted our exports, and in which the commercial world has an interest scarcely less than our own. This common interest of the producer and consumer can only be interrupted by an exterior force, which should obstruct its transmission to foreign markets—a course of conduct which would be as unjust toward us as it would be detrimental to the manufacturing and commercial interests abroad. Should reason guide the action of the government from which we have separated, a policy so detrimental to the civilized world, the Northern States included, could not be dictated by even the strongest desire to inflict injury upon us; but, if otherwise, a terrible responsibility will rest upon it, and the suffering of millions will bear testimony to the folly and wickedness of our aggressors. In the meantime, there will remain to us, besides the ordinary means before suggested, the well-known resources for retaliation upon the commerce of an enemy.

Experience in public stations, of subordinate grade to this which your kindness has conferred, has taught me that care, and toil, and disappointment, are the price of official elevation. You will see many errors to forgive, many deficiencies to tolerate, but you shall not find in me either a want of zeal or fidelity to the cause that is to me highest in hope and of most enduring affection. Your generosity has bestowed upon me an undeserved distinction—one which I neither sought nor desired. Upon the continuance of that sentiment, and upon your wisdom and patriotism, I rely to direct and support me in the performance of the duty required at my hands.

We have changed the constituent parts, but not the system of our government. The constitution formed by our fathers is that of these Confederate States, in their exposition of it; and, in the judicial construction it has received, we have a light which reveals its true meaning.

Thus instructed as to the just interpretation of the instrument, and ever remembering that all officies are but trusts held for the people, and that delegated powers are to be strictly construed, I will hope, by due diligence in the performance of my duties, though I may disappoint your expectations, yet to retain, when retiring, something of the goodwill and confidence which welcomed my entrance into office.

It is joyous, in the midst of perilous times, to look around upon a people united in heart, where one purpose of high resolve animates and actuates the whole—where the sacrifices to be made are not weighed in the balance against honor, and right, and liberty, and equality. Obstacles may retard—they cannot long prevent—the progress of a movement sanctified by its justices, and sustained by a virtuous people. Reverently let us invoke the God of our fathers to guide and protect us in our efforts to perpetuate the principles which by His blessing, they were able to vindicate, establish, and transmit to their posterity, and with a continuance of His favor, ever gratefully acknowledged, we may hopefully look forward to success, peace, and to prosperity.

ABRAHAM LINCOLN
A Just and Lasting Peace

With the beaten Confederate armies in retreat and the rebellion collapsing, Abraham Lincoln opened his second term of office on March 4, 1865, with the short speech that follows, which has become one of the classical utterances of American political history. Anxious now to reunite a divided country, bringing a lofty vision of forgiveness and understanding to a nation inflamed by the passions of a bloody civil war, Lincoln called for a peace "with malice toward none; with charity for all. . . ." Six weeks later he was dead of an assassin's bullet, and the nation was plunged into the problems of reconstruction of the

FROM "Second Inaugural Address," by Abraham Lincoln, in *Inaugural Addresses of the Presidents of the United States from George Washington 1789 to Harry S. Truman 1949* (Washington, D.C.: H. D. No. 540, 1952), pp. 117–18.

Union. But the slaves had been freed and the Union preserved. Lincoln has been made the subject of many American poems, but the impact of his death and of the Civil War upon the country has nowhere been more profoundly and beautifully depicted than in Whitman's "When Lilacs Last in the Dooryard Bloom'd."

At this second appearing to take the oath of the Presidential office there is less occasion for an extended address than there was at the first. Then a statement somewhat in detail of a course to be pursued seemed fitting and proper. Now, at the expiration of four years, during which public declarations have been constantly called forth on every point and phase of the great contest which still absorbs the attention and engrosses the energies of the nation, little that is new could be presented. The progress of our arms, upon which all else chiefly depends, is as well known to the public as to myself, and it is, I trust, reasonably satisfactory and encouraging to all. With high hope for the future, no prediction in regard to it is ventured.

On the occasion corresponding to this four years ago all thoughts were anxiously directed to an impending civil war. All dreaded it, all sought to avert it. While the inaugural address was being delivered from this place, devoted altogether to *saving* the Union without war, insurgent agents were in the city seeking to *destroy* it without war—seeking to dissolve the Union and divide effects by negotiation. Both parties deprecated war; but one of them would *make* war rather than let the nation survive; and the other would *accept* war rather than let it perish, and the war came.

One eighth of the whole population were colored slaves, not distributed generally over the Union, but localized in the southern part of it. These slaves constituted a peculiar and powerful interest. All knew that this interest was somehow the cause of the war. To strengthen, perpetuate, and extend this interest was the object for which the insurgents would rend the Union even by war, while the Government claimed no right to do more than to restrict the territorial enlargement of it. Neither party expected for the war the magnitude or the duration which it has already attained. Neither anticipated that the *cause* of the conflict might cease with or even before the conflict itself should cease. Each looked for an easier triumph, and a result less fundamental and astounding. Both read the same Bible and pray to the same God, and each invokes His aid against the other. It may seem strange that any men should dare to ask a just God's assistance in wringing their bread from the sweat of other men's faces, but let us judge not, that we be not judged. The prayers of both could not be answered. That of neither has been answered fully. The Almighty has His own purposes. "Woe unto the world because of offences; for it must needs be that offences come; but woe to that man by whom the offence cometh." If we shall suppose that American Slavery is one of those offences which, in the providence of God, must needs come, but which, having continued through His appointed time, He now wills to remove, and that He gives to both North and South this terrible war as the woe due to those by whom the offence came, shall we discern therein any departure from those divine attributes which the believers in a living God always ascribe to Him? Fondly do we hope, fervently do we pray, that this mighty scourge of war may speedily pass away. Yet, if God wills that it continue until all the wealth piled by the bondsman's two hundred and fifty years of unrequited toil shall be sunk, and until every drop of blood drawn with the lash shall be paid by another drawn with the sword, as was said three thousand years ago, so still it must be said, "The judgments of the Lord are true and righteous altogether."

With malice toward none, with charity for all, with firmness in the right as God gives us to see the right, let us strive on to finish the work we are in, to bind up the nation's wounds, to care for him who shall have borne the battle and for his widow and his orphan, to do all which may achieve and cherish a just and lasting peace among ourselves and with all nations.

ROBERT E. LEE
To Avoid the Useless Sacrifice

On April 9, 1865, General Robert E. Lee (1807–1870) surrendered the remnants of the Confederate Army of Northern Virginia to Major General U. S. Grant at Appomattox Court House, Virginia. Though other Confederate forces were still in existence, Lee's surrender meant the end of the Confederacy. For almost three years he had fought off repeated Union assaults, and in his last campaign from the Wilderness to Petersburg, Union battle losses alone had amounted to more troops than Lee's entire army. But now the lines at Petersburg had been broken, large segments of Lee's army had been cut off and surrounded, his supplies had been captured, and there was no hope of escape. Lee asked his adjutant, Colonel Charles Marshall, to prepare a farewell order; when it was ready, he edited it, cut out a paragraph he thought might keep alive ill-feeling, then had it copied and distributed.

FROM General Order No. 9, HQ, Army of Northern Virginia, 10 April 1865.

Hd. qrs. Army of N. Va.
April 10, 1865

General Orders
No. 9

After four years of arduous service marked by unsurpassed courage and fortitude, the Army of Northern Virginia has been compelled to yield to overwhelming numbers and resources.

I need not tell the brave survivors of so many hard fought battles, who have remained steadfast to the last, that I have consented to this result from no distrust of them; but feeling that valor and devotion could accomplish nothing that could compensate for the loss that must have attended the continuance of the contest, I determined to avoid the useless sacrifice of those whose past services have endeared them to their countrymen.

By the terms of the agreement, officers and men can return to their homes and remain until exchanged. You will take with you the satisfaction that proceeds from the consciousness of duty faithfully performed; and I earnestly pray that a Merciful God will extend to you His blessing and protection.

With an unceasing admiration of your constancy and devotion to your Country, and a grateful remembrance of your kind and generous consideration for myself, I bid you all an affectionate farewell.

(Sgd) R. E. Lee

Genl.

9

THE GILDED AGE

The Civil War marked, in American life and culture, a dividing force which seemed in retrospect to have changed America from one kind of nation into another. Perhaps the enormous blood-letting of the war made Americans wary of idealism and skeptical about moral abstractions; perhaps the triumph of industrial capitalism that the war certainly brought about meant that the way was now open for unimpeded money-making—whatever the causes, something had happened that was not pleasant to contemplate. As Lionel Trilling describes it, "we cannot disregard the testimony of men so diverse as Henry Adams, Walt Whitman, William Dean Howells, and Mark Twain himself, to mention but a few of the many who were in agreement on this point. All spoke of something that had gone out of American life after the war, some simplicity, some innocence, some peace. . . . The difference was in the public attitude, in the things that were now accepted and made respectable in the national ideal. It was, they all felt, connected with new emotions about money." The pursuit of the Almighty Dollar, never a pastime, now became not simply necessary but altogether glorious. The heroes of the 1870's, 1880's, and 1890's were the big business operators, the financial tycoons who dealt in the millions. Wall Street became an everyday byword. Life in the cities became the national norm. What Mark Twain termed "The Gilded Age" was in full sway.

It was a period, too, when there was widespread misery among the urban and rural poor, and very little protection for them against the unbridled forces of industrial capitalism. The philosophy of the day was that of self-help; the evolutionary discoveries of Charles Darwin had been adapted to fit society, and life was viewed in terms of the survival of the fittest. Any attempt to regulate the working of finance capitalism, to block monopolistic combinations as being against the public interest, was considered interference with natural evolutionary processes. The strong would and should survive; the weak would go to the wall; and society would ultimately be the better for it. Government had no right to interfere in the working out of this process. It was the day of laissez-faire. As Jim Fisk, Jr., remarked after one financial escapade in which he had made some highly dubious financial moves, "Nothing is lost save honor!"

The selections that follow illustrate some of the dominant attitudes of the period.

JIM FISK
It Was Each Man Drag Out His Own Corpse

In 1869 two Wall Street speculators, Jay Gould (1836–1892) and Jim Fisk (1834–1872), made one of the more audacious moves in the history of American finance. The two of them, who controlled the Erie Railroad, tried to corner the gold market. To do this they needed assurance that the U.S. Treasury would not sell any of its gold reserves, and working through President U. S. Grant's brother-in-law, Abel R. Corbin, they thought they had arranged it. Several times the two of them entertained the innocent Grant, who was always impressed by wealth, and they believed that Grant was in agreement with their opinion that the "good of the republic" was best served by having gold pegged at a high figure. As the price rose steadily, there was panic on Wall Street, and widespread indignation in the public press. Gould, growing nervous about Grant's attitude, had a letter sent to the President, who was on vacation in western Pennsylvania. Grant, annoyed, merely accepted Gould's letter without comment. The courier then telegraphed back this message: "Message delivered all right." Somewhere along the line a telegraph operator inserted a period, so that the message read "Message delivered. All right." It was a costly error. When Grant realized what was going on, he had his wife write to Corbin, telling him to stop speculating in gold. Gould realized what would happen, so he began quietly selling his gold while the uninformed Fisk continued buying. On Black Friday, September 24, 1869, the bubble burst; the Treasury began selling gold, prices collapsed, and there was widespread panic. Eventually Gould, who had recouped his losses, settled up with Fisk, and the two of them made a profit on the whole transaction. Subsequently both were

FROM Testimony of James Fisk, Jr., before Congressional Committee, *Gold Panic Investigation, Report No. 31, House of Representatives, 41st Congress, 2nd Session,* 1870, pp. 168–69, 171–76.

called to testify before a Congressional investigating committee. Fisk's testi-
mony gives a remarkable insight into the attitudes of the leading financial
barons of the Gilded Age. Fisk was shot to death several years later by a jeal-
ous rival for the affections of his mistress. Gould went on to control the Union
Pacific, the Kansas Pacific, and other railroads. The nature of a typical post-
Civil War financier and speculator would later be given definitive fictional
representation in two novels by Theodore Dreiser, The Financier *and* The
Titan.

Washington, D.C., January 22, 1870.

James Fisk, Jr., sworn and examined.

By the Chairman:

Question. State your residence, place of business, and occupation.—Answer.
I live at 313 West Twenty-third street, New York. My business is railroading,
steamboating, and I suppose I may add speculating.

Q. Were you familiar with the course of gold during the last summer and
fall?—A. Yes, sir.

Q. Were you particularly familiar with the course of gold during the week
in September commonly known as the gold panic week?—A. Yes, sir.

Q. Were you engaged in either buying, selling, or loaning gold through
yourself or others during these days?—A. Yes, sir.

Q. With whom were you associated?—A. With no one. I think that all the
interests I had were personal. That question, however, may admit of some explanation on my part. I could say that no one was interested with me personally, or I might convey a clearer impression to the committee of my exact position by going into an explanation. At the outset, I may say that the transactions
of Mr. Gould and myself are joint, and that our usual custom is to have no one
else with us. At the time he started in to purchase gold, if I recollect right, he
was with some other parties, perhaps with Woodward and Kimber, in the
street. They spoke to me about it, and he said, I think, something to me about
buying some gold. I replied that I did not believe in it; that I believed the pressure was against us on the street. At that time I was called away for three or
four days; and when I came back, he had started in with Messrs. Kimber and
Woodward, as I understood, and had commenced buying at about 37 or 38.
You have had Mr. Gould before this committee, and have probably ascertained
that he is a rather peculiar man. Gold having settled down to 35, and I not
having cared to touch it he was a little sensitive on the subject, feeling as if he
would rather take his losses without saying anything about it. It went along in
that way for three or four weeks, when one day he said to me, "Don't you
think gold has got to the bottom?" I replied, that I did not see the profit in
buying gold unless you have got into a position where you can command the
market. He then said he had bought quite a large amount of gold, and I
judged from his conversation that he wanted me to go into the movement and
help strengthen the market. Upon that I went into the market and bought. I

should say that was about the 15th or 16th of September. I bought at that time about seven or eight millions, I think. As I said, our custom has been, in all transactions with which we have been connected, to make up a settlement and divide the results, whatever they are. This, I think, is the only case in which that was not done. It so happened that I started out with Heath & Co. The transactions of Smith, Gould & Martin, owing to the excitement that occurred, I think have never been fully settled. At any rate, Mr. Gould and I have never passed a word as to whether I was to be interested in his profits or losses, and there was no understanding that I was or was not. When the settlement is made in full, if there should be a loss, I should be very glad to help him to bear it, and if there are any profits I should not say no to a proposition to divide them with him; that is not my nature. I came into this movement simply to strengthen the market. I came in individually, and placed my own margins. There was no understanding between us any more than a general understanding that we did business together.

Q. Did you buy gold through any other house than that of Heath & Co.?— A. Some of my gold must have gone into the house of Smith, Gould, Martin & Co., and perhaps Carver may have had some; I think it probable that he did.

Q. How much did you buy, or order to be bought, during the week of the panic?—A. I should think the aggregate of gold that I bought for myself during that week was, perhaps, ten or twelve millions.

Q. Do you know Mr. Corbin?—A. Yes, sir.

Q. Did you transact any business for him during these days?—A. I did not.

Q. Did he have any interest in your operations so far as you know?—A. Not in mine. I know of an interest that he had in the market from information which I derived from him, and from information which I derived from Mr. Gould. . . .

Q. Please state in your own way what your object was in pursuing the policy you did?—A. Before my starting in for the purchase of this gold, and as far back as the time when General Grant went to Boston on the occasion of the peace jubilee, which was in June, he went over on one of our boats, and we went with him.

We have employed on the Erie road some twenty thousand men, all told; a stock of eight hundred locomotives, with the other equipments of the road on a corresponding scale. I am aware of no way in which these men and equipments can be used to advantage unless the crops come forward from the West. The actual amount of transportation due us on the moving of the crops would be about three and a half million dollars. Now if these crops should be held over and come on late in the spring, they would come right on the transportation of the mercantile people, when we could not carry the whole of them, and they would seek other channels, canals, &c., while we would lose the benefit; or, again, if they came forward very early in the fall, it would be at a time when we were doing a large business in package goods for the merchants, which pays better remunerative prices than produce. Our policy, therefore, is to encourage the crops to move forward at a time when other trade is quiet. I have been with the Erie road now some three years, and during my connection with it in the falls of 1866, 1867, and 1868, while the crops have been coming forward, gold has ranged from 41 to 45, and our freights were full all the time. When we began to figure at the precise position in which we were in regard to these freights for the last fall, we found that unless our western produce moved eastward early, the foreign market would be supplied from the Mediterranean, the Black Sea, and all that section of country. We had lying upon our table advices of three hundred sail of vessels with wheat, on its way from these waters. Our cars were at that time doing a fair package business, but we were doing none of this produce trade at all. It was of vital consequence that our large railroad stock and steamers running from Buffalo for us should get this trade started. If we could have this produce trade of three and a half millions, with all the facilities we had for carrying it, about a couple of millions would be clear money, which in carrying on our road is too large an item to let go if we could help it.

So that on our passage over to Boston with General Grant, we endeavored to ascertain what his position in regard to the finances was. We went down to supper about nine o'clock, intending while we were there to have this thing pretty thoroughly talked up, and, if possible, to relieve him from any idea of putting the price of gold down, for if his policy was such as to permit gold to go down to twenty-five, our transportation would have been snapped right up. We talked there until about half-past twelve. When we first commenced to talk, I could see that he was for returning to a specie basis. I remember the remark he made that we might as well tap the bubble at once as at any other time, saying that it had got to come to that. That was in the first part of the conversation. He entered into the conversation with a good deal of spirit, and I made up my mind that he was individually paying a good deal of attention to the finances, which he would to a certain extent control, so far as the action of the government was concerned. That being his idea, it looked as if it was the policy which we should have to work up to in the fall. I know that when we got to Boston, Mr. Gould and myself made up our minds that the prospect did not look promising.

When we got back to New York the next thing we did was to write to Mr. Boutwell something in regard to the matter. I think it was some time in August that General Grant started to go to Newport. I then went down to see him. I had seen him before, but not feeling so thoroughly acquainted as I desired for this purpose, I took a letter of introduction from Mr. Gould, in which it was written that there were three hundred sail of vessels then on the Mediterranean from the Black Sea, with grain to supply the Liverpool market. Gold was then about 34. If it continued at that price we had very little chance of carrying forward the crop during the fall. I know that we felt very nervous about it. I talked with General Grant on the subject, and endeavored, as far as I could, to convince him that his policy was one that would only bring destruction on us all. He then asked me when we should have an interview, and we agreed upon the time. He said "During that time I will see Mr. Boutwell, or have him there." Now, then, gold had continued to go down until it sold for 130 or 132, though when the crops began to move forward I knew that gold would work up again without the necessity of buying to bring it up. I did not like the looks of affairs then. It was upon that theory that Mr. Gould had commenced to purchase gold. I told him that I did not think the skies looked clear enough to go into that operation, but he started to buy gold with a firm conviction that there was a short interest in the market, and I have no other idea than that it was his conviction that he could put up gold to 45 if he felt any sort of confidence that he would not come into competition with gold sold by the government. The theory was that it was safe to buy gold for the purpose of putting up the price, to enable us to secure this transportation for our road, and in the course of the operation we would get rid of our gold without loss; but the thing began to look scary to me, and I did not go into the transaction until I considered that Mr. Gould was undertaking to carry a pretty heavy burden, when I said that of course my entire resources were at his disposal. There was never any understanding regarding there being any corner in gold, nor had I ever had a word with any human being, except Mr. Corbin, on this subject. Mr. Gould started in again on the 17th of September, and seeing his position I said, "I will join you." During the week before there had been a little coldness between us, which did not often exist, for the reason that he had taken upon himself a pretty heavy load, which he did not want me to share, and, therefore, he was not in the habit of saying anything about it. I remember the morning I started in that I illustrated his position by the story of a man who goes out on a spring morning to yoke his oxen. Putting the great elm bow on the neck of Brindle, and holding the other end of the yoke, he undertakes, by main force, to carry the yoke and draw Brindle over until he can yoke Star, and I described Mr. Gould as being in pretty much the same condition. He had a very heavy load to carry. He would not have invited me to help him, but I concluded I would help him to draw Brindle over. In the first place, however, I wanted to ascertain exactly how he stood, and I said to him: "How much gold have you got?" I said to him that it was my firm conviction that if we bought gold up the government would unload their gold onto us. Said he, "That is all fixed. I suppose you have seen nothing to convince you of that fact." General Grant was then in the city. It has always been our policy never to mix in politics unless it is in our business, but Mr. Gould said to me that morning: "This matter is all tied up; Butterfield is all right; Corbin has got Butterfield all right, and Corbin has got Grant fixed all right." That, in his opinion, they were interested together. That was a point I had not taken into consideration. I did presume that Mr. Corbin had prevailed upon General Grant to make him believe that 45 was the proper point at which to carry off this crop. Up to that time I did not believe that General Grant, or anybody connected with him, had any interest in the movement whatever, but it startled me when it was suggested that Grant was in this movement, and I determined to go right around and see Corbin. I had known him before through a son-in-law of his, by the name of Catherwood, whom I had met in railroading, but I said to Mr. Gould: "You give me a letter to him, so that he will talk confidentially with me." He did so and I went to see Mr. Corbin. When I met him he talked very shy about the matter at first, but finally came right out and told me that Mrs. Grant had an interest; that five hundred thousand of gold had been taken by Mr. Gould at 31 and 32, which had been sold at 37; that Mr. Corbin held for himself about two millions of gold, five hundred thousand of which was for Mrs. Grant, and five hundred thousand for Porter.

Q. Was that General Porter?—A. I did not ask whether he was a general or not; I remember the name of Porter. This was given out very slow. He let out just as fast as I did. When he found that Mr. Gould had told me about the same thing, I said: "Now, I have had nothing to do with your transactions in one way or the other; but you can make your pathway clear and straight by emptying it all out to me, because Mr. Gould and myself stand together. We have no secrets from each other. We have embarked in a scheme that looks like one of large magnitude. Mr. Gould has lost, as the thing stands now, and it looks as if it might be pretty serious business before getting it straight again. The whole success depends on whether the government will unload onto us or not." He says: "You need not have the least fear." I said: "I want to know whether what Mr. Gould has told me is true. I want to know whether you have sent this $25,000 to Washington, as he states." He then told me that he had sent it; that Mr. Gould had sold $500,000 of gold belonging to Mrs. Grant, which cost 33, for 37, or something in that neighborhood, leaving a balance in her favor of about $27,000, and that a check for $25,000 had been sent. Said I, "Mr. Corbin, what can you show me that goes still further than your talk?" "O, well," the old man said, "I cannot show you anything; but," said he, "this is all right." He talked freely, and repeated, "I tell you it is all right." When I went away from there I made up my mind that Corbin had told me the truth. Whether he had taken money or not—whether he had lied about that part of it or not—I made up my mind that, either through speculation or for the good of the country in moving these crops, the sale of gold which was to have taken place within two or three weeks, in October, was stopped for October, either upon one basis or the other; either from motives of personal interest or for the best welfare of the country. I came out with that conclusion. In the evening Mr. Corbin came round to the Opera House, and I had another interview with him there.

Q. Fix that date, as near as you can.—A. I should say, if it did not occur on Sunday, that it was about the 21st of September. It was either Monday or Tuesday night. We talked that evening, and Mr. Gould went home with him that night. In the morning, when Mr. Gould came down, I was over the river, and came into the office about 1 o'clock in the afternoon, but had no recourse with Mr. Gould until about 1 o'clock. We were then doing our business on Wall street through the telegraph from our office to Wall street. I asked Mr. Gould if he had seen Mr. Corbin that morning. He said: "Yes, everything is all right. If Butterfield gives any information we will get it in time to get out. I am to see Corbin again to night. I think I can give you some more information to night, after I see him." It seems that when he started to go home that night he stopped in at Corbin's house, when he went up or when he came back; anyhow, he came into the office about 8 o'clock in the evening. Says he to me, "Who is the most confidential man you have got?" I said: "It all depends upon what his mission is." He says: "I want a man who is a quick traveler; says nothing, but passes right along." Said I, "I will give you Chapin." I sent for Chapin. I said to him, "Chapin, I want you to-morrow morning to be at Corbin's house at half-past six. You will there receive a letter from him directed to General Grant, at Washington, Pennsylvania. I want you to leave on the eight-o'clock train, traveling as fast as you can, and not stop until you lay that letter in his hands. Wait until he reads the letter. Drive directly from there to the nearest telegraph office (it seems that Washington is several miles from the railroads) and telegraph back to me whether the letter is satisfactory, if you can do so without conveying that intelligence to anybody else." I then told Chapin, "You are boarding at a private house; I will send another man to call you, so that you will positively not be late." My brother-in-law went up in the morning, saw that Chapin was called, took him in a carriage at half-past six, and went to Corbin's house; rang the bell; Corbin came down, and, as Chapin says, delivered him the letter. He took it, went over the Pennsylvania Central to Pittsburg, left the railroad the next night and drove to Washington, arriving there about half-past seven in the morning, I should judge. He sent in his card immediately, saying that he was a special messenger from Mr. Corbin. General Grant came in, opened the letter and read it, and said, as he was going out, "You wait a few minutes." General Grant went out, and in a few minutes returned and said, "All right." Chaplin drove to the nearest telegraph office, according to instructions, and we got a telegram about 1 o'clock, "Delivered. All right."

I then had one evening another interview with Corbin. We were feeling a little nervous about the position we were then in. I said to Corbin, I hoped everything was all for the best. But, said I, "If we should miss—if the government should sell this gold, it would certainly be a serious matter." Corbin then said to me, "I want you to talk with my wife." Mrs. Corbin came into the room. I had been introduced to Mrs. Corbin before. The thing had gone beyond the matter of mere courtesy with anybody I met there. That was the first time I had seen her in reference to this transaction. We sat down and talked the matter over quite fully. I did not cover any matters up. I took it for granted that they had bought gold, and that they had as much interest in the matter as I had. She made this remark: "I know there will be no gold sold by the government; I am quite positive there will be no gold sold; for this is a chance of a lifetime for us; you need not have any uneasiness whatever."

I had a phantom ahead of me all the time that this real gold would come out. I was well aware that we had bought all the gold there was in New York, and had no fear about that coming back on us. The gold we were then buying in Wall street was phantom gold, and could give us no trouble.

I started away on the strength of that conversation, and I think it was on the morning of Thursday we left our carriage back of the post office, and when we came up to get into the carriage, as I came along up street, we stopped right below Duncan & Shearman's office. Mr. Gould says to me, "Old Corbin feels troubled and nervous about some gold; he wants a hundred thousand dollars;" and said Mr. Gould to me, "What do you think of it?" Said I, "If he wants a hundred thousand dollars to feed out to parties in interest, he had better have it." I think this was on the afternoon of Thursday. Mr. Gould asked if that didn't look as if there might be some blow up. I said, "If he wants that money to deal out to people, and it will help to strengthen our position in regard to this gold, we will give him one hundred or two hundred thousand." "Well," said he, "do as you please." I told him I would go and get the money; and I went immediately to Smith, Gould, Martin & Co., got a check for a hundred thousand dollars, and brought it and gave it to Mr. Gould in the carriage. Mr. Gould said he would stop there when he went home that night and give it to him.

I was not aware but what Mr. Corbin had received that hundred thousand dollars until the afternoon of Friday, after the blow up, when I said to Mr. Gould, "I'll be damned if that old scoundrel shall have that hundred thousand dollars; I will stop the payment of that check." Mr. Gould replied, "He has not got it; I have got it." I told him I was glad of that; there was that much saved, anyhow. Mr. Gould said Corbin had the twenty-five thousand dollar check, but he (Gould) had the hundred thousand one in his pocket.

I went down to the neighborhood of Wall street Friday morning, and the history of that morning you know. When I got back to our office you can imagine I was in no enviable state of mind, and the moment I got up street that afternoon I started right round to old Corbin's to rake him out. I went into the room, and sent word that Mr. Fisk wanted to see him in the dining-room. I was too mad to say anything civil, and when he came into the room, said I, "You damned old scoundrel, do you know what has happened?" This was, of course, after everything had blown up. Said I, "Do you know what you have done here, you and your people?" He began to wring his hands, and "Oh," he says, "this is a horrible position; are you ruined?" I said I didn't know whether I was or not; and I asked him again if he knew what had happened. He had been crying, and said he had just heard; that he had been sure everything was all right; but that something had occurred entirely different from what he had anticipated: Said I, "That don't amount to anything; we know that gold ought not to be at 31, and that it would not be but for such performances as you have had this last week; you knew damned well it would not if you had not failed." I knew that somebody had run a saw right into us, and said I, "This whole damned thing has turned out just as I told you it would; I considered the whole party a pack of cowards;" and I expected that when we came to clear our hands they would sock it right into us. I said to him, "I don't know whether you have lied or not, and I don't know what ought to be done with you."

He was on the other side of the table, weeping and wailing, and I was gnashing my teeth. "Now," he says, "you must quiet yourself." I told him I didn't want to be quiet; I had no desire to ever be quiet again, and probably never should be quiet again. He says, "But, my dear sir, you will lose your reason." Says I, "Speyers has already lost his reason; reason has gone out of everybody but me." I continued, "Now what are you going to do; you have got us into this thing, and what are you going to do to get out of it?" He says, "I don't know; I will go and get my wife." I said, "Get her down here." The soft talk was all over. He went upstairs and they returned, "tottling" into the room, looking older than Stephen Hopkins. His wife and he both looked like death. He was tottling just like that. (Illustrated by a trembling movement of the body.)

Finally I said, "Here is the position of the matter. We are forty miles down the Delaware, and we don't know where we are. I don't know but we may be rich; but it looks devilish like as if we were poor. You have got us into this scrape, and now what is going to be done?" She said she could not think this had been done with the President's consent. She thought Boutwell had done it in violation of the strict orders of the President not to sell gold. Said I, "That don't help matters at all. I can't tell you where we stand." We had sold large amounts of gold, which I was afraid would not go out. "Now, Mr. Corbin, what do you mean to do?" The old man straightened up in front of the table and said, "I will go down to Washington, and lay it at their door; I will fathom this thing." Said I, "When will you go—to-night?" "No," he said, "they had both been abed all day, and could not go that night; but," said he, "we will be in Washington Sunday morning; we will ride all night Saturday night, and go to the Executive Mansion Sunday morning. You stand right still until Monday morning, and we will stop all sales of gold. We will mend up the matter; bind up the wounds, and all will be right."

I had made up my mind that Corbin's influence was pretty well played out, but I thought that the further off he was the happier I should be, and so I recommended him to go. He came down Saturday night, as I afterward heard, and came back Sunday night, spending the day at the mansion. I have never seen him from that day to this. Of course matters took such a turn that it was no use. It was each man drag out his own corpse. Get out of it as well as you can.

WILLIAM GRAHAM SUMNER
The Burdens of the Good-for-Nothing

Human society is a struggle for survival, in which the same principles apply as in other phases of the evolutionary process whereby higher forms evolve from lower, and less adaptable species perish. Such was the gospel of Social Darwinism, of which a leading proponent in the years after the Civil War was William Graham Sumner (1840–1910), professor of political and social science at Yale University. In the following excerpt from his famous lecture "The Forgotten Man," Sumner cautions against coddling the "weak"—by which he meant the idle poor—in the name of social justice. The phrase "The Forgotten Man" was later to be used by President Franklin Delano Roosevelt, but in a way that would have horrified Sumner.

There is some sort of a poetical and metaphysical notion of liberty afloat in men's minds which some people dream about but which nobody can define. In popular language it means that a man may do as he has a mind to. When people get this notion of liberty into their heads and combine with it the notion that they live in a free country and ought to have liberty, they sometimes make strange demands upon the state. If liberty means to be able to do as you have a mind to, there is no such thing in this world. Can the Czar of Russia do as he has a mind to? Can the Pope do as he has a mind to? Can the President of the United States do as he has a mind to? Can Rothschild do as he has a mind to? Could a Humboldt or a Faraday do as he had a mind to? Could a Shakespeare or a Raphael do as he had a mind to? Can a tramp do as he has a mind to? Where is the man, whatever his station, possessions, or talents, who can get any such liberty? There is none. There is a doctrine floating about in our literature that we are born to the inheritance of certain rights. That is another glorious dream, for it would mean that there was something in this world which we got for nothing. But what is the truth? We are born into no right whatever but what has an equivalent and corresponding duty right alongside of it. There is no such thing on this earth as something for nothing. Whatever we inherit of wealth, knowledge, or institutions from the past has been paid for by the labor and sacrifice of preceding generations; and the fact that these gains are carried on, that the race lives and that the race can, at least within some cycle, accumulate its gains, is one of the facts on which civilization rests. The law of the conservation of energy

FROM "The Forgotten Man," by William Graham Sumner, in *The Forgotten Man and Other Essays,* ed. Albert Galloway Keller (New Haven: Yale University Press, 1943). Reprinted by permission of Yale University Press.

is not simply a law of physics; it is a law of the whole moral universe, and the order and truth of all things conceivable by man depends upon it. If there were any such liberty as that of doing as you have a mind to, the human race would be condemned to everlasting anarchy and war as these erratic wills crossed and clashed against each other. True liberty lies in the equilibrium of rights and duties, producing peace, order, and harmony. As I have defined it, it means that a man's right to take power and wealth out of the social product is measured by the energy and wisdom which he has contributed to the social effort.

Now if I have set this idea before you with any distinctness and success, you see that civil liberty consists of a set of civil institutions and laws which are arranged to act as impersonally as possible. It does not consist in majority rule or in universal suffrage or in elective systems at all. These are devices which are good or better just in the degree in which they secure liberty. The institutions of civil liberty leave each man to run his career in life in his own way, only guaranteeing to him that whatever he does in the way of industry, economy, prudence, sound judgment, etc., shall redound to his own welfare and shall not be diverted to someone else's benefit. Of course it is a necessary corollary that each man shall also bear the penalty of his own vices and his own mistakes. If I want to be free from any other man's dictation, I must understand that I can have no other man under my control.

Now with these definitions and general conceptions in mind, let us turn to the special class of facts to which, as I said at the outset, I invite your attention. We see that under a régime of liberty and equality before the law, we get the highest possible development of independence, self-reliance, individual energy, and enterprise, but we get these high social virtues at the expense of the old sentimental ties which used to unite baron and retainer, master and servant, sage and disciple, comrade and comrade. We are agreed that the son shall not be disgraced even by the crime of the father, much less by the crime of a more distant relative. It is a humane and rational view of things that each life shall stand for itself alone and not be weighted by the faults of another, but it is useless to deny that this view of things is possible only in a society where the ties of kinship have lost nearly all the intensity of poetry and romance which once characterized them. The ties of sentiment and sympathy also have faded out. We have come, under the régime of liberty and equality before the law, to a form of society which is based not on status, but on free contract. Now a society based on status is one in which classes, ranks, interests, industries, guilds, associations, etc., hold men in permanent relations to each other. Custom and prescription create, under status, ties, the strength of which lies in sentiment. Feeble remains of this may be seen in some of our academical societies to-day, and it is unquestionably a great privilege and advantage for any man in our society to win an experience of the sentiments which belong to a strong and close association, just because the chances for such experience are nowadays very rare. In a society based on free contract, men come together as free and independent parties to an agreement which is of mutual advantage. The relation is rational, even rationalistic. It is not poetical. It does not exist from use and custom, but for reasons given, and it does not endure by prescription but ceases when the reason for it ceases. There is no sentiment in it at all. The fact is that, under the régime of liberty and equality before the law, there is no place for sentiment in trade or politics as public interests. Sentiment is thrown back into private life, into personal relations, and if ever it comes into a public discussion of an impersonal and general public question it always produces mischief.

Now you know that "the poor and the weak" are continually put forward as objects of public interest and public obligation. In the appeals which are made, the terms "the poor" and "the weak" are used as if they were terms of exact definition. Except the pauper, that is to say, the man who cannot earn his living or pay his way, there is no possible definition of a poor man. Except a man who is incapacitated by vice or by physical infirmity, there is no definition of a weak man. The paupers and the physically incapacitated are an inevitable charge on society. About them no more need be said. But the weak who constantly arouse the pity of humanitarians and philanthropists are the shiftless, the imprudent, the negligent, the impractical, and the inefficient, or they are the idle, the intemperate, the extravagant, and the vicious. Now the troubles of these persons are constantly forced upon public attention, as if they and their interests deserved especial consideration, and a great portion of all organized and unorganized effort for the common welfare consists in attempts to relieve these classes of people. I do not wish to be understood now as saying that nothing ought to be done for these people by those who are stronger and wiser. That is not my point. What I want to do is to point out the thing which is overlooked and the error which is made in all these charitable efforts. The notion is accepted as if it were not open to any question that if you help the inefficient and vicious you may gain something for society or you may not, but that you lose nothing. This is a complete mistake. Whatever capital you divert to the support of a shiftless and good-for-nothing person is so much diverted from some other employment, and that means from somebody else. I would spend any conceivable amount of zeal and eloquence if I possessed it to try to make people grasp this idea. Capital is force. If it goes one way it cannot go another. If you give a loaf to a pauper you cannot give the same loaf to a laborer. Now this other man who would have got it but for the charitable sentiment which bestowed it on a worthless member of society is the Forgotten Man. The philanthropists and humanitarians have their minds all full of the wretched and miserable whose case appeals to compassion, attacks the sympathies, takes possession of the imagination, and excites the emotions. They push on towards the quickest and easiest remedies and they forget the real victim.

Now who is the Forgotten Man? He is the simple, honest laborer, ready to earn his living by productive work. We pass him by because he is independent, self-supporting, and asks no favors. He does not appeal to the emotions or excite the sentiments. He only wants to make a contract and fulfill it, with respect on both sides and favor on neither side. He must get his living out of the capital of the country. The larger the capital is, the better living he can get. Every particle of capital which is wasted on the vicious, the idle, and the shiftless is so much taken from the capital available to reward the independent and productive laborer. But we stand with our backs to the independent and productive laborer all the time. We do not remember him because he makes no clamor; but I appeal to you whether he is not the man who ought to be remembered first of all, and whether, on any sound social theory, we ought not to protect him against the burdens of the good-for-nothing. In these last years I have read hundreds of articles and heard scores of sermons and speeches which were really glorifications of the good-for-nothing, as if these were the charge of society, recommended by right reason to its care and protection. We are addressed all the time as if those who are respectable were to blame because some are not so, and as if there were an obligation on the part of those who have done their duty towards those who have not done their duty. Every man is bound to take care of himself and his family and to do his share in the work of society. It is totally false that one who has done so is bound to bear the care and charge of those who are wretched because they have not done so. The silly popular notion is that the beggars live at the expense of the rich, but the truth is that those who eat and produce not, live at the expense of those who labor and produce. The next time that you are tempted to subscribe a dollar to a charity, I do not tell you not to do it, because after you have fairly considered the matter, you may think it right to do it, but I do ask you to stop and remember the Forgotten Man and understand that if you put your dollar in the savings bank it will go to swell the capital of the country which is available for division amongst those who, while they earn it, will reproduce it with increase. . . .

MARK TWAIN /
CHARLES DUDLEY WARNER
According to Our Surveys, a Million
Would Do It

In 1873 Mark Twain (Samuel L. Clemens, 1835–1910) and Charles Dudley Warner (1829–1900) collaborated on a novel, The Gilded Age, *notable today*

FROM The Gilded Age, by Mark Twain and Charles Dudley Warner (Hartford, Conn.: American Publishing Co., 1873), pp. 186–93.

*because of the high comedy with which the business, industrial, and political
mores of post-Civil War America are so neatly burlesqued. Especially in the
chapters written by Twain, chronicling the imaginative planning and dreaming of one Colonel Beriah Sellers, does the modern reader gain a feeling for
the optimistic, threadbare romanticizing of the doctrine of Getting Ahead In
Life that seems to typify the era. Here Colonel Sellers interests a United States
Senator in internal improvements for the town of Hawkeye.*

The visit of Senator Abner Dilworthy was an event in Hawkeye. When a
Senator, whose place is in Washington moving among the Great and guiding
the destinies of the nation, condescends to mingle among the people and accept the hospitalities of such a place as Hawkeye, the honor is not considered
a light one. All parties are flattered by it and politics are forgotten in the presence of one so distinguished among his fellows.

Senator Dilworthy, who was from a neighboring state, had been a Unionist
in the darkest days of his country, and had thriven by it, but was that any
reason why Col. Sellers, who had been a confederate and had not thriven by
it, should give him the cold shoulder?

The Senator was the guest of his old friend Gen. Boswell, but it almost appeared that he was indebted to Col. Sellers for the unreserved hospitalities of
the town. It was the large hearted Colonel who, in a manner, gave him the
freedom of the city.

"You are known here, sir," said the Colonel, "and Hawkeye is proud of
you. You will find every door open, and a welcome at every hearthstone. I
should insist upon your going to my house, if you were not claimed by your
older friend Gen. Boswell. But you will mingle with our people, and you will
see here developments that will surprise you."

The Colonel was so profuse in his hospitality that he must have made the
impression upon himself that he had entertained the Senator at his own mansion during his stay; at any rate, he afterwards always spoke of him as his
guest, and not seldom referred to the Senator's relish of certain viands on his
table. He did, in fact, press him to dine upon the morning of the day the
Senator was going away.

Senator Dilworthy was large and portly, though not tall—a pleasant spoken
man, a popular man with the people.

He took a lively interest in the town and all the surrounding country, and
made many inquiries as to the progress of agriculture, of education, and of
religion, and especially as to the condition of the emancipated race.

"Providence," he said, "has placed them in our hands, and although you
and I, General, might have chosen a different destiny for them, under the
Constitution, yet Providence knows best."

"You can't do much with 'em," interrupted Col. Sellers. "They are a speculating race, sir, disinclined to work for white folks without security, planning

how to live by only working for themselves. Idle, sir, there's my garden just a ruin of weeds. Nothing practical in 'em."

"There is some truth in your observation, Colonel, but you must educate them."

"You educate the niggro and you make him more speculating than he was before. If he won't stick to any industry except for himself now, what will he do then?"

"But, Colonel, the negro when educated will be more able to make his speculations fruitful."

"Never, sir, never. He would only have a wider scope to injure himself. A niggro has no grasp sir. Now, a white man can conceive great operations, and carry them out; a niggro can't."

"Still," replied the Senator, "granting that he might injure himself in a worldly point of view, his elevation through education would multiply his chances for the hereafter—which is the important thing after all, Colonel. And no matter what the result is, we must fulfill our duty by this being."

"I'd elevate his soul," promptly responded the Colonel; "that's just it; you can't make his soul too immortal, but I wouldn't touch *him,* himself. Yes, sir! make his soul immortal, but don't disturb the niggro as he is."

Of course one of the entertainments offered the Senator was a public reception, held in the court house, at which he made a speech to his fellow citizens. Col. Sellers was master of ceremonies. He escorted the band from the city hotel to Gen. Boswell's; he marshalled the procession of Masons, of Odd Fellows, and of Firemen, the Good Templars, the Sons of Temperance, the Cadets of Temperance, the Daughters of Rebecca, the Sunday School children, and citizens generally, which followed the Senator to the court house; he bustled about the room long after every one else was seated, and loudly cried "Order!" in the dead silence which preceded the introduction of the Senator by Gen. Boswell. The occasion was one to call out his finest powers of personal appearance, and one he long dwelt on with pleasure.

This not being an edition of the *Congressional Globe* it is impossible to give Senator Dilworthy's speech in full. He began somewhat as follows:—

"Fellow citizens: It gives me great pleasure to thus meet and mingle with you, to lay aside for a moment the heavy duties of an official and burdensome station, and confer in familiar converse with my friends in your great state. The good opinion of my fellow citizens of all sections is the sweetest solace in all my anxieties. I look forward with longing to the time when I can lay aside the cares of office—" ["dam sight," shouted a tipsy fellow near the door. Cries of "put him out."]

"My friends, do not remove him. Let the misguided man stay. I see that he is a victim of that evil which is swallowing up public virtue and sapping the foundation of society. As I was saying, when I can lay down the cares of office and retire to the sweets of private life in some such sweet, peaceful, intelligent, wide-awake and patriotic place as Hawkeye (applause). I have traveled much, I have seen all parts of our glorious union, but I have never seen a lovelier village than yours, or one that has more signs of commercial and industrial and religious prosperity—(more applause)."

The Senator then launched into a sketch of our great country, and dwelt for an hour or more upon its prosperity and the dangers which threatened it.

He then touched reverently upon the institutions of religion, and upon the necessity of private purity, if we were to have any public morality. "I trust," he said, "that there are children within the sound of my voice," and after some remarks to them, the Senator closed with an apostrophe to "the genius of American Liberty, walking with the Sunday School in one hand and Temperance in the other up the glorified steps of the National Capitol."

Col. Sellers did not of course lose the opportunity to impress upon so influential a person as the Senator the desirability of improving the navigation of Columbus river. He and Mr. Brierly took the Senator over to Napoleon and opened to him their plan. It was a plan that the Senator could understand without a great deal of explanation, for he seemed to be familiar with the like improvements elsewhere. When, however, they reached Stone's Landing the Senator looked about him and inquired,

"Is this Napoleon?"

"This is the nucleus, the nucleus," said the Colonel, unrolling his map. "Here is the deepo, the church, the City Hall and so on."

"Ah, I see. How far from here is Columbus River? Does that stream empty—"

"That, why, that's Goose Run. Thar ain't no Columbus, thout'n it's over to Hawkeye," interrupted one of the citizens, who had come out to stare at the strangers. "A railroad come here last summer, but it haint been here no mo'."

"Yes, sir," the Colonel hastened to explain, "in the old records Columbus River is called Goose Run. You see how it sweeps round the town—forty-nine miles to the Missouri; sloop navigation all the way pretty much, drains this whole country; when it's improved steamboats will run right up here. It's got to be enlarged, deepened. You see by the map, Columbus River. This country must have water communication!"

"You'll want a considerable appropriation, Col. Sellers."

"I should say a million; is that your figure Mr. Brierly."

"According to our surveys," said Harry, "a million would do it; a million spent on the river would make Napoleon worth two millions at least."

"I see," nodded the Senator. "But you'd better begin by asking only for two or three hundred thousand, the usual way. You can begin to sell town lots on that appropriation, you know."

The Senator, himself, to do him justice, was not very much interested in the country or the stream, but he favored the appropriation, and he gave the Colonel and Mr. Brierly to understand that he would endeavor to get it through. Harry, who thought he was shrewd and understood Washington, suggested an interest.

But he saw that the Senator was wounded by the suggestion.

"You will offend me by repeating such an observation," he said. "Whatever I do will be for the public interest. It will require a portion of the appropriation for necessary expenses, and I am sorry to say that there are members who will have to be seen. But you can reckon upon my humble services."

This aspect of the subject was not again alluded to. The Senator possessed himself of the facts, not from his observation of the ground, but from the lips of Col. Sellers, and laid the appropriation scheme away among his other plans for benefiting the public.

It was on this visit also that the Senator made the acquaintance of Mr. Washington Hawkins, and was greatly taken with his innocence, his guileless manner and perhaps with his ready adaptability to enter upon any plan proposed.

Col. Sellers was pleased to see this interest that Washington had awakened, especially since it was likely to further his expectations with regard to the Tennessee lands; the Senator having remarked to the Colonel, that he delighted to help any deserving young man, when the promotion of a private advantage could at the same time be made to contribute to the general good. And he did not doubt that this was an opportunity of that kind.

The result of several conferences with Washington was that the Senator proposed that he should go to Washington with him and become his private secretary and the secretary of his committee; a proposal which was eagerly accepted.

The Senator spent Sunday in Hawkeye and attended church. He cheered the heart of the worthy and zealous minister by an expression of his sympathy in his labors, and by many inquiries in regard to the religious state of the region. It was not a very promising state, and the good man felt how much lighter his task would be, if he had the aid of such a man as Senator Dilworthy.

"I am glad to see, my dear sir," said the Senator, "that you give them the doctrines. It is owing to a neglect of the doctrines, that there is such a fearful falling away in the country. I wish that we might have you in Washington—as chaplain, now, in the senate."

The good man could not but be a little flattered, and if sometimes, thereafter, in his discouraging work, he allowed the thought that he might perhaps be called to Washington as chaplain of the Senate, to cheer him, who can wonder. The Senator's commendation at least did one service for him, it elevated him in the opinion of Hawkeye.

Laura was at church alone that day, and Mr. Brierly walked home with her. A part of their way lay with that of General Boswell and Senator Dilworthy, and introductions were made. Laura had her own reasons for wishing to know the Senator, and the Senator was not a man who could be called indifferent to charms such as hers. That meek young lady so commended herself to him in the short walk, that he announced his intentions of paying his respects to her the next day, an intention which Harry received glumly; and when the Senator was out of hearing he called him "an old fool."

"Fie," said Laura, "I do believe you are jealous, Harry. He is a very pleasant man. He said you were a young man of great promise."

The Senator did call next day, and the result of his visit was that he was confirmed in his impression that there was something about him very attractive to ladies. He saw Laura again and again during his stay, and felt more and more the subtle influence of her feminine beauty, which every man felt who came near her.

Harry was beside himself with rage while the Senator remained in town; he declared that women were always ready to drop any man for higher game; and he attributed his own ill-luck to the Senator's appearance. The fellow was in fact crazy about her beauty and ready to beat his brains out in chagrin. Perhaps Laura enjoyed his torment, but she soothed him with blandishments that increased his ardor, and she smiled to herself to think that he had, with all his protestations of love, never spoken of marriage. Probably the vivacious fellow never had thought of it. At any rate when he at length went away from Hawkeye he was no nearer it. But there was no telling to what desperate lengths his passion might not carry him.

Laura bade him good bye with tender regret, which, however, did not disturb her peace or interfere with her plans. The visit of Senator Dilworthy had become of more importance to her, and it by and by bore the fruit she longed for, in an invitation to visit his family in the National Capital during the winter session of Congress.

ELBERT HUBBARD
It Is the Survival of the Fittest

Few publications have enjoyed the vogue of an inspirational tract entitled "A Message to Garcia," written by Elbert Hubbard (1856–1915) for his magazine, The Philistine, for March, 1899. Based on the successful delivery of a military message to the Cuban insurgent leader Iniguez Garcia by an American officer, Hubbard's sermon extolled the virtues of initiative and intelligent obedience to instructions, and was reprinted by American businesses and distributed to their employees in the hundreds of thousands of copies.

FROM *A Message to Garcia,* by Elbert Hubbard (East Aurora, N.Y.: The Roycrofters, 1899), pp. 1–11.

In all this Cuban business there is one man stands out on the horizon of my memory like Mars at perihelion. When war broken out between Spain and the United States, it was very necessary to communicate quickly with the leader of the Insurgents. Garcia was somewhere in the mountain fastnesses of Cuba—no one knew where. No mail or telegraph message could reach him. The President must secure his co-operation, and quickly. What to do!

Some one said to the President, "There is a fellow by the name of Rowan will find Garcia for you, if anybody can." Rowan was sent for and was given a letter to be delivered to Garcia. How "the fellow by the name of Rowan" took the letter, sealed it up in an oilskin pouch, strapped it over his heart, in four days landed by night off the coast of Cuba from an open boat, disappeared into the jungle, and in three weeks came out on the other side of the Island, having traversed a hostile country on foot, and delivered his letter to Garcia— are things I have no special desire now to tell in detail. The point that I wish to make is this: McKinley gave Rowan a letter to be delivered to Garcia; Rowan took the letter and did not ask, "Where is he at?" By the Eternal! there is a man whose form should be cast in deathless bronze and the statue placed in every college of the land. It is not book-learning young men need, nor instruction about this and that, but a stiffening of the vertebrae which will cause them to be loyal to a trust, to act promptly, concentrate their energies: do the thing—"Carry a message to Garcia."

General Garcia is dead now, but there are other Garcias. No man who has endeavored to carry out an enterprise where many hands were needed, but has been well-nigh appalled at times by the imbecility of the average man—the inability or unwillingness to concentrate on a thing and do it.

Slipshod assistance, foolish inattention, dowdy indifference, and half-hearted work seem the rule; and no man succeeds, unless by hook or crook or threat he forces or bribes other men to assist him; or mayhap, God in His goodness performs a miracle, and sends him an Angel of Light for an assistant. You, reader, put this matter to a test: You are sitting now in your office—six clerks are within call. Summon any one and make this request: "Please look in the encyclopedia and make a brief memorandum for me concerning the life of Correggio."

Will the clerk quietly say, "Yes, sir," and go do the task?

On your life he will not. He will look at you out of a fishy eye and ask one or more of the following questions: Who was he? Which encyclopedia? Where is the encyclopedia? Was I hired for that? Don't you mean Bismarck? What's the matter with Charlie doing it? Is he dead? Is there any hurry? Shall I bring you the book and let you look it up yourself? What do you want to know for?

And I will lay you ten to one that after you have answered the questions, and explained how to find the information, and why you want it, the clerk will go off and get one of the other clerks to help him try to find Garcia—and then come back and tell you there is no such man. Of course I may lose my bet, but according to the Law of Average I will not.

Now, if you are wise, you will not bother to explain to your "assistant" that Correggio is indexed under the C's, not in the K's, but you will smile very sweetly and say, "Never mind," and go look it up yourself.

And this incapacity for independent action, this moral stupidity, this infirmity of the will, this unwillingness to cheerfully catch hold and lift—these are the things that put pure Socialism so far into the future. If men will not act for themselves, what will they do when the benefit of their effort is for all? A first mate with knotted club seems necessary; and the dread of getting "the bounce" Saturday night holds many a worker to his place.

Advertise for a stenographer, and nine out of ten who apply can neither spell nor punctuate—and do not think it necessary to.

Can such a one write a letter to Garcia?

"You see that bookkeeper," said a foreman to me in a large factory.

"Yes; what about him?"

"Well, he's a fine accountant, but if I'd send him up-town on an errand, he might accomplish the errand all right, and on the other hand, might stop at four saloons on the way, and when he got to Main Street would forget what he had been sent for."

Can such a man be entrusted to carry a message to Garcia?

We have recently been hearing much maudlin sympathy expressed for the "downtrodden denizens of the sweat-shop" and the "homeless wanderer searching for honest employment," and with it all often go many hard words for the men in power.

Nothing is said about the employer who grows old before his time in a vain attempt to get frowsy ne'er-do-wells to do intelligent work; and his long, patient striving with "help" that does nothing but loaf when his back is turned. In every store and factory there is a constant weeding-out process going on. The employer is continually sending away "help" that have shown their incapacity to further the interests of the business, and others are being taken on.

No matter how good times are, this sorting continues: only if times are hard and work is scarce, the sorting is done finer—but out and forever out the incompetent and unworthy go. It is the surival of the fittest. Self-interest prompts every employer to keep the best—those who can carry a message to Garcia.

I know one man of really brilliant parts who has not the ability to manage a business of his own, and yet who is absolutely worthless to any one else, because he carries with him constantly the insane suspicion that his employer is oppressing, or intending to oppress, him. He can not give orders; and he will not receive them. Should a message be given him to take to Garcia, his answer would probably be, "Take it yourself!"

Tonight this man walks the streets looking for work, the wind whistling through his threadbare coat. No one who knows him dare employ him, for he is a regular firebrand of discontent. He is impervious to reason, and the only thing that can impress him is the toe of a thick-soled Number Nine boot.

Of course I know that one so morally deformed is no less to be pitied than a physical cripple; but in our pitying let us drop a tear, too, for the men who are striving to carry on a great enterprise, whose working hours are not limited by the whistle, and whose hair is fast turning white through the struggle to hold in line dowdy indifference, slipshod imbecility, and the heartless ingratitude which, but for their enterprise, would be both hungry and homeless.

Have I put the matter too strongly? Possibly I have; but when all the world has gone a-slumming I wish to speak a word of sympathy for the man who succeeds—the man who, against great odds, has directed the efforts of others, and having succeeded, finds there's nothing in it: nothing but bare board and clothes. I have carried a dinner-pail and worked for day's wages, and I have also been an employer of labor, and I know there is something to be said on both sides. There is no excellence, per se, in poverty; rags are no recommendation; and all employers are not rapacious and high-handed, any more than all poor men are virtuous.

My heart goes out to the man who does his work when the "boss" is away, as well as when he is at home. And the man who, when given a letter for Garcia, quietly takes the missive, without asking any idiotic questions, and with no lurking intention of chucking it into the nearest sewer, or of doing aught else but deliver it, never gets "laid off," nor has to go on a strike for higher wages. Civilization is one long anxious search for just such individuals. Anything such a man asks shall be granted. His kind is so rare that no employer can afford to let him go. He is wanted in every city, town and village—in every office, shop, store and factory.

The world cries out for such: he is needed, and needed badly—the man who can carry A MESSAGE TO GARCIA.

ANDREW CARNEGIE
Eureka! We Have Found It!

Andrew Carnegie (1835–1919), industrialist and philanthropist, recounts here the beginnings of a success story which seemed to typify the ideals and ambitions of post-Civil War America. Rising from honest poverty by diligence and intelligence, he attained a commanding position in the steel industry. Then Carnegie sold his interests to the combination that became the United

FROM *The Gospel of Wealth and Other Timely Essays,* by Andrew Carnegie (New York: The Century Co., 1900), pp. xi–xxii.

States Steel Corporation, and devoted his latter days to the disposal of his immense fortune through charity and philanthropy.

You know how people moan about poverty as being a great evil, and it seems to be accepted that if people had only plenty of money and were rich, they would be happy and more useful, and get more out of life.

As a rule, there is more genuine satisfaction, a truer life, and more obtained from life in the humble cottages of the poor than in the palaces of the rich. I always pity the sons and daughters of rich men, who are attended by servants, and have governesses at a later age, but am glad to remember that they do not know what they have missed.

They have kind fathers and mothers, too, and think that they enjoy the sweetness of these blessings to the fullest: but this they cannot do; for the poor boy who has in his father his constant companion, tutor, and model, and in his mother—holy name!—his nurse, teacher, guardian angel, saint, all in one, has a richer, more precious fortune in life than any rich man's son who is not so favored can possibly know, and compared with which all other fortunes count for little.

It is because I know how sweet and happy and pure the home of honest poverty is, how free from perplexing care, from social envies and emulations, how loving and how united its members may be in the common interest of supporting the family, that I sympathize with the rich man's boy and congratulate the poor man's boy; and it is for these reasons that from the ranks of the poor so many strong, eminent, self-reliant men have always sprung and always must spring.

If you will read the list of the immortals who "were not born to die," you will find that most of them have been born to the precious heritage of poverty.

It seems, nowadays, a matter of universal desire that poverty should be abolished. We should be quite willing to abolish luxury, but to abolish honest, industrious, self-denying poverty would be to destroy the soil upon which mankind produces the virtues which enable our race to reach a still higher civilization than it now possesses.

I come now to the third step in my apprenticeship, for I had already taken two, as you see—the cotton factory and then the bobbin factory; and with the third—the third time is the chance, you know—deliverance came. I obtained a situation as messenger boy in the telegraph office of Pittsburg when I was fourteen. Here I entered a new world.

Amid books, newspapers, pencils, pens and ink and writing-pads, and a clean office, bright windows, and the literary atmosphere, I was the happiest boy alive.

My only dread was that I should some day be dismissed because I did not know the city; for it is necessary that a messenger boy should know all the firms and addresses of men who are in the habit of receiving telegrams. But I was a stranger in Pittsburg. However, I made up my mind that I would learn to repeat successively each business house in the principal streets, and was soon able to shut my eyes and begin at one side of Wood Street, and call every firm successively to the top, then pass to the other side and call every firm to the bottom. Before long I was able to do this with the business streets generally. My mind was then at rest upon that point.

Of course every messenger boy wants to become an operator, and before the operators arrive in the early mornings the boys slipped up to the instruments and practised. This I did, and was soon able to talk to the boys in the other offices along the line, who were also practising.

One morning I heard Philadelphia calling Pittsburg, and giving the signal, "Death message." Great attention was then paid to "death messages," and I thought I ought to try to take this one. I answered and did so, and went off and delivered it before the operator came. After that the operators sometimes used to ask me to work for them.

Having a sensitive ear for sound, I soon learned to take messages by the ear, which was then very uncommon—I think only two persons in the United States could then do it. Now every operator takes by ear, so easy it is to follow and do what any other boy can—if you only have to. This brought me into notice, and finally I became an operator, and received the, to me, enormous recompense of twenty-five dollars per month—three hundred dollars a year!

This was a fortune—the very sum that I had fixed when I was a factory-worker as the fortune I wished to possess, because the family could live on three hundred dollars a year and be almost or quite independent. Here it was at last! But I was soon to be in receipt of extra compensation for extra work.

The six newspapers of Pittsburg received telegraphic news in common. Six copies of each despatch were made by a gentleman who received six dollars per week for the work, and he offered me a gold dollar every week if I would do it, of which I was very glad indeed, because I always liked to work with news and scribble for newspapers.

The reporters came to a room every evening for the news which I had prepared, and this brought me into most pleasant intercourse with these clever fellows, and besides, I got a dollar a week as pocket-money, for this was not considered family revenue by me.

I think this last step of doing something beyond one's task is fully entitled to be considered "business." The other revenue, you see, was just salary obtained for regular work; but here was a little business operation upon my own account, and I was very proud indeed of my gold dollar every week.

The Pennsylvania Railroad shortly after this was completed to Pittsburg, and that genius, Thomas A. Scott, was its superintendent. He often came to the telegraph office to talk to his chief, the general superintendent, at Altoona, and I became known to him in this way.

When that great railway system put up a wire of its own, he asked me to be his clerk and operator; so I left the telegraph office—in which there is great danger that a young man may be permanently buried, as it were—and became connected with the railways.

The new appointment was accompanied by what was, to me, a tremendous increase of salary. It jumped from twenty-five to thirty-five dollars per month. Mr. Scott was then receiving one hundred and twenty-five dollars per month, and I used to wonder what on earth he could do with so much money.

I remained for thirteen years in the service of the Pennsylvania Railroad Company, and was at last superintendent of the Pittsburg division of the road, successor to Mr. Scott, who had in the meantime risen to the office of vice-president of the company.

One day Mr. Scott, who was the kindest of men, and had taken a great fancy to me, asked if I had or could find five hundred dollars to invest.

Here the business instinct came into play. I felt that as the door was opened for a business investment with my chief, it would be wilful flying in the face of providence if I did not jump at it; so I answered promptly:

"Yes, sir; I think I can."

"Very well," he said, "get it; a man has just died who owns ten shares in the Adams Express Company which I want you to buy. It will cost you fifty dollars per share, and I can help you with a little balance if you cannot raise it all."

Here was a queer position. The available assets of the whole family were not five hundred dollars. But there was one member of the family whose ability, pluck, and resource never failed us, and I felt sure the money could be raised somehow or other by my mother.

Indeed, had Mr. Scott known our position he would have advanced it himself; but the last thing in the world the proud Scot will do is to reveal his poverty and rely upon others. The family had managed by this time to purchase a small house and pay for it in order to save rent. My recollection is that it was worth eight hundred dollars.

The matter was laid before the council of three that night, and the oracle spoke: "Must be done. Mortgage our house. I will take the steamer in the morning for Ohio, and see uncle, and ask him to arrange it. I am sure he can." This was done. Of course her visit was successful—where did she ever fail?

The money was procured, paid over; ten shares of Adams Express Company stock was mine; but no one knew our little home had been mortgaged "to give our boy a start."

Adams Express stock then paid monthly dividends of one per cent, and the first check for five dollars arrived. I can see it now, and I well remember the signature of "J. C. Babcock, Cashier," who wrote a big "John Hancock" hand.

The next day being Sunday, we boys—myself and my ever-constant companions—took our usual Sunday afternoon stroll in the country, and sitting down in the woods, I showed them this check, saying, "Eureka! We have found it."

Here was something new to all of us, for none of us had ever received anything but from toil. A return from capital was something strange and new.

How money could make money, how, without any attention from me, this mysterious golden visitor should come, led to much speculation upon the part of the young fellows, and I was for the first time hailed as a "capitalist."

You see, I was beginning to serve my apprenticeship as a business man in a satisfactory manner.

A very important incident in my life occurred when, one day in a train, a nice, farmer-looking gentleman approached me, saying that the conductor had told him I was connected with the Pennsylvania Railroad, and he would like to show me something. He pulled from a small green bag the model of the first sleeping-car. This was Mr. Woodruff, the inventor.

Its value struck me like a flash. I asked him to come to Altoona the following week, and he did so. Mr Scott, with his usual quickness, grasped the idea. A contract was made with Mr. Woodruff to put two trial cars on the Pennsylvania Railroad. Before leaving Altoona Mr. Woodruff came and offered me an interest in the venture, which I promptly accepted. But how I was to make my payments rather troubled me, for the cars were to be paid for in monthly instalments after delivery, and my first monthly payment was to be two hundred and seventeen dollars and a half.

I had not the money, and I did not see any way of getting it. But I finally decided to visit the local banker and ask him for a loan, pledging myself to repay at the rate of fifteen dollars per month. He promptly granted it. Never shall I forget his putting his arm over my shoulder, saying, "Oh, yes, Andy; you are all right!"

I then and there signed my first note. Proud day this; and surely now no one will dispute that I was becoming a "business man." I had signed my first note, and, most important of all,—for any fellow can sign a note,—I had found a banker willing to take it as "good."

My subsequent payments were made by the receipts from the sleeping-cars, and I really made my first considerable sum from this investment in the Woodruff Sleeping-car Company, which was afterward absorbed by Mr. Pullman—a remarkable man whose name is now known over all the world.

Shortly after this I was appointed superintendent of the Pittsburg division, and returned to my dear old home, smoky Pittsburg. Wooden bridges were then used exclusively upon the railways, and the Pennsylvania Railroad was experimenting with a bridge built of cast-iron. I saw that wooden bridges would not do for the future, and organized a company in Pittsburg to build iron bridges.

Here again I had recourse to the bank, because my share of the capital was twelve hundred and fifty dollars, and I had not the money; but the bank lent it to me, and we began the Keystone Bridge Works, which proved a great success. This company built the first great bridge over the Ohio River, three hundred feet span, and has built many of the most important structures since.

This was my beginning in manufacturing; and from that start all our other works have grown, the profits of one building the other. My "apprenticeship" as a business man soon ended, for I resigned my position as an officer of the Pennsylvania Railroad Company to give exclusive attention to business.

I was no longer merely an official working for others upon a salary, but a full-fledged business man working upon my own account.

I never was quite reconciled to working for other people. At the most, the railway officer has to look forward to the enjoyment of a stated salary, and he has a great many people to please; even if he gets to be president, he has sometimes a board of directors who cannot know what is best to be done; and even if this board be satisfied, he has a board of stockholders to criticize him, and as the property is not his own he cannot manage it as he pleases.

I always liked the idea of being my own master, of manufacturing something and giving employment to many men. There is only one thing to think of manufacturing if you are a Pittsburger, for Pittsburg even then had asserted her supremacy as the "Iron City," the leading iron-and-steel-manufacturing city in America.

So my indispensable and clever partners, who had been my boy companions, I am delighted to say,—some of the very boys who had met in the grove to wonder at the five-dollar check,—began business, and still continue extending it to meet the ever-growing and ever-changing wants of our most progressive country, year after year.

Always we are hoping that we need expand no farther; yet ever we are finding that to stop expanding would be to fall behind; and even to-day the successive improvements and inventions follow each other so rapidly that we see just as much yet to be done as ever.

When the manufacturer of steel ceases to grow he begins to decay, so we must keep on extending. The result of all these developments is that three pounds of finished steel are now bought in Pittsburg for two cents, which is cheaper than anywhere else on the earth, and that our country has become the greatest producer of iron in the world.

And so ends the story of my apprenticeship and graduation as a business man.

THEODORE DREISER
They Could Not Organize Then, and They Are Not Organized Now

In 1894 a young newspaper reporter, Theodore Dreiser (1871–1945), went to work for the Pittsburgh Dispatch. He visited the steel milling districts about

REPRINTED by permission of The World Publishing Company from *A Book About Myself*, by Theodore Dreiser, pp. 399–405. Copyright © 1922 by Boni & Liveright, Inc., 1949 by Mrs. Theodore Dreiser.

the city, controlled by Andrew Carnegie, and saw the effects of the bloody Homestead strikes of two years before, in which Pinkerton detectives and 8,000 National Guard troops had broken up an attempt by the Amalgamated Association of Iron and Steel Workers to organize the steel workers. Dreiser later went on to New York City, and in 1900 published Sister Carrie, *his first novel. In 1922 he published* A Book About Myself, *in which he described his stay in Pittsburgh.*

I went with him first to Homestead, then to some tenements there, later to some other mill districts nearer Pittsburgh, the names of which I have forgotten. What astonished me, in so far as the steel mills were concerned, was the large number of furnaces going at once, the piles, mountains, of powdered iron ore ready to be smelted, the long lines of cars, flat, box and coal cars, and the nature and size and force of the machinery used to roll steel. The work, as he or his friends the bosses showed me, was divided between the "front" and the "back." Those working at the front of the furnace took care of the molten ore and slag which was being "puddled." The men at the back, the stock and yard men, filled huge steel buckets or "skips" suspended from traveling cranes with ore, fuel and limestone, all of which was piled near at hand; this material was then trundled to a point over the mouth of the melting-vats, as they were called, and "released" via a movable bottom. At this particular plant I was told that the machinery for handling all this was better than elsewhere, the company being richer and more progressive. In some of the less progressive concerns the men filled carts with raw material and then trundled them around to the front of a hoist, which was at the back of the furnace, where they were lifted and dumped into the furnaces. But in this mill all a man had to do to fill a steel bucket with raw material was to push one of those steel buckets suspended from a trolley under a chute and pull a rod, when the "stock" tumbled into it. From these it was trundled, by machinery, to a point over the furnace. The furnaces were charged or fed constantly by feeders working in twelve-hour shifts, so that there was little chance to rest from their labors. Their pay was not more than half of that paid to the men at the "front" because it was neither so hard nor so skillful, although it looked hard enough to me.

The men at the front, the puddlers, were the labor princes of this realm and yet among the hardest worked. A puddling or blast furnace was a brick structure like an oven, about seven feet high and six feet square, with two compartments, one a receptacle into which pigiron was thrown, the other a fuel chamber where the melting heat was generated. The drafts were so arranged that the flame swept from the fuel chamber directly upon the surface of the iron. From five to six hundred pounds of pigiron were put into each furnace at one time, after which it was closed and sufficient heat applied to melt down the iron. Then the puddler began to work it with an iron rod through a hole in the furnace door, so as to stir up the liquid and bring it in contact with the air. As the impurities became separated from the iron and rose to the top as slag, they were tipped out through a center notch. As it became freer from impurities, a constantly higher temperature was required to keep the iron in a liquid condition. Gradually it began to solidify in granules, much as butter forms in churning. Later it took on or was worked into large malleable balls or lumps or rolls like butter, three to any given "charge" or furnace. Then, while still in a comparatively soft but not molten condition, these were taken out and thrown across a steel floor to a "taker" to be worked by other machinery and other processes.

Puddling was a full-sized man's job. There were always two, and sometimes three, to a single furnace, and they took turns at working the metal, as a rule ten minutes to a turn. No man could stand before a furnace and perform that backbreaking toil continually. Even when working by spells a man was often nearly exhausted at the end of his spell. As a rule he had to go outside and sit on a bench, the perspiration running off him. The intensity of the heat in those days (1893) was not as yet relieved by the device of shielding the furnace with water-cooled plates. The wages of these men was in the neighborhood of three dollars a day, the highest then paid. Before the great strike it had been more.

But the men who most fascinated me were the "roughers" who, once the puddler had done his work and thrown his lump of red-hot iron out upon an open hearth, and another man had taken it and thrown it to a "rougher," fed it into a second machine which rolled or beat it into a more easily handled and workable form. The exact details of the process escape me now, but I remember the picture they presented in those hot, fire-lighted, noisy and sputtering rooms. Agility and even youth were at a premium, and a false step possibly meant death. I remember watching two men in the mill below Mt. Washington, one who pulled out billet after billet from furnace after furnace and threw them along the steel floor to the "rougher," and the latter, who, dressed only in trousers and a sleeveless flannel shirt, the sweat pouring from his body and his muscles standing out in knots, took these same and, with the skill and agility of a tight-rope performer, tossed them into the machine. He was constantly leaping about thrusting the red billets which came almost in a stream into or between the first pair of rolls for which they were intended. And yet before he could turn back there was always another on the floor behind him. The rolls into which he fed these billets were built in a train, side by side in line, and as they went through one pair they had to be seized by a "catcher" and shoved back through the next. Back and forth, back and forth they went at an ever increasing speed, until the catcher at the next to the last pair of rolls, seizing the end of the rod as it came through, still red-hot, described with it a fiery circle bending it back again to enter the last roll, from which it passed into water. It was wonderful.

And yet these men were not looked upon as anything extraordinary. While the places in which they worked were metal infernos and their toil of the most intense and exacting character, they were not allowed to organize to better their condition. The recent great victory of the steel magnates had settled that. In that very city and elsewhere, these magnates were rolling in wealth. Their profits were tumbling in so fast that they scarcely knew what to do with them. Vast libraries and universities were being built with their gifts. Immense mansions were crowded with art and historic furniture. Their children were being sent to special schools to be taught how to be ladies and gentlemen in a democracy which they condemned; and on the other hand, these sweating men were being denied an additional five or ten cents an hour and the right to organize. If they protested or attempted to drive out imported strike-breakers they were fired and State or Federal troops were called in to protect the mills. They could not organize then, and they are not organized now.

My friend Martyn, who was intensely sympathetic toward them, was still more sympathetic toward the men who were not so skillful, mere day laborers who received from one dollar to one-sixty-five at a time when two a day was too little to support any one. He grew melodramatic as he told me where these men lived and how they lived, and finally took me in order that I might see for myself. Afterward, in the course of my reportorial work, I came upon some of these neighborhoods and individuals, and since they are all a part of the great fortune-building era, and illustrate how democracy works in America, and how some great fortunes were built, I propose to put down here a few pictures of things that I saw. Wages varied from one to one-sixty-five a day for the commonest laborer, three and even four a day for the skilled worker. Rents, or what the cheaper workers, who constituted by far the great number, were able to pay, varied from two-fifteen per week, or eight-sixty per month, to four-seventy-two per week, or twenty per month.

And the type of places they could secure for this! I recall visiting a two-room tenement in a court, the character of which first opened my eyes to the type of home these workers endured. This court consisted of four sides with an open space in the center. Three of these sides were smoke-grimed wooden houses three stories in height; the fourth was an ancient and odorous wooden stable, where the horses of a contractor were kept. In the center of this court stood a circular wooden building or lavatory with ten triangular compartments, each opening into one vault or cesspool. Near this was one hydrant, the only water-supply for all these homes or rooms. These two conveniences served twenty families, Polish, Hungarian, Slavonic, Jewish, Negro, of from three to five people each, living in the sixty-three rooms which made up the three grimy sides above mentioned. There were twenty-seven children in these rooms, for whom this court was their only playground. For twenty housewives this was the only place where they could string their wash-lines. For twenty tired, sweaty, unwashed husbands this was, aside from the saloon, the only near and neighborly recreation and companionship center. Here of a sweltering summer night, after playing cards and drinking beer, they would frequently stretch themselves to sleep.

But this was not all. As waste pipes were wanting in the houses, heavy tubs of water had to be carried in and out, and this in a smoky town where a double amount of washing and cleaning was necessary. When the weather permitted, the heavy washes were done in the yard. Then the pavement of this populous court, covered with tubs, wringers, clothes baskets and pools of soapy water, made a poor playground for children. In addition to this, these lavatories must be used, and in consequence a situation was created which may be better imagined than explained. Many of the front windows of these apartments looked down on this center, which was only a few yards from the kitchen windows, creating a neat, sanitary and uplifting condition. While usually only two families used one of these compartments, in some other courts three or four families were compelled to use one, giving rise to indifference and a sense of irresponsibility for their condition. While all the streets had sewers and by borough ordinance these outside vaults must be connected with them, still most of them were flushed only by waste water, which flowed directly into them from the yard faucet. When conditions became unbearable the vaults were washed out with a hose attached to the hydrant, but in winter, when there was danger of freezing, this was not always possible. There was not one indoor closet in any of these courts.

But to return to the apartment in question. The kitchen was steaming with vapor from a big washtub set on a chair in the middle of the room. The mother, who had carried the water in, was trying to wash and at the same time keep the older of her two babies from tumbling into the tub of scalding water that was standing on the floor. On one side of the room was a huge puffy bed, with one feather tick to sleep on and another for covering. Near the window was a sewing-machine, in a corner a melodeon, and of course there was the inevitable cookstove, upon which was simmering a pot of soup. To the left, in the second room, were one boarder and the man of the house asleep. Two boarders, so I learned, were at work, but at night would be home to sleep in the bed now occupied by one boarder and the man of the house. The little family and their boaders, taken to help out on the rent, worked and lived so in order that Mr. Carnegie might give the world one or two extra libraries with his name plastered on the front, and Mr. Frick a mansion on Fifth Avenue.

It was to Martyn and his interest that I owed still other views. He took me one day to a boardinghouse in which lived twenty-four people, all in two rooms, and yet, to my astonishment and confusion, it was not so bad as that other court, so great apparently is the value of intimate human contact. Few of the very poor day laborers, as Martyn explained to me, who were young and unmarried, cared how they lived so long as they lived cheaply and could save a little. This particular boardinghouse in Homestead was in a court such as I have described, and consisted of two rooms, one above the other, each measuring perhaps 12x20. In the kitchen at the time was the wife of the boarding boss cooking dinner. Along one side of the room was an oilcloth-covered table with a plank bench on each side; above it was a rack holding a long row of white cups, and a shelf with tin knives and forks. Near the up-to-date range, the only real piece of furniture in the room, hung the buckets in which all mill men carried their noon or midnight meals. A crowd of men were lounging cheerfully about, talking, smoking and enjoying life, one of them playing a concertina. They were making the most of a brief spell before their meal and departure for work. In the room above, as the landlord cheerfully showed us, were double iron bedsteads set close together and on them comfortables neatly laid.

In these two rooms lived, besides the boarding boss and his wife, both stalwart Bulgarians, and their two babies, twenty men. They were those who handled steel billets and bars, unloaded and loaded trains, worked in cinder pits, filled steel buckets with stock, and what not. They all worked twelve hours a day, and their reward was this and what they could save over and above it out of nine-sixty per week. Martyn said a good thing about them at the time: "I don't know how it is. I know these people are exploited and mis-used. The mill-owners pay them the lowest wages, the landlords exploit these boardinghouse keepers as well as their boarders, and the community which they make by their work don't give a damn for them, and yet they are happy, and I'll be hanged if they don't make me happy. It must be that just work is happiness," and I agreed with him. Plenty of work, something to do, the ability to avoid the ennui of idleness and useless, pensive, futile thought! . . .

10

POPULIST
AND LABOR UNREST

Prices maintained a high level for several years following the Civil War; then they began falling. In the Midwest and the South the drop in farm prices meant widespread misery. Farms were mortgaged; further declines brought sweeping foreclosures. Railroads, upon which farmers were dependent to carry their crops to market, charged discriminatory rates. Money was scarce, bank rates were appallingly high. Eventually farmers began to organize politically, first as Grangers, then as Populists. They captured control of the legislatures of various states, and enacted laws regulating railroad rates and limiting bank interest; in many instances the United States Supreme Court declared such laws unconstitutional. In 1891 farmers, workers and small businessmen organized a third party, the Populist Party; in the election of the next year the Populist candidate received more than a million popular and 22 electoral votes, carrying four states.

Meanwhile, in the large cities, living conditions were crowded and unsanitary, slums were everywhere, and wages were low. In many instances large industrial concerns reduced wages, and attempts at protest were met with armed strikebreakers and importation of immigrant laborers. On several occasions the federal government intervened with troops to protect the property of factory owners against the actions of striking workmen. Labor unions, in particular the Knights of Labor, sought to organize workers, but were bitterly combatted. By 1896, when William Jennings Bryan received the Democratic nomination for President against Republican William McKinley, conditions were very bad.

Then rising farm prices and wages and greater prosperity in the late 1890's began easing matters, and a further crisis was averted.

The selections that follow illustrate the nature of farm and labor protest during the 1890's.

POPULIST PARTY
A Vast Conspiracy Against Mankind

In 1892 the Populist Party nominated James B. Weaver of Iowa for President and James G. Field of Virginia for Vice-President. They campaigned on a party platform written by Ignatius Donnelly (1831–1901), a politician and newspaper editor who during the previous decade had also published several novels. The Populist platform called for free coinage of silver at a ratio of 16 to 1 with gold; a national currency issued by the federal government only; government ownership of all transportation and communication lines; a graduated income tax; a postal savings system; direct election of U.S. Senators; a shorter working day for industry; and restrictions on further immigration. Many of these highly "radical" demands have long since become law.

Assembled upon the 116th anniversary of the Declaration of Independence, the People's Party of America, in their first national convention, invoking upon their action the blessing of Almighty God, put forth in the name and on behalf of the people of this country, the following preamble and declaration of principles:

Preamble

The conditions which surround us best justify our co-operation; we meet in the midst of a nation brought to the verge of moral, political, and material ruin. Corruption dominates the ballot-box, the Legislatures, the Congress, and touches even the ermine of the bench. The people are demoralized; most of the States have been compelled to isolate the voters at the polling places to prevent universal intimidation and bribery. The newspapers are largely subsidized or muzzled, public opinion silenced, business prostrated, homes covered with mortgages, labor impoverished, and the land concentrating in the hands of capitalists. The urban workmen are denied the right to organize for self-protection, imported pauperized labor beats down their wages, a hireling standing army, unrecognized by our laws, is established to shoot them down, and they are rapidly degenerating into European conditions. The fruits of the

FROM "Populist Party Platform," *The World Almanac for 1893* (New York: The Press Publishing Co., 1893), pp. 83–85.

toil of millions are boldly stolen to build up colossal fortunes for a few, unprecedented in the history of mankind; and the possessors of these, in turn, despise the Republic and endanger liberty. From the same prolific womb of governmental injustice we breed the two great classes—tramps and millionaires.

The national power to create money is appropriated to enrich bond-holders; a vast public debt payable in legal-tender currency has been funded into gold-bearing bonds, thereby adding millions to the burdens of the people.

Silver, which has been accepted as coin since the dawn of history, has been demonetized to add to the purchasing power of gold by decreasing the value of all forms of property as well as human labor, and the supply of currency is purposely abridged to fatten usurers, bankrupt enterprise, and enslave industry. A vast conspiracy against mankind has been organized on two continents, and it is rapidly taking possession of the world. If not met and overthrown at once it forebodes terrible social convulsions, the destruction of civilization, or the establishment of an absolute despotism.

We have witnessed for more than a quarter of a century the struggles of the two great political parties for power and plunder, while grievous wrongs have been inflicted upon the suffering people. We charge that the controlling influences dominating both these parties have permitted the existing dreadful conditions to develop without serious effort to prevent or restrain them. Neither do they now promise us any substantial reform. They have agreed together to ignore, in the coming campaign, every issue but one. They propose to drown the outcries of a plundered people with the uproar of a sham battle over the tariff, so that capitalists, corporations, national banks, rings, trusts, watered stock, the demonetization of silver and the oppressions of the usurers may all be lost sight of. They propose to sacrifice our homes, lives, and children on the altar of mammon; to destroy the multitude in order to secure corruption funds from the millionaires.

Assembled on the anniversary of the birthday of the nation, and filled with the spirit of the grand general and chief who established our independence, we seek to restore the government of the Republic to the hands of the "plain people," with which class it originated. We assert our purposes to be identical with the purposes of the National Constitution; to form a more perfect union and establish justice, insure domestic tranquillity, provide for the common defence, promote the general welfare, and secure the blessings of liberty for ourselves and our posterity.

We declare that this Republic can only endure as a free government while built upon the love of the people for each other and for the nation; that it cannot be pinned together by bayonets; that the Civil War is over, and that every passion and resentment which grew out of it must die with it, and that we must be in fact, as we are in name, one united brotherhood of free men.

Our country finds itself confronted by conditions for which there is no precedent in the history of the world; our annual agricultural productions amount to billions of dollars in value, which must, within a few weeks or months, be exchanged for billions of dollars' worth of commodities consumed in their production; the existing currency supply is wholly inadequate to make this exchange; the results are falling prices, the formation of combines and rings, the impoverishment of the producing class. We pledge ourselves that if given power we will labor to correct these evils by wise and reasonable legislation, in accordance with the terms of our platform.

We believe that the power of government—in other words, of the people—should be expanded (as in the case of the postal service) as rapidly and as far as the good sense of an intelligent people and the teachings of experience shall justify, to the end that oppression, injustice, and poverty shall eventually cease in the land.

While our sympathies as a party of reform are naturally upon the side of every proposition which will tend to make men intelligent, virtuous, and temperate, we nevertheless regard these questions, important as they are, as secondary to the great issues now pressing for solution, and upon which not only our individual prosperity but the very existence of free institutions depend; and we ask all men to first help us to determine whether we are to have a republic to administer before we differ as to the conditions upon which it is to be administered, believing that the forces of reform this day organized will never cease to move forward until every wrong is righted and equal rights and equal privileges securely established for all the men and women of this country.

Platform

We declare, therefore—

First.—That the union of the labor forces of the United States this day consummated shall be permanent and perpetual; may its spirit enter into all hearts for the salvation of the Republic and the uplifting of mankind.

Second.—Wealth belongs to him who creates it, and every dollar taken from industry without an equivalent is robbery. "If any will not work, neither shall he eat." The interests of rural and civil labor are the same; their enemies are identical.

Third.—We believe that the time has come when the railroad corporations will either own the people or the people must own the railroads; and should the government enter upon the work of owning and managing all railroads, we should favor an amendment to the constitution by which all persons engaged in the government service shall be placed under a civil-service regulation of the most rigid character, so as to prevent the increase of the power of the national administration by the use of such additional government employes.

Finance.—We demand a national currency, safe, sound, and flexible issued by the general government only, a full legal tender for all debts, public and private, and that without the use of banking corporations; a just, equitable, and efficient means of distribution direct to the people, at a tax not to exceed

2 per cent per annum, to be provided as set forth in the sub-treasury plan of the Farmers' Alliance, or a better system; also by payments in discharge of its obligations for public improvements.

1. We demand free and unlimited coinage of silver and gold at the present legal ratio of 16 to 1.

2. We demand that the amount of circulating medium be speedily increased to not less than $50 per capita.

3. We demand a graduated income tax.

4. We believe that the money of the country should be kept as much as possible in the hands of the people, and hence we demand that all State and national revenues shall be limited to the necessary expenses of the government, economically and honestly administered.

5. We demand that postal savings banks be established by the government for the safe deposit of the earnings of the people and to facilitate exchange.

Transportation.—Transportation being a means of exchange and a public necessity, the government should own and operate the railroads in the interest of the people. The telegraph and telephone, like the post-office system, being a necessity for the transmission of news, should be owned and operated by the government in the interest of the people.

Land.—The land, including all the natural sources of wealth, is the heritage of the people, and should not be monopolized for speculative purposes, and alien ownership of land should be prohibited. All land now held by railroads and other corporations in excess of their actual needs, and all lands now owned by aliens should be reclaimed by the government and held for actual settlers only.

Expression of Sentiments

Your Committee on Platform and Resolutions beg leave unanimously to report the following:

Whereas, Other questions have been presented for our consideration, we hereby submit the following, not as a part of the Platform of the People's Party, but as resolutions expressive of the sentiment of this Convention:

1. *Resolved,* That we demand a free ballot and a fair count in all elections, and pledge ourselves to secure it to every legal voter without Federal intervention, through the adoption by the States of the unperverted Australian or secret ballot system.

2. *Resolved,* That the revenue derived from a graduated income tax should be applied to the reduction of the burden of taxation now levied upon the domestic industries of this country.

3. *Resolved,* That we pledge our support to fair and liberal pensions to ex-Union soldiers and sailors.

4. *Resolved,* That we condemn the fallacy of protecting American labor under the present system, which opens our ports to the pauper and criminal

classes of the world and crowds out our wage-earners; and we denounce the present ineffective laws against contract labor, and demand the further restriction of undesirable emigration.

5. *Resolved,* That we cordially sympathize with the efforts of organized workingmen to shorten the hours of labor, and demand a rigid enforcement of the existing eight-hour law on Government work, and ask that a penalty clause be added to the said law.

6. *Resolved,* That we regard the maintenance of a large standing army of mercenaries, known as the Pinkerton system, as a menace to our liberties, and we demand its abolition; and we condemn the recent invasion of the Territory of Wyoming by the hired assassins of plutocracy, assisted by Federal Officers.

7. *Resolved,* That we commend to the favorable consideration of the people and the reform press the legislative system known as the initiative and referendum.

8. *Resolved,* That we favor a constitutional provision limiting the office of President and Vice-President to one term, and providing for the election of Senators of the United States by a direct vote of the people.

9. *Resolved,* That we oppose any subsidy or national aid to any private corporation for any purpose.

10. *Resolved,* That this convention sympathizes with the Knights of Labor and their righteous contest with the tyrannical combine of clothing manufacturers of Rochester, and declare it to be a duty of all who hate tyranny and oppression to refuse to purchase the goods made by the said manufacturers, or to patronize any merchants who sell such goods.

EUGENE V. DEBS
I Answer a Thousand Times, NO!

The efforts of working men's organizations to press demands against industrial concerns for better pay and more favorable working conditions were savagely resisted. In late June, 1894, the American Railway Union, under Eugene V. Debs (1855–1926), went on strike with a boycott on Pullman cars, tying up all middle-western railroads, and 3,400 men were sworn in as special deputies to keep trains running. When violence broke out, President Grover Cleveland sent federal troops to restore order, safeguard the mail, and protect interstate commerce. On July 2 an injunction was issued by a federal court, forbidding interference with the mails or with interstate commerce. Debs was jailed for contempt of court, and the strike was broken. Deb's proclamation the next summer, when the U.S. Supreme Court affirmed his jail sentence and thus

FROM "Proclamation to American Railway Union," in *The New York Times* (June 3, 1895).

legalized the granting of injunctions for strike-breaking, called upon "the members of the American Railway Union to stand by their order. In God's own good time we will make the despot's prison, where innocent men suffer, monumental." The proclamation follows. Debs' life and personality are vividly depicted in John Dos Passos' U.S.A.

Terre Haute, Ind., June 1, 1895.

Sirs and Brothers—A cruel wrong against our great and beloved order, perpetrated by Wm. A. Woods, United States Circuit Judge, has been approved by the United States Supreme Court, and from under its shadow I address this communication to you; but though prison walls frown upon myself and others whom you chose as officials, I assure you that neither despondency nor despair has taken the place of the courage which has characterized us and our order since the storms of persecution first began to beat upon us. Hope has not deserted us. Our faith in the future of our great order is as strong as when our banners waved triumphantly over the Great Northern from St. Paul to the coast. Our order is still the undaunted friend of the toiling masses and our battle-cry now, as ever, is the emancipation of labor from degrading, starving and enslaving conditions. We have not lost faith in the ultimate triumph of truth over perjury, of justice over wrong, however exalted may be the stations of those who perpetrate the outrages.

I need not remind you, comrades of the American Railway Union, that our order in the pursuit of the right was confronted with a storm of opposition such as never beat upon a labor organization in all time. Its brilliant victory on the Great Northern and its gallant championship of the unorganized employes of the Union Pacific had aroused the opposition of every railroad corporation in the land.

To crush the American Railway Union was the one tie that united them all in the bonds of vengeance; it solidified the enemies of labor into one great association, one organization which, by its fabulous wealth, enabled it to bring into action resources aggregating billions of money and every appliance that money could purchase. But in this supreme hour the American Railway Union, undaunted, put forth its efforts to rescue Pullman's famine-cursed wage slaves from the grasp of an employer as heartless as a stone, as remorseless as a savage and as unpitying as an incarnate fiend. The battle fought in the interest of starving men, women and children stands forth in the history of Labor's struggles as the great "Pullman Strike." It was a battle on the part of the American Railway Union fought for a cause as holy as ever aroused the courage of brave men; it was a battle in which upon one side were men thrice armed because their cause was just, but they fought against the combined power of corporations which by the use of money could debauch justice, and, by playing the part of incendiary, bring to their aid the military power of the government, and this solidified mass of venality, venom and vengeance constituted the foe against which the American Railway Union fought Labor's greatest battle for humanity.

What has been your reward for your splendid courage and manifold sacrifices? Our enemies say they are summed up in the one word "defeat." They point to the battlefield and say: "Here is where the host of the American Railway Union went down before the confederated enemy of labor." They point to the spot where Miles' serried soldiery stood with drawn swords, tramping steeds and shotted guns to kill innocent men whose only crime was devotion to wretched men and women, the victims of Pullman's greed. They designate the places where the minions of a despotic judge, the thieves and thugs, taken from Chicago slums, transformed into deputy marshals and armed with clubs and pistols, went forth to murder indiscriminately and to arouse the vengeance of the people by incendiary fires, and they point to the General Managers' Association, the Nero of the occasion, whose pitiless enmity of labor would have glorified in widespread conflagration rather than permitted a strike in the interest of famishing men, women and children, to have succeeded; and such disasters, say the enemies of labor, are the rewards of the courage of the A.R.U. men, a courage as invincible as was ever displayed by Spartans, and which makes Pullman's Labor Thermopylæ to live in history as long as the right has a defender in the ranks of American workingmen.

Brothers of the American Railway Union, even in defeat our rewards are grand beyond expression, rewards which come only to brave men, the consciousness of noble deeds performed in the holy cause of labor's emancipation. Cowards, the fawning, sycophantic poltroons of power, never knew the thrills of joy that reward the heroes of battle fought in the interest of the oppressed.

> Once to ev'ry man and nation comes a moment to decide,
> In the strife of Truth and Falsehood, for the good or evil side.

The American Railway Union did decide. It espoused the cause of justice. It furrowed the land deeper with its plows of Truth and Courage than had fallen to the lot of any other labor organization since time began, and the seeds of emancipation which it sowed broadcast are germinating and a new era is destined to dawn upon labor.

Truth it is that the "Sons of brutish Force and Darkness," who have "drenched the earth with blood," chuckle over their victories. They point to the black-listed heroes of the American Railway Union, idle and poor, and count upon their surrender. Their hope is that our order will disband; that persecution, poverty and prison will do the work. These gory-handed enemies of our order expect to put out our lodge fires, silence our battle cries, disrobe ourselves of courage and manhood, permit them to place their ironshod hoofs on our neck and sink us to fathomless depths of degradation and make the American Railway Union the synonym of all things the most detestable.

Can they do it? In the presence of prison doors and prison bars and weary months of incarceration. I answer a thousand times, NO! In the grasp of despotic power, as infamous and as cruel as ever blackened the records of Russia, I treat with ineffable scorn the power that without trial sends me and my official associates of the American Railway Union to prison. I do not believe, nor will I believe, that my brothers, beloved of our great order, will throw their courage away and join the ranks of the enemy, while their comrades, the victims of worse than Russian vengeance, are suffering in prison.

In Russia, the land of the autocrat, liberty is unknown. In that thrice damned country liberty and justice, free speech and free press and trial by jury are banished, and a trail of blood and tears from the palace of the despot to prison and to death, made by men and women whose only crime is a desire for freedom, tell their doom; and yet in Russia imprisonment, torture and death only increase the ranks of men and women who cry, "Give me liberty or give me death."

In Russia, the victim of autocratic displeasure is denied a trial by a jury of his peers. Wm. A. Woods carries out the Russian practice. In Russia the doomed man or woman is arraigned before the supreme despot or one of his numerous satraps. Truth, justice, mercy are forever exiled, hope disappears and only words of satanic cruelty are uttered. Age, sex, character, innocence, name and condition count for nothing. It is enough to know that the brave soul yearned for freedom, and the penalty of exile, imprisonment, torture or death is inflicted, and it has come to this at last in the United States of America, that the law of injunction is the will of a despot, and by the exercise of this Russian power American Railway Union officials go to prison and the hope is that by the exercising of this power the American Railway Union will be crushed.

At this supreme juncture I call upon the members of the American Railway Union to stand by their order. In God's own good time we will make the despot's prison, where innocent men suffer, monumental. We will link them with the legends and lore of labor's struggles to be read by our children and our children's children when Bartholdi's goddess of liberty with her torch enlightening the world has succumbed to the ravages of time.

> Count me o'er earth's chosen heroes—they were souls that stood alone.
> (While the men they agonized for threw the contumelious stone)
> Stood serene and down the future saw the golden beam incline
> To the side of perfect justice, mastered by their faith divine.
> By one man's plain truth to manhood and to God's supreme design.

WILLIAM JENNINGS BRYAN
You Shall Not Crucify Mankind
Upon a Cross of Gold

In 1896 the Populists appeared to have captured the Democratic Party. They nominated for president a Nebraska Congressman, William Jennings Bryan (1860–1925), after his electrifying speech on the wording of the party platform plank regarding the free coinage of silver. Bryan ran for President three times, but never came closer to winning than in 1896. In the long run, some historians contend, Bryan's nomination meant that the Democratic Party had subsumed the Populists, rather than vice versa. Bryan remained a vocal figure in American political life for thirty more years, but he never again attained the oratorical heights reached in the peroration to his famous "Cross of Gold" speech, given below. The poet Vachel Lindsay has depicted Bryan's impact in his poem, "Bryan, Bryan, Bryan, Bryan."

Mr. Chairman and Gentlemen of the Convention: I would be presumptuous, indeed, to present myself against the distinguished gentlemen to whom you have listened if this were a mere measuring of abilities; but this is not a contest between persons. The humblest citizen in all the land, when clad in the armor of a righteous cause, is stronger than all the hosts of error. I come to speak to you in defense of a cause as holy as the cause of liberty—the cause of humanity.

When this debate is concluded, a motion will be made to lay upon the table the resolution offered in commendation of the administration, and also the resolution offered in condemnation of the administration. We object to bringing this question down to the level of persons. The individual is but an atom; he is born, he acts, he dies; but principles are eternal; and this has been a contest over a principle.

Never before in the history of this country has there been witnessed such a contest as that through which we have just passed. Never before in the history of American politics has a great issue been fought out as this issue has been, by the voters of a great party. On the fourth of March, 1895, a few Democrats, most of them members of Congress, issued an address to the Democrats of the nation, asserting that the money question was the paramount issue of the hour; declaring that a majority of the Democratic party had the right to control the action of the party on this paramount issue; and concluding with

FROM *The First Battle*, by William J. Bryan (Chicago: W. B. Conkey Co., 1896), pp. 199–206.

the request that the believers in the free coinage of silver in the Democratic party should organize, take charge of, and control the policy of the Democratic party. Three months later, at Memphis, an organization was perfected, and the silver Democrats went forth openly and courageously proclaiming their belief, and declaring that, if successful, they would crystallize into a platform the declaration which they had made. Then began the conflict. With a zeal approaching the zeal which inspired the crusaders who followed Peter the Hermit, our silver Democrats went forth from victory unto victory until they are now assembled, not to discuss, not to debate, but to enter up the judgment already rendered by the plain people of this country. In this contest brother has been arrayed against brother, father against son. The warmest ties of love, acquaintance and association have been disregarded; old leaders have been cast aside when they have refused to give expression to the sentiments of those whom they would lead, and new leaders have sprung up to give direction to this cause of truth. Thus has the contest been waged, and we have assembled here under as binding and solemn instructions as were ever imposed upon representatives of the people.

We do not come as individuals. As individuals we might have been glad to compliment the gentleman from New York (Senator Hill), but we know that the people for whom we speak would never be willing to put him in a position where he could thwart the will of the Democratic party. I say it was not a question of persons; it was a question of principle, and it is not with gladness, my friends, that we find ourselves brought into conflict with those who are now arrayed on the other side.

The gentleman who preceded me (ex-Governor Russell) spoke of the State of Massachusetts; let me assure him that not one present in all this convention entertains the least hostility to the people of the State of Massachusetts, but we stand here representing people who are the equals, before the law, of the greatest citizens in the State of Massachusetts. When you (turning to the gold delegates) come before us and tell us that we are about to disturb your business interests, we reply that you have disturbed our business interests by your course.

We say to you that you have made the definition of a business man too limited in its application. The man who is employed for wages is as much a business man as his employer; the attorney in a country town is as much a business man as the corporation counsel in a great metropolis; the merchant at the cross-roads store is as much a business man as the merchant of New York; the farmer who goes forth in the morning and toils all day—who begins in the spring and toils all summer—and who by the application of brain and muscle to the natural resources of the country creates wealth, is as much a business man as the man who goes upon the board of trade and bets upon the price of grain; the miners who go down a thousand feet into the earth, or climb two thousand feet upon the cliffs, and bring forth from their hiding places the precious metals to be poured into the channels of trade are as much business men as the few financial magnates who, in a back room, corner the money of the world. We come to speak for this broader class of business men.

Ah, my friends, we say not one word against those who live upon the Atlantic coast, but the hardy pioneers who have braved all the dangers of the wilderness, who have made the desert to blossom as the rose—the pioneers away out there (pointing to the West), who rear their children near to Nature's heart, where they can mingle their voices with the voices of the birds—out there where they have erected schoolhouses for the education of their young, churches where they praise their Creator, and cemeteries where rest the ashes of their dead—these people, we say, are as deserving of the consideration of our party as any people in this country. It is for these that we speak. We do not come as aggressors. Our war is not a war of conquest; we are fighting in the defense of our homes, our families, and posterity. We have petitioned, and our petitions have been scorned; we have entreated, and our entreaties have been disregarded; we have begged, and they have mocked when our calamity came. We beg no longer; we entreat no more; we petition no more. We defy them.

The gentleman from Wisconsin has said that he fears a Robespierre. My friends, in this land of the free you need not fear that a tyrant will spring up from among the people. What we need is an Andrew Jackson to stand, as Jackson stood, against the encroachments of organized wealth.

They tell us that this platform was made to catch votes. We reply to them that changing conditions make new issues; that the principles upon which Democracy rests are as everlasting as the hills, but that they must be applied to new conditions as they arise. Conditions have arisen, and we are here to meet those conditions. They tell us that the income tax ought not to be brought in here; that it is a new idea. They criticise us for our criticism of the Supreme Court of the United States. My friends, we have not criticised; we have simply called attention to what you already know. If you want criticisms, read the dissenting opinions of the court. There you will find criticisms. They say that we passed an unconstitutional law; we deny it. The income tax law was not unconstitutional when it was passed; it was not unconstitutional when it went before the Supreme Court for the first time; it did not become unconstitutional until one of the judges changed his mind, and we cannot be expected to know when a judge will change his mind. The income tax is just. It simply intends to put the burdens of government justly upon the backs of the people. I am in favor of an income tax. When I find a man who is not willing to bear his share of the burdens of the government which protects him, I find a man who is unworthy to enjoy the blessings of a government like ours.

They say that we are opposing national bank currency; it is true. If you will read what Thomas Benton said, you will find he said that, in searching history, he could find but one parallel to Andrew Jackson; that was Cicero, who destroyed the conspiracy of Cataline and saved Rome. Benton said that Cicero only did for Rome what Jackson did for us when he destroyed the bank conspiracy and saved America. We say in our platform that we believe that the right to coin and issue money is a function of government. We believe it. We believe that it is a part of sovereignty, and can no more with safety be delegated to private individuals than we could afford to delegate to private individuals the power to make penal statutes or levy taxes. Mr. Jefferson, who was once regarded as good Democratic authority, seems to have differed in opinion from the gentleman who has addressed us on the part of the minority. Those who are opposed to this proposition tell us that the issue of paper money is a function of the bank, and that the Government ought to go out of the banking business. I stand with Jefferson rather than with them, and tell them, as he did, that the issue of money is a function of government, and that the banks ought to go out of the governing business. . . .

And now, my friends, let me come to the paramount issue. If they ask us why it is that we say more on the money question than we say upon the tariff question, I reply that, if protection has slain its thousands, the gold standard has slain its tens of thousands. If they ask us why we do not embody in our platform all the things that we believe in, we reply that when we have restored the money of the Constitution all other necessary reforms will be possible; but that until this is done there is no other reform that can be accomplished.

Why is it that within three months such a change has come over the country? Three months ago, when it was confidently asserted that those who believe in the gold standard would frame our platform and nominate our candidates, even the advocates of the gold standard did not think that we could elect a president. And they had good reason for their doubt, because there is scarcely a State here today asking for the gold standard which is not in the absolute control of the Republican party. But note the change. Mr. McKinley was nominated at St. Louis upon a platform which declared for the maintenance of the gold standard until it can be changed into bimetallism by international agreement. Mr. McKinley was the most popular man among the Republicans, and three months ago everybody in the Republican party prophesied his election. How is today? Why, the man who was once pleased to think that he looked like Napoleon—that man shudders today when he remembers that he was nominated on the anniversary of the battle of Waterloo. Not only that, but as he listens he can hear with ever-increasing distinctness the sound of the waves as they beat upon the lonely shores of St. Helena.

Why this change? Ah, my friends, is not the reason for the change evident to any one who will look at the matter? No private character, however pure, no personal popularity, however great, can protect from the avenging wrath of an indignant people a man who will declare that he is in favor of fastening the gold standard upon this country, or who is willing to surrender the right of self-government and place the legislative control of our affairs in the hands of foreign potentates and powers.

We go forth confident that we shall win. Why? Because upon the paramount issue of this campaign there is not a spot of ground upon which the enemy will dare to challenge battle. If they tell us that the gold standard is a good thing, we shall point to their platform and tell them that their platform pledges the party to get rid of the gold standard and substitute bimetallism. If the gold standard is a good thing, why try to get rid of it? I call your attention to the fact that some of the very people who are in this convention today and who tell us that we ought to declare in favor of international bimetallism— thereby declaring that the.gold standard is wrong and that the principle of bimetallism is better—these very people four months ago were open and avowed advocates of the gold standard, and were then telling us that we could not legislate two metals together, even with the aid of all the world. If the gold standard is a good thing, we ought to declare in favor of its retention and not in favor of abandoning it; and if the gold standard is a bad thing why should we wait until other nations are willing to help us to let go? Here is the line of battle, and we care not upon which issue they force the fight; we are prepared to meet them on either issue or on both. If they tell us that the gold standard is the standard of civilization, we reply to them that this, the most enlightened of all the nations of the earth, has never declared for a gold standard and that both the great parties this year are declaring against it. If the gold standard is the standard of civilization, why, my friends, should we not have it? If they come to meet us on that issue we can present the history of our nation. More than that; we can tell them that they will search the pages of history in vain to find a single instance where the common people of any land have ever declared themselves in favor of the gold standard. They can find where the holders of fixed investments have declared for a gold standard, but not where the masses have.

Mr. Carlisle said in 1878 that this was a struggle between "the idle holders of idle capital" and "the struggling masses, who produce the wealth and pay the taxes of the country;" and, my friends, the question we are to decide is: Upon which side will the Democratic party fight; upon the side of "the idle holders of idle capital" or upon the side of "the struggling masses?" That is the question which the party must answer first, and then it must be answered by each individual hereafter. The sympathies of the Democratic party, as shown by the platform, are on the side of the struggling masses who have ever been the foundation of the Democratic party. There are two ideas of government. There are those who believe that, if you will only legislate to make the well-to-do prosperous, their prosperity will leak through on those below. The Democratic idea, however, has been that if you legislate to make the masses prosperous, their prosperity will find its way up through every class which rests upon them.

You come to us and tell us that the great cities are in favor of the gold standard; we reply that the great cities rest upon our broad and fertile prairies. Burn down your cities and leave our farms, and your cities will spring up again as if by magic; but destroy our farms and the grass will grow in the streets of every city in the country.

My friends, we declare that this nation is able to legislate for its own people on every question, without waiting for the aid or consent of any other nation on earth; and upon that issue we expect to carry every State in the Union. I shall not slander the inhabitants of the fair State of Massachusetts nor the inhabitants of the State of New York by saying that, when they are confronted with the proposition, they will declare that this nation is not able to attend to its own business. It is the issue of 1776 over again. Our ancestors, when but three millions in number, had the courage to declare their political independence of every other nation; shall we, their descendants, when we have grown to seventy millions, declare that we are less independent than our forefathers? No, my friends, that will never be the verdict of our people. Therefore, we care not upon what lines the battle is fought. If they say bimetallism is good, but that we cannot have it until other nations help us, we reply that, instead of having a gold standard because England has, we will restore bimetallism, and then let England have bimetallism because the United States has it. If they dare to come out in the open field and defend the gold standard as a good thing, we will fight them to the uttermost. Having behind us the producing masses of this nation and the world, supported by the commercial interests, the laboring interests, and the toilers everywhere, we will answer their demand for a gold standard by saying to them: You shall not press down upon the brow of labor this crown of thorns, you shall not crucify mankind upon a cross of gold.

WILLIAM ALLEN WHITE
Whoop It Up for the Ragged Trousers

A young Kansas newspaper editor, William Allen White (1868–1944), burst into national prominence in 1896 with an editorial in the Emporia Gazette, *entitled "What's the Matter with Kansas?" It was a scathing indictment of Populism and the Democratic Party platform of that election, and was widely reprinted, playing no inconsiderable part in the defeat of the Bryan candidacy that November. White later became a liberal Republican of national distinction, as well as a novelist and essayist, and his ultimate position in Republican politics was far removed from the forces with which he had allied himself in 1896. More searching depictions than White's of the plight of rural Midwesterners may be found in the literature of the late nineteenth and early twentieth centuries, and especially in the writings of Hamlin Garland, Carl Sandburg, and Edgar Lee Masters.*

FROM "What's the Matter with Kansas?" by William Allen White, *The New York Times*, October 7, 1896, p. 9.

Today the Kansas Department of Agriculture sent out a statement which indicates that Kansas has gained less than 2,000 people in the past year. There are about 125,000 families in this State, and there were about 10,000 babies born in Kansas, and yet so many people have left the State that the natural increase is cut down to less than 2,000 net. This has been going on for eight years. If there had been a high brick wall around the state eight years ago and not a soul had been admitted or permitted to leave, Kansas would be 500,000 souls better off than she is today. And yet the Nation has increased in population. In five years 10,000,000 people have been added to the National population—yet instead of gaining a share of this—say 500,000—Kansas has apparently been a plague spot, and in the very garden of the world has lost population by the ten thousands every year.

Not only has she lost population, but she has lost wealth. Every moneyed man in the State who could get out without loss has gone. Every month in every community sees some one who has a little money pick up and leave the State. This has been going on for eight years. Money is being drained out all the time. In towns where ten years ago there were three or four or half a dozen money-lending concerns, stimulating industry by furnishing capital there is now none, or one or two that are looking after the interest and principal already outstanding. No one brings any money into Kansas any more. What community knows over one or two men who have moved in with more than $5,000 in the last three years? And what community cannot count half a score of men in that time who have left, taking all the money they could scrape together?

Yet the Nation has grown rich: other states have increased in population and wealth—other neighboring States. Missouri has gained nearly 2,000,000, while Kansas has been losing 500,000. Nebraska has gained in wealth and population, while Kansas has gone down hill. Colorado has gained every way, while Kansas has lost every way since 1888.

What is the matter with Kansas?

There is no substantial city in the State. Every big town save one has lost in population. Yet Kansas City, Omaha, Lincoln, St. Louis, Colorado Springs, Denver, Sedalia, the cities of the Dakotas, St. Paul and Minneapolis—all cities and towns in the West—have steadily grown. Take up the Government blue book and you will see that Kansas is virtually off the map. Two or three little scrabby Consular places in yellow-fever-stricken communities that do not aggregate 10,000 a year are all the recognition Kansas has. Nebraska draws about $100,000; little North Dakota draws $50,000; Oklahoma doubles Kansas; Missouri leaves her a thousand miles behind; Colorado is almost seven times greater than Kansas—the whole West is ahead of Kansas.

Take it by any standard you please, Kansas is not in it.

Go east, and you hear them laugh at Kansas; go West, and they sneer at her; go South and they "cuss" her; go North and they have forgotten her. Go into any crowd of intelligent people gathered anywhere on the globe, and you will find the Kansas man on the defensive. The newspaper columns and magazine pages, once devoted to praise of the State, to boastful facts and startling figures concerning her resources, are now filled with cartoons, jibes and Pefferian speeches. Kansas just naturally isn't in the civilized world. She has traded places with Arkansas and Timbuctoo.

What's the matter with Kansas?

We all know; yet here we are at it again. We have an old mossback Jacksonian, who snorts and howls because there is a bathtub in the State House; we are running that old jay for Governor. We have another shabby, wild-eyed, rattle-brained fanatic who has said openly in a dozen speeches that "the rights of the user are paramount to the rights of the owner"; we are running him for Chief Justice, so that capital will come tumbling over itself to get into the State. We have raked the ash heap of human failure in the State and have found an old hoopskirt of a man who has failed as a business man, who has failed as an editor, who has failed as a preacher and we are going to run him for Congressman at Large. He will help the looks of the Kansas delegation in Washington. Then we have discovered a kid without a law practice, and have decided to vote for him as Attorney General. Then, for fear some hint that the State had become respectable might percolate through the civilized portions of the nations, we have decided to send three of four harpies out lecturing, telling the people that Kansas is raising hell and letting corn go to weeds.

Oh, this is a State to be proud of! We are a people who can hold up our heads! What we need here is less money, less capital, fewer white shirts and brains, fewer men with business judgment, and more of these fellows who boast that they are "just ordinary old clodhoppers, but they know more in a minute about finance than John Sherman." We need more men who are "posted," who can bellow about the crime of '73, who hate prosperity, and who think that because a man believes in National honor, that he is a tool of Wall Street. We have had a few of them, some 150,000 but we want more.

We need several thousand gibbering idiots to scream about the "Great Red Dragon" of Lombard Street. We don't need population, we don't need wealth, we don't need well-dressed men on the streets, we don't need standing in the Nation, we don't need cities on these fertile prairies; you bet we dont! What we are after is the money power. Because we have become poorer and ornerier and meaner than a spavined, distempered mule, we, the people of Kansas, propose to kick. We don't care to build up; we wish to tear down.

"There are two ideas of government," said our noble Bryan at Chicago. "There are those who believe that if you just legislate to make the well-to-do prosperous, their prosperity will leak through on those below. The Democratic idea has been that if you legislate to make the masses prosperous their prosperity will find its way up and through every class and rest upon us." That's the stuff! Give the prosperous man the dickens. Legislate the thriftless man into ease, whack the stuffing out of the creditors, and tell the debtors who borrowed money five years ago, when the money in circulation was more general than it is now, that the contraction of the currency gives him a right to repudiate. Whoop it up for the ragged trousers; put the lazy, greasy fizzle, who can't pay his debts, on an altar, and bow down and worship him. Let the State ideal be high. What we need is not the respect of our fellowmen, but a chance to get something for nothing.

Oh, yes, Kansas is a great state. Here are people fleeing from it by the score every day, capital going out of the state by the hundreds of dollars; and every industry except farming paralyzed, and that crippled, because its products have to go across the ocean before they can find a laboring man at work who can afford to buy them. Let's don't stop this year. Let's drive all the decent, self-respecting men out of the state. Let's keep the old clodhoppers who know it all. Let's encourage the man who is "posted." He can talk, and what we need is not mill hands to eat our meat, nor factory hands to eat our wheat, nor cities to oppress the farmer by consuming his butter and eggs and chickens and produce; what Kansas needs is men who can talk, who have large leisure to argue the currency question while their wives wait at home for that nickel's worth of bluing.

What's the matter with Kansas?

Nothing under the shining sun. She is losing her wealth, population and standing. She has got her statesmen, and the money power is afraid of her. Kansas is all right. She has started in to raise hell, as Mrs. Lease advised, and she seems to have an over production. But that doesn't matter. Kansas never did believe in diversified crops. Kansas is all right. There is absolutely nothing wrong with Kansas. "Every prospect pleases and only man is vile."

11

OUR BROTHER IN BLACK

The slaves had been freed. Now millions of Negroes were left in the South, most of them penniless and without any property, many of them illiterate, with no skills save what they had learned in plantation days. Five years of Reconstruction in the South had seen them gain some political power, but they did not know how to use or keep it, and once federal troops were removed from the South and white governments had regained control, the Negroes were generally helpless. Northern philanthropy and state funds had set up schools, but these were poor and ineffective. Nor was there much money available to help them in the white South, for the war had left the region impoverished and threadbare. Under the Bourbon governments that the white South set up when federal occupation ended, Negroes were allowed to vote and given token political recognition, but illiteracy and ignorance made them easy prey, and there was widespread corruption and vote buying. Lower and middle-class whites resented the manipulation of Negro votes by the Bourbons, and with slavery gone, the economic rivalry between poor whites and Negroes became intense. Throughout the South political pressure arose for disfranchisement of the Negro, and by various kinds of discriminatory legislation as well as terrorism and intimidation, including night ridings and lynchings, Negroes were prevented from voting. During the latter half of the nineteenth century the Negro's plight grew steadily worse, and the first several decades of the twentieth century saw little or no relief. In this situation of degradation and despair, Negro leaders nevertheless worked patiently and untiringly to educate their people and prepare them for a day when they would receive greater freedom.

The selections that follow show various attitudes and issues on the

248

Negro question during the post-Civil War years and the early twentieth century.

JAMES S. PIKE
All Modern History Does Not Furnish a Parallel

After the Civil War the various Southern states elected governors and Congressmen, and prepared to re-enter the Union. The Republican-dominated U.S. Congress, however, would not have it so. It refused to seat the Southern delegates, and, outraged by the harsh Black Codes passed by Southern states, abolished the state governments and set up a series of Military Districts throughout the South. Most Southern whites were themselves disfranchised, and new state governments were established, elected principally by Negroes. "Carpetbaggers" —Northerners who came South after the War, Scalawags, and Negroes controlled the governments, their status guaranteed by federal troops. The history of the Reconstruction is still a hotly debated subject; there was graft, corruption, and ignorance, though probably not quite as much as Southerners claimed then and later. In many instances the state constitutions adopted by the Reconstruction legislatures have remained the basis of government in the Southern states. Northern public opinion, however, increasingly moved away from the idea that the white South should be kept out of power, and by 1876 all federal troops had been withdrawn from the South. Important in convincing the North that the South was being mistreated were such books as The Prostrate State, *by a former Republican and Abolitionist, James S. Pike (1811–1882), an excerpt from which follows. Pike visited Reconstruction South Carolina as a newspaperman, and wrote a book urging that the Southern white people be allowed to govern themselves.*

The Reconstruction period has been the subject of much fiction, including works by John W. DeForest, Albion Tourgee, Thomas Nelson Page, George Washington Cable, and William Faulkner.

Among the significant peculiarities to be observed in Columbia is the presence of United States troops. They occupy barracks on the outskirts of the town, in a pleasant quarter, where they drill daily, where the flag always floats, and where military music is heard at sunset. Among the airs often played is that which refers to the late John Brown, of Ossawattomie. The gentle reminder contained in that piece of music seems to be particularly superfluous

FROM *The Prostrate State: South Carolina Under Negro Government,* by James S. Pike (New York: D. Appleton and Co., 1874), pp. 79–84.

during the sessions of the present South Carolina Legislature. For if any thing would demonstrate the fact that the soul of that immortal person is marching on, it would be the living presence of that body of legislators. But the music seems to create no ripple of discontent. It is a favorite pastime of the "Gig Society" of Columbia to drive every evening to the parade-grounds and listen to such strains as the band chooses to discourse. Out of the multitude no one runs away at the sound of John Brown's name. The military have no terrors for this community, and their presence is welcomed rather than deprecated. They are not regarded in the light of an offensive symbol of authority; the money they spend and the music they make are considered a good deal more than an offset for any sentimental objections that it might be fancied their presence would excite.

Near by the parade-grounds are the college buildings of the University of South Carolina. Before the war their walls sheltered some two hundred students. Their young blood was fired by the first tap of the drum, and they all rushed to the field. They have not come back. What was to be a pastime proved a stern reality. The buildings look worn and desolate, and only a handful of scholars and a few poorly-paid professors remain. In execution of the steady purpose of putting the blacks on an equality with the whites, a measure was passed at this session to throw open the library to the colored students of the Normal School, and to take one of the college buildings for its uses. And in pursuance of the same purpose a majority of the trustees of the college were recently chosen by the same Legislature from the ranks of the blacks. In this case it was color rather than qualification for the post that was sought. This destroys the usefulness of the college so far as the white youth are concerned, as the young aristocratic blood of the State will decline the proposed amalgamation. The movement will eventuate in the substantial destruction of the university, as the black population will afford an inadequate supply of students. It is a damaging blow to the interests of education in the State, and a significant step in the process of Africanization. But, even if the college could be allowed to remain in the hands of the whites, such is their stripped condition that it would be difficult to maintain its former prosperity. Still, it would have afforded to the youth of the State a sort of domestic intellectual holding-ground, of great service during the present transition stage. Its capture by the blacks is a useless humiliation to the whites, since its advantages will now be lost to both races. It does great evil and it does no good. It is an attack upon the prejudices of the whites from no other motive than desire of domination. Rather than relinquish the opportunity to control the college, the blacks are willing to destroy it. The class of whites that support institutions of learning naturally decline enforced intellectual association with the new masters of South Carolina, and we judge will not be accounted particularly fastidious for this peculiarity.

In whatever direction we turn our eyes, we find such details of the operation of this anomalous government confronting us that we are provoked to speculations and comparisons impossible to repress. We know that changes of government often shove one set of men from their stools in order that their seats may be occupied by rivals. Thus the Huguenots, after Henry IV. of France; thus the Stuarts of England; thus the elder and the later Bourbons of St.-Germain, were overthrown. The philosophical student of history sympathizes comparatively little with the lamentations over such and like mutations. The successful and the vanquished stand upon the same general plane of equality. At the worst, it is but hereditary rank giving way to plebeian energy and intellect. It is no worse than the genuine force of Nature in any instance, that conquers and assumes control. But it does this by virtue of its own intrinsic power. It does it through the God-given prerogative of capacity and strength of character. Above all, it does it of its own motion, and by dint of its own exertion. And when the result is accomplished, civilization has received no backward set. In all modern history there has been no substitution of ignorance for knowledge, of barbarism for cultivation, of stolidity for intelligence, of incapacity for skill, of vice and corruption for probity and virtue, in the revolutions and changes that have taken place. The transitions, however trying to individuals and dynasties, have been on the same general plane of equality to the eye of history, have been in the general interest of civilization, and they do not startle us by offensive or shocking peculiarities or degradations. But it is altogether otherwise in the case of South Carolina. Here is one to which all modern history does not furnish a parallel. The changes here experienced have been accomplished by outside forces. The result has not been produced by a wrestle between two powers, in which the stronger has thrown and taken the place of the weaker. The strong has put the weak under foot, but has withdrawn itself after placing upon the neck of its prostrate foe the yoke of an ignoble and an incompetent crowd. They reign and rule by virtue of no merit, no intelligence, no prowess, no capacity of their own, but by means of an alien and borrowed authority only. Obedience is enforced by a power foreign to the instrument that inflicts the humiliation. It is not the rule of intrinsic strength; it is the compulsive power of the Federal authority at Washington. But for that, the forces of civilization would readjust themselves and overturn the present artificial arrangement.

The State really bears a foreign yoke; not one imposed by its own people, or by an authority which has arisen of itself among themselves. And this is the anomaly of the situation. It is a so-called democracy sustained by external force. In other words, it is a government that the intelligent public opinion of the State would overthrow if left to itself. It may be called self-government, or democratic government, but in no just sense is it either. It is a government which in the very nature of things could never rise to control, of itself, in any community. It is not an outgrowth of power and authority in the regular order. It is a hybrid born of unnatural connections, offensive alike to God and man; and, wherever the retributive responsibility of it fairly belongs, it is clear that it does not belong to the generation now rising upon the stage of action in the South, and who alone will be in the near future the sole victims of its oppressions. And this is the class whose just rights must be considered, whose hardships must be mitigated and removed by the power which holds the actual control of the situation, or another and yet another political and social convulsion will inevitably ensue, till disorder and revolution become chronic in our affairs. Not till absolute justice is established can we look for peace and tranquillity in our political system anywhere.

ATTICUS G. HAYGOOD
Wise People Never Make These Issues

It took considerable courage in the South of the 1870's and 1880's to advocate better treatment for Negroes. Thus a Georgia Methodist minister, Atticus G. Haygood (1839–1896), president of Emory College, was strongly criticized for his book Our Brother In Black *(1881), in which he urged greater Negro educational and economic opportunities. Haygood's book, however, was brought to the attention of the Northern philanthropists who were organizing the Slater Fund, with the result that Haygood was made general agent for the fund in its work of encouraging Negro colleges in the South to emphasize industrial training for Negroes. For ten years Haygood dispensed patronage to those schools whose work he approved, among them Tuskegee Institute in Alabama, whose president, Booker T. Washington, would soon become a figure of national prominence and influence.*

The modern reader will note that Haygood's views in the excerpt from Our Brother in Black *which follows, however radical they may have seemed in the 1880's, definitely implied white supremacy and rigid social segregation.*

I propose this question to myself: How must I, a white man, and my neighbor, Daniel Martin, a black man treat each other? He is my neighbor living with his family near me; he is my friend also, in whom I can trust; more, he has been a servant in my household for six full years. Daniel is a citizen; more than that, he is a man; the law made him a citizen, God made him a man. I am as much bound by eternal righteousness to deal fairly with Daniel Martin in all things, as with the worthy man and cultured Christian minister whose garden joins mine. And, let it not be overlooked, Daniel Martin is as much bound as I am to deal righteously in all the relations that bind us together. I may, because I have larger opportunity, owe more duty to him than he owes to me, but the nature of the obligation is the same.

FROM *Our Brother in Black,* by Atticus G. Haygood (Nashville, Tenn.: Southern Methodist Publishing House, 1881), pp. 185–88.

Does any man with a particle of sense suppose that any law can provide for all the relations that exist between Daniel Martin and me? Divine law never proceeds upon this sort of literalism in statutory enactment, that every possible duty must be named and weighed and timed and measured. When human law makes the attempt it fails always. The infinitely varied adjustments of human life make mere statutory solutions of such questions impossible. And there is another reason besides the endless variety of occasions and circumstances; if it were possible to provide for every duty by statute, there would be no place left for our personal development in good conscience and moral life.

If mere laws cannot guide and restrain Daniel Martin and me, (and both of us need guidance and restraint,) how are we to manage our seemingly difficult case? Here is our first mistake; it is not a difficult case at all, except we make it so by want of sense and of a good conscience. There is no trouble whatever, provided we two men have the right spirit in our hearts; provided, also, that we have good sense in our heads. Daniel and I have just one thing to do; we must plant ourselves squarely and sincerely on the "Sermon on the Mount." On this basis we will get on with little thought or need of outside help to the end of a long chapter.

In the course of time Daniel and I will have various business relations. (There is no discount, be it observed, in the matter of "caste" for business connections. "Business is business," unless it be in teaching his children to read!) I want Daniel's muscle, his experience in a line of things, and his integrity; he wants my money, my confidence, my friendship, and now and then when he "gets in a pinch," a little "advance," or other extra help. Some day he will have something to sell that I wish to buy; I will have something to sell that he wishes to buy; and so on to the end of our natural lives. How are we to manage? Just as two white men who wish to do right would do; just as two black men who wish to do right would do. We are each to do in all our dealings with each other the fair and honest thing. This is all there is in it. With this difference, if I wrong him, taking advantage of his ignorance, or weakness, or dependence, of any thing peculiar to his condition that gives me the advantage of him, I am all the viler for using my advantage unrighteously. It is doubly mean for the white man to wrong a negro. And this is recognized broadly in the proverbial phrase by which some superlatively despicable person is described in all parts of the South: "He is mean enough to cheat a negro."

"But," says the irrepressible one, be he Northern or Southern, "how about the social question?" This question indicates a sort of hysteria. But if you must be answered, it is easy: Daniel Martin never asks any thing of me as to social life that I am not willing to give. I respect him in his place; he respects me in my place. He is master in his house, (except when his wife gets the upper hand,) I am master in mine, (all exceptions understood.) No test that brought embarrassment to me or mortification to him ever occurred, or ever will. Wise people never make these issues; they do not come up spontaneously, not once in a thousand times. In his capacity as servant, Daniel Martin will make fires, clean shoes, and do other such things. Were I living in New York or London, and Daniel were what he is, or any other man in similar relations to me, I should expect him to do the same things, so long as they are included in our bargain, and he is paid for his work. But I do not ask him to sit at the table with my guests, or to entertain company in the parlor after tea. He does not wish such association. *Ask him.* He has just about the same social recognition in my house that a man of all work has in other decent and well-ordered households.

There never was a subject so much discussed that has so little in it, except it may be the invention of perpetual motion. It gives no trouble to either race when let alone. People of good sense, good breeding, and of unmeddlesome temper, do let it alone.

HENRY WOODFIN GRADY
Uttermost Justice and Abiding Friendship

In December, 1889, the editor of the Atlanta, Ga., Constitution, *Henry Woodfin Grady (1830–1889), made a celebrated address in Boston in which he called for Northern understanding of the South's race problem. Grady's speech is a remarkable specimen of "enlightened" American opinion on the Negro question in the 1880's and 1890's; he urged the Southerner's love of the Negro, called for good-will, praised the reconciliation of the sections, and championed the industrialization of the South. His speech came at a time when pressure for disfranchisement of the Negro in the South was becoming irresistible, and when the traditional social and economic barriers were being made into state law all over the South. Grady died shortly after returning home from his speech. Across the desk from Grady in the* Consititution *offices worked another editorialist, Joel Chandler Harris, whose "Uncle Remus" stories glorified the old plantation days before the War even while Grady extolled the virtues of the industrial New South.*

Happy am I that this mission has brought my feet at last to press New England's historic soil and my eyes to the knowledge of her beauty and her thrift. Here, within touch of Plymouth Rock and Bunker Hill—where Webster thundered and Longfellow sang, Emerson thought and Channing preached—here in the cradle of American letters and almost of American liberty, I hasten to make the obeisance that every American owes New England when first he stands uncovered in her mighty presence. Strange apparition!

FROM "The Race Problem," by Henry W. Grady, in *Modern Eloquence,* ed. Thomas B. Reed (Philadelphia: John D. Morris and Co., 1900), Vol. II, pp. 534–38, 547–50.

This stern and unique figure—carved from the ocean and the wilderness—its majesty kindling and growing amid the storms of winter and of wars—until at last the gloom was broken, its beauty disclosed in the sunshine, and the heroic workers rested at its base—while startled kings and emperors gazed and marveled that from the rude touch of this handful cast on a bleak and unknown shore, should have come the embodied genius of human government and the perfected model of human liberty! God bless the memory of those immortal workers, and prosper the fortunes of their living sons—and perpetuate the inspiration of their handiwork. . . .

Far to the South, Mr. President, separated from this section by a line— once defined in irrepressible difference, once traced in fratricidal blood, and now, thank God, but a vanishing shadow—lies the fairest and richest domain of this earth. It is the home of a brave and hospitable people. There is centered all that can please or prosper humankind. A perfect climate above a fertile soil yields to the husbandman every product of the temperate zone. There, by night the cotton whitens beneath the stars, and by day the wheat locks the sunshine in its bearded sheaf. In the same field the clover steals the fragrance of the wind, and the tobacco catches the quick aroma of the rains. There are mountains stored with exhaustless treasures; forests—vast and primeval; and rivers that, tumbling or loitering, run wanton to the sea. Of the three essential items of all industries—cotton, iron, and wood—that region has easy control. In cotton, a fixed monopoly—in iron, proven supremacy—in timber, the reserve supply of the Republic. From this assured and permanent advantage, against which artificial conditions cannot much longer prevail, has grown an amazing system of industries. Not maintained by human contrivance of tariff or capital, afar off from the fullest and cheapest source of supply, but resting in Divine assurance, within touch of field and mine and forest—not set amid costly farms from which competition has driven the farmer in despair, but amid cheap and sunny lands, rich with agriculture, to which neither season nor soil has set a limit—this system of industries is mounting to a splendor that shall dazzle and illumine the world. That, sir, is the picture and the promise of my home—a land better and fairer than I have told you, and yet but fit setting in its material excellence, for the loyal and gentle quality of its citizenship. Against that, sir, we have New England, recruiting the Republic from its sturdy loins, shaking from its overcrowded hives new swarms of workers, and touching this land all over with its energy and its courage. And yet—while in the Eldorado of which I have told you but fifteen per cent of its lands are cultivated, its mines scarcely touched, and its population so scant that, were it set equidistant, the sound of the human voice could not be heard from Virginia to Texas—while on the threshold of nearly every house in New England stands a son, seeking, with troubled eyes, some new land in which to carry his modest patrimony, the strange fact remains that in 1880 the South had fewer northern-born citizens than she had in 1870—fewer in '70 than in '60. Why is this? Why is it, sir, though the sectional line be now but a mist that the breath may dispel, fewer men of the North have crossed it over to the South, than when it was crimson with the best blood of the Republic, or even when the slave-holder stood guard every inch of its way?

There can be but one answer. It is the very problem we are now to consider. The key that opens that problem will unlock to the world the fairest half of this Republic, and free the halted feet of thousands whose eyes are already kindling with its beauty. Better than this, it will open the hearts of brothers for thirty years estranged, and clasp in lasting comradeship a million hands now withheld in doubt. Nothing, sir, but this problem and the suspicions it breeds, hinders a clear understanding and a perfect union. Nothing else stands between us and such love as bound Georgia and Massachusetts at Valley Forge and Yorktown, chastened by the sacrifices at Manassas and Gettysburg, and illumined with the coming of better work and a nobler destiny than was ever wrought with the sword or sought at the cannon's mouth.

If this does not invite your patient hearing to-night—hear one thing more. My people, your brothers in the South—brothers in blood, in destiny, in all that is best in our past and future—are so beset with this problem that their very existence depends upon its right solution. Nor are they wholly to blame for its presence. The slave-ships of the Republic sailed from your ports, the slaves worked in our fields. You will not defend the traffic, nor I the institution. But I do hereby declare that in its wise and humane administration in lifting the slave to heights of which he had not dreamed in his savage home, and giving him a happiness he has not yet found in freedom, our fathers left their sons a saving and excellent heritage. In the storm of war this institution was lost. I thank God as heartily as you do that human slavery is gone forever from the American soil. But the free man remains. With him a problem without precedent or parallel. Note its appalling conditions. Two utterly dissimilar races on the same soil—with equal political and civil rights—almost equal in numbers, but terribly unequal in intelligence and responsibility—each pledged against fusion—one for a century in servitude to the other, and freed at last by a desolating war, the experiment sought by neither but approached by both with doubt—these are the conditions. Under these, adverse at every point, we are required to carry these two races in peace and honor to the end. . . .

The love we feel for that race, you cannot measure nor comprehend. As I attest it here, the spirit of my old black mammy, from her home up there, looks down to bless, and through the tumult of this night steals the sweet music of her croonings as thirty years ago she held me in her black arms and led me smiling into sleep. This scene vanishes as I speak, and I catch a vision of an old Southern home with its lofty pillars, and its white pigeons fluttering down through the golden air. I see women with strained and anxious faces, and children alert yet helpless. I see night come down with its dangers and its apprehensions, and in a big homely room I feel on my tired head the touch of loving hands—now worn and wrinkled, but fairer to me yet than the hands of mortal woman, and stronger yet to lead me than the hands of mortal man—as they lay a mother's blessing there, while at her knees—the truest altar I yet have found—I thank God that she is safe in her sanctuary, because her slaves, sentinel in the silent cabin, or guard at her chamber door, put a black man's loyalty between her and danger.

I catch another vision. The crisis of battle—a soldier struck, staggering, fallen. I see a slave, scuffling through the smoke, winding his black arms about the fallen form, reckless of hurtling death—bending his trusty face to catch the words that tremble on the stricken lips, so wrestling meantime with agony that he would lay down his life in his master's stead. I see him by the weary bedside, ministering with uncomplaining patience, praying with all his humble heart that God will lift his master up, until death comes in mercy and in honor to still the soldier's agony and seal the soldier's life. I see him by the open grave, mute, motionless, uncovered, suffering from the death of him who in life fought against his freedom. I see him, when the mound is heaped and the great drama of his life is closed, turn away, and with downcast eyes and uncertain step start out into new and strange fields, faltering, struggling, but moving on, until his trembling figure is lost in the light of this better and brighter day. And from the grave comes a voice saying: "Follow him! Put your arms about him in his need, even as he put his about me. Be his friend as he was mine." And out into this new world—strange to me as to him, dazzling, bewildering both—I follow! And may God forget my people—when they forget these!

Whatever the future may hold for them, whether they plod along in the servitude from which they have never been lifted since the Cyrenian was laid hold upon by the Roman soldiers, and made to bear the cross of the fainting Christ—whether they find homes again in Africa, and thus hasten the prophecy of the psalmist, who said: "And suddenly Ethiopia shall hold out her hands unto God"—whether for ever dislocated and separate, they remain a weak people, beset by stronger, and exist, as the Turk, who lives in the jealousy rather than in the conscience of Europe—or whether in this miraculous Republic they break through the caste of twenty centuries, and, belying universal history, reach the full stature of citizenship, and in peace maintain it—we shall give them uttermost justice and abiding friendship. . . .

Such, Mr. President, is this problem as we see it, such is the temper in which we approach it, such the progress made. What do we ask of you? First, patience; out of this alone can come perfect work. Second, confidence; in this alone can you judge fairly. Third, sympathy; in this you can help us best. Fourth, give us your sons as hostages. When you plant your capital in millions, send your sons that they may know how true are our hearts and may help to swell the Caucasian current until it can carry without danger this black infusion. Fifth, loyalty to the Republic—for there is sectionalism in loyalty as in estrangement. This hour little needs the loyalty that is loyal to one section and yet holds the other in enduring suspicion and estrangement.

Give us the broad and perfect loyalty that loves and trusts Georgia alike with Massachusetts—that knows no South, no North, no East, no West, but endears with equal and patriotic love every foot of our soil, every State of our Union.

A mighty duty, sir, and mighty inspiration impels every one of us tonight to lose in patriotic consecration whatever estranges, whatever divides. We, sir, are Americans—and we stand for human liberty. The uplifting force of the American idea is under every throne on earth. France, Brazil—these are our victories. To redeem the earth from kingcraft and oppression—this is our mission! And we shall not fail. God has sown in our soil the seed of His millennial harvest, and He will not lay the sickle to the ripening crop until His full and perfect day has come. Our history, sir, has been a constant and expanding miracle from Plymouth Rock and Jamestown all the way—ay, even from the hour when, from the voiceless and trackless ocean, a new world rose to the sight of the inspired sailor. As we approach the fourth centennial of that stupendous day—when the old world will come to marvel and to learn amid our gathered treasures—let us resolve to crown the miracles of our past with the spectacle of a Republic compact, united, indissoluble in the bonds of love—loving from the lakes to the gulf—the wounds of war healed in every heart as on every hill, serene and resplendent at the summit of human achievement and earthly glory, blazing out the path and making clear the way up which all the nations of the earth must come in God's appointed time!

PLESSY v. *FERGUSON*
Legislation Is Powerless to Eradicate Racial Instincts

In Plessy v. Ferguson, *163 U.S. 537 (1896), the Supreme Court of the United States formally ratified the "separate but equal" doctrine whereby Southern state laws placing the Negro in a separate social status were declared constitutional. Plessy, who was one-eighth Negro, refused to be evicted from a seat in a railroad coach reserved for white people, and was imprisoned for violating a Louisiana statute decreeing "separate but equal" accommodations for the races. Justice Henry Billings Brown (1836–1913) delivered the majority opinion of the Court, from which only Justice John Marshall Harlan, grandfather of the present Supreme Court Justice, dissented.*

By the Fourteenth Amendment, all persons born or naturalized in the United States, and subject to the jurisdiction thereof, are made citizens of the United States and of the State wherein they reside; and the States are forbidden from

FROM *Plessy v. Ferguson,* 163 U.S. 537 (1896).

making or enforcing any law which shall abridge the privileges or immunities of citizens of the United States, or shall deprive any person of life, liberty, or property without due process of law, or deny to any person within their jurisdiction the equal protection of the laws. . . .

The object of the amendment was undoubtedly to enforce the absolute equality of the two races before the law, but in the nature of things it could not have been intended to abolish distinctions based upon color, or to enforce social, as distinguished from political equality, or a commingling of the two races upon terms unsatisfactory to either. Laws permitting, and even requiring, their separation in places where they are liable to be brought into contact do not necessarily imply the inferiority of either race to the other, and have been generally, if not universally, recognized as within the competency of the state legislatures in the exercise of their police power. The most common instance of this is connected with the establishment of separate schools for white and colored children, which has been held to be a valid exercise of the legislative power even by courts of States where the political rights of the colored race have been longest and most earnestly enforced.

. . . It is claimed by the plaintiff in error that, in any mixed community, the reputation of belonging to the dominant race, in this instance the white race, is *property,* in the same sense that a right of action, or of inheritance, is property. Conceding this to be so, for the purposes of this case, we are unable to see how this statute deprives him of, or in any way affects his right to, such property. If he be a white man and assigned to a colored coach, he may have his action for damages against the company for being deprived of his so-called property. Upon the other hand, if he be a colored man and be so assigned, he has been deprived of no property, since he is not lawfully entitled to the reputation of being a white man.

In this connection, it is also suggested by the learned counsel for the plaintiff in error that the same argument that will justify the state legislature in requiring railways to provide separate accommodations for the two races will also authorize them to require separate cars to be provided for people whose hair is of a certain color, or who are aliens, or who belong to certain nationalities, or to enact laws requiring colored people to walk upon one side of the street, and white people upon the other, or requiring white men's houses to be painted white, and colored men's black, or their vehicles or business signs to be of different colors, upon the theory that one side of the street is as good as the other, or that a house or vehicle of one color is as good as one of another color. The reply to all this is that every exercise of the police power must be reasonable, and extend only to such laws as are enacted in good faith for the promotion of the public good, and not for the annoyance or oppression of a particular class. . . .

So far, then, as a conflict with the Fourteenth Amendment is concerned, the case reduces itself to the question whether the statute of Louisiana is a reasonable regulation, and with respect to this there must necessarily be a large discretion on the part of the legislature. In determining the question of reasonableness it is at liberty to act with reference to the established usages, customs, and traditions of the people, and with a view to the promotion of their comfort, and the preservation of the public peace and good order. Gauged by this standard, we cannot say that a law which authorizes or even requires the separation of the two races in public conveyances is unreasonable, or more obnoxious to the Fourteenth Amendment than the acts of Congress requiring separate schools for colored children in the District of Columbia, the constitutionality of which does not seem to have been questioned, or the corresponding acts of state legislatures.

We consider the underlying fallacy of the plaintiff's argument to consist in the assumption that the enforced separation of the two races stamps the colored race with a badge of inferiority. If this be so, it is not by reason of anything found in the act, but solely because the colored race chooses to put that construction upon it. The argument necessarily assumes that if, as has been more than once the case, and is not unlikely to be so again, the colored race should become the dominant power in the state legislature, and should enact a law in precisely similar terms, it would thereby relegate the white race to an inferior position. We imagine that the white race, at least, would not acquiesce in this assumption. The argument also assumes that social prejudices may be overcome by legislation, and that equal rights cannot be secured to the Negro except by an enforced commingling of the two races. We cannot accept this proposition. If the two races are to meet upon terms of social equality, it must be the result of natural affinities, a mutual appreciation of each other's merits, and a voluntary consent of individuals. As was said by the Court of Appeals of New York in *People* v. *Gallagher,* 93 N.Y. 438, 448, "this end can neither be accomplished nor promoted by laws which conflict with the general sentiment of the community upon whom they are designed to operate. When the government, therefore, has secured to each of its citizens equal rights before the law and equal opportunities for improvement and progress, it has accomplished the end for which it was organized and performed all of the functions respecting social advantages with which it is endowed." Legislation is powerless to eradicate racial instincts or to abolish distinctions based upon physical differences, and the attempt to do so can only result in accentuating the difficulties of the present situation. If the civil and political rights of both races be equal one cannot be inferior to the other civilly or politically. If one race be inferior to the other socially, the Constitution of the United States cannot put them upon the same plane.

BOOKER T. WASHINGTON
As Separate as the Fingers, Yet One as the Hand

Booker T. Washington (1856–1915) was the first great Negro leader to emerge after the Civil War. Born in slavery, Washington managed to secure an education, and in the 1880's was chosen to found Tuskegee Institute, a training school for Negroes in Alabama. Working with almost no funds, he developed Tuskegee into a center for Negro education, and with his Atlanta Exposition speech of 1895, the text of which follows, he achieved national attention. Recognizing the precarious position of the Negro in the South and in the nation, Washington pursued a policy of striving for economic gains for the Negro people, while carefully avoiding political and social agitation. Though his policy seemed conservative and submissive to many Negro leaders, it is doubtful that at the time he could have worked more successfully for improved Negro status had he pursued a different course. His Atlanta speech sets forth his philosophy, his tactics, and his objectives. More than a half-century later a onetime Tuskegee student, Ralph Ellison, would write a novel, The Invisible Man, in which the school that Washington founded would be depicted in a very different light.

MR. PRESIDENT AND GENTLEMEN OF THE BOARD OF DIRECTORS AND CITIZENS

One-third of the population of the South is of the Negro race. No enterprise seeking the material, civil, or moral welfare of this section can disregard this element of our population and reach the highest success. I but convey to you, Mr. President and Directors, the sentiment of the masses of my race when I say that in no way have the value and manhood of the American Negro been more fittingly and generously recognized than by the managers of this magnificent Exposition at every stage of its progress. It is a recognition that will do more to cement the friendship of the two races than any occurrence since the dawn of our freedom.

Not only this, but the opportunity here afforded will awaken among us a new era of industrial progress. Ignorant and inexperienced, it is not strange that in the first years of our new life we began at the top instead of at the bottom; that a seat in Congress or the state legislature was more sought than real estate or industrial skill; that the political convention of stump speaking had more attractions than starting a dairy farm or truck garden.

FROM "Atlanta Exposition Speech," in *Up From Slavery*, by Booker T. Washington (New York: Doubleday, Doran, 1901), pp. 218–25.

A ship lost at sea for many days suddenly sighted a friendly vessel. From the mast of the unfortunate vessel was seen a signal, "Water, water; we die of thirst!" The answer from the friendly vessel at once came back, "Cast down your bucket where you are." A second time the signal, "Water, water; send us water!" ran up from the distressed vessel, and was answered, "Cast down your bucket where you are." And a third and fourth signal for water was answered, "Cast down your bucket where you are." The captain of the distressed vessel, at last heeding the injunction, cast down his bucket, and it came up full of fresh, sparkling water from the mouth of the Amazon River. To those of my race who depend on bettering their condition in a foreign land or who underestimate the importance of cultivating friendly relations with the Southern white man, who is their next-door neighbour, I would say: "Cast down your bucket where you are"—cast it down in making friends in every manly way of the people of all races by whom we are surrounded.

Cast it down in agriculture, mechanics, in commerce, in domestic service, and in the professions. And in this connection it is well to bear in mind that whatever other sins the South may be called to bear, when it comes to business, pure and simple, it is in the South that the Negro is given a man's chance in the commercial world, and in nothing is this Exposition more eloquent than in emphasizing this chance. Our greatest danger is that in the great leap from slavery to freedom we may overlook the fact that the masses of us are to live by the productions of our hands, and fail to keep in mind that we shall prosper in proportion as we learn to dignify and glorify common labour and put brains and skill into the common occupations of life; shall prosper in proportion as we learn to draw the line between the superficial and the substantial, the ornamental gewgaws of life and the useful. No race can prosper till it learns that there is as much dignity in tilling a field as in writing a poem. It is at the bottom of life we must begin, and not at the top. Nor should we permit our grievances to overshadow our opportunities.

To those of the white race who look to the incoming of those of foreign birth and strange tongue and habits for the prosperity of the South, were I permitted I would repeat what I say to my own race, "Cast down your bucket where you are." Cast it down among the eight millions of Negroes whose habits you know, whose fidelity and love you have tested in days when to have proved treacherous meant the ruin of your firesides. Cast down your bucket among these people who have, without strikes and labour wars, tilled your fields, cleared your forests, builded your railroads and cities, and brought forth treasures from the bowels of the earth, and helped make possible this magnificent representation of the progress of the South. Casting down your bucket among my people, helping and encouraging them as you are doing on these grounds, and to education of head, hand, and heart, you will find that they will buy surplus land, make blossom the waste places in your fields, and run your factories. While doing this, you can be sure in the future, as in the past, that you and your families will be surrounded by the most patient, faithful, law-abiding, and unresentful people that the world has seen. As we have proved our loyalty to you in the past, in nursing your children, watching by the sick-bed of your mothers and fathers, and often following them with tear-dimmed eyes to their graves, so in the future, in our humble way, we shall stand by you with a devotion that no foreigner can approach, ready to lay down our lives, if need be, in defence of yours, interlacing our industrial, commercial, civil, and religious life with yours in a way that shall make the interests of both races one. In all things that are purely social we can be as separate as the fingers, yet one as the hand in all things essential to mutual progress.

There is no defence or security for any of us except in the highest intelligence and development of all. If anywhere there are efforts tending to curtail the fullest growth of the Negro, let these efforts be turned into stimulating, encouraging, and making him the most useful and intelligent citizen. Effort or means so invested will pay a thousand per cent interest. These efforts will be twice blessed—"blessing him that gives and him that takes."

There is no escape through law of man or God from the inevitable:—

> The laws of changeless justice bind
> Oppressor with oppressed;
> And close as sin and suffering joined
> We march to fate abreast.

Nearly sixteen millions of hands will aid you in pulling the load upward, or they will pull against you the load downward. We shall constitute one-third and more of the ignorance and crime of the South, or one-third its intelligence and progress; we shall contribute one-third to the business and industrial prosperity of the South, or we shall prove a veritable body of death, stagnating, depressing, retarding every effort to advance the body politic.

Gentlemen of the Exposition, as we present to you our humble effort at an exhibition of our progress, you must not expect overmuch. Starting thirty years ago with ownership here and there in a few quilts and pumpkins and chickens (gathered from miscellaneous sources), remember the path that has led from these to the inventions and production of agricultural implements, buggies, steam-engines, newspapers, books, statuary, carving, paintings, the management of drug-stores and banks, has not been trodden without contact with thorns and thistles. While we take pride in what we exhibit as a result of our independent efforts, we do not for a moment forget that our part in this exhibition would fall far short of your expectations but for the constant help that has come to our educational life, not only from the Southern states, but especially from Northern philanthropists, who have made their gifts a constant stream of blessing and encouragement.

The wisest among my race understand that the agitation of questions of social equality is the extremest folly, and that progress in the enjoyment of all the privileges that will come to us must be the result of severe and constant struggle rather than of artificial forcing. No race that has anything to contribute to the markets of the world is long in any degree ostracized. It is important and right that all privileges of the law be ours, but it is vastly more important that we be prepared for the exercises of these privileges. The opportunity to earn a dollar in a factory just now is worth infinitely more than the opportunity to spend a dollar in an opera-house.

In conclusion, may I repeat that nothing in thirty years has given us more hope and encouragement, and drawn us so near to you of the white race, as this opportunity offered by the Exposition; and here bending, as it were, over the altar that represents the results of the struggles of your race and mine, both starting practically empty-handed three decades ago, I pledge that in your effort to work out the great and intricate problem which God has laid at the doors of the South, you shall have at all times the patient, sympathetic help of my race; only let this be constantly in mind, that, while from representations in these buildings of the product of field, of forest, of mine, of factory, letters, and art, much good will come, yet far above and beyond material benefits will be that higher good, that, let us pray God, will come, in a blotting out of sectional differences and racial animosities and suspicions, in a determination to administer absolute justice, in a willing obedience among all classes to the mandates of law. This, this, coupled with our material prosperity, will bring into our beloved South a new heaven and a new earth.

W. E. B. DUBOIS
A Mobbed and Mocked and
Murdered People

More militant Negro leaders were in the making. W. E. Burghardt DuBois (1868–1963), Massachusetts-born and Harvard-educated, never acquiesced in the view that Negro claims to social and political equality could be set aside. In 1898, following an election in which the Negro voter was effectively disfranchised, four days of race rioting took place in Atlanta, Georgia, in which a number of Negroes were killed by white mobs. DuBois wrote "A Litany at Atlanta" to mark the occasion. He also took the lead in organizing Negroes in the North to work against discrimination and inequality, and throughout the several decades that followed was a leader in the fight for Negro rights. It was DuBois's outlook, not Washington's, that would characterize the fiction

FROM "A Litany At Atlanta," in *Darkwater*, by W. E. Burghardt DuBois (New York: Harcourt, Brace and Co., 1921), pp. 25–28.

of such twentieth-century American writers as Ralph Ellison, James Baldwin, Richard Wright, and others.

O Silent God, Thou whose voice afar in mist and mystery hath left our ears an-hungered in these fearful days—
   Hear us, good Lord!
   Listen to us, Thy children: our faces dark with doubt are made a mockery in Thy Sanctuary. With uplifted hands we front Thy Heaven, O God, crying:
   We beseech Thee to hear us, good Lord!
   We are not better than our fellows, Lord; we are but weak and human men. When our devils do deviltry, curse Thou the doer and the deed,—curse them as we curse them, do to them all and more than ever they have done to innocence and weakness, to womanhood and home.
   Have mercy upon us, miserable sinners!
   And yet, whose is the deeper guilt? Who made these devils? Who nursed them in crime and fed them on injustice? Who ravished and debauched their mothers and their grandmothers? Who bought and sold their crime and waxed fat and rich on public iniquity?
   Thou knowest, good God!
   Is this Thy Justice, O Father, that guile be easier than innocence and the innocent be crucified for the guilt of the untouched guilty?
   Justice, O Judge of men!
   Wherefore do we pray? Is not the God of the Fathers dead? Have not seers seen in Heaven's halls Thine hearsed and lifeless form stark amidst the black and rolling smoke of sin, where all along bow bitter forms of endless dead?
   Awake, Thou that sleepest!
   Thou art not dead, but flown afar, up hills of endless light, through blazing corridors of suns, where worlds do swing of good and gentle men, of women strong and free—far from the cozenage, black hypocrisy, and chaste prostitution of this shameful speck of dust!
   Turn again, O Lord; leave us not to perish in our sin!
   From lust of body and lust of blood,—
   Great God, deliver us!
   From lust of power and lust of gold,—
   Great God, deliver us!
   From the leagued lying of despot and of brute,—
   Great God, deliver us!
   A city lay in travail, God our Lord, and from her loins sprang twin Murder and Black Hate. Red was the midnight; clang, crack, and cry of death and fury filled the air and trembled underneath the stars where church spires pointed silently to Thee. And all this was to sate the greed of greedy men who hide behind the veil of vengeance!
   Bend us Thine ear, O Lord!

In the pale, still morning we looked upon the deed. We stopped our ears and held our leaping hands, but they—did they not wag their heads and leer and cry with bloody jaws: *Cease from Crime!* The word was mockery, for thus they train a hundred crimes while we do cure one.

Turn again our captivity, O Lord!

Behold this maimed and broken thing, dear God; it was an humble black man, who toiled and sweat to save a bit from the pittance paid him. They told him: *Work and Rise!* He worked. Did this man sin? Nay, but someone told how someone said another did—one whom he had never seen nor known. Yet for that man's crime this man lieth maimed and murdered, his wife naked to shame, his children to poverty and evil.

Hear us, O heavenly Father!

Doth not this justice of hell stink in Thy nostrils, O God? How long shall the mounting flood of innocent blood roar in Thine ears and pound in our hearts for vengeance? Pile the pale frenzy of blood-crazed brutes, who do such deeds, high on Thine Altar, Jehovah Jireh, and burn it in hell forever and forever!

Forgive us, good Lord; we know not what we say!

Bewildered we are and passion-tossed, mad with the madness of a mobbed and mocked and murdered people; straining at the armposts of Thy throne, we raise our shackled hands and charge Thee, God, by the bones of our stolen fathers, by the tears of our dead mothers, by the very blood of Thy crucified Christ: What meaneth this? Tell us the plan; give us the sign!

Keep not Thou silent, O God!

Sit not longer blind, Lord God, deaf to our prayer and dumb to our dumb suffering. Surely Thou, too, art not white, O Lord, a pale, bloodless, heartless thing!

Ah! Christ of all the Pities!

Forgive the thought! Forgive these wild, blasphemous words! Thou art still the God of our black fathers and in Thy Soul's Soul sit some soft darkenings of the evening, some shadowings of the velvet night.

But whisper—speak—call, great God, for Thy silence is white terror to our hearts! The way, O God, show us the way and point us the path!

Whither? North is greed and South is blood; within, the coward, and without, the liar. Whither? To death?

Amen! Welcome, dark sleep!

Whither? To life? But not this life, dear God, not this. Let the cup pass from us, tempt us not beyond our strength, for there is that clamoring and clawing within, to whose voice we would not listen, yet shudder lest we must,—and it is red. Ah! God! It is a red and awful shape.

Selah!

In yonder East trembles a star.

Vengeance is Mine; I will repay, saith the Lord!

Thy Will, O Lord, be done!
  Kyrie Eleison!
Lord, we have done these pleading, wavering words.
  We beseech Thee to hear us, good Lord!
We bow our heads and hearken soft to the sobbing of women and little children.
  We beseech Thee to hear us, good Lord!
Our voices sink in silence and in night.
  Hear us, good Lord!
In night, O God of a godless land!
  Amen!
In silence, O Silent God.
  Selah!

W. E. B. DUBOIS
Except by Silence

In 1910 DuBois left his post at Atlanta University to become Director of Publications and Research of the newly formed National Association for the Advancement of Colored People, and editor of a new magazine, The Crisis. *In editorial after editorial he attacked the notion that the Negro should be patient and conciliatory, and should refrain from vigorous protest of any and all abridgements of his civil rights as a citizen. A typical editorial is that in* The Crisis *for May, 1914, in which DuBois replied to a letter from a friend, Charles F. Dole, urging him to play down statements of bitterness over the mistreatment of Negroes in the South. DuBois's militancy led him in the direction of socialism, and at the age of 93 he joined the Communist Party. He became a citizen of Ghana in 1963 and died in that country.*

We publish very gladly Mr. Dole's criticism of THE CRISIS, because of our deep respect for the writer and because he voices a real and vital disagreement with our policy which is continually, in one way or another, coming to expression. It is briefly this thesis: "Don't antagonize, don't be bitter; say the conciliatory thing; make friends and do not repel them; insist on and emphasize the cheerful and good and dwell as little as possible on wrong and evil."

THE CRISIS does not believe in this policy so far as the present status of the American Negro problem is concerned. We could imagine many social

FROM "The Philosophy of Mr. Dole," by W. E. B. DuBois, in *The Crisis*, Vol. VIII (May, 1914), pp. 24–26.

problems, and many phases in a particular problem, when the watchful waiting, the tactfully conciliatory attitude would be commendable and worth while.
At other times it would be suicidal and this, in our opinion, is one of the
times.

It was ever so. When the Hebrew prophets cried aloud there were respectable persons by the score who said:

"Unfortunate exaggeration!"

"Unnecessary feeling!"

"Ungodly bitterness!"

Yet the jeremiads were needed to redeem a people. When the abolitionists
began, not simply to say, but to act as if slavery were a "covenant with hell,"
there were plenty of timid souls "on the fence, hesitating," who scrambled
down hastily on the popular side and were willing to lynch Garrison and
ostracize Phillips.

All this might be beside the mark if we had not already tried Mr. Dole's
prescriptions. For now nearly twenty years we have made of ourselves mudsills
for the feet of this Western world. We have echoed and applauded every
shameful accusation made against 10,000,000 victims of slavery. Did they call
us inferior half-beasts? We nodded our simple heads and whispered: "We is."
Did they call our women prostitutes and our children bastards? We smiled
and cast a stone at the bruised breasts of our wives and daughters. Did they
accuse of laziness 4,000,000 sweating, struggling laborers, half paid and cheated
out of much of that? We shrieked: "Ain't it so?" We laughed with them at
our color, we joked at our sad past, and we told chicken stories to get alms.

And what was the result? We got "friends." I do not believe any people
ever had so many "friends" as the American Negro to-day! He has nothing
but "friends" and may the good God deliver him from most of them, for they
are like to lynch his soul.

What is it to be a friend of the Negro? It is to believe in anything for him
except, perhaps, total and immediate annihilation. Short of that, good and kind
friends of colored folk believe that he is, in Mr. Dooley's charming phrase,
"aisily lynched," and ought to be occasionally. Even if 2,662 accused black
people have been publicly lynched, burned and multilated in twenty-eight
years (not to mention the murder of perhaps 10,000 other black folk), our
friends think we ought not to disturb the good President of these United
States because *"the wonder is that there is so little killing!"*

It is the old battle of the better and the best. The worst foes of Negro manhood to-day are those compromising friends who are willingly satisfied with
even less than half a loaf. They want the Negro educated; but the South objects to Negro colleges. Oh, very well, then, high schools; but the South objects
to "literary" training for "niggers!" Dear, dear! Then "industrial" training;
but the South objects to training any considerable number of Negroes for industry; it wants them for menial service. Very well, train them as servants
and field hands—anything as long as it is "education!" Then we and THE

CRISIS rise and say: *"But——"* Our friends raise deprecating hands; they adjust the sofa pillows, shade the light, and say: "Now, now! *Give them the benefit of the doubt!"*

Or we clamor for the right to vote. "Of course you should vote," say our friends. "But," says the South, "they are too ignorant and inexperienced; we will vote for them." "Excellent," cry our friends, "vote for them and guard them in their civil rights." "What's this?" asks the South. "We mean their economic rights," say our friends glibly, "their right to work and get property." "Yes," answers the South calmly, "the right to work, and we'll work them." *"But——"* cries THE CRISIS and the black man who has been worked long enough. "Sh!" answer our friends. *"You'll halt the procession!"*

That's precisely what we intend to do. For twenty-five years we have let the procession go by until the systematic denial of manhood rights to black men in America is the crying disgrace of the century. We have wrongs, deep and bitter wrongs. There are local and individual exceptions; there are some mitigating circumstances; there is much to be excused; there is much to be said; and yet for the great mass of 10,000,000 Americans of Negro descent these things are true:

We are denied education.

We are driven out of the Church of Christ.

We are forced out of hotels, theatres and public places.

We are publicly labeled like dogs when we travel.

We can seldom get decent employment.

We are forced down to the lowest wage scale.

We pay the highest rent for the poorest homes.

We cannot buy property in decent neighborhoods.

We are held up to ridicule in the press and on the platform and stage.

We are disfranchised.

We are taxed without representation.

We are denied the right to choose our friends or to be chosen by them, but must publicly announce ourselves as social pariahs or be suggestively kicked by the *Survey.*

In law and custom our women have no rights which a white man is bound to respect.

We cannot get justice in the courts.

We are lynched with impunity.

We are publicly, continuously and shamefully insulted from the day of our birth to the day of our death.

And yet we are told not to be "self-conscious"; to lie about the truth in order to make it "come true;" to grapple with the "philosophy of evolution;" and not to make people "feel ugly" by telling them "ugly facts."

Few admire Mr. Dole, personally, more than the editor of THE CRISIS. Mr. Dole is the type of what the American of the future may be: fine in feeling, delicate in touch, sensitive to the subtle beauties of the world. But Mr. Dole's feet never walked the way we tread. He does not know—he cannot conceive this darker world of insult, repression, hunger and murder. He and Charles William Eliot and Woodrow Wilson and millions of others have given no encouragement to lynching, except by silence!

Except by silence!

EXCEPT BY SILENCE!

Who ever tried harder than the Negro and his "friends" to use the lie for social betterment? We have lied about the South so strenuously that this may account for the persistent blackness of our faces. Oh, yes: the South is the true, tried friend of Negroes; the South wants them educated; the South detests lynching; the South loves black mammies and buries them handsomely; the little playful antics of mobs are but ebullitions of Anglo-Saxon energy or at worst the faults of "poor white trash," who do not count. Moreover, those who dispute these statements are either meddling white Northerners or impudent Negroes who want to marry white women.

All of this we black folk and our "friends" have been saying glibly and frequently. We were lying, and we knew we were lying, *to make the "falsehood come true;"* but did the world know this? Did we not lull this nation to false security and fatuous insensibility? And is the uneasiness of our friends at the plain talk of THE CRISIS the cause of ugly feeling or the necessary result of ridiculous lies? How far may we indeed meddle with the truth? Where is the boundary line between getting people "to come and believe" what is untrue and telling them on your honor that black is white? We have a sincere desire to see a little brochure by Mr. Dole—with hand-made paper, deckle edged and privately printed—on "The Uses of the Lie as a Means of Social Salvation." We would like to distribute a few copies in Heaven among Mr. Dole's Puritan ancestors and listen to the ensuing profanity.

It is the palpable evasions of our friends, and our earnest friends like Mr. Dole, that are most discouraging. When we protest at the plain insult of "negro," Mr. Dole answers that we do not capitalize "white". But white is not the correlative of Negro, as Mr. Dole knows right well. "Black" and "colored" are the correlatives to "white," while Negro is used exactly as the words Malay or German or Jew or Indian are used. To refuse a word so used capitalization is a petty and usually a deliberate insult.

Humanity is progressing toward an ideal; but not, please God, solely by men who sit in cloistered ease, hesitate from action and seek sweetness and light; rather we progress today, as in the past, by the soul-torn strength of those who can never sit still and silent while the disinherited and the damned clog our gutters and gasp their lives out on our front porches. These are the men who go down in the blood and dust of battle. They say ugly things to an ugly world. They spew the lukewarm fence straddlers out of their mouths, like God of old; they cry aloud and spare not; they shout from the housetops, and they make this world so damned uncomfortable with its nasty burden of evil that it tries to get good and does get better.

Evolution is evolving the millennium, but one of the unescapable factors in evolution are the men who hate wickedness and oppression with perfect hatred, who will not equivocate, will not excuse, and will be heard. With the sainted spirits of such as these THE CRISIS would weakly but earnestly stand and cry in the world's four corners of the way; and it claims no man as friend who dare not stand and cry with it.

WINFIELD H. COLLINS
Meeting Extraordinary Conditions with Extraordinary Means

The despair of Negro intellectuals such as W. E. B. DuBois over the hope of the Negro's ever receiving justice and equality during the first several decades of the twentieth century can be understood when one encounters some of the writings of white men on the subject. In the year 1915, there were 99 lynchings of Negroes in the South. In a book entitled The Truth About Lynching and the Negro, In Which the Author Pleads that the South Be Made Safe for the White Race, *published three years later, one Winfield H. Collins, of Maryland, defends lynching on various grounds—including the contention that Negroes rather enjoy the prominence that comes to them while being hanged, and feel no such degradation as a white man might under similar circumstances! He cites several newspaper reports as "proof."*

The belief of the average white man of the South that lynching is the most effective way of dealing with the Negro for his crime against white women also seems to be borne out by the statistics: In 1892–3, 88 Negroes were lynched for rape; in 1901–2, 59; while for the four years 1911–14, only 43. That this great reduction in rape cases and lynchings was not due to legal executions is shown by the fact that during the same time but 36 Negroes were legally executed, only 12 of these being for the four years 1911–14. Thus as a consequence of a reduction in the crime of rape by Negroes is noted a great reduction in the lynching of Negroes,—from 287 in 1892–3; 185, 1901–2; 129, 1906–7; to 91 for 1913–14.

However, during 1915 and 1916, 104 Negroes were lynched in the South as compared with 91 for 1913 and 1914. The increased number lynched for rape is very marked: being only 13 for 1913 and 1914, but twice the number, or 26, for 1915 and 1916. During the former two years, also, 6 Negroes were legally hanged for rape as compared to 12 for the latter. The proportion re-

FROM *The Truth About Lynching and the Negro in the South*, by Winfield H. Collins (New York: Neale Publishing Co., 1918), pp. 54–61.

mains the same: thus during 1913 and 1914, 19 Negroes in the South were put to death for rape as compared with 38 for 1915 and 1916.

Although the legal execution of 12 Negroes in the South for rape during 1915 and 1916 may show a tendency to allow the law to take its course in such cases, may not the above statistics also indicate that when for a few years but few lynchings occurred, especially for the crime of rape, that the effect of such immediate and fearful punishment—consisting of burning as it sometimes does—gradually fades from the mind of the Negro inclined to such crime, with a great increase of rape as a consequence?

Again, in extenuation of lynching, it is important to observe, that, as a result of most crimes against the body, such as murder, but little, if any, humiliation attaches. But it is quite different in rape cases. Not only is there often great physical injury, but also an unutterable humiliation. Our civilization teaches that one should hold certain personal rights and considerations even more dear than life itself. To have in mind such ideas and live up to them measures our reach above lower peoples. That this feeling or spirit should be encouraged, rather than risk its check, is not to be questioned. Therefore, the average Southern white man does not believe that the innocent rape victim of a Negro should be obliged to endure further humiliation incident upon her appearance in a court of law.

In this connection, a set of resolutions published by those who lynched a Negro at Annapolis, Md., in 1875, are interesting. These resolutions, which set forth the causes of the act, were drawn up before the lynching took place and show serious consideration. I quote:

Fellow Citizens: In view of the fact that we are about to take into our hands the sword of justice to do to death one who is now incarcerated in our county jail, it is meet that we should give some reason for the purpose we hope to consummate. First, then: While we can but honor the deep feeling of interest manifested by those who are the proper guardians of our lives, our property, and our honor; and while we, as true and loyal citizens of the State of Maryland, and of Anne Arundel County, do bend to the supreme majesty of the law and acknowledge trials by jury as the very arch-stone in the grand edifice of human rights, still we know the vilest criminal is accorded the same rights under the law that belong to the petty thief, nor can this devil incarnate, should he claim his rights, be denied the privilege of a change of venue, such a circumstance might probably rob the gallows of its due and foil the aims of the law. Before God we believe in the existence of a higher code than that which is dignified by the great seal of a Commonwealth and that the high and holy time to exercise it is when the chastity of our women is tarnished by the foul breath of an imp from hell and the sanctity of our homes invaded by a demon.

Secondly, admitting that in the event of a trial by a jury he shall be hanged— a highly probable result—yet would his execution be as illegal as though done by a band of wronged citizens; for must not a juror be a peer, and with a mind free of bias, and where can a man be found competent to try this case? Who can be found of his level, and who that has heard has not already convicted him in his mind? At best, that which would be done under the semblance of law would be a *more sham* by force of all the circumstances connected with this horrible deed, and if under the law the penalty is death, and we know the deed was committed by him—we claim that there is no moral difference in the means of destroying him, and we act upon this conviction.

Thirdly, we are not willing that the victim shall be dragged into court to tell over and over again the story of her terrible wrongs, or that her name shall be entered upon the records of our criminal jurisprudence for future reference.[1]

Further comment on this lynching is unnecessary—unless indirectly: the Negro, child of Africa, but lately removed from the jungle, because of the necessity of the habitat of his origin, has had developed in him by nature, possibly, stronger sexual passion than is to be found in any other race.[2] But he is infinitely lacking in the high mental, moral, and emotional qualities that are especially characteristic of the Anglo-Saxon, and it is a grievous mistake to attribute such high qualities to him. When proper restraint is removed from the Negro he gets beyond bounds. The Anglo-Saxon, indeed, or members of that race, has a way of meeting extraordinary conditions with extraordinary means—hence lynching in order to hold in check the Negro in the South.

Indeed, a country occupied by two races so widely apart in origin, characteristics, and development as the whites and Negroes of the Southern States— one race of the highest mental endowments and culture, the other of the lowest—one having a civilization that reaches back hundreds, if not thousand, of years, the other in the early dawn of civilization—might reasonably have two codes of law suited, as nearly as possible, to each race, respectively.

A mode of punishment that would be out of place as to the white man may be well suited to the Negro. Small-pox is not to be treated as chicken-pox. Barbarous criminals require barbarous laws. The innocent and law-abiding citizens of a State have rights as well as the criminals—at least, the right to protection from the criminals. But let some crafty scoundrel finally get in jail, and he will be flooded with letters of consolation and sympathy from sentimental women and soft-headed men.[3] And let some Negro brute, guilty of rape, suffer the punishment he so richly deserved at the hands of an outraged community, and one would think, if he considered the bitter censure from distant quarters, that the foundations of the government were being undermined, or that a poor lamb was set upon by a pack of howling wolves, thirsting for its blood, but not a word of commiseration for the family, or the victim, of the fiendish Negro's unbridled bestiality.

Moreover, instead of a Negro's being overawed by the solemn deliberations of a court, rather, as he is the center of interest, he all but enjoys it. For once in

---

[1] *Baltimore American,* June 15, 1875.
[2] To make up for the high death rate.
[3] Joliet, Ill., Sept. 10 (1917), *Riot in State Prison.* Rioters numbered about fifty. Had become angered at impositions of restrictions. "Among the privileges previously enjoyed by the convicts was an almost unlimited correspondence with sentimental women."—*Washington* (D.C.) *Star,* Sept. 10, 1917.

his life he finds himself in a position of prominence. It would be contrary to the Negro nature if he were not somewhat elated at being the object of so much attention. Even were this not the case, he has no such appreciation of his degradation as the white man feels under similar circumstances. Indeed, it would sometimes appear as almost a triumphal procession for him from the time he gets in jail until he reaches the gallows. The two quotations below may help to justify this idea:

Joe Clark, colored, . . . was hanged at this place on Friday forenoon, in the presence of about 3,000 persons, mostly Negroes. Clark spoke about fifteen minutes, giving a detailed account of the murder and fully confessing the crime. He advised all present to live an upright life. . . . After he had shaken hands with his friends the trap was sprung, and thus the sentence of the court was duly executed. Clark's last request was that the *black cap be kept off, so that all might see how easy he could meet death.*[4]

The second one is taken from accounts of the execution at Denton, Md., of "Wish" Shepperd, colored, for the outrage of a fifteen-year-old white girl.[5]

He told his spiritual advisers that he had a message for the public: "Tell all the young men to avoid the fate that awaits me by joining the church and attending its service." [Evidently inspired by his preacher advisers] . . . He slumbered soundly, the guards noticed, and awoke early this morning apparently indifferent to his doom. . . . With a firm step he accompanied the officers and his spiritual advisers to the scaffold which was erected near the Choptank River. Passing *undismayed* through the throng which had gathered along the way from the prison *to the gallows. His gaze* passed fearlessly around surveying the people.

[4] Taken from *Richmond Enquirer*, May 4, 1775.
[5] *Baltimore Sun*, August 27–28, 1915.

12

Commerce Follows the Flag

At the time of the Civil War the United States held no colonial territory outside the continental limits. It had not participated in the establishment of colonies in Africa, Asia, and the Pacific. The Monroe Doctrine had long since informed European powers that the United States did not regard the Western Hemisphere as a place for further colonization. When France had taken advantage of the Civil War to place a puppet emperor on the throne of Mexico, the United States sent an army of 50,000 troops to the border as soon as the war was over, and issued an ultimatum, whereupon Napoleon III withdrew his soldiers and the regime collapsed.

Soon, however, the United States began some expansion of its own. Naval bases were set up in Samoa and Cuba. A bill calling for the annexation of Santo Domingo was defeated in Congress only after long debate. American industries sought world markets, and the American Navy was deployed on two oceans. Americans in Hawaii overthrew the native government in 1893, under the protection of U.S. warships; seven years later annexation was approved by Congress.

In 1898 came the decisive move. Cuba had for some time been in rebellion against Spain, and American sympathies lay with the insurgents. The U.S. Battleship *Maine,* anchored in Havana harbor, was blown up by a mine, whereupon hostility to Spain reached fever pitch, and on April 20 war was declared. Quickly the U.S. Pacific fleet under Admiral Dewey destroyed the Spanish fleet in the Philippines. American troops were landed in Cuba, and shortly afterward the main Spanish fleet was destroyed at Santiago Bay. Spain sued for peace. Cuba was granted its independence, with an American naval base established at Guantanamo Bay. Puerto Rico was annexed. A protectorate was set up over the Philippines. Wake Island and a portion of Samoa in the Pacific Ocean were acquired. When attempts to negotiate a treaty with Colombia to permit the digging of a canal across the Isthmus of Panama failed, U.S. warships stood by while a group of Panamanians revolted, then prevented the Colombian government from landing troops to suppress the revolt. With the new Republic of Panama a treaty was quickly signed, and work on the canal begun. The United States of America was now a world power.

Our new role was hailed by many; there was great pride in the far-flung dominion of the United States flag. But others viewed the new imperialism with distrust, and saw our actions in the Philippines and elsewhere as a violation of all that America represented.

The selections that follow illustrate several attitudes toward the United States as a colonial power. Some of the comments are not without their relevance today. In retrospect, however, this much seems evident: regardless of whether or not our colonial activities were desirable, American interests and American involvement would and could no longer stop at the ocean shore. Difficult though it was for the American people to accept the fact, we were in the wide world to stay. The resulting "rediscovery" of Europe was to have enormous influence on the literature of twentieth-century American writers.

CAPTAIN A. T. MAHAN
Along This Path a Great Commerce Will Travel

One of the most influential books in the rise of imperialistic sentiment in the years after the Civil War was The Influence of Sea Power Upon History *(1890), by Captain A. T. Mahan (1840–1914). Mahan's view of the role of naval power in determining the destinies of nations was important both to the United States and to other nations, where his work was also widely read. In the excerpt that follows, Mahan points out the necessity for American bases in the Caribbean, and in succeeding years, especially after the building of the*

FROM *The Influence of Sea Power Upon History, 1660–1783* by Capt. A. T. Mahan (Boston: Little, Brown, 1894), pp. 33–35.

Panama Canal, his views prevailed. The naval station at Guantanamo Bay, Cuba, is one legacy of the Mahan outlook. (Meanwhile, in a very different way, the novelist Henry James was at work on his probing inquiries into the impact of the international role upon Americans.)

Circumstances have caused the Mediterranean Sea to play a greater part in the history of the world, both in a commercial and a military point of view, than any other sheet of water of the same size. Nation after nation has striven to control it, and the strife still goes on. Therefore a study of the conditions upon which preponderance in its waters has rested, and now rests, and of the relative military values of different points upon its coasts, will be more instructive than the same amount of effort expended in another field. Furthermore, it has at the present time a very marked analogy in many respects to the Caribbean Sea,—an analogy which will be still closer if a Panama canal-route ever be completed. A study of the strategic conditions of the Mediterranean, which have received ample illustration, will be an excellent prelude to a similar study of the Caribbean, which has comparatively little history.

The second remark bears upon the geographical position of the United States relatively to a Central-American canal. If one be made, and fulfil the hopes of its builders, the Caribbean will be changed from a terminus, and place of local traffic, or at best a broken and imperfect line of travel, as it now is, into one of the great highways of the world. Along this path a great commerce will travel, bringing the interests of the other great nations, the European nations, close along our shores, as they have never been before. With this it will not be so easy as heretofore to stand aloof from international complications. The position of the United States with reference to this route will resemble that of England to the Channel, and of the Mediterranean countries to the Suez route. As regards influence and control over it, depending upon geographical position, it is of course plain that the centre of the national power, the permanent base,[1] is much nearer than that of other great nations. The positions now or hereafter occupied by them on island or mainland, however strong, will be but outposts of their power; while in all the raw materials of military strength no nation is superior to the United States. She is, however, weak in a confessed unpreparedness for war; and her geographical nearness to the point of contention loses some of its value by the character of the Gulf coast, which is deficient in ports combining security from an enemy with facility for repairing war-ships of the first class, without which ships no country can pretend to control any part of the sea. In case of a contest for supremacy in the Caribbean, it seems evident from the depth of the South Pass of the Mississippi, the nearness of New Orleans, and the advantages of the Mississippi Valley for water transit, that the main effort of the country

---

[1] By a base of permanent operations "is understood a country whence come all the resources, where are united the great lines of communication by land and water, where are the arsenals and armed posts."

must pour down that valley, and its permanent base of operations be found there. The defence of the entrance to the Mississippi, however, presents peculiar difficulties; while the only two rival ports, Key West and Pensacola, have too little depth of water, and are much less advantageously placed with reference to the resources of the country. To get the full benefit of superior geographical position, these defects must be overcome. Furthermore, as her distance from the Isthmus, though relatively less, is still considerable, the United States will have to obtain in the Caribbean stations fit for contingent, or secondary, bases of operations; which by their natural advantages, susceptibility of defence, and nearness to the central strategic issue, will enable her fleets to remain as near the scene as any opponent. With ingress and egress from the Mississippi sufficiently protected, with such outposts in her hands, and with the communications between them and the home base secured, in short, with proper military preparation, for which she has all necessary means, the preponderance of the United States on this field follows, from her geographical position and her power, with mathematical certainty.

THEODORE ROOSEVELT
In Accordance With Our Settled Principles of Conduct

Theodore Roosevelt (1858–1919), as President of the United States, took the lead in helping to create conditions whereby the United States was enabled to complete a treaty with the newly formed Republic of Panama in 1903 which made possible the building of a ship canal across the Isthmus of Panama. For a time Roosevelt contemplated seizing Panama from the Republic of Colombia after that government rejected the Hay-Herran Convention calling for a canal across what was then Colombian territory. On November 3, 1903, when the province of Panama rose in revolt against Colombia and declared itself independent, Roosevelt had already ordered American warships to maintain "free and uninterrupted transit" across the Isthmus, effectively prevented suppression of the revolt by refusing to allow the Colombian government to land troops to put down the rebellion. Here is Roosevelt's version of what happened.

So far from there having been too much foresight about the revolution on the part of the American Government, this plain official account by a naval officer of what occurred on November 4 showed that the American Government had, if anything, delayed too long its orders for the movement of American war-

FROM *Fear God and Take Your Own Part,* by Theodore Roosevelt (New York: George H. Doran Co., 1916), pp. 328–33. Reprinted by permission of Theodore Roosevelt III.

ships to Panama, and that it was only the coolness and gallantry of forty-two marines and sailors in the face of ten times their number of armed foes that prevented the carrying out of the atrocious threat of the Colombian commander. In accordance with our settled principles of conduct we refused to allow the transportation of troops across the Isthmus by either the Colombians or the Panamanians, so as to prevent bloodshed and interference with traffic.

No one connected with this Government had any part in preparing, inciting or encouraging the revolution on the Isthmus of Panama. Save from the reports of our military and naval officers given in full in the message of the President to the Senate, and from the official reports in the Department of State, no one connected with the Government had any previous knowledge of the revolution except such as was accessible to any person of ordinary intelligence who read the newspapers and kept up a current acquaintance with public affairs.

Secretary of State John Hay stated officially at the time:

The action of the President in the Panama matter is not only in the strictest accordance with the best precedents of our public policy, but it was the only course he could have taken in compliance with our treaty rights and obligations.

I saw at the time very many men, Americans, natives of Panama, and Europeans, all of whom told me that they believed a revolution was impending, and most of whom asked me to take sides one way or the other. The most noted of these men whom I now recollect seeing was Mr. Bunau-Varilla. He, however, did not ask me to take sides one way or the other. To no one of these men did I give any private assurance of any kind one way or the other, referring them simply to my published declarations and acts.

For some reason certain newspapers have repeatedly stated that Mr. Nelson Cromwell was responsible for the revolution. I do not remember whether Mr. Nelson Cromwell was or was not among my callers during the months immediately preceding the revolution. But if he was I certainly did not discuss with him anything connected with the revolution. I do not remember his ever speaking to me about the revolution until after it occurred, and my understanding was, and is, that he had nothing whatever to do with the revolutionary movement which actually took place.

There were, as I have said, various revolutionary movements on foot in the Isthmus, and it was my understanding that there was considerable jealousy among the instigators of these movements as to which one would come off first and would be effective. On information received after the event, I believed then, and believe now, that the revolutionary movement which actually succeeded was the one with which Mr. Bunau-Varilla was connected. He was sent by the Government of Panama as Minister to this country as soon as Panama became an independent state, and he then made no secret of the fact that he had been one of those who had organized the successful revolution;

precisely as was the case with the President and other officials of the new republic. Neither did Mr. Bunau-Varilla make any secret of the fact that in acting as he did he was influenced both by his indignation as a resident of Panama at the Colombian treatment of Panama, and also by his indignation as a Frenchman at the Colombian proposal to blackmail the company, and if it would not submit to blackmail, then to confiscate its possessions.

In view of this double attitude of the Colombian Government, an attitude of tyranny toward Panama and of robbery toward the French company, Mr. Bunau-Varilla conceived it to be his duty to do all he could to aid the natives of Panama in throwing off the yoke of Colombia. I believe his attitude was entirely proper, alike from the standpoint of his duty as a resident of Panama, from the standpoint of his duty as a Frenchman to the investors and property holders of the French company, and from the standpoint of his duty as a citizen of the world. But until after the event I had no knowledge of his activities save the knowledge possessed by all intelligent men who had studied the affairs of the Isthmus. I gave him no aid or encouragement. My attitude was open to the knowledge of all; it was set forth with minute accuracy in my message to Congress.

No one connected with the American Government instigated the revolution. I thought that a revolution might very probably occur, but so far from fomenting it I was at the time, as has repeatedly been made public since, preparing my message on the basis that it would be necessary for us openly to take possession of the Isthmus in view of the scandalous conduct of Colombia. However, the fact that the revolution occurred and that the independent republic of Panama was actually seated on the Isthmus, rendered it unnecessary for me to send in this original draft of my message.

Even had I desired to foment a revolution—which I did not—it would have been wholly unnecessary for me to do so. The Isthmus was seething with revolution. Any interference from me would have had to take the shape of preventing a revolution, not of creating one. All the people residing on the Isthmus ardently desired the revolution. The citizens of Panama desired it. Every municipal council, every governmental body the citizens themselves could elect or control, demanded and supported it. When the revolution had occurred, and was successful, and Panama was an independent republic, I certainly did prevent Colombia from carrying on a bloody war on the Isthmus in the effort to overthrow the revolutionists. I certainly did refuse to do what Colombia requested, that is, to use the Army and Navy of the United States against our friends in the interests of the foes who had just been trying to blackmail us. We were solemnly pledged to keep transit across the Isthmus open. Again and again we had landed forces in time of revolutionary disturbance to secure this object. If Colombia had attempted the reconquest of the Isthmus, there would have been a far more bloody contest than ever before on the Isthmus, and the only way by which that contest could have been carried on would have been by using the railroad line and interrupting transit across the Isthmus.

It is therefore perfectly true that I prevented any attempt by Colombia to land troops on the Isthmus and plunge the Isthmus into a long drawn-out and bloody war. What I did then was as plainly my duty as it would be the duty of the President to act in a similar manner now. Panama was an independent republic *de facto* then just as she is now. Colombia had not a particle more right to land troops and conquer her then than she has now. If I was wrong in preventing Colombia from making an effort by a long drawn-out and bloody war to reconquer the Isthmus in 1903, then it would be a wrong to prevent her from making a similar effort at reconquest now. . . .

FINLEY PETER DUNNE
Th' Proudest Anglo-Saxon Name in th' County Roscommon

In the person of Mr. Dooley, Irish-born tavern-keeper of Archey Road in Chicago, Finley Peter Dunne (1867–1936) created one of America's most astute and amusing commentators on the foibles of his fellow-countrymen. For several decades Mr. Dooley's rich Irish brogue provided monologues on the political and social scene in the United States and abroad. Here Mr. Dooley delivers himself of some views on the celebrated Anglo-Saxon race which, according to some commentators, was destined to lead the world out of darkness into light—at considerable financial profit. Dialect such as Dunne's has now gone so much out of fashion that modern readers find it difficult to read. Yet in the nineteenth century, dialect and intentional misspelling were among the most popular forms of American humor. The Uncle Remus *tales are another example.*

"Well," said Mr. Dooley, "I see be th' pa-apers that th' snow-white pigeon iv peace have tied up th' dogs iv war. It's all over now. All we've got to do is to arrest th' pathrites an' make th' reconcenthradios pay th' stamp tax, an' be r-ready f'r to take a punch at Germany or France or Rooshia or anny counthry on th' face iv th' globe.

"An' I'm glad iv it. This war, Hinnissy, has been a gr-reat sthrain on me. To think iv th' suffrin' I've endured! F'r weeks I lay awake at nights fearin' that th' Spanish ar-rmadillo'd lave the Cape Verde Islands, where it wasn't,

FROM "On the Anglo-Saxon," *Mr. Dooley in Peace and War*, by Finley Peter Dunne (Boston: Small, Maynard and Co., 1898), pp. 53–57.

an' take th' thrain out here, an' hur-rl death an' desthruction into me little store. Day be day th' pitiless exthries come out an' beat down on me. Ye hear iv Teddy Rosenfelt plungin' into ambus-cades an' Sicrity iv Wars; but d'ye hear iv Martin Dooley, th' man behind th' guns, four thousan' miles behind thim, an' willin' to be further? They ar-re no bokays f'r me. I'm what Hogan calls wan iv th' mute, ingloryous heroes iv th' war; an' not so dam mute, ayther. Some day, Hinnissy, justice'll be done me, an' th' likes iv me; an', whin th' story iv a gr-reat battle is written, they'll print th' kilt, th' wounded, th' missin', an' th' seryously disturbed. An' thim that have bore thimsilves well an' bravely an' paid th' taxes an' faced th' deadly newspa-apers without flinchin' 'll be advanced six pints an' given a chanst to tur-rn jack f'r th' game.

"But me wurruk ain't over jus' because Mack has inded th' war an' Teddy Rosenfelt is comin' home to bite th' Sicrety iv War. You an' me, Hinnissy, has got to bring on this here Anglo-Saxon 'lieance. An Anglo-Saxon, Hinnissy, is a German that's forgot who was his parents. They're a lot iv thim in this counthry. There must be as manny as two in Boston: they'se wan up in Maine, an' another lives at Bogg's Ferry in New York State, an' dhrives a milk wagon. Mack is an Anglo-Saxon. His folks come fr'm th' County Armagh, an' their naytional Anglo-Saxon hymn is 'O'Donnell Aboo.' Teddy Rosenfelt is another Anglo-Saxon. An' I'm an Anglo-Saxon. I'm wan iv th' hottest Anglo-Saxons that iver come out iv Anglo-Saxony. Th' name iv Dooley has been th' proudest Anglo-Saxon name in th' County Roscommon f'r many years.

"Schwartzmeister is an Anglo-Saxon, but he doesn't know it, an' won't till some wan tells him. Pether Bowbeen down be th' Frinch church is formin' th' Circle Francaize Anglo-Saxon club, an' me ol' frind Dominigo that used to boss th' Ar-rchey R-road wagon whin Callaghan had th' sthreet conthract will march at th' head iv th' Dago Anglo-Saxons whin th' time comes. There ar-re twinty thousan' Rooshian Jews at a quarther a vote in th' Sivinth Ward; an', ar-rmed with rag hooks, they'd be a tur-r-ble thing f'r anny inimy iv th' Anglo-Saxon 'lieance to face. Th' Bohemians an' Pole Anglo-Saxons may be a little slow in wakin' up to what th' pa-apers calls our common hurtage, but ye may be sure they'll be all r-right whin they're called on. We've got together an Anglo-Saxon 'lieance in this wa-ard, an' we're goin' to ilict Sarsfield O'Brien prisidint, Hugh O'Neill Darsey vice-prisidint, Robert Immitt Clancy sicrety, an' Wolfe Tone Malone three-asurer. O'Brien'll be a good wan to have. He was in the Fenian r-raid, an' his father carrid a pike in forty-eight. An' he's in th' Clan. Besides, he has a sthrong pull with th' Ancient Ordher iv Anglo-Saxon Hibernyans.

"I tell ye, whin th' Clan an' th' Sons iv Sweden an' th' Banana Club an' th' Circle Francaize an' th' Pollacky Benivolent Society an' th' Rooshian Sons of Dinnymite an' th' Benny Brith an' th' Coffee Clutch that Schwartzmeister r-runs an' th' Tur-rnd'ye-mind an' th' Holland society an' th' Afro-Americans an' th' other Anglo-Saxons begin f'r to raise their Anglo-Saxon battlecry, it'll

be all day with th' eight or nine people in th' wurruld that has th' misfortune
iv not bein' brought up Anglo-Saxons."

"They'se goin' to be a debate on th' 'lieance at th' ninety-eight picnic at
Ogden's gr-rove," said Mr. Hennessy.

"P'r'aps," said Mr. Dooley, sweetly, "ye might like to borry th' loan iv an
ice-pick."

MARK TWAIN
We Have Debauched America's Honor

*Imperialism was strongly opposed by an articulate section of American public
opinion, including America's best-known writer and humorist, "Mark Twain"
(Samuel L. Clemens, 1835–1910). Twain thought our role in the Cuban war
quite defensible, but our subsequent annexation of the Philippine Islands he
likened to the behavior of the British in South Africa, the Germans in China,
the Russians in Asia, and the French on several continents. Here, in an excerpt
from an essay entitled "To the Person Sitting in Darkness," he delivers a
savage attack on those Americans who would help assume the White Man's
Burden.*

The Blessings-of-Civilization Trust, wisely and cautiously administered, is a
Daisy. There is more money in it, more territory; more sovereignty, and other
kinds of emolument, than there is in any other game that is played. But
Christendom has been playing it badly of late years, and must certainly suffer
by it, in my opinion. She has been so eager to get every stake that appeared
on the green cloth, that the People who Sit in Darkness have noticed it—they
have noticed it, and have begun to show alarm. They have become suspicious
of the Blessings of Civilization. More—they have begun to examine them. This
is not well. The Blessings of Civilization are all right, and a good commercial
property; there could not be a better, in a dim light. In the right kind of a
light, and at a proper distance, with the goods a little out of focus, they furnish
this desirable exhibit to the Gentlemen who Sit in Darkness: Love, Justice,
Gentleness, Christianity, Protection to the Weak, Temperance, Law and Order,
Liberty, Equality, Honorable Dealing, Mercy Education—and so on.

There. Is it good? Sir, it is pie. It will bring into camp any idiot that sits
in darkness anywhere. But not if we adulterate it. It is proper to be emphatic
upon that point. This brand is strictly for Export—apparently. *Apparently.*

FROM "To the Person Sitting in Darkness," by Mark Twain, *North American Review*, Vol.
CLXXII (February, 1901), pp. 165–66, 169–76.

Privately and confidentially, it is nothing of the kind. Privately and confidentially, it is merely an outside cover, gay and pretty and attractive, displaying the special patterns of our Civilization which we reserve for Home Consumption, while *inside* the bale is the Actual Thing that the Customer Sitting in Darkness buys with his blood and tears and land and liberty. That Actual Thing is, indeed, Civilization, but it is only for Export. Is there a difference between the two brands? In some of the details, yes.

We all know that the Business is being ruined. The reason is not far to seek. It is because our Mr. McKinley, and Mr. Chamberlain, and the Kaiser, and the Czar and the French have been exporting the Actual Thing *with the outside cover left off.* This is bad for the Game. It shows that these new players of it are not sufficiently acquainted with it. . . .

. . . by and by comes America, and our Master of the Game plays it badly —plays it as Mr. Chamberlain was playing it in South Africa. It was a mistake to do that; also, it was one which was quite unlooked for in a Master who was playing it so well in Cuba. In Cuba, he was playing the usual and regular *American* game, and it was winning, for there is no way to beat it. The Master, contemplating Cuba, said: "Here is an oppressed and friendless little nation which is willing to fight to be free; we go partners, and put up the strength of seventy million sympathizers and the resources of the United States: play!" Nothing but Europe combined could call that hand: and Europe cannot combine on anything. There, in Cuba, he was following our great traditions in a way which made us very proud of him, and proud of the deep dissatisfaction which his play was provoking in Continental Europe. Moved by a high inspiration, he threw out those stirring words which proclaimed that forcible annexation would be "criminal aggression;" and in that utterance fired another "shot heard round the world." The memory of that fine saying will be outlived by the remembrance of no act of his but one—that he forgot it within the twelvemonth, and its honorable gospel along with it.

For, presently, came the Philippine temptation. It was strong; it was too strong, and he made that bad mistake: he played the European game, the Chamberlain game. It was a pity; it was a great pity, that error; that one grievous error, that irrevocable error. For it was the very place and time to play the American game again. And at no cost. Rich winnings to be gathered in, too; rich and permanent; indestructible; a fortune transmissible forever to the children of the flag. Not land, not money, no dominion—no, something worth many times more than that dross: our share, the spectacle of a nation of long harassed and persecuted slaves set free through our influence; our posterity's share, the golden memory of that fair deed. The game was in our hands. If it had been played according to the American rules, Dewey would have sailed away from Manila as soon as he had destroyed the Spanish fleet— after putting up a sign on shore guaranteeing foreign property and life against damage by the Filipinos, and warning the Powers that interference with the emancipated patriots would be regarded as an act unfriendly to the United

States. The Powers cannot combine, in even a bad cause, and the sign would not have been molested.

Dewey could have gone about his affairs elsewhere, and left the competent Filipino army to starve out the little Spanish garrison and send it home, and the Filipino citizens to set up the form of government they might prefer, and deal with the friars and their doubtful acquisitions according to Filipino ideas of fairness and justice—ideas which have since been tested and found to be of as high an order as any that prevail in Europe or America.

But we played the Chamberlain game, and lost the chance to add another Cuba and another honorable deed to our good record.

The more we examine the mistake, the more clearly we perceive that it is going to be bad for the Business. The Person Sitting in Darkness is almost sure to say: "There is something curious about this—curious and unaccountable. There must be two Americas: one that sets the captive free, and one that takes a once-captive's new freedom away from him, and picks a quarrel with him with nothing to found it on; then kills him to get his land."

The truth is, the Person Sitting in Darkness *is* saying things like that; and for the sake of the Business we must persuade him to look at the Philippine matter in another and healthier way. We must arrange his opinions for him. I believe it can be done; for Mr. Chamberlain has arranged England's opinion of the South African matter, and done it most cleverly and successfully. He presented the facts—some of the facts—and showed those confiding people what the facts meant. He did it statistically, which is a good way. He used the formula: "Twice 2 are 14, and 2 from 9 leaves 35." Figures are effective; figures will convince the elect.

Now, my plan is a still bolder one than Mr. Chamberlain's, though apparently a copy of it. Let us be franker than Mr. Chamberlain; let us audaciously present the whole of the facts, shirking none, then explain them according to Mr. Chamberlain's formula. This daring truthfulness will astonish and dazzle the Person Sitting in Darkness, and he will take the Explanation down before his mental vision has had time to get back into focus. Let us say to him:

"Our case is simple. On the 1st of May, Dewey destroyed the Spanish fleet. This left the Archipelago in the hands of its proper and rightful owners, the Filipino nation. Their army numbered 30,000 men, and they were competent to whip out or starve out the little Spanish garrison; then the people could set up a government of their own devising. Our traditions required that Dewey should now set up his warning sign, and go away. But the Master of the Game happened to think of another plan—the European plan. He acted upon it. This was, to send out an army—ostensibly to help the native patriots put the finishing touch upon their long and plucky struggle for independence, but really to take their land away from them and keep it. That is, in the interest of Progress and Civilization. The plan developed, stage by stage, and quite satisfactorily. We entered into a military alliance with the trusting Filipinos, and they hemmed in Manila on the land side, and by their valuable help the place, with its garrison of 8,000 or 10,000 Spaniards, was captured—a thing which we could not have accomplished unaided at that time. We got their help by—by ingenuity. We knew they were fighting for their independence, and that they had been at it for two years. We knew they supposed that we also were fighting in their worthy cause—just as we had helped the Cubans fight for Cuban independence—and we allowed them to go on thinking so. *Until Manila was ours and we could get along without them.* Then we showed our hand. Of course, they were surprised—that was natural; surprised and disappointed; disappointed and grieved. To them it looked un-American; uncharacteristic; foreign to our established traditions. And this was natural, too; for we were only playing the American Game in public—in private it was the European. It was neatly done, very neatly, and it bewildered them. They could not understand it; for we had been so friendly—so affectionate, even—with those simple-minded patriots! We, our own selves, had brought back out of exile their leader, their hero, their hope, their Washington—Aguinaldo; brought him in a warship, in high honor, under the sacred shelter and hospitality of the flag; brought him back and restored him to his people, and got their moving and eloquent gratitude for it. Yes, we had been so friendly to them, and had heartened them up in so many ways! We had lent them guns and ammunition; advised with them; exchanged pleasant courtesies with them; placed our sick and wounded in their kindly care; intrusted our Spanish prisoners to their humane and honest hands; fought shoulder to shoulder with them against "the common enemy" (our own phrase); praised their courage, praised their gallantry, praised their mercifulness, praised their fine and honorable conduct; borrowed their trenches, borrowed strong positions which they had previously captured from the Spaniards; petted them, lied to them—officially proclaiming that our land and naval forces came to give them their freedom and displace the bad Spanish Government—fooled them, used them until we needed them no longer; then derided the sucked orange and threw it away. We kept the positions which we had beguiled them of; by and by, we moved a force forward and overlapped patriot ground—a clever thought, for we needed trouble, and this would produce it. A Filipino soldier, crossing the ground, where no one had a right to forbid him, was shot by our sentry. The badgered patriots resented this with arms, without waiting to know whether Aguinaldo, who was absent, would approve or not. Aguinaldo did not approve; but that availed nothing. What we wanted, in the interest of Progress and Civilization, was the Archipelago, unencumbered by patriots struggling for independence; and War was what we needed. We clinched our opportunity. It is Mr. Chamberlain's case over again—at least in its motive and intention; and we played the game as adroitly as he played it himself."

At this point in our frank statement of fact to the Person Sitting in Darkness, we should throw in a little trade taffy about the Blessings of Civilization—for a change, and for the refreshment of his spirit—then go on with our tale:

"We and the patriots having captured Manila, Spain's ownership of the Archipelago and her sovereignty over it were at an end—obliterated—annihilated—not a rag or shred of either remaining behind. It was then that we conceived the divinely humorous idea of *buying* both of these specters from Spain! [It is quite safe to confess this to the Person Sitting in Darkness, since neither he nor any other sane person will believe it.] In buying those ghosts for twenty millions, we also contracted to take care of the friars and their accumulations. I think we also agreed to propagate leprosy and smallpox, but as to this there is doubt. But it is not important; persons afflicted with the friars do not mind other diseases.

"With our Treaty ratified, Manila subdued, and our Ghosts secured, we had no further use for Aguinaldo and the owners of the Archipelago. We forced a war, and we have been hunting America's guest and ally through the woods and swamps ever since."

At this point in the tale, it will be well to boast a little of our war work and our heroisms in the field, so as to make our performance look as fine as England's in South Africa; but I believe it will not be best to emphasize this too much. We must be cautious. Of course, we must read the war telegrams to the Person, in order to keep up our frankness; but we can throw an air of humorousness over them, and that will modify their grim eloquence a little, and their rather indiscret exhibitions of gory exultation. Before reading to him the following display heads of the dispatches of November 18, 1900, it will be well to practice on them in private first, so as to get the right tang of lightness and gayety into them:

"ADMINISTRATION WEARY OF PROTRACTED HOSTILITIES!"
"REAL WAR AHEAD FOR FILIPINO REBELS!"*

"WILL SHOW NO MERCY!"
"KITCHENER'S PLAN ADOPTED!"

Kitchener knows how to handle disagreeable people who are fighting for their homes and their liberties, and we must let on that we are merely imitating Kitchener, and have no national interest in the matter, further than to get ourselves admired by the Great Family of Nations, in which august company our Master of the Game has bought a place for us in the back row.

Of course, we must not venture to ignore our General MacArthur's reports—oh, why do they keep on printing those embarrassing things?—we must drop them trippingly from the tongue and take the chances:

During the last ten months our losses have been 268 killed and 750 wounded; Filipino loss, *three thousand two hundred and twenty-seven killed,* and 694 wounded.

* "Rebels!" Mumble that funny word—don't let the Person catch it distinctly.

We must stand ready to grab the Person Sitting in Darkness, for he will swoon away at this confession saying: "Good God! those 'niggers' spare their wounded, and the Americans massacre theirs!"

We must bring him to, and coax him and coddle him, and assure him that the ways of Providence are best, and that it would not become us to find fault with them; and then, to show him that we are only imitators, not originators, we must read the following passage from the letter of an American soldier lad in the Philippines to his mother, published in *Public Opinion,* of Decorah, Iowa, describing the finish of a victorious battle: "We never left one alive. If one was wounded, we would run our bayonets through him."

Having now laid all the historical facts before the Person Sitting in Darkness, we should bring him to again, and explain them to him. We should say to him:

"They look doubtful, but in reality they are not. There have been lies; yes, but they were told in a good cause. We have been treacherous; but that was only in order that real good might come out of apparent evil. True, we have crushed a deceived and confiding people; we have turned against the weak and the friendless who trusted us; we have stamped out a just and intelligent and well-ordered republic; we have stabbed an ally in the back and slapped the face of a guest; we have bought a Shadow from an enemy that hadn't it to sell; we have robbed a trusting friend of his land and his liberty; we have invited our clean young men to shoulder a discredited musket and do bandits' work under a flag which bandits have been accustomed to fear, not to follow; we have debauched America's honor and blackened her face before the world; but each detail was for the best. We know this. The Head of every State and Sovereignty in Christendom and ninety per cent. of every legislative body in Christendom, including our Congress and our fifty State legislatures, are members not only of the church, but also of the Blessings-of-Civilization Trust. This world-girdling accumulation of trained morals, high principles, and justice cannot do an unright thing, an unfair thing, an ungenerous thing, an unclean thing. It knows what it is about. Give yourself no uneasiness; it is all right."

Now then, that will convince the Person. You will see. It will restore the Business. Also, it will elect the Master of the Game to the vacant place in the Trinity of our national gods; and there on their high thrones the Three will sit, age after age, in the people's sight, each bearing the Emblem of his service: Washington, the Sword of the Liberator; Lincoln, the Slave's Broken Chains; the Master, the Chains Repaired.

It will give the Business a splendid new start. You will see.

Everything is prosperous, now; everything is just as we should wish it. We have got the Archipelago, and we shall never give it up. Also, we have every reason to hope that we shall have an opportunity before very long to slip out of our congressional contract with Cuba and give her something better in the place of it. It is a rich country, and many of us are already beginning to see that the contract was a sentimental mistake. But now—right now— is the best time to do some profitable rehabilitating work—work that will set us up and make us comfortable, and discourage gossip. We cannot conceal from ourselves that, privately, we are a little troubled about our uniform. It is one of our prides; it is acquainted with honor; it is familiar with great deeds and noble; we love it, we revere it; and so this errand it is on makes us uneasy. And our flag—another pride of ours, our chiefest! We have worshiped it so; and when we have seen it in far lands—glimpsing it unexpectedly in that strange sky, waving its welcome and benediction to us—we have caught our breath, and uncovered our heads, and couldn't speak, for a moment, for the thought of what it was to us and the great ideals it stood for. Indeed, we *must* do something about these things; we must not have the flag out there, and the uniform. They are not needed there; we can manage in some other way. . . . And as for a flag for the Philippine Province, it is easily managed. We can have a special one—our States do it: we can have just our usual flag, with the white stripes painted black and the stars replaced by the skull and crossbones. . . .

By help of these suggested amendments, Progress and Civilization in that country can have a boom, and it will take in the Persons who are Sitting in Darkness, and we can resume Business at the old stand.

13

MUCKRAKERS
AND THE
NEW FREEDOM

W hile the nation was expanding
and becoming an industrial and business society, that activity itself
seemed to satisfy the American demand for action and progress. But
when, around the turn of the century, the new society settled into a smug
acceptance of its own gains and values, the inevitable and necessary reaction began. The equally essential American demand for individual freedom and the just society asserted itself in a variety of reform movements,
both of idea and fact, as we have already noted in Sections 10 and 11 of
this book.

Theodore Roosevelt became President upon the death of McKinley
and turned to "busting the trusts" which had long been the mainstay of
his own Republican party. And, then, a Democratic President, Woodrow
Wilson, called for a "New Freedom" (see his inaugural address in Section 1), in which the individual would regain his proper stature even in
an industrial society growing larger, more powerful, and more impersonal day by day. A new tension developed between the economic power
structure of America and the government, and by extension between
Big Business and the bulk of the American people. Muckrakers began
to write, exposing the excesses and disgraces of the business world. Their
writings were popular successes and were followed by serious demands
for reform and regulation. The labor movement took on new life, both
within the established unions and the new International Workers of the

World—the radical and utterly idealistic "Wobblies." The tone of the country became one of reaction, of a turning away, and as well of a positive demand for a restoration of those individual rights and privileges which had vanished or at least diminished during the period of industrial expansion.

The new pragmatic philosophy of William James and John Dewey re-emphasized Emerson's belief in the individual discovery of truth apart from dogma and accepted ideas. A reaction against mechanistic materialism, this philosophical movement reasserted personal dignity and spiritual value in the face of the forces of conformity and strictly material values.

American naturalism became a major literary force, not as detached and "scientifically objective" as Zola's naturalism, but passionately concerned with the loss of human freedom in a world of economic chance. Howells, Crane, Norris, Dreiser, Herrick, Sinclair, and many others focused their attention on the little man at the bottom of the economic pile, the forgotten man in an era of industrial and financial giants. Social realism, a literary mode essentially alien to the American idealistic and aesthetic literary tradition, flowered before the war with a strength and progressive vigor which it was to lose later, for Babbitt and the small businessman of the 1920's did not inspire the same sort of vigorous opposition as did Gould and Fisk and the Wall Street tycoons.

Even if its essential impulse was negative, the period had much of the vitality and spirit of earlier days; these were angry voices raised against the vices of the system, but they were not voices alien to hope and the dream of progress. In the following pieces, both that anger and its accompanying idealism are exhibited, from the muckraker's protests to Woodrow Wilson's committing the nation to world politics in a war to make the world "safe for democracy."

THEODORE ROOSEVELT
There Are Real and Grave Evils

Theodore Roosevelt, historian, cow-puncher, explorer, soldier, and twenty-sixth President of the United States, coined the term "muckrakers" to describe those

FROM "First Annual Message to Congress," December 3, 1901, by Theodore Roosevelt, in *A Compilation of the Messages and Papers of the Presidents, 1789–1904*, ed. James D. Richardson, rev. and enl. by G. R. Devitt (Washington, D.C.: Bureau of National Literature and Art, 1904), Vol. X, pp. 421–25.

journalists of the 1900's who dedicated their efforts to exposing public and private corruption, but it was his administration which first employed the weight of federal authority against monopolistic business abuses. He dissolved the Northern Securities Company, and gained a considerable reputation for "trust busting." However, he distinguished between "good" and "bad" trusts, and in actuality he prosecuted comparatively few of them. The first really effective government action against monopoly would not come until the New Freedom of Woodrow Wilson came into power. Roosevelt's first message to Congress expresses his views on the trusts.

The tremendous and highly complex industrial development which went on with ever-accelerated rapidity during the latter half of the nineteenth century brings us face to face, at the beginning of the twentieth, with very serious social problems. The old laws, and the old customs which had almost the binding force of law, were once quite sufficient to regulate the accumulation and distribution of wealth. Since the industrial changes which have so enormously increased the productive power of mankind, they are no longer sufficient.

The growth of cities has gone on beyond comparison faster than the growth of the country, and the upbuilding of the great industrial centers has meant a startling increase, not merely in the aggregate of wealth, but in the number of very large individual, and especially of very large corporate, fortunes. The creation of these great corporate fortunes has not been due to the tariff nor to any other governmental action, but to natural causes in the business world, operating in other countries as they operate in our own.

The process has aroused much antagonism, a great part of which is wholly without warrant. . . . The captains of industry who have driven the railway systems across this continent, who have built up our commerce, who have developed our manufactures, have on the whole done great good to our people. Without them the material development of which we are so justly proud could never have taken place. Moreover, we should recognize the immense importance of this material development by leaving as unhampered as is compatible with the public good the strong and forceful men upon whom the success of business operations inevitably rests. The slightest study of business conditions will satisfy any one capable of forming a judgment that the personal equation is the most important factor in a business operation; that the business ability of the man at the head of any business concern, big or little, is usually the factor which fixes the gulf between striking success and hopeless failure.

An additional reason for caution in dealing with corporations is to be found in the international commercial conditions of today. The same business conditions which have produced the great aggregations of corporate and individual wealth have made them very potent factors in international commercial competition. Business concerns which have the largest means at their disposal and are managed by the ablest men are naturally those which take the lead in the strife for commercial supremacy among the nations of the world. America has only just begun to assume that commanding position in the international business world which we believe will more and more be hers. It is of the utmost importance that this position be not jeopardized, especially at a time when the overflowing abundance of our own natural resources and the skill, business energy, and mechanical aptitude of our people make foreign markets essential. Under such conditions it would be most unwise to cramp or to fetter the youthful strength of our Nation.

Moreover, it cannot too often be pointed out that to strike with ignorant violence at the interests of one set of men almost inevitably endangers the interests of all. The fundamental rule in our national life—the rule which underlies all others—is that, on the whole, and in the long run, we shall go up or down together. Disaster to great business enterprises can never have its effects limited to the men at the top. It spreads throughout and while it is bad for everybody, it is worst for those farthest down. The capitalist may be shorn of his luxuries; but the wage-worker may be deprived of even bare necessities.

The mechanism of modern business is so delicate that extreme care must be taken not to interfere with it in a spirit of rashness or ignorance. Many of those who have made it their vocation to denounce the great industrial combinations which are popularly, although with technical inaccuracy, known as "trusts", appeal especially to hatred and fear. These are precisely the two emotions, particularly when combined with ignorance, which unfit men for the exercise of cool and steady judgment. In facing new industrial conditions, the whole history of the world shows that legislation will generally be both unwise and ineffective unless undertaken after calm inquiry and with sober self-restraint. Much of the legislation directed at the trusts would have been exceedingly michievous had it *not* also been entirely ineffective. . . .

All this is true; and yet it is also true that there are real and grave evils, one of the chief being overcapitalization because of its many baleful consequences; and a resolute and practical effort must be made to correct these evils. . . .

It is no limitation upon property rights or freedom of contract to require that when men receive from government the privilege of doing business under corporate form, which frees them from individual responsibility, and enables them to call into their enterprises the capital of the public, they shall do so upon absolutely truthful representations as to the value of the property in which the capital is to be invested. Corporations engaged in interstate commerce should be regulated if they are found to exercise a license working to the public injury. It should be as much the aim of those who seek for social betterment to rid the business world of crimes of cunning as to rid the entire body politic of crimes of violence. Great corporations exist only because they are created and safeguarded by our institutions; and it is therefore our right and our duty to see that they work in harmony with these institutions.

The first essential in determining how to deal with the great industrial combinations is knowledge of the facts—publicity. In the interest of the public, the government should have the right to inspect and examine the working of the great corporations engaged in interstate business. Publicity is the only sure remedy which we can now invoke. What further remedies are needed in the way of governmental regulation, or taxation, can only be determined after publicity has been obtained, by process of law, and in the course of administration. The first requisite is knowledge, full and complete—knowledge which may be made public to the world. . . .

The large corporations, commonly called trusts, though organized in one State, always do business in many States, often doing very little business in the State where they are incorporated. There is utter lack of uniformity in the State laws about them; and as no State has any exclusive interest in or power over their acts, it has in practice proved impossible to get adequate regulation through State action. Therefore, in the interest of the whole people, the nation should, without interfering with the power of the States in the matter itself, also assume power of supervision and regulation over all corporations doing an interstate business. This is especially true where the corporation derives a portion of its wealth from the existence of some monopolistic element or tendency in its business. There would be no hardship in such supervision; banks are subject to it, and in their case it is now accepted as a simple matter of course. . . .

When the Constitution was adopted, at the end of the eighteenth century, no human wisdom could foretell the sweeping changes, alike in industrial and political conditions, which were to take place by the beginning of the twentieth century. At that time it was accepted as a matter of course that the several States were the proper authorities to regulate, so far as was then necessary, the comparatively insignificant and strictly localized corporate bodies of the day. The conditions are now wholly different and wholly different action is called for. I believe that a law can be framed which will enable the National Government to exercise control along the lines above indicated; profiting by the experience gained through the passage and administration of the Interstate Commerce Act. If, however, the judgment of the Congress is that it lacks the constitutional power to pass such an act, then a constitutional amendment should be submitted to confer the power. . . .

UPTON SINCLAIR
No Tiniest Particle of Organic Matter Was Wasted

In 1906 Upton Sinclair (1878–) published a novel entitled The Jungle. *Though no great work of literary art, it presented a thorough and gruesome exposé of conditions in the Chicago meat-packing industry. Brutality and disease were rampant; working conditions were deplorable. The impact of* The Jungle *was swift; President Theodore Roosevelt asked Sinclair to come to the White House, and soon afterward ordered an investigation which culminated in the Pure Food Act of 1906. The prolific Sinclair wrote dozens of other books, most of them exposing unsavory conditions and activities; an ardent Socialist, he almost won the governorship of California in 1934 with his "End Poverty in California" program.*

There were two hundred and fifty miles of track within the yards, their guide went on to tell them. They brought about ten thousand head of cattle every day, and as many hogs, and half as many sheep—which meant some eight or ten million live creatures turned into food every year. One stood and watched, and little by little caught the drift of the tide, as it set in the direction of the packing-houses. There were groups of cattle being driven to the chutes, which were roadways about fifteen feet wide, raised high above the pens. In these chutes the stream of animals was continuous; it was quite uncanny to watch them, pressing on to their fate, all unsuspicious—a very river of death. Our friends were not poetical, and the sight suggested to them no metaphors of human destiny; they thought only of the wonderful efficiency of it all. The chutes into which the hogs went climbed high up—to the very top of the distant buildings; and Jokubas explained that the hogs went up by the power of their own legs, and then their weight carried them back through all the processes necessary to make them into pork.

"They don't waste anything here," said the guide, and then he laughed and added a witticism, which he was pleased that his unsophisticated friends should take to be his own: "They use everything about the hog except the squeal." In front of Brown's General Office building there grows a tiny plot of grass, and this, you may learn, is the only bit of green thing in Packingtown; likewise this jest about the hog and his squeal, the stock in trade of all the guides, is the one gleam of humor that you will find there.

After they had seen enough of the pens, the party went up the street to

FROM *The Jungle*, by Upton Sinclair (New York: Doubleday Page and Co., 1906), pp. 38–47.

the mass of buildings which occupy the centre of the yards. These buildings, made of brick and stained with innumberable layers of Packingtown smoke, were painted all over with advertising signs, from which the vistor realized suddenly that he had come to the home of many of the torments of his life. It was here that they made those products with the wonders of which they pestered him so—by placards that defaced the landscape when he travelled, and by staring advertisements in the newspapers and magazines—by silly little jingles that he could not get out of his mind, and gaudy pictures that lurked for him around every street corner. Here was where they made Brown's Imperial Hams and Bacon, Brown's Dressed Beef, Brown's Excelsior Sausages! Here was the headquarters of Durham's Pure Leaf Lard, of Durham's Breakfast Bacon, Durham's Canned Beef, Potted Ham, Devilled Chicken, Peerless Fertilizer!

Entering one of the Durham buildings, they found a number of other visitors waiting; and before long there came a guide, to escort them through the place. They make a great feature of showing strangers through the packing-plants, for it is a good advertisement. But ponas Jokubas whispered maliciously that the visitors did not see any more than the packers wanted them to.

They climbed a long series of stairways outside of the building, to the top of its five or six stories. Here were the chute, with its river of hogs, all patiently toiling upward; there was a place for them to rest to cool off, and then through another passageway they went into a room from which there is no returning for hogs.

It was a long, narrow room, with a gallery along it for visitors. At the head there was a great iron wheel, about twenty feet in circumference, with rings here and there along its edge. Upon both sides of this wheel there was a narrow space, into which came the hogs at the end of their journey; in the midst of them stood a great burly negro, bare-armed and bare-chested. He was resting for the moment, for the wheel had stopped while men were cleaning up. In a minute or two, however, it began slowly to revolve, and then the men upon each side of it sprang to work. They had chains which they fastened about the leg of the nearest hog, and the other end of the chain they hooked into one of the rings upon the wheel. So, as the wheel turned, a hog was suddenly jerked off his feet and borne aloft.

At the same instant the ear was assailed by a most terrifying shriek; the visitors started in alarm, the women turned pale and shrank back. The shriek was followed by another, louder and yet more agonizing—for once started upon that journey, the hog never came back; at the top of the wheel he was shunted off upon a trolley, and went sailing down the room. And meantime another was swung up, and then another, and another, until there was a double line of them, each dangling by a foot and kicking in frenzy—and squealing. The uproar was appalling, perilous to the ear-drums; one feared there was too much sound for the room to hold—that the walls must give way or the ceiling crack. There were high squeals and low squeals, grunts, and wails of agony;

there would come a momentary lull, and then a fresh outburst, louder than ever, surging up to a deafening climax. It was too much for some of the visitors—the men would look at each other, laughing nervously, and the women would stand with hands clenched, and the blood rushing to their faces, and the tears starting in their eyes.

Meantime, heedless of all these things, the men upon the floor were going about their work. Neither squeals of hogs nor tears of visitors made any difference to them; one by one they hooked up the hogs, and one by one with a swift stroke they slit their throats. There was a long line of hogs, with squeals and life-blood ebbing away together; until at last each started again, and vanished with a splash into a huge vat of boiling water.

It was all so very businesslike that one watched it fascinated. It was pork-making by machinery, pork-making by applied mathematics. And yet somehow the most matter-of-fact person could not help thinking of the hogs; they were so innocent, they came so very trustingly; and they were so very human in their protests—and so perfectly within their rights! They had done nothing to deserve it; and it was adding insult to injury, as the thing was done here, swinging them up in this cold-blooded, impersonal way, without a pretence at apology, without the homage of a tear. Now and then a visitor wept, to be sure; but this slaughtering-machine ran on, visitors or no visitors. It was like some horrible crime committed in a dungeon, all unseen and unheeded, buried out of sight and of memory.

One could not stand and watch very long without becoming philosophical, without beginning to deal in symbols and similes, and to hear the hog-squeal of the universe. Was it permitted to believe that there was nowhere upon the earth, or above the earth, a heaven for hogs, where they were requited for all this suffering? Each one of these hogs was a separate creature. Some were white hogs, some were black; some were brown, some were spotted; some were old, some were young; some were long and lean, some were monstrous. And each of them had an individuality of his own, a will of his own, a hope and a heart's desire; each was full of self-confidence, of self-importance, and a sense of dignity. And trusting and strong in faith he had gone about his business, the while a black shadow hung over him and a horrid Fate waited in his pathway. Now suddenly it had swooped upon him, and had seized him by the leg. Relentless, remorseless, it was; all his protests, his screams, were nothing to it—it did its cruel will with him, as if his wishes, his feelings, had simply no existence at all; it cut his throat and watched him gasp out his life. And now was one to believe that there was nowhere a god of hogs, to whom this hog-personality was precious, to whom these hog-squeals and agonies had a meaning? Who would take this hog into his arms and comfort him, reward him for his work well done, and show him the meaning of his sacrifice? Perhaps some glimpse of all this was in the thoughts of our humble-minded Jurgis, as he turned to go on with the rest of the party, and muttered: "Dieve—but I'm glad I'm not a hog!" . . .

The carcass hog was scooped out of the vat by machinery, and then it fell to the second floor, passing on the way through a wonderful machine with numerous scrapers, which adjusted themselves to the size and shape of the animal, and sent it out at the other end with nearly all of its bristles removed. It was then again strung up by machinery, and sent upon another trolley ride; this time passing between two lines of men, who sat upon a raised platform, each doing a certain single thing to the carcass as it came to him. One scraped the outside of a leg; another scraped the inside of the same leg. One with a swift stroke cut the throat; another with two swift strokes severed the head, which fell to the floor and vanished through a hole. Another made a slit down the body; a second opened the body wider; a third with a saw cut the breast-bone; a fourth loosened the entrails; a fifth pulled them out—and they also slid through a hole in the floor. There were men to scrape each side and men to scrape the back; there were men to clean the carcass inside, to trim it and wash it. Looking down this room, one saw, creeping slowly, a line of dangling hogs a hundred yards in length; and for every yard there was a man, working as if a demon were after him. At the end of this hog's progress every inch of the carcass had been gone over several times; and then it was rolled into the chilling room, where it stayed for twenty-four hours, and where a stranger might lose himself in a forest of freezing hogs.

Before the carcass was admitted here, however, it had to pass a government inspector, who sat in the doorway and felt of the gland in the neck for tuberculosis. This government inspector did not have the manner of a man who was worked to death; he was apparently not haunted by a fear that the hog might get by him before he had finished his testing. If you were a sociable person, he was quite willing to enter into conversation with you, and to explain to you the deadly nature of the ptomaines which are found in tubercular pork; and while he was talking with you you could hardly be so ungrateful as to notice that a dozen carcasses were passing him untouched. This inspector wore a blue uniform, with brass buttons, and he gave an atmosphere of authority to the scene, and, as it were, put the stamp of official approval upon the things which were done in Durham's.

Jurgis went down the line with the rest of the visitors, staring open-mouthed, lost in wonder. He had dressed hogs himself in the forest of Lithuania; but he had never expected to live to see one hog dressed by several hundred men. It was like a wonderful poem to him, and he took it all in guilelessly—even to the conspicuous signs demanding immaculate cleanliness of the employees. Jurgis was vexed when the cynical Jokubas translated these signs with sarcastic comments, offering to take them to the secret-rooms where the spoiled meats went to be doctored.

The party descended to the next floor, where the various waste materials were treated. Here came the entrails, to be scraped and washed clean for sausage-casings; men and women worked here in the midst of a sickening stench, which caused the vistors to hasten by, gasping. To another room came all the scraps to be "tanked," which meant boiling and pumping off the grease to make soap and lard; below they took out the refuse, and this, too, was a region in which the visitors did not linger. In still other places men were engaged in cutting up the carcasses that had been through the chilling rooms. First there were the "splitters," the most expert workmen in the plant, who earned as high as fifty cents an hour, and did not a thing all day except chop hogs down the middle. Then there were "cleaver men," great giants with muscles of iron; each had two men to attend him—to slide the half carcass in front of him on the table, and hold it while he chopped it, and then turn each piece so that he might chop it once more. His cleaver had a blade about two feet long, and he never made but one cut; he made it so neatly, too, that his implement did not smite through and dull itself—there was just enough force for a perfect cut, and no more. So through various yawning holes there slipped to the floor below—to one room hams, to another forequarters, to another sides of pork. One might go down to this floor and see the pickling-rooms, where the hams were put into vats, and the great smoke-rooms, with their airtight iron doors. In other rooms they prepared salt-pork—there were whole cellars full of it, built up in great towers to the ceiling. In yet other rooms they were putting up meat in boxes and barrels, and wrapping hams and bacon in oiled paper, sealing and labelling and sewing them. From the doors of these rooms went men with loaded trucks, to the platform where freight cars were waiting to be filled; and one went there and realized with a start that he had come at last to the ground floor of this enormous building.

Then the party went across the street to where they did the killing of beef— where every hour they turned four or five hundred cattle into meat. Unlike the place they had left, all this work was done on one floor, and instead of there being one line of carcasses which moved to the workmen, there were fifteen or twenty lines, and the men moved from one to another of these. This made a scene of intense activity, a picture of human power wonderful to watch. It was all in one great room, like a circus amphitheater, with a gallery for visitors running over the center.

Along one side of the room ran a narrow gallery, a few feet from the floor, into which gallery the cattle were driven by men with goads which gave them electric shocks. Once crowded in here, the creatures were prisoned, each in a separate pen, by gates that shut, leaving them no room to turn around, and while they stood bellowing and plunging, over the top of the pen there leaned one of the "knockers," armed with a sledge hammer, and watching for a chance to deal a blow. The room echoed with the thuds in quick succession, and the stamping and kicking of the steers. The instant the animal had fallen, the "knocker" passed on to another; while a second man raised a lever, and the side of the pen was raised, and the animal, still kicking and struggling, slid out to the "killing bed." Here a man put shackles about one leg, and pressed another lever, and the body was jerked up into the air. There were fifteen or twenty such pens, and it was a matter of only a couple of minutes to knock fifteen or twenty cattle and roll them out. Then once more the gates were opened, and another lot rushed in; and so out of each pen there rolled a steady stream of carcasses, which the men upon the killing-beds had to get out of the way.

The manner in which they did this was something to be seen and never forgotten. They worked with furious intensity, literally upon the run—at a pace with which there is nothing to be compared except a football game. It was all highly specialized labor, each man having his task to do; generally this would consist of only two or three specific cuts, and he would pass down the line of fifteen or twenty carcasses, making these cuts upon each. First there came the "butcher," to bleed them; this meant one swift stroke, so swift that you could not see it—only the flash of the knife; and before you could realize it, the man had darted on to the next line, and a stream of bright red was pouring out upon the floor. This floor was half an inch deep with blood, in spite of the best efforts of men who kept shoveling it through holes; it must have made the floor slippery, but no one could have guessed this by watching the men at work.

The carcass hung for a few minutes to bleed; there was no time lost, however, for there were several hanging in each line, and one was always ready. It was let down to the ground, and there came the "headsman," whose task it was to sever the head, with two or three swift strokes. Then came the "floorsman," to make the first cut in the skin; and then another to finish ripping the skin down the center; and then half a dozen more in swift succession, to finish the skinning. After they were through, the carcass was again swung up, and while a man with a stick examined the skin, to make sure that it had not been cut, and another rolled it up and tumbled it through one of the inevitable holes in the floor, the beef proceeded on its journey. There were men to cut it, and men to gut it and scrape it clean inside. There were some with hoses which threw jets of boiling water upon it, and others who removed the feet and added the final touches. In the end, as with the hogs, the finished beef was run into the chilling room, to hang its appointed time.

The visitors were taken there and shown them, all neatly hung in rows, labelled conspicuously with the tags of the government inspectors—and some, which had been killed by a special process, marked with the sign of the "kosher" rabbi, certifying that it was fit for sale to the orthodox. And then the visitors were taken to the other parts of the building, to see what became of each particle of the waste material that had vanished through the floor; and to the pickling-rooms, and the salting-rooms, the canning-rooms, and the packing rooms, where choice meat was prepared for shipping in refrigerator-cars, destined to be eaten in all the four corners of civilization. Afterward they went outside, wandering about among the mazes of buildings in which was done the work auxiliary to this great industry. There was scarcely a thing needed in the business that Durham and Company did not make for themselves. There was a great steam-power plant and an electricity plant. There was a barrel factory, and a boiler-repair shop. There was a building to which the grease was piped, and made into soap and lard, and then there was a factory for making lard cans, and another for making soap boxes. There was a building in which the bristles were cleaned and dried, for the making of hair cushions and such things; there was a building where the skins were dried and tanned, there was another where heads and feet were made into glue, and another where bones were made into fertilizer. No tiniest particle of organic matter was wasted in Durham's. Out of the horns of the cattle they made combs, buttons, hair-pins, and imitation ivory; out of the shin bones and other big bones they cut knife and tooth-brush handles, and mouthpieces for pipes; out of the hoofs they cut hair-pins and buttons, before they made the rest into glue. From such things as feet, knuckles, hide clippings and sinews came such strange and unlikely products as gelatin, isinglass, and phosphorus, bone-black, shoe-blacking and bone-oil. They had curled-hair works for the cattle tails, and a "wool-pullery" for the sheep skins; they made pepsin from the stomachs of the pigs, and albumen from the blood, and violin strings from the ill-smelling entrails. When there was nothing else to be done with a thing, they first put it into a tank and got out of it all the tallow and grease, and then they made it into fertilizer. All these industries were gathered into buildings near by, connected by galleries and railroads with the main establishment; and it was estimated that they had handled nearly a quarter of a billion of animals since the founding of the plant by the elder Durham a generation and more ago. If you counted with it the other big plants—and they were now really all one—it was, so Jokubas informed them, the greatest aggregation of labor and capital ever gathered in one place. It employed thirty thousand men; it supported directly two hundred and fifty thousand people in its neighborhood, and indirectly it supported half a million. It sent its products to every country in the civilized world, and it furnished the food for no less than thirty million people!

LINCOLN STEFFENS
The People Are Not Innocent

A leading figure among the muckrakers was Lincoln Steffens (1866–1936). Writing for McClure's, the *American* Magazine *and* Everybody's, *he specialized in revealing corruption in municipal government and its tie-in with business. His first book,* The Shame of the Cities, *contained a collection of his revealing magazine inquiries into the power structure of various American metropolises. In his Introduction, an excerpt from which follows, he places*

FROM *The Shame of the Cities,* by Lincoln Steffens (New York: McClure, Phillips & Co., 1904), pp. 9–19.

the blame for municipal corruption on those who made it possible; the voters themselves.

In the twentieth-century life in the large city became an important theme in American literature and has continued so. Beginning with William Dean Howells, Stephen Crane and Theodore Dreiser, the list of American writers who have dealt with life in the metropolis has been long and distinguished, including John Dos Passos, Thomas Wolfe, James T. Farrell, F. Scott Fitzgerald, Hart Crane, Saul Bellow, Bernard Malamud, Norman Mailer, and many others.

But do the people want good government? Tammany says they don't. Are the people honest? Are the people better than Tammany? Are they better than the merchant and the politician? Isn't our corrupt government, after all, representative?

President Roosevelt has been sneered at for going about the country preaching as a cure for our American evils, good conduct in the individual, simple honesty, courage, and efficiency. "Platitudes!" the sophisticated say. Platitudes? If my observations have been true, the literal adoption of Mr. Roosevelt's reform scheme would result in a revolution, more radical and terrible to existing institutions from the Congress to the Church, from the bank to the ward organization, than socialism or even than anarchy. Why, that would change all of us—not alone our neighbors, not alone the grafters, but you and me.

No, the contemned methods of our despised politics are the master methods of our braggart business, and the corruption that shocks us in public affairs we practice ourselves in our private concerns. There is no essential difference between the pull that gets your wife into society or for your book a favorable review, and that which gets a heeler into office, a thief out of jail, and a rich man's son on the board of directors of a corporation; none between the corruption of a labor union, a bank, and a political machine; none between a dummy director of a trust and the caucus-bound member of a legislature; none between a labor boss like Sam Parks, a boss of banks like John D. Rockefeller, a boss of railroads like J. P. Morgan, and a political boss like Matthew S. Quay. The boss is not a political, he is an American institution, the product of a freed people that have not the spirit to be free.

And it's all a moral weakness; a weakness right where we think we are strongest. Oh, we are good—on Sunday, and we are "fearfully patriotic" on the Fourth of July. But the bribe we pay to the janitor to prefer our interests to the landlord's, is the little brother of the bribe passed to the alderman to sell a city street, and the father of the air-brake stock assigned to the president of a railroad to have this life-saving invention adopted on his road. And as for graft, railroad passes, saloon and bawdy-house blackmail, and watered stock, all these belong to the same family. We are pathetically proud of our democratic institutions and our republican form of government, of our grand Constitution and our just laws. We are a free and sovereign people, we govern ourselves and the government is ours. But that is the point. We are responsible, not our leaders, since we follow them. We *let* them divert our loyalty from the United States to some "party"; we *let* them boss the party and turn our municipal democracies into autocracies and our republican nation into a plutocracy. We cheat our government and we let our leaders loot it, and we let them wheedle and bribe our sovereignty from us. True, they pass for us strict laws, but we are content to let them pass also bad laws, giving away public property in exchange; and our good, and often impossible, laws we allow to be used for oppression and blackmail. And what can we say? We break our own laws and rob our own government, the lady at the customhouse, the lyncher with his rope, and the captain of industry with his bribe and his rebate. The spirit of graft and of lawlessness is the American spirit.

And this shall not be said? Not plainly? William Travers Jerome, the fearless District Attorney of New York says, "You can say anything you think to the American people. If you are honest with yourself you may be honest with them, and they will forgive not only your candor, but your mistakes." This is the opinion, and the experience too, of an honest man and a hopeful democrat. Who says the other things? Who says "Hush," and "What's the use?" and "ALL's well," when all is rotten? It is the grafter; the coward, too, but the grafter inspires the coward. The doctrine of "addition, division, and silence" is the doctrine of graft. "Don't hurt the party," "Spare the fair fame of the city," are boodle yells. The Fourth of July oration is the "front" of graft. There is no patriotism in it, but treason. It is part of the game. The grafters call for cheers for the flag, "prosperity," and "the party," just as a highway man commands "hands up," and while we are waving and shouting, they float the flag from the nation to the party, turn both into graft factories, and prosperity into a speculative boom to make "weak hands," as the Wall Street phràse has it, hold the watered stock while the strong hands keep the property. "Blame us, blame anybody, but praise the people," this, the politician's advice, is not the counsel of respect for the people, but of contempt. By just such palavering as courtiers play upon the degenerate intellects of weak kings, the bosses, political, financial, and industrial are befuddling and befooling our sovereign American citizenship; and—likewise—they are corrupting it.

And it is corruptible, this citizenship. "I know what Parks is doing," said a New York union workman, "but what do I care. He has raised my wages. Let him have his graft!" And the Philadelphia merchant says the same thing: "The party leaders may be getting more than they should out of the city, but that doesn't hurt me. It may raise taxes a little, but I can stand that. The party keeps up the protective tariff. If that were cut down, my business would be ruined. So long as the party stands pat on that, I stand pat on the party."

The people are not innocent. That is the only "news" in all the journalism of these articles, and no doubt that was not new to many observers. It was to me. When I set out to describe the corrupt systems of certain typical cities, I meant to show simply how the people were deceived and betrayed. But in the very first study—St. Louis—the startling truth lay bare that corruption was not merely political; it was financial, commercial, social; the ramifications of boodle were so complex, various, and far-reaching, that one mind could hardly grasp them, and not even Joseph W. Folk, the tireless prosecutor, could follow them all. . . . When I went next to Minneapolis alone, I could see more independently, without respect for persons, and there were traces of the same phenomenon. The first St. Louis article was called "Tweed Days in St. Louis," and though the "better citizen" received attention the Tweeds were the center of interest. In "The Shame of Minneapolis," the truth was put into the title; it was the Shame of Minneapolis; not of the Ames administration, not of the Tweeds, but of the city and its citizens. . . . In Pittsburgh also the people was the subject, and though the civic spirit there was better, the extent of the corruption throughout the social organization of the community was indicated. But it was not till I got to Philadelphia that the possibilities of popular corruption were worked out to the limit of humiliating confession. That was the place for such a study. There is nothing like it in the country, except possibly, in Cincinnati. Philadelphia certainly is not merely corrupt, but corrupted, and this was made clear. Philadelphia was charged up to—the American citizen.

It was impossible in the space of a magazine article to cover in any one city all the phases of municipal government, so I chose cities that typified most strikingly some particular phase or phases. Thus as St. Louis exemplified boodle; Minneapolis, police graft; Pittsburg, a political and industrial machine; and Philadelphia, general civic corruption; so Chicago was an illustration of reform, and New York of good government. All these things occur in most of these places. There are, and long have been, reformers in St. Louis, and there is to-day police graft there. Minneapolis has had boodling and council reform, and boodling is breaking out there again. Pittsburg has general corruption, and Philadelphia a very perfect political machine. Chicago has police graft and a low order of administrative and general corruption which permeates business, labor, and society generally. As for New York, the metropolis might exemplify almost anything that occurs anywhere in American cities, but no city has had for many years such a good administration as was that of Mayor Seth Low.

That which I have made each city stand for, is that which it had most highly developed. It would be absurd to seek for organized reform in St. Louis, for example, with Chicago next door; or for graft in Chicago with Minneapolis so near. After Minneapolis, a description of administrative corruption in Chicago would have seemed like a repetition. Perhaps it was not just to treat only the conspicuous element in each situation. But why should I be just? I was not judging; I arrogated to myself no such function. I was not writing about Chicago for Chicago, but for the other cities, so I picked out what light each had for the instruction of the others. But, if I was never complete, I never exaggerated. Every one of those articles was an understatement, especially where the conditions were bad, and the proof thereof is that while each article seemed to astonish other cities, it disappointed the city which was its subject. . . .

This is all very unscientific, but then, I am not a scientist. I am a journalist. I did not gather with indifference all the facts and arrange them patiently for permanent preservation and laboratory analysis. I did not want to preserve, I wanted to destroy the facts. My purpose was no more scientific than the spirit of my investigation and reports; it was, as I said above, to see if the shameful facts, spread out in all their shame, would not burn through our civic shamelessness and set fire to American pride. That was the journalism of it. I wanted to move and to convince. That is why I was not interested in all the facts, sought none that was new, and rejected half those that were old. I often was asked to expose something suspected. I couldn't and why should I? Exposure of the unknown was not my purpose. The people: what they will put up with, how they are fooled, how cheaply they are bought, how dearly sold, how easily intimidated, and how led, for good or for evil—that was the inquiry, and so the significant facts were those only which everybody in each city knew, and of these, only those which everybody in every other town would recognize, from their common knowledge of such things, to be probable. But these, understated, were charged always to the guilty persons when individuals were to blame, and finally brought home to the people themselves, who, having the power, have also the responsibility, they and those they respect, and those that guide them.

JOE HILL
Pie in the Sky When You Die

Labor unions, notably the American Federation of Labor, were coming to be respectable in the 1900's, but great masses of industrial workers were without union representation. The I.W.W.—Industrial Workers of the World, known as the Wobblies—attempted to fill the need. Undoubtedly the I.W.W. was radical, with an anarchistic-socialist program demanding the revolutionary overthrow of capitalism through political and economic means. But it was hardly the destructive, violent organization that its foes claimed. In World War I, because of its antiwar stand, it was suppressed, many of its leaders were jailed, and its membership dropped off from more than 100,000 to some

FROM *Rebel Voices, An I. W. W. Anthology*, ed. Joyce C. Kornbluth (Ann Arbor: Univ. of Michigan Press, 1964), pp. 140–41, 145–46. Reprinted by permission of the Industrial Workers of the World, Chicago, Ill.

10,000. The I.W.W. was the first "singing union"; its members sang labor, anti-company songs as they went on strike. The moving spirit in the singing was the legendary Joe Hill. Born Joel Haaglund, he came to the United States from Sweden about 1901, and wrote many lyrics for the I.W.W. Songbooks before he was shot to death in 1915 for an alleged murder. Here are several of Joe Hill's songs.

THERE IS POWER IN A UNION

(Tune: "There Is Power in the Blood")

Would you have freedom from wage slavery,
· Then join in the grand Industrial band;
Would you from mis'ry and hunger be free,
Then come! Do your share, like a man.

Chorus:

There is pow'r, there is pow'r
In a band of workingmen,
When they stand hand in hand,
That's a pow'r, that's a pow'r
That must rule in every land—
One Industrial Union Grand.

Would you have mansions of gold in the sky,
And live in a shack, way in the back?
Would you have wings up in heaven to fly?
And starve here with rags on your back?

If you've had "nuff" of "the blood of the lamb"
Then join in the grand Industrial band;
If, for a change, you would have eggs and ham,
Then come! Do your share, like a man.

If you like sluggers to beat off your head,
Then don't organize, all unions despise,
If you want nothing before you are dead,
Shake hands with your boss and look wise.

Come all ye workers, from every land,
Come join in the grand Industrial band,
Then we our share of this earth shall demand.
Come on! Do your share, like a man.

NEARER MY JOB TO THEE

(*Tune: "Nearer My God to Thee"*)

Nearer my job to thee,
Nearer with glee,
Three plunks for the office fee,
But my fare is free.
My train is running fast,
I've got a job at last,
Nearer my job to thee
Nearer to thee.

Arrived where my job should be,
Nothing in sight I see,
Nothing but sand, by gee,
Job went up a tree.
No place to eat or sleep,
Snakes in the sage brush creep.
Nero a saint would be,
Shark, compared to thee.

Nearer to town! each day
(Hiked all the way),
Nearer that agency,
Where I paid my fee,
And when that shark I see
You'll bet your boots that he
Nearer his god shall be.
Leave that to me.

IT'S A LONG WAY DOWN TO THE SOUPLINE

Bill Brown was just a working man like others of his kind.
   He lost his job and tramped the streets when work was hard to find.
The landlord put him on the stem, the bankers kept his dough,
   And Bill heard everybody sing, no matter where he'd go:

Chorus

It's a long way down to the soupline,
It's a long way to go.
It's a long way down to the soupline
And the soup is thin I know.

Good-bye good old pork chops,
Farewell beefsteak rare;
It's a long, long way down to the soupline,
But my soup is there.

So Bill and sixteen million men responded to the call
  To force the hours of labor down and thus make jobs for all.
They picketed the industries and won the four-hour day
  And organized a General Strike so men don't have to say:

Chorus

The workers own the factories now, where jobs were once destroyed
  By big machines that filled the world with hungry unemployed.
They all own homes, they're living well, they're happy, free and strong,
  But millionaires wear overalls and sing this little song:

Chorus

MY LAST WILL

My will is easy to decide,
For there is nothing to divide.
My kin don't need to fuss and moan—
"Moss does not cling to rolling stone."

My body?—Oh!—If I could choose,
I would to ashes it reduce,
And let the merry breezes blow
My dust to where some flowers grow.

Perhaps some fading flower then
Would come to life and bloom again.
This is my last and final will.
Good luck to all of you,

JOE HILL

WOODROW WILSON
The World Must Be Made Safe for Democracy

Overseas, World War I raged. At first President Woodrow Wilson called upon Americans to be "neutral in thought and deed," but gradually the United States was drawn closer to war. Wilson won a second term as President in 1916, on the slogan "he kept us out of war." However, the resumption of unrestricted submarine warfare by Germany in 1917 which resulted in the sinking of American ships, and the revelation of a telegram from the German government to Mexico proposing an alliance against the United States if war broke out, forced Wilson's hand. On April 2, 1917, he addressed Congress and asked for an American declaration of war against Germany, declaring that "the world must be made safe for democracy." With passage of the War Resolution by the House of Representatives (April 4) and the Senate (April 6), America was in the war, and its role as a world power officially confirmed. The subsequent impact on American life and literature was profound.

. . . When I addressed the Congress on the twenty-sixth of February last I thought that it would suffice to assert our neutral rights with arms, our right to use the seas against unlawful interference, our right to keep our people safe against unlawful violence. But armed neutrality, it now appears, is impracticable. Because submarines are in effect outlaws when used as the German submarines have been used against merchant shipping, it is impossible to defend ships against their attacks as the law of nations has assumed that merchantmen would defend themselves against privateers or cruisers, visible craft giving chase upon the open sea. It is common prudence in such circumstances, grim necessity indeed, to endeavour to destroy them before they have shown their own intention. They must be dealt with upon sight, if dealt with at all. The German Government denies the right of neutrals to use arms at all within the areas of the sea which it has proscribed, even in the defense of rights which no modern publicist has ever before questioned their right to defend. The intimation is conveyed that the armed guards which we have placed on our merchant ships will be treated as beyond the pale of law and subject to be dealt with as pirates would be. Armed neutrality is ineffectual enough at best; in such circumstances and in the face of such pretensions it is worse than ineffectual; it is likely only to produce what it was meant to prevent; it is practically certain

FROM "Address to Congress Advising that Germany's Course Be Declared War against the United States," by Woodrow Wilson, Senate Document No. 5, *Congressional Record,* Vol. 55, 103–104. U.S. Govt. P. O., 1917.

to draw us into the war without either the rights or the effectiveness of belligerents. There is one choice we cannot make, we are incapable of making: we will not choose the path of submission and suffer the most sacred rights of our nation and our people to be ignored or violated. The wrongs against which we now array ourselves are no common wrongs; they cut to the very roots of human life.

With a profound sense of the solemn and even tragical character of the step I am taking and of the grave responsibilities which it involves, but in unhesitating obedience to what I deem my constitutional duty, I advise that the Congress declare the recent course of the Imperial German Government to be in fact nothing less than war against the government and people of the United States; that it formally accept the status of belligerent which has thus been thrust upon it; and that it take immediate steps not only to put the country in a more thorough state of defense but also to exert all its power and employ all its resources to bring the Government of the German Empire to terms and end the war. . . .

I shall take the liberty of suggesting, through the several executive departments of the Government, for the consideration of your committees, measures for the accomplishment of the several objects I have mentioned. I hope that it will be your pleasure to deal with them as having been framed after very careful thought by the branch of the Government upon which the responsibility of conducting the war and safeguarding the nation will most directly fall.

While we do these things, these deeply momentous things, let us be very clear, and make very clear to all the world what our motives and our objects are. My own thought has not been driven from its habitual and normal course by the unhappy events of the last two months, and I do not believe that the thought of the nation has been altered or clouded by them. I have exactly the same things in mind now that I had in mind when I addressed the Senate on the twenty-second of January last; the same that I had in mind when I addressed the Congress on the third of February and on the twenty-sixth of February. Our object now, as then, is to vindicate the principles of peace and justice in the life of the world as against selfish and autocratic power and to set up amongst the really free and self-governed peoples of the world such a concert of purpose and of action as will henceforth ensure the observance of those principles. Neutrality is no longer feasible or desirable where the peace of the world is involved and the freedom of its peoples, and the menace to that peace and freedom lies in the existence of autocratic governments backed by organized force which is controlled wholly by their will, not by the will of their people. We have seen the last of neutrality in such circumstances. We are at the beginning of an age in which it will be insisted that the same standards of conduct and of responsibility for wrong done shall be observed among nations and their governments that are observed among the individual citizens of civilized states.

We have no quarrel with the German people. We have no feeling towards them but one of sympathy and friendship. It was not upon their impulse that their government acted in entering this war. It was not with their previous knowledge or approval. It was a war determined upon as wars used to be determined upon in the old, unhappy days when peoples were nowhere consulted by their rulers and wars were provoked and waged in the interest of dynasties or of little groups of ambitious men who were accustomed to use their fellow men as pawns and tools. Self-governed nations do not fill their neighbour states with spies or set the course of intrigue to bring about some critical posture of affairs which will give them an opportunity to strike and make conquest. Such designs can be successfully worked out only under cover and where no one has the right to ask questions. Cunningly contrived plans of deception or aggression, carried, it may be, from generation to generation, can be worked out and kept from the light only within the privacy of courts or behind the carefully guarded confidences of a narrow and privileged class. They are happily impossible where public opinion commands and insists upon full information concerning all the nation's affairs.

A steadfast concert for peace can never be maintained except by a partnership of democratic nations. No autocratic government could be trusted to keep faith within it or observe its covenants. It must be a league of honour, a partnership of opinion. Intrigue would eat its vitals away; the plottings of inner circles who could plan what they would and render account to no one would be a corruption seated at its very heart. Only free peoples can hold their purpose and their honour steady to a common end and prefer the interests of mankind to any narrow interest of their own.

Does not every American feel that assurance has been added to our hope for the future peace of the world by the wonderful and heartening things that have been happening within the last few weeks in Russia? Russia was known by those who knew it best to have been always in fact democratic at heart, in all the vital habits of her thought, in all the intimate relationships of her people that spoke their natural instinct, their habitual attitude towards life. The autocracy that crowned the summit of her political structure, long as it had stood and terrible as was the reality of its power, was not in fact Russian in origin, character, or purpose; and now it has been shaken off and the great, generous Russian people have been added in all their naive majesty and might to the forces that are fighting for freedom in the world, for justice, and for peace. Here is a fit partner for a League of Honour.

One of the things that has served to convince us that the Prussian autocracy was not and could never be our friend is that from the very outset of the present war it has filled our unsuspecting communities and even our offices of government with spies and set criminal intrigues everywhere afoot against our national unity of counsel, our peace within and without, our industries and our commerce. Indeed it is now evident that its spies were here even before the war began; and it is unhappily not a matter of conjecture but a fact proved in our courts of justice that the intrigues which have more than once come perilously near to disturbing the peace and dislocating the industries of the country have been carried on at the instigation, with the support, and even under the personal direction of official agents of the Imperial Government accredited to the Government of the United States. Even in checking these things and trying to extirpate them we have sought to put the most generous interpretation possible upon them because we knew that their source lay, not in any hostile feeling or purpose of the German people towards us (who were, no doubt, as ignorant of them as we ourselves were), but only in the selfish designs of a Government that did what it pleased and told its people nothing. But they have played their part in serving to convince us at last that that Government entertains no real friendship for us and means to act against our peace and security at its convenience. That it means to stir up enemies against us at our very doors the intercepted note to the German Minister at Mexico City is eloquent evidence.

We are accepting this challenge of hostile purpose because we know that in such a government, following such methods, we can never have a friend; and that in the presence of its organized power, always lying in wait to accomplish we know not what purpose, there can be no assured security for the democratic governments of the world. We are now about to accept gauge of battle with this natural foe to liberty and shall, if necessary, spend the whole force of the nation to check and nullify its pretensions and its power. We are glad, now that we see the facts with no veil of false pretense about them, to fight thus for the ultimate peace of the world and for the liberation of its peoples, the German peoples included; for the rights of nations great and small and the privilege of men everywhere to choose their way of life and of obedience. The world must be made safe for democracy. Its peace must be planted upon the tested foundations of political liberty. We have no selfish ends to serve. We desire no conquest, no dominion. We seek no indemnities for ourselves, no material compensation for the sacrifices we shall freely make. We are but one of the champions of the rights of mankind. We shall be satisfied when those rights have been made as secure as the faith and the freedom of nations can make them. . . .

14

The 1920's

A general disillusionment following the war and President Wilson's failure to win American approval of the League of Nations marked the temporary end of the spirit of the "New Freedom" and a waning of the social progressivism of the prewar years. The 1920's in America constituted the brief period of ascendancy of the ideas and life style of the American Midwest, both in its stifling moral puritanism and small-business mentality and the particular reaction to that atmosphere by young people who escaped into a variety of exiles, both physical and spiritual. It is the period of Babbittry and prohibition and the business ethic ("time is money"), but it is also the era of flappers, speakeasies, and gangsters, and a new literature of alienation and loss. The Republican Presidents, Harding, Coolidge, and Hoover, are perfect examples of the ruling order, uncommitted to any clear ideals or beliefs other than a desire to maintain "normalcy" and not to rock the boat. Edna St. Vincent Millay, with her candle lit at both ends, and Sinclair Lewis, bitterly ridiculing those whom Emerson would have called the "goodies" of the American middle class, represent the other extreme, the one ignoring American life in a bohemian denial of its importance and even existence, and the other futilely striking out at its hollowness and smug complacency.

The typical Midwestern fictional hero leaves home, searching for the American dream elsewhere after realizing the futility of ever finding it in the society from which he sprang, as in Sherwood Anderson's *Winesburg, Ohio* or Floyd Dell's *Moon-Calf* or the early stories of Hemingway. The society had failed its writers and also the American idealistic spirit which had always made those writers earlier feel themselves to be a real and vital part of American life. The writer was spiritually in exile,

313

whether at home or away. American life seemed cut off from its past and its heritage; think of Fitzgerald's Gatsby looking in vain for Benjamin Franklin's American dream, or the Compsons in Faulkner's *The Sound and the Fury*, or Thomas Wolfe's young Gulliver hungry for the American spirit in experience. When the Emersonian or Poe traditions survived, they did so in a darker context, in a pragmatic realism in which individuals found spiritual and moral victory only in material defeat, as in the late long poems of Robinson or the novels of Ellen Glasgow. In an odd way, this state of exile produced a body of American literature with an artistic subtlety which had been too often lacking since before the Civil War, but it was a hard literature, open-eyed and honest in a painful way, born out of an end to innocence in a new America in which idea and art and the everyday world were no longer in harmony.

The 1920's were the jazz age, but the liveliness was as negative as the liquor was bootleg. These years brought out into the open a split in American life which is still all too painfully apparent. The following pieces document the surface and some of the unsettled depths of that time of contrasts. The Depression would end this era and begin a new one of revolution. The 1920's and the Midwestern small town were, oddly and inappropriately enough, the *ancien régime* against which that revolution would be directed. Normalcy was the unreal quiet before the deluge.

THE VOLSTEAD ACT
The Use of Intoxicating Liquor as a Beverage

Immediately after World War I, the people of the United States of America embarked upon a "noble experiment," the outlawing of the drinking of intoxicating beverages. On October 28, 1919, Congress passed the Volstead Act, over the veto of President Woodrow Wilson, as the 18th Amendment to the Constitution. Introduced by Congressman Andrew Joseph Volstead of Minnesota (1860–1947), it prohibited the sale of any beverage containing more than ½ of 1 per cent of alcohol. Enforcing it was another matter; throughout the 1920's there was widespread bootlegging and rum-running, and the result was gangsterism and corruption. Finally, in 1933, it was repealed, and regulation

FROM "The Volstead Act: Oct. 28, 1919," in *The Statutes At Large of the United States from May, 1919 to March, 1921*. 66th Congress, Session I, ch. 85 (1919). XLI, pt. 1 (Washington: U.S. Govt. P. O., 1921), pp. 305–06, 308, 310–11, 313–17.

of alcoholic consumption was left to the states. Before then, however, F. Scott Fitzgerald would immortalize the bootlegger in The Great Gatsby.

Be it Enacted. . . . That the short title of this Act shall be the "National Prohibition Act."

Title I
To Provide for the Enforcement of War Prohibition

The term "War Prohibition Act" used in this Act shall mean the provisions of any Act or Acts prohibiting the sale and manufacture of intoxicating liquors until the conclusion of the present war and thereafter until the termination of demobilization, the date of which shall be determined and proclaimed by the President of the United States. The words "beer, wine, or other intoxicating malt or vinous liquors" in the War Prohibition Act shall be hereafter construed to mean any such beverages which contain one-half of 1 per centum or more of alcohol by volume: . . .

SEC. 2. The Commissioner of Internal Revenue, his assistants, agents, and inspectors, shall investigate and report violations of the War Prohibition Act to the United States attorney for the district in which committed, who shall be charged with the duty of prosecuting, subject to the direction of the Attorney General, the offenders as in the case of other offenses against laws of the United States; and such Commissioner of Internal Revenue, his assistants, agents, and inspectors may swear out warrants before United States commissioners or other officers or courts authorized to issue the same for the apprehension of such offenders, and may, subject to the control of the said United States attorney, conduct the prosecution at the committing trial for the purpose of having the offenders held for the action of a grand jury. . . .

Title II
Prohibition of Intoxicating Beverages

SEC. 3. No person shall on or after the date when the eighteenth amendment to the Constitution of the United States goes into effect, manufacture, sell, barter, transport, import, export, deliver, furnish or possess any intoxicating liquor except as authorized in this Act, and all the provisions of this Act shall be liberally construed to the end that the use of intoxicating liquor as a beverage may be prevented.

Liquor for nonbeverage purposes and wine for sacramental purposes may be manufactured, purchased, sold, bartered, transported, imported, exported, delivered, furnished and possessed, but only as herein provided and the commissioner may, upon application, issue permits therefor: *Provided,* That nothing in this Act shall prohibit the purchase and sale of warehouse receipts covering distilled spirits on deposit in Government bonded warehouses, and no special tax liability shall attach to the business of purchasing and selling such warehouse receipts. . . .

SEC. 6. No one shall manufacture, sell, purchase, transport, or prescribe any liquor without first obtaining a permit from the commissioner so to do, except that a person may, without a permit, purchase and use liquor for medicinal purposes when prescribed by a physician as herein provided, and except that any person who in the opinion of the commissioner is conducting a bona fide hospital or sanatorium engaged in the treatment of persons suffering from alcoholism, may, under such rules, regulations, and conditions as the commissioner shall prescribe, purchase and use, in accordance with the methods in use in such institution, liquor, to be administered to the patients of such institution under the direction of a duly qualified physician employed by such institution.

All permits to manufacture, prescribe, sell, or transport liquor, may be issued for one year, and shall expire on the 31st day of December next succeeding the issuance thereof: . . . Permits to purchase liquor shall specify the quantity and kind to be purchased and the purpose for which it is to be used. No permit shall be issued to any person who within one year prior to the application therefor or issuance thereof shall have violated the terms of any permit issued under this Title or any law of the United States or of any State regulating traffic in liquor. No permit shall be issued to anyone to sell liquor at retail, unless the sale is to be made through a pharmacist designated in the permit and duly licensed under the laws of his State to compound and dispense medicine prescribed by a duly licensed physician. No one shall be given a permit to prescribe liquor unless he is a physician duly licensed to practice medicine and actively engaged in the practice of such profession.

Nothing in this title shall be held to apply to the manufacture, sale, transportation, importation, possession, or distribution of wine for sacramental purposes, or like religious rites, except section 6 (save as the same requires a permit to purchase) and section 10 hereof, and the provisions of this Act prescribing penalties for the violation of either of said sections. No person to whom a permit may be issued to manufacture, transport, import, or sell wines for sacramental purposes or like religious rites shall sell, barter, exchange, or furnish any such to any person not a rabbi, minister of the gospel, priest, or an officer duly authorized for the purpose by any church or congregation, nor to any such except upon an application duly subscribed by him, which application, authenticated as regulations may prescribe, shall be filed and preserved by the seller. The head of any conference or diocese or other ecclesiastical jurisdiction may designate any rabbi, minister, or priest to supervise the manufacture of wine to be used for the purposes and rites in this section mentioned, and the person so designated may, in the discretion of the commissioner, be granted a permit to supervise such manufacture.

SEC. 7. No one but a physician holding a permit to prescribe liquor shall issue any prescription for liquor. And no physician shall prescribe liquor unless after careful physical examination of the person for whose use such prescription is sought, or if such examination is found impracticable, then upon the best information obtainable, he in good faith believes that the use of such liquor as a medicine by such person is necessary and will afford relief to him from some known ailment. Not more than a pint of spiritous liquor to be taken internally shall be prescribed for use by the same person within any period of ten days and no prescription shall be filled more than once. Any pharmacist filling a prescription shall at the time indorse upon it over his own signature the word "canceled," together with the date when the liquor was delivered, and then make the same a part of the record that he is required to keep as herein provided.

Every physician who issues a prescription for liquor shall keep a record, alphabetically arranged in a book prescribed by the commissioner, which shall show the date of issue, amount prescribed, to whom issued, the purpose or ailment for which it is to be used, and directions for use, stating the amount and frequency of the dose. . . .

SEC. 18. It shall be unlawful to advertise, manufacture, sell, or possess for sale any utensil, contrivance, machine, preparation, compound, tablet, substance, formula direction, recipe advertised, designed, or intended for use in the unlawful manufacture of intoxicating liquor. . . .

SEC. 21. Any room, house, building, boat, vehicle, structure, or place where intoxicating liquor is manufactured, sold, kept, or bartered in violation of this title, and all intoxicating liquor and property kept and used in maintaining the same, is hereby declared to be a common nuisance, and any person who maintains such a common nuisance shall be guilty of a misdemeanor and upon conviction thereof shall be fined not more than $1,000 or be imprisoned for not more than one year, or both. . . .

SEC. 25. It shall be unlawful to have or possess any liquor or property designed for the manufacture of liquor intended for use in violating this title or which has been so used, and no property rights shall exist in any such liquor or property. . . . No search warrant shall issue to search any private dwelling occupied as such unless it is being used for the unlawful sale of intoxicating liquor, or unless it is in part used for some business purposes such as a store, shop, saloon, restaurant, hotel, or boarding house. . . .

SEC. 29. Any person who manufactures or sells liquor in violation of this title shall for a first offense be fined not more than $1,000, or imprisoned not exceeding six months, and for a second or subsequent offense shall be fined not less than $200 nor more than $2,000 and be imprisoned not less than one month nor more than five years.

Any person violating the provisions of any permit, or who makes any false record, report, or affidavit required by this title, or violates any of the provisions of this title, for which offense a special penalty is not prescribed, shall be fined for a first offense not more that $500; for a second offense not less than

$100 nor more than $1,000, or be imprisoned not more than ninety days; for any subsequent offense he shall be fined not less than $500 and be imprisoned not less than three months nor more than two years. . . .

SEC. 33. After February 1, 1920, the possession of liquors by any person not legally permitted under this title to possess liquor shall be prima facie evidence that such liquor is kept for the purpose of being sold, bartered, exchanged, given away, furnished, or otherwise disposed of in violation of the Provisions of this title. . . . But it shall not be unlawful to possess liquors in one's private dwelling while the same is occupied and used by him as his dwelling only and such liquor need not be reported, provided such liquors are for use only for the personal consumption of the owner thereof and his family residing in such dwelling and of his bona fide guests when entertained by him therein; and the burden of proof shall be upon the possessor in any action concerning the same to prove that such liquor was lawfully acquired, possessed, and used. . . .

WARREN G. HARDING
We Must Strive for Normalcy to Reach Stability

Warren Gamaliel Harding (1865–1923), elected President of the United States in 1920 to succeed Woodrow Wilson, produced an inaugural address that seemed fittingly to usher in the public life of the 1920's. It contained, in H. L. Mencken's words, "the damnedest bosh that even he has perpetrated." Included were these syntactical gems: "There was no American failure to resist the attempted reversion of civilization." "Our supreme task is the resumption of our onward, normal way." "We need a rigid yet sane economy." "We must strive for normalcy to reach stability." "We have mistaken unpreparedness to embrace it to be a challenge of the reality," and "the earth is thirsting for the cup of good will, understanding is its fountain source." Harding lasted only a little more than two years in the White House; he died while on a speaking tour at San Francisco, and shortly afterward his Secretary of the Interior and Attorney-General were exposed on charges of corruption and fraud. If Warren were a girl, his father once said, he would always be in a family way, because he didn't know how to say "no." In Thomas Wolfe's Of Time and the River, *the attitude of "leading citizens" to the Harding-Cox presidential campaign is*

FROM Inaugural Address, by Warren G. Harding, in *Inaugural Addresses of the Presidents of the United States from George Washington, 1789, to Harry S. Truman, 1949.* 82nd Congress, 2nd Session, House Doc. No. 540 (Washington: U.S. Govt. P. O., 1952), pp. 197–203.

vividly portrayed. Harding is also the subject of a savagely satirical poem by E. E. Cummings.

MY COUNTRYMEN:

When one surveys the world about him after the great storm, noting the marks of destruction and yet rejoicing in the ruggedness of the things which withstood it, if he is an American he breathes the clarified atmosphere with a strange mingling of regret and new hope. We have seen a world passion spend its fury, but we contemplate our Republic unshaken, and hold our civilization secure. Liberty—liberty within the law—and civilization are inseparable, and though both were threatened we find them now secure; and there comes to Americans the profound assurance that our representative government is the highest expression and surest guaranty of both.

Standing in this presence, mindful of the solemnity of this occasion, feeling the emotions which no one may know until he senses the great weight of responsibility for himself, I must utter my belief in the divine inspiration of the founding fathers. Surely there must have been God's intent in the making of this new-world Republic. Ours is an organic law which had but one ambiguity, and we saw that effaced in a baptism of sacrifice and blood, with union maintained, the Nation supreme, and its concord inspiring. We have seen the world rivet its hopeful gaze on the great truths on which the founders wrought. We have seen civil, human, and religious liberty verified and glorified. In the beginning the Old World scoffed at our experiment; today our foundations of political and social belief stand unshaken, a precious inheritance to ourselves, an inspiring example of freedom and civilization to all mankind. Let us express renewed and strengthened devotion, in grateful reverence for the immortal beginning, and utter our confidence in the supreme fulfillment. . . .

Today, better than ever before, we know the aspirations of humankind, and share them. We have come to a new realization of our place in the world and a new appraisal of our Nation by the world. The unselfishness of these United States is a thing proven; our devotion to peace for ourselves and for the world is well established; our concern for preserved civilization has had its impassioned and heroic expression. There was no American failure to resist the attempted reversion of civilization; there will be no failure today or tomorrow. . . .

Mankind needs a world-wide benediction of understanding. It is needed among individuals, among peoples, among governments, and it will inaugurate an era of good feeling to mark the birth of a new order. In such understanding men will strive confidently for the promotion of their better relationships and nations will promote the comities so essential to peace.

We must understand that ties of trade bind nations in closest intimacy, and none may receive except as he gives. We have not strengthened ours in accordance with our resources or our genius, notably on our own continent, where a galaxy of Republics reflects the glory of new-world democracy, but in the new order of finance and trade we mean to promote enlarged activities and seek expanded confidence.

Perhaps we can make no more helpful contribution by example than prove a Republic's capacity to emerge from the wreckage of war. While the world's embittered travail did not leave us devastated lands nor desolated cities, left no gaping wounds, no breast with hate, it did involve us in the delirium of expenditure, in expanded currency and credits, in unbalanced industry, in unspeakable waste, and disturbed relationships. While it uncovered our portion of hateful selfishness at home, it also revealed the heart of America as sound and fearless, and beating in confidence unfailing. . . .

Our supreme task is the resumption of our onward, normal way. Reconstruction, readjustment, restoration—all these must follow. I would like to hasten them. If it will lighten the spirit and add to the resolution with which we take up the task, let me repeat for our Nation, we shall give no people just cause to make war upon us; we hold no national prejudices; we entertain no spirit of revenge; we do not hate; we do not covet; we dream of no conquest, nor boast of armed prowess. . . .

We can reduce the abnormal expenditures, and we will. We can strike at war taxation, and we must. We must face the grim necessity, with full knowledge that the task is to be solved, and we must proceed with a full realization that no statute enacted by man can repeal the inexorable laws of nature. Our most dangerous tendency is to expect too much of government, and at the same time do for it too little.

We contemplate the immediate task of putting our public household in order. We need a rigid and yet sane economy, combined with fiscal justice, and it must be attended by individual prudence and thrift, which are so essential to this trying hour and reassuring for the future.

The business world reflects the disturbance of war's reaction. Herein flows the lifeblood of material existence. The economic mechanism is intricate and its parts interdependent, and has suffered the shocks and jars incident to abnormal demands, credit inflations, and price upheavals. The normal balances have been impaired, the channels of distribution have been clogged, the relations of labor and management have been strained. We must seek the readjustment with care and courage. Our people must give and take. Prices must reflect the receding fever of war activities. Perhaps we never shall know the old levels of wages again, because war invariably readjusts compensations, and the necessaries of life will show their inseparable relationship, but we must strive for normalcy to reach stability. All the penalties will not be light, nor evenly distributed. There is no way of making them so. There is no instant step from disorder to order. We must face a condition of grim reality, charge off our losses and start afresh. It is the oldest lesson of civilization. I would like government to do all it can to mitigate; then, in understanding, in mutuality of interest, in concern for the common good, our tasks will be solved. No altered system will work a miracle. Any wild experiment will only add to the confusion. Our best assurance lies in efficient administration of our proven system.

The forward course of the business cycle is unmistakable. Peoples are turning from destruction to production. Industry has sensed the changed order and our own people are turning to resume their normal, onward way. The call is for productive America to go on. I know that Congress and the Administration will favor every wise Government policy to aid the resumption and encourage continued progress.

I speak for administrative efficiency, for lightened tax burdens, for sound commercial practices, for adequate credit facilities, for sympathetic concern for all agricultural problems, for the omission of unnecessary interference of Government with business, for an end to Government's experiment in business, and for more efficient business in Government administration. With all of this must attend a mindfulness of the human side of all activities, so that social, industrial, and economic justice will be squared with the purposes of a righteous people.

With the nation-wide induction of womanhood into our political life, we may count upon her intuitions, her refinements, her intelligence, and her influence to exalt the social order. We count upon her exercise of the full privileges and the performance of the duties of citizenship to speed the attainment of the highest state.

I wish for an America no less alert in guarding against dangers from within than it is watchful against enemies from without. Our fundamental law recognizes no class, no group, no section; there must be none in legislation or administration. The supreme inspiration is the common weal. Humanity hungers for international peace, and we crave it with all mankind. My most reverent prayer for America is for industrial peace, with its rewards, widely and generally distributed, amid the inspirations of equal opportunity. No one justly may deny the equality of opportunity which made us what we are. We have mistaken unpreparedness to embrace it to be a challenge of the reality, and due concern for making all citizens fit for participation will give added strength of citizenship and magnify our achievement.

If revolution insists upon overturning established order, let other peoples make the tragic experiment. There is no place for it in America. When World War threatened civilization we pledged our resources and our lives to its preservation, and when revolution threatens we unfurl the flag of law and order and renew our consecration. Ours is a constitutional freedom where the popular will is the law supreme and minorities are sacredly protected. Our revisions, reformations, and evolutions reflect a deliberate judgment and an orderly progress, and we mean to cure our ills, but never destroy or permit destruction by force.

I had rather submit our industrial controversies to the conference table in advance than to a settlement table after conflict and suffering. The earth is thirsting for the cup of good will, understanding is its fountain source. I would like to acclaim an era of good feeling amid dependable prosperity and all the blessings which attend.

It has proved again and again that we cannot, while throwing our markets open to the world, maintain American standards of living and opportunity, and hold our industrial eminence in such unequal competition. There is a luring fallacy in the theory of banished barriers of trade, but preserved American standards require our higher production costs to be reflected in our tariffs on imports. Today, as never before, when peoples are seeking trade restoration and expansion, we must adjust our tariffs to the new order. We seek participation in the world's exchanges, because therein lies our way to widened influence and the triumphs of peace. We know full well we cannot sell where we do not buy, and we cannot sell successfully where we do not carry. Opportunity is calling not alone for the restoration, but for a new era in production, transportation and trade. We shall answer it best by meeting the demand of a surpassing home market, by promoting self-reliance in production, and by bidding enterprise, genius, and efficiency to carry our cargoes in American bottoms to the marts of the world.

We would not have an America living within and for herself alone, but we would have her self-reliant, independent, and ever nobler, stronger, and richer. Believing in our higher standards, reared through constitutional liberty and maintained opportunity, we invite the world to the same heights. But pride in things wrought is no reflex of a completed task. Common welfare is the goal of our national endeavor. Wealth is not inimical to welfare; it ought to be its friendliest agency. There never can be equality of rewards or possessions so long as the human plan contains varied talents and differing degrees of industry and thrift, but ours ought to be a country free from the great blotches of distressed poverty. We ought to find a way to guard against the perils and penalties of unemployment. We want an America of homes, illumined with hope and happiness, where mothers, freed from the necessity for long hours of toil beyond their own doors, may preside as befits the hearthstone of American citizenship. We want the cradle of American childhood rocked under conditions so wholesome and so hopeful that no blight may touch it in its development, and we want to provide that no selfish interest, no material necessity, no lack of opportunity shall prevent the gaining of that education so essential to best citizenship. . . .

Service is the supreme commitment of life. I would rejoice to acclaim the era of the Golden Rule and crown it with the autocracy of service. I pledge an administration wherein all the agencies of Government are called to serve, and ever promote an understanding of Government purely as an expression of the popular will.

One cannot stand in this presence and be unmindful of the tremendous

responsibility. The world upheaval has added heavily to our tasks. But with
the realization comes the surge of high resolve, and there is reassurance in
belief in the God-given destiny of our Republic. If I felt that there is to be
sole responsibility in the Executive for the America of tomorrow I should
shrink from the burden. But here are a hundred millions, with common concern and shared responsibility, answerable to God and country. The Republic
summons them to their duty, and I invite co-operation. . . .

H. L. MENCKEN
So Complete a Drying-up of a Civilization

*One of the wittiest and most often-quoted essays by Henry Louis Mencken
(1880–1956), leading literary critic and commentator on American life in the
twentieth century, was "The Sahara of the Bozart," in which he castigated the
intellectual and artistic shortcomings of the South. Published first in 1917, it
was revised for inclusion in* Prejudices: Second Series, *in 1920. Almost as if its
publication had invoked the spirits out of the deep, there developed in the
1920's a flowering of literature in the South that ever since has dominated the
American literary scene.*

> Alas, for the South! Her books have grown fewer—
> She never was much given to literature.

In the lamented J. Gordon Coogler, author of these elegaic lines, there was
the insight of a true poet. He was the last bard of Dixie, at least in the legitimate line. Down there a poet is now almost as rare as an oboe-player, a dry-
point etcher or a metaphysician. It is, indeed, amazing to contemplate so vast
a vacuity. One thinks of the interstellar spaces, of the colossal reaches of the
now mythical ether. Nearly the whole of Europe could be lost in that stupendous region of fat farms, shoddy cities and paralyzed cerebrums: one could
throw in France, Germany and Italy, and still have room for the British Isles.
And yet, for all its size and all its wealth and all the "progress" it babbles of,
it is almost as sterile, artistically, intellectually, culturally, as the Sahara Desert.
There are single acres in Europe that house more first-rate men than all the
states south of the Potomac; there are probably single square miles in America.
If the whole of the late Confederacy were to be engulfed by a tidal wave to-
morrow, the effect upon the civilized minority of men in the world would be

FROM "The Sahara of the Bozart," in *Prejudices: Second Series,* by H. L. Mencken (New York:
Alfred A. Knopf, 1920), pp. 136–54. Copyright 1920 by Alfred A. Knopf, Inc. and renewed
1948 by H. L. Mencken. Reprinted from *A Mencken Chrestomathy,* by H. L. Mencken, by permission of the publisher.

but little greater than that of a flood on the Yang-tse-kiang. It would be impossible in all history to match so complete a drying-up of a civilization.

I say a civilization because that is what, in the old days, the South had, despite the Baptist and Methodist barbarism that reigns down there now. More, it was a civilization of manifold excellence—perhaps the best that the Western Hemisphere has ever seen—undoubtedly the best that These States have ever seen. Down to the middle of the last century, and even beyond, the main hatchery of ideas on this side of the water was across the Potomac bridges. The New England shopkeepers and theologians never really developed a civilization; all they ever developed was a government. They were, at their best, tawdry and tacky fellows, oafish in manner and devoid of imagination; one searches the books in vain for mention of a salient Yankee gentleman; as well look for a Welsh gentleman. But in the south there were men of delicate fancy, urbane instinct and aristocratic manner—in brief, superior men—in brief, gentry. To politics, their chief diversion, they brought active and original minds. It was there that nearly all the political theories we still cherish and suffer under came to birth. It was there that the crude dogmatism of New England was refined and humanized. It was there, above all, that some attention was given to the art of living—that life got beyond and above the state of a mere infliction and became an exhilarating experience. A certain noble spaciousness was in the ancient southern scheme of things. The *Ur*-Confederate had leisure. He liked to toy with ideas. He was hospitable and tolerant. He had the vague thing that we call culture.

But consider the condition of his late empire today. The picture gives one the creeps. It is as if the Civil War stamped out every last bearer of the torch, and left only a mob of peasants on the field. One thinks of Asia Minor, resigned to Armenians, Greeks and wild swine, of Poland abandoned to the Poles. In all that gargantuan paradise of the fourth-rate there is not a single picture gallery worth going into, or a single orchestra capable of playing the nine symphonies of Beethoven, or a single opera-house, or a single theater devoted to decent plays, or a single public monument (built since the war) that is worth looking at, or a single workshop devoted to the making of beautiful things. Once you have counted Robert Loveman (an Ohioan by birth) and John McClure (an Oklahoman) you will not find a single southern poet above the rank of a neighborhood rhymester. Once you have counted James Branch Cabell (a lingering survivor of the *ancien régime:* a scarlet dragonfly imbedded in opaque amber) you will not find a single southern prose writer who can actually write. And once you have—but when you come to critics, musical composers, painters, sculptors, architects and the like, you will have to give it up, for there is not even a bad one between the Potomac mud-flats and the Gulf. Nor an historian. Nor a sociologist. Nor a philosopher. Nor a theologian. Nor a scientist. In all these fields the south is an awe-inspiring blank—a brother to Portugal, Serbia and Esthonia.

Consider, for example, the present estate and dignity of Virginia—in the great days indubitably the premier American state, the mother of Presidents and statesmen, the home of the first American university worthy of the name, the *arbiter elegantiarum* of the western world. Well, observe Virginia to-day. It is years since a first rate man, save only Cabell, has come out of it; it is years since an idea has come out of it. The old aristocracy went down the red gullet of war; the poor white trash are now in the saddle. Politics in Virginia are cheap, ignorant, parochial, idiotic; there is scarcely a man in office above the rank of a professional job-seeker; the political doctrine that prevails is made up of hand-me-downs from the bumpkinry of the Middle West—Bryanism, Prohibition, vice crusading, all that sort of filthy claptrap; the administration of the law is turned over to professors of Puritanism and espionage; a Washington or a Jefferson, dumped there by some act of God, would be denounced as a scoundrel and jailed overnight. Elegance, *esprit,* culture? Virginia has no art, no literature, no philosophy, no mind or aspiration of her own. Her education has sunk to the Baptist seminary level; not a single contribution to human knowledge has come out of her colleges in twenty-five years; she spends less than half upon her common schools, *per capita,* than any northern state spends. In brief, an intellectual Gobi or Lapland. Urbanity, *politesse,* chivalry? Go to! It was in Virginia that they invented the device of searching for contraband whisky in women's underwear. . . . There remains, at the top, a ghost of the old aristocracy, a bit wistful and infinitely charming. But it has lost all its old leadership to fabulous monsters from the lower depths; it is submerged in an industrial plutocracy that is ignorant and ignominious. The mind of the state, as it is revealed to the nation, is pathetically naïve and inconsequential. It no longer reacts with energy and elasticity to great problems. It has fallen to the bombastic trivialities of the camp-meeting and the chautauqua. Its foremost exponent—if so flabby a thing may be said to have an exponent—is a statesman whose name is synonymous with empty words, broken pledges and false pretenses. One could no more imagine a Lee or a Washington in the Virginia of to-day than one could imagine a Huxley in Nicaragua.

I choose the Old Dominion, not because I disdain it, but precisely because I esteem it. It is, by long odds, the most civilized of the southern states, now as always. It has sent a host of creditable sons northward; the stream kept running into our own time. Virginians, even the worst of them, show the effects of a great tradition. They hold themselves above other southerners, and with sound pretension. If one turns to such a commonwealth as Georgia the picture becomes far darker. There the liberated lower orders of whites have borrowed the worst commercial bounderism of the Yankee and superimposed it upon a culture that, at bottom, is but little removed from savagery. Georgia is at once the home of the cotton-mill sweater and of the most noisy and vapid sort of chamber of commerce, of the Methodist parson turned Savonarola and of the lynching bee. A self-respecting European, going there to live, would not only find intellectual stimulation utterly lacking; he would actually feel a certain insecurity, as if the scene were the Balkans or the China Coast. The Leo Frank affair was no isolated phenomenon. It fitted into its frame very snugly. It was a natural expression of Georgian notions of truth and justice. There is a state with more than half the area of Italy and more populaton than either Denmark or Norway, and yet in thirty years it has not produced a single idea. Once upon a time a Georgian printed a couple of books that attracted notice, but immediately it turned out that he was little more than an amanuensis for the local blacks—that his works were really the products, not of ·white Georgia, but of black Georgia. Writing afterward *as* a white man, he swiftly subsided into the fifth rank. And he is not only the glory of the literature of Georgia; he is, almost literally, the whole of the literature of Georgia—nay, of the entire art of Georgia.

Virginia is the best of the south to-day, and Georgia is perhaps the worst. The one is simply senile; the other is crass, gross, vulgar and obnoxious. Between lies a vast plain of mediocrity, stupidity, lethargy, almost of dead silence. In the north, of course, there is also grossness, crassness, vulgarity. The north, in its way, is also stupid and obnoxious. But nowhere in the north is there such complete sterility, so depressing a lack of all civilized gesture and aspiration. One would find it difficult to unearth a second rate city between the Ohio and the Pacific that isn't struggling to establish an orchestra, or setting up a little theater, or going in for an art gallery, or making some other effort to get into touch with civilization. These efforts often fail, and sometimes they succeed rather absurdly, but under them there is at least an impulse that deserves respect, and that is the impulse to seek beauty and to experiment with ideas, and so to give the life of every day a certain dignity and purpose. You will find no such impulse in the south. There are no committees down there cadging subscriptions for orchestras; if a string quartet is ever heard there, the news of it has never come out; an opera troupe, when it roves the land, is a nine days' wonder. The little theater movement has swept the whole country, enormously augmenting the public interest in sound plays, giving new dramatists their chance, forcing reforms upon the commercial theater. Everywhere else the wave rolls high—but along the line of the Potomac it breaks upon a rock-bound shore. There is no little theater beyond. There is no gallery of pictures. No artist ever gives exhibitions. No one talks of such things. No one seems to be interested in such things.

As for the cause of this unanimous torpor and doltishness, this curious and almost pathological estrangement from everything that makes for a civilized culture, I have hinted at it already, and now state it again. The south has simply been drained of all its best blood. The vast blood-letting of the Civil War half exterminated and wholly paralyzed the old aristocracy, and so left the land to the harsh mercies of the poor white trash, now its masters. The war, of course, was not a complete massacre. It spared a decent number of first-rate southerners—perhaps even some of the very best. Moreover, other countries, notably France and Germany, have survived far more staggering butcheries, and even showed marked progress thereafter. But the war not only cost a great many valuable lives; it also brought bankruptcy, demoralization and despair in its train—and so the majority of the first-rate southerners that were left, broken in spirit and unable to live under the new dispensation, cleared out. A few went to South America, to Egypt, to the Far East. Most came north. They were fecund; their progeny is widely dispersed, to the great benefit of the north. A southerner of good blood almost always does well in the north. He finds, even in the big cities, surroundings fit for a man of condition. His peculiar qualities have a high social value, and are esteemed. He is welcomed by the codfish aristocracy as one palpably superior. But in the south he throws up his hands. It is impossible for him to stoop to the common level. He cannot brawl in politics with the grandsons of his grandfather's tenants. He is unable to share their fierce jealousy of the emerging black—the cornerstone of all their public thinking. He is anæsthetic to their theological and political enthusiasms. He finds himself an alien at their feasts of soul. And so he withdraws into his tower, and is heard of no more. Cabell is almost a perfect example. His eyes, for years, were turned toward the past; he became a professor of the grotesque genealogizing that decaying aristocracies affect; it was only by a sort of accident that he discovered himself to be an artist. The south is unaware of the fact to this day; it regards Woodrow Wilson and Col. John Temple Graves as much finer stylists, and Frank L. Stanton as an infinitely greater poet. If it has heard, which I doubt, that Cabell has been hoofed by the Comstocks, it unquestionably views that assault as a deserved rebuke to a fellow who indulges a lewd passion for fancy writing, and is a covert enemy to the Only True Christianity.

What is needed down there, before the vexatious public problems of the region may be intelligently approached, is a survey of the population by competent ethnologists and anthropologists. The immigrants of the north have been studied at great length, and any one who is interested may now apply to the Bureau of Ethnology for elaborate data as to their racial strains, their stature and cranial indices, their relative capacity for education, and the changes that they undergo under American *Kultur*. But the older stocks of the south, and particularly the emancipated and dominant poor white trash, have never been investigated scientifically, and most of the current generalizations about them are probably wrong. For example, the generalization that they are purely Anglo-Saxon in blood. This I doubt very seriously. The chief strain down there, I believe, is Celtic rather than Saxon, particularly in the hill country. French blood, too, shows itself here and there, and so does Spanish, and so does German. The last-named entered from the northward, by way of the limestone belt just east of the Alleghenies. Again, it is very likely that in some parts of the south a good many of the plebeian whites have more than a trace of negro blood. Interbreeding under concubinage produced some very light half-breeds at an early day, and no doubt appreciable numbers of them went over into the white race by the simple process of changing their abode. Not long ago I read a curious article by an intelligent negro, in which he stated that it is easy for a very light negro to pass as white in the south on account of the fact that large numbers of southerners accepted as white have distinctly negroid features. Thus it becomes a delicate and dangerous matter for a train conductor or a hotel-keeper to challenge a suspect. But the Celtic strain is far more obvious than any of these others. It not only makes itself visible in physical stigmata— *e. g.,* leanness and dark coloring—but also in mental traits. For example, the religious thought of the south is almost precisely identical with the religious thought of Wales. There is the same naïve belief in an anthropomorphic Creator but little removed, in manner and desire, from an evangelical bishop; there is the same submission to an ignorant and impudent sacerdotal tyranny, and there is the same sharp contrast between doctrinal orthodoxy and private ethics. Read Caradoc Evans' ironical picture of the Welsh Wesleyans in his preface to "My Neighbors," and you will be instantly reminded of the Georgia and Carolina Methodists. The most booming sort of piety, in the south, is not incompatible with the theory that lynching is a benign institution. Two generations ago it was not incompatible with an ardent belief in slavery.

It is highly probable that some of the worst blood of western Europe flows in the veins of the southern poor whites, now poor no longer. The original strains, according to every honest historian, were extremely corrupt. Philip Alexander Bruce (a Virginian of the old gentry) says in his "Industrial History of Virginia in the Seventeenth Century" that the first native-born generation was largely illegitimate. "One of the most common offenses against morality committed in the lower ranks of life in Virginia during the seventeenth century," he says, "was bastardy." The mothers of these bastards, he continues, were chiefly indentured servants, and "had belonged to the lowest class in their native country." Fanny Kemble Butler, writing of the Georgia poor whites of a century later, described them as "the most degraded race of human beings claiming an Anglo-Saxon origin that can be found on the face of the earth—filthy, lazy, ignorant, brutal, proud, penniless savages." The Sunday-school and the chautauqua, of course, have appreciably mellowed the descendants of these "savages," and their economic progress and rise to political power have done perhaps even more, but the marks of their origin are still unpleasantly plentiful. Every now and then they produce a political leader who puts their secret notions of the true, the good and the beautiful into plain words, to the amazement and scandal of the rest of the country. That amazement is turned into downright incredulity when news comes that his platform has got him high office, and that he is trying to execute it.

In the great days of the south the line between the gentry and the poor whites was very sharply drawn. There was absolutely no intermarriage. So far as I know there is not a single instance in history of a southerner of the upper class marrying one of the bondwomen described by Mr. Bruce. In other societies characterized by class distinctions of that sort it is common for the lower class to be improved by extra-legal crosses. That is to say, the men of the upper class take women of the lower class as mistresses, and out of such unions spring the extraordinary plebeians who rise sharply from the common level, and so propagate the delusion that all other plebeians would do the same thing if they had the chance—in brief, the delusion that class distinctions are merely economic and conventional, and not congenital and genuine. But in the south the men of the upper classes sought their mistresses among the blacks, and after a few generations there was so much white blood in the black women that they were considerably more attractive than the unhealthy and bedraggled women of the poor whites. This preference continued into our own time. A southerner of good family once told me in all seriousness that he had reached his majority before it ever occurred to him that a white woman might make quite as agreeable a mistress as the octaroons of his jejune fancy. If the thing has changed of late, it is not the fault of the southern white man, but of the southern mulatto women. The more sightly yellow girls of the region, with improving economic opportunities, have gained self-respect, and so they are are no longer as willing to enter into concubinage as their grand-dams were.

As a result of this preference of the southern gentry for mulatto mistresses there was created a series of mixed strains containing the best white blood of the south, and perhaps of the whole country. As another result the poor whites went unfertilized from above, and so missed the improvement that so constantly shows itself in the peasant stocks of other countries. It is a commonplace that nearly all negroes who rise above the general are of mixed blood, usually with the white predominating. I know a great many negroes, and it would be hard for me to think of an exception. What is too often forgotten is that this white blood is not the blood of the poor whites but that of the old gentry. The mulatto girls of the early days despised the poor whites as creatures distinctly inferior to negroes, and it was thus almost unheard of for such a girl to enter into relations with a man of that sumerged class. This aversion was based upon a sound instinct. The southern mulatto of to-day is a proof of it. Like all other half-breeds he is an unhappy man, with disquieting tendencies toward anti-social habits of thought, but he is intrinsically a better animal than the pure-blooded descendant of the old poor whites, and he not infrequently demonstrates it. It is not by accident that the negroes of the south are making faster progress, economically and culturally, than the masses of the whites. It is not by accident that the only visible æsthetic activity in the south is wholly in their hands. No southern composer has ever written music so good as that of half a dozen white-black composers who might be named. Even in politics, the negro reveals a curious superiority. Despite the fact that the race question has been the main political concern of the southern whites for two generations, to the practical exclusion of everything else, they have contributed nothing to its discussion that has impressed the rest of the world so deeply and so favorably as three or four books by southern negroes.

Entering upon such themes, of course, one must resign one's self to a vast misunderstanding and abuse. The south has not only lost its old capacity for producing ideas; it has also taken on the worst intolerance of ignorance and stupidity. Its prevailing mental attitude for several decades past has been that of its own hedge ecclesiastics. All who dissent from its orthodox doctrines are scoundrels. All who presume to discuss its ways realistically are damned. I have had, in my day, several experiences in point. Once, after I had published an article on some phase of the eternal race question, a leading southern newspaper replied by printing a column of denunciation of my father, then dead nearly twenty years—a philippic placarding him as an ignorant foreigner of dubious origin, inhabiting "the Baltimore ghetto" and speaking a dialect recalling that of Weber & Fields—two thousand words of incandescent nonsense, utterly false and beside the point, but exactly meeting the latter-day southern notion of effective controversy. Another time, I published a short discourse on lynching, arguing that the sport was popular in the south because the backward culture of the region denied the populace more seemly recreations. Among such recreations I mentioned those afforded by brass bands, symphony orchestras, boxing matches, amateur athletic contests, shoot-the-chutes, roof gardens, horse races, and so on. In reply another great southern journal denounced me as a man "of wineshop temperament, brass-jewelry tastes and pornographic predilections." In other words, brass bands, in the south, are classed with brass jewelry, and both are snares of the devil! To advocate setting up symphony orchestras is pornography! . . . Alas, when the touchy southerner attempts a greater urbanity, the result is often even worse. Some time ago a colleague of mine printed an article deploring the arrested cultural development of Georgia. In reply he received a number of protests from patriotic Georgians, and all of them solemnly listed the glories of the state. I indulge in a few specimens:

Who has not heard of Asa G. Candler, whose name is synonymous with Coca-Cola, a Georgia product?

The first Sunday-school in the world was opened in Savannah.

Who does not recall with pleasure the writings of . . . Frank L. Stanton, Georgia's brilliant poet?

Georgia was the first state to organize a Boy's Corn Club in the South—Newton county, 1904.

The first to suggest a common United Daughters of the Confederacy badge was Mrs. Raynes, of Georgia.

The first to suggest a state historian of the United Daughters of the Confederacy was Mrs. C. Helen Plane (Macon convention, 1896).

The first to suggest putting to music Heber's "From Greenland's Icy Mountains" was Mrs. F. R. Goulding, of Savannah.

And so on, and so on. These proud boasts came, remember, not from obscure private persons, but from "Leading Georgians"—in one case, the state historian. Curious sidelights upon the ex-Confederate mind! Another comes from a stray copy of a negro paper. It describes an ordinance lately passed by the city council of Douglas, Ga., forbidding any trousers presser, on penalty of forfeiting a $500 bond, to engage in "pressing for both white and colored." This in a town, says the negro paper, where practically all of the white inhabitants have "their food prepared by colored hands," "their babies cared for by colored hands," and "the clothes which they wear right next to their skins washed in houses where negroes live"—houses in which the said clothes "remain for as long as a week at a time." But if you marvel at the absurdity, keep it dark! A casual word, and the united press of the south will be upon your trail, denouncing you bitterly as a scoundrelly Yankee, a Bolshevik Jew, an agent of the Wilhelm-strasse. . . .

Obviously, it is impossible for intelligence to flourish in such an atmosphere. Free inquiry is blocked by the idiotic certainties of ignorant men. The arts, save in the lower reaches of the gospel hymn, the phonograph and the chautauqua harangue, are all held in suspicion. The tone of public opinion is set by an upstart class but lately emerged from industrial slavery into commermercial enterprise—the class of "hustling" business men, of "live wires," of commercial club luminaries, of "drive" managers, of forward-lookers and right-thinkers—in brief, of third-rate southerners inoculated with all the worst traits of the Yankee sharper. One observes the curious effects of an old tradition of truculence upon a population now merely pushful and impudent, of an old tradition of chivalry upon a population now quite without imagination. The old repose is gone. The old romanticism is gone. The philistinism of the new type of town-boomer southerner is not only indifferent to the ideals of the old south; it is positively antagonistic to them. That philistinism regards human life, not as an agreeable adventure, but as a mere trial of rectitude and efficiency. It is overwhelmingly utilitarian and moral. It is inconceivably hollow and obnoxious. What remains of the ancient tradition is simply a certain charming civility in private intercourse—often broken down, alas, by the hot rages of Puritanism, but still generally visible. The southerner, at his worst, is never quite the surly cad that the Yankee is. His sensitiveness may betray him into occasional bad manners, but in the main he is a pleasant fellow—hospitable, polite, good-humored, even jovial. . . . But a bit absurd. . . . A bit pathetic.

ROGER W. BABSON
The Most Interesting Connection Between Religion and Prosperity

"The business of America," declared President Calvin Coolidge, "is business." The 1920's were a period in which business reigned supreme, and the businessman was the nation's ideal. An advertising man, Bruce Barton, wrote a biography of Christ in which he demonstrated that He was a good businessman. Roger W. Babson (1875–1967), financial analyst and prognosticator, produced a book entitled Religion and Business, *and another entitled* Prayers for the Business Man. *"The religion of the future," he declared in the former, "will work to have all people healthy, happy, and prosperous; it will strive to have a hundred Standard Oils instead of one . . ." (Cf. Charles Chauncy, p. 45; "We were made for business.") In the excerpt that follows, from* Religion and Business, *Babson discusses wealth, prosperity, and God. Sinclair Lewis's Babbitt would have read the following passage with much satisfaction.*

The Question of Wealth

As heretofore stated, Jesus had no interest in property as such. He continually emphasized that life consisteth not in the abundance of things which a man possesseth, but rather in the intangibles; such as health, happiness, and independence, which latter is very dependent on prosperity. Hence, He always closed His appeals with the promise that if we would be saturated with the Service Idea, we would automatically become prosperous.

Jesus never objected to wealth as such, but rather He objected to dependence on wealth, as in the case of the man who decided to retire from business so as to "eat, drink, and be merry." He also objected to the vast difference that exists between different people under different circumstances. This was emphasized by John the Baptist when he said:

Make ye ready the way of the Lord, make His paths straight. Every valley shall be filled, and every mountain and hill shall be brought low; and the crooked shall become straight, and the rough ways smooth, and all flesh shall see the salvation of God.

Jesus would not object to millionaires as such, but He would object very strongly to any system which would result in having only a few millionaires and the rest of the people poor. The more millionaires we have, the better off

FROM *Religion and Business*, by Roger W. Babson (New York: The Macmillan Co., 1920), pp. 121–25.

people are, provided these men make their money by producing and by increasing the total wealth of the community. Those who make their wealth by increasing the total wealth of the community are a blessing to the community. We want more of such people. Those, however, who secure their wealth only from others, like the gambler, are a menace to the community.

This means that every dollar which we secure by making the community better and richer is right in the sight of God; but every dollar which we secure by methods which do not add to the health, happiness, and prosperity of the community is dishonestly secured.

The importance of this statement cannot be over-emphasized. Doubtless its non-recognition by the church has kept many bad men in and many good men out. If our churches would lay more stress on this fundamental teaching and less stress on theological questions, the churches and the nations would be very much better off to-day.

The churches should doubtless do some house cleaning. Many men should change their occupations or get out of the church. Many women should do something useful or else get out of the church.

Religion and Prosperity

A further study shows the most interesting connection between religion and prosperity. Were inheritances and government interferences eliminated, the most truly religious men would gradually but surely acquire the wealth of the earth. The truly religious are those who best observe the laws of God and seek continually to render the best service. Prosperity naturally gravitates to such people. They cannot be held down.

For instance, the farmer who gets the largest crops per acre has the most profit left at the end of the season. If he is a religious man, instead of wasting this profit on himself and family, he will invest it in more land. Thus, the succeeding year he has more acres to till. This process continues from year to year and he naturally becomes the owner of the largest farm in the community. Thus, if the laws of nature are allowed to work freely, the wealth of the world automatically gravitates to those who can most efficiently use and conserve it.

Trouble comes only when men, after securing their wealth, become careless, indifferent, and indulgent. As pride and haughtiness precede destruction, so trouble automatically follows indifference. The inheritance laws doubtless interfere with this natural process, as an industrious, thrifty, religious farmer may be followed by a worthless, indifferent son. Even under these conditions, however, the nation is better off to have the property left to such a son than to have it left to the state. If the son is careless, he will soon lose control of the property and it will pass into the hands of some one else who is better able to take care of it; but if it went to the state, it would continue to be the property of the state, even though inefficiently and extravagantly handled by the state.

What is true of farming is true also of all the great industries. If nature is allowed to take its course, we can be sure that the results will be for the best. Of course this was not always true, as man has passed through various stages. In the first stage the victory went to the fighter; in the second stage, it went to the talker; but in the present final stage, the victory is going to the producer. Hence, the best religion is the religion which will produce the most.

Just a word of warning to those good-hearted people who are crazy over democracy. It is very much better to talk and vote than it is to fight and kill. Let no one think, however, that our democracy is in any final shape. Jesus did not say much about democracy because He knew of its weaknesses. Jesus said very little about economic or sociological affairs. He believed that religious communities can get on all right without socialism; while even socialism cannot succeed excepting as people are filled with the religious spirit. Jesus' economic teachings are best expressed by the Parable of the Talents. In choosing the men for the leaders, He did not suggest that they be chosen by voting. Jesus never appealed to sympathy nor popularity. The determining factor in His method of selecting people was the amount that they had produced with what they had been given. The man who had produced ten pounds was given rule over ten cities; the man who had produced five pounds was given rule over five cities; but the man who had wrapped his pound in a napkin and produced nothing, had to give up that pound to the one who had produced ten.

Those who have property must cease depending on property, for as we depend on our wealth we become self-satisfied, inefficient, and weak. We must continually keep in mind that we have our wealth only in trust and we must not use it for self-gratification, display, or in any way that will make others dissatisfied or unhappy. Our only justification for holding property is that we are using it to create more property, as did the man with the ten talents.

Those business men, however, who are filled with the vision of service are great blessings to the community and should be encouraged from every point of view. All attempts to present the pleasing side of religion are very harmful. Some preachers rail against the rich to please the poor; while other preachers defend the rich in order to please the rich. Both policies are wrong and harmful. It is demoralizing to appeal to popularity in any way. Riches are neither right nor wrong by themselves. It all depends on how they are secured and how they are used. The religion of the future will work to have all people healthy, happy, and prosperous; it will strive to have a hundred Standard Oils instead of one; it will seek to have an automobile owned by every family instead of by only a few; it will extol, instead of depreciate, both men and property. On the other hand, the coming religion will make most careful distinctions as to how wealth is secured and how it is used. Those who secure their wealth without making the community better and richer or those who use it in an ostentatious way to make others unhappy, will be frowned upon. The church which finally survives will be that church which teaches its people to produce, at the same time continually emphasizing that the production must be in the interests of the group as a whole. A study of history strongly suggests that this will be some branch of the Christian church.

H. L. MENCKEN
He Liked People Who Sweated Freely

The obituary that Henry Louis Mencken (1880–1956) composed upon the death of William Jennings Bryan (1860–1925) has become one of the classic works of vituperation in American journalism. Sardonic, witty, thoroughly rationalistic and urban in his outlook, Mencken covered the Scopes evolution trial in Dayton, Tennessee, in which the aging Bryan served as chief spokesman for the Fundamentalist interpretation of the Bible, and therefore of the state's prosecution of Scopes for violating a Tennessee statute forbidding the teaching of evolution in public schools. When Bryan died shortly after the trial, Mencken penned an obituary for the Baltimore Evening Sun, *which he later reworked for use in his magazine,* The American Mercury.

Has it been duly marked by historians that William Jennings Bryan's last secular act on this globe of sin was to catch flies? A curious detail, and not without its sardonic overtones. He was the most sedulous fly-catcher in American history, and in many ways the most successful. His quarry, of course, was not *Musca domestica* but *Homo neandertalensis.* For forty years he tracked it with coo and bellow, up and down the rustic backways of the Republic. Wherever the flambeaux of Chautauqua smoked and guttered, and the bilge of idealism ran in the veins, and Baptist pastors damned the brooks with the sanctified, and men gathered who were weary and heavy laden, and their wives who were full of Peruna and as fecund as the shad (*Alosa sapidissima*), there the indefatigable Jennings set up his traps and spread his bait. He knew every country town in the South and West, and he could crowd the most remote of them to suffocation by simply winding his horn. The city proletariat, transiently flustered by him in 1896, quickly penetrated his buncombe and would have no more of him; the cockney gallery jeered him at every Democratic national convention for twenty-five years. But out where the grass grows high, and the horned cattle dream away the lazy afternoons, and men still fear the powers and principalities of the air—out there between the cornrows he held his old puissance to the end. There was no need of beaters to drive in his game. The news that he was coming was enough. For miles the

FROM "In Memoriam: W. J. B.," in *A Mencken Chrestomathy* (New York: Alfred A. Knopf, 1949), pp. 243–48. Copyright 1926 by Alfred A. Knopf, Inc. and renewed 1954 by H. L. Mencken. Reprinted from *A Mencken Chrestomathy*, by H. L. Mencken, by permission of the publisher.

flivver dust would choke the roads. And when he rose at the end of the day
to discharge his Message there would be such breathless attention, such a rapt
and enchanted ecstasy, such a sweet rustle of amens as the world had not
known since Johann fell to Herod's ax.

There was something peculiarly fitting in the fact that his last days were
spent in a one-horse Tennessee village, beating off the flies and gnats, and that
death found him there. The man felt at home in such simple and Christian
scenes. He liked people who sweated freely, and were not debauched by the
refinements of the toilet. Making his progress up and down the Main street
of little Dayton, surrounded by gaping primates from the upland valleys of the
Cumberland Range, his coat laid aside, his bare arms and hairy chest shining
damply, his bald head sprinkled with dust—so accoutred and on display, he
was obviously happy. He liked getting up early in the morning, to the tune
of cocks crowing on the dunghill. He liked the heavy, greasy victuals of the
farmhouse kitchen. He liked country lawyers, country pastors, all country
people. He liked country sounds and country smells.

I believe that this liking was sincere—perhaps the only sincere thing in the
man. His nose showed no uneasiness when a hillman in faded overalls and
hickory shirt accosted him on the street, and besought him for light upon
some mystery of Holy Writ. The simian gabble of the cross-roads was not
gabble to him, but wisdom of an occult and superior sort. In the presence of
city folks he was palpably uneasy. Their clothes, I suspect, annoyed him, and
he was suspicious of their too delicate manners. He knew all the while that
they were laughing at him—if not at his baroque theology, then at least at his
alpaca pantaloons. But the yokels never laughed at him. To them he was not
the huntsman but the prophet, and toward the end, as he gradually forsook
mundane politics for more ghostly concerns, they began to elevate him in their
hierarchy. When he died he was the peer of Abraham. His old enemy, Wilson,
aspiring to the same white and shining robe, came down with a thump. But
Bryan made the grade. His place in Tennessee hagiography is secure. If the
village barber saved any of his hair, then it is curing gall-stones down there
today.

But what label will he bear in more urbane regions? One, I fear, of a far
less flattering kind. Bryan lived too long, and descended too deeply into the
mud, to be taken seriously hereafter by fully literate men, even of the kind
who write schoolbooks. There was a scattering of sweet words in his funeral
notices, but it was no more than a response to conventional sentimentality. The
best verdict the most romantic editorial writer could dredge up, save in the
humorless South, was to the general effect that his imbecilities were excused
by his earnestness—that under his clowning, as under that of the juggler of
Notre Dame, there was the zeal of a steadfast soul. But this was apology, not
praise; precisely the same thing might be said of Mary Baker G. Eddy. The
truth is that even Bryan's sincerity will probably yield to what is called, in
other fields, definitive criticism. Was he sincere when he opposed imperialism
in the Philippines, or when he fed it with deserving Democrats in Santo

Domingo? Was he sincere when he tried to shove the Prohibitionists under the table, or when he seized their banner and began to lead them with loud whoops? Was he sincere when he bellowed against war, or when he dreamed of himself as a tin-soldier in uniform, with a grave reserved at Arlington among the generals? Was he sincere when he fawned over Champ Clark, or when he betrayed Clark? Was he sincere when he pleaded for tolerance in New York, or when he bawled for the faggot and the stake in Tennessee?

This talk of sincerity, I confess, fatigues me. If the fellow was sincere, then so was P. T. Barnum. The word is disgraced and degraded by such uses. He was, in fact, a charlatan, a mountebank, a zany without sense or dignity. His career brought him into contact with the first men of his time; he preferred the company of rustic ignoramuses. It was hard to believe, watching him at Dayton, that he had traveled, that he had been received in civilized societies, that he had been a high officer of state. He seemed only a poor clod like those around him, deluded by a childish theology, full of an almost pathological hatred of all learning, all human dignity, all beauty, all fine and noble things. He was a peasant come home to the barnyard. Imagine a gentleman, and you have imagined everything that he was not. What animated him from end to end of his grotesque career was simply ambition—the ambition of a common man to get his hand upon the collar of his superiors, or, failing that, to get his thumb into their eyes. He was born with a roaring voice, and it had the trick of inflaming half-wits. His whole career was devoted to raising those half-wits against their betters, that he himself might shine.

His last battle will be grossly misunderstood if it is thought of as a mere exercise in fanaticism—that is, if Bryan the Fundamentalist Pope is mistaken for one of the bucolic Fundamentalists. There was much more in it than that, as everyone knows who saw him on the field. What moved him, at bottom, was simply hatred of the city men who had laughed at him so long, and brought him at last to so tatterdemalion an estate. He lusted for revenge upon them. He yearned to lead the anthropoid rabble against them, to punish them for their execution upon him by attacking the very vitals of their civilization. He went far beyond the bounds of any merely religious frenzy, however inordinate. When he began denouncing the notion that man is a mammal even some of the hinds at Dayton were agape. And when, brought upon Clarence Darrow's cruel hook, he writhed and tossed in a very fury of malignancy, bawling against the veriest elements of sense and decency like a man frantic—when he came to that tragic climax of his striving there were snickers among the hinds as well as hosannas.

Upon that hook, in truth, Bryan committed suicide, as a legend as well as in the body. He staggered from the rustic court ready to die, and he staggered from it ready to be forgotten, save as a character in a third-rate farce, witless and in poor taste. It was plain to everyone who knew him, when he came to Dayton, that his great days were behind him—that, for all the fury of his hatred, he was now definitely an old man, and headed at last for silence. There was a vague, unpleasant manginess about his appearance; he somehow seemed dirty, though a close glance showed him as carefully shaven as an actor, and clad in immaculate linen. All the hair was gone from the dome of his head, and it had begun to fall out, too, behind his ears, in the obscene manner of Samuel Gompers. The resonance had departed from his voice; what was once a bugle blast had become reedy and quavering. Who knows that, like Demosthenes, he had a lisp? In the old days, under the magic of his eloquence, no one noticed it. But when he spoke at Dayton it was always audible.

When I first encountered him, on the sidewalk in front of the office of the rustic lawyers who were his associates in the Scopes case, the trial was yet to begin, and so he was still expansive and amiable. I had printed in the *Nation,* a week or so before, an article arguing that the Tennessee anti-evolution law, whatever its wisdom, was at least constitutional—that the yahoos of the State had a clear right to have their progeny taught whatever they chose, and kept secure from whatever knowledge violated their superstitions. The old boy professed to be delighted with the argument, and gave the gaping bystanders to understand that I was a publicist of parts. Not to be outdone, I admired the preposterous country shirt that he wore—sleeveless and with the neck cut very low. We parted in the manner of two ambassadors.

But that was the last touch of amiability that I was destined to see in Bryan. The next day the battle joined and his face became hard. By the end of the week he was simply a walking fever. Hour by hour he grew more bitter. What the Christian Scientists call malicious animal magnetism seemed to radiate from him like heat from a stove. From my place in the courtroom, standing upon a table, I looked directly down upon him, sweating horribly and pumping his palm-leaf fan. His eyes fascinated me; I watched them all day long. They were blazing points of hatred. They glittered like occult and sinister gems. Now and then they wandered to me, and I got my share, for my reports of the trial had come back to Dayton, and he had read them. It was like coming under fire.

Thus he fought his last fight, thirsting savagely for blood. All sense departed from him. He bit right and left, like a dog with rabies. He descended to demagogy so dreadful that his very associates at the trial table blushed. His one yearning was to keep his yokels heated up—to lead his forlorn mob of imbeciles against the foe. That foe, alas, refused to be alarmed. It insisted upon seeing the whole battle as a comedy. Even Darrow, who knew better, occasionally yielded to the prevailing spirit. One day he lured poor Bryan into the folly I have mentioned: his astounding argument against the notion that man is a mammal. I am glad I heard it, for otherwise I'd never believe it. There stood the man who had been thrice a candidate for the Presidency of the Republic— there he stood in the glare of the world, uttering stuff that a boy of eight would laugh at. The artful Darrow led him on: he repeated it, ranted for it, bellowed it in his cracked voice. So he was prepared for the final slaughter. He came into life a hero, a Galahad, in bright and shining armor. He was passing out a poor mountebank.

15

THE CRASH

The Great Depression not only ended the old ideas of the business utopia, but it began a social revolution in America which is still very much in progress. The suffering of the Depression, both physical and mental, brought the people of the nation together with a set of common ideals and desires as they had not been since before the Civil War. Emerson's old idea of the free individual had been long corrupted by the business ideal of "rugged individualism," and it was reinterpreted in the 1930's in the idea of community action to free the individual within the inescapable community. There were those who, like the Agrarians, sought a return to the purity of the older ideals, but the majority of Americans demanded a new world that could only be formed by community action. Franklin D. Roosevelt's "New Deal" was the political expression of the revolution in thinking, and his political following was a coalition of workers and farmers, small businessmen and intellectuals, a new union of those who had seemed so far apart in the 1920's. Roosevelt revived Wilson's ideas of a "New Freedom" by extending the federal government's activity into all phases of American life. The society organized as the government began to tend to the public welfare in a way that it apparently could not do without that organization.

The old literature of protest gained a new vigor with the infusion of the ideals of community action. John Steinbeck's *The Grapes of Wrath* and *In Dubious Battle* were muckraking novels but with a strong sense of idealism and optimism. The movement of ideas in the 1930's was toward a rediscovery of what Hemingway was to find in John Donne, that "No man is an *Iland,* intire of it selfe." Much of the bitterness and helplessness of the 1920's remained, but the American traditional belief in the efficacy of action clearly began to reassert itself.

Politically the country was splintered to the right and left, but Roosevelt's New Deal gave the social revolution a practical and effective mode of realization. The Depression was an American trauma, but one which created its own cure even as it left deep and lasting scars.

The following five pieces give some of the shock and impact of the Depression and also a statement of the new ideals which grew from that shock.

FREDERICK LEWIS ALLEN
You Might Notice That a Great Many Shops Were Untenanted

The stock market crash of October, 1929, marked the end of "normalcy" and the boom market and unrestrained speculation of the Coolidge and Hoover administrations. It was also the beginning of the Great Depression, which cast a dark shadow of suffering across American life for a decade. Frederick Lewis Allen (1890–1954), an American social historian and magazine editor, describes the depression at its worst in 1932. In this chapter from his social history of the 1930's, Since Yesterday, *he captures the feeling of spiritual collapse which accompanied the economic failure. He calls the chapter appropriately "Black Depression."*

Statistics are bloodless things.

To say that during the year 1932, the cruelest year of the Depression, the average number of unemployed people in the country was 12½ million by the estimates of the National Industrial Conference Board, a little over 13 million by the estimates of the American Federation of Labor, and by other estimates (differently arrived at, and defining unemployment in various ways) anywhere from 8½ to 17 million—to say this is to give no living impression of the jobless men going from office to office or from factory gate to factory gate; of the disheartening inevitability of the phrase, "We'll let you know if anything shows up"; of men thumbing the want ads in cold tenements, spending fruitless hours, day after day and week after week, in the sidewalk crowds before the employment offices; using up the money in the savings bank, borrowing

FROM *Since Yesterday*, by Frederick Lewis Allen (New York: Harper & Brothers, 1940), pp. 57–64. Copyright 1939, 1940 by Harper & Brothers. Reprinted by permission of Harper & Row, Publishers, Incorporated.

on their life insurance, selling whatever possessions could be sold, borrowing from relatives less and less able to lend, tasting the bitterness of inadequacy, and at last swallowing their pride and going to apply for relief—if there was any to be got. (Relief money was scarce, for charitable organizations were hard beset and cities and towns had either used up their available funds or were on the point of doing so.)

A few statistical facts and estimates are necessary, however, to an understanding of the scope and impact of the Depression. For example:—

Although the amount of money paid out in interest during the year 1932 was only 3.5 per cent less than in 1929, according to the computations of Dr. Simon Kuznets for the National Bureau of Economic Research, on the other hand the amount of money paid out in salaries had dropped 40 per cent, dividends had dropped 56.6 per cent, and wages had dropped 60 per cent. (Thus had the debt structure remained comparatively rigid while other elements in the economy were subjected to fierce deflation.)

Do not imagine, however, that the continuation of interest payments and the partial continuation of dividend payments meant that business as a whole was making money. Business as a whole lost between five and six billion dollars in 1932. (The government figure for all the corporations in the country— 451,800 of them—was a net deficit of $5,640,000,000.) To be sure, most of the larger and better-managed companies did much better than that. E. D. Kennedy's figures for the 960 concerns whose earnings were tabulated by Standard Statistics—mostly big ones whose stock was active on the Stock Exchange— show that these 960 leaders had a collective profit of over a third of a billion. Yet one must add that "better managed" is here used in a special sense. Not only had labor-saving devices and speed-ups increased the output per man-hour in manufacturing industries by an estimated 18 per cent since 1929, but employees had been laid off in quantity. Every time one of the giants of industry, to keep its financial head above water, threw off a new group of workers, many little corporations roundabout sank further into the red.

While existing businesses shrank, new ones were not being undertaken. The total of domestic corporate issues—issues of securities floated to provide capital for American corporations—had dropped in 1932 to just about *one twenty-fourth* of the 1929 figure.

But these cold statistics give us little sense of the human realities of the economic paralysis of 1932. Let us try another approach.

Walking through an American city, you might find few signs of the Depression visible—or at least conspicuous—to the casual eye. You might notice that a great many shops were untenanted, with dusty plate-glass windows and signs indicating that they were ready to lease; that few factory chimneys were smoking; that the streets were not so crowded with trucks as in earlier years, that there was no uproar of riveters to assail the ear, that beggars and panhandlers were on the sidewalks in unprecedented numbers (in the Park Avenue district of New York a man might be asked for money four or five times in a ten-block walk). Traveling by railroad, you might notice that the trains were shorter, the Pullman cars fewer—and that fewer freight trains were on the line. Traveling overnight, you might find only two or three other passengers in your sleeping car. (By contrast, there were more filling stations by the motor highways than ever before, and of all the retail businesses in "Middletown" only the filling stations showed no large drop in business during the black years; for although few new automobiles were being bought, those which would still stand up were being used more than ever—to the dismay of the railroads.)

Otherwise things might seem to you to be going on much as usual. The major phenomena of the Depression were mostly negative and did not assail the eye.

But if you knew where to look, some of them would begin to appear. First, the breadlines in the poorer districts. Second, those bleak settlements ironically known as "Hoovervilles" in the outskirts of the cities and on vacant lots— groups of makeshift shacks constructed out of packing boxes, scrap iron, anything that could be picked up free in a diligent combing of the city dumps: shacks in which men and sometimes whole families of evicted people were sleeping on automobile seats carried from auto-graveyards, warming themselves before fires of rubbish in grease drums. Third, the homeless people sleeping in doorways or on park benches, and going the rounds of the restaurants for leftover half-eaten biscuits, piecrusts, anything to keep the fires of life burning. Fourth, the vastly increased number of thumbers on the highways, and particularly of freight-car transients on the railroads: a huge army of drifters ever on the move, searching half-aimlessly for a place where there might be a job. According to Jonathan Norton Leonard, the Missouri Pacific Railroad in 1929 had "taken official cognizance" of 13,745 migrants; by 1931 the figure had already jumped to 186,028. It was estimated that by the beginning of 1933, the country over, there were a million of these transients on the move. Forty-five thousand had passed through El Paso in the space of six months; 1,500 were passing through Kansas City every day. Among them were large numbers of young boys, and girls disguised as boys. According to the Children's Bureau, there were 200,000 children thus drifting about the United States. So huge was the number of freight-car hoppers in the Southwest that in a number of places the railroad police simply had to give up trying to remove them from the trains: there were far too many of them.

Among the comparatively well-to-do people of the country (those, let us say, whose pre-Depression incomes had been over $5,000 a year) the great majority were living on a reduced scale, for salary cuts had been extensive, especially since 1931, and dividends were dwindling. These people were discharging servants, or cutting servants' wages to a minimum, or in some cases "letting" a servant stay on without other compensation than board and lodging. In many pretty houses, wives who had never before—in the revealing current phrase—"done their own work" were cooking and scrubbing. Husbands were wearing the old suit longer, resigning from the golf club, deciding, perhaps, that this year the family couldn't afford to go to the beach for the summer, paying seventy-five cents for lunch instead of a dollar at the restaurant or thirty-five instead of fifty at the lunch counter. When those who had flown high with the stock market in 1929 looked at the stockmarket page of the newspapers nowadays their only consoling thoughts (if they still had any stock left) was that a judicious sale or two would result in such a capital loss that they need pay no income tax at all this year.

Alongside these men and women of the well-to-do classes whose fortunes had been merely reduced by the Depression were others whose fortunes had been shattered. The crowd of men waiting for the 8:14 train at the prosperous suburb included many who had lost their jobs, and were going to town as usual not merely to look stubbornly and almost hopelessly for other work but also to keep up a bold front of activity. (In this latter effort they usually succeeded: one would never have guessed, seeing them chatting with their friends as train-time approached, how close to desperation some of them had come.) There were architects and engineers bound for offices to which no clients had come in weeks. There were doctors who thought themselves lucky when a patient paid a bill. Mrs. Jones, who went daily to her stenographic job, was now the economic mainstay of her family, for Mr. Jones was jobless and was doing the cooking and looking after the children (with singular distaste and inefficiency). Next door to the Joneses lived Mrs. Smith, the widow of a successful lawyer: she had always had a comfortable income, she prided herself on her "nice things," she was pathetically unfitted to earn a dollar even if jobs were to be had; her capital had been invested in South American bonds and United Founders stock and other similarly misnamed "securities," and now she was completely dependent upon hand-outs from her relatives, and didn't even have carfare in her imported pocketbook.

The Browns had retreated to their "farmhouse" in the country and were trying to raise crops on its stony acres; they talked warmly about primal simplicities but couldn't help longing sometimes for electric light and running hot water, and couldn't cope with the potato bugs. (Large numbers of city dwellers thus moved to the country, but not enough of them engaged in real farming to do more than partially check the long-term movement from the farms of America to the cities and towns.) It was being whispered about the community that the Robinson family, though they lived in a $40,000 house and had always spent money freely, were in desperate straights: Mr. Robinson had lost his job, the house could not be sold, they had realized on every asset at their command, and now they were actually going hungry—though their house still looked like the abode of affluence.

Further down in the economic scale, particularly in those industrial communities in which the factories were running at twenty per cent of capacity or had closed down altogether, conditions were infinitely worse. Frederick E. Croxton's figures, taken in Buffalo, show what was happening in such communities: out of 14,909 persons of both sexes willing and able to work, his house-to-house canvassers found in November, 1932, that 46.3 per cent were fully employed, 22.5 per cent were working part time, and as many as 31.2 per cent were unable to find jobs. In every American city, quantities of families were being evicted from their inadequate apartments; moving in with other families till ten or twelve people would be sharing three or four rooms; or shivering through the winter in heatless houses because they could afford no coal, eating meat once a week or not at all. If employers sometimes found that former employees who had been discharged did not seem eager for re-employment ("They won't take a job if you offer them one!"), often the reason was panic: a dreadful fear of inadequacy which was one of the Depression's commonest psycho-pathological results. A woman clerk, offered piecework after being jobless for a year, confessed that she almost had not dared to come to the office, she had been in such terror lest she wouldn't know where to hang her coat, wouldn't know how to find the washroom, wouldn't understand the boss's directions for her job.

For perhaps the worst thing about this Depression was its inexorable continuance year after year. Men who have been sturdy and self-respecting workers can take unemployment without flinching for a few weeks, a few months, even if they have to see their families suffer; but it is different after a year . . . two years . . . three years. . . . Among the miserable creatures curled up on park benches or standing in dreary lines before the soup kitchens in 1932 were men who had been jobless since the end of 1929.

At the very bottom of the economic scale the conditions may perhaps best be suggested by two brief quotations. The first, from Jonathan Norton Leonard's *Three Years Down,* describes the plight of Pennsylvania miners who had been put out of company villages after a blind and hopeless strike in 1931: "Reporters from the more liberal metropolitan papers found thousands of them huddled on the mountainsides, crowded three or four families together in one-room shacks, living on dandelions and wild weed-roots. Half of them were sick, but no local doctor would care for the evicted strikers. All of them were hungry and many were dying of those providential diseases which enable welfare authorities to claim that no one has starved." The other quotation is from Louise V. Armstrong's *We Too Are the People,* and the scene is Chicago in the late spring of 1932:—

"One vivid, gruesome moment of those dark days we shall never forget. We saw a crowd of some fifty men fighting over a barrel of garbage which had been set outside the back door of a restaurant. American citizens fighting for scraps of food like animals!" . . .

MALCOLM COWLEY
This Threat Would Pass and Be Forgotten

In the summer of 1932 a "Bonus Expeditionary Force" of some eleven thousand veterans assembled in and around Washington to bring pressure to bear on the Congress to act for veterans' relief. In 1931 Congress had voted, despite and over President Hoover's veto, to permit veterans to borrow from the government as much as 50 percent of the face value of their bonus certificates, but the leaders of the Bonus Army insisted that the veterans were still being only half paid. The House passed on July 15, 1932, the Patman Bonus Bill which said that if the government could not pay the veterans in any other way, it should issue fiat money. When the Senate rejected this bill, the Bonus Army stayed on in Washington living in a village of huts of their own construction. About half of the Army left when Congress agreed to pay the way home for legitimate veterans, but the rest were driven out of Washington by army troops under General MacArthur using tear gas and fixed bayonets. President Hoover claimed that the military had overstepped its bounds, but the deed was done— unarmed American citizens were assaulted by armed soldiers of the American army. Malcolm Cowley (1898–   ) wrote the following essay for The New Republic, *which reflects the emotional shock which was felt across the country and gives a cool appraisal of the results of the events.*

When the veterans of the Bonus Army first tried to escape, they found that the bridges into Virginia were barred by soldiers and the Maryland roads blocked against them by state troopers. They wandered from street to street or sat in ragged groups, the men exhausted, the women with wet handkerchiefs laid over their smarting eyes, the children waking from sleep to cough and whimper from the tear gas in their lungs. The flames behind them were climbing into the night sky. About four in the morning, as rain began to fall, they were allowed to cross the border into Maryland, on condition that they moved as rapidly as possible into another state.

The veterans were expected to disperse to their homes—but most of them had no homes, and they felt that their only safety lay in sticking together. Somehow the rumor passed from group to group that the mayor of Johnstown had invited them to his city. And they cried, as they rode toward Pennsylvania or marched in the dawn twilight along the highways, "On to Johnstown."

Their shanties and tents had been burned, their personal property destroyed, except for the few belongings they could carry on their backs; many of their

FROM "The Flight of the Bonus Army," by Malcolm Cowley, in *The New Republic*, Vol. LXXII (August 17, 1932), pp. 13–15. Reprinted by permission of the author.

families were separated, wives from husbands, children from parents. Knowing all this, they still did not appreciate the extent of their losses. Two days before, they had regarded themselves, and had thought the country regarded them, as heroes trying to collect a debt long overdue. They had boasted about their months or years of service, their medals, their wounds, their patriotism in driving the Reds out of their camp; they had nailed an American flag to every hut. When threatened with forcible eviction, they answered that no American soldier would touch them: hadn't a detachment of Marines (consisting, some said, of twenty-five or thirty men, though others claimed there were two whole companies) thrown down its arms and refused to march against them? But the infantry, last night, had driven them out like so many vermin. Mr. Hoover had announced that "after months of patient indulgence, the government met overt lawlessness as it always must be met if the cherished processes of self-government are to be preserved." Mr. Hoover and his subordinates, in their eagerness to justify his action, were about to claim that the veterans were Red radicals, that they were the dregs of the population, that most of them had criminal records and, as a final insult, that half of them weren't veterans at all.

They would soon discover the effect of these official libels. At Somerset, on the Lincoln Highway, some of them asked for food. "We can't give you any," said a spokesman for the businessmen. "The President says that you're rebels—don't you understand? You're all outlaws now." A veteran's wife and children were refused admission to a hotel, even though they offered to pay for a room in advance. At Johnstown the wealthier citizens were dismayed to hear of their arrival. Possibly half the workmen in the city were unemployed; a fifth or a sixth of the population was in need of charity. Ten thousand hungry people were a threat in themselves, but the editor of The Johnstown Tribune was about to conjure up new terrors. He wrote:

Johnstown faces a crisis. It must prepare to protect itself from the Bonus Army concentrating here at the invitation of Mayor Eddie McCloskey. . . .
In any group of the size of the Bonus Army, made up of men gathered from all parts of the country, without discipline, without effective leadership in a crisis, without any attempt on the part of those leaders to check up the previous records of the individuals who compose it, there is certain to be a mixture of undesirables—thieves, plug-uglies, degenerates. . . . The community must protect itself from the criminal fringe of the invaders.
Booster clubs, community organizations of every sort, volunteer organizations if no sectional group is available, should get together in extraordinary sessions and organize to protect property, women and possibly life.
It is no time for halfway measures. . . .

The heroes of 1918, now metamorphosed into "thieves, plug-uglies, degenerates," were preparing to gather in the outskirts of the city, in the camp site offered them at Ideal Park. And the leading citizens, aided by the state police, were planning to use any means short of violence to keep them from reaching it. Mr. Hoover's proclamation had done its work.

At Jennerstown is a barracks of the Pennsylvania State Police, looking for all the world like a fashionable roadhouse. In front of the barracks is a traffic light. The road ahead leads westward over Laurel Hill and Chestnut Ridge; the right-hand road leads nineteen miles northward into Johnstown. It was the task of the state troopers to keep the Bonus Army moving west over the mountains, toward Ligonier and the Ohio border.

In half an hour on Saturday morning, I saw more than a thousand veterans pass through Jennerstown—that is, more than fifty trucks bearing an average of twenty men apiece. Later I was told that the procession continued at irregular intervals until Sunday evening. The troopers would wait at the intersection, twenty men on their motorcycles like a school of swift gray sharks, till they heard that a convoy was approaching; then they would dart off to meet it in a cloud of dust and blue gasoline smoke, with their hats cutting the air like so many fins. One of the troopers stayed behind to manipulate the traffic light. As the trucks came nearer, he would throw a switch that changed it into a mere yellow blinker, so that all of them could shoot past the intersection without slacking speed. They were full of ragged men, kneeling, standing unsteadily, clinging to the sideboards; there was no room to sit down. Behind each truck rode a trooper, and there were half a dozen others mingled with the crowd that watched from in front of a filling station.

The contrast between these homeless veterans, hatless, coatless, unshaven, half-starved—most of them hadn't eaten or slept for thirty-six hours, a few hadn't had so much as a drink of water—and the sleekly uniformed, well-nourished troopers who were herding them past their destination, produced a sharp effect on the crowd of backwoods farmers, who otherwise cared little about the Bonus March.

"Hey, buddies," they shouted, "turn right, turn right. Johnstown"—pointing northward—"Johnstown." The hungry men smiled and waved at them uncomprehendingly.

But a few had seen that something was wrong, that they were being carried beyond their meeting place. They tried to pass the word from truck to truck, above the roar of the motors. As they went bowling through the level village street, there was no way of escape; but just beyond Jennerstown, the road climbs steeply up Laurel Hill; the drivers shifted into second gear—and promptly lost half their passengers. The others, those who received no warning or let themselves be cowed by the troopers, were carried westward. The following week I met a New York veteran who hadn't escaped from the convoy till it passed the Ohio line. A Negro from Washington, a resident of the city for thirty years—he wasn't a bonus marcher at all, but made the mistake of walking through Anacostia in his shirt sleeves—was arrested, piled into a truck, and carried all the way to Indianapolis before he managed to tell his story to a reporter.

As for the veterans who escaped at Jennerstown, they lay by the roadside utterly exhausted. Their leaders had been arrested, dispersed, or else had betrayed them; their strength had been gnawed away by hunger or lack of sleep; they hoped to reunite and recuperate in a new camp, but how to reach it they did not know. For perhaps twenty minutes, they dozed there hopelessly. Then—and I was a witness of this phenomenon—a new leader would stand forth from the ranks. He would stop a motorist, learn the road to Johnstown, call the men together, give them their instructions—and the whole group would suddenly obey a self-imposed discipline. As they turned northward at the Jennerstown traffic light, one of them would shout, "We're going back!" and perhaps half a dozen would mumble in lower voices, "We're gonna get guns and go back to Washington."

Mile after mile we passed the ragged line as we too drove northward to the camp at Ideal Park. We were carrying two of the veterans, chosen from a group of three hundred by a quick informal vote of their comrades. One was a man gassed in the Argonne and tear-gassed at Anacostia; he breathed with an effort, as if each breath would be his last. The other was a man with family troubles; he had lost his wife and six children during the retreat from Camp Marks and hoped to find them in Johnstown. He talked about his service in France, his three medals, which he refused to wear, his wounds, his five years in a government hospital. "If they gave me a job," he said, "I wouldn't care about the bonus."

The sick man, as we passed one group of veterans after another, pointed northward and said in an almost inaudible voice, "This way, comrades, this way. Comrades, this way," till his head fell back and he lapsed into a feverish sleep.

It seemed the ragged line would never end. Here the marchers were stumbling under the weight of their suitcases and blanket rolls, here they were clustered round a farmhouse pump, here a white man was sharing the burden of a crippled Negro, here white and Negro together were snoring in a patch of shade. The road curled downward into the valley where Johnstown swelters between steep hills. On either side of us were fields of golden grain, cut and stacked for the threshers; a moment later we were winding through a forest. It was a landscape not unlike the high hills north of the River Aisne. In that other country, fifteen years before, I had seen gaunt men coming out of the trenches half-dead with fatigue, bending under the weight of their equipment. The men on the Johnstown road that day were older, shabbier, but somehow more impressive: they were volunteers, fighting a war of their own. "And don't forget it, Buddy," one of them shouted as the car slowed down, "we've enlisted for the duration."

At Ideal Park, where the new camp was being pitched, there was the same determination, combined with a hysteria caused by sudden relief from tension. A tall man with a tear-streaked face was marching up and down. "I used to be a hundred-percenter," he said, "but now I'm a Red radical. I had an American flag, but the damned tin soldiers burned it. Now I don't ever want to see a flag again. Give me a gun and I'll go back to Washington."—"That's right, Buddy," said a woman looking up from her two babies, who lay on a dirty quilt in the sun. A cloud of flies hovered above them. Another man was reading the editorial page of a Johnstown paper. He shouted, "Let them come here and mow us down with machine guns. We won't move this time."—"That's right, Buddy," said the woman again. A haggard face—eyes bloodshot, skin pasty white under a three days' beard—suddenly appeared at the window of our car. "Hoover must die," said the face ominously. "You know what this means?" a man shouted from the other side. "This means revolution."—"Yes, you're damned right it means revolution."

But a thousand homeless veterans, or fifty thousand, don't make a revolution. This threat would pass and be forgotten, like the other threat that was only half concealed in the Johnstown editorial. Next day the bonus leaders would come, the slick guys in leather puttees; they would make a few speeches and everything would be smoothed over. They would talk of founding a new Fascist order of Khaki Shirts, but this threat, too, can be disregarded: a Fascist movement, to succeed in this country, must come from the middle classes and be respectable. No, if any revolution results from the flight of the Bonus Army, it will come from a different source, from the government itself. The army in time of peace, at the national capital, has been used against unarmed citizens —and this, with all it threatens for the future, is a revolution in itself.

TWELVE SOUTHERNERS
An Undistinguished Replica of the Usual Industrial Community

In the turmoil immediately following the Crash, a book appeared. Though written while Business had still seemed as healthy as ever, it now spoke with peculiar appropriateness. Entitled I'll Take My Stand *(1930), it was written by Twelve Southerners, and it called for a restoration in the South of an agrarian society, and the repudiation of the "New South" idea of progress through industrialization. Though for a few years it was a topic of controversy, Agrarianism was not considered by most Southerners as a realistic program of action, and the Depression proved only a temporary setback in the region's accelerating industrialization and urbanization. Yet as an image of the good society, and a rebuke to the materialism of the twentieth century, what the Agrarians said has continued to interest readers and to stir up controversy. Their group included such poets, critics, and novelists as John Crowe Ransom, Donald Davidson, Allen Tate, Robert Penn Warren, John Gould Fletcher,*

FROM *I'll Take My Stand*, by Twelve Southerners (New York: Harper & Brothers, 1962), pp. xix–xxx. Copyright 1930, by Harper & Brothers; renewed 1958, by Donald Davidson. Reprinted by permission of Harper & Row, Publishers, Incorporated.

and Stark Young, as well as a number of prominent Southern historians,
political scientists, and other scholars. They prefaced I'll Take My Stand *with*
a Statement of Principles, to which all acceded, and which is reproduced below.

The authors contributing to this book are Southerners, well acquainted with
one another and of similar tastes, though not necessarily living in the same
physical community, and perhaps only at this moment aware of themselves as
a single group of men. By conversation and exchange of letters ·over a number
of years it had developed that they entertained many convictions in common,
and it was decided to make a volume in which each one should furnish his
views upon a chosen topic. This was the general background. But background
and consultation as to the various topics were enough; there was to be no
further collaboration. And so no single author is responsible for any view
outside his own article. It was through the good fortune of some deeper
agreement that the book was expected to achieve its unity. All the articles
bear in the same sense upon the book's title-subject: all tend to support a
Southern way of life against what may be called the American or prevailing
way; and all as much as agree that the best terms in which to represent the
distinction are contained in the phrase, Agrarian *versus* Industrial.

But after the book was under way it seemed a pity if the contributors,
limited as they were within their special subjects, should stop short of showing
how close their agreements really were. On the contrary, it seemed that they
ought to go on and make themselves known as a group already consolidated
by a set of principles which could be stated with a good deal of particularity.
This might prove useful for the sake of future reference, if they should undertake any further joint publication. It was then decided to prepare a general
introduction for the book which would state briefly the common convictions
of the group. This is the statement. To it every one of the contributors in this
book has subscribed.

Nobody now proposes for the South, or for any other community in this
country, an independent political destiny. That idea is thought to have been
finished in 1865. But how far shall the South surrender its moral, social, and
economic autonomy to the victorious principle of Union? That question
remains open. The South is a minority section that has hitherto been jealous
of its minority right to live its own kind of life. The South scarcely hopes to
determine the other sections, but it does propose to determine itself, within
the utmost limits of legal action. Of late, however, there is the melancholy fact
that the South itself has wavered a little and show signs of wanting to join
up behind the common or American industrial ideal. It is against that tendency that this book is written. The younger Southerners, who are being
converted frequently to the industrial gospel, must come back to the support
of the Southern tradition. They must be persuaded to look very critically at

the advantages of becoming a "new South" which will be only an undistinguished replica of the usual industrial community.

But there are many other minority communities opposed to industrialism, and wanting a much simpler economy to live by. The communities and private persons sharing the agrarian tastes are to be found widely within the Union. Proper living is a .matter of the intelligence and the will, does not depend on the local climate or geography, and is capable of a definition which is general and not Southern at all. Southerners have a filial duty to discharge to their own section. But their cause is precarious and they must seek alliances with sympathetic communities everywhere. The members of the present group would be happy to be counted as members of a national agrarian movement.

Industrialism is the economic organization of the collective American society. It means the decision of society to invest its economic resources in the applied sciences. But the word science has acquired a certain sanctitude. It is out of order to quarrel with science in the abstract, or even with the applied sciences when their applications are made subject to criticism and intelligence. The capitalization of the applied sciences has now become extravagant and uncritical; it has enslaved our human energies to a degree now clearly felt to be burdensome. The apologists of industrialism do not like to meet this charge directly; so they often take refuge in saying that they are devoted simply to science! They are really devoted to the applied sciences and to practical production. Therefore it is necessary to employ a certain skepticism even at the expense of the Cult of Science, and to say, It is an Americanism, which looks innocent and disinterested, but really is not either.

The contribution that science can make to a labor is to render it easier by the help of a tool or a process, and to assure the laborer of his perfect economic security while he is engaged upon it. Then it can be performed with leisure and enjoyment. But the modern laborer has not exactly received this benefit under the industrial regime. His labor is hard, its tempo is fierce, and his employment is insecure. The first principle of a good labor is that it must be effective, but the second principle is that it must be enjoyed. Labor is one of the largest items in the human career; it is a modest demand to ask that it may partake of happiness.

The regular act of applied science is to introduce into labor a labor-saving device or a machine. Whether this is a benefit depends on how far it is advisable to save the labor. The philosophy of applied science is generally quite sure that the saving of labor is a pure gain, and that the more of it the better. This is to assume that labor is an evil, that only the end of labor or the material product is good. On this assumption labor becomes mercenary and servile, and it is no wonder if many forms of modern labor are accepted without resentment though they are evidently brutalizing. The act of labor as one of the happy functions of human life has been in effect abandoned, and is practiced solely for its rewards.

Even the apologists of industrialism have been obliged to admit that some economic evils follow in the wake of the machines. These are such as over-production, unemployment, and a growing inequality in the distribution of wealth. But the remedies proposed by the apologists are always homeopathic. They expect the evils to disappear when we have bigger and better machines, and more of them. Their remedial programs, therefore, look forward to more industrialism. Sometimes they see the system righting itself spontaneously and without direction: they are Optimists. Sometimes they rely on the benevolence of capital, or the militancy of labor, to bring about a fairer division of the spoils: they are Coöperationists or Socialists. And sometimes they expect to find super-engineers, in the shape of Boards of Control, who will adapt production to consumption and regulate prices and guarantee business against fluctuations: they are Sovietists. With respect to these last it must be insisted that the true Sovietists or Communists—if the term may be used here in the European sense—are the Industrialists themselves. They would have the government set up an economic super-organization, which in turn would become the government. We therefore look upon the Communist menace as a menace indeed, but not as a Red one; because it is simply according to the blind drift of our industrial development to expect in America at last much the same economic system as that imposed by violence upon Russia in 1917.

Turning to consumption, as the grand end which justifies the evil of modern labor, we find that we have been deceived. We have more time in which to consume, and many more products to be consumed. But the tempo of our labors communicates itself to our satisfactions, and these also become brutal and hurried. The constitution of the natural man probably does not permit him to shorten his labor-time and enlarge his consuming-time indefinitely. He has to pay the penalty in satiety and aimlessness. The modern man has lost his sense of vocation.

Religion can hardly expect to flourish in an industrial society. Religion is our submission to the general intention of a nature that is fairly inscrutable; it is the sense of our rôle as creatures within it. But nature industrialized, transformed into cities and artificial habitations, manufactured into commodities, is no longer nature but a highly simplified picture of nature. We receive the illusion of having power over nature, and lose the sense of nature as something mysterious and contingent. The God of nature under these conditions is merely an amiable expression, a superfluity, and the philosophical understanding ordinarily carried in the religious experience is not there for us to have.

Nor do the arts have a proper life under industrialism, with the general decay of sensibility which attends it. Art depends, in general, like religion, on a right attitude to nature; and in particular on a free and disinterested observation of nature that occurs only in leisure. Neither the creation nor the understanding of works of art is possible in an industrial age except by some local and unlikely suspension of the industrial drive.

The amenities of life also suffer under the curse of a strictly-business or industrial civilization. They consist in such practices as manners, conversation, hospitality, sympathy, family life, romantic love—in the social exchanges which reveal and develop sensibility in human affairs. If religion and the arts are founded on right relations of man-to-nature, these are founded on right relations of man-to-man.

Apologists of industrialism are even inclined to admit that its actual processes may have upon its victims the spiritual effects just described. But they think that all can be made right by extraordinary educational efforts, by all sorts of cultural institutions and endowments. They would cure the poverty of the contemporary spirit by hiring experts to instruct it in spite of itself in the historic culture. But salvation is hardly to be encountered on that road. The trouble with the life-pattern is to be located at its economic base, and we cannot rebuild it by pouring in soft materials from the top. The young men and women in colleges, for example, if they are already placed in a false way of life, cannot make more than an inconsequential acquaintance with the arts and humanities transmitted to them. Or else the understanding of these arts and humanities will but make them the more wretched in their own destitution.

The "Humanists" are too abstract. Humanism, properly speaking, is not an abstract system, but a culture, the whole way in which we live, act, think, and feel. It is a kind of imaginatively balanced life lived out in a definite social tradition. And, in the concrete, we believe that this, the genuine humanism, was rooted in the agrarian life of the older South and of other parts of the country that shared in such a tradition. It was not an abstract moral "check" derived from the classics—it was not soft material poured in from the top. It was deeply founded in the way of life itself—in its tables, chairs, portraits, festivals, laws, marriage customs. We cannot recover our native humanism by adopting some standard of taste that is critical enough to question the contemporary arts but not critical enough to question the social and economic life which is their ground.

The tempo of the industrial life is fast, but that is not the worst of it; it is accelerating. The ideal is not merely some set form of industrialism, with so many stable industries, but industrial progress, or an incessant extension of industrialization. It never proposes a specific goal; it initiates the infinite series. We have not merely capitalized certain industries; we have capitalized the laboratories and inventors, and undertaken to employ all the labor-saving devices that come out of them. But a fresh labor-saving device introduced into an industry does not emancipate the laborers in that industry so much as it evicts them. Applied at the expense of agriculture, for example, the new processes have reduced the part of the population supporting itself upon the soil to a 'smaller and smaller fraction. Of course no single labor-saving process is fatal; it brings on a period of unemployed labor and unemployed capital, but soon a new industry is devised which will put them both to work again, and a new commodity is thrown upon the market. The laborers were sufficiently embarrassed in the meantime, but, according to the theory, they will eventually be taken care of. It is now the public which is embarrassed; it feels obligated to purchase a commodity for which it had expressed no desire, but it is invited to make its budget equal to the strain. All might yet be well, and stability and comfort might again obtain, but for this: partly because of industrial ambitions and partly because the repressed creative impulse must break out somewhere, there will be a stream of further labor-saving devices in all industries, and the cycle will have to be repeated over and over. The result is an increasing disadjustment and instability.

It is an inevitable consequence of industrial progress that production greatly outruns the rate of natural consumption. To overcome the disparity, the producers, disguised as the pure idealists of progress, must coerce and wheedle the public into being loyal and steady consumers, in order to keep the machines running. So the rise of modern advertising—along with its twin, personal salesmanship—is the most significant development of our industrialism. Advertising means to persuade the consumers to want exactly what the applied sciences are able to furnish them. It consults the happiness of the consumer no more than it consulted the happiness of the laborer. It is the great effort of a false economy of life to approve itself. But its task grows more difficult every day.

It is strange, of course, that a majority of men anywhere could ever as with one mind become enamored of industrialism: a system that has so little regard for individual wants. There is evidently a kind of thinking that rejoices in setting up a social objective which has no relation to the individual. Men are prepared to sacrifice their private dignity and happiness to an abstract social ideal, and without asking whether the social ideal produces the welfare of any individual man whatsoever. But this is absurd. The responsibility of men is for their own welfare and that of their neighbors; not for the hypothetical welfare of some fabulous creature called society.

Opposed to the industrial society is the agrarian, which does not stand in particular need of definition. An agrarian society is hardly one that has no use at all for industries, for professional vocations, for scholars and artists, and for the life of cities. Technically, perhaps, an agrarian society is one in which agriculture is the leading vocation, whether for wealth, for pleasure, or for prestige—a form of labor that is pursued with intelligence and leisure, and that becomes the model to which the other forms approach as well as they may. But an agrarian regime will be secured readily enough where the superfluous industries are not allowed to rise against it. The theory of agrarianism is that the culture of the soil is the best and most sensitive of vocations, and that therefore it should have the economic preference and enlist the maximum number of workers.

These principles do not intend to be very specific in proposing any practical measures. How may the little agrarian community resist the Chamber of Commerce of its county seat, which is always trying to import some foreign industry that cannot be assimilated to the life-pattern of the community? Just what must the Southern leaders do to defend the traditional Southern life? How may the Southern and the Western agrarians unite for effective action? Should the agrarian forces try to capture the Democratic party, which historically is so closely affiliated with the defense of individualism, the small community, the state, the South? Or must the agrarians—even the Southern ones—abandon the Democratic party to its fate and try a new one? What legislation could most profitably be championed by the powerful agrarians in the Senate of the United States? What anti-industrial measures might promise to stop the advances of industrialism, or even undo some of them, with the least harm to those concerned? What policy should be pursued by the educators who have a tradition at heart? These and many other questions are of the greatest importance, but they cannot be answered here.

For, in conclusion, this much is clear: If a community, or a section, or a race, or an age, is groaning under industrialism, and well aware that it is an evil dispensation, it must find the way to throw it off. To think that this cannot be done is pusillanimous. And if the whole community, section, race, or age thinks it cannot be done, then it has simply lost its political genius and doomed itself to impotence.

FRANKLIN D. ROOSEVELT
We Must Act and Act Quickly

The election of Franklin D. Roosevelt (1882–1945) to the presidency in 1932 saved the nation from a crisis of spirit as well as beginning its recovery from

FROM "Inaugural Address, March 4, 1933" by Franklin D. Roosevelt in *Inaugural Addresses of the Presidents of the United States from George Washington, 1789, to Harry S. Truman, 1949.* 82nd Congress, 2nd Session, House Doc. No. 540, pp. 225–28.

the economic crisis of the depression. Not only was there general despair and loss of faith in the economic policies of the years of Republican "normalcy," but there was strong reaction against the very system of government. Revolutionary movements of right and left began to gain some of the power in America that they were developing in Europe, while there was no strong voice speaking with any real conviction in support of the American institutions which were in such turmoil. Roosevelt's campaign had been relatively conservative, for he was depending upon Hoover's vast unpopularity to give him the votes of the discontented. His inaugural address, however, opened the drive of the New Deal to create a social revolution within the fabric of the present system even while it repaired the economic structure. He asked for "action, and action now," but always for action in the larger American idealistic tradition in which "Happiness lies not in the mere possession of money" but rather "in the joy of achievement, in the thrill of creative effort." He brought what Emerson would have called "the party of hope" back into the mainstream of American life, and he established as the central principle of American society the twentieth century idea of motion as the essence of being, replacing the Victorian belief in progress in an orderly but static world.

I am certain that my fellow Americans expect that on my induction into the Presidency I will address them with a candor and a decision which the present situation of our Nation impels. This is preeminently the time to speak the truth, the whole truth, frankly and boldly. Nor need we shrink from honestly facing conditions in our country today. This great Nation will endure as it has endured, will revive and will prosper. So, first of all, let me assert my firm belief that the only thing we have to fear is fear itself—nameless, unreasoning, unjustified terror which paralyzes needed efforts to convert retreat into advance. In every dark hour of our national life a leadership of frankness and vigor has met with that understanding and support of the people themselves which is essential to victory. I am convinced that you will again give that support to leadership in these critical days.

In such a spirit on my part and on yours we face our common difficulties. They concern, thank God, only material things. Values have shrunken to fantastic levels; taxes have risen; our ability to pay has fallen; government of all kinds is faced by serious curtailment of income; the means of exchange are frozen in the currents of trade; the withered leaves of industrial enterprise lie on every side; farmers find no markets for their produce; the savings of many years in thousands of families are gone.

More important, a host of unemployed citizens face the grim problem of existence, and an equally great number toil with little return. Only a foolish optimist can deny the dark realities of the moment.

Yet our distress comes from no failure of substance. We are stricken by no plague of locusts. Compared with the perils which our forefathers conquered because they believed and were not afraid, we have still much to be thankful for. Nature still offers her bounty and human efforts have multiplied it. Plenty is at our doorstep, but a generous use of it languishes in the very sight of the supply. Primarily this is because rulers of the exchange of mankind's goods have failed, through their own stubbornness and their own incompetence, have admitted their failure, and have abdicated. Practices of the unscrupulous money changers stand indicted in the court of public opinion, rejected by the hearts and minds of men.

True they have tried, but their efforts have been cast in the pattern of an outworn tradition. Faced by failure of credit they have proposed only the lending of more money. Stripped of the lure of profit by which to induce our people to follow their false leadership, they have resorted to exhortations, pleading tearfully for restored confidence. They know only the rules of a generation of self-seekers. They have no vision, and when there is no vision the people perish.

The money changers have fled from their high seats in the temple of our civilization. We may now restore that temple to the ancient truths. The measure of the restoration lies in the extent to which we apply social values more noble than mere monetary profit.

Happiness lies not in the mere possession of money; it lies in the joy of achievement, in the thrill of creative effort. The joy and moral stimulation of work no longer must be forgotten in the mad chase of evanescent profits. These dark days will be worth all they cost us if they teach us that our true destiny is not to be ministered unto but to minister to ourselves and to our fellow men.

Recognition of the falsity of material wealth as the standard of success goes hand in hand with the abandonment of the false belief that public office and high political position are to be valued only by the standards of pride of place and personal profit; and there must be an end to a conduct in banking and in business which too often has given to a sacred trust the likeness of callous and selfish wrongdoing. Small wonder that confidence languishes, for it thrives only on honesty, on honor, on the sacredness of obligations, on faithful protection, on unselfish performance; without them it cannot live.

Restoration calls, however, not for changes in ethics alone. This Nation asks for action, and action now.

Our greatest primary task is to put people to work. This is no unsolvable problem if we face it wisely and courageously. It can be accomplished in part by direct recruiting by the Government itself, treating the task as we would treat the emergency of a war, but at the same time, through this employment, accomplishing greatly needed projects to stimulate and reorganize the use of our natural resources.

Hand in hand with this we must frankly recognize the overbalance of population in our industrial centers and, by engaging on a national scale in a re-distribution, endeavor to provide a better use of the land for those best fitted for the land. The task can be helped by definite efforts to raise the values of agricultural products and with this the power to purchase the output of our cities. It can be helped by preventing realistically the tragedy of the growing loss through foreclosure of our small homes and our farms. It can be helped by insistence that the Federal, State, and local governments act forthwith on the demand that their cost be drastically reduced. It can be helped by the unifying of relief activities which today are often scattered, uneconomical, and unequal. It can be helped by national planning for and supervision of all forms of transportation and of communications and other utilities which have a definitely public character. There are many ways in which it can be helped, but it can never be helped merely by talking about it. We must act and act quickly.

Finally, in our progress toward a resumption of work we require two safeguards against a return of the evils of the old order: there must be a strict supervision of all banking and credits and investments, so that there will be an end to speculation with other people's money; and there must be provision for an adequate but sound currency.

These are the lines of attack. I shall presently urge upon a new Congress in special session detailed measures for their fulfillment, and I shall seek the immediate assistance of the several States.

Through this program of action we address ourselves to putting our own national house in order and making income balance outgo. Our international trade relations, though vastly important, are in point of time and necessity secondary to the establishment of a sound national economy. I favor as a practical policy the putting of first things first. I shall spare no effort to restore world trade by international economic readjustment, but the emergency at home cannot wait on that accomplishment.

The basic thought that guides these specific means of national recovery is not narrowly nationalistic. It is the insistence, as a first consideration, upon the interdependence of the various elements in and parts of the United States—a recognition of the old and permanently important manifestation of the American spirit of the pioneer. It is the way to recovery. It is the immediate way. It is the strongest assurance that the recovery will endure.

In the field of world policy I would dedicate this Nation to the policy of the good neighbor—the neighbor who resolutely respects himself and, because he does so, respects the rights of others—the neighbor who respects his obligations and respects the sanctity of his agreements in and with a world of neighbors.

If I read the temper of our people correctly, we now realize as we have never realized before our interdependence on each other; that we cannot merely take but we must give as well; that if we are to go forward, we must move as a trained and loyal army willing to sacrifice for the good of a common discipline, because without such discipline no progress is made, no leadership becomes effective. We are, I know, ready and willing to submit our lives and property to such discipline because it makes possible a leadership which aims at a larger good. This I propose to offer, pledging that the larger purposes will bind upon us all as a sacred obligation with a unity of duty hitherto evoked only in time of armed strife.

With this pledge taken, I assume unhesitatingly the leadership of this great army of our people dedicated to a disciplined attack upon our common problems.

Action in this image and to this end is feasible under the form of government which we have inherited from our ancestors. Our Constitution is so simple and practical that it is possible always to meet extraordinary needs by changes in emphasis and arrangement without loss of essential form. That is why our constitutional system has proved itself the most superbly enduring political mechanism the modern world has produced. It has met every stress of vast expansion of territory, of foreign wars, of bitter internal strife, of world relations.

It is to be hoped that the normal balance of executive and legislative authority may be wholly adequate to meet the unprecedented task before us. But it may be that an unprecedented demand and need for undelayed action may call for temporary departure from that normal balance of public procedure.

I am prepared under my constitutional duty to recommend the measures that a stricken nation in the midst of a stricken world may require. These measures, or such other measures as the Congress may build out of its experience and wisdom, I shall seek, within my constitutional authority, to bring to speedy adoption.

But in the event that the Congress shall fail to take one of these two courses, and in the event that the national emergency is still critical, I shall not evade the clear course of duty that will then confront me. I shall ask the Congress for the one remaining instrument to meet the crisis—broad Executive power to wage a war against the emergency, as great as the power that would be given to me if we were in fact invaded by a foreign foe.

For the trust reposed in me I will return the courage and the devotion that befit the time. I can do no less.

We face the arduous days that lie before us in the warm courage of national unity; with the clear consciousness of seeking old and precious moral values; with the clean satisfaction that comes from the stern performance of duty by old and young alike. We aim at the assurance of a rounded and permanent national life.

We do not distrust the future of essential democracy. The people of the United States have not failed. In their need they have registered a mandate that they want direct, vigorous action. They have asked for discipline and direction under leadership. They have made me the present instrument of their wishes. In the spirit of the gift I take it.

In this dedication of a Nation we humbly ask the blessing of God. May He protect each and every one of us. May He guide me in the days to come.

DAVID E. LILIENTHAL
The Tennessee Was Kept in Hand

*The Tennessee Valley Authority, a large network of dams along the Tennessee
River designed for flood control and the production of cheap electrical power,
was one of the most tangible results of the New Deal's drive for action, for it
transformed not only the society of the valley but the face of the land itself.
David E. Lilienthal (1899–   ) was named by President Roosevelt in 1933
one of three directors of the TVA. As chairman of the Authority from 1941
to 1946, he fought in most of the bitter battles both within the TVA and with
its opponents, all the while insisting on nonpolitical administration. In the
opening chapters of his book,* TVA: Democracy on the March, *Lilienthal gives
an account of the hopes and successes of the TVA. It is a testament of faith
in builders and technicians, who can create a new world when they have
"imagination and faith." His is a belief in man's ability to* make *himself better
and better, as opposed to the twenties' belief that man* gets *better and better
by the natural order of things. Recently there have been several interesting
novels about the coming of the TVA, including Madison Jones' A Buried
Land and Robert Penn Warren's Flood.*

This is an entirely different region from what it once was. You can see the
change almost everywhere you go. You can see it in the copper lines strung
along back country roads, in the fresh paint on the houses those electric lines
were built to serve. You can see it in new electric water pumps in the farm-
yards, in the community refrigerators at the crossroads, in the feed grinders in
the woodsheds. You can see the factories that stand today where there were
worn-out cotton fields and rows of tenant shacks a few years ago. You can see
new houses, by the thousands, on the edges of the towns—new houses of the
men who take away as much cash from a few trips to the payroll window as
they used to earn in a year.

You can see the change best of all if you have flown down the valley from
time to time, as I have done so frequently. From five thousand feet the great
change is unmistakable. There it is, stretching out before your eyes, a moving
and exciting picture. You can see the undulation of neatly terraced hillsides,
contrived to make the beating rains "walk, not run, to the nearest exit"; you
can see the grey bulk of the dams, stout marks across the river now deep blue,
no longer red and murky with its hoard of soil washed from the eroding land.

FROM *TVA: Democracy on the March* by David E. Lilienthal (New York: Harper & Brothers,
1953) pp. 8–16. Copyright 1944, 1953 by David E. Lilienthal. Reprinted by permission of Harper
& Row, Publishers, Incorporated.

You can see the barges with their double tows of goods to be unloaded at new river terminals. And marching toward every point on the horizon you can see the steel crisscross of electric transmission towers, a twentieth-century tower standing in a cove beside an eighteenth-century mountain cabin, a symbol and a summary of the change. These are among the things you can see as you travel through the Tennessee Valley today. And on every hand you will also see the dimensions of the job yet to be done, the problem and the promise of the valley's future.

A technical man will observe much that will interest him, for the Tennessee Valley Authority represents a substantial technical achievement, a record written over a wide area in concrete and steel, and in land revived and forests renewed. Here one can see what modern science can do in a few years to change the face of the earth and the waters. That technical story has been recorded with painstaking care and great detail and published in the many volumes of scientific reports by TVA's engineers, agronomists, town builders, chemists, biologists, foresters, public health experts, architects.

These technical reports will interest the experts. The average citizen will measure the change through reports of another kind: in the records of new private industries established in the valley, of failing enterprises revived, more money in people's hands, fewer tax delinquencies, increased bank deposits, a greater volume of buying at the stores—trends clearly established before the war. The citizen may read of the change in records of new public library service or state parks established where none had been before, more hospitals, new county health units, less tuberculosis and malaria and other "low income diseases." He may read of the number of miles of lines built to bring power to the farms of the area and the rapid increase in the amount of electricity used by the people—unprecedented in this country. He may reflect on the better quality of food produced and the increased yield per acre on the land, or analyze the ton-miles of traffic increase on the river. He may figure the potential value of the millions of seedlings planted in farm woodland and forest. He may see the newly created "Great Lakes of the South," the beauty of their thousands of miles of wooded shoreline unmarred, deep blue waters set among high mountains and abounding with game fish.

Such sights and such records reflect the ways in which, as this beautiful valley has changed, the lives of several million fellow Americans have also changed.

The story of the change begins with the river. On the map the river's five mountain tributaries, each a considerable stream—the French Broad, the Holston, the Hiwassee, the Little Tennessee, the Clinch—are clearly set off from the broad main stem, the Tennessee itself, a major river of great volume, fed by the heaviest rainfall in eastern America. The map shows that main stem as a deep crescent, its source and eastern tip in the Appalachian Mountains, the dip of the crescent slicing off the northern third of Alabama, the western tip arching northward through the flat red lands of western Tennessee and

Kentucky., The river flows not in one general direction, but in three; it moves southward first, then its middle course is westward, and its lower reaches turn back toward the north. A river that "flows up the map," as visitors to TVA almost invariably remark, seems to be water flowing perversely uphill, making its way more than 650 miles from Knoxville in Tennessee, in sight of the virgin timber in the Great Smoky Mountains, the highest peaks in eastern North America, to Paducah in the lowlands of Kentucky where across the broad Ohio you can see the fields of Illinois.

The valley through which the river flows actually lies in seven historic states of the Old South: the western part of the seacoast states of North Carolina and Virginia; the northern parts of Georgia, Alabama, and Mississippi; the western half of Kentucky from its southern jointure with Tennessee north to the Ohio River; and almost of the whole of the wide reaches of the state of Tennessee. Less exactly, the region reaches from the mountains about Asheville west to the sluggish Mississippi at Memphis, and north and south from the old steamboat whistle landings on Ohio's shores to the cotton fields of Mississippi and the flambeau of the furnaces at Birmingham—an area all told about the size of England and Scotland, with a population of about 6,000,000 persons.

This is the river system that thirty dams of the TVA integrated system now control and have put to work for the people. To do that job twenty new dams, several among the largest in America, were designed and constructed. Five dams already existing have been improved and modified. Five more major dams owned by a private corporation are, by agreement, operated as a part of the system. One of TVA's carpenters, a veteran who worked on seven of these dams, described this to me as "one hell of a big job of work." I cannot improve on that summary. It is the largest job of engineering and construction ever carried out by any single organization in all our history.

In heat and cold, in driving rain and under the blaze of the August sun, tens of thousands of men have hewed and blasted and hauled with their teams and tractors, clearing more than 175,000 acres of land, land that the surface of the lakes now covers. They have built or relocated more than 1300 miles of highway and almost 200 miles of railroad. With thousands of tons of explosives and great electric shovels they have excavated over 30,000,000 cubic yards of rock and earth to prepare the foundations of these dams—an excavation large enough to bury twenty Empire State buildings. To hold the river the men of the TVA have poured and placed concrete, rock fill, and earth in a total quantity of 113 million cubic yards.

To comprehend these figures requires a few comparisons. This 113 million cubic yards of material is more than twelve times the bulk of the seven great pyramids of Egypt. Of these materials, the concrete alone poured into the TVA dams is two and a half times as much as used in all the locks and structures of the Panama Canal; is four times as much as in Hoover Dam; 1,200,000 cubic yards greater than in the Grand Coulee Dam; would build more than seven dams as large as Soviet Russia's great Dneiper Dam. The Grand Coulee Dam is the largest single masonry structure yet built, and Hoover Dam the second largest. Hoover was in the process of construction for five years and took the combined efforts of six of our largest private building contractor firms. Grand Coulee took eight years to build, and ten major private construction firms were engaged on it.

Thirty-five Hoover dams or ten Grand Coulee dams could have been built with the total materials required for completion of this valley's dams, the work of a single organization. The TVA's employees in 1942 were simultaneously designing and building a dozen dams and improving four others, were erecting the South's largest steam electric plant, and building large chemical and munitions factories, with a total of 40,000 men and women at work.

A decade later, in 1952, a total of 21,000 men and women were at work building two dams, installing ten additional generators in existing dams, and erecting six huge coal-burning electric generating plants, some of which will be among the largest in the world.

The work of the builders has made of the river a highway that is carrying huge amounts of freight over its deep watercourses. In 1952 more than 800 million ton-miles of traffic moved through locks, designed in co-operation with the Army Corps of Engineers and operated by them, which raise the barges from one lake's level to another. In 1928 only a little more than 46 million ton-miles of traffic moved on the river; in 1933 the figure was 32 million. This was mostly sand and gravel moving in short hauls between adjacent areas, and some forest products.

Today huge modern towboats, powered by great Diesel engines, move up and down the channel, pushing double columns of barges, and the cargo is no longer limited to raw materials. Billets of steel and cotton goods come from Birmingham headed north, grain from the Midwest, millions of gallons of gasoline, oil, machinery, merchandise, automobiles, military vehicles. In 1951, with more than 580 million ton-miles carried, savings were $8,000,000.

Quiet cotton towns of yesterday are now busy river ports. And, as always has been true of water transportation, new industries are rising along its course. Millions of dollars have been invested, and thousands of jobs created as new grain elevators, flour mills, and oil terminals have been erected along the river's banks.

At Decatur, Alabama, on land where farmers once raised corn and cotton, ocean-going cargo vessels slipped down the ways into Wheeler Lake during the War and thence to their North Atlantic job. After the war, self-propelled barges were built there for use on the Rhine River in Europe, as well as barges for the inland waterways of the U.S.

And on these lakes are thousands of new pleasure craft of every kind—costly yachts, sailboats, homemade skiffs. Ten thousand miles of shoreline—more than the total of the seacoast line of the United States on the Atlantic, the Pacific, and the Gulf of Mexico—are available for the recreation of the people. Thousands of acres along the shore are devoted to public parks, operated by the states, by counties, and by cities. More than 225 boat docks serve the needs of fishermen from all parts of the United States.

There is far more fishing on the new lakes than there was on these same rivers before the dams were built—one hundred times more on the storage reservoirs and thirty times as intensive on the mainstream reservoirs. About half of the increase was due to dropping the traditional idea of a "closed season," and encouraging fishing any time of the year. Careful studies showed that not more than 10 per cent of the available fish "crop" is being harvested annually, hence a closed season was unnecessary. In 1952 sports fishermen alone are estimated to have taken some 8,000,000 pounds of fish from the streams, while commercial operations yielded nearly 2,000,000 pounds of fish and 10,000 tons of mussel shells.

Before the men of the Tennessee Valley built these dams, flooding was a yearly threat to every farm and industry, every town and village and railroad on the river's banks, a barrier to progress. Today there is security from that annual danger in the Tennessee Valley. When local protective works have been erected at Chattanooga this region will be completely safe, even against a flood bigger than anything in recorded history. A measure of protection resulting from the Tennessee's control extends even beyond this valley; for no longer will the Tennessee send her torrents at flood crest to add what might be fatal inches to top the levees and spread desolation on the lower Ohio and the Mississippi.

In others of the earth's thousand valleys people live under the shadow of fear that each year their river will bring upon them damage to their property, suffering, and death. Here the people are safe. In the winter of 1942 torrents came ranging down this valley's two chief tributaries, in Tennessee and Virginia. Before the river was controlled this would have meant a severe flood; the machinery of vital war industries down the river at Chattanooga would have stopped, under several feel of water, with over a million dollars of direct damage resulting.

But in 1942 it was different. Orders went out from the TVA office of central control to every tributary dam. The message came flashing to the operator in the control room at Hiwassee Dam, deep in the mountains of North Carolina: "Hold back all the water of the Hiwassee River. Keep it out of the Tennessee." The operator pressed a button. Steel gates closed. The water of that tributary was held. To Cherokee Dam on the Holston went the message: "Keep back the flow of the Holston." To Chickamauga Dam just above the industrial danger spot at Chattanooga: "Release water to make room for the waters from above."

Day by day till the crisis was over the men at their control instruments at each dam in the system received their orders. The rate of water release from every tributary river was precisely controlled. The Tennessee was kept in hand. There was no destruction, no panic, no interruption of work. Most of the water, instead of wrecking the valley, actually produced a benefit in power, when later it was released through the turbines.

By 1945, two more large tributary and two more main Tennessee River reservoirs had been completed. January, 1946, brought water flows that without the river's new safeguards would have been a great and disastrous flood, the fifth largest ever to occur at Chattanooga. TVA reservoirs reduced the crest by more than ten feet. In the next two years, 1947 and 1948, the crests of potentially the sixth and seventh largest floods were similarly reduced; the saving in actual damage averted in Chattanooga alone in these three floods was more than $36 million.

Back of the orders from the water dispatcher to the men who operate the dams is an elaborate system of reporting rainfall and gauging the flow of streams so the height of waters can be predicted for days in advance. To the head of the TVA forecasting division, from all over the watershed, from every tributary stream, from three hundred stations, by teletype, telephone, and short-wave radio come reports of the river's "stages" i.e., its height. Here, for example, is one of the messages that came from H. S. Barker near Mendota, in Virginia, during the critical days of the 1942 flood: "River three feet eighty-four hundredths raining rainfall one seventeen hundredths inches." That is, river stage was 3.84 feet; it was raining at the time; the rainfall during the past twenty-four hours was 1.17 inches.

Reports come in from hundreds of remote rain-gauge stations, telephoned in by a farmer's wife, a crossroad store merchant, a woodsman. From well-nigh inaccessible mountain streams ingenious TVA-made devices send in their reports by shortwave radio without human intervention. And all the reports are combined and interpreted by engineers, so that they know almost exactly how much water will be swelling the river the next day and the next. Yesterday's reports are checked with today's and revised tomorrow, and the best technical judgment is sent to the river control room: just how much water is being added to the rivers flow in the French Broad, the Holston, the Clinch, the Hiwassee.

The operating orders go out, turning water off or on to meet the demands of the crisis along a watercourse from the headwaters of the Tennessee to the Gulf, almost as long as the Mississippi from its headwaters to New Orleans. The Tennessee River throughout its length is controlled, as water is retained at one dam, released at another. This valley has been made safe.

This is not true of other river valleys. Here, for example, is a press association dispatch of May 13, 1943:

Swollen creeks and rivers flooded more than one million acres of low-lying farm-lands in six states Thursday, burying spring crops, blocking highways and taking at least seven lives.

High water left hundreds of farm families homeless as flood crests rolled downstream in Arkansas, Oklahoma, Kansas, Missouri, Indiana, and Illinois. . . .

As the river crest moved downstream Army engineers retreated before it, abandoning levee after levee as the hopelessness of combating the flood became apparent.

A few days later this summary appeared in the New York *Times* (May 27, 1943):

During May muddy waters have submerged 3,926,000 acres in Illinois, Missouri, Arkansas, Oklahoma, Kansas and Indiana, routed 160,000 persons and caused twenty-one deaths in the worst floods in the midlands since 1937, when the Ohio and Mississippi Valley disaster made more than 1,000,000 persons homeless and took 466 lives.

The story of one year's disaster after another in the floods of the Missouri Valley has become a familiar and sorry tale, culminating—though unhappily not necessarily ending—in the Missouri Valley floods of 1950 and 1951. Taken together these constitute a major national disaster; and for a country so advanced in engineering, soil technology, and management as ours, a national disgrace as well.

In the technically retarded or undeveloped parts of the world one comes to expect much the same kind of story of the devastation of man's works by floods. Here, for example, is a newspaper account from New Delhi, India, dated August 7, 1943:

Approximately 10,000 Indians were drowned in the past week by floodwaters of the Khari River which swept suddenly through nearly 100 villages. Nearly a sixth of the tiny British Province of Ajmer-Merwara was under water.

And in the fall of 1943 came that flood's horrible sequel: famine.

No major river in the world is so fully controlled as the Tennessee, no other river works so hard for the people, for the force that used to spend itself so violently is today turning giant waterwheels. The turbines and generators in the TVA powerhouses have transformed it into electric energy. And this is the river's greatest yield.

16

THE SHADOW
OF
TOTALITARIANISM

Growing behind and through all the effort and activity of the domestic social revolution was an understanding that America's problems could no longer be considered to stop at the oceans of the East and West. Europe was suffering from the same economic crisis and finding different solutions: Mussolini and Fascism in Italy, Hitler and Nazism in Germany, Stalin and his tough, nationalistic form of Communism in Russia. War is a solution for many internal difficulties, and Mussolini said, "Three cheers for war in general." And Japan was fighting on the Asian mainland to create a Greater East Asia Co-Prosperity Sphere. The Spanish Civil War broke out in 1936, a bloody preview of the larger conflict to follow. The world was moving toward another world war; everyone knew it, but no one seemed to be able to do anything about it.

In America, Roosevelt won re-election in 1940 both on the strength of his New Deal program and also on a pledge to keep America out of "foreign wars," but he knew that the war brewing and then exploding around the world could not long remain a foreign war. He saw America as an "arsenal for democracy," and he began to aid the allied nations in every way he could. The sense of unity following the crash began to break up as Americans began to seek ways out of a new war. Isolationism and the attempt to be no more than the arsenal of democracy both failed, and America entered World War II from which it would emerge as the dominant world power in a new world in which no nation would ever again be able to separate its domestic from its foreign affairs.

The following eight pieces outline the changing tone of American life in the shadow of totalitarianism, from the leftist ideals of the American writers and young men who went to Spain to support the Loyalist cause, to President Truman's hard and totally practical decision to drop the atomic bomb on Japan to end the war. Like the Civil War, this war changed America radically; it also changed the world of which America was now so inextricably a part. These selections give some idea of what it was like to be a part of that change.

MALCOLM COWLEY
The Explosions Are Becoming Less Frequent

In 1936, General Francisco Franco led a semifascistic revolution against the republican government of Spain; this was the Spanish Civil War which lasted until 1938 when the Republic was finally overthrown after a brutal and bloody conflict. The war had large international complications, for Hitler and Mussolini both gave considerable aid to Franco's forces, while Stalin gave some aid to the Loyalists. Young liberal and idealistic young men came from all over the world to fight on the side of the Republic in International Brigades, among which were the American Lincoln and Washington battalions of the XVth brigade formed in February, 1937. It was the first direct military confrontation between the forces of right and left, of fascism and republicanism, and as such it was a vicious and very real rehearsal for World War II. Many writers were drawn to Spain to fight and take part in the war effort in whatever capacity they could. Ernest Hemingway wrote and narrated the film, "The Spanish Earth," which was an effective piece of moral propaganda for the Republic. Malcolm Cowley, in the piece below, tells of a writers' conference in Madrid in 1937 and captures much of the intellectual ferment of the period and much of the hopelessness which was already becoming the dominant tone in a world on the brink of war. The outstanding American work about the Spanish Civil War, Hemingway's For Whom the Bell Tolls, *also deals with much the same material.*

FROM "Offensive on Two Fronts," by Malcolm Cowley, *The New Republic*, Vol. LXXXXII (September 15, 1937), pp. 152–55. Copyright 1937 by Editorial Publications. Renewal copyright 1965 by Malcolm Cowley. Reprinted by permission of the author.

A few hours after we first arrived in Valencia, I had begun hearing that the republican army would soon be taking the offensive. A photographer drew us aside to whisper an important piece of news to Dick Mowrer. He had ridden down from Madrid in an army truck. Along a back road he passed more than ten miles of guns—big guns—and tanks that were waiting for darkness to move up to the front. There was more artillery on that one road than he had seen during his first six months in Spain. At Albacete he had heard that all but the most seriously wounded were being evacuated from the American hospitals in order to make room for new cases. The government was planning a big push; there was absolutely no doubt of it.

Later that evening there was a reception at the headquarters of the Spanish writers' union, the Alianza. I talked with a Dutch writer named Jef Last, tall, thin, tired, and fragile-looking, who had been fighting on the Madrid front for more than ten months and was now a captain in the Spanish regular army. He explained to me why it was that the republican troops had so far been unable to carry out a general offense. When their attacks reached a point within four hundred yards of the enemy lines, the problem was how to maintain superiority of fire. It couldn't be done without automatic rifles or light machine guns, whereas the Loyalists had only heavy machine guns and army rifles. Sometimes, by sacrificing their men, they made important gains in spite of their faulty equipment, but they had so far lacked the reserve forces that would have enabled them to withstand a counter attack; that was why they had to retreat from La Granja after a really brilliant advance. . . . He paused for a moment, as if shaking off his fatigue. "But we have now some light machine guns. We are making reserve forces, a great number. The next time, it will be different—and the next time will be sooner than you expect."

I crossed to another corner of the room, where I had recognized an English novelist now serving as a political officer with the International Brigades. He wanted to talk about the new Spanish army. "The young conscripts," he said "are actually better soldiers than the first volunteers. They have less dash, perhaps, and less political consciousness, but they hate the Fascists just as much and they are more amendable to discipline. Very soon they'll get a chance to show their fighting qualities." He lowered his voice. "They may be going into the lines at this very moment."

Walking home through the darkened streets, we were stopped by a man whom I had known in New York as a reporter out of a job. At present he was working for the American hospital in Albacete. He told us that the photographer had been right about the evacuation of all the lightly wounded; they were being sent to rest homes farther in the rear. What was more, the director of the hospital had been asked to prepare for handling sixteen hundred new cases every day until further notice. We could guess what that meant. . . .

Everybody in Spain seemed to know something new about the offensive. Even Queipo de Llano had mentioned it in one of his facetious broadcasts from Seville. He had begged the Loyalists to hurry because, he said, the Moors were waiting to gobble them up. That is the way with military plans in Spain: the whole world hears about them, including the general staff of the opposing army. But this time, surprisingly, there was a difference. Nobody knew just where the attack would take place, and nobody knew just when.

I didn't think much about it during the long drive to Madrid. There were troops and guns on the road, but not in any unusual numbers. The Madrid evening papers of July 5 had no exciting news. I decided that the rumors had been false, or that the offensive was going to be delayed. But early next morning, at the door of the hotel, I heard a peculiar low throbbing and booming that was almost like a thunderstorm in the next county. It suggested something else besides—the rumble of the guns as you heard it in 1917, when it was carried to Paris by a northeasterly wind. The Loyalist offensive had opened on the Sierra front.

The same morning the writers' international congress convened for its first session in Madrid.

There were two reasons why it was meeting in this beleaguered town. One of these was a matter of simple and almost routine courtesy. At the first writers' congress, held in Paris two years before, the Spanish delegates had invited their colleagues to hold a second congress in Madrid. They had repeated the invitation in London, at a meeting of the executive committee in June, 1936, just a month before the military revolt; and this time it had been formally accepted. In one sense, you could say that they were merely keeping an engagement. In another sense they were of course doing much more. This civil war transformed into an international war has engaged the sympathies of writers in all countries; and there is no doubt that most of them have taken the government side. To hold a literary congress in Madrid was a means of stating this fact; it was a means of telling the Spanish writers and soldiers that they were not fighting alone.

The first plans were announced in the Paris papers of November 6—that is, on the day that Franco's Moors were fighting in the Madrid streets. During the next eight months, the city was under fire and short of food; the congress had to be postponed more than once. Always the date of it had to be kept secret, for fear that Franco would provide his own reception committee. Invitations had to be carefully issued for fear of admitting provocators or spies or simple trouble-makers—since what would be an amusing literary scandal in New York or Paris might have dangerous echoes in a country at war, especially in view of the Anarchist-Trotskyist uprising in Barcelona. There were all sorts of difficulties growing out of the non-intervention agreement. The British delegates as originally chosen were refused passports by their Foreign Office, which leans toward the Fascists. A new delegation had to be named and smuggled across the border. The German exiles were afraid of carrying passports with a Spanish visa; they might be barred from returning to France or Austria. The hardships of travel in the war zone made it physically impossible for some of the older writers, like Heinrich Mann. His brother Thomas was ill in Switzerland.

Considering all these obstacles—and considering, too, the natural individualism and indiscipline of literary people—it is a wonder to me that the congress ever assembled in Paris, or got itself across the border after only a few hours of delay, or traveled for several hundred miles along Spanish roads reserved for military traffic. Once in Madrid, it made a pretty impressive showing. There were seventy-five or eighty delegates from twenty-eight countries scattered over the world from China and Iceland to Chile. Latin America was strongly represented. There was a fair sprinkling of men and women with international reputations—from France, Malraux and Benda and Chamson; from England, Stephen Spender and Sylvia Townsend Warner; from the Soviet Union, Tolstoy, Fadayev and Ehrenbourg; from Denmark, Hans Anderson Nexö. They were joined by a Spanish delegation that included Bergamin (a Catholic, head of the writers' alliance), Alvarez del Vayo (till recently Foreign Minister) and Machado and Alberti (regarded as the two great Spanish poets, since the death of Garcia Lorca). They were also joined by writers from the International Brigades: Ludwig Renn, Gustav Regler, Ralph Bates. Here were people whose books I had admired or argued about. Meeting them in Madrid, I could look forward to an interchange of experience, observation, theory. . . .

But the congress in Madrid encountered another difficulty that had not been foreseen. Loyalist Spain, during its battles with Moors and Germans and Italians, has become intensely and justifiably proud of itself as a nation. It doesn't want the mere pity of well meaning foreigners: it wants their admiration and it wants material aid. In the meantime it is determined to fight its own battles. The Spanish government officials who dealt with the congress were for the most part writers themselves; in any case they were men of broad culture concerned with literary problems. But in their preoccupation with the civil war, they could not help regarding the congress as an offensive on the cultural front. As such it was less important than the military offensive that had opened west of Madrid.

I don't mean to say that the writers were urged to think or speak on any given topics. Nobody guided the course of the discussion. But in the air of this really heroic city trying to free itself from an eight-months' siege, it was almost impossible to talk about literary questions—about realism or the nature of the contemporary hero or the problem of creating novels for and by the working class. Instead people talked about the immediate struggle, often in terms of political slogans. Sometimes the discussion was very nearly drowned out by the sound of the guns.

This martial atmosphere was strongest at the two meetings in Madrid on July 6. They were held under the honorary chairmanship of General Miaja, the commander-in-chief. Soldiers stood guard at either side of the platform; in the intense heat I could see the sweat rolling down their foreheads and making them blink their eyes. A good military band played selections, but played them too often; during each rendition of the "International" and the new Spanish anthem, we stood at attention, raising our clenched fists. Speakers succeeded one another on the rostrum, under the glare of the searchlights—a Cuban Negro poet, a German exile, a Bulgarian once condemned to death and released after eight years in prison, a Pole from the Dombrowski Battalion, a Frenchman from the Marty Battalion, a whole parade of nations to say in their different languages that the Spaniards were fighting our fight, that we were with them in body and spirit.

I remember the appearance of the speakers much better than anything they said. There was Stephen Spender, tall, slim, with wavy hair, a shirt open at the neck and a general look of being Shelley astray in the twentieth century; there was Julien Benda, short, with gray bangs that made him resemble a seated statue of the Emperor Augustus; there was thin, dark, elusive José Bergamín; there was Alexis Tolstoy, plump, bald-crowned, bearing with him an aura of success, of two million copies sold in Soviet Russia and translations all over the world; there was Sylvia Townsend Warner looking like a very pleasantly daft English spinster (say her own Lolly Willowes); there was Ludwig Renn, very tall, with his eyes smiling behind steel-rimmed spectacles and his head cocked to one side as if he were always leaning down to catch an inaudible voice from the world of shorter men; there were Vishnievski and Stavski, the roaring boys from Moscow—the first looking like a jolly sailor on shore leave, which is exactly what he was; the second six feet tall and three feet broad, with a huge nose a low forehead and ears standing straight out from his skull, which was completely shaven, so that he had the air of being a convict in a Mack Sennett comedy—but such a friendly convict that everybody grinned at him and shook his enormous hand. . . .

Thinking back on the writers there, I feel that they had a common quality of warmth and humanness—almost of recklessness—that set them apart from any other large group of writers I have seen together. In their own countries they were men of individual ideas. Even here in this meeting behind the trenches, some of them were saying keen or moving or subtle things, as I discovered afterwards when reading the reports of their speeches; but I was distracted by the heat and the confusion of tongues; all I caught for the moment were the patriotic slogans—and I have a very low capacity for listening to patriotic slogans. In my notebook I find the record of a dialogue with Sylvia Townsend Warner, half in my handwriting, half in hers:

M.C.—"*Abajo fascismo! Viva el proletario español! Salud!*" As used by the last speaker these belong in the aw nuts department. He used them to get a hand.

S.T.W.—The Spanish are too damned taken up with their own affairs to care for German anti-fascism. So the German baited his remarks, which referred to his own national struggle.

M.C.—But when you see those French writers going out for a smoke, you realize that he's been baiting for moths with moth balls and for mosquitoes with eucalyptus oil.

S.T.W.—Not all writers are well disciplined.
M.C.—Writers' congresses usually go on in the lobby.
S.T.W.—Did you hear that *bomb?*

The bomb put an end to our dialogue for the moment—and besides, the next speaker turned out to be much more interesting. Before the end of his address, there was an interruption of a more welcome sort. A detachment of soldiers rushed up to the platform carrying two Fascist banners taken at Brunete, and the uniform of a captured Fascist colonel, and a whole handful of women's gold lockets which this same colonel had appropriated in the course of a raid on the civilian population. The soldiers announced that an advance of sixteen kilometers had been made since daybreak. Their offensive —the other offensive—was succeeding beyond expectations.

And our offensive too, went better on the following days. Back in Valencia, on July 10, there was an extraordinarily fine meeting at which Fernando de los Rios paid a tribute to his dead friend, the poet Lorca. Louis Aragon at a later meeting in Paris, read an important paper in defense of literary national-ism. In the end the congress was not without literary results, though it was more important as a demonstration of international solidarity. But that is running considerably ahead of my story.

Madrid, July 6.—We dine late in the evening, after the second meeting. The writer-delegates from the International Brigades are full of high spirits. For us, this congress is a serious business; for them, it is a magical escape into civilian life and the company of pretty women. They wheel a little piano into the center of the room and begin to play all their marching songs, including an interminable series of parodies on "La Cucaracha." The big hotel is shaking at every chorus. Suddenly I notice that the waiters are closing the windows and pulling down the shutters. The lights go out one by one; the last chorus dies. In the silence we can hear a shell bursting only a few hundred yards away; then another that seems nearer.

Gradually—in utter darkness now, except for the glowing tips of cigarettes —we are herded to the lower floors of the hotel, to wait until the bombardment has ended. Here are a hundred sedentary people, civilians, bookmen; most of them are under fire for the first time. They react in different fashions. One nice Frenchwoman runs up to me and insists that I must keep Anna Louise Strong from going into the street and getting killed—speaking with the sort of brave calm that verges on hysteria. Others seem totally indifferent. Going down the stairs I stumble into one group arguing in French about André Gide's trip to the Soviet Union, saying nothing new with great eloquence. For my own part I feel a curious elation, which undoubtedly is shared by others. It had seemed a little cheap to come as tourists to this city that had suffered so much. Now at last we are partly justified by sharing its dangers.

The explosions are becoming less frequent. A group of us, including Anna

Louise Strong and all the English delegates, go out into the street and watch the ambulances clanging past. A big fire is burning two blocks away, on the Puerta del Sol, and we decide to go down and look at it. There isn't much to see. The flames burn with a cold light, almost like a magnesium flare. The firemen work in absolute silence. And this conflagration in the heart of a city is watched by no one—by no one except two policemen on duty and half a dozen timid British and American writers peering round the corner so as to be safe from steel fragments.

The end of the world, I think, will be like this—not a sudden immense catastrophe but a slow attrition, as in Madrid: a building burned at night, another building demolished, a street car wrecked, a shop closed because the owner is dead—not a great disaster but an accumulation of small disasters, while people carry on their business and try to repair the damage, never quite fast enough to keep up with the attacks of the enemy. The end of the world will be like this—and I am sure that even during the last months there will be writers, deeply stirred, who will hold congresses at which the discussions will be inflated with martial hope and eventually drowned out by the guns.

FRANKLIN D. ROOSEVELT
The Hand That Held the Dagger

On June 10, 1940, Italy, which had hitherto been attempting to stay out of the war and even to mediate a peace, succumbed to the pressures of the German Foreign Office and attacked France. President Roosevelt was to speak at the graduation ceremonies at the University of Virginia that day, and he used the occasion to denounce the Italian attack, to describe American isolationism as "the nightmare of a people lodged in prison," and to define the social revolution of the New Deal as only a part of "national defense itself." Although a major weapon in his re-election campaign of 1940 was that he had "kept us out of war," Roosevelt was clearly stating in this speech that he was supporting "the opponents of force" with the material resources of the nation and that he was preparing the nation for the eventuality of war. The domestic drive of the New Deal took second place from this time on to foreign affairs as America entered into world politics on a large scale for the first time since Wilson's unsuccessful attempt to lead the country into participation in the League of Nations.

FROM "Address at University of Virginia," by Franklin D. Roosevelt, *Congressional Record*, Vol. 86, Pt. 16 (Washington, D.C.: U.S. Govt. P. O., 1940), pp. 3740–41.

President Newcomb, my friends of the University of Virginia,

I notice by the program that I am asked to address the classes of 1940. I avail myself of that privilege, but I also take this very apt occasion to speak to many other classes, classes that have graduated through all the years, classes that are still in the period of study, classes not alone of the schools of learning of the Nation, but classes that· have come up through the great schools of experience; in other words, a cross section, a cross section just as you who graduate today are a cross section of the Nation as a whole.

Every generation of young men and women in America has questions to ask the world. Most of the time they are the simple but nevertheless difficult questions, questions of work to do, opportunities to find, ambitions to satisfy.

But every now and again in the history of the Republic a different kind of question presents itself—a question that asks, not about the future of an individual or even of a generation, but about the future of the country, the future of the American people.

There was such a time at the beginning of our history—at the beginning of our history as a Nation. Young people asked themselves in those days what lay ahead, not for themselves, but for the new United States.

There was such a time again in the seemingly endless years of the War Between the States. Young men and young women on both sides of the line asked themselves, not what trades or professions they would enter, what lives they would make, but what was to become of the country they had known.

There is such a time again today. Again today the young men and the young women of America ask themselves with earnestness and with deep concern this same question: "What is to become of the country we know?"

Now they ask it with even greater anxiety than before. They ask, nôt only what the future holds for this Republic, but what the future holds for all peoples and all nations that have been living under democratic forms of Government, under the free institutions of a free people.

It is understandable to all of us that they should ask this question. They read the words of those who are telling them that the ideal of individual liberty, the ideal of free franchise, the ideal of peace through justice is a decadent ideal. They read the word and hear the boast of those who say that a belief in force—force directed by self-chosen leaders—is the new and vigorous system which will overrun the earth. They have seen the ascendancy of this philosophy of force in nation after nation where free institutions and individual liberties were once maintained.

It is natural and understandable that the younger generation should first ask itself what the extension of the philosophy of force to all the world would lead to ultimately. We see today, for example, in stark reality some of the consequences of what we call the machine age.

Where control of machines has been retained in the hands of mankind as a whole, untold benefits have accrued to mankind. For mankind was then the master and the machine was the servant.

But in this new system of force the mastery of the machine is not in the hands of mankind. It is in the control of infinitely small groups of individuals who rule without a single one of the democratic sanctions that we have known. The machine in hands of irresponsible conquerors becomes the master; mankind is not only the servant; it is the victim too. Such mastery abandons with deliberate contempt all of the moral values to which even this young country for more than three hundred years has been accustomed and dedicated.

Surely the new philosophy proves from month to month that it could have no possible conception of the way of life or the way of thought of a nation whose origins go back to Jamestown and Plymouth Rock.

And conversely, neither those who spring from that ancient stock nor those who have come hither in later years can be indifferent to the destruction of freedom in their ancestral lands across the sea.

Perception of danger, danger to our institutions may come slowly or it may come with a rush and a shock as it has to the people of the United States in the past few months. This perception of danger, danger in a world-wide area—it has come to us clearly and overwhelmingly—we perceive the peril in a world-wide arena—an arena that may become so narrowed that only the Americas will retain the ancient faiths.

Some indeed still hold to the now somewhat obvious delusion that we of the United States can safely permit the United States to become a lone island, a lone island in a world dominated by the philosophy of force.

Such an island may be the dream of those who still talk and vote as isolationists. 'Such an island represents to me and to the overwhelming majority of Americans today a helpless nightmare, the helpless nightmare of a people without freedom; yes, the nightmare of a people lodged in prison, handcuffed, hungry, and fed through the bars from day to day by the contemptuous, unpitying masters of other continents.

It is natural also that we should ask ourselves how now we can prevent the building of that prison and the placing of ourselves in the midst of it.

Let us not hesitate—all of us—to proclaim certain truths. Overwhelmingly we, as a nation—and this applies to all the other American nations—are convinced that military and naval victory for the gods of force and hate would endanger the institutions of democracy in the western world, and that equally, therefore, the whole of our sympathies lies with those nations that are giving their lifeblood in combat against these forces.

The people and the Government of the United States have seen with the utmost regret and with grave disquiet the decision of the Italian Government to engage in the hostilities now raging in Europe.

More than 3 months ago the Chief of the Italian Government sent me word that because of the determination of Italy to limit, so far as might be possible, the spread of the European conflict, more than 200,000,000 people in the region of the Mediterranean had been enabled to escape the suffering and the devastation of war.

I informed the Chief of the Italian Government that this desire on the part of Italy to prevent the war from spreading met with full sympathy and response on the part of the Government and the people of the United States, and I expressed the earnest hope of this Government and of this people that this policy on the part of Italy might be continued. I made it clear that in the opinion of the Government of the United States any extension of hostilities in the region of the Mediterranean might result in a still greater enlargement of the scene of the conflict, the conflict in the Near East and in Africa, and that if this came to pass no one could foretell how much greater the theater of the war eventually might become.

Again on a subsequent occasion, not so long ago, recognizing that certain aspirations of Italy might form the basis of discussions among the powers most specifically concerned, I offered, in a message addressed to the Chief of the Italian Government, to send to the Governments of France and of Great Britain such specific indications of the desires of Italy to obtain readjustments with regard to her position as the Chief of the Italian Government might desire to transmit through me. While making it clear that the Government of the United States in such an event could not and would not assume responsibility for the nature of the proposals submitted nor for agreements which might thereafter be reached, I proposed that if Italy would refrain from entering the war I would be willing to ask assurances from the other powers concerned that they would faithfully execute any agreement so reached and that Italy's voice in any future peace conference would have the same authority as if Italy had actually taken part in the war, as a belligerent.

Unfortunately, to the regret of all of us and the regret of humanity, the Chief of the Italian Government was unwilling to accept the procedure suggested and he has made no counter proposal.

This Government directed its efforts to doing what it could to work for the preservation of peace in the Mediterranean area, and it likewise expressed its willingness to endeavor to cooperate with the Government of Italy when the appropriate occasion arose for the creation of a more stable world order, through the reduction of armaments, and through the construction of a more liberal international economic system which would assure to all powers equality of opportunity in the world's markets and in the securing of raw materials on equal terms.

I have likewise, of course, felt it necessary in my communications to Signor Mussolini to express the concern of the Government of the United States because of the fact that any extension of the war in the region of the Mediterranean would inevitably result in great prejudice to the ways of life and government and to the trade and commerce of all the American Republics.

The Government of Italy has now chosen to preserve what it terms its "freedom of action" and to fulfill what it states are its promises to Germany.

In so doing it has manifested disregard for the rights and security of other nations, disregard for the lives of the peoples of those nations which are directly threatened by this spread of the war, and has evidenced its unwilling-ness to find the means through pacific negotiations for the satisfaction of what it believes are its legitimate aspirations.

On this tenth day of June 1940, the hand that held the dagger has struck it into the back of its neighbor.

On this tenth day of June 1940, in this university, founded by the first great American teacher of democracy, we send forth our prayers and our hopes to those beyond the seas who are maintaining with magnificent valor their battle for freedom.

In our, in our unity—in our American unity—we will pursue two obvious and simultaneous courses; we will extend to the opponents of force the material resources of this Nation, and at the same time, we will harness and speed up the use of those resources in order that we ourselves in the Americas may have equipment and training equal to the task of any emergency and every defense.

All roads leading to the accomplishment of these objectives must be kept clear of obstructions. We will not slow down or detour. Signs and signals call for speed—full speed ahead.

Yes, it is right that each new generation should ask questions. But in recent months the principal question has been somewhat simplified. Once more the future of the Nation, the future of the American people is at stake.

We need not and we will not in any way abandon our continuing effort to make democracy work within our borders. Yes; we still insist on the need for vast improvements in our own social and economic life.

But that, that is a component part of national defense itself.

The program unfolds swiftly, and into that program will fit the responsi-bility and the opportunity of every man and women in the land to preserve his and her heritage in days of peril.

I call for effort, courage, sacrifice, devotion. Granting the love of freedom, all of these are possible.

And—the love of freedom is still fierce, still steady in the Nation today.

CHARLES A. LINDBERGH
Now We Are Being Led Toward War

In 1940 after the fall of France, the large sentiment for American isolation from Europe's problems and Europe's war reached its height in this country. Geog-raphy, it was urged, would protect America from Hitler even if Germany won

FROM "Strength and Peace: Our Frontiers Do Not Lie in Europe," by Col. Charles A. Lindbergh, *Vital Speeches of the Day*, Vol. VII (November 1, 1940), pp. 42–43.

the war, and American youth should not have to be sacrificed when national security was not at stake. Certainly the sense of futility following Germany's return to power after having lost the "war to end war" had a great deal to do with the wide appeal of isolationist sentiment. If the first war had won nothing, why should another be expected to gain any more? The isolationist camp drew support from all points of the political spectrum, ranging from Norman Thomas, the head of the American Socialist Party, to senators like Burton K. Wheeler, Robert La Follette and Gerald P. Nye, to the various cryptofascist groups of the American right. The America First Committee became the focal point of the isolationist opposition to President Roosevelt's international policies. Among the arguments advanced was that intervention in the war against Nazi Germany would leave Europe open to the menace of Soviet Russia. Colonel Charles A. Lindbergh (1902–   ), the aviator who had flown nonstop to Paris, became one of the most outspoken members of that committee. This speech, delivered on the radio, October 13, 1940, is a typical example of the isolationist argument, the strength of which was to be put to the test and found lacking in the presidential election the following month when Roosevelt received nearly 55 percent of the vote.

I come before you tonight to enter a plea for American independence. It is amazing that one should have to plead for American independence in a nation with a heritage such as ours; in a nation which in its infancy revolted against foreign control, and whose people have fought time and time again against the armies and interference of the Old World. Yet the independence and the destiny of America were never more in jeopardy than they are today.

During the first century and a quarter of our existence as a free and independent people we opposed, and opposed successfully, all the major powers in Europe. At the same time that our forefathers pushed through the wilderness to the Pacific they forced, one after another, England, France and Spain to discontinue their interference with American affairs.

We won our independence from England when we were a nation of less than 4,000,000 people. We numbered only 10,000,000 when the Monroe Doctrine was established. With a population of 35,000,000, even though we had just emerged from four years of civil war, we made France remove her invading armies from Mexico. Later in the century, with a population of 75,000,000 we forced Spain to withdraw entirely from the New World.

Why, then, with 130,000,000 people, are we being told that we must give up our independent position, that our frontiers lie in Europe and that our destiny will be decided by European armies fighting upon European soil? What has happened to this nation that it fears in maturity the forces that it conquered in its youth? What change has come over us? Where is the blood of such leaders as Washington, Jefferson and Lincoln; blood that stood firm on American soil against the threats, the armies and the navies of the greatest empires on earth?

What we lack today is the type of leadership that made us a great nation; the type that turned adversity and hardship into virility and success. No one doubts that we are in the midst of a world crisis. No one denies that our defenses are weak, that our debt is great, that dissatisfaction is rising among us. We do not question the need for rearmament, for reform, for a better economic system.

What we do question is the leadership that has brought these conditions upon us. We question that the men who were unable to foresee these conditions in time to avoid them, who could not foresee the war in time to prepare for it, who refused to believe the reports of rearming abroad when there was still time to take action, are now competent to carry this nation successfully through a period of great crisis.

Under their leadership we have alienated the most powerful military nations of both Europe and Asia, at a time when we ourselves are unprepared for action, and while the people of our nation are overwhelmingly opposed to war.

There is no question about the fundamental courage and solidarity of Americans when our national welfare is at stake. There is no division among us about the defense of our own country. We have always been ready to fight against the interference of foreign powers in our affairs. If need be, we are ready to die for the independence of America, as our forefathers have died before us when necessity arose.

On a clearly American issue we stand a united nation. It is only when we are asked to take part in the quarrels of foreign countries that we divide; only when we are asked to merge our destiny with that of other lands; only when an attempt is made to transfer loyalty for America to loyalty for some other nation.

The fact is today that we are divided; we have not confidence in our leaders. We have not confidence in their efficiency or in their judgment.

Instead of a Washington warning us against the wiles of foreign influence and excessive partiality for any nation, we are told that our frontiers lie in Europe.

Instead of a Lincoln telling us that if danger ever reach us it must spring up amongst us, and that it cannot come from abroad, we are informed that we may be invaded from the ice-bound mountains of Greenland; and by fleets of non-existent transatlantic bombers.

We find the same men who have led us to the greatest national debt in our history now telling us that as a nation we are weak and unprepared; that we must appropriate more billions of dollars and devote more years of time to building up our military forces. These same leaders who have failed to solve even our peace-time problems, who have a consistent record of promise followed by failure, now ask us to put ourselves in their hands again as they lead us steadily toward that climax of all political failure—war.

They do not tell us openly what their intentions are. They say we should leave our decisions and our destiny to specialists—to their particular specialists

—to the same specialists who have made us a weakened nation in the center of an antagonistic world.

They harangue us about "democracy," yet they leave us with less knowledge of the direction in which we are headed than if we were citizens of a "totalitarian" State. We are told that we are being prepared to defend America at the same time that orders are placed for the type and quantity of armament that would be used for a war in Europe.

We do not need untold thousands of military aircraft unless we intend to wage a war abroad. What we do need is a thoroughly modern and efficient Air Corps, trained, equipped and maintained for the specific mission of American defense. What we need even more, however, is balanced action, a clear-cut plan and a consistent attitude.

Adequate defense does not necessitate this alarm and confusion. With intelligent leadership, we could have built an impregnable defense for America without disturbing seriously our national life and industry. We have already spent more than enough money to have done this.

With an Army, a Navy and an Air Corps of high quality and reasonable size, we could have maintained our position with safety at home and respect abroad. But today, while we listen to talk of aircraft, guns and battleships, couched in figures so astronomical that they compare only to our national debt, we find ourselves in confusion at home, and under ridicule abroad.

The same thing is happening to us that happened to England and France. We have been led to debt and weakness, and now we are being led toward war. Instead of building their own national strength, the peacetime leaders of England and France told their people that security lay abroad, that the best way to defend their own countries was to fight for Poland. They followed this advice and failed.

Now we in America are being told under similar circumstances, and by leaders of similar caliber that our security lies abroad; that the best way to defend our own country is to defend England. All the lessons of Europe have passed unheeded before us. The effort that should have been devoted to the welfare of our own nation has been spread ineffectively over the difficulties of other parts of the world. The attention that should have been concentrated on the defense of America has been divided by a controversy over what part we should take in the wars of Europe.

If we desire strength, and freedom, and independence for our country, the first step must be to assure ourselves of leadership which is entirely and unequivocally American. When a man is drafted to serve in the armed forces of our country, he has the right to know that his government has the independent destiny of America as its objective, and that he will not be sent to fight in the wars of a foreign land.

The doctrine that we must enter the wars of Europe, in order to defend America, will be fatal to our nation if we follow it.

FRANKLIN D. ROOSEVELT
A World Founded Upon Four Essential Human Freedoms

In his State of the Union Address of January 6, 1941, President Roosevelt attempted to define more clearly his new understanding of America as the "arsenal of democracy" in a time of extreme peril. The speech was designed to rally the various forces of American life into a patriotic unity, working together with wartime cooperation at a time when the country was not yet at war. More important, however, was Roosevelt's expansion of the social and political ideals of the New Deal into an expression of a global policy based upon the securing for all of "four essential human freedoms": freedom of speech and expression, freedom of worship, freedom from want, and freedom from fear. The conclusion of the speech exhibits Roosevelt's recognition that the social revolution depended upon the whole world and that no one nation could achieve its successful resolution alone.

As men do not live by bread alone, they do not fight by armaments alone. Those who man our defenses, and those behind them who build our defenses, must have the stamina and courage which come from unshakable belief in the manner of life which they are defending. The mighty action which we are calling for cannot be based on a disregard of all things worth fighting for.

The Nation takes great satisfaction and much strength from the things which have been done to make its people conscious of their individual stake in the preservation of democratic life in America. Those things have toughened the fiber of our people, have renewed their faith and strengthened their devotion to the institutions we make ready to protect.

Certainly this is no time to stop thinking about the social and economic problems which are the root cause of the social revolution which is today a supreme factor in the world.

There is nothing mysterious about the foundations of a healthy and strong democracy. The basic things expected by our people of their political and economic systems are simple. They are:

Equality of opportunity for youth and for others.

Jobs for those who can work.

Security for those who need it.

The ending of special privilege for the few.

The preservation of civil liberties for all.

FROM "Annual Message, 1941" by Franklin D. Roosevelt, *Congressional Record,* Vol. 87, Pt. I (Washington, D.C.: U.S. Govt. P. O., 1941), pp. 46–47.

The enjoyment of the fruits of scientific progress in a wider and constantly rising standard of living.

These are the simple, basic things that must never be lost sight of in the turmoil and unbelievable complexity of our modern world. The inner and abiding strength of our economic and political systems is dependent upon the degree to which they fulfill these expectations.

Many subjects connected with our social economy call for immediate improvement.

As examples:

We should bring more citizens under the coverage of old-age pensions and unemployment insurance.

We should widen the opportunities for adequate medical care.

We should plan a better system by which persons deserving or needing gainful employment may obtain it.

I have called for personal sacrifice. I am assured of the willingness of almost all Americans to respond to that call.

A part of the sacrifice means the payment of more money in taxes. In my Budget message I recommend that a greater portion of this great defense program be paid for from taxation than we are paying today. No person should try, or be allowed, to get rich out of this program; and the principle of tax payments in accordance with ability to pay should be constantly before our eyes to guide our legislation.

If the Congress maintains these principles, the voters, putting patriotism ahead of pocketbooks, will give you their applause.

In the future days, which we seek to make secure, we look forward to a world founded upon four essential human freedoms.

The first is freedom of speech and expression everywhere in the world.

The second is freedom of every person to worship God in his own way everywhere in the world.

The third is freedom from want, which, translated into world terms, means economic understandings which will secure to every nation a healthy peacetime life for its inhabitants everywhere in the world.

The fourth is freedom from fear—which, translated into world terms, means a world-wide reduction of armaments to such a point and in such a thorough fashion that no nation will be in a position to commit an act of physical aggression against any neighbor—anywhere in the world.

That is no vision of a distant millennium. It is a definite basis for a kind of world attainable in our time and generation. That kind of world is the very antithesis of the so-called new order of tyranny which the dictators seek to create with the crash of a bomb.

To that new order we oppose the greater conception—the moral order. A good society is able to face schemes of world domination and foreign revolutions alike without fear.

Since the beginning of our American history we have been engaged in change—in a perpetual peaceful revolution—a revolution which goes on stead-ily, quietly adjusting itself to changing conditions—without the concentration camp or the quick lime in the ditch. The world order which we seek is the cooperation of free countries, working together in a friendly, civilized society.

This Nation has placed its destiny in the hands and heads and hearts of its millions of free men and women; and its faith in freedom under the guidance of God. Freedom means the supremacy of human rights everywhere. Our support goes to those who struggle to gain those rights or keep them. Our strength is in our unity of purpose.

To that high concept there can be no end save victory.

FRANKLIN D. ROOSEVELT
The Character of the Onslaught Against Us

The argument between isolationism and internationalism which had been settled in great part by Roosevelt's impressive victory in the 1940 elections was silenced once and for all by the Japanese attack on the American naval base at Pearl Harbor in Hawaii on the morning of December 7, 1941. President Roosevelt addressed Congress on Monday the eighth of December, asking that a state of war be declared between the United States and Japan. The speech speaks for itself and for the righteous anger which was to dominate American life for the war years to follow.

Yesterday, December 7, 1941—a date which will live in infamy—the United States of America was suddenly and deliberately attacked by naval and air forces of the Empire of Japan.

The United States was at peace with that nation and, at the solicitation of Japan, was still in conversation with its Government and its Emperor looking toward the maintenance of peace in the Pacific. Indeed, 1 hour after Japanese air squadrons had commenced bombing in Oahu, the Japanese Ambassador to the United States and his colleague delivered to our Secretary of State a formal reply to a recent American message. And while this reply stated that it seemed useless to continue the existing diplomatic negotiations, it contained no threat or hint of war or armed attack.

It will be recorded that the distance of Hawaii from Japan makes it obvious that the attack was deliberately planned many days or even weeks ago. During the intervening time the Japanese Government has deliberately sought to deceive the United States by false statements and expressions of hope for continued peace.

FROM "Address to the Congress, December 8, 1941" by Franklin D. Roosevelt, *Congressional Record*, Vol. 87, No. 9 (Washington, D.C.: U.S. Govt. P. O., 1941), pp. 9504–05.

The attack yesterday on the Hawaiian Islands has caused severe damage to American naval and military forces. Very many American lives have been lost. In addition American ships have been reported torpedoed on the high seas between San Francisco and Honolulu.

Yesterday the Japanese Government also launched an attack against Malaya.

Last night Japanese forces attacked Hong Kong.

Last night Japanese forces attacked Guam.

Last night Japanese forces attacked the Philippine Islands.

Last night the Japanese attacked Wake Island.

This morning the Japanese attacked Midway Island.

Japan has therefore undertaken a surprise offensive extending throughout the Pacific area. The facts of yesterday speak for themselves. The people of the United States have already formed their opinions and well understand the implications to the very life and safety of our Nation.

As Commander in Chief of the Army and Navy I have directed that all measures be taken for our defense.

But always will we remember the character of the onslaught against us.

No matter how long it may take us to overcome this premeditated invasion, the American people in their righteous might will win through to absolute victory.

I believe I interpret the will of the Congress and of the people when I assert that we will not only defend ourselves to the uttermost but will make very certain that this form of treachery shall never endanger us again.

Hostilities exist. There is no blinking at the fact that our people, our territory, and our interests are in grave danger.

With confidence in our armed forces—with the unbounded determination of our poeple—we will gain the inevitable triumph, so help us God.

I ask that the Congress declare that, since the unprovoked and dastardly attack by Japan on Sunday, December 7, a state of war has existed between the United States and the Japanese Empire.

WENDELL WILLKIE
We Must Win Not Only the War, But Also the Peace

Wendell Willkie (1892–1944) was the Republican candidate for president in 1940. After his defeat, he visited England, the Near East, Russia, and China as President Roosevelt's personal representative. Although he had opposed the

FROM *One World,* by Wendell L. Willkie (New York: Simon and Schuster, 1943), pp. 196–98, 201–06. Reprinted by permission of Philip H. Willkie, trustee for Wendell Willkie Fund.

New Deal, Willkie was a strong supporter of Roosevelt's foreign policy and his ideals as exemplified by the four freedoms. Upon his return to America, he wrote One World, *and turned his attention to freeing the Republican Party from what he saw as the bonds of isolationism. In the concluding chapter of* One World, *he saw the war as a revolutionary war which would create a new and necessarily closer world, marked especially by an economically unified Europe and a new importance for the nations of Asia. The only possibility for peace was, as he saw it, in the creation of a world society free of economic imperialism as well as military conquest, one "in which men and women the world around can live and grow invigorated by independence and freedom."* One World *is marred by an excessive optimism, but that optimism also gives it much of its prophetic vigor.*

It was only a short time ago—less than a quarter of a century—that the allied nations gained an outstanding victory over the forces of conquest and aggression then led by imperial Germany.

But the peace that should have followed that war failed primarily because no joint objectives upon which it could be based had been arrived at in the minds of the people, and therefore no world peace was possible. The League of Nations was created full-blown; and men and women, having developed no joint purpose, except to defeat a common enemy, fell into capricious arguments about its structural form. Likewise, it failed because it was primarily an Anglo-French-American solution, retaining the old colonial imperialisms under new and fancy terms. It took inadequate account of the pressing needs of the Far East, nor did it sufficiently seek solution of the economic problems of the world. Its attempts to solve the world's problems were primarily political. But political internationalism without economic internationalism is a house built upon sand. For no nation can reach its fullest development alone.

Our own history furnishes, I believe, another clue to our failure. One of our most obvious weaknesses, in the light of what is going on today, is the lack of any continuity in our foreign policy. Neither major party can claim to have pursued a stable or consistent program of international cooperation even during the relatively brief period of the last forty-five years. Each has had its season of world outlook—sometimes an imperialistic one—and each its season of strict isolationism, the Congressional leadership of the party out of power usually, according to accepted American political practice, opposing the program of the party in power, whatever it might be.

For years many in both parties have recognized that if peace, economic prosperity, and liberty itself were to continue in this world, the nations of the world must find a method of economic stabilization and co-operative effort.

These aspirations at the end of the First World War, under the presidency of Woodrow Wilson, produced a program of international co-operation intended to safeguard all nations against military aggression, to protect racial minorities, and to give the oncoming generation some confidence that it could go about its affairs without a return of the disrupting and blighting scourge of war. Whatever we may think about the details of that program, it was definite, affirmative action for world peace. We cannot state positively just how effective it might have proved had the United States extended to it support, influence, and active participation.

But we do know that we tried the opposite course and found it altogether futile. We entered into an era of strictest detachment from world affairs. Many of our public leaders, Democratic and Republican, went about the country proclaiming that we had been tricked into the last war, that our ideals had been betrayed, that never again should we allow ourselves to become entangled in world politics which would inevitably bring about another armed outbreak. We were blessed with natural barriers, they maintained, and need not concern ourselves with the complicated and unsavory affairs of an old world beyond our borders. . . .

I am satisfied that the American people never deliberately and intentionally turned their backs on a program for international co-operation. Possibly they would have preferred changes in the precise Versailles covenant, but not complete aloofness from the efforts of other nations. They were betrayed by leaders without convictions who were thinking in terms of group vote catching and partisan advantage.

If our withdrawal from world affairs after the last war was a contributing factor to the present war and to the economic instability of the past twenty years—and it seems plain that it was—a withdrawal from the problems and responsibilities of the world after this war would be sheer disaster. Even our relative geographical isolation no longer exists.

At the end of the last war, not a single plane had flown across the Atlantic. Today that ocean is a mere ribbon, with airplanes making regular scheduled flights. The Pacific is only a slightly wider ribbon in the ocean of the air, and Europe and Asia are at our very doorstep.

America must choose one of three courses after this war: narrow nationalism, which inevitably means the ultimate loss of our own liberty; international imperialism, which means the sacrifice of some other nation's liberty; or the creation of a world in which there shall be an equality of opportunity for every race and every nation. I am convinced the American people will choose, by overwhelming majority, the last of these courses. To make this choice effective, we must win not only the war, but also the peace, and we must start winning it now.

To win this peace three things seem to me necessary—first, we must plan now for peace on a world basis; second, the world must be free, politically and economically, for nations and for men, that peace may exist in it; third, America must play an active, constructive part in freeing it and keeping its peace.

When I say that peace must be planned on a world basis, I mean quite literally that it must embrace the earth. Continents and oceans are plainly only parts of a whole, seen, as I have seen them, from the air. England and America are parts. Russia and China, Egypt, Syria and Turkey, Iraq and Iran are also parts. And it is inescapable that there can be no peace for any part of the world unless the foundations of peace are made secure throughout all parts of the world.

This cannot be accomplished by mere declarations of our leaders, as in an Atlantic Charter. Its accomplishment depends primarily upon acceptance by the peoples of the world. For if the failure to reach international understanding after the last war taught us anything it taught us this: even if war leaders apparently agree upon generalized principles and slogans while the war is being fought, when they come to the peace table they make their own interpretations of their previous declarations. So unless today, while the war is being fought, the people of the United States and of Great Britain and of China, and of all the other United Nations, fundamentally agree on their purposes, fine and idealistic expressions of hope such as those of the Atlantic Charter will live merely to mock us as have Mr. Wilson's Fourteen Points. The Four Freedoms will not be accomplished by the declarations of those momentarily in power. They will become real only if the people of the world forge them into actuality.

When I say that in order to have peace this world must be free, I am only reporting that a great process has started which no man—certainly not Hitler—can stop. Men and women all over the world are on the march, physically, intellectually, and spiritually. After centuries of ignorant and dull compliance, hundreds of millions of people in eastern Europe and Asia have opened the books. Old fears no longer frighten them. They are no longer willing to be Eastern slaves for Western profits. They are beginning to know that men's welfare throughout the world is interdependent. They are resolved, as we must be, that there is no more place for imperialism within their own society than in the society of nations. The big house on the hill surrounded by mud huts has lost its awesome charm.

Our Western world and our presumed supremacy are now on trial. Our boasting and our big talk leave Asia cold. Men and women in Russia and China and in the Middle East are conscious now of their own potential strength. They are coming to know that many of the decisions about the future of the world lie in their hands. And they intend that these decisions shall leave the peoples of each nation free from foreign domination, free for economic, social, and spiritual growth.

Economic freedom is as important as political freedom. Not only must people have access to what other peoples produce, but their own products must in turn have some chance of reaching men all over the world. There will be no peace, there will be no real development, there will be no economic stability, unless we find the method by which we can begin to break down the unnecessary trade barriers hampering the flow of goods. Obviously, the sudden and uncompromising abolition of tariffs after the war could only result in disaster. But obviously, also, one of the freedoms we are fighting for is freedom to trade.

I know there are many men, particularly in America, where our standard of living exceeds the standard of living in the rest of the world, who are genuinely alarmed at such a prospect, who believe that any such process will only lessen our own standard of living. The reverse of this is true.

Many reasons may be assigned for the amazing economic development of the United States. The abundance of our national resources, the freedom of our political institutions, and the character of our population have all undoubtedly contributed. But in my judgment the greatest factor has been the fact that by the happenstance of good fortune there was created here in America the largest area in the world in which there were no barriers to the exchange of goods and ideas.

And I should like to point out to those who are fearful one inescapable fact. In view of the astronomical figures our national debt will assume by the end of this war, and in a world reduced in size by industrial and transportation developments, even our present standard of living in America cannot be maintained unless the exchange of goods flows more freely over the whole world. It is also inescapably true that to raise the standard of living of any man anywhere in the world is to raise the standard of living by some slight degree of every man everywhere in the world.

Finally, when I say that this world demands the full participation of a self-confident America, I am only passing on an invitation which the peoples of the East have given us. They would like the United States and the other United Nations to be partners with them in this grand adventure. They want us to join them in creating a new society of independent nations, free alike of the economic injustices of the West and the political malpractices of the East. But as partners in that great new combination they want us neither hesitant, incompetent, nor afraid. They want partners who will not hesitate to speak out for the correction of injustice anywhere in the world.

Our allies in the East know that we intend to pour out our resources in this war. But they expect us now—not after the war—to use the enormous power of our giving to promote liberty and justice. Other peoples, not yet fighting, are waiting no less eagerly for us to accept the most challenging opportunity of all history—the chance to help create a new society in which men and women the world around can live and grow invigorated by independence and freedom.

ERNIE PYLE
The Night They Brought
Captain Waskow Down

The war itself, apart from ideals and political necessities, was, like all wars, ugly. Ernie Pyle (1900–1945) wrote about the war from the enlisted man's point of view, toughly, honestly, and even sentimentally. He, like so many of the soldiers he wrote about, died in action, killed by Japanese machine gun fire. In his book, Brave Men, *he tells of the death of Captain Henry T. Waskow and the impact of his death upon his men. It is not the account of men fighting and dying for anything, but in its understanding and sympathy with the common soldier in the everyday circumstances, it is very much a part of the mood of the 1930's and 1940's with the emphasis on the common man as doer and hero.*

The impact of the war on civilian Americans serving as soldiers in the fighting forces became the subject of numerous novels and poems, including work by Karl Shapiro, Norman Mailer, Irwin Shaw, Randall Jarrell, Peter Viereck, James Dickey, Howard Nemerov, Joseph Heller, and many others.

In this war I have known a lot of officers who were loved and respected by the soldiers under them. But never have I crossed the trail of any man as beloved as Captain Henry T. Waskow, of Belton, Texas.

Captain Waskow was a company commander in the Thirty-sixth Division. He had led his company since long before it left the States. He was very young, only in his middle twenties, but he carried in him a sincerity and a gentleness that made people want to be guided by him.

"After my father, he came next," a sergeant told me.

"He always looked after us," a soldier said. "He'd go to bat for us every time."

"I've never known him to do anything unfair," another said.

I was at the foot of the mule trail the night they brought Captain Waskow down. The moon was nearly full, and you could see far up the trail, and even partway across the valley below.

Dead men had been coming down the mountain all evening, lashed onto the backs of mules. They came lying belly-down across the wooden pack-saddles, their heads hanging down on one side, their stiffened legs sticking out awkwardly from the other, bobbing up and down as the mules walked.

The Italian mule skinners were afraid to walk beside dead men, so Ameri-

FROM *Brave Men,* by Ernie Pyle (New York: Henry Holt and Company, 1944), pp. 106–07. Copyright 1943, 1944 by Scripps Howard Newspaper Alliance and Holt, Rinehart and Winston, Inc. Reprinted by permission of Holt, Rinehart and Winston, Inc.

cans had to lead the mules down that night. Even the Americans were reluctant to unlash and lift off the bodies when they got to the bottom, so an officer had to do it himself and ask others to help.

I don't know who that first one was. You feel small in the presence of dead men, and you don't ask silly questions.

They slid him down from the mule, and stood him on his feet for a moment. In the half-light he might have been merely a sick man standing there leaning on the others. Then they laid him on the ground in the shadow of the stone wall alongside the road. We left him there beside the road that first one, and we all went back into the cowshed and sat on water cans or lay on the straw, waiting for the next batch of mules.

Somebody said the dead soldier had been dead for four days, and then nobody said anything more about it. We talked soldier talk for an hour or more; the dead man lay all alone, outside in the shadow of the wall.

Then a soldier came into the cowshed and said there were some more bodies outside. We went out into the road. Four mules stood there in the moonlight, in the road where the trail came down off the mountain. The soldiers who led them stood there waiting.

"This one is Captain Waskow," one of them said quietly.

Two men unlashed his body from the mule and lifted it off and laid it in the shadow beside the stone wall. Other men took the other bodies off. Finally, there were five lying end to end in a long row. You don't cover up dead men in the combat zones. They just lie there in the shadows until somebody comes after them.

The unburdened mules moved off to their olive grove. The men in the road seemed reluctant to leave. They stood around, and gradually I could sense them moving, one by one, close to Captain Waskow's body. Not so much to look, I think, as to say something in finality to him and to themselves. I stood close by and I could hear.

One soldier came and looked down, and he said out loud, "God damn it!" That's all he said, and then he walked away.

Another one came, and he said, "God damn it to hell anyway!" He looked down for a few last moments and then turned and left.

Another man came. I think he was an officer. It was hard to tell officers from men in the dim light, for everybody was bearded and grimy. The man looked down into the dead captain's face and then spoke directly to him, as though he were alive, "I'm sorry, old man."

Then a soldier came and stood beside the officer and bent over, and he too spoke to his dead captain, not in a whisper but awfully tenderly, and he said, "I sure am sorry, sir."

Then the first man squatted down, and he reached down and took the captain's hand, and he sat there for a full five minutes holding the dead hand in his own and looking intently into the dead face. And he never uttered a sound all the time he sat there.

Finally he put the hand down. He reached over and gently straightened the points of the captain's shirt collar, and then he sort of rearranged the tattered edges of the uniform around the wound, and then he got up and walked away down the road in the moonlight, all alone.

The rest of us went back into the cowshed, leaving the five dead men lying in a line end to end in the shadow of the low stone wall. We lay down on the straw in the cowshed, and pretty soon we were all asleep.

HARRY S TRUMAN
A Harnessing of the Basic Power of the Universe

On August 2, 1939, Albert Einstein wrote President Roosevelt a letter that marked the beginning of the atomic age as a political and moral fact as well as a scientific one. "Some recent work by E. Fermi and L. Szilard, which has been communicated to me in manuscript," he wrote, "leads me to expect that the element uranium may be turned into a new and important source of energy in the immediate future. Certain aspects of the situation which has arisen seem to call for watchfulness and, if necessary, quick action on the part of the Administration." In 1939 Roosevelt set up an advisory committee on uranium, and by May, 1943 the research phase of the project was ended. The first atomic bomb was exploded in the desert of New Mexico on July 16, 1945.

President Truman (1884–   ), faced with intelligence reports that an invasion of Japan would cost a staggering number of American casualties and a nearly genocidal number of Japanese deaths, decided to use the atomic bomb on Japan. The Japanese were warned but refused to heed the warnings, and on August 6, 1945 an atomic bomb was dropped on the city of Hiroshima. Another one followed on the city of Nagasaki on August 9. By August 15, the Japanese accepted the surrender terms offered by the allied governments. President Truman's act opened a new era of world politics and strategies that has marked all American thinking and writing since that time. It was a moral and necessary decision which he has never regretted, but it did move the world into a new condition in which international cooperation became no longer a dream to be desired, but a necessity for the future of civilization and perhaps even humanity itself. The following is President Truman's message to the American people which revealed to them both the existence and use of the new weapon and also a real awareness of the tremendous responsibility involved. It was a moment requiring greatness to which Truman responded solemnly and well.

Sixteen hours ago an American airplane dropped one bomb on Hiroshima, an important Japanese Army base. That bomb had more power than 20,000 tons

FROM *The New York Times* (August 7, 1945), p. 4.

of TNT. It had more than two thousand times the blast power of the British "Grand Slam" which is the largest bomb ever yet used in the history of warfare.

The Japanese began the war from the air at Pearl Harbor. They have been repaid manyfold. And the end is not yet. With this bomb we have now added a new and revolutionary increase in destruction to supplement the growing power of our armed forces. In their present form these bombs are now in production and even more powerful forms are in development.

It is an atomic bomb. It is a harnessing of the basic power of the universe. The force from which the sun draws its powers has been loosed against those who brought war to the Far East.

Before 1939, it was the accepted belief of scientists that it was theoretically possible to release atomic energy. But no one knew any practical method of doing it. By 1942, however, we knew that the Germans were working feverishly to find a way to add atomic energy to the other engines of war with which they hoped to enslave the world. But they failed. We may be grateful to Providence that the Germans got the V-1's and the V-2's late and in limited quantities and even more grateful that they did not get the atomic bomb at all.

The battle of the laboratories held fateful risks for us as well as the battles of the air, land and sea, and we have now won the battle of the laboratories as we have won the other battles.

Beginning in 1940, before Pearl Harbor, scientific knowledge useful in war was pooled between the United States and Great Britain, and many priceless helps to our victories have come from that arrangement. Under that general policy the research on the atomic bomb was begun. With American and British scientists working together, we entered the race of discovery against the Germans.

The United States had available a large number of scientists of distinction in the many needed areas of knowledge. It had the tremendous industrial and financial resources necessary for the project and they could be devoted to it without undue impairment of other vital war work. In the United States the laboratory work and the production plants, on which a substantial start had already been made, would be out of reach of enemy bombing, while at the time Britain was exposed to constant air attack and was still threatened with the possibility of invasion.

For these reasons Prime Minister Churchill and President Roosevelt agreed that it was wise to carry on the project here. We now have two great plants and many lesser works devoted to the production of atomic power. Employment during peak construction numbered 125,000, and over 65,000 individuals are even now engaged in operating the plants. Many have worked there for two and a half years. Few know what they have been producing. They see great quantities of material going in and they see nothing coming out of these plants, for the physical size of the explosive charge is exceedingly small. We have spent two billion dollars on the greatest scientific gamble in history—and won.

But the greatest marvel is not the size of the enterprise, its secrecy, or its cost, but the achievement of scientific brains in putting together infinitely complex pieces of knowledge held by many men in different fields of science into a workable plan. And hardly less marvelous has been the capacity of industry to design, and of labor to operate, the machines and methods to do things never done before so that the brain child of many minds came forth in physical shape and performed as it was supposed to do.

Both science and industry worked under the direction of the United States Army, which achieved a unique success in managing so diverse a problem in the advancement of knowledge in an amazingly short time. It is doubtful if such another combination could be got together in the world. What has been done is the greatest achievement of organized science in history. It was done under high pressure and without failure.

We are now prepared to obliterate more rapidly and completely every productive enterprise the Japanese have above ground in any city. We shall destroy their docks, their factories and their communications. Let there be no mistake; we shall completely destroy Japan's power to make war.

It was to spare the Japanese people from utter destruction that the ultimatum of July 26 was issued at Potsdam. Their leaders promptly rejected that ultimatum. If they do not now accept our terms they may expect a rain of ruin from the air, the like of which has never been seen on this earth. Behind this air attack will follow sea and land forces in such numbers and power as they have not yet seen and with the fighting skill of which they are already well aware. . . .

The fact that we can release atomic energy ushers in a new era in man's understanding of nature's forces. Atomic energy may, in the future, supplement the power that now comes from coal, oil, and falling water, but at present it cannot be produced on a basis to compete with them commercially. Before that comes there must be a long period of intensive research.

It has never been the habit of the scientists of this country or the policy of this Government to withhold from the world scientific knowledge. Normally, therefore, everything about the work with atomic energy would be made public.

But under present circumstances it is not intended to divulge the terminal processes of production or all the military applications, pending further examination of possible methods of protecting us and the rest of the world from the danger of sudden destruction.

I shall recommend that the Congress of the United States consider promptly the establishment of an appropriate commission to control the production and use of atomic power within the United States. I shall give further consideration and make further recommendations to the Congress as to how atomic power can become a powerful and forceful influence toward the maintenance of world peace.

17

OLD PROBLEMS
AND NEW

Γhe electronic age, the atomic age, call it what you will, the period following World War II has been one of speed, change, and complexity. The world is much smaller because of technological advance, but it has more people and more nations in it. Divided by a cold war which is itself enormous, complex and mutable, the modern world escapes definition and even very good description.

In America, the 1950's were a decade of tension and fear despite the quiet presidential air of Dwight Eisenhower. Senator Joe McCarthy was at the center of a period of almost hysterical fear of the "Communist menace from within" at the same time that Eisenhower was easily elected on a platform of "Peace, Progress and Prosperity." The Korean conflict initiated Americans to a new era of limited wars with obscure and long-range objectives, perhaps necessary in a way that most of America's wars had not been, but not the kind of wars to inspire intense patriotic fervor and sacrifice. The literature of the 1950's was also tortured and darkly "existential," attempting to capture a sense of the absurdity of life in a world grown too complex to understand, much less cope with effectively. Even the social revolution, despite the Supreme Court's major decision ending school segregation, seemed to reach a sluggish and confused end. Liberals and conservatives alike were dissatisfied and demanding action to escape the malaise which they, of course, attributed to widely different causes.

The election of John F. Kennedy to the presidency in 1960 was emblematic of a change, of a new vigor rising out of a younger generation with new goals and ideals. His death, if anything, gave the social revolution a new impetus founded in guilt and a shock which led to understanding. President Johnson's administration revived the social revolution at a rapid pace. Literature in the 1960's also took on a new vigor and a new imaginative and inventive quality. Neither social realism nor the existential realism of the 1950's seemed to suffice; the younger writers began to turn back to Poe's example but with a new and wildly comic quality. Activity, motion, free experience, these became again the watchwords of the American consciousness.

And it has not proven easy. War, violence, injustice, and impatience have marred Johnson's administration, its high aims and its real achievements. The world is too large for easy solutions or quick ones, but the direction, for all the faltering and all the discontent, seems to be set. Einstein defined the very nature of the world as motion and change, and modern American society reflects that new understanding of the way things are. Because of our frontier beginnings and the idealistic sources of so much of our thinking, we can perhaps live more naturally in this new world than many older nations and cultures. In any case, the motion may be confused, but it does appear to be a forward movement; the "party of hope" does appear to be at the source of the motion. No revolution is easy, and action is always hard to follow if it is complex. Nevertheless, the experience of America is continuing, still vital, still progressive in the best sense, still striving for the free society in which the individual can find and make his own truth even in the complex community of his fellow Americans.

These selections in this last section suggest some of the texture of these times. The rest is for you to find around you.

CHARTER OF THE UNITED NATIONS
To Unite Our Strength to Maintain International Peace

The name "United Nations" was coined by President Roosevelt in 1941 to describe the countries fighting against the Axis nations. More than a century before, however, the poet Byron had used it as a name for the Allies at the Battle of Waterloo: "Here, where the sword united nations drew, Our country-

FROM *The United Nations Conference on International Organization: Selected Documents* (Washington, D.C.: U.S. Govt. P.O., 1946), pp. 943–44.

men were warring on that day!" (Childe Harold's Pilgrimage) *In 1942 the term was first officially used, when twenty-six nations signed a Declaration by the United Nations to fight together and not to make separate peace. During the war, the idea of a new international peace-keeping organization to replace the defunct League of Nations developed, and in 1945 the founding conference was held in San Francisco from April to June. The Preamble and first chapter, "Purposes and Principles," of the Charter of the United Nations written at that conference express the hopes and purposes of the organization. In the new atomic age, the need for such a forum of international discussion and mutual action became imperative. Whether it will ultimately prove successful is yet to be proven, but the principles of the Charter, subscribed to by practically every nation in the world, do perhaps explain one reason why the Cold War has not yet exploded into a real global war.*

WE THE PEOPLE OF THE UNITED NATIONS
DETERMINED

to save succeeding generations from the scourge of war, which twice in our lifetime has brought untold sorrow to mankind, and

to reaffirm faith in fundamental human rights, in the dignity and worth of the human person, in the equal rights of men and women and of nations large and small, and

to establish conditions under which justice and respect for the obligations arising from treaties and other sources of international law can be maintained, and

to promote social progress and better standards of life in larger freedom,

AND FOR THESE ENDS

to practice tolerance and live together in peace with one another as good neighbors, and

to unite our strength to maintain international peace and security, and

to ensure, by the acceptance of principles and the institution of methods, that armed force shall not be used, save in the common interest, and

to employ international machinery for the promotion of the economic and social advancement of all peoples,

HAVE RESOLVED TO COMBINE OUR EFFORTS
TO ACCOMPLISH THESE AIMS

Accordingly, our respective Governments, through representatives assembled in the city of San Francisco, who have exhibited their full powers found to be in good and due form, have agreed to the present Charter of the United

Nations and do hereby establish an international organization to be known as the United Nations.

CHAPTER I

Purposes and Principles

Article 1

The Purposes of the United Nations are:

1. To maintain international peace and security, and to that end: to take effective collective measures for the prevention and removal of threats to the peace, and for the suppression of acts of aggression or other breaches of the peace, and to bring about by peaceful means, and in conformity with the principles of justice and international law, adjustment or settlement of international disputes or situations which might lead to a breach of the peace;

2. To develop friendly relations among nations based on respect for the principle of equal rights and self-determination of peoples, and to take other appropriate measures to strengthen universal peace;

3. To achieve international cooperation in solving international problems of an economic, social, cultural, or humanitarian character, and in promoting and encouraging respect for human rights and for fundamental freedoms for all without distinction as to race, sex, language, or religion; and

4. To be a center for harmonizing the actions of nations in the attainment of these common ends.

Article 2

The Organization and its Members, in pursuit of the Purposes stated in Article 1, shall act in accordance with the following Principles.

1. The Organization is based on the principle of the sovereign equality of all its Members.

2. All Members, in order to ensure to all of them the rights and benefits resulting from membership, shall fulfil in good faith the obligations assumed by them in accordance with the present Charter.

3. All Members shall settle their international disputes by peaceful means in such a manner that international peace and security, and justice, are not endangered.

4. All Members shall refrain in their international relations from the threat or use of force against the territorial integrity or political independence of any state, or in any other manner inconsistent with the Purposes of the United Nations.

5. All Members shall give the United Nations every assistance in any action it takes in accordance with the present Charter, and shall refrain from giving assistance to any state against which the United Nations is taking preventive or enforcement action.

6. The Organization shall ensure that states which are not Members of the United Nations act in accordance with these Principles so far as may be necessary for the maintenance of international peace and security.

7. Nothing contained in the present Charter shall authorize the United Nations to intervene in matters which are essentially within the domestic jurisdiction of any state or shall require the Members to submit such matters to settlement under the present Charter; but this principle shall not prejudice the application of enforcement measures under Chapter VII.

GUNNAR MYRDAL
What Really Matters to Him Is
His Treatment at Home

World War II not only ended the moves for world domination of Germany and Japan, but it also changed the social structure of the world. It marked the beginning of the end of the British Empire and the other lesser colonial powers, and it brought the desire for national independence to the nations of Africa and Asia. In the United Nations and the other circles of diplomacy, former master and slave would now sit on a level as representatives of sovereign states. In America, the race problem and the question of civil rights became the most important social issue in a nation successfully out of the Depression and clearly the richest and most powerful in the world. For the Carnegie Corporation, Gunnar Myrdal (1898–), the Swedish economist and sociologist, headed a study of the American Negro, and his An American Dilemma *was a thorough and brilliant examination of the Negro's situation in America. In the concluding chapter, he discusses the impact of the war and of the new America which* "can never more regard its Negroes as a patient, submissive minority." *He examines the question in the larger context of world affairs, and he sees the Negro problem as* "not only America's greatest failure but also America's incomparably great opportunity for the future." *Subsequently a host of Negro and white novelists and poets have come along to document Myrdal's analysis in works of imaginative literature.*

. . . In the South three generations ago white people had for their defense a consistent and respectable theory, endorsed by the church and by all sciences, printed in learned books and periodicals, and expounded by the South's great

FROM *An American Dilemma,* by Gunnar Myrdal, with the assistance of Richard Sterner and Arnold Rose (New York: Harper & Brothers, 1944), Vol. 2, pp. 1002–08, 1021–22. Copyright 1944, 1962 by Harper & Row Publishers, Incorporated. Reprinted by permission of Harper & Row, Publishers, Incorporated.

statesmen in the Capitol at Washington. The Negro's subordinate status was a principle integrated into a whole philosophy of society and of human life. The Negro was a completely different species of mankind: undeveloped, "child like," amoral, and much less endowed with intellectual capacities than the white man; he was meant by the Creator to be a servant forever; if kept in his "place" he was useful or at least tolerable, and there he was also happy; "social equality" was unthinkable as it implied intermarriage which would destroy the white race and Anglo-Saxon civilization. Much of this theory—which acquired an elaborate structure to satisfy the specific needs to justify discrimination in various spheres of life—remained through Reconstruction, and it was again hailed in the Restoration of white supremacy. Indeed, much of it remained until a couple of decades ago. But now it is almost destroyed for upper class and educated people. Its maintenance among lower class and uneducated people meets increasing difficulties. *The gradual destruction of the popular theory behind race prejudice is the most important of all social trends in the field of interracial relations.*

It is significant that today even the white man who defends discrimination frequently describes his motive as "prejudice" and says that it is "irrational." The popular beliefs rationalizing caste in America are no longer intellectually respectable. They can no longer, therefore, be found in current books, newspapers or public speeches. They live a surreptitious life in thoughts and private remarks. There we have had to hunt them when studying the matter in this inquiry. When they were thus drawn out into the open they looked shabby and ashamed of themselves. Everybody who has acquired a higher education knows that they are wrong. Most white people with a little education also have a hunch that they are wrong. There is today a queer feeling of *credo quia absurdum* hovering over the whole complex of popular beliefs sustaining racial discrimination. This makes the prejudiced white man nearly as pathetic as his Negro victim.

The white man is thus in the process of losing confidence in the theory which gave reason and meaning to his way of life. And since he has not changed his life much, he is in a dilemma. This change is probably irreversible and cumulative. It is backed by the American Creed. The trend of psychology, education, anthropology, and social science is toward environmentalism in the explanation of group differences, which means that the racial beliefs which defended caste are being torn away. It also means, by implication, that the white majority group in power is accused of being the cause of the Negro's deficiencies and unhappiness. Authority and respectability are no longer supporting the popular beliefs. The beliefs are no longer nourished from above. Instead they are increasingly fought. There is a considerable time-lag between what is thought in the higher and in the lower social classes. But as time passes the lower social strata also will change their beliefs. These ideas are spread by the advance of education.

All of this is important. People want to be rational, and they want to feel that they are good and righteous. They want to have the society they live in, and their behavior in this society, explained and justified to their conscience. And now their theory is being torn to pieces; its expression is becoming recognized as a mark of ignorance.

On the other side of the caste gulf the development leads to increased bitterness. To the Negro the white man's trouble with his conscience cannot but seem to be insincerity or something worse. The Negro protest is rising, spurred by the improvement in education. The Negro group is being permeated by the democratic and equalitarian values of the American culture. Since at the same time there has been increasing separation between the two groups, Negroes are beginning to form a self-conscious "nation within the nation," defining ever more clearly their fundamental grievances against white America.

America can never more regard its Negroes as a patient, submissive minority. Negroes will continually become less well "accommodated." They will organize for defense and offense. They will be more and more vociferous. They will watch their opportunities ever more keenly. They will have a powerful tool in the caste struggle against white America: the glorious American ideals of democracy, liberty, and equality to which America is pledged not only by its political Constitution but also by the sincere devotion of its citizens. The Negroes are a minority, and they are poor and suppressed, but they have the advantage that they can fight wholeheartedly. The whites have all the power, but they are split in their moral personality. Their better selves are with the insurgents. The Negroes do not need any other allies.

This moral process had proceeded far when the Second World War broke out.

This War is an ideological war fought in defense of democracy. The totalitarian dictatorships in the enemy countries had even made the ideological issue much sharper in this War than it was in the First World War. Moreover, in this War the principle of democracy had to be applied more explicitly to race. Fascism and nazism are based on a racial superiority dogma—not unlike the old hackneyed American caste theory—and they came to power by means of racial persecution and oppression. In fighting fascism and nazism, America had to stand before the whole world in favor of racial tolerance and cooperation and of racial equality. It had to denounce German racialism as a reversion to barbarism. It had to proclaim universal brotherhood and the inalienable human freedoms. The fact that the Japanese utilize anti-white feelings in Asia and elsewhere made it even more necessary to stress the racial equality principle.

In the internal political struggle before America became involved in the War, the isolationalists had worked up the idea that there was much to improve at home without trying to improve the rest of the world. They did not disdain even to point to the injustices inflicted upon the Negro; many isolationists to the left put the Negro cause to the forefront. A Georgia senator who had made a lengthy talk about the danger to democracy abroad was challenged by an isolationist co-senator with the question whether the fight for democracy should not begin in Georgia. The plight of the Negro sharecropper and the presence of peonage and lynching were brought up to stress the unsolved tasks at home and to win Negro sympathies for the isolationist cause. One permanent result of this pre-war discussion was that, in this War, the promises to establish the full democratic liberties, not only abroad but also in America, played an even more prominent role than in the First World War. . . .

In the twenty years between the two World Wars the general level of education of the American Negroes had become considerably higher, and so had their capacity for democracy. The Negro press had become better equipped, and it reached farther. The Negro organizations had grown in strength. The national Negro leaders had become firmer, and they were more resentful. This time they were not willing cheerfully to postpone their complaints until the War was over. The elderly Du Bois renounced with bitterness the credulous advice he once gave his people in the First World War to "close ranks." In this new War the Negro leaders advertised freely—and sometimes provocatively—the danger of a low morale among Negroes.

In this War there was a "colored" nation on the other side—Japan. And that nation started out by beating the white Anglo-Saxons on their own ground. The smoldering revolt in India against British rule had significance for the American Negroes, and so had other "color" incidents in the world conflict: the wavering sympathies of several native populations in the Dutch and British possessions in the Pacific, the mistrust against Great Britain among the Arab peoples, the first abandonment of Ethiopia, and the ambiguity of the plans for the colonial chessboard of Africa. Even unsophisticated Negroes began to see vaguely a color scheme in world events, although their thoughts are usually not yet organized in a definite pattern. . . .

The loyalty of the American Negro in war and peace is, however, proverbial. The only thing Negroes ask for is to be accepted as Americans. The American Constitution is even dearer to them than to their white compatriots. They are more unreservedly anti-fascist. Few American Negroes want the Axis powers to win the War. But this is not much of an issue to Negroes, as they, about as much as white Americans, are convinced of the invincibility of their country. Negroes have never doubted the strength and resourcefulness of the whites. Even more, they know that America offers more possibility of democracy, even for themselves, than do the Axis nations. . . .

But it is quite common that Negroes feel a satisfaction in the temporary adversities and want the War to become as serious a matter as possible to the white people in power. There have been reports that poor Negro sharecroppers in the South sometimes indulge in dreams of a Japanese army marching through the South and killing off a number of "crackers." They do not want them to land in the North, though, and they certainly do not want them to stay. But much more common is a glowing ill-concealed satisfaction over the war adversities on various fronts. Practically every issue of any Negro newspaper gives proof of this attitude. It must be conceded that Negroes have also some good rational reasons for this feeling. . . .

A white commentator complained some months ago that the Negro press is something of a fifth column. He received the unanimous and angry answer in all Negro papers that this is exactly contrary to the truth. Negroes are standing only for the democratic principles, to defend which America is waging war. They are dissatisfied because these principles are ignored in America itself. They are just the opposite of war dodgers and traitors: they pray to have the right to fight and die for their country and to work in the war industries, but they are excluded. They can, with new reason, point to the inconsistency between American ideals and practices, as does one of their wisest editors, Elmer A. Carter: ". . . this strange and curious picture, this spectacle of America at war to preserve the ideal of government by free men, yet clinging to the social vestiges of the slave system." This ideological attack is so clear-cut and simple and so obviously to the point that it appeals even to the least educated Negro. The cause of the American Negro has supreme logical strength. And the Negro is better prepared than ever before in his history to fight for it. . . .

But these consequences of the present course of America's and the world's history should not be recorded only in terms of compelling forces. The bright side is that the conquering of color caste in America is America's own innermost desire. This nation early laid down as the moral basis for its existence the principles of equality and liberty. However much Americans have dodged this conviction, they have refused to adjust their laws to their own license. Today, more than ever, they refuse to discuss systematizing their caste order to mutual advantage, apparently because they most seriously mean that caste is wrong and should not be given recognition. They stand warmheartedly against oppression in all the world. When they are reluctantly forced into war, they are compelled to justify their participation to their own conscience by insisting that they are fighting against aggression and for liberty and equality.

America feels itself to be humanity in miniature. When in this crucial time the international leadershp passes to America, the great reason for hope is that this country has a national experience of uniting racial and cultural diversities and a national theory, if not a consistent practice, of freedom and equality for all. What America is constantly reaching for is democracy at home and abroad. The main trend in its history is the gradual realization of the American Creed.

In this sense the Negro problem is not only America's greatest failure but also America's incomparably great opportunity for the future. If America should follow its own deepest convictions, its well-being at home would be increased directly. At the same time America's prestige and power abroad would rise immensely. The century-old dream of American patriots, that America should give to the entire world its own freedoms and its own faith, would come true. America can demonstrate that justice, equality and cooperation are possible between white and colored people.

In the present phase of history this is what the world needs to believe. Mankind is sick of fear and disbelief, of pessimism and cynicism. It needs the youthful moralistic optimism of America. But empty declarations only deepen cynicism. Deeds are called for. If America in actual practice could show the world a progressive trend by which the Negro became finally integrated into modern democracy, all mankind would be given faith again—it would have reason to believe that peace, progress and order are feasible. And America would have a spiritual power many times stronger than all her financial and military resources—the power of the trust and support of all good people on earth. *America is free to choose whether the Negro shall remain her liability or become her opportunity.*

WILLIAM FAULKNER
To Help Man Endure by Lifting His Heart

When Nathaniel Hawthorne spoke of the unpardonable sin of a writer as allowing himself to "swerve aside from the truth of the human heart," he was stating a central moral and aesthetic belief of the major American literary and philosophical tradition. By the use of impulse and imagination, the important American writers of the nineteenth century sought an essential truth which lay not in the world of physical fact but in the human spirit, mind and heart. Although he wrote, at least in surfaces, in a "realistic" manner, William Faulkner (1897–1962) was clearly of that central American literary tradition, as is his Nobel Prize address, delivered in 1950 in the early years of the Cold War when, as he put it, modern men were all suffering from "a general and universal physical fear," the fear of personal death and the death of mankind itself in atomic war. In this brief speech, Faulkner restates Hawthorne's belief that the writer's subject is the human heart and that his faith in the human spirit and his artistic affirmation of that spirit will, indeed, help man "endure and prevail."

I feel that this award was not made to me as a man, but to my work—a life's work in the agony and sweat of the human spirit, not for glory and least of all for profit, but to create out of the materials of the human spirit something which did not exist before. So this award is only mine in trust. It will not be difficult to find a dedication for the money part of it commensurate with the purpose and significance of its origin. But I would like to do the same with the acclaim too, by using this moment as a pinnacle from which I might be

FROM "Address upon Receiving the Nobel Prize for Literature," by William Faulkner. Reprinted from *The Faulkner Reader*, Copyright 1954 by William Faulkner (Random House, Inc.).

listened to by the young men and women already dedicated to the same anguish and travail, among whom is already that one who will some day stand here where I am standing.

Our tragedy today is a general and universal physical fear so long sustained by now that we can even bear it. There are no longer problems of the spirit. There is only the question: When will I be blown up? Because of this the young man or woman writing today has forgotten the problems of the human heart in conflict with itself which alone can make good writing because only that is worth writing about, worth the agony and the sweat.

He must learn them again. He must teach himself that the basest of all things is to be afraid; and, teaching himself that, forget it forever, leaving no room in his workshop for anything but the old verities and truths of the heart, the old universal truths lacking which any story is ephemeral and doomed—love and honor and pity and pride and compassion and sacrifice. Until he does so, he labors under a curse. He writes not of love but of lust, of defeats in which nobody loses anything of value, of victories without hope and, worst of all, without pity or compassion. His griefs grieve on no universal bones, leaving no scars. He writes not of the heart but of the glands.

Until he relearns these things, he will write as though he stood among and watched the end of man. I decline to accept the end of man. It is easy enough to say that man is immortal simply because he will endure: that when the last ding-dong of doom has clanged and faded from the last worthless rock hanging tideless in the last red and dying evening, that even then there will still be one more sound: that of his puny inexhaustible voice, still talking. I refuse to accept this. I believe that man will not merely endure: he will prevail. He is immortal, not because he alone among creatures has an inexhaustible voice, but because he has a soul, a spirit capable of compassion and sacrifice and endurance. The poet's, the writer's, duty is to write about these things. It is his privilege to help man endure by lifting his heart, by reminding him of the courage and honor and hope and pride and compassion and pity and sacrifice which have been the glory of his past. The poet's voice need not merely be the record of man, it can be one of the props, the pillars to help him endure and prevail.

JOSEPH McCARTHY
I Have in My Hand 57 Cases

The tensions of the Cold War which followed immediately upon the conclusion of World War II were difficult for Americans, so new to the world of

FROM *Major Speeches and Debates of Senator Joe McCarthy Delivered in the United States Senate 1950–1951* (Washington, D.C.: U.S. Govt. P.O., 1952), pp. 7–14.

international power politics and the atomic era, to understand. Although the Truman administration, with such innovations as the Truman doctrine, the Marshall Plan, the Point Four Program, the Berlin airlift and the formation of NATO, was handling the Cold War with considerable success and securing Western Europe against Russian control, the fall of the Chiang Kai-shek government to the Communists in China and the general atmosphere of fear and tension caused a wave of hysteria and despair to be the dominant tone of the 1950's, even during the relatively placid years of Eisenhower's presidency. Senator Joseph R. McCarthy (1908–1957) became the grand inquisitor of a new Red hunt, and "McCarthyism," as a method of purging the government of "subversives," gained an international repute. McCarthy burst upon the scene with this speech, which he delivered in Wheeling, West Virginia, in February, 1950. In it, he claimed to have proof of fifty-seven members of the State Department "who would appear to be either card carrying members or certainly loyal to the Communist party." This number later rose and diminished, but the list was never made public. Although his power was later to be broken by a Senate "condemnation" in 1954, he was the dominant force, at least negatively, in American politics for the first half of the decade, and his assault on "Communists" subverting America from within kept the nation's attention away from the complex problems of maintaining an international balance of power and from the growing internal problems arising from racial injustice and a hard core of poverty beneath the surfaces of affluence.

Five years after a world war has been won, men's hearts should anticipate a long peace, and men's minds should be free from the heavy weight that comes with war. But this is not such a period—for this is not a period of peace. This is a time of the "cold war." This is a time when all the world is split into two vast, increasingly hostile armed camps—a time of a great armaments race.

Today we can almost physically hear the mutterings and rumblings of an invigorated god of war. You can see it, feel it, and hear it all the way from the hills of Indochina, from the shores of Formosa, right over into the very heart of Europe itself.

The one encouraging thing is that the "mad moment" has not yet arrived for the firing of the gun or the exploding of the bomb which will set civilization about the final task of destroying itself. There is still a hope for peace if we finally decide that no longer can we safely blind our eyes and close our ears to those facts which are shaping up more and more clearly. And that is that we are now engaged in a show-down fight—not the usual war between nations for land areas or other material gains, but a war between two diametrically opposed ideologies.

The great difference between our western Christian world and the atheistic Communist world is not political, ladies and gentlemen, it is moral. There are other differences, of course, but those could be reconciled. For instance, the Marxian idea of confiscating the land and the factories and running the entire economy as a single enterprise is momentous. Likewise, Lenin's invention of the one-party police state as a way to make Marx's idea work is hardly less momentous.

Stalin's resolute putting across of these two ideas, of course, did much to divide the world. With only those differences, however, the East and the West could most certainly still live in peace.

The real, basic difference, however, lies in the religion of immoralism—invented by Marx, preached feverishly by Lenin, and carried to unimaginable extremes by Stalin. This religion of immoralism, if the Red half of the world wins—and well it may—this religion of immoralism will more deeply wound and damage mankind than any conceivable economic or political system.

Karl Marx dismissed God as a hoax, and Lenin and Stalin have added in clear-cut, unmistakable language their resolve that no nation, no people who believe in a God, can exist side by side with their communistic state.

Karl Marx, for example, expelled people from his Communist Party for mentioning such things as justice, humanity, or morality. He called this soulful ravings and sloppy sentimentality.

While Lincoln was a relatively young man in his late thirties, Karl Marx boasted that the Communist specter was haunting Europe. Since that time, hundreds of millions of people and vast areas of the world have fallen under Communist domination. Today, less than 100 years after Lincoln's death, Stalin brags that this Communist specter is not only haunting the world, but is about to completely subjugate it.

Today we are engaged in a final, all-out battle between communistic atheism and Christianity. The modern champions of communism have selected this as the time. And, ladies and gentlemen, the chips are down—they are truly down. . . .

At war's end we were physically the strongest nation on earth and, at least potentially, the most powerful intellectually and morally. Ours could have been the honor of being a beacon in the desert of destruction, a shining living proof that civilization was not yet ready to destroy itself. Unfortunately, we have failed miserably and tragically to arise to the opportunity.

The reason why we find ourselves in a position of impotency is not because our only powerful potential enemy has sent men to invade our shores, but rather because of the traitorous actions of those who have been treated so well by this Nation. It has not been the less fortunate or members of minority groups who have been selling this Nation out, but rather those who have had all the benefits that the wealthiest nation on earth has had to offer—the finest homes, the finest college education, and the finest jobs in Government we can give.

This is glaringly true in the State Department. There the bright young men who are born with silver spoons in their mouths are the ones who have been worst. . . .

I have in my hand 57 cases of individuals who would appear to be either card carrying members or certainly loyal to the Communist Party, but who nevertheless are still helping to shape our foreign policy.

One thing to remember in discussing the Communists in our Government is that we are not dealing with spies who get 30 pieces of silver to steal the blueprints of a new weapon. We are dealing with a far more sinister type of activity because it permits the enemy to guide and shape our policy. . . .

This brings us down to the case of one Alger Hiss who is important not as an individual any more, but rather because he is so representative of a group in the State Department. It is unnecessary to go over the sordid events showing how he sold out the Nation which had given him so much. Those are rather fresh in all of our minds.

However, it should be remembered that the facts in regard to his connection with this international Communist spy ring were made known to the then Under Secretary of State Berle 3 days after Hitler and Stalin signed the Russo-German alliance pact. At that time one Whittaker Chambers—who was also part of the spy ring—apparently decided that with Russia on Hitler's side, he could no longer betray our Nation to Russia. He gave Under Secretary of State Berle—and this is all a matter of record—practically all, if not more, of the facts upon which Hiss' conviction was based.

Under Secretary Berle promptly contacted Dean Acheson and received word in return that Acheson (and I quote) "could vouch for Hiss absolutely"—at which time the matter was dropped. And this, you understand, was at a time when Russia was an ally of Germany. This condition existed while Russia and Germany were invading and dismembering Poland, and while the Communist groups here were screaming "war monger" at the United States for their support of the allied nations.

Again in 1943, the FBI had occasion to investigate the facts surrounding Hiss' contacts wtih the Russian spy ring. But even after that FBI report was submitted, nothing was done.

Then late in 1948—on August 5—when the Un-American Activities Committee called Alger Hiss to give an accounting, President Truman at once issued a Presidential directive ordering all Government agencies to refuse to turn over any information whatsoever in regard to the Communist activities of any Government employee to a congressional committee.

Incidentally, even after Hiss was convicted—it is interesting to note that the President still labeled the exposé of Hiss as a "red herring."

If time permitted, it might be well to go into detail about the fact that Hiss was Roosevelt's chief adviser at Yalta when Roosevelt was admittedly in ill health and tired physically and mentally, and when, according to the Secretary of State, Hiss and Gromyko drafted the report on the conference. . . .

Of the results of this conference, Arthur Bliss Lane of the State Department had this to say: "As I glanced over the document, I could not believe my eyes. To me, almost every line spoke of a surrender to Stalin."

As you hear this story of high treason, I know that you are saying to yourself, "Well, why doesn't the Congress do something about it?" Actually, ladies and gentlemen, one of the important reasons for the graft, the corruption, the dishonesty, the disloyalty, the treason in high Government positions —one of the most important reasons why this continues is a lack of moral uprising on the part of the 140,000,000 American people. In the light of history, however, this is not hard to explain.

It is the result of an emotional hang-over and a temporary moral lapse which follows every war. It is the apathy to evil which people who have been subjected to the tremendous evils of war feel. As the people of the world see mass murder, the destruction of defenseless and innocent people, and all of the crime and lack of morals which go with war, they become numb and apathetic. It has always been thus after war.

However, the morals of our people have not been destroyed. They still exist. This cloak of numbness and apathy has only needed a spark to rekindle them. Happily, this spark has finally been supplied.

As you know, very recently the Secretary of State proclaimed his loyalty to a man guilty of what has always been considered as the most abominable of all crimes—of being a traitor to the people who gave him a position of great trust. The Secretary of State in attempting to justify his continued devotion to the man who sold out the Christian world to the atheistic world, referred to Christ's Sermon on the Mount as a justification and reason therefor, and the reaction of the American people to this would have made the heart of Abraham Lincoln happy.

When this pompous diplomat in striped pants, with a phony British accent, proclaimed to the American people that Christ on the Mount endorsed communism, high treason, and betrayal of a sacred trust, the blasphemy was so great that it awakened the dormant indignation of the American people.

He has lighted the spark which is resulting in a moral uprising and will end only when the whole sorry mess of twisted, warped thinkers are swept from the national scene so that we may have a new birth of national honesty and decency in Government.

ADLAI E. STEVENSON
Let Us Also Favor Free Enterprise for the Mind

As Senator McCarthy's excessive attack on Communists in government grew ever larger, including an assault on former General, Secretary of State and

FROM *Major Campaign Speeches of Adlai E. Stevenson* (New York: Random House, 1953), pp. 19–22. Copyright 1953 by Random House, Inc. Reprinted by permission of the publisher.

Secretary of Defense George C. Marshall, politicians became afraid to speak out against McCarthy or the anti-Communist hysteria. In the presidential campaign of 1952, the Republican candidate, Dwight D. Eisenhower, avoided the issue entirely, although the Vice-Presidential candidate, Richard Nixon, did refer to the Roosevelt and Truman administrations as "twenty years of treason." Governor Adlai E. Stevenson of Illinois (1900–1965), the Democratic candidate, did speak up, however, in one of the first speeches of his campaign to the American Legion Convention in New York on August 27. He spoke of the "climate of fear" which was the "tragedy of our day," and he warned against men "who use 'patriotism' as a club for attacking other Americans." His speech proved to be politically inexpedient, but he was one of the few American politicians who dared speak out against the fear of internal subversion, and by doing so he won the trust and devotion of a generation of younger Americans. He also restated the American belief in the efficacy of purposive action even in a world of disorder and danger: "I believe that man stands on the eve of his greatest day. I know, too, that that day is not a gift but a prize; that we shall not reach it until we have won it."

We talk a great deal about patriotism. What do we mean by patriotism in the context of our times? I venture to suggest that what we mean is a sense of national responsibility which will enable America to remain master of her power—to walk with it in serenity and wisdom, with self-respect and the respect of all mankind; a patriotism that puts country ahead of self; a patriotism which is not short, frenzied outbursts of emotion, but the tranquil and steady dedication of a lifetime. The dedication of a lifetime—these are words that are easy to utter, but this is a mighty assignment. For it is often easier to fight for principles than to live up to them.

Patriotism, I have said, means putting country before self. This is no abstract phrase, and unhappily, we find some things in American life today of which we cannot we proud.

Consider the groups who seek to identify their special interests with the general welfare. I find it sobering to think that their pressures might one day be focused on me. I have resisted them before and I hope the Almighty will give me the strength to do so again and again. And I should tell you—my fellow Legionnaires—as I would tell all other organized groups, that I intend to resist pressures from veterans, too, if I think their demands are excessive or in conflict with the public interest, which must always be the paramount interest.

Let me suggest, incidentally, that we are rapidly becoming a nation of veterans. If we were all to claim a special reward for our service, beyond that to which specific disability or sacrifice has created a just claim, who would be left to pay the bill? After all, we are Americans first and veterans second, and the best maxim for any administration is still Jefferson's "Equal rights for all, special privileges for none."

True patriotism, it seems to me, is based on tolerance and a large measure of humility.

There are men among us who use "patriotism" as a club for attacking other Americans. What can we say for the self-styled patriot who thinks that a Negro, a Jew, a Catholic, or a Japanese-American is less an American than he? That betrays the deepest article of our faith, the belief in individual liberty and equality which has always been the heart and soul of the American idea.

What can we say for the man who proclaims himself a patriot—and then for political or personal reasons attacks the patriotism of faithful public servants? I give you, as a shocking example, the attacks which have been made on the loyalty and the motives of our great wartime Chief of Staff, General Marshall. To me this is the type of "patriotism" which is, in Dr. Johnson's phrase, "the last refuge of scoundrels."

The anatomy of patriotism is complex. But surely intolerance and public irresponsibility cannot be cloaked in the shining armor of rectitude and righteousness. Nor can the denial of the right to hold ideas that are different—the freedom of man to think as he pleases. To strike freedom of the mind with the fist of patriotism is an old and ugly subtlety.

And the freedom of the mind, my friends, has served America well. The vigor of our political life, our capacity for change, our cultural, scientific and industrial achievements, all derive from free inquiry, from the free mind—from the imagination, resourcefulness and daring of men who are not afraid of new ideas. Most of us favor free enterprise for business. Let us also favor free enterprise for the mind. For, in the last analysis, we would fight to the death to protect it. Why is it, then, that we are sometimes slow to detect, or are indifferent to, the dangers that beset it?

Many of the threats to our cherished freedoms in these anxious, troubled times arise, it seems to me, from a healthy apprehension about the communist menace within our country. Communism is abhorrent. It is strangulation of the individual; it is death for the soul. Americans who have surrendered to this misbegotten idol have surrendered their right to our trust. And there can be no secure place for them in our public life.

Yet, as I have said before, we must take care not to burn down the barn to kill the rats. All of us, and especially patriotic organizations of enormous influence like the American Legion, must be vigilant in protecting our birthright from its too zealous friends while protecting it from its evil enemies.

The tragedy of our day is the climate of fear in which we live, and fear breeds repression. Too often sinister threats to the Bill of Rights, to freedom of the mind, are concealed under the patriotic cloak of anti-communism.

I could add, from my own experience, that it is never necessary to call a man a communist to make political capital. Those of us who have undertaken to practice the ancient but imperfect art of government will always make enough mistakes to keep our critics well supplied with standard ammunition. There is no need for poison gas.

Another feature of our current scene that I think invites a similar restraint is the recurrent attacks in some communities upon our public schools.

There is no justification for indiscriminate attacks on our schools, and the sincere, devoted, and by no means overpaid teachers who labor in them. If there are any communist teachers, of course they should be excluded, but the task is not one for self-appointed thought police or ill-informed censors. As a practical matter, we do not stop communist activity in this way. What we do is give the communists material with which to defame us. And we also stifle the initiative of teachers and depreciate the prestige of the teaching profession which should be as honorable and esteemed as any among us.

Let me now, in my concluding words, inquire with you how we may affirm our patriotism in the troubled yet hopeful years that are ahead.

The central concern of the American Legion—the ideal which holds it together—the vitality which animates it—is patriotism. And those voices which we have heard most clearly and which are best remembered in our public life have always had the accent of patriotism.

It was always accounted a virtue in a man to love his country. With us it is now something more than a virtue. It is a necessity, a condition of survival. When an American says that he loves his country, he means not only that he loves the New England hills, the prairies glistening in the sun, the wide and rising plains, the great mountains, and the sea. He means that he loves an inner air, an inner light in which freedom lives and in which a man can draw the breath of self-respect.

Men who have offered their lives for their country know that patriotism is not the *fear* of something, it is the *love* of something. Patriotism with us is not the hatred of Russia; it is the love of this Republic and of the ideal of liberty of man and mind in which it was born, and to which this Republic is dedicated.

With this patriotism—patriotism in its large and wholesome meaning—America can master its power and turn it to the noble cause of peace. We can maintain military power without militarism; political power without oppression; and moral power without compulsion or complacency.

The road we travel is long, but at the end lies the grail of peace. And in the valley of peace we see the faint outlines of a new world, fertile and strong. It is odd that one of the keys to abundance should have been handed to civilization on a platter of destruction. But the power of the atom to work evil gives only the merest hint of its power for good.

I believe that man stands on the eve of his greatest day. I know, too, that that day is not a gift but a prize; that we shall not reach it until we have won it. . . .

BROWN v. *BOARD OF EDUCATION*
With All Deliberate Speed

In 1954, the Senate condemnation of Senator McCarthy broke the hold the internal anti-Communist crusade had on the American attention, and the Supreme Court decision in the case of Brown *v.* Board of Education *delivered on May 17 gave Americans a new and more valid internal problem to concentrate on. This decision and the opinion delivered by Chief Justice Earl Warren (1891–) was the dramatic beginning of the successful Civil Rights movement of the 1960's, which in turn led to a broader Negro revolution and the revival of the even larger social revolution of the New Deal during the administration of President Johnson. By striking down school segregation, the Supreme Court broke down the first and largest barrier between the present static and essentially unjust system and a newer, more open society in which most of the old barriers would begin to fall. By saying that school desegregation should proceed "with all deliberate speed," the court attempted to bring about the radical changes gradually, which led to the slow legal battles in the South in the latter half of the 1950's but which also prepared a climate for the general acceptance of the strong Civil Rights Law of 1964.*

These cases come to us from the States of Kansas, South Carolina, Virginia, and Delaware. They are premised on different facts and different local conditions, but a common legal question justifies their consideration together in this consolidated opinion.

In each of the cases, minors of the Negro race, through their legal representatives, seek the aid of the courts in obtaining admission to the public schools of their community on a nonsegregated basis. In each instance, they had been denied admission to schools attended by white children under laws requiring or permitting segregation according to race. This segregation was alleged to deprive the plaintiffs of the equal protection of the laws under the Fourteenth Amendment. In each of the cases other than the Delaware case, a three-judge federal district court denied relief to the plaintiffs on the so-called "separate but equal" doctrine announced by this Court in *Plessy* v. *Ferguson,* 163 U. S. 537. Under that doctrine, equality of treatment is accorded when the races are provided substantially equal facilities, even though these facilities be separate. In the Delaware case, the Supreme Court of Delaware adhered to that doctrine, but ordered that the plaintiffs be admitted to the white schools because of their superiority to the Negro schools.

The plaintiffs contend that segregated public schools are not "equal" and

FROM *United States Reports,* Vol. 347 (Washington, D.C.: U.S. Govt. P.O., 1954), pp. 486–96.

cannot be made "equal," and that hence they are deprived of the equal protection of the laws. Because of the obvious importance of the question presented, the Court took jurisdiction. Argument was heard in the 1952 Term, and reargument was heard this Term on certain questions propounded by the Court.

Reargument was largely devoted to the circumstances surrounding the adoption of the Fourteenth Amendment in 1868. It covered exhaustively consideration of the Amendment in Congress, ratification by the states, then existing practices in racial segregation, and the views of proponents and opponents of the Amendment. This discussion and our own investigation convince us that, although these sources cast some light, it is not enough to resolve the problem with which we are faced. At best, they are inconclusive. The most avid proponents of the post-War Amendments undoubtedly intended them to remove all legal distinctions among "all persons born or naturalized in the United States." Their opponents, just as certainly, were antagonistic to both the letter and the spirit of the Amendments and wished them to have the most limited effect. What others in Congress and the state legislatures had in mind cannot be determined with any degree of certainty.

An additional reason for the inconclusive nature of the Amendment's history, with respect to segregated schools, is the status of public education at that time. In the South, the movement toward free common schools, supported by general taxation, had not yet taken hold. Education of white children was largely in the hands of private groups. Education of Negroes was almost nonexistent, and practically all of the race were illiterate. In fact, any education of Negroes was forbidden by law in some states. Today, in contrast, many Negroes have achieved outstanding success in the arts and sciences as well as in the business and professional world. It is true that public school education at the time of the Amendment had advanced further in the North, but the effect of the Amendment on Northern States was generally ignored in the congressional debates. Even in the North, the conditions of public education did not approximate those existing today. The curriculum was usually rudimentary; ungraded schools were common in rural areas; the school term was but three months a year in many states; and compulsory school attendance was virtually unknown. As a consequence, it is not surprising that there should be so little in the history of the Fourteenth Amendment relating to its intended effect on public education.

In the first cases in this Court construing the Fourteenth Amendment, decided shortly after its adoption, the Court interpreted it as proscribing all state-imposed discriminations against the Negro race. The doctrine of "separate but equal" did not make its appearance in this Court until 1896 in the case of *Plessy* v. *Ferguson, supra,* involving not education but transportation. American courts have since labored with the doctrine for over half a century. In this Court, there have been six cases involving the "separate but equal" doctrine in the field of public education. In *Cumming* v. *County Board of*

Education, 175 U. S. 528, and *Gong Lum* v. *Rice,* 275 U. S. 78, the validity of the doctrine itself was not challenged. In more recent cases, all on the graduate school level, inequality was found in that specific benefits enjoyed by white students were denied to Negro students of the same educational qualifications. *Missouri ex rel. Gaines* v. *Canada,* 305 U. S. 337; *Sipuel* v. *Oklahoma,* 332 U. S. 631; *Sweatt* v. *Painter,* 339 U. S. 629; *McLaurin* v. *Oklahoma State Regents,* 339 U. S. 637. In none of these cases was it necessary to reexamine the doctrine to grant relief to the Negro plaintiff. And in *Sweatt* v. *Painter, supra,* the Court expressly reserved decision on the question whether *Plessy* v. *Ferguson* should be held inapplicable to public education.

In the instant cases, that question is directly presented. Here, unlike *Sweatt* v. *Painter,* there are findings below that the Negro and white schools involved have been equalized, or are being equalized, with respect to buildings, curricula qualifications and salaries of teachers, and other "tangible" factors. Our decision, therefore, cannot turn on merely a comparison of these tangible factors in the Negro and white schools involved in each of the cases. We must look instead to the effect of segregation itself on public education.

In approaching this problem, we cannot turn the clock back to 1868 when the Amendment was adopted, or even to 1896 when *Plessy* v. *Ferguson* was written. We must consider public education in the light of its full development and its present place in American life throughout the Nation. Only in this way can it be determined if segregation in public schools deprives these plaintiffs of the equal protection of the laws.

Today, education is perhaps the most important function of state and local governments. Compulsory school attendance laws and the great expenditures for education both demonstrate our recognition of the importance of education to our democratic society. It is required in the performance of our most basic public responsibilities, even service in the armed forces. It is the very foundation of good citizenship. Today it is a principal instrument in awakening the child to cultural values, in preparing him for later professional training, and in helping him to adjust normally to his environment. In these days, it is doubtful that any child may reasonably be expected to succeed in life if he is denied the opportunity of an education. Such an opportunity, where the state has undertaken to provide it, is a right which must be made available to all on equal terms.

We come then to the question presented: Does segregation of children in public schools solely on the basis of race, even though the physical facilities and other "tangible" factors may be equal, deprive the children of the minority group of equal educational opportunities? We believe that it does.

In *Sweatt* v. *Painter, supra,* in finding that a segregated law school for Negroes could not provide them equal educational opportunities, this Court relied in large part on "those qualities which are incapable of objective measurement but which make for greatness in a law school." In *McLaurin* v. *Oklahoma State Regents, supra,* the Court, in requiring that a Negro admitted to a white graduate school be treated like all other students, again resorted to intangible considerations: " . . . his ability to study, to engage in discussions and exchange views with other students, and, in general, to learn his profession." Such considerations apply with added force to children in grade and high schools. To separate them from others of similar age and qualifications solely because of their race generates a feeling of inferiority as to their status in the community that may affect their hearts and minds in a way unlikely ever to be undone. The effect of this separation on their educational opportunities was well stated by a finding in the Kansas case by a court which nevertheless felt compelled to rule against the Negro plaintiffs:

> Segregation of white and colored children in public schools has a detrimental effect upon the colored children. The impact is greater when it has the sanction of the law; for the policy of separating the races is usually interpreted as denoting the inferiority of the negro group. A sense of inferiority affects the motivation of a child to learn. Segregation with the sanction of law, therefore, has a tendency to [retard] the educational and mental development of negro children and to deprive them of some of the benefits they would recive in a racial[ly] integrated school system.

Whatever may have been the extent of psychological knowledge at the time of *Plessy* v. *Ferguson,* this finding is amply supported by modern authority. Any language in *Plessy* v. *Ferguson* contrary to this finding is rejected.

We conclude that in the field of public education the doctrine of "separate but equal" has no place. Separate educational facilities are inherently unequal. Therefore, we hold that the plaintiffs and others similarly situated for whom the actions have been brought are, by reason of the segregation complained of, deprived of the equal protection of the laws guaranteed by the Fourteenth Amendment. . . .

JOHN F. KENNEDY
We All Breathe the Same Air

The election of John F. Kennedy (1917–1963) as President after the eight-year administration of Dwight Eisenhower gave the nation a new style of youthfulness and vigor which was reflected in the arts as well as in the government. This new vigor and the national traumatic shock resulting from Kennedy's assassination on November 22, 1963, are perhaps the most vivid recollections of his brief presidency, but what is more likely to prove the most lasting result of

FROM *Public Papers of the Presidents of the United States: John F. Kennedy* (Washington: U.S. Govt. P.O., 1963), pp. 460–62.

his administration was his attempt to achieve a new flexibility in the Cold War and a new understanding with the Soviet Union. Although the Cuban invasion and Kennedy's meeting with Khrushchev in Vienna were both, in varying degree, failures, his later efforts proved more and more successful, culminating in the signing of a treaty prohibiting nuclear tests in the atmosphere in July, 1963. In this speech delivered at the American University on June 10, 1963, he states clearly his desire for a real peace "as the necessary rational end of rational men." This desire for a coming to peaceful terms with the Soviet Union coupled with a controlled use of force in the Cuban missile crisis laid the ghost of McCarthyism and established a new and more subtle American approach to international affairs which, despite the confusion of conflicting opinion surrounding the Vietnam conflict, is still operating today.

"There are few earthly things more beautiful than a university," wrote John Masefield, in his tribute to English universities—and his words are equally true today. He did not refer to spires and towers, to campus greens and ivied walls. He admired the splendid beauty of the university, he said, because it was "a place where those who hate ignorance may strive to know, where those who perceive truth may strive to make others see."

I have, therefore, chosen this time and this place to discuss a topic on which ignorance too often abounds and the truth is too rarely perceived—yet it is the most important topic on earth: world peace.

What kind of peace do I mean? What kind of peace do we seek? Not a *Pax Americana* enforced on the world by American weapons of war. Not the peace of the grave or the security of the slave. I am talking about genuine peace, the kind of peace that makes life on earth worth living, the kind that enables men and nations to grow and to hope and to build a better life for their children—not merely peace for Americans, but peace for all men and women—not merely peace in our time, but peace for all time.

I speak of peace because of the new face of war. Total war makes no sense in an age when great powers can maintain large and relatively invulnerable nuclear forces and refuse to surrender without resort to those forces. It makes no sense in an age when a single nuclear weapon contains almost ten times the explosive force delivered by all of the allied air forces in the Second World War. It makes no sense in an age when the deadly poisons produced by a nuclear exchange would be carried by the wind and water and soil and seed to the far corners of the globe and to generations yet unborn.

Today the expenditure of billions of dollars every year on weapons acquired for the purpose of making sure we never need to use them is essential to keeping the peace. But surely the acquisition of such idle stockpiles—which can only destroy and never create—is not the only, much less the most efficient, means of assuring peace.

I speak of peace, therefore, as the necessary rational end of rational men. I realize that the pursuit of peace is not as dramatic as the pursuit of war—and frequently the words of the pursuer fall on deaf ears. But we have no more urgent task.

Some say that it is useless to speak of world peace or world law or world disarmament—and that it will be useless until the leaders of the Soviet Union adopt a more enlightened attitude. I hope they do. I believe we can help them do it. But I also believe that we must re-examine our own attitude—as individuals and as a Nation—for our attitude is as essential as theirs. And every graduate of this school, every thoughtful citizen who despairs of war and wishes to bring peace, should begin by looking inward—by examining his own attitude toward the possibilities of peace, toward the Soviet Union, toward the course of the cold war, and toward freedom and peace here at home.

First: let us examine our attitude toward peace itself. Too many of us think it is impossible. Too many think it unreal. But that is a dangerous, defeatist belief. It leads to the conclusion that war is inevitable—that mankind is doomed—that we are gripped by forces we cannot control.

We need not accept that view. Our problems are man-made—therefore, they can be solved by man. And man can be as big as he wants. No problem of human destiny is beyond human beings. Man's reason and spirit have often solved the seemingly unsolvable—and we believe they can do it again.

I am not referring to the absolute, infinite concept of universal peace and good will of which some fantasies and fanatics dream. I do not deny the value of hopes and dreams, but we merely invite discouragement and incredulity by making that our only and immediate goal.

Let us focus instead on a more practical, more attainable peace—based not on a sudden revolution in human nature but on a gradual evolution in human institutions—on a series of concrete actions and effective agreements which are in the interest of all concerned. There is no single, simple key to this peace— no grand or magic formula to be adopted by one or two powers. Genuine peace must be the product of many nations, the sum of many acts. It must be dynamic, not static, changing to meet the challenge of each new generation. For peace is a process—a way of solving problems.

With such a peace, there will still be quarrels and conflicting interests, as there are within families and nations. World peace, like community peace, does not require that each man love his neighbor—it requires only that they live together in mutual tolerance, submitting their disputes to a just and peaceful settlement. And history teaches us that enmities between nations, as between individuals, do not last forever. However fixed our likes and dislikes may seem, the tide of time and events will often bring surprising changes in the relations between nations and neighbors.

So let us persevere. Peace need not be impracticable, and war need not be inevitable. By defining our goal more clearly, by making it seem more manageable and less remote we can help all peoples to see it, to draw hope from it, and to move irresistibly toward it.

Second: let us re-examine our attitude toward the Soviet Union. It is discouraging to think that their leaders may actually believe what their propagandists write. It is discouraging to read a recent authoritative Soviet text on *Military Strategy* and find, on page after page, wholly baseless and incredible claims—such as the allegation that "American imperialist circles are preparing to unleash different types of wars . . . that there is a very real threat of preventive war being unleashed by American imperialists against the Soviet Union . . . [and that] the political aims of the American imperialists are to enslave economically and politically the European and other capitalist countries... [and] to achieve world domination . . . by means of aggressive wars."

Truly as it was written long ago: "The wicked flee when no man pursueth." Yet it is sad to read these Soviet statements—to realize the extent of the gulf between us. But it is also a warning—a warning to the American people not to fall into the same trap as the Soviets, not to see only a distorted and desperate view of the other side, not to see conflict as inevitable, accommodation as impossible, and communication as nothing more than an exchange of threats.

No government or social system is so evil that its people must be considered as lacking in virtue. As Americans, we find Communism profoundly repugnant as a negation of personal freedom and dignity. But we can still hail the Russian people for their many achievements—in science and space, in economic and industrial growth, in culture and in acts of courage.

Among the many traits the peoples of our two countries have in common, none is stronger than our mutual abhorrence of war. Almost unique, among the major world powers, we have never been at war with each other. And no nation in the history of battle ever suffered more than the Soviet Union suffered in the course of the Second World War. At least 20 million lost their lives. Countless millions of homes and farms were burned or sacked. A third of the nation's territory, including nearly two-thirds of its industrial base, was turned into a wasteland—a loss equivalent to the devastation of this country east of Chicago.

Today, should total war ever break out again—no matter how—our two countries would become the primary targets. It is an ironical but accurate fact that the two strongest powers are the two in the most danger of devastation. All we have built, all we have worked for, would be destroyed in the first 24 hours. And even in the cold war, which brings burdens and dangers to so many countries, including this Nation's closest allies—our two countries bear the heaviest burdens. For we are both devoting massive sums of money to weapons that could be better devoted to combating ignorance, poverty and disease. We are both caught up in a vicious and dangerous cycle in which suspicion on one side breeds suspicion on the other, and new weapons beget counterweapons.

In short, both the United States and its allies, and the Soviet Union and its allies, have a mutually deep interest in a just and genuine peace and in halting the arms race. Agreements to this end are in the interests of the Soviet Union as well as ours—and even the most hostile nations can be relied upon to accept and keep those treaty obligations, and only those treaty obligations, which are in their own interest.

So let us not be blind to our differences—but let us also direct attention to our common interests and to the means by which those differences can be resolved. And if we cannot end now our differences, at least we can help make the world safe for diversity. For, in the final analysis, our most basic common link is that we all inhabit this planet. We all breathe the same air. We all cherish our children's future. And we are all mortal.

Third: let us reexamine our attitude toward the cold war, remembering that we are not engaged in a debate, seeking to pile up debating points. We are not here distributing blame or pointing the finger of judgment. We must deal with the world as it is, and not as it might have been had the history of the last 18 years been different.

We must, therefore, persevere in the search for peace in the hope that constructive changes within the Communist bloc might bring within reach solutions which now seem beyond us. We must conduct our affairs in such a way that it becomes in the Communists' interest to agree on a genuine peace. Above all, while defending our own vital interests, nuclear powers must avert those confrontations which bring an adversary to a choice of either a humiliating retreat or a nuclear war. To adopt that kind of course in the nuclear age would be evidence only of the bankruptcy of our policy—or of a collective death wish for the world.

To secure these ends, America's weapons are nonprovocative, carefully controlled, designed to deter and capable of selective use. Our military forces are committed to peace and disciplined in self-restraint. Our diplomats are instructed to avoid unnecessary irritants and purely rhetorical hostility.

For we can seek a relaxation of tensions without relaxing our guard. And, for our part, we do not need to use threats to prove that we are resolute. We do not need to jam foreign broadcasts out of fear our faith will be eroded. We are unwilling to impose our system on any unwilling people—but we are willing and able to engage in peaceful competition with any people on earth.

Meanwhile, we seek to strengthen the United Nations, to help solve its financial problems, to make it a more effective instrument of peace, to develop it into a genuine world security system—a system capable of resolving disputes on the basis of law, of insuring the security of the large and the small and of creating conditions under which arms can finally be abolished. . . .

LYNDON B. JOHNSON
The Time of the Great American Breakthrough

The shock and national guilt following President Kennedy's assassination enabled his successor, President Lyndon B. Johnson (1908–   ) to press through Congress many of the social reforms, such as a strong civil rights bill, which Kennedy had tried and failed to have enacted into law. The landslide election of Johnson in 1964 marked the rebirth of the social revolution of the New Deal, and the first year of his administration in his own right saw the enactment into law of more important pieces of social legislation than any similar time in the history of the republic. In his book, My Hope for America, *Johnson stated briefly the principles and hopes of his political philosophy, and especially in this chapter, "Toward the Great Society," he expressed his belief in the total commitment of the federal government to the creation of a "Great Society," by the elimination of poverty and ignorance and disease by means of massive government action, even to the point of government support of the arts through the creation of the National Foundation for the Arts and Humanities. The pace may have later been slowed by the demands of war and the tone may have been different, but the social revolution of 1932 was restored to full and real vitality in 1964.*

Franklin Delano Roosevelt once prophesied, "One day a generation may possess this land, blessed beyond anything we now know, blessed with those things—material and spiritual—that make man's life abundant. If that is the fashion of your dreaming then I say: 'Hold fast to your dream. America needs it.'"

Franklin D. Roosevelt and John F. Kennedy are gone. But our people still dream their dreams and we will carry on.

Old hopes have been reached and new horizons beckon us. This remains the land of the Great Experiment. The American story in the history of life on this planet is just beginning.

Forty years ago I left my high school diploma at home and headed west to seek the fame and fortune that I knew America offered. Almost two years later I came back to Johnson City, with empty hands and empty pockets. I came back because I realized that the place to begin was the place that I had been all the time.

Here, at this time, is the starting point of the path that leads to the future.

FROM *My Hope for America,* by Lyndon B. Johnson (New York: Random House, 1964), pp. 49–60. © Copyright 1964 by Random House, Inc. Reprinted by permission.

Our society can be a place where we will raise our families, free from the dark shadow of war and suspicion among nations. It can be a place where our children will grow up knowing that success in life depends only on his ability and not on the color of his skin, or the creed of his religion, or the region of his birth. It can be a place where America is growing not only richer and stronger but happier and wiser. For whatever the strength of our arms, or whatever the size of our economy, we will not be a great nation unless we pursue excellence.

The purpose of protecting the life of our Nation and preserving the liberty of our citizens is to pursue the happiness of our people. Our success in that pursuit is the test of our success as a nation. For a century we labored to settle and to subdue a continent. For half a century we called upon unbounded invention and untiring industry to create an order of plenty for all of our people. The challenge of the next half century is whether we have the wisdom to use that wealth to enrich and elevate our national life, and to advance the quality of our American civilization.

Imagination, initiative, and indignation will determine whether we build a society where progress is the servant of our needs—or a society where old values and new visions are buried under unbridled growth. We have the opportunity to move, not only toward the rich society and the powerful society, but upward to the Great Society.

The Great Society rests on abundance and liberty for all. It demands an end to poverty and racial injustice. But that is just the beginning. The Great Society is a place where every child can find knowledge to enrich his mind and to enlarge his talents. It is a place where leisure is a welcome chance to build and reflect, not a feared cause of boredom and restlessness. It is a place where the city of man serves not only the needs of the body and the demands of commerce, but the desire for beauty and the hunger for community.

It is a place where man can renew contact with nature. It is a place which honors creation for its own sake and for what it adds to the understanding of the race. It is a place where men are more concerned with the quality of their goals than the quantity of their goods. But most of all, the Great Society is not a safe harbor, a resting place, a final objective, a finished work. It is a challenge constantly renewed, beckoning us toward a destiny where the meaning of our lives matches the marvelous products of our labor.

There are three central places where we must begin to build the Great Society—in our cities, in our countryside and in our classrooms.

Many living today will see the time, perhaps fifty years from now, when there will be four hundred million Americans, four fifths of them in urban areas. In the remainder of this century, urban population will double, city land will double, and we will have to build homes, highways, and facilities equal to all those built since this country was first settled. In the next forty years we must rebuild the entire urban United States.

Aristotle said, "Men come together in cities in order to live, but they remain together in order to live the good life."

It is harder and harder to live the good life in American cities today. The catalogue of ills is long. There is the decay of the centers and the despoiling of the suburbs. There is not enough housing for our people or transportation for our traffic. Open land is vanishing and old landmarks are violated. Worst of all, expansion is eroding the precious and time-honored values of community with neighbors and communion with nature. The loss of these values breeds loneliness and boredom and indifference.

Our society will never be great until our cities are great. Today the frontier of imagination and innovation is inside those cities and not beyond their borders. New experiments are already going on. It will be our task to make the American city a place where future generations will come, not only to live, but to live the good life.

A second place where we begin to build the Great Society is in our countryside. We have always prided ourselves on being not only America the strong and America the free but America the beautiful. Today that beauty is in danger. The water we drink, the food we eat, the very air that we breathe, are threatened wtih pollution. Our parks are overcrowded, our seashores overburdened. Green fields and dense forests are disappearing.

A few years ago we were greatly concerned about the Ugly American. Today we must act to prevent an Ugly America.

Once the battle is lost, once our natural splendor is destroyed, it can never be recaptured. And once man can no longer walk with beauty or wonder at nature, his spirit will wither and his sustenance be wasted.

A third place to build the Great Society is in the classrooms of America. There our children's lives will be shaped. Our society will not be great until every young mind is set free to scan the farthest reaches of thought and imagination.

We are still far from that goal. Today, eight million adult Americans have not finished five years of school. Nearly fifty-four million—more than one quarter of all America—have not even finished high school. Each year more than a hundred thousand high school graduates, with proven ability, do not enter college because they cannot afford it.

If we cannot educate today's youth, what will we do in 1970 when elementary school enrollment will be five million greater than in 1960? High school enrollment will rise by five million. College enrollment will increase by more than three million.

In many places, classrooms are overcrowded and curricula are outdated. Most of our qualified teachers are underpaid, and many of our paid teachers are unqualified. We must give every child a place to sit and a teacher to learn from. Poverty must not be a bar to learning, and learning must offer an escape from poverty.

But more classrooms and more teachers are not enough. We must seek an educational system which grows in quality as well as in size. This means better training for our teachers. It means preparing youth to enjoy their hours of leisure as well as their hours of labor. It means exploring new techniques of teaching to find new ways to stimulate the love of learning and the capacity for creation.

These are three of the central issues of the Great Society. While our government has many programs directed at those issues, I do not pretend that we have the full answer to those problems. But I do promise this: We are going to assemble the best thought and the broadest knowledge from all over the world to find those answers for America.

We hear it said from time to time that the day of the individual is passing. We are told that this is the age of the oversized organization—of big business, of big unions, of big government. We hear that the individual is being smothered by giant concentrations of power. We are told that the individual can count for little in the era of The Organization Man.

Earlier generations also prophesied that the individual had reached his final frontier. Our ancestors complained bitterly when the West was won, leaving no new avenues of adventure or escape. At the turn of the century, prophets were predicting that men would be devoured by the monster corporation. During the dreary Depression years, some concluded that the future, if there were a future, belonged to the totalitarian society.

History has a habit of upsetting dire calculations. I believe that the pessimistic prophecies about our future are mistaken. We can shape a destiny in which the individual finds rich rewards.

This statement of faith is not based on an idle dream. As machines increasingly bring release from manual toil, I foresee little leisure for those who work with their minds. We have big problems ahead—and challenging times demand creative thinking.

Unless we stimulate individual enterprise, unless we regard individual accomplishment, we will be the servants and not the masters of change.

In education, we must provide higher learning for all who qualify. But we must also encourage the excellence which inspires a talented student to enlarge the limits of his capacity.

In science, achievement requires many technicians working in concert. But we must never forget the tradition of the solitary genius—the Newton, the Einstein, the Fermi—who tests the free range of his own curiosity.

In art, we welcome the growth of mass markets for books, painting, and sculpture. But we must also seek to nourish the artistic talent which has not yet achieved a buying public.

In the humanities, we must ensure that centers of liberal learning are not neglected as new knowledge nourishes the practical studies.

In all areas of public and private enterprise, we must understand that important ideas cannot be fashioned on an assembly line. The wit who told us that a camel was a horse designed by a committee deserves a medal.

We can and we must set priorities for individual accomplishment, and avoid mediocrity as the standard of success. These are wise and proper cautions to protect and promote individual expression in America.

At the same time, let us not call forth phantom fears about 'what the future holds. One of these fears often raised is that government has become a major menace to individual liberty. This is not so.

Does government subvert our freedom through the Social Security system which guards our people against destitution when they are too old to work? Does government undermine our freedom by bringing electricity to the farm, by controlling floods, or by ending bank failures? Is freedom lessened by efforts to abate pollution in our streams, by efforts to gain knowledge of the causes of heart disease and cancer, or by efforts to strengthen competition and the free market? Is freedom really diminished by banning the sale of harmful drugs, by providing school lunches for our children, by preserving our wilderness areas, or by improving the safety of our airways? Is freedom betrayed when in 1964 we redeem in full a pledge made a century ago by the Emancipation Proclamation?

The truth is—far from crushing the individual, government at its best liberates him from the enslaving forces of his environment. For, as Thomas Jefferson said, "The care of human life and happiness, and not their destruction, is the first and only legitimate object of good government."

A compassionate government keeps faith with the trust of the people and cherishes the future of their children. Through compassion for the plight of one individual, government fulfills its purpose as the servant of all the people.

Let me state clearly what I mean by "government." I do not mean just the politicians, technicians, and experts in Washington. I do not mean only the agencies that make up the Federal system, or the departments and bureaus of state government or local municipalities. I include every citizen. For as Aristotle said, "If liberty and equality . . . are chiefly to be found in democracy, they will be best attained when all persons alike share in the government to the utmost."

We have in this country a government which derives its power from the consent of the governed—from the people. From those same people must come the dreams, the faith, the hopes, and the works which fashion the great purpose of government. From the people must come the private compassion and the personal commitment by which struggles for justice and wars against poverty are won.

Because our government is the sum total of the people it serves, the choices that we personally make, the courses that we personally follow, the contests that we personally join—these will finally decide the real character of this country.

I do not doubt history's verdict. I believe that thirty years from now Americans will look back upon these 1960s as the time of the great American Breakthrough—toward the victory of peace over war; toward the victory of prosperity over poverty; toward the victory of human rights over human wrongs: toward the victory of enlightened minds over darkness.

MALCOLM X
My Friends Today Are Black, Brown, Red, Yellow and *White*

After the success of Johnson's civil rights legislation in Congress, the Negro civil rights movement predictably began to lose much of its unity and divide into factions like any other large political group. The militant wing of the movement began to call for a Negro revolution and for Black Nationalism and Black Power. Their goals were and are ill-defined, but the central impulse toward Negro autonomy, economically and politically, proved to be strong and deeply felt, especially in the huge Negro ghettos in the large Northern cities, where violence of unusual intensity for America began to break out. The militant movement takes as its heroes three men: Marcus Garvey, the Negro militant leader who had called for "Africa for the Africans" and for American Negroes to return to Africa, W. E. B. DuBois, an essay and poem of whose appears in Section 11, and Malcolm X (1925–1965), the articulate and exciting Black Muslim leader who was murdered after leaving that organization and striking out on his own to build a working black revolutionary movement in America. Near the end of his life, after a trip to Mecca which had broadened his horizons in many ways, Malcolm X maintained his belief in a Black Nationalist movement, but he had grown to understand that his objectives did not preclude an understanding with the whites of America even if there could never be a genuine integration of the Negro into white society. These pages from his autobiography reveal both his militancy and his hope that there could be solutions. It expresses the Negro demand for justice as well as the traditional American faith in "humanism and moral responsibility."

I kept having all kinds of troubles trying to develop the kind of Black Nationalist organization I wanted to build for the American Negro. Why Black Nationalism? Well, in the competitive American society, how can there ever be any white-black solidarity before there is first some black solidarity? If you will remember, in my childhood I had been exposed to the Black Nationalist teachings of Marcus Garvey—which, in fact, I had been told had led to my father's

FROM *The Autobiography of Malcolm X*, by Malcolm X, with the assistance of Alex Haley (New York: Grove Press, 1965), pp. 374–77. Reprinted by permission of Grove Press, Inc., and Hutchinson Publishing Group Ltd, London. Copyright © 1964 by Alex Haley and Malcolm X. Copyright © 1965 by Alex Haley and Betty Shabazz.

murder. Even when I was a follower of Elijah Muhammad, I had been strongly aware of how the Black Nationalist political, economic and social philosophies had the ability to instill within black men the racial dignity, the incentive, and the confidence that the black race needs today to get up off its knees, and to get on its feet, and get rid of its scars, and to take a stand for itself.

One of the major troubles that I was having in building the organization that I wanted—an all-black organization whose ultimate objective was to help create a society in which there could exist honest white-black brotherhood—was that my earlier public image, my old so-called "Black Muslim" image, kept blocking me. I was trying to gradually reshape that image. I was trying to turn a corner, into a new regard by the public, especially Negroes; I was no less angry than I had been, but at the same time the true brotherhood I had seen in the Holy World had influenced me to recognize that anger can blind human vision.

Every free moment I could find, I did a lot of talking to key people whom I knew around Harlem, and I made a lot of speeches saying: "True Islam taught me that it takes *all* of the religious, political, economic, psychological, and racial ingredients, or characteristics, to make the Human Family and the Human Society complete.

"Since I learned the *truth* in Mecca, my dearest friends have come to include *all* kinds—some Christians, Jews, Buddhists, Hindus, agnostics, and even atheists! I have friends who are called capitalists, Socialists, and Communists! Some of my friends are moderates, conservatives, extremists—some are even Uncle Toms! My friends today are black, brown, red, yellow, and *white!*"

I said to Harlem street audiences that only when mankind would submit to the One God who created all—only then would mankind even approach the "peace" of which so much *talk* could be heard . . . but toward which so little *action* was seen.

I said that on the American racial level, we had to approach the black man's struggle against the white man's racism as a human problem, that we had to forget hypocritical politics and propaganda. I said that both races, as human beings, had the obligation, the responsibility, of helping to correct America's human problem. The well-meaning white people, I said, had to combat, actively and directly, the racism in other white people. And the black people had to build within themselves much greater awareness that along with equal rights there had to be the bearing of equal responsibilities.

I knew, better than most Negroes, how many white people truly wanted to see American racial problems solved. I knew that many whites were as frustrated as Negroes. I'll bet I got fifty letters some days from white people. The white people in meeting audiences would throng around me, asking me, after I had addressed them somewhere, "What *can* a sincere white person do?"

When I say that here now, it makes me think about that little co-ed I told you about, the one who flew from her New England college down to New

York and came up to me in the Nation of Islam's restaurant in Harlem, and I told her that there was "nothing" she could do. I regret that I told her that. I wish that now I knew her name, or where I could telephone her, or write to her, and tell her what I tell white people now when they present themselves as being sincere, and ask me, one way or another, the same thing that she asked.

The first thing I tell them is that at least where my own particular Black Nationalist organization, the Organization of Afro-American Unity, is concerned, they can't *join* us. I have these very deep feelings that white people who want to join black organizations are really just taking the escapist way to salve their consciences. By visibly hovering near us, they are "proving" that they are "with us." But the hard truth is this *isn't* helping to solve America's racist problem. The Negroes aren't the racists. Where the really sincere white people have got to do their "proving" of themselves is not among the black *victims,* but out on the battle lines of where America's racism really *is*—and that's in their own home communities; America's racism is among their own fellow whites. That's where the sincere whites who really mean to accomplish something have got to work.

Aside from that, I mean nothing against any sincere whites when I say that as members of black organizations, generally whites' very presence subtly renders the black organization automatically less effective. Even the best white members will slow down the Negroes' discovery of what they need to do, and particularly of what they can do—for themselves, working by themselves, among their own kind, in their own communities.

I sure don't want to hurt anybody's feelings, but in fact I'll even go so far as to say that I never really trust the kind of white people who are always so anxious to hang around Negroes, or to hang around in Negro communities. I don't trust the kind of whites who love having Negroes always hanging around them. I don't know—this feeling may be a throwback to the years when I was hustling in Harlem and all of those red-faced, drunk whites in the afterhours clubs were always grabbing hold of some Negroes and talking about "I just want you to know you're just as good as I am—" And then they got back in their taxicabs and black limousines and went back downtown to the places where they lived and worked, where no blacks except servants had better get caught. But, anyway, I know that every time that whites join a black organization, you watch, pretty soon the blacks will be leaning on the whites to support it, and before you know it a black may be up front with a title, but the whites, because of their money, are the real controllers.

I tell sincere white people, "Work in conjunction with us—each of us working among our own kind." Let sincere white individuals find all other white people they can who feel as they do—and let them form their own all-white groups, to work trying to convert other white people who are thinking and acting so racist. Let sincere whites go and teach nonviolence to white people!

We will completely respect our white co-workers. They will deserve every credit. We will give them every credit. We will meanwhile be working among our own kind, in our own black communities—showing and teaching black men in ways that only other black men can—that the black man has got to help himself. Working separately, the sincere white people and sincere black people actually will be working together.

In our mutual sincerity we might be able to show a road to the salvation of America's very soul. It can only be salvaged if human rights and dignity, in full, are extended to black men. Only such real meaningful actions as those which are sincerely motivated from a deep sense of humanism and moral responsibility can get at the basic causes that produce the racial explosions in America today. Otherwise, the racial explosions are only going to grow worse. Certainly nothing is ever going to be solved by throwing upon me and other so-called black "extremists" and "demagogues" the blame for the racism that is in America.

Sometimes, I have dared to dream to myself that one day, history may even say that my voice—which disturbed the white man's smugness, and his arrogance, and his complacency—that my voice helped to save America from a grave, possibly even a fatal catastrophe. . . .